When should I travel to get the best airfare?
Where do I go for answers to my travel questions?
What's the best and easiest way to plan and book my trip?

www.frommers.travelocity.com

Frommer's, the travel guide leader, has teamed up with **Travelocity.com**, the leader in online travel, to bring you an in-depth, easy-to-use resource designed to help you plan and book your trip online.

At **www.frommers.travelocity.com**, you'll find free online updates about your destination from the experts at Frommer's plus the outstanding travel planning and purchasing features of Travelocity.com. Travelocity.com provides reservations capabilities for 95 percent of all airline seats sold, more than 47,000 hotels, and over 50 car rental companies. In addition, Travelocity.com offers more than 2,000 exciting vacation and cruise packages. Travelocity.com puts you in complete control of your travel planning with these and other great features:

> **Expert travel guidance from Frommer's** - over 150 writers reporting from around the world!

> **Best Fare Finder** - an interactive calendar tells you when to travel to get the best airfare

> **Fare Watcher** - we'll track airfare changes to your favorite destinations

> **Dream Maps** - a mapping feature that suggests travel opportunities based on your budget

> **Shop Safe Guarantee** - 24 hours a day / 7 days a week live customer service, and more!

Whether traveling on a tight budget, looking for a quick weekend getaway, or planning the trip of a lifetime, Frommer's guides and Travelocity.com will make your travel dreams a reality. You've bought the book, now book the trip!

Also available from Wiley

Beyond Disney: The Unofficial Guide to Universal, SeaWorld, and the Best of Central Florida

Inside Disney: The Incredible Story of Walt Disney World and the Man Behind the Mouse

Mini Las Vegas: The Pocket-Sized Unofficial Guide to Las Vegas

Mini-Mickey: The Pocket-Sized Unofficial Guide to Walt Disney World

The Unofficial Guide to Bed & Breakfasts in California

The Unofficial Guide to Bed & Breakfasts in the Northwest

The Unofficial Guide to Bed & Breakfasts in the Southeast

The Unofficial Guide to Branson, Missouri

The Unofficial Guide to California with Kids

The Unofficial Guide to Chicago

The Unofficial Guide to Cruises

The Unofficial Guide to Disneyland

The Unofficial Guide to Disneyland Paris

The Unofficial Guide to Florida with Kids

The Unofficial Guide to the Great Smoky and Blue Ridge Region

The Unofficial Guide to Golf Vacations in the Eastern U.S.

The Unofficial Guide to Hawaii

The Unofficial Guide to London

The Unofficial Guide to Miami and the Keys

The Unofficial Guide to the Mid-Atlantic with Kids

The Unofficial Guide to New England and New York with Kids

The Unofficial Guide to New Orleans

The Unofficial Guide to New York City

The Unofficial Guide to Paris

The Unofficial Guide to San Francisco

The Unofficial Guide to Skiing in the West

The Unofficial Guide to the Southeast with Kids

The Unofficial Guide to Walt Disney World

The Unofficial Guide to Walt Disney World for Grown-Ups

The Unofficial Guide to Walt Disney World with Kids

The Unofficial Guide to Washington, D.C.

The Unofficial Guide to the World's Best Diving Vacations

the Unofficial Guide® to

Bed & Breakfasts and Country Inns in New England

2nd Edition

Lea Lane

Wiley Publishing, Inc.

To Chaim: great man, great love

Please note that prices fluctuate in the course of time, and travel information changes under the impact of many factors that influence the travel industry. We therefore suggest that you write or call ahead for confirmation when making your travel plans. Every effort has been made to ensure the accuracy of information throughout this book and the contents of this publication are believed correct at the time of printing. Nevertheless, the publishers cannot accept responsibility for errors or omissions or for changes in details given in this guide or for the consequences of any reliance on the information provided by the same. Assessments of attractions and so forth are based upon the author's own experience and therefore, descriptions given in this guide necessarily contain an element of subjective opinion, which may not reflect the publisher's opinion or dictate a reader's own experience on another occasion. Readers are invited to write to the publisher with ideas, comments, and suggestions for future editions. Your safety is important to us, so we encourage you to stay alert and be aware of your surroundings. Keep a close eye on cameras, purses, and wallets, all favorite targets of thieves and pickpockets.

Published by Wiley Publishing, Inc.
909 Third Avenue
New York, NY 10022

Produced by Menasha Ridge Press
Published by Wiley Publishing, Inc., New York, NY

ISBN 0-7645-6502-8
ISSN 1521-4931

Manufactured in the United States of America
10 9 8 7 6 5 4 3 2

Second edition

Contents

List of Maps

About the Author and Illustrator

Lea Lane has written about New England inns and bed-and-breakfasts in consumer guidebooks including Birnbaum USA, *The Zagat Hotel Survey,* and trade publications including *Star Service.* She was a columnist for Gannett Suburban Papers, managing editor of "Travel Smart" newsletter, has co-authored a book on cruises, and contributes to publications including *The New York Times, The Miami Herald, Fodor's Belgium and Luxembourg, Fodor's Naples and the Amalfi Coast,* and *The Unofficial Guide to New York City.*

Born and raised in New York City, Giselle Simons received her Bachelor of Fine Arts degree from Cornell University. She currently lives on Manhattan's Upper West Side, where she works as an illustrator, architectural design drafter, and graphic designer. She is caretaker to a dog, two cats, an increasing number of fish, and her husband, Jeff.

Acknowledgments

This book is a labor of love, with an emphasis on both words. Hundreds of lodgings have been visited numerous times over the past 25 years.

This team effort starts with tourism departments and innkeepers who answered endless questions, patiently opening their properties for inspection. For this *Unofficial Guide,* I am especially grateful to research associates Dian Larkin and Allyson Shames for their diligence and skills, and Catherine Rose, for her help with this edition. Deep appreciation to Bob Sehlinger, Molly Merkle, Russell Helms, and the staff at Menasha Ridge Press for gentle, effective, and wise editorial support. Also, thanks to Erin Willder, Caroline Carr, Jan Mucciarone, Barry Kerrigan, and Dawn Charlton for helping getting the book in order. Thanks also to all those who assisted and provided leads on new and interesting properties whether or not they were chosen to appear in the book. These stalwart researchers include Jane Peters, Janine Thomson, Dave Feibusch, Susan Pavleck, Judy Jacobs, Stan Jacobs, Carol Levy, Steve Levy, Stuart Bussey, Gloria Meisel, Sylvia Erlich, Randall Lane, Jen Reingold, Gayle Conran, Cary Lane, Louise Shames, and Chaim Stern.

And a special thank you to my Aunt Hilda, an independent woman and lover of things beautiful and delicious for all of her 87 years. She introduced me to travel and the pleasures of New England inns and B&Bs, early on, ahead of the game. Because of her, I have been able to follow the development of some of these properties for decades.

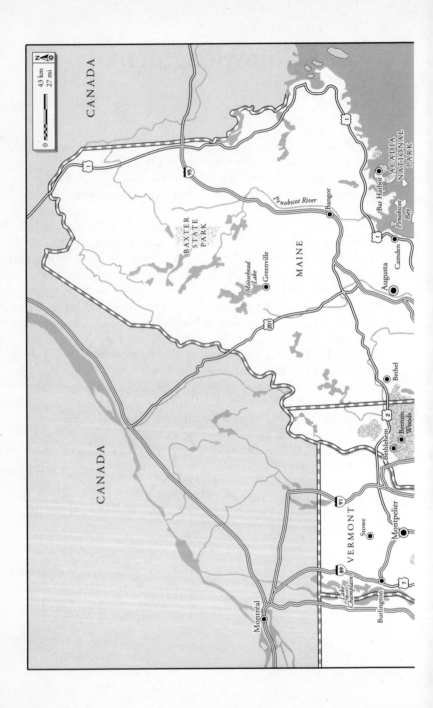

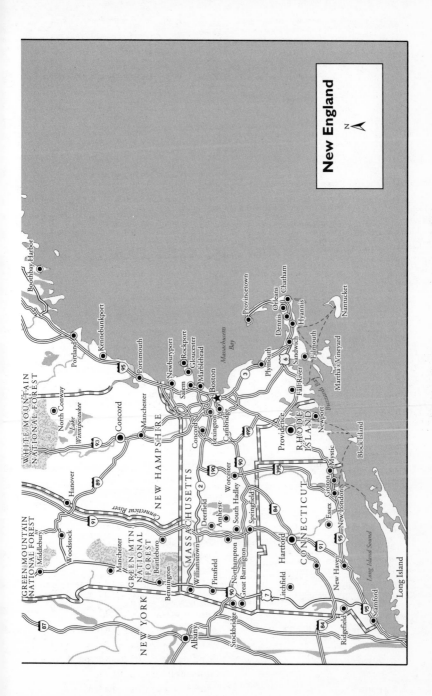

New England

N

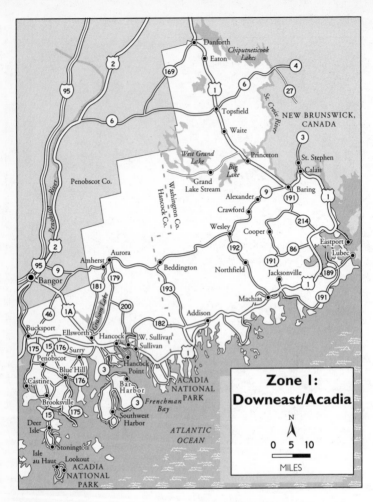

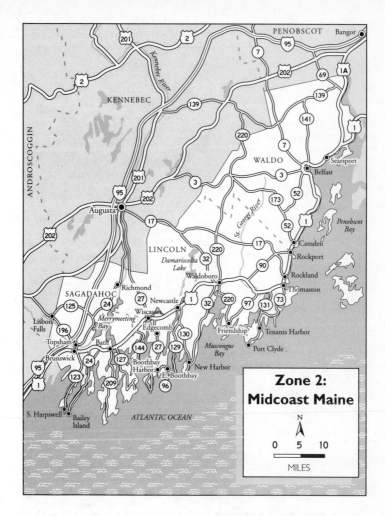

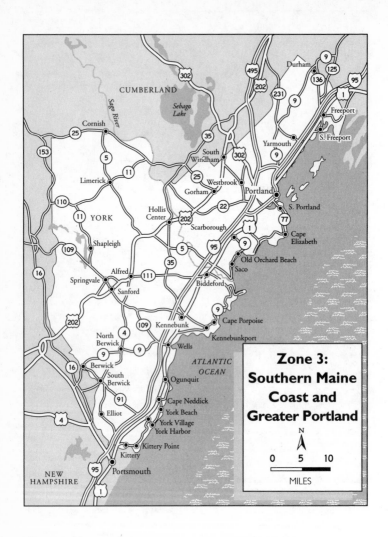

Zone 3:
Southern Maine
Coast and
Greater Portland

N

0   5   10

MILES

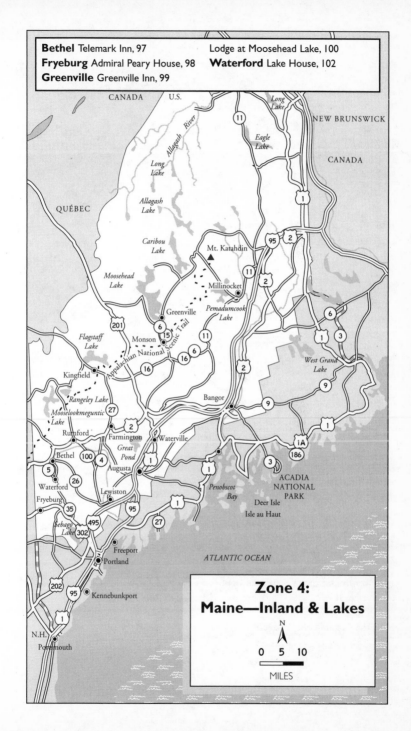

Bethel Telemark Inn, 97   Lodge at Moosehead Lake, 100
Fryeburg Admiral Peary House, 98   Waterford Lake House, 102
Greenville Greenville Inn, 99

Zone 4:
Maine—Inland & Lakes

N

0   5   10

MILES

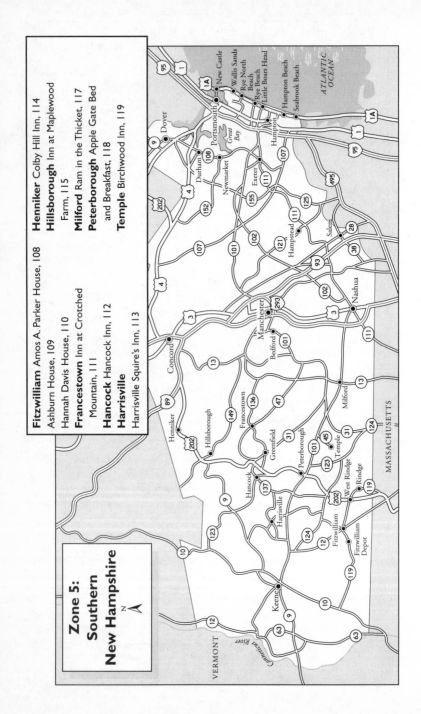

Zone 5: Southern New Hampshire

N

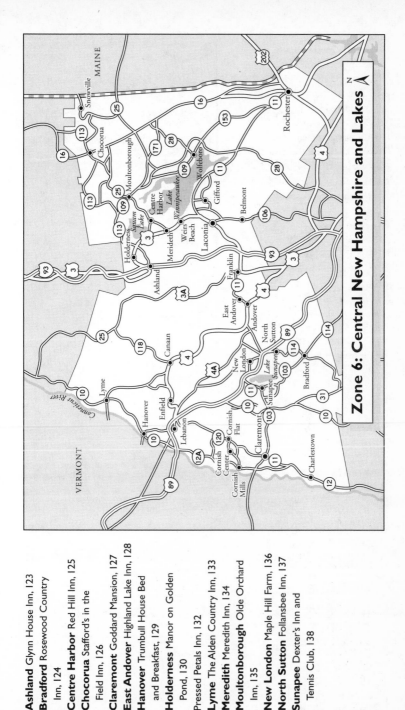

Zone 6: Central New Hampshire and Lakes

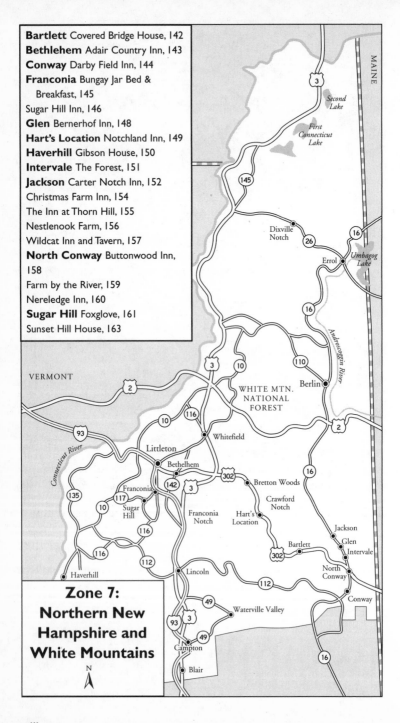

MAINE

Second
Lake

First
Connecticut
Lake

145

Dixville
Notch

26

16

Errol

Umbagog
Lake

16

VERMONT

2

3

10

110

Androscoggin River

WHITE MTN.
NATIONAL
FOREST

Berlin

10

116

93

Connecticut River

10

Littleton

Whitefield

2

16

Bethlehem

302

135

Franconia

142

3

Bretton Woods

117

Sugar
Hill

116

Franconia
Notch

Hart's
Location

Crawford
Notch

Jackson

Glen

116

112

Haverhill

Lincoln

302

Bartlett

Intervale

North
Conway

112

Conway

49

Waterville Valley

93

3

16

49

Campton

Blair

**Zone 7:
Northern New
Hampshire and
White Mountains**

N

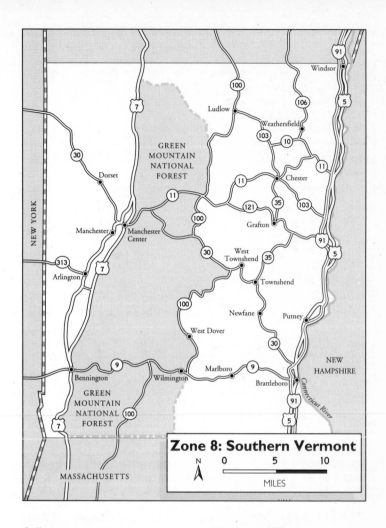

Zone 8: Southern Vermont

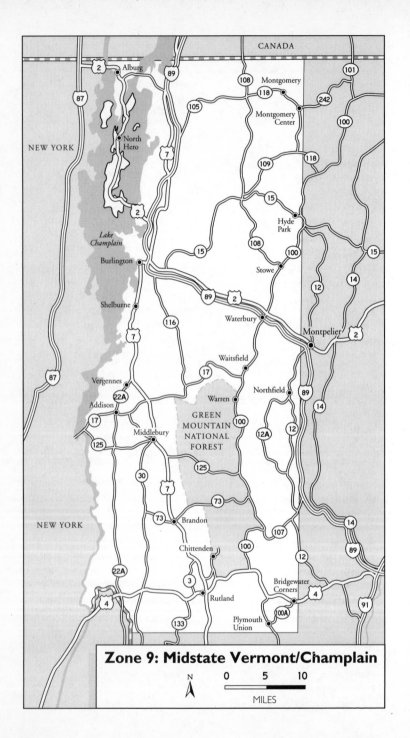

Zone 9: Midstate Vermont/Champlain

N

0 5 10

MILES

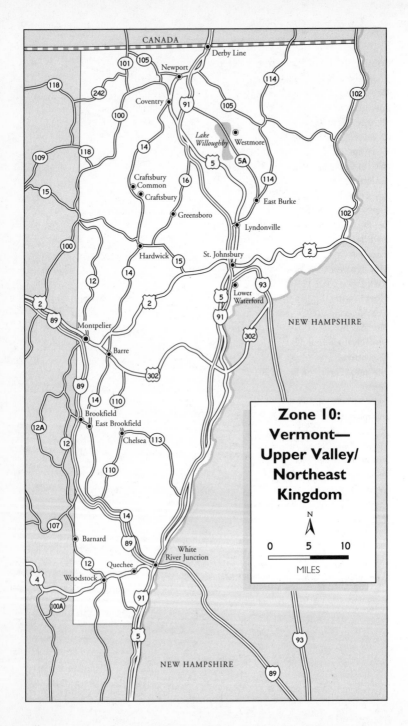

Zone 10:
Vermont—
Upper Valley/
Northeast
Kingdom

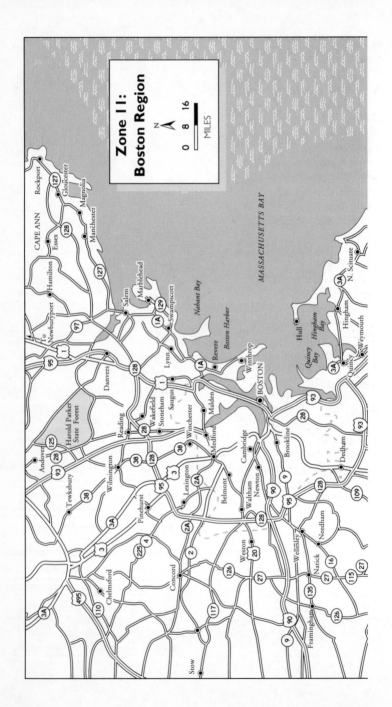

Zone 11:
Boston Region

N

0   8   16
MILES

MASSACHUSETTS BAY

CAPE ANN

Rockport
Gloucester
Magnolia
Manchester
Essex
Hamilton
Newburyport
To
Danvers
Marblehead
Salem
Swampscott
Lynn
Nahant Bay
Revere
Boston Harbor
Winthrop
BOSTON
Hull
Hingham Bay
Quincy Bay
Hingham
Weymouth
Quincy
N. Scituate
Wakefield
Stoneham
Saugus
Winchester
Malden
Medford
Cambridge
Brookline
Dedham
Reading
Wilmington
Belmont
Waltham
Newton
Needham
Andover
Tewksbury
Pinehurst
Lexington
Weston
Wellesley
Natick
Framingham
Harold Parker State Forest
Chelmsford
Concord
Stow

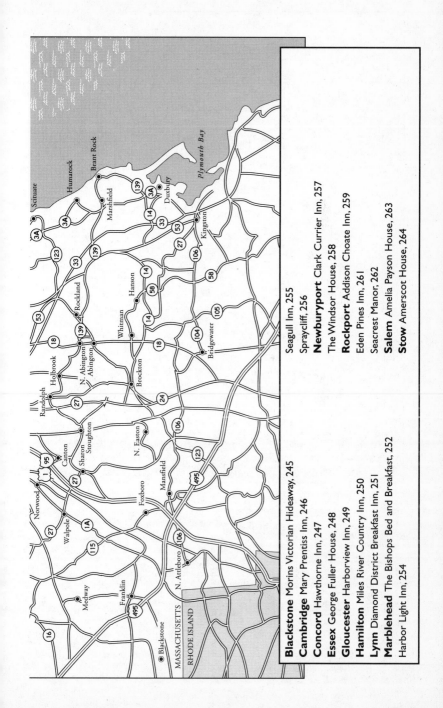

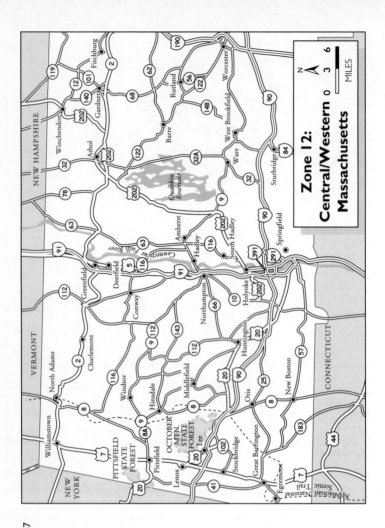

Zone 12:
Central/Western
Massachusetts

MILES
0 3 6

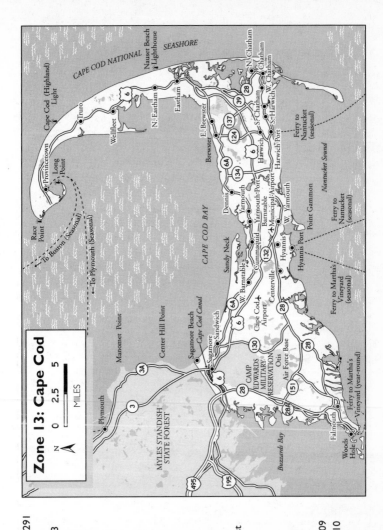

Zone 13: Cape Cod

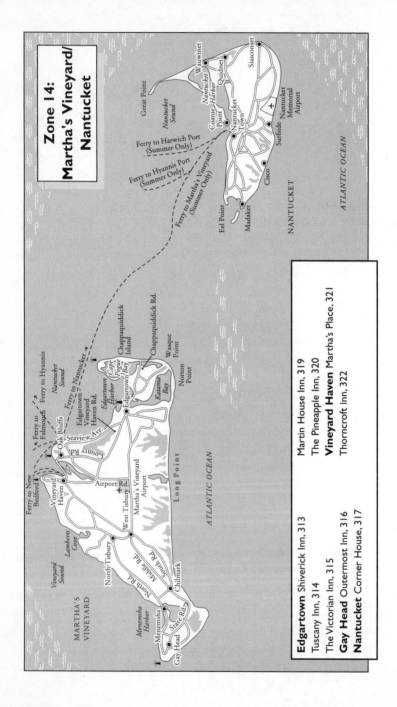

Zone 14:
Martha's Vineyard/
Nantucket

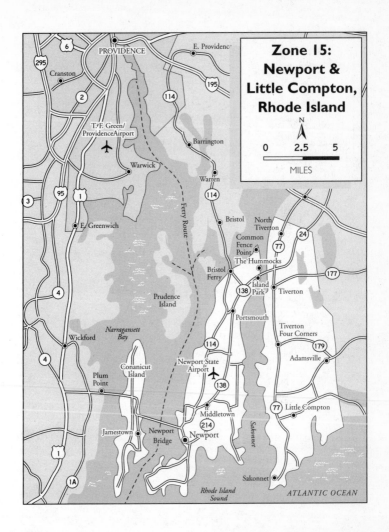

Zone 15:
Newport &
Little Compton,
Rhode Island

N

0   2.5   5

MILES

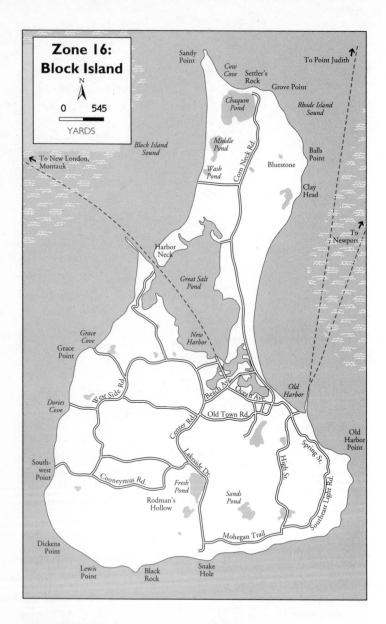

Zone 16: Block Island

N

0   545

YARDS

To Point Judith

Sandy Point

Cow Cove

Settler's Rock

Grove Point

Chaqun Pond

Rhode Island Sound

Middle Pond

Balls Point

Block Island Sound

Corn Neck Rd.

Bluestone

Wash Pond

Clay Head

To New London, Montauk

Harbor Neck

Great Salt Pond

To Newport

Grace Cove

New Harbor

Grace Point

Beach Ave.

Ocean Ave.

Old Harbor

Dories Cove

West Side Rd.

Old Town Rd.

South-west Point

Center Rd.

Old Harbor Point

Cooneymus Rd.

Lakeside Dr.

Fresh Pond

Sands Pond

High St.

Spring St.

Southeast Light Rd.

Rodman's Hollow

Dickens Point

Mohegan Trail

Lewis Point

Black Rock

Snake Hole

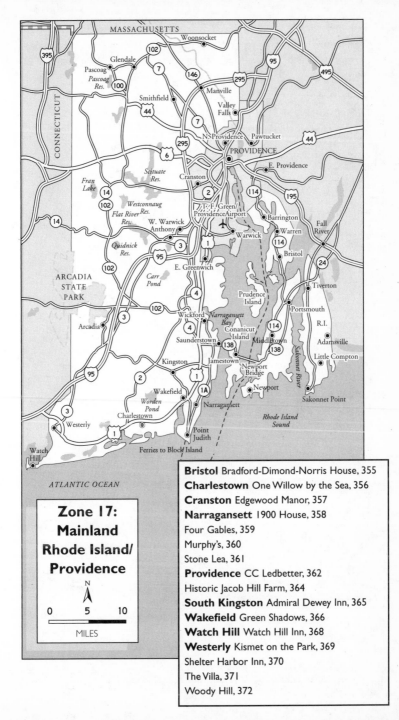

MASSACHUSETTS

CONNECTICUT

Woonsocket

395

Glendale
Pascoag
Pascoag Res.
100
102
7
146
95
495

Smithfield
44
Manville
Valley Falls
295
7

295
6

N. Providence
PROVIDENCE
Pawtucket
44

E. Providence

Scituate Res.
Cranston
2
114

Fran Lake
14
102
Westconnaug Res.
Flat River Res.
W. Warwick
Anthony
T.F. Green/Providence Airport
114
195

14

Quidnick Res.
95
3
Warwick
Barrington
Warren
114
Bristol
Fall River

ARCADIA STATE PARK
102
Carr Pond
E. Greenwich
24

3
102
Wickford
4
Narragansett Bay
Prudence Island
Tiverton
Portsmouth
R.I.

Arcadia
4
Saunderstown
Conanicut Island
138
Middletown
114
138
Adamsville
Little Compton

95
2
Kingston
Jamestown
1
Newport Bridge
Sakonnet River

Wakefield
1A
Newport
Sakonnet Point

Worden Pond
Charlestown
Narragansett

3
Westerly
Rhode Island Sound

Watch Hill
1
Point Judith
Ferries to Block Island

ATLANTIC OCEAN

Zone 17: Mainland Rhode Island/ Providence

N
↑

0   5   10

MILES

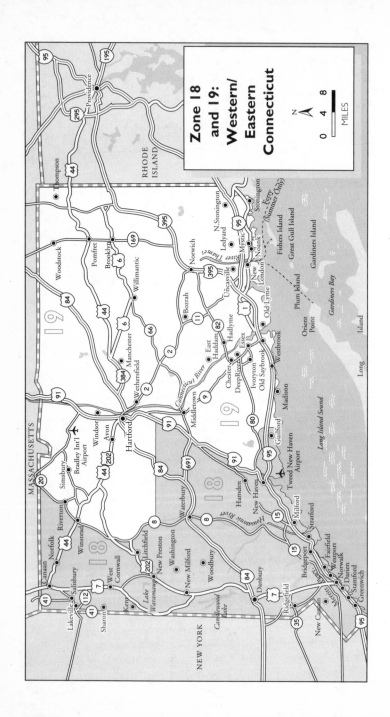

Zone 18 and 19:
Western/
Eastern
Connecticut

N

0 4 8
MILES

The Best of New England

TOP 30 OVERALL*

Five Stars ★★★★★
1. Inn at the Round Barn Farm
2. Captain Lord Mansion
3. Adair Country Inn
4. Inn at Shelburne Farms
5. Inn on the Common
6. Manor on Golden Pond
7. Rabbit Hill Inn
8. Norumbega
9. Elm Tree Cottage
10. Cliffside Inn
11. White Barn Inn
12. Inn at Saw Mill Farm
13. Pitcher Inn
14. Inn at National Hall
15. Blantyre
16. Mayflower Inn
17. Twin Farms

Four-and-a-Half Stars ★★★★½
18. Baldwin Hill Farm
19. Country Garden Inn
20. Edson Hill Manor
21. Eden Pines Inn
22. Bungay Jar Bed & Breakfast
23. Edgewood Manor
24. Cornucopia of Dorset
25. Blue Hill Inn
26. 1661 Inn
27. Bufflehead Cove Inn
28. Baldwin Place Inn
29. Bay Beach Bed and Breakfast
30. Boulders Inn

TOP 30 BY ROOM QUALITY*

1. Twin Farms
2. Blantyre
3. Inn at National Hall
4. Inn at the Round Barn Farm
5. Pitcher Inn
6. Rabbit Hill Inn
7. Adair Country Inn
8. Captain Lord Mansion
9. Elm Tree Cottage
10. Inn at Saw Mill Farm
11. Jackson House Inn
12. Mayflower Inn
13. White Barn Inn
14. Inn at Ormsby Hill
15. Lodge at Moosehead Lake
16. Manor on Golden Pond
17. Pomegranate
18. Wynstone
19. Bay Beach Bed and Breakfast
20. Cliffside Inn
21. Edgewood Manor
22. Field Farm Guest House
23. Ivy Lodge
24. Nannau-Seaside
25. Notchland Inn
26. Pilgrim's Inn
27. Angel Hill
28. Blue Hill Inn
29. Captain Jefferds Inn
30. Gibson House

*See pp. 9–11 for ratings criteria.

TOP VALUES

Heermansmith Farm Inn

Homeport Inn

Weston House

Ram in the Thicket

1900 House

Birchwood Inn

Morins Victorian Hideaway

Covered Bridge House

Ashburn House

Apple Gate Bed and Breakfast

Somerset House

Chester Bulkley House

Murphy's

Amos A. Parker House

BOAT-AND-BREAKFASTS

Maine

Schooner Stephen Taber

Connecticut

Stonecroft

BUDGET ACCOMMODATIONS

Some rooms rent for $75 or less

Maine

Bagley House

East Wind Inn & Meeting House

Edwards' Harborside Inn

Homeport Inn

Kingsleigh Inn 1904

Manor House

Nellie Littlefield House

Oakland House

Pleasant Bay

Weston House

New Hampshire

Apple Gate Bed and Breakfast

Birchwood Inn

Carter Notch Inn

Covered Bridge House

Farm by the River

Goddard Mansion

Hannah Davis House

Inn at Crotched Mountain

Inn at Maplewood Farm

Maple Hill Farm

Nereledge Inn

Olde Orchard Inn

Vermont

Black Lantern Inn

Heermansmith Farm Inn

Somerset House

Strong House Inn

Ten Acres Lodge

Massachusetts

Allen House Victorian Inn

Corner House

Martin House Inn

Morins Victorian Hideaway

Rhode Island

1661 Inn

1900 House

C C Ledbetter

Four Gables

Green Shadows

Hotel Manisses

Jailhouse Inn

One Willow by the Sea

Sheffield House

Connecticut

The French Bulldog Bed & Breakfast
  and Antiques

Ram in the Thicket

DINNER SERVED

Maine

Blue Hill Inn
Captain Lindsey House
Crocker House Country Inn
East Wind Inn & Meeting House
Gosnold Arms
Greenville Inn
Hartstone Inn
Hartwell House
Inn on the Harbor
Keeper's House
Lake House
Lodge at Moosehead Lake
Newcastle Inn
Oakland House
Pilgrim's Inn
Schooner Stephen Taber
Telemark Inn
Weatherby's Fisherman's Resort
Weston House
White Barn Inn

New Hampshire

Adair Country Inn
Alden Country Inn
Bernerhof Inn
Birchwood Inn
Christmas Farm Inn
Colby Hill Inn
Darby Field Inn
Dexter's Inn and Tennis Club
Follansbee Inn
Foxglove
Hancock Inn
Inn at Crotched Mountain
Inn at Thorn Hill
Manor on Golden Pond
Notchland Inn
Ram in the Thicket
Red Hill Inn
Stafford's in the Field Inn
Sugar Hill Inn
Sunset Hill House
Wild Cat Inn and Tavern

Vermont

Black Lantern Inn
Edson Hill Manor
Four Columns Inn
Governor's Inn
Heermansmith Farm Inn
Inn at Mountain View Farm
Inn at Ormsby Hill
Inn at Saw Mill Farm
Inn at Shelburne Farms
Inn at the Round Barn Farm
Inn at Weathersfield
Inn on the Common
Jackson House Inn
Juniper Hill Inn
Lilac Inn
North Hero House Country Inn
October Country Inn
Pitcher Inn
Rabbit Hill Inn
Reluctant Panther
Rowell's Inn
Shire Inn
Ten Acres Lodge
Tulip Tree Inn
Twin Farms
West Hill House
Wildflower Inn
Willough Vale Inn
Windham Hill Inn

Massachusetts

Blantyre
Deerfield Inn
Mary Prentiss Inn
Outermost Inn

Rhode Island

Hotel Manisses
Shelter Harbor Inn
Watch Hill Inn

Connecticut

Bee and Thistle Inn
Boulders Inn

Connecticut (*continued*)
Elms Inn
Gelston Inn
Homestead Inn (Greenwich)
Inn at National Hall
Lakeview Inn
Mayflower Inn

Old Lyme Inn
Roger Sherman Inn
Silvermine Tavern
Simsbury 1820 House
Three Chimneys Inn
Toll Gate Hill
Under Mountain Inn

FARM OR RURAL SETTING

Maine
Bagley House
Cod Cove Farm
Pleasant Bay
Squire Tarbox Inn
Telemark Inn
Weatherby's Fisherman's Resort

New Hampshire
Apple Gate Bed and Breakfast
Bungay Jar Bed & Breakfast
Farm by the River
The Forest
Harrisville Squire's Inn
Inn at Crotched Mountain
Inn at Maplewood Farm
Maple Hill Farm
Nestlenook Farm
Olde Orchard Inn
Rosewood Country Inn
Sugar Hill Inn

Vermont
Cornwall Orchards
Edson Hill Manor
Heermansmith Farm Inn
Inn at Mountain View Farm
Inn at Round Barn Farm
Inn at Shelburne Farms
Inn at Weathersfield
Inn at Woodchuck Hill Farm
Maple Leaf Inn
October Country Inn
Shire Inn
Strong House Inn
Ten Acres Lodge

Ten Bends on the River
Tulip Tree Inn
Twin Farms
Whitford House Inn
Wildflower Inn
Windham Hill Inn

Massachusetts
Amerscot House
Applegate
Baldwin Hill Farm
Blantyre
Field Farm Guest House
Historic Merrell Inn
Miles River Country Inn
River Bend Farm

Rhode Island
Historic Jacob Hill Farm
The Roost
Woody Hill

Connecticut
Angel Hill
Applewood Farms Inn
Boulders Inn
Elias Child House
Friendship Valley Inn
Hearthside Farm
Lord Thompson Manor
Mayflower Inn
Merrywood
Silvermine Tavern
Stonecroft
Toll Gate Hill
Under Mountain Inn

FAMILY-ORIENTED

Maine
Goose Cove Lodge
Island View Inn
Keeper's House
Pleasant Bay
Schooner Stephen Taber (teenagers)
Telemark Inn
Weatherby's Fisherman's Resort

New Hampshire
Christmas Farm Inn
Covered Bridge House
Darby Field Inn
Dexter's Inn and Tennis Club
Goddard Mansion
Inn at Crotched Mountain
Maple Hill Farm
Nereledge Inn
Olde Orchard Inn
Ram in the Thicket
Sunset Hill House
Trumbull House Bed and Breakfast

Vermont
Cornwall Orchards
Edson Hill Manor
Heermansmith Farm Inn
Hickory Ridge House
Hugging Bear Inn
Inn at Mountain View Farm
Inn at Shelburne Farms

Inn on the Common
North Hero House Country Inn
October Country Inn
Ten Bends on the River
Whitford House Inn
Wildflower Inn
Woodstocker

Massachusetts
Field Farm Guest House
Mary Prentiss Inn
Over Look Inn
Windflower

Rhode Island
1661 Inn
Jailhouse Inn
Shelter Harbor Inn
Watch Hill Inn

Connecticut
Brigadoon
Chester Bulkley House
Elms Inn
Gelston Inn
Homestead Inn (New Milford)
Inn at National Hall
Old Lyme Inn
Roger Sherman Inn
Silvermine Tavern
Toll Gate Hill

GHOSTS

These inns boast friendly ghosts.

Maine
Crocker House Country Inn

Vermont
Willard Street Inn

Massachusetts
Deerfield Inn

Rhode Island
Stone Lea

Connecticut
Inn at Lafayette

GROUPS, CONFERENCES, AND/OR WEDDINGS
EASILY ACCOMMODATED

Check individual profiles for the one that suits your needs.

Maine

Bagley House
Captain Jefferds Inn
Captain Lord Mansion
Crocker House Country Inn
East Wind Inn & Meeting House
Five Gables Inn
Flying Cloud
Goose Cove Lodge
Hartwell House
Inn at Portsmouth Harbor
Lake House
Manor House
Oakland House
Old Fort Inn
Weatherby's Fisherman's Resort

New Hampshire

Adair Country Inn
Alden Country Inn
Buttonwood Inn
Carter Notch Inn
Christmas Farm Inn
Colby Hill Inn
Dexter's Inn and Tennis Club
The Forest
Foxglove
Gibson House
Goddard Mansion
Harrisville Squire's Inn
Highland Lake Inn
Inn at Crotched Mountain
Maple Hill Farm
Nestlenook Farm
Olde Orchard Inn
Pressed Petals Inn
Ram in the Thicket
Red Hill Inn
Rosewood Country Inn
Stafford's in the Field Inn

Sunset Hill House
The Inn at Thorn Hill
Trumbull House Bed and Breakfast
Wildcat Inn and Tavern

Vermont

Andrie Rose Inn
Four Columns Inn
Green Trails Inn
Hickory Ridge House
Inn at Ormsby Hill
Inn at Weathersfield
Jackson House Inn
Juniper Hill Inn
Lilac Inn
Maple Leaf Inn
North Hero House Country Inn
Northfield Inn
Somerset House
Strong House Inn
Ten Bends on the River
The Pitcher Inn
Thomas Mott Homestead
Tulip Tree Inn
Twin Farms
West Hill House
Whitford House Inn
Wildflower Inn
Windham Hill Inn

Massachusetts

Amerscot House
Augustus Snow House
Blantyre
Captain Freeman Inn
Clark Currier Inn
Cyrus Kent House Inn
Dunscroft-by-the-Sea
Harbor Light Inn
Hawthorne Inn

GROUPS, CONFERENCES, AND/OR WEDDINGS EASILY ACCOMMODATED *(continued)*

Massachusetts (continued)
Mary Prentiss Inn
Mary Rockwell Stuart House
Miles River Country Inn
Over Look Inn
Seagull Inn
Fernbrook Inn
Walker House
Wedgewood Inn
Whalewalk Inn
Windflower
Windsor House

Rhode Island
1855 Marshall Slocum Guest House
Admiral Dewey Inn

Four Gables
Francis Malbone House
Hotel Manisses
Ivy Lodge
Kismet on the Park
The Roost
Savana's Inn
Stone Lea
Victorian Ladies Inn
Watch Hill Inn
Woody Hill
Connecticut
Boulders Inn

HISTORIC

This list includes only those inns that are 200 years old, or older.

Maine
Bagley House
Captain Jefferds Inn
Flying Cloud
Harpswell Inn
Lake House
Pilgrim's Inn
Squire Tarbox Inn

New Hampshire
Amos A. Parker House
Birchwood Inn
Christmas Farm Inn
Colby Hill Inn
Dexter's Inn and Tennis Club
Farm by the River
Hancock Inn
Highland Lake Inn
Nereledge Inn
Olde Orchard Inn
Stafford's in the Field Inn
Sugar Hill Inn

Vermont
1811 House
Cornwall Orchards
Inn at Blush Hill
Inn at Ormsby Hill
Inn at Weathersfield
Inn at Woodchuck Hill Farm
Inn on Covered Bridge Green
Rabbit Hill Inn
Wildflower Inn

Massachusetts
Amerscot House
Clark Tavern Inn
Corner House
Harbor Light Inn
Historic Merrell Inn
Miles River Country Inn
River Bend Farm
Saltbox
Windsor House

Rhode Island

Bradford-Dimond-Norris House
C C Ledbetter
Clarkston
Francis Malbone House
Historic Jacob Hill Farm
Jailhouse Inn

Connecticut

Bee and Thistle Inn
Brigadoon

Cobbscroft
Elias Child House
Elms Inn
Friendship Valley Inn
Hearthside Farm
Homestead Inn
Old Mystic Inn
Red Brook Inn
Roger Sherman Inn
Silvermine Tavern
Toll Gate Hill

ISLAND SETTING

Maine

Keeper's House

Massachusetts

Corner House
Martha's Place
Martin House Inn
Outermost Inn
Pineapple Inn
Shiverick Inn
Thorncroft Inn

Tuscany Inn
Victorian Inn

Rhode Island

1661 Inn
Blue Dory Inn
Hotel Manisses
Sea Breeze Inn
Sheffield House
Weather Bureau Inn

MOUNTAIN SETTING

Maine

Telemark Inn

New Hampshire

Adair Country Inn
Bernerhof Inn
Bungay Jar Bed & Breakfast
Darby Field Inn
Farm by the River
Foxglove
Inn at Crotched Mountain
Inn at Thorn Hill
Nereledge Inn
Notchland Inn
Sugar Hill Inn
Sunset Hill House

Vermont

Andrie Rose Inn

Black Lantern Inn
Cornwall Orchards
Edson Hill Manor
Inn at Blush Hill
Inn at Mountain View Farm
Maple Leaf Inn
Pitcher Inn
Rabbit Hill Inn
Siebeness
Strong House Inn
Ten Acres Lodge
Ten Bends on the River
Tulip Tree Inn
Twin Farms
West Hill House
Whitford House Inn
Willough Vale Inn
Windham Hill Inn

MOUNTAIN SETTING (continued)

Massachusetts
Field Farm Guest House
River Bend Farm
Connecticut

Boulders Inn
Hilltop Haven
White Hart Inn

NO CREDIT CARDS

Maine
Harbor Hill
Keeper's House
Weston House

Seacrest Manor
Walker House

Rhode Island
1900 House

New Hampshire
Amos A. Parker House
Birchwood Inn
Inn at Crotched Mountain

Elm Tree Cottage
Green Shadows
Kismet on the Park
Murphy's
One Willow By The Sea
Stone Lea
Woody Hill

Massachusetts
Bed and Breakfast of Sagamore Beach
Cliffwood Inn
Fernbrook Inn
Morins Victorian Hideaway
River Bend Farm

Connecticut
Gibson House
Hilltop Haven
Palmer Inn

PETS ALLOWED

The following properties accept pets at least somewhere on their property. Many still have restrictions, so call ahead. Always let a host know ahead of time if you plan to bring a pet.

Maine
Balance Rock Inn By-The-Sea
Captain Jefferds Inn
East Wind Inn & Meeting House
Harbor Hill
Hartstone Inn
Inn at Bath
Island View Inn
Weatherby's Fisherman's Resort
White Hart Inn

New Hampshire
Ashburn House
Inn at Crotched Mountain
Olde Orchard Inn
Ram in the Thicket

Vermont
Four Columns Inn
Hugging Bear Inn
Inn on the Common
Ten Acres Lodge
Whitford House Inn

Massachusetts
Clark Tavern Inn
Field Farm Guest House
Harborview Inn
Over Look Inn
Victorian Inn
Walker House
Windsor House

Rhode Island
Four Gables

Connecticut
Applewood Farms Inn
Hearthside Farm

Silvermine Tavern
Sound Reach
Toll Gate Hill

ROMANTIC

Maine
Balance Rock Inn By-the-Sea
Bufflehead Cove Inn
Lake House
Norumbega

New Hampshire
Gibson House
Hannah Davis House
Inn at Thorn Hill
Nestlenook Farm
Sugar Hill Inn

Vermont
Cornucopia of Dorset
Inn at Ormsby Hill
Juniper Hill Inn
Maple Leaf Inn
Rabbit Hill Inn
Shire Inn
Strong House Inn
Twin Farms
Willough Vale Inn

Massachusetts
Acworth Inn
Allen House Victorian Inn

Augustus Snow House
Captain Freeman Inn
Dunscroft-by-the-Sea
Martha's Place
Mary Rockwell Stuart House
Shiverick Inn
Spraycliff
Thorncroft Inn
Wildflower Inn

Rhode Island
Elm Tree Cottage
Hydrangea House Inn
Old Beach Inn
The Villa
Wynstone

Connecticut
Angel Hill
Boulders Inn
Elias Child House
House of 1833
Linden House
Lord Thompson Manor
Riverwind
Steamboat Inn
Stonecroft

RUSTIC

Maine
Goose Cove Lodge
Inn at Bay Ledge
Keeper's House
Lodge at Moosehead Lake
Telemark Inn
Weatherby's Fisherman's Resort

New Hampshire
Bungay Jar Bed & Breakfast
Stafford's in the Field Inn

Vermont
Heermansmith Farm Inn

RUSTIC *(continued)*

Rhode Island
The Roost

Connecticut
Sound Reach

SOLO-ORIENTED

These accommodations are good for solo travelers because they have communal breakfasts, friendly hosts, and many activities on site.

Maine
Admiral Peary House
Bagley House
Captain Jefferds Inn
Captain Lindsey House
Cod Cove Farm
Five Gables Inn
Flying Cloud
Harbor View Inn at Newcastle
Harpswell Inn
Hartwell House
Hawthorn Inn
Homeport Inn
Inn at Canoe Point
Linekin Bay Bed & Breakfast
Manor House
Oakland House
Pomegranate
Schooner Stephen Taber
Telemark Inn
Trellis House
Weston House
White House

New Hampshire
Ashburn House
Follansbee Inn
Glynn House Inn
Goddard Mansion
Hannah Davis House
Harrisville Squire's Inn
Highland Lake Inn
Meredith Inn
Olde Orchard Inn
Rosewood Country Inn
Wildcat Inn and Tavern

Vermont
Charleston House
Inn on Covered Bridge Green
Inn on the Common
Northfield Inn
Thomas Mott Homestead
Tulip Tree Inn
West Hill House
Windham Hill Inn

Massachusetts
Bay Beach Bed and Breakfast
Bed and Breakfast of Sagamore Beach
Field Farm Guest House
Hawthorne Inn
Honeysuckle Hill Bed and Breakfast
Inn at Lewis Bay
Martin House Inn
Mostly Hall
Pineapple Inn
River Bend Farm
Walker House

Rhode Island
1855 Marshall Slocum Guest House
Admiral Dewey Inn
Blue Dory Inn
Bradford-Dimond-Norris House
Cliffside Inn
Four Gables
Hotel Manisses
Ivy Lodge
Murphy's
The Roost
Savana's Inn
Victorian Ladies Inn
Woody Hill

Connecticut

Antiques & Accomodations
Applewood Farms Inn
Chester Bulkley House
Cobbscroft
Elias Child House

House of 1833
Lakeview Inn
Manor House
Merrywood
Palmer Inn
Three Chimneys Inn

SMOKING ALLOWED

These accommodations allow smoking somewhere in the house. Check the profiles for details.

Maine

Balance Rock Inn By-The-Sea
East Wind Inn & Meeting House
Goose Cove Lodge
Gosnold Arms
Greenville Inn
Oakland House
Weatherby's Fisherman's Resort

New Hampshire

Ashburn House
Christmas Farm Inn
Glynn House Inn
Harrisville Squire's Inn
Ram in the Thicket
Red Hill Inn

Massachusetts

Outermost Inn

Rhode Island

Blue Dory Inn
Hotel Manisses
Shelter Harbor Inn
The Villa

Connecticut

Applewood Farms Inn
Lakeview Inn
Roger Sherman Inn
Silvermine Tavern

SWIMMING POOL

Maine

Balance Rock Inn By-The-Sea
Inn at Bay Ledge
John Peters Inn
Old Fort Inn
White Barn Inn

New Hampshire

Bernerhof Inn
Buttonwood Inn
Dexter's Inn and Tennis Club
The Forest
Inn at Crotched Mountain
Inn at Thorn Hill
Manor on Golden Pond
Ram in the Thicket

Red Hill Inn
Sunset Hill House

Vermont

Edson Hill Manor
Four Columns Inn
Inn at Saw Mill Farm
Inn on the Common
Inn at Round Barn Farm
Juniper Hill Inn
October Country Inn
Siebeness
Ten Acres Lodge
Wildflower Inn
Windham Hill Inn

SWIMMING POOL *(continued)*

Massachusetts
Addison Choate Inn
Applegate
Baldwin Hill Farm
Blantyre
Brook Farm Inn
Clark Tavern Inn
Cliffwood Inn
Field Farm Guest House
Gables Inn

Harbor Light Inn
Morins Victorian Hideaway
Windflower

Rhode Island
Historic Jacob Hill Farm
The Villa
Woody Hill

Connecticut
Mayflower Inn

THREE ROOMS OR LESS

Maine
Harbor View Inn at Newcastle
Pleasant Bay

Vermont
Birchwood Bed and Breakfast
Ten Bends on the River

Massachusetts
Amerscot House
Bed and Breakfast of Sagamore Beach
Bishops Bed and Breakfast
Clark Tavern Inn
Morins Victorian Hideaway
Saltbox
Seagull Inn

Rhode Island
1900 House
Four Gables
Green Shadows
Murphy's
One Willow By The Sea
The Roost

Connecticut
Elias Child House
Hearthside Farm
Hilltop Haven
Merrywood
Rosewood Meadow
Sound Reach

TWENTY ROOMS OR MORE

Maine
Captain Lord Mansion
Castine Inn
East Wind Inn & Meeting House
Goose Cove Lodge
White Barn Inn

New Hampshire
Christmas Farm Inn
Manor on Golden Pond
Red Hill Inn
Sunset Hill House

Vermont
Andrie Rose Inn
Edson Hill Manor
Inn at Saw Mill Farm
Inn at Shelburne Farms
North Hero House Country Inn
Wildflower Inn
Windham Hill Inn

Massachusetts
Blantyre
Deerfield Inn

Massachusetts *(continued)*
  Harbor Light Inn
  Mary Prentiss Inn

Rhode Island
  1661 Inn
  Jailhouse Inn
  Shelter Harbor Inn

Connecticut
  Homestead Inn
  Mayflower Inn
  Simsbury 1820 House
  Toll Gate Hill
  White Hart Inn

WATERSIDE

Maine
  Balance Rock Inn By-The-Sea
  Bufflehead Cove Inn
  East Wind Inn & Meeting House
  Edward's Harborside Inn
  Five Gables Inn
  Greenville Inn
  Goose Cove Lodge
  Harbor Hill
  Harpswell Inn
  Inn at Bay Ledge
  Inn at Canoe Point
  Inn at Sunrise Point
  Inn on the Harbor
  Island View Inn
  John Peters Inn
  Keeper's House
  Lake House
  Lodge at Moosehead Lake
  Nannau-Seaside
  Oakland House
  Pleasant Bay, Addison
  Schooner Stephen Taber
  Ullikana
  Weatherby's Fisherman's Resort

New Hampshire
  Covered Bridge House
  Follansbee Inn
  Highland Lake Inn
  Manor on Golden Pond
  Nestlenook Farm
  Notchland Inn

Vermont
  Green Trails Inn
  Inn at Shelburne Farms
  North Hero House Country Inn
  Ten Bends on the River
  Thomas Mott Homestead
  Willard Street Inn
  Willough Vale Inn

Massachusetts
  Bay Beach Bed and Breakfast
  Bed and Breakfast of Sagamore Beach
  Bishops Bed and Breakfast
  Diamond District Breakfast Inn
  Dunscroft-by-the-Sea
  Eden Pines Inn
  George Fuller House
  Harborview Inn
  Historic Merrell Inn
  Miles River Country Inn
  Morins Victorian Hideaway
  Outermost Inn
  Scargo Manor Bed and Breakfast
  Seagull Inn
  Spraycliff

Rhode Island
  1661 Inn
  Cliffside
  Elm Tree Cottage
  Four Gables
  Sea Breeze Inn
  Stone Lea

WATERSIDE *(continued)*

Rhode Island *(continued)*
Watch Hill Inn
Weather Bureau Inn

Connecticut
Bee and Thistle Inn
Boulders Inn

French Bulldog Bed & Breakfast
   and Antiques
Lakeview Inn
Silvermine Tavern
Stonecroft
Steamboat Inn

Introduction

How Come "Unofficial"?

The book in your hands is part of a unique travel and lifestyle guidebook series begun in 1985 with *The Unofficial Guide to Walt Disney World.* That guide, a comprehensive, behind-the-scenes, hands-on prescription for getting the most out of a complex amusement park facility, spawned a series of like titles: *The Unofficial Guide to Chicago, The Unofficial Guide to New Orleans,* and so on. Today, dozens of *Unofficial Guides* help millions of savvy readers navigate some of the world's more complex destinations and situations.

The *Unofficial Guides to Bed & Breakfasts and Country Inns in New England* continues the tradition of insightful, incisive, cut-to-the-chase information, presented in an accessible, easy-to-use format. Unlike in some popular books, no property can pay to be included—those reviewed are solely our choice. And we don't simply rehash the promotional language of these establishments. We visit the good, the bad, and the quirky. We finger the linens, chat with the guests, and sample the scones. We screen hundreds of lodgings, affirming or debunking the acclaimed, discovering or rejecting the new and the obscure. In the end, we present detailed profiles of the lodgings we feel represent the best of the best, select lodgings representing a broad range of prices and styles within each geographic region.

We also include introductions for each state and zone to give you an idea of the nearby general attractions; these introductions also feature helpful phone numbers and websites for further, open-ended information. Area maps with the properties marked help you pinpoint your general destination. And detailed "best of" lists (see pp. xxxiv–xlviii) help you look up properties by categories and lead you to places that best fit your needs.

With *The Unofficial Guides to Bed & Breakfasts and Country Inns,* we strive to help you find the perfect lodging for every trip. This guide is unofficial because we answer to no one but you.

Letters, Comments, and Questions from Readers

We expect to learn from our mistakes, as well as from the input of our readers, and to improve with each book and edition. Many of those who use the *Unofficial Guides* write to us to ask questions, make comments, or share their own discoveries and lessons learned. We appreciate all such input, both positive and critical, and encourage our readers to continue writing. Readers' comments and observations will contribute immeasurably to the improvement of revised editions of the *Unofficial Guides.*

How to Write the Author

Lea Lane
The Unofficial Guide to Bed & Breakfasts and Country Inns in New England
P.O. Box 43673
Birmingham, AL 35243

When you write, be sure to put your return address on your letter as well as on the envelope—they may get separated. And remember, our work takes us out of the office for long periods of research, so forgive us if our response is delayed. If you prefer, use our email address, unofficialguides@ menasharidge.com.

What Makes It a Bed-and-Breakfast or Inn?

Comparing the stale, sterile atmosphere of most hotels and motels to the typical bed-and-breakfast experience—cozy guestroom, intimate parlor, friendly hosts, fresh-baked cookies, a delicious breakfast—why stay anywhere *other than* a bed-and-breakfast or inn? But this isn't a promotional piece for the bed-and-breakfast/country inn life; they are not hotels. Here are some of the differences:

A bed-and-breakfast or country inn, as we define it, is a small property— from about 3 to 25 guestrooms (with a few exceptions), with hosts around, a distinct personality, individually decorated rooms, and breakfast included in the price (again, with a few exceptions). Many of these smaller properties have owners living right there; in others, the owners are nearby, a phone call away. **For our purposes, the only difference between an inn and a bed-and-breakfast is that the inn serves dinner on a regular basis.**

Recently, the bed-and-breakfast and small inn trade has taken off—with mixed results. This growth, for the most part, has taken place on both fronts: the low and high end. As bed-and-breakfasts gain popularity, anyone with a spare bedroom can pop an ad in the Yellow Pages for "Billy's Bedroom B&B." These enterprises generally lack professionalism, don't keep regular hours or days of operation, are often unlicensed, and were avoided in this guide.

On the other end of the spectrum are luxury premises with more amenities than the finest hotels. Whether historic homes or lodgings built to be bed-and-breakfasts or inns, interiors are posh, baths are private and *en suite,* and breakfasts are gourmet affairs. In-room whirlpool tubs and fireplaces are *de rigueur,* and extras range from in-room refrigerators (perhaps stocked with champagne) to complimentary high tea to free use of state-of-the-art recreational equipment to . . . the list goes on! (One longtime innkeeper, whose historic home was tidily and humbly maintained by hours of elbow grease and common sense, dubbed this new state of affairs "the amenities war.")

The result is an industry in which a simple homestay bed-and-breakfast with a shared bath and common rooms can be a budget experience, while a new, upscale bed-and-breakfast can be the luxury venue of a lifetime.

Who Stays at Bed-and-Breakfasts and Inns?

American travelers are finally catching on to what Europeans have known for a long time. Maybe it's a backlash against a cookie-cutter, strip-mall landscape, or longing for a past that maybe never was, and for an idealized, short-term interaction with others. Maybe it's a need for simple pleasures in a world over-the-top with theme parks and high-tech wonders. Who can say for sure?

The bed-and-breakfast trade has grown so large that it includes niches catering to virtually every need. Some bed-and-breakfasts and small inns are equipped to help travelers conduct business, others provide turn-down service and fresh flowers by the honeymooners' canopied bed, and still others offer amenities for reunions or conferences. Whatever your needs, there is a bed-and-breakfast or small inn tailored to your expectations. The challenge, and one this guide was designed to help you meet, is sifting through the choices until you find the perfect place.

Romantics

More and more, properties are establishing at least one room or suite with fireplace, whirlpool, canopied king, and the trappings of romance. Theme rooms can also be especially fun for fantasizing. Always check out the privacy factor. Sometimes a property that caters to families has a carriage house in the back, or a top-floor room away from the others. If an inn allows children under 16, don't be surprised if it's noisy; look for ones that are for older children or adults only.

Families

Face it Moms and Dads: rumpled surroundings will sometimes have to be accepted where children are welcome. You may have to give up pristine décor and breakfast tea served in bone china for the relaxed, informal mood, but on the upside, you won't have to worry as much about Caitlin or Michael knocking over the Wedgwood collection on the sideboard.

When an establishment says kids are "welcome," that usually means a really kid-friendly place. Check the age restrictions. If your children are under-aged but well-behaved, let the host know; often they will make exceptions. (But be sure it's true—other guests are counting on it.) On the flip side, honeymooners or other folks who might prefer common areas free of crayons, and breakfasts without sugar-frosted confetti, may want to look elsewhere.

Generally, bed-and-breakfasts are not ideal for high-action kids. But if your children enjoy games, puzzles, books, a chance for quiet pleasures and meeting others; if they don't need TVs, and can be counted on to be thoughtful and follow instructions ("whisper before 9 a.m.," "don't put your feet on the table"), you and your kids can have a wonderful experience together—and so can the rest of the guests.

Business Travelers

For individual business travelers, bed-and-breakfasts and small inns are becoming much more savvy at anticipating your needs, but in differing degrees. While phone lines and data ports are fairly common, they vary from one bed-and-breakfast to another. Some say they offer data ports when in fact they have two phone jacks in every room but only one phone line servicing the entire property. This can be fine for a three-room inn in the off-season, but if you're trying to conduct business, look for properties with private lines and/or dedicated data ports. If in doubt, ask. Rooms are often available with desks, but these also vary, particularly in surface area and quality of lighting. If this is an important feature, ask for specifics and make sure you secure a room with a desk when you reserve.

Some establishments even offer couriers, secretarial support, and laundry/dry cleaning. And for business travelers who don't have time to take advantage of a leisurely and sumptuous breakfast, hosts often provide an early-morning alternative, sometimes continental, sometimes full.

Finally, there are the intangibles to consider. After the sterile atmosphere of the trade show, meeting hall, or boardroom, a small inn or bed-and-breakfast with a friendly host, a plate of cookies, and a fine dinner are nice to come home to.

The atmosphere is also a plus for business meetings or seminars: the relaxed surroundings are conducive to easy-going give and take. During the week when guestrooms are often available, bed-and-breakfasts and small inns are usually eager to host business groups. Discounts are often included and special services such as catering and equipment are offered if you rent the entire property. But forget weekends; these properties are still tourist-oriented.

Independents

If you are on your own, small lodgings are ideal. Look for a place with single rates, and even if a special rate isn't listed, you can often negotiate a small discount. If you want some interaction, just sit in the parlor, lounge, or common rooms, and talk to people before meals. Most of the time if you're friendly and interested, you'll get an invite to join someone at a table. You could talk to the innkeepers about this even before you arrive, and they might fix you up with friendly folks. (And if you are traveling with others, invite a single to join you.) As for breakfast, communal tables are perfect for singles. Note our profiles to choose properties with that in mind.

Groups

Whether you are part of a wedding, reunion, or just a group of people who want to travel together, an inn or bed-and-breakfast is a delightful place to stay. The atmosphere is special, your needs are taken care of in a personal way, the grounds are most often spacious and lovely, and in the evening you can all retire in close proximity. (Remember the Alan Alda movie, *The Four Seasons,* filmed at one of our New England inns?) It's especially fun when you take over the whole place—so you may want to choose an especially small property if that's your goal.

Those with Special Needs

Look in our entries for mention of disabled facilities or access. Then call for details to determine just how extensive the accessibility is. Remember also that these houses are usually quite old, and owners of a small bed-and-breakfast will not have a team of accessibility experts on retainer, so be specific with your questions. If doorways must be a certain width to accommodate a wheelchair or walker, know how many inches before you call; if stairs are difficult for Great Aunt Agnes, don't neglect to find out how many are present outside, as well as inside. And if a property that seems otherwise special doesn't seem to have facilities, perhaps you can patch things together, such as a room on the first floor. Realistically, though, most of these properties were built with many stairs and steps, and are situated on hilltops or in rural terrain—so you will have to choose very carefully.

If you suffer from allergies or aversions, talk it over when you book and a good innkeeper will make every attempt to accommodate you. As for food, if you request a special meal and give enough notice, you can often get what you like. That's one of the joys of a small, personalized property.

You and Your Hosts

Hosts are the heart of your country inn or bed-and-breakfast experience and color all aspects of the stay. They can make or break a property, and sometimes an unassuming place will be the most memorable of all because of the care and warmth of the hosts. Typically, they are well versed in navigating the area, and can be a wealth of "insider information" on restaurants, sightseeing, and the like.

While many—most, in these guides—hosts live on the premises, they often have designed or remodeled their building so that their living quarters are separate. Guests often have their own living room, den, parlor, and sitting room; you may be sharing with other guests, but not so much with your hosts. The degree of interaction between host families and guests varies greatly; we try to give a feel for the extremes in the *Comments* section of each profile. In most cases, hosts are accessible but not intrusive; they will swing through the common areas and chat a bit, but are sensitive to guests' need for privacy. But sometimes hosts are in another building altogether; in the other extreme, you are intimately sharing living space with your hosts. This intimate, old-style bed-and-breakfast arrangement is called a "homestay." We try to note this.

In short, most of our hosts are gracious in accommodating travelers' needs, and many are underpinning their unique small lodging with policies and amenities from hotel-style lodgings. But bed-and-breakfasts and small inns are not The Sheraton, and being cognizant of the differences can make your experience more pleasant.

Planning Your Visit

When You Choose

If you're not sure where you want to travel, browse through our listings. Maybe from an introduction or from a description of a property, you'll find something to spark your interest.

If you know you are going to a certain location, note the properties in that zone, and then read the entries. You can also call for brochures or take a further look at websites, especially to see rooms or to book directly.

We've provided a listing of some useful websites; others categorized by state and region are in their respective section introductions.

HELPFUL WEBSITES

www.virtualcities.com	www.bbchannel.com
www.bbonline.com	www.bnbcity.com
www.bnbinns.com	www.epicurious.com
www.getawayguides.com	www.innbook.com
www.inns.com	www.innsnorthamerica.com
www.johansens.com	www.relaischateaux.fr/[name of inn]
www.travel.com/accom/bb/usa	www.travelguide.com
www.trip.com	www.triple1.com
www.virtualcities.com	

When You Book

Small properties usually require booking on your own. Some travel agents will help you out on this but may charge a fee, because many small properties don't give travel agent commissions. The fastest, easiest way to book is through the Internet or through a reservation service, but if you have special needs or questions, we suggest contacting properties directly to get exactly what you want.

Ask about any special needs or requirements, and make sure your requests are clear. Most of these properties are not designed for people in wheelchairs, so be sure to ask ahead of time if you need that accessibility. Specify what's important to you—privacy, king-size bed, fireplace, tub versus shower, view, first-floor access. A host won't necessarily know what you want, so make sure you decide what is important—writing it down will help you remember. Note the room you want by name, or ask for the "best" room, if you're not sure. Remember to ask about parking conditions—does the property have off-street parking or will you have to find a place on the street? And if air-conditioning is a must for you, always inquire—some bed-and-breakfasts do not have it.

Verify prices and conditions, and any factors or amenities that are important to you. The best time to call is in the early afternoon, before new guests arrive for the day and when hosts have the most free time. Book as soon as possible; for weekends and holidays, preferred properties could be filled a year or more in advance.

A Word about Negotiating Rates

Negotiating a good rate can be more straightforward at a bed-and-breakfast or country inn than at a hotel. For starters, the person on the other end of the line will probably be the owner and will have the authority to offer you a discount. Secondly, the bed-and-breakfast/inn owner has a smaller number of rooms and guests to keep track of than does a hotel manager and won't have to do a lot of checking to know that something is available. Also, because the number of rooms is small, each room is more important. In a bed-and-breakfast or inn with four rooms, the rental of each room increases the occupancy rate by 25%.

To get the best rate, just ask. If the owner expects a full house, you'll probably get a direct and honest "no deal." On the other hand, if there are rooms and you are sensitive about price, perhaps you'll get a break. In either event, be polite and don't make unreasonable requests. If you are overbearing or contentious on the phone, the proprietor may suddenly discover no rooms available.

Some Considerations

Like snowflakes, no two bed-and-breakfasts are alike. Some are housed in historic homes or other buildings (churches, fraternal halls, barns, castles . . . !). Some are humble and cozy, some are grand and opulent. Some are all in one building, while others are scattered among individual, free-standing units. Some offer a breakfast over which you'll want to linger for hours, others . . . well, others make a darn good muffin. Small lodgings are less predictable than hotels and motels, but can be much more interesting. A few aficionados have discovered that "interesting" sometimes comes at a price. This guide takes the "scary" out of "interesting" and presents only places that meet a certain standard of cleanliness, predictability, and amenities. However, there are certain questions and issues common to bed-and-breakfasts and country inns that first-time visitors should consider:

Choosing Your Room

Check out your room before lugging your luggage (not having elevators is usually part of the charm). This is standard procedure at small properties, and saves time and trouble should you prefer another room. When a guest room has an open door, it usually means the proud innkeeper wants you to peek. You may just find a room that you like better than the one you are assigned, and it may be available, so ask.

Bathrooms

Americans are picky about their potties. While the traditional (sometimes referred to as "European-style") bed-and-breakfast set-up involved several bedrooms sharing a bath, this is becoming less common. Even venerable Victorians are being remodeled to include private baths. In fact, many bed-and-breakfasts and inns offer ultra-luxurious bath facilities, including jetted tubs, dual vanities, and so forth. Our advice is not to reject shared bath facilities out of hand as these can be excellent values. Do check the bedroom-to-bath ratio, however. Two rooms sharing a bath can be excellent; three or more can be problematic with a full house.

Security

Many small properties have property locks and room locks as sophisticated as those at hotels and motels. Others do not. For the most part, inns with 3½ stars or more have quality locks throughout the premises. (Many with lower rankings do as well.) Beyond locks, however, most bed-and-breakfasts provide an additional measure of security in that they are small properties, generally in a residential district, and typically with live-in hosts on the premises. Single female travelers might find a measure of security in coming "home" to a facility like this as opposed to a 150-room hotel with a cardlock system but God-knows-what lurking in the elevator.

Privacy

At a hotel, you can take your key and hole up in solitude for the duration of your stay. It's a little harder at a bed-and-breakfast, especially if you take part in a family-style breakfast (although many inns offer the option of an early continental breakfast if you're pressed for time or feeling antisocial, and some offer en suite breakfast service—these options are noted in the profiles). Most hosts we've met are very sensitive to guests' needs for privacy, and seem to have a knack for being as helpful or as unobtrusive as you wish. If privacy is hard to achieve at a given property, we've noted that in the profile.

Autonomy

Most bed-and-breakfasts provide a key to the front door and/or an unlocked front door certain hours of the day. While you might be staying in a family-style atmosphere, you are seldom subject to rules such as a curfew. (A few properties request that guests be in by a specific time; these policies are noted and rare.) Some places have "quiet hours," usually from about 10 or 11 p.m. until about 7 a.m. Such policies tend to be in place when properties lack sufficient sound insulation, and are noted in the profile. Generally, higher ratings tend to correspond with better sound insulation.

What the Ratings Mean

We have organized this book so that you can get a quick idea of each property by checking out the ratings, reading the information at the beginning of each entry and then, if you're interested, reading the more detailed overview of each property. Obviously ratings are subjective, and people of good faith (and good taste) can and do differ. But you'll get a good, relative idea, and the ability to quickly compare properties.

Overall Rating   The overall ratings are represented by stars, which range in number from one to five and represent our opinion of the quality of the property as a whole. It corresponds something like this:

★★★★★	The Best
★★★★½	Excellent
★★★★	Very Good
★★★½	Good
★★★	Good enough
★★½	Fair
★★	Not so good
★½	Barely Acceptable
★	Unacceptable

The overall rating for the bed-and-breakfast or country inn experience includes all factors of the property including guest rooms and also public rooms, food, facilities, grounds, maintenance, hosts and something we'll called "specialness," for lack of a better phrase. Many times it involves the personalities and personal touches of the hosts.

Some properties have fairly equal star levels for all of these things, but most have some qualities that are better than others. Also, large, ambitious properties that serve dinner would tend to have a slightly higher star rating for the same level of qualities than a smaller property (the difference, say, between a great novel and a great short story; the larger it is the harder it is to pull off, hence the greater the appreciation). Yet a small property can earn five stars with a huge dose of "specialness."

Overall ratings and room quality ratings do not always correspond. While guest rooms may be spectacular, the rest of the inn may be average, or vice versa. Generally though, we've found through the years that a property is usually consistently good, or bad, throughout.

Room Quality Rating   Using the star system, the quality ratings represent our opinion of the quality of the guest rooms and bathrooms only. For the room quality ratings we factored in view, size, closet space, bedding, seating, desks, lighting, soundproofing, comfort, bathrooms (or lack), style, privacy, soundproofing, decor, "taste," and other intangibles. A really great private bathroom with a claw-foot tub and antique table might bring up the rating of an otherwise average room. Conversely, poor maintenance or lack of good lighting will lower the rating of a spacious, well-decorated room. Sometimes a few rooms are really special while others are standard, and we have averaged these, where possible. It's difficult to codify this, but all factors are weighed, and the grades seem to come up easily, something like this:

★★★★★	Excellent
★★★★	Very Good
★★★	Good
★★	Acceptable
★	Poor

Value Rating   The value ratings—also using the star system—are a combination of the overall and room quality ratings, divided by the cost of an average guest room. They are an indication rather than a scientific formulation—a general idea of value for money. If getting a good deal means the most to you, choose a property by looking at the value rating. Otherwise, the numbers and stars are better indicators of a satisfying experience. An inn or bed and breakfast rating ★★★★★ in all categories (value, room quality, and overall rating) would be ideal, but most often, you'll find a ★★★ value, and you are getting your money's worth. If a wonderful property is fairly priced, it may only get a ★★★ value rating, but you still might prefer the experience to an average property that gets an ★★★★★ value rating.

Price   Our price range is the lowest-priced room in low season to the highest-priced room in high season. The range does not usually include specially priced times such as holidays and foliage season. It is a room rate, based on double occupancy, and assumes that breakfast is included. It does not assume that other meals are included in the rate. However, be sure to check the inn's Food & Drink category. If meals other than breakfast are included in your room rate, we will have noted MAP, which stands for the hotel industry's standard Modified American Plan, in the Food & Drink category. Lodgings where MAP is applicable offer breakfast and dinner in the room rate. Unless specifically noted, prices quoted in the formats do not include gratuities or state taxes, which can be fairly steep. Gratuities are optional; use your own discretion. Prices change constantly, so check before booking.

The Profiles Clarified

The bulk of information about properties is straightforward, but much of it is in abbreviated style, so the following clarifications may help. They are arranged in the order they appear in the profile format.

Many of the properties in this book have similar names or even the same name; for example, there are two Homestead Inns in Connecticut, one in New Milford and one in Greenwich. Town names, too, can be strikingly similar. Make sure you don't confuse properties or town names when selecting an inn.

Location

First, check the map for location. Our directions are designed to give you a general idea of the property's location. For more complete directions, call the property when you are in town.

Building

This category denotes the design and architecture of the building. Many of the properties in the *Unofficial Guides* are historically and architecturally interesting. Here are a few architectural terms you may want to brush up on, in no particular order: Painted Lady, hip-roof, Colonial, Federal, Queen Ann, Doric column, Shingle, King's Lumber, Pumpkin Pine, Bird's Eye Maple, Tiger Maple, Rumford fireplace, Georgian, Victorian, Arts and Crafts, English Aesthetic, Eastlake, Greek Revival, Gingerbread, 12-over-12 windows, claw-foot tub. The more you know the jargon, the better you can select the property you want.

Food & Drink

For food and drink, we offer a taste of the inn or bed-and-breakfast, so to speak. Most properties go all out to fill you up at breakfast, so that you could easily skip lunch (factor that into the value). In some areas, however, the tourist board regulates that properties can only serve a continental breakfast without a hot dish. Note whether we state "full breakfast," if that experience is paramount. In most cases, a bed-and-breakfast breakfast—even a continental—tends to include more homemade items, greater selection, and greater care in presentation.

In this category, what we call "specialties" are really typical dishes, which may not always be served, but should give you a good idea of the cuisine. And a very few bed-and-breakfasts and inns do not include the breakfast in the price. However, it is almost always offered as an option.

Many inns and bed-and-breakfasts offer afternoon tea, snacks or sherry or pre-dinner wine and cheese. If a property offers tea in the afternoon, we have noted so in this Food & Drink category by just stating "tea." Note that if an inn offers meals to the public as well as guests, the atmosphere becomes less personal. Also, if have noted MAP in this category, it means that the inn offers meals other than breakfast as part of the room rate.

Some inns provide alcoholic beverages to guests, some forbid consumption of alcohol—either extreme is noted in the inn's profile. The norm is that alcohol consumption is a private matter, and guests may bring and consume their own, if they do so respectfully. Glassware is generally provided. Bed-and-breakfasts are not well suited to drunkenness and partying.

A diet and a bed-and-breakfast or small inn go together about as well as a haystack and a lighted match. Come prepared to eat. If calories matter, a bed-and-breakfast will give you less guilt than an inn, as breakfast can easily last till an afternoon snack, and for dinner you can go lightly. Inns make that much, much harder, as often the prices for dinner are built in, and even when they aren't the aromas will lure even the most disciplined calorie-counter to the dining room. Dinners are usually served charmingly, with flowers, candlelight, crystal, silver, and so forth. Some bed-and-breakfasts will serve dinner on request, and we included that info when it was available.

Most properties are sensitive to dietary needs and preferences, but need to be warned of this in advance. When you make your reservation, be sure to explain if you are living with diabetes, have a wheat- or dairy-intolerance, are a vegetarian/vegan, or are otherwise restricted. Many proprietors pride themselves on accommodating special diets.

Recreation

We do not usually spell out whether the activities noted in the format are on-site. With some exceptions, assume that golf, tennis, fishing, canoeing, downhill skiing, and the like are not on-site (since these are small properties, not resorts). Assume that games and smaller recreational activities are on the property. But there are exceptions, so ask.

Amenities & Services

These blend a bit. Generally, amenities include extras such as swimming pools and games, or services such as business support and turning down beds in the evening. Business travelers should note if any services are mentioned, also if there are public rooms, group discounts, and so forth to back them up. Almost all bed-and-breakfasts and inns can provide advice regarding touring, restaurants, and local activities; many keep maps and brochures on hand.

Deposit

Unless otherwise noted, "refund" usually means "minus a service charge," which varies from $10 or so to 50% or more. The more popular the property, usually the more deposit you'll have to put down, and the further ahead. When canceling after the site's noted policy, most will still refund, less a fee, if the room is re-rented. Check back on this.

Discounts

Discounts may extend to singles, long-stay guests, kids, seniors, packages, groups and extra people in a room, even though not listed in the text. It doesn't hurt to ask, as these sorts of things are especially flexible in small establishments, mid-week, off-season, last-minute, when innkeepers may want to fill their rooms.

Credit Cards

For those properties that do accept credit cards (we note those that do not), we've listed credit cards accepted with the following codes:

V	VISA	MC	MasterCard
AE	American Express	D	Discover
DC	Diner's Club International	CB	Carte Blanche

Check-in/Out

As small operators, most bed-and-breakfast hosts need to know approximately when you'll be arriving. Many have check-in periods (specified in the profiles) during which the hosts or staff will be available to greet you. Most can accommodate arrival beyond their stated check-in period, but need to be advised so they can arrange to be home or get a key to you. Think about it—they have to buy groceries and go to the kids' soccer games and get to doctors' appointments just like you. And they have to sleep sometime. Don't show up at 11:30 p.m. and expect a smiling bellhop—the same person who lets you in is probably going to be up at 5 or 6 a.m. slicing mushrooms for your omelet!

Check-in times are often flexible, but, as with any commercial lodging, check-out times can be critical, as the innkeeper must clean and prepare your room for incoming guests. If you need to stay longer, ask and you'll often get an extension. Sometimes, a host will let you leave your bags and enjoy the common areas after check-out, as long as you vacate your room.

Please take cancellation policies seriously. A "no-show" is not a cancellation! If an establishment has a seven-day, or 72-hour, or whatever, cancellation policy, you are expected to call and cancel your reservation prior to that time, or you could be liable for up to the full amount of your reserved stay. After all, a four-unit bed-and-breakfast has lost 25% of its revenue if you arbitrarily decide not to show up.

Smoking

We've indicated in the inn's profile if smoking is banned outright, or if there are designated rooms where it's allowed. Usually it's fine to smoke outside, what with the excellent ventilation, but ask your hosts before you light up. Be mindful, too, of how you dispose of the butts—when you flick them into a nearby shrub, it's likely that your hosts, not some sanitation team, will be plucking them out next week.

Pets

We have not mentioned most of the inn-house pets in the profiles, as this situation changes even more frequently than most items. Many properties have pets on the premises. Don't assume that because an establishment does not allow guests to bring pets that pets aren't around. Dogs and cats and birds (and monkeys, pigs, goats, llamas, etc.) are often around. If you foresee a problem with this, be sure to clarify "how around," before booking. If properties allow pets, we have noted this, but most do not. And if you can't bear to leave your own beloved Fido or Miss Kitty for long periods, and want to stay in an inn that does not allow them, good innkeepers often know of reputable boarding facilities nearby.

Open

Properties often claim they are open all year, but they can close at any time; at the last minute for personal reasons or if business is slow. Similarly, properties that close during parts of the year may open specially for groups. If you can get a bunch of family or friends together, it's a great way to stay at popular inns and bed-and-breakfasts that would be otherwise hard to book. And remember, in low-season things slow down, dinners may not be served, and even when some properties are "open," they may be half-closed.

An Important Note

Facts and situations change constantly in the small-lodging business. Innkeepers get divorced, prices go up, puppies arrive, chefs quit in the middle of a stew, and rooms get redecorated, upgraded and incorporated. So use this format as a means to get a good overall idea of the property, and then inquire when you book about the specific details that matter most. Changes will definitely occur, so check to be sure.

Making the Most of Your Stay

Once you're settled in, it's a good idea to scope out the entire place, or you may not realize until too late that your favorite book was on the shelf, or that an old-fashioned swing would have swung you into the moonlight on a warm evening. If you are alone in the inn, it can feel like the property is yours (and that, in fact, is a good reason to go midweek or off-season).

Do take advantage of the special charms of these lodgings: the fireplace, the piano, other guests, the gardens. What makes a bed-and-breakfast or inn experience an integral part of a trip are small moments that can become cherished memories.

Did you love it? You can perhaps duplicate in your daily life some of the touches that made the experience special, whether it was warm towels, an early weekend breakfast by candlelight, or a special recipe for stuffed French toast. Hosts usually enjoy sharing ideas and recipes.

A country inn or bed-and-breakfast, perhaps set in a village or town where at least a few blocks retain a look of history and often grace, encourages you to relax, lie back, unwind, open up, read, talk, get romantic, dream, slow down, look up at the stars and down at the grass, smell the coffee—and of course, the roses climbing on the pergola or lining the walkway. These small lodgings are stress-busters, far away from sitcoms and fast food and the media mania *du jour*. They are cozy places to settle into and curl up with a book, or a honey, or a dream. Or, if you must, a laptop and a cell phone.

New England Bed-and-Breakfasts and Country Inns

The six New England states seem to have more small inns and bed-and-breakfasts than anywhere else in the country. And some of them, for sure, are among the best in the world. Properties are scattered from the shores of Connecticut, Rhode Island, and Massachusetts's Cape and islands to the isolated peninsulas of Maine; from New Hampshire and Vermont mountaintops to the historic cities of Hartford, Providence, Newport, Portland, and Boston. By beaches, streams, greens, glittering lakes, hardwood forests, in picture-perfect hamlets, or rolling, stone-walled pastures—you're never very far from special lodging in this magnificent, historic region.

The character of these properties reflects the character of New England. You'll find sea captains' houses, some crammed to their mahogany rafters with world treasures; turreted Victorian "Painted Ladies" in mauve and cream and bottle green and rose with wraparound porches, where prosperous folks from another age used to gossip and rock on summer evenings; and farmhouse parlors that still overlook awesome views of fields and beyond.

From thousands of possibilities we have listed 600 properties throughout the New England area. We have chosen to profile 300 of them, not only well-known classics, but also new, interesting, odd, and unusual ones. Bed-and-breakfasts and inns in this *Unofficial Guide* include a lighthouse with an outhouse, a hand-hewn log cabin, Sinclair Lewis' farm (perhaps the most luxurious small inn in the world), and a schooner that plies the Maine coast. One bed-and-breakfast has 8,000 teddy bears, another a theme of apples throughout; one has its own in-house radio station, another, a room dedicated to Princess Di; and many harbor (usually friendly) ghosts.

Whether lavish summer cottages and mansions or spare saltboxes and basic old houses, most have a long, sometimes fascinating history. Lodgings were once weather bureaus, jails, barns, general stores, mills, factories, museums, taverns, churches, post offices, or schools, and some still are horse, goat, dairy, or llama farms. Even the little bed-and-breakfasts that may seem "nothing special" were carefully selected for something special—whether it is one luxurious room, a great view, a convenient location, delicious food, a warm host, or a unique feature.

In a great inn or bed-and-breakfast everything just seems to come together effortlessly, but a huge amount of work is needed, from maintenance to decoration and food preparation. The innkeepers are key. Over the years, we have seen properties go from average to great, and back. New hosts can turn a loser into a winner, or can take away the charm of a property even when everything seems the same on the surface.

That stereotypical New England reserve occasionally shows up in property innkeepers, but most are engaging and helpful. Most work full-time at hosting, but many are part of a couple in which one partner works at another job. Some innkeep from Bora Bora with a manager on site, but most owners are right there, and the smaller the property, the more likely you are to interact, if that's your choice.

In this group of 300 profiled properties, our innkeepers include a former pro football player, an FBI agent, a soap opera actor, a former U.S. Congressman, feminists, a director of a New York ballet company, a mailman, opera singers, socialites, CEOs, poets, painters, musicians, sports enthusiasts, James Taylor's brother, Matt Damon's cousin, and so on. Their hobbies and collections and cooking abilities vary widely, and we've tried to mention them if we think you'd be interested. City folk, people from all over the country, and locals—all have the goal of hospitality, and some are truly gifted at it.

Returning to an inn after a crisp autumn day, welcomed by a friendly host; enjoying lobster soufflé and glass of chardonnay by a crackling fire; retiring to a canopied four-poster under hand-sewn down quilts; waking up to the smell of blueberry muffins, bacon, and brewing coffee; and the warmth of fellow travelers—these are as much a delight of a trip to New England as the blazing leaves or a steepled church on a village green. Indeed, the lodging at the end of the day can be an end in itself.

Some Background on New England Small Lodgings

Venerable New England lodgings like The Hawthorne Inn have been around since Nathaniel Hawthorne himself (who lived across the road). But in the past, where you stayed wasn't why you went. People vacationed all summer at resorts in Maine or went to lodges in Vermont or motels on the Cape for a couple of weeks, but short getaways weren't in style, and "long weekends" were concepts of the future.

But many artisans and youth who traveled the world in the 1960s and 1970s came back to New England and opened bed-and-breakfasts like the ones they stayed in overseas (maybe with a craft workshop in the attic or barn, in which to build handmade furnishings and art). Then there were the professionals who dropped out of the rat race to open an inn or bed-and-breakfast in a gentrified old house or building, with a goal of family togetherness and a laid-back life.

Today, the newest legion of bed-and-breakfast and country-inn owners—sophisticated and particular, many with hotel or cooking school backgrounds—are taking the small lodging experience to new, sophisticated, and even fantasy levels and creating an art form as varied as jazz. But the talent, artistry, and personality of the great innkeepers are a constant refrain.

Ten Reasons to Get Out and Go

"Beauty is its own excuse for being," wrote local boy Ralph Waldo Emerson, who knew his way around these parts. We'd add, "The place to stay is its own excuse for going"—the only reason you need to drive around New England is to arrive at the place you are staying.

But some of you may need a more motivating prompt to get up and out in New England. State tourist boards offer free material about each area, and the Internet has much information as well. Here are a few more excuses to get going:

1. Shop. This part of the country is crammed with antiques, crafts, and discount outlets. Save your special-occasion, decorating, or holiday shopping for these excursions. Empty your car's trunk, and load up.

2. Retrace history. This is, after all, where the Pilgrims landed and the American Revolution began. This is where the Underground Railway hid slaves, and ship captains and merchants made fortunes and then created art colonies and wealthy enclaves, and where farmers and millworkers toiled. Read up on the history of the area, and visit historic sites.

3. Experience the full glory of seasons. Fall color here, one of the greatest concentrations in the world, is justly famous, and draws leaf-peeping visitors in crowds throughout late September and October. But summer in Maine and at the beaches of Connecticut, Rhode Island, and Massachusetts and winter in Vermont and New Hampshire are just as definitive. Spring is chancy and short in New England, with a spring mud season that is messy. But we love maple-sugar tapping in April and the hatchlings and buds and the roaring brooks and the empty trails and back roads. It's the best time for birding, fishing, biking, and shopping uncrowded stores. And the best time to get a room at popular bed-and-breakfasts and inns.

4. Make a college tour. Just for fun. Some of the most beautiful campuses in the world are in New England. From Harvard Yard to Bennington's artsy campus, from Amherst to UConn to Brown to Wesleyan, Smith, and Wellesley—just walking them gives you opportunity for nostalgia and dreams. The towns are charming. Museums are frequent: Williams and Yale are especially notable. Architecture on campuses is some of the best and most interesting in the country. And bed-and-breakfasts and inns are often a walk away from the campuses, so you can cut down on driving.

5. Study and note the flora and fauna. Bird or whale watch. Study the geology and collect examples of different rocks. Learn the state flowers and animals. Lupines in Maine, rose hips on Cape Cod, hydrangeas in Newport—each area has its specialty.

6. Seek out your favorite recreation, whether it's skiing, golf, water sports, horseback riding, hunting. New England has it. At a minimum, you can bike or walk.

7. Learn about architecture and furnishings, and see how many styles you can find.

8. Enjoy a local festival. Americana is charming, and in New England, local fairs, meets, swaps, and parades celebrate it throughout the year.

9. Meet people. Staying at a bed-and-breakfast or inn is one of the nicest, easiest ways to talk to others, even make friends. Just be open, ask questions, smile.

10. Be an unofficial Unofficial correspondent. Look out for new or special properties not profiled in the book. If you provide us with five new lodgings that we choose to visit and write about in the next edition, we'll credit you and send a copy when the edition is published. That's reason enough to get out into the gorgeous New England countryside.

A Few of My Favorite Things

This is a highly personal and short list of specific pleasures from bed-and-breakfasts and country inns of New England.

Property Names

- A Little Dream
- Mostly Hall
- Night with a Native
- The Ram in the Thicket
- Tootsies

- Bungay Jar
- Mucky Duck
- Outermost Inn
- The White House
- Ullikana

Special Dishes

- Pan-roasted buffalo with mustard-maple demi glacé, The Inn on the Common, Craftsbury Common, Vermont
- Stuffed corn with scrambled eggs, Harborview, Newcastle, Maine
- Sunflower crêpes with pansy butter, Wildflower Inn, Falmouth, Massachusetts
- Earl Grey mousse with laurel syrup, The Castine Inn, Castine, Maine

Miscellany

- Newburyport, Massachusetts: A fine hidden gem of an old whaling port, just north of Boston; the commuter train has arrived, so be sure to see it before it becomes too exurban
- The Tamworth area of New Hampshire: The drive through the forest and by the old playhouse
- The view of the bay from the Inn at Canoe Point, Bar Harbor, Maine
- The first sight of Norumbega, Camden, Maine

- The citrus colors of the breakfast room, Gibson House, Haverhill Corners, New Hampshire
- The bathroom with the crystal sink, Elm Tree Cottage, Newport, Rhode Island
- The willow bed under the starry ceiling, Cod Cove Farm, Edgecomb, Maine
- The pricey perfection, Twin Farms, Barnard, Vermont
- The clip-clop of horse-drawn carriages outside the window at The Deerfield Inn, Deerfield, Massachusetts
- The gift of the heart-shaped pillow and the gentility at Rabbit Hill Inn, Waterford, Vermont
- Room diaries—comments from aspiring romance writers and star-crossed guests
- The Mallard Room at the Pitcher Inn, Warren, Vermont
- The Matisse Room at The Pomegranate Inn, Portland, Maine
- Gardens at Miles Country Inn, Hamilton, Massachusetts
- Wood-burning fireplaces that crackle, hiss, splatter, flare up, and die out
- Claw-foot tubs (bring your own bath gel, just in case)

Maine

Maine is the first state to greet each day as the sun touches the summit of **Cadillac Mountain** in **Acadia,** and it reaches farthest into the icy Atlantic, inviting crystal waters into hundreds of bays, harbors, inlets and coves, with 33,000 square miles, 6,000 lakes, and 240 miles of dipping, curving Atlantic coastline, twisting and turning to equal 3,000 miles of oceanfront.

The state name derives from "mainland," and perhaps this rock-solid nature explains the legendary temperament of Maine's permanent residents: down-to-earth. Descendants of French, Acadian, Russian, Swedish, German, and Scottish settlers live here today, but the first residents were the Abnakis, woodland Algonquin Indians. Religious holidays, ethnic festivals, and fairs observe a variety of traditions and cultures.

Many summer visitors return for generations, dancing to the tune of the motto, "We're not here for a long time. We're here for a good time." Couples pulled by heartstring ties often return to marry in white-steepled churches or oceanfront inns, atop mountains or afloat on windjammers.

This "Pine Tree State" is indeed green throughout the year, and summertime colors of red-cracked lobster, gray rocks, and blue water are clichés come true. But locals treasure what the "summer people" never see—the golds, oranges, yellows, and reds of fall and the white grace and power of a Maine winter.

Quiet **Aroostock County** occupies the entire northern corner of the state bordering Canada. Residents celebrate their agrarian roots with festivals and fairs, and you can bike alongside flowering potato fields in this rural county with nearly 2,000 lakes, rivers and streams, and miles of wooded and cleared trails. You can also fish, canoe, and hike the northern **Appalachian Trail,** cross-country ski or snowmobile, or drive any portion of a 5-hour, 204-mile fall foliage tour.

Inland is mountainous and wild, with excellent whitewater rafting on the **Penobscot River** and on **The Forks** in the state capital, **Augusta.** You can hike mile-high **Mt. Katahdin** or trails in **White Mountain National Forest,** view the largest moose population in the state around **Baxter State Park** and **Moosehead Lake,** or drive on scenic Route 201.

Acadia National Park on **Mount Desert Island** has streams, islands, lakes, mountains, and forests plus hiking and miles of carriage trails built and donated by the Rockefellers. Downeast coves protect authentic fishing villages such as **Stonington;** sleepy artist/native enclaves like **Deer Isle, Isle au Haut,** and the **Cranberry Islands;** quietly glamorous **Bar Harbor;** and quaint villages like **Castine** and **Blue Hill,** where antiquing and touring reign supreme.

Greater Portland and **Casco Bay** sparkle with **Monhegan Island,** historic forts, sandy beaches, lighthouses, and shopping at **Freeport's L.L. Bean Outlet.** The Southern Maine Coast and Midcoast tourism zones offer Atlantic-edge favorites: touring, antiquing, outlet shopping in **Kittery,** lobster pounds (where the crustaceans are hauled in, boiled and eaten on the spot), ocean activities and nature adventures on sandy beaches and rocky shores. Summering spots include the **Yorks, Ogunquit, Kennebunkport, Bath, the Boothbays, Wiscasset, Searsport, Camden,** and **Camden Harbor.**

April through October is traditionally visitors season; high season starts around mid-June. In early summer, arm yourself with a good insect repellent to ward off black flies and other biting bugs. September is a great month to get away. Peak prices and minimum-stay requirements may apply through foliage season, but you'll find fewer crowds and, usually, wonderful weather.

Much of tourist Maine closes or limits operation during winter months, particularly near the coast. Inland areas often offer winter activities, but check for lodging and dining availability. Walking deserted streets past closed restaurants and shops can be a letdown if you're expecting the full tourist experience. But the dramatic winter beauty offered by this most natural New England state compensates—if you bundle up.

FOR MORE INFORMATION

Maine State Ferry Service (207) 596-2202
Many islands are accessible only through private boat operators

Maine Web Pages

www.state.me.us   www.visitmaine.com
www.mainetourism.com   www.maineguide.com

Maine Farm Vacation B&B Association (207) 797-5540
Maine Innkeepers Association (207) 773-7670

Downeast/Acadia

Downeast is actually up north, coastally speaking, and Downeast Acadia occupies the large, northeastern coastal corner of the state. The term derives from the era of summer hotels, when guests arrived by the boatload, literally. The prevailing coastal winds out of the northwest made the trip from Boston to Bar Harbor an easy voyage, with the wind at one's back traveling east. Over time, "downwind" translated into "downeast."

This easternmost point in the country has Maine's most striking coastline, with waves crashing against rocky precipices and wind whistling through stalwart pines. Peninsulas thrust into the Atlantic, sheltering harbors, coves, bays, and inlets. Ocean vistas are balanced by activities, including the "world's fastest lobster boat races" in **Jonesport** on Independence Day. You can enjoy fresh-off-the-boat lobster, look for whales and adorable puffins, sail, take a tour cruise, kayak, canoe, fish, hunt, climb, hike, bike, and more.

Writers and artists in the early 1800s were inspired by 22-square-mile **Acadia National Park** on glacier-carved **Mt. Desert Island.** The morning sun rises first here, at **Cadillac Mountain,** on the highest point on the Atlantic north of Brazil. The ocean smashing against granite cliffs at **Somes Sound** and **Thunderhole,** and crescent-shaped **Sand Beach** are typical sights of the coast and tiny offshore islands. Horse-drawn carriages may no longer be allowed along the over 50 miles of carriage trails donated by the Rockefellers, but bikers and walkers are welcome.

To go international, ferry or drive across the bridge from **Lubec, Maine,** to **New Brunswick, Canada,** for **Campobello Island,** the longtime summer residence of Franklin D. Roosevelt. The 2,600-acre natural area includes the Roosevelt home, walking trails, gardens, scenic vistas and observation areas, and beaches. **West Quoddy Head Lighthouse** in Lubec can be visited by car and is one of 20 accessible lighthouses of the state's 63.

Blue Hill, Castine, Stonington, Northeast and Southwest Harbors, Hancock Point, Little Deer Isle and Deer Isle, the Cranberry Islands, Vinalhaven Island, and **Isle au Haut** offer antiquing, lobster boats, fine dining, and several authentic fishing economies. The famous **Haystack Mountain School of Crafts** on Deer Isle has put the little island on the crafts lovers' map.

Finally, pricey, see-and-be-seen **Bar Harbor** on **Mount Desert Island,** still summer home to many rich and powerful, was part of the "Gilded Age" overflow. Cars are no longer banned within the town, which hosts throngs of summer visitors. The entrance to **Acadia National Park,** art galleries, museums, varied dining choices, concerts and fairs, the town pier, and the July and August **Bar Harbor Music Festival** are among the draws. Stick around long enough to walk from Bar Harbor to Bar Island at low tide.

Many of the mansions and summer retreats in this area have become exceptional small inns and bed-and-breakfasts. Summer bookings are hard to come by. Plan way ahead, especially for weekends, or come midweek and off-season when the crowds have thinned.

FOR MORE INFORMATION

Bar Harbor Chamber of Commerce (207) 288-5103; Fax: (207) 288-2565
email: visitors@barharborinfo.com
www.barharborinfo.com

Mt. Desert Chamber of Commerce (207) 276-5040; Acadia (207) 288-3338

Deer Isle/Stonington Area (207) 348-6124
email: deerisle@acadia.net
www.deerislemaine.com

East Penobscot Bay Association (East Penobscot, Deer Isle, Stonington)
email: info@penobscotbay.com.

Ellsworth Area (Blue Hill, Castine, Deer Isle, Schoodic Peninsula) (207) 667-5584
email: eacc@downeast.net
www.downeast.net/acadia or www.ellsworthme.com

Southwest Harbor Chamber of Commerce (207) 244-9264 or (800) 423-9264
Fax: (207) 244-4185

PLEASANT BAY, Addison

OVERALL ★★★★ | ROOM QUALITY ★★★★ | VALUE ★★★★ | PRICE $50–100

A really kid-friendly site, this informal bed-and-breakfast allows guests, young and old, to play with the wooly llamas and even take the them for walks. Here you are far from the crowds with water views, easy access to nature, and peace and quiet. Joan and Lee raised six children in New Hampshire and then traveled north, cleared this land, and built a comfortable, free-flowing house for themselves, family, and guests. They enjoy chatting about farming, canoeing, music, birding, gardening and, of course, their llamas.

SETTING & FACILITIES

Location Follow signs from Rt. 1 in Columbia; on tidal river
Near Ocean, nature preserves, Pleasant River, vineyard and winery, Acadia Nat'l Park, Campobello, Canada (international park, site of FDR's summer home)
Building 1988 Cape/Colonial
Grounds Rural; llama farm; water frontage; hiking trails

Public Space Library, DR, family room, kitchen
Food & Drink Full breakfast; specialties: popover fruit pancake, fresh farm eggs, maple syrup or preserves
Recreation Bird watching, puffin- and whale-watching cruises, canoeing, kayaking
Amenities & Services Boat mooring, cots and cribs, limited disabled access

ACCOMMODATIONS

Units 4 guest rooms
All Rooms Water view, spacious
Some Rooms Private bath (2), shared bath (2), carpet, hardwoods
Bed & Bath Beds vary; full baths

Favorites Rooms w/ priv. bath, upstairs, water view
Comfort & Decor Art prints, quilts. Comfortable, pretty. Simple and family-friendly.

RATES, RESERVATIONS, & RESTRICTIONS

Deposit Mastercard, Visa, or 50%; 7-day cancellation policy.
Discounts Singles
Credit Cards V, MC
Check-in/Out Open
Smoking Outdoors only
Pets No; B & B has animals
Kids Welcome
Minimum Stay None

Open All year
Hosts Joan and Leon Yeaton
386 West Side Rd. P.O. Box 222
Addison, ME 04606
(207) 483-4490
Fax: (207) 483-4653
pleasantbay@nemaine.com
www.nemaine.com/pleasantbay

BALANCE ROCK INN BY-THE-SEA, Bar Harbor

OVERALL ★★★½ | ROOM QUALITY ★★★★ | VALUE ★ | PRICE $95–575

Overlooking the huge, precariously tipped rock it's named for, this hybrid seems a bit like a balancing act itself—an old-fashioned small hotel that's a bed-and-breakfast at heart. Set in a former summer house, with modern add-ons, it is on the fashionable, historic shore-path walk along the ocean, next door to residential mansions. The property seems isolated, but the busy Bar Harbor area is actually only a couple of blocks away. Furnishings are dramatic, decorated by a former theatrical manager. Focus is on stunning central pool and terrace, but when kids are splashing, things can get decidedly unromantic in this otherwise romantic setting.

SETTING & FACILITIES

Location Rt. 3 to Bar Harbor, left on Main St., right onto Albert Meadow Near Ocean, Acadia National Park, 2-block walk to Bar Harbor
Building Traditional 1903 mansion of the summer-cottage genre, refurbished and expanded
Grounds Expansive oceanside gardens and lawns, heated pool overlooking ocean, Frenchman Bay views
Public Space Entrance hall w/ grand staircase, parlor
Food & Drink Full buffet breakfast in dining room, early-riser tea/coffee w/ paper; full afternoon tea; full bar
Recreation Water sports, touring, hiking, biking, golf, tennis, whale watching, horseback riding, local cultural events
Amenities & Services Gym in carriage house, cots, off-street parking, on-premises gift shop. Concierge, turndown service on request

ACCOMMODATIONS

Units 14 guest rooms, 3 luxury suites
All Rooms Bath, TV, phone, individual heat/AC control
Some Rooms Water view, fireplace, sauna or whirlpool, sitting area, separate living area, kitchen, private deck/balcony
Bed & Bath Luxury bedding, some canopy, four-poster beds; marble baths
Favorites Rooms in original house, w/ deck and views
Comfort & Decor Luxurious European ambiance. Plush carpet, reproduction wall and window coverings, English-print floral fabrics, Queen Anne furnishings. Good lighting and large window views. Rooms vary in size. Dramatic.

RATES, RESERVATIONS, & RESTRICTIONS

Deposit Full payment 1–2 nights, 2 nights deposit for a 3-night stay, 50% longer stays; must cancel 10 days in advance
Discounts Custom packages, off-season, 3rd person
Credit Cards V, AE, MC, D
Check-in/Out 3/11
Smoking In certain rooms

Smoking In certain rooms
Pets Well-behaved pets in limited numbers; check
Kids Not permitted.
Minimum Stay None
Open May–Oct.
Hosts Nancy Cloud and Mike Miles
21 Albert Meadow

Bar Harbor, ME 04609
(800) 753-0494 or (207) 288-2610
Fax: (207) 288-5534
2barharbor@aol.com or
barhbrinns@aol.com
www.barharborvacations.com
www.balancerockinn.com

INN AT BAY LEDGE, Bar Harbor

OVERALL ★★★★½ | ROOM QUALITY ★★★★★ | VALUE ★★ | PRICE $150–350

Sipping a lemonade slush and nibbling homemade cookies on the sun porch overlooking Frenchman Bay, life looks pretty tranquil indeed. But 80 feet below the cliff are dramatic ledges and caves to explore. The decor is rustic-sophisticated and may seem more like Northern California than Maine, but whatever or wherever, this original bed-and-breakfast is romantic and beautiful—and unique in these traditional Downeast parts. Early season rates are much lower.

SETTING & FACILITIES

Location half-mile off Rt. 3; 5 miles before Bar Harbor
Near Penobscot Bay, Acadia Nat'l Park, Bar Harbor
Building Lodge-style, 3 cottages
Grounds Sun porch overlooks Frenchman Bay, stairs down cliff face to secluded rocky beach, heated outdoor pool w/ water view
Public Space Common rooms, porch, sitting room w/ TV/VCR
Food & Drink Full breakfast; specialties: cranberry and cashew granola, crab Benedict; refreshments; beer and wine for purchase
Recreation Visiting caves, boating, biking, kayaking, touring
Amenities & Services Common sauna and steam shower

ACCOMMODATIONS

Units 7 guest rooms, 3 cottages
All Rooms Bath
Some Rooms Water view, priv. deck; all cottages have a fireplace
Bed & Bath Antique beds, king or queen; feather bedding, down comforters, damask sheets; some whirlpool tubs
Favorites Room 7—spacious, full view of bay, four-poster carved canopy king, whirlpool; Room 10—most priv., queen canopy, view from deck; Cottages—privacy
Comfort & Decor Designer fabrics, antiques in main building; cottages are casual country w/ wicker, very priv.; spacious, charming, immaculate.

RATES, RESERVATIONS, & RESTRICTIONS

Deposit 2 nights; must cancel 14 days in advance
Credit Cards V, MC
Check-in/Out 3/11
Smoking No
Pets No; B&B has dogs
Kids Over 16
Minimum Stay 2 nights in season

Open May–mid-Oct.
Hosts Jeani and Jack Ochtera
1385 Sand Point Rd.
Bar Harbor, ME 04609
(207) 288-4204
Fax: (207) 288-5573
www.innatbayledge.com

THE INN AT CANOE POINT, Bar Harbor

OVERALL ★★★★½ | ROOM QUALITY ★★★★ | VALUE ★★½ | PRICE $90–285

What a gorgeous setting and view, with harbor seal, fox, and bald eagle sightings common through big windows. The outside is wisely allowed to dominate the pale sophistication within. The affable hosts were formerly computer execs on Long Island and owned and operated the nearby Kingsleigh Inn. Their warmth has added oomph to this gabled, stucco-and-fieldstone fairytale cottage on the water's edge. Ask Maine innkeepers for a short list of their favorites, and it usually includes this bed-and-breakfast. Book way ahead.

SETTING & FACILITIES

Location Just past entrance to Acadia Nat'l Park on Mount Desert Island, 2 mi. from Bar Harbor on Frenchman Bay
Near Bar Harbor, Acadia Nat'l Park
Building 1889 Tudor-style home
Grounds Rocky shoreline; 2 acres of wilderness; gravel beach
Public Space LR, wraparound deck, 2nd common room
Food & Drink 4-course communal breakfast, refreshments (e.g., chocolate chip cookies)

Recreation Water sports, rock climbing, golf, carriage rides, XC skiing, snowshoeing
Amenities & Services Guest refrigera-tor, irons, rentals for activities, special occasions, recipes, can reserve entire property

ACCOMMODATIONS

Units 3 guest rooms, 2 suites
All Rooms Bath, water view, air conditioning, radio
Some Rooms 2 rooms share a deck, fireplace (1), priv. entrance (1), suites sitting area
Bed & Bath Queens, 1 king; all with tub and shower, robes, hairdryers
Favorites Master Suite—sitting area, queen four-poster, view, shared deck; Garret Suite—sloped attic ceilings, 3rd-floor views; Garden Room—small, romantic, priv. entrance, whirlpool tub, window walls
Comfort & Decor Uncluttered, comfortable, stylish. Mix of wicker, overstuffed love seats, eaves, contemporary w/ some antique pieces. Some rooms small, but views add dimension. Minimal decoration, maximal views.

RATES, RESERVATIONS, & RESTRICTIONS

Deposit 1 night at least; refund w/ 21-day notice
Credit Cards V, MC, D
Check-in/Out 2–8/11
Smoking No
Pets No
Kids Over 16
Minimum Stay None

Open Feb.–Dec.
Hosts Nancy and Tom Cervelli
Rt. 3, Eden St., Box 216
Bar Harbor, ME 04609
(207) 288-9511
Fax: (207) 288-2870
info@innatcanoepoint.com
www.innatcanoepoint.com

MANOR HOUSE, Bar Harbor

OVERALL ★★★★½ | ROOM QUALITY ★★★★★ | VALUE ★★★ | PRICE $65–225

Originally a summer home to several generations of Colonel Foster's family, this solid, many-gabled clapboard has a circular driveway and gingerbread cottages. It is a Victorian beauty without fussiness and clutter. Guests sign in on a stunning antique desk and are pampered from there. The talented innkeeper is a former banker with an eye for color and great period antiques. He keeps his bed-and-breakfast literally gleaming for first-timers and repeaters who appreciate dark woods, small prints, and constant care—and who don't need to put their feet up.

SETTING & FACILITIES

Location On tree-lined residential street; from Ellsworth take Rt. 3 to Bar Harbor, left onto West St.

Near Ocean, Bar Island, Porcupine Islands, Acadia Nat'l Park, Frenchman Bay

Building 1887 22-room, 3-story Queen Anne Victorian; 2 garden cottages

Grounds Parklike 1+ acres, gardens

Public Space Veranda, foyer, DR, sitting room, 3rd-floor sitting room w/ TV

Food & Drink Full communal buffet breakfast; specialty: bread pudding w/ apple-cider sauce; afternoon tea

Recreation Harbor, beach activities; kayaking, trails, rock climbing, fishing, antiquing

Amenities & Services Fax, guest refrigerator, baby grand piano, irons, binoculars, special celebrations, beach towels, recipes, meeting facilities up to 20, entire property can be reserved

ACCOMMODATIONS

Units 8 guest rooms, 9 suites

All Rooms Bath, antiques, lace curtain

Some Rooms Garden view, fireplace, sitting area, AC. Chauffeur's cottage priv. entrance, fireplace, wet bar, sitting room, refrigerators. Garden cottages priv., fireplace, sitting area, porch, TV, whirlpool tubs

Bed & Bath Bed sizes vary, some elaborate antique beds; some hall access, some showers only

Favorites Room 5—largest, sitting area, charming, Oriental rug, fireplace

Comfort & Decor Period wallcoverings, lighting fixtures. Victorian nooks and corners. Chauffeur's cottage w/ stained glass and skylights. Cottages w/ porches, small, BR/sitting area in one. Beamed cathedral ceilings, commercial grade carpet, wicker furnishings, minimal decoration.

RATES, RESERVATIONS, & RESTRICTIONS

Deposit 2 nights; refund w/ 14-day notice.

Discounts 3rd person

Credit Cards V, AE, MC, D

Check-in/Out 3–9/1030; can stay till 1130 w/ arrangement

Smoking No

Pets No; inn has dog, Sheltie, not permitted in guest rooms

Kids Over 12

Minimum Stay 2 nights

Open April 15–Nov. 15

Host Malcolm "Mac" Noyes
106 West St.
Bar Harbor, ME 04609
(800) 437-0088 or (207) 288-3759
Fax: (207) 288-2974
manor@acadia.net
www.barharbormanorhouse.com

NANNAU-SEASIDE, Bar Harbor

OVERALL ★★★★½ | ROOM QUALITY ★★★★★ | VALUE ★★★ | PRICE $125–175

This lovely, secluded 20-room mansion was once home to the mother of the family who still lives next door. It's a solid example of an extravagant turn-of-the-century shingle-style summer cottage peculiar to the New England coastline. Vikki, an art history major, decorated this much-loved home in tasteful English Aesthetic furnishings, accented with imported William Morris fabrics and wallcoverings and deep, rich colors. Serene and private, the site is convenient to Bar Harbor restaurants and activities, and yet overlooks its own little rocky beach.

SETTING & FACILITIES

Location Compass Harbor, Mt. Desert Island; in Bar Harbor south on Main St. (Rt. 3), 1 mi. south of town, small sign at head of long driveway on left
Near 100 yards from Frenchman Bay, Acadia Nat'l Park hiking trails from property, short drive to Bar Harbor
Building 1904 shingle-style mansion, Tudor overtones
Grounds 5 wooded acres; screened porch, gardens; terrace, picnic area; fields; wooded path to bay, priv. rocky beach

Public Space Entrance hall; LR, sitting area, TV area, games/writing table; parlor/library; DR; screened porch
Food & Drink Full breakfast; specialties: Danish with fruit compote, almond French toast, personalized omelets, garden vegetables; early riser coffee
Recreation Sailing, kayaking, cruises, biking, golf, tennis, whale watching, horses, beach activities, local events, hiking
Amenities & Services Beach, games, croquet court, maps, fax

ACCOMMODATIONS

Units 4 guest rooms, 2 suites
All Rooms Bath, writing desk, water view, ambiance lighting
Some Rooms Fireplace
Bed & Bath Queen, twin beds; full baths, some claw-foot soaking tubs, handheld showerheads, some marble vanities, 1 hall access, bathrobes provided
Favorites Room 1—most spacious,

views, bay window, fireplace, plush carpet; Room 4—best 2-BR suite for families, companions
Comfort & Decor Spacious rooms, generous sitting areas. Reproduction turn-of-the-century wallcoverings, fabrics by William Morris. Artwork. Elegant window treatments. 3rd-floor rooms smallest. Casual, stylish, luxurious, immaculate.

RATES, RESERVATIONS, & RESTRICTIONS

Deposit 2 nights; refund w/ 21-day notice
Discounts Singles, 3rd person
Credit Cards V, MC

Check-in/Out 4–7/11
Smoking No
Pets No
Kids w/ prior arrangement

Minimum Stay 2 nights; 3 nights holiday weekends in high season
Open June–Oct
Hosts Vikki and Ron Evers
396 Main St., Box 710

Bar Harbor, ME 04609-0710
(207) 288-5575
Fax: (207) 288-5421
www.nannau.com

ULLIKANA, Bar Harbor

OVERALL ★★★★½ | ROOM QUALITY ★★★★ | VALUE ★★½ | PRICE $140–250

As offbeat as its mysterious name, this former summer cottage near Balance Rock is seemingly isolated. Who knows what Alpheus Hardy, who built and named it, would have thought of the magic of French-Canadian host Helene, whose bold colors and decorative touches appear where you least expect them. If you enjoy whimsy, surprise, and striking design you'll love the mix-and-match—and not-match—that unfolds all around. Breakfasts are just as creative. If you're more traditional, the talented and warm hosts also own a lovely, newly refurbished mansion-turned-bed-and-breakfast across the field. But this one is the tour de force.

SETTING & FACILITIES

Location I block off Main St., behind the Bar Harbor Banking & Trust, overlooking the water
Near Waterfront, town of Bar Harbor, Acadia Nat'l Park
Building 1885 Tudor-style mansion
Grounds Minimal; fountain, terrace over-

looks harbor
Public Space Huge foyer, parlors, DR, terrace.
Food & Drink Full breakfast; specialties: raspberry soup w/ sorbet and blueberries, apple popovers; refreshments

Recreation Water sports, biking, golf, tennis, whale watching, hiking

Amenities & Services Art and book collection, games, French spoken

ACCOMMODATIONS

Units 10 guest rooms
All Rooms Bath, whimsical/offbeat decor
Some Rooms Fireplace, priv. deck, sitting area; furnishings from France; add'l beds
Bed & Bath Bed sizes vary; iron, brass beds; some soaking tubs, hall access
Favorites Room 5—spacious, deck, fire-

place, striking red-and-white wall-paper, coordinating fabrics, king and daybed, hall access to priv. bath
Comfort & Decor Surprising color, design. Filled with original paintings, puppets, kilim rugs, wicker. Some rooms spacious, some under eaves, all comfy. Reading lamps.

RATES, RESERVATIONS, & RESTRICTIONS

Deposit Refund w/ 21-day notice
Discounts 3rd person
Credit Cards V, MC
Check-in/Out 3/11
Smoking No
Pets No
Kids Over 12

Minimum Stay None
Open May–Oct.
Hosts Helene Harton and Roy Kasindorf
16 The Field
Bar Harbor, ME 04609
(207) 288-9552; Fax: (207) 288-3682

BLUE HILL INN, Blue Hill

OVERALL ★★★★½ | ROOM QUALITY ★★★★★ | VALUE ★★ | PRICE $138–265

Delectable aromas wafting from the kitchen into the blue-stenciled, Colonial common rooms clue you in to the culinary delights that await. The inn was featured in a PBS cooking series (the chef grows 20 varieties of potatoes!), and it has won the *Wine Spectator* Award for Excellence several times. This understated winner is loaded with warmth and authentic, old-fashioned delights. Blue Hill is relatively quiet even at the height of summer, and this great, authentic inn is reputedly one of the oldest continuously operating in New England.

SETTING & FACILITIES

Location Rt. 15 from Bucksport or 172 from Ellsworth to Blue Hill; on residential street 2 blocks from harbor
Near Blue Hill Bay, kayaking center, artisan community, Acadia Nat'l Park, Castine, Blue Hill Falls, Deer Isle
Building 1830 Federal clapboard; Cape House, luxury suite
Grounds 1-acre lawn, gardens, old elms, apple trees
Public Space DR, small library, LR/parlor
Food & Drink Full breakfast with fresh fruit and choice of several entrées, communal on request; hors d'oeuvres; refreshments; Four wine dinners open to guests and public by reservation; liquor license, extensive wine list; picnic lunches, food preferences noted
Recreation Tennis, fishing, boating, sailing, kayaking, summer chamber music in garden
Amenities & Services Fax, copier, modem, irons, beach towels, postcards, twice-daily maid, meetings (25), group reservations, wheelchair access in some rooms

ACCOMMODATIONS

Units 10 guest rooms, 2 suites
All Rooms Bath, sitting area, alarm clock
Some Rooms Fireplace; phone; suites sitting room, AC; wheelchair access; Cape House priv. deck
Bed & Bath Some antique beds, sizes vary, luxury bedding; robes provided; hairdryers; some showers only
Favorites Room 10—fireplace, antique queen bed; Cape House suite—open, airy, king canopy bed, fireplace, kitchen; private deck
Comfort & Decor Attention to detail, good lighting. Hand-hewn beams, cathedral ceilings, pine floors, large windows. Add'l beds for families. Comfortable. Some rooms charmingly rustic, some formally Federal. All furnished w/ antiques.

RATES, RESERVATIONS, & RESTRICTIONS

Deposit 1 night, 50% longer stays; refund w/ 14-day notice
Discounts Custom pkgs., off-season extended stays, singles
Credit Cards V, AE, MC
Check-in/Out 2–5/1030, possible to stay until 1130
Smoking No
Pets No
Kids Over 13
Minimum Stay 2 nights on weekends
Open Mid-May–Nov.
Hosts Mary and Don Hartley
Union St., Box 403
Blue Hill, ME 04614
(800) 826-7415 or (207) 374-2844
Fax: (207) 374-2829
bluehillin@hotmail.com
bluehillinn.com

JOHN PETERS INN, Blue Hill

OVERALL ★★★★½ | ROOM QUALITY ★★★★ | VALUE ★★★ | PRICE $105–175

Neither TVs nor room keys are available at this romantic bed-and-breakfast at the water's edge, and you won't need them. You can walk down to the pebble beach, swim, sail away for the day, or just hole up with a book in front of a fire. Romantic and away from it all, in surroundings of meadows sloping to the sea, you can relax here, and mull about which breakfast delicacy Barbara will be preparing next in the glass-walled porch. Classical music, blue water, a quaint town—these are simple, deep pleasures to be savored.

SETTING & FACILITIES

Location Rt. 1 to Rt. 15 to Blue Hill, follow signs
Near Walk to Village of Blue Hill, 15 minutes to Deer Isle, 1 hr. to Acadia Nat'l Park, Camden, Bar Harbor
Building 1815 plantation-style mansion, carriage house
Grounds 25 shorefront acres on Blue Hill Bay
Public Space LR, sun porch, deck
Food & Drink Elaborate breakfast on sun porch or in DR; specialties: cantaloupe w/ strawberry sorbet, lobster omelet; honeymoon suite, breakfast in bed option
Recreation Day excursions, biking, swimming, kayaking, canoeing, windjammer cruises, summer events, touring Blue Hill pottery and crafts shops, antiquing
Amenities & Services In-ground pool, canoe and small sailboat for guest use, 2 boat moorings, chamber music recitals, grand piano

ACCOMMODATIONS

Units 8 guest rooms in main house, 6 in carriage house
All Rooms Bath
Some Rooms Working fireplace, bay view, wet bar, kitchen, deck, sitting area, room for 3rd person, phone
Bed & Bath Beds vary

Favorites Westport Room—barn beams, kitchen, living/dining area, deck; Surrey Room—elegant and comfortable w/ working fireplace and sitting area; Blue Hill Room—fireplace, priv. deck, king bed, wet bar
Comfort & Decor Country comfort.

Rooms gracious and large. Colonial antiques, cherry hardwood floors, polished wood furnishings, rocking chairs. Quaint touches in wallcoverings, fabrics, and lace curtains. Fresh flowers. Good lighting.

RATES, RESERVATIONS, & RESTRICTIONS

Deposit Will hold room w/ credit card; refund w/ 14-day notice
Discounts 3rd person
Credit Cards V, MC
Check-in/Out 2–9/11ish
Smoking No
Pets No; inn has an aged Welsh terrier, DOC (DisObedientCanine)
Kids Permitted, check

Minimum Stay 2 nights weekends
Open May–Oct.
Hosts Barbara and Rick Seeger
Peters Point, Box 916
Blue Hill, ME 04614
(207) 374-2116
jpi@downeast.net
www.johnpetersinn.com

OAKLAND HOUSE SEASIDE RESORT, Brooksville

OVERALL ★★★★ | ROOM QUALITY ★★★★ | VALUE ★½ | PRICE $75–500

The land was deeded to Jim's forebears by King George in the 1700s. Nanny and Gramp Herrick, Jim's great-grandparents, were the original hosts, over 100 years ago, when the property was a vacation stop for guests arriving by steamboat to Eggemoggin Reach. This venerable complex (also known as Shore Oaks Seaside Inn, Vacation Cottages & Country Dining) is the kind of old-fashioned New England resort that is dying out. Groups, families, and vacationers who long for a comfortable seaside getaway with fine food won't go wrong. Families prefer cottages; couples and singles, the inn—which keeps everyone happy.

SETTING & FACILITIES

Location On the shore of East Penobscot Bay in Brooksville; Rt. 15, 12 min. east of Blue Hill, follow Oakland House signs
Near Blue Hill, Castine, Deer Isle, Acadia Nat'l Park
Building Original mansard Victorian homestead, now restaurant; main building, the Seaside Inn, 1907 rustic; Arts and

Crafts–style expanded cottage, recently renovated; vacation cottages; barn
Grounds 50 acres, .5 mile of oceanfront; dock, boat moorings, ocean and lake beaches, wooded areas, gardens, tidal pools
Public Space Rustic parlor; well-stocked library; DR; front porch overlooks ocean, lighthouse

Food & Drink (MAP) Full breakfast in high season, communal or separate; 5-course dinner, lunch for fee; specialty: lobster picnic on beach, weekly in summer; wine and beer available

Recreation Golf, biking, day cruises, trails, water sports; bald eagle, moose, and seal sightings

Amenities & Services Fax, games, meetings, weddings, seminars

ACCOMMODATIONS

Units 10 guest rooms; 15 cottages
All Rooms Heat controls, local directory w/ stories, events, and attractions
Some Rooms priv. bath (7), shared (3); view, fireplace or wood-burning stove; cottages w/ LR and kitchen; limited disabled access
Bed & Bath Beds vary; some baths, showers only
Favorites Lone Pine Cottage—log cabin, fully renovated w/ porch, fireplace, ocean views, kitchen, office, phone, satellite

TV/VCR, housekeeping. At inn, Room 4, Annie's Room—artisan-crafted bed, 5 windows w/ views, large full bathroom; Room 6—moss and white room, 2 double beds, fireplace, views of sunset.
Comfort & Decor Arts and Crafts, and Victorian pieces. Airy white window treatments. Cottages along shore vary in style and decor, w/ claw-foot tub, kitchen. All comfortable. TVs and phones deliberately excluded, but can request.

RATES, RESERVATIONS, & RESTRICTIONS

Deposit Arranged at reservation; check cancellation policy
Discounts Singles, 3rd person, pkgs.
Credit Cards V, MC
Check-in/Out 2 inn, 4 cottages/11
Smoking Outside at inn, permitted in cottages
Pets No pets
Kids Over 14 in inn; all ages in cottages unless specified; childcare available by advance arrangement.

Minimum Stay 2 nights in inn; cottages, weekly
Open All year, limited availability in winter
Hosts Sally and Jim Littlefield
Herrick Rd., Box 435
Brooksville, ME 04617
(800) 359-RELAX(7352) or
(207) 359-8521
jim@oaklandhouse.com

CASTINE INN, Castine

OVERALL ★★★★ | ROOM QUALITY ★★★ | VALUE ★★½ | PRICE $90–215

On a quiet peninsula in a pretty, sleepy sailing port, this old-fashioned inn is, like The Hartstone Inn in Camden (run by a similarly talented, young couple), worth a visit for the cuisine at least. Award-winning owner-chef Tom honed his skills at many great restaurants, including Bouley in New York City. The mural in the dining room and other original touches remain special. The ambitious hosts are slowly upgrading the faded and simple guest rooms to match the sublime food, so when booking, ask for one that's been refurbished.

SETTING & FACILITIES

Location In the heart of Castine village, a block from the water
Near Penobscot Bay w/ offshore islands, Acadia Nat'l Park, Castine town square
Building Late-Victorian clapboard. Built in 1898 as an inn.
Grounds Small Victorian gardens, brook w/ bridge, benches, walkways, stone walls, rose gardens
Public Space Front hall, sitting room, pub, DR, wraparound porch
Food & Drink Full breakfast, specialties: goat-cheese omelets, apple bread French toast; creative dinners, including cheese course, focus on local, organic products; open to public, liquor license, pub
Recreation Kayaking, sailing, island tours, beach activities, biking, whale watching, horses, fishing, local cultural events
Amenities & Services Sauna, games, fax, modem, French spoken, maps, recipes, irons

ACCOMMODATIONS

Units 16 guest rooms, 3 suites (up to 4 people)
All Rooms Bath, fan
Some Rooms Water view, reading chair
Bed & Bath Queen/twin, one four-poster; robes, some showers only, cast-iron tub
Favorites Room 11—cherry four-poster, views, antique tub, glass shower; 3rd-floor rooms facing water offer best views
Comfort & Decor Bright, airy, simply furnished, functional, Small. Old-fashioned and uninspired, except for brighter refurbished rooms with floral coordinates, armoires, desks

RATES, RESERVATIONS, & RESTRICTIONS

Deposit 1 night, checks only; refund w/ 10-day notice
Discounts Singles, add'l person
Credit Cards V, MC
Check-in/Out 3/11
Smoking No
Pets No
Kids Over 8
Minimum Stay 2 nights July–August, other holiday weekends, special event weekends
Open May–Oct.
Hosts Amy and Tom Gutow
Box 41
Castine, ME 04421
(207) 326-4365
Fax: (207) 326-4570
relax@castineinn.com

PILGRIM'S INN, *Deer Isle*

OVERALL ★★★★½ | ROOM QUALITY ★★★★ | VALUE ★★½ | PRICE $150–245

This Pilgrim continues its progress, with new carriage-house accommodations and ever-changing menus. The artsy-craftsy village has provided inspiration within, and offers interesting browsing at numerous galleries. Built by Squire Ignatius Haskell in 1793 in fashionable Newburyport,

Massachusetts, the house with spare, stylish rooms was transported up to this isolated fishing port at his demanding bride's request. Thank you, Mrs. Haskell.

SETTING & FACILITIES

Location On Penobscot Bay; Rt 15 S to Deer Isle Village, turn right onto Main St. (Sunset Rd., 15A), drive 1 block; inn on left, opposite harbor

Near Camden Hills State Park, nature conservatory, Northwest Harbor, ocean, Stonington fishing village, Acadia Nat'l Park, Islands, Haystack School of Crafts

Building 1793 country home and cottage

Grounds Lawns slope to large tidal pond, nature habitat

Public Space Common room, DR

Food & Drink Full breakfast; cocktails and hors d'oeuvre hour; dinner avail. in season; specialty: rosemary tenderloin of pork in phyllo, w/ shiitakes, lentils, apricot chutney, and Dijon Cote Du Rhone sauce.

Recreation Hiking, biking, kayaking, bird watching, touring

Amenities & Services Gift shop, bikes, books, events sponsored by inn. Limited disabled access.

ACCOMMODATIONS

Units 13 guest rooms, 2 apts.

All Rooms Antiques, hardwood floors, luxurious furnishings. Cottage apts. priv. deck, LR w/ sofa beds, BR, queen bed, kitchen, DR, full bath

Some Rooms priv. bath (10), shared bath (3)

Bed & Bath Beds vary

Favorites Ginny's cottage—living area, cast-iron stove, kitchenette, TV, deck;

Room 5—four-poster, water views, hardwoods

Comfort & Decor Main building, period luxury, antiques. Cottages, airy, romantic. Wainscot paneling, hardwoods, wicker, windows. Great water views from 3rd-floor rooms. Sizes vary widely from huge in cottages to cozy (Room 12, smallest).

RATES, RESERVATIONS, & RESTRICTIONS

Deposit Check w/ inn

Discounts Add'l person(s) in July/August, pkgs.; weekly rates for cottage apts.

Credit Cards V, MC

Check-in/Out 5/11

Smoking No

Pets No

Kids All ages in cottage; over 10 in main building

No-No's Dinner w/out reservations

Minimum Stay Varies according to season

Open All year

Hosts Dan and Michelle Brown

Box 69 Main Street

Deer Isle, ME 04627

(207) 348-6615 or (888) 778-7505

Fax: (207) 348-7769

innkeeper@pilgrimsinn.com

www.Pilgrimsinn.com

WESTON HOUSE, Eastport

OVERALL ★★★½ | ROOM QUALITY ★★★ | VALUE ★★★★★ | PRICE $65–80

John James Audubon stayed here on his way to Labrador, but most travelers don't get this far northeast. For breakfast, you may find a cute fish puff pastry filled with smoked salmon and dill (not surprisingly, Jett operates a catering business). The friendly innkeepers cater to guests' whims, and for holidays they love to decorate their classic house and prepare special fare and favors. If you can accept shared bathrooms and enjoy an out-of-the-way location, this sweet bed-and-breakfast offers good value and quiet pleasures.

SETTING & FACILITIES

Location Rt. 1 to ME Highway 190, to Eastport, on a wooded hill
Near Roosevelt's Campobello Island, St. Andrews by the Sea, St. Croix River, Moosehorn Nat'l Wildlife Preserve; Old Sow, world's second-largest whirlpool
Building Stately 1810 hilltop Federal
Grounds Country gardens, porch, gazebo, bay views
Public Space Spacious; divided kitchen, sitting area; DR; LR
Food & Drink Full breakfast, communal; specialty: pancakes w/ hot apricot brandy sauce, bacon curls; seasonal brunch; sherry, tea; picnic lunches and candlelight dinners w/ reservation; setups for BYOB
Recreation Whale or bird watching, beach/water activities, golf, biking, horses; summer events; ferry to Campobello; day trips
Amenities & Services Irons, cordless phone, fax, lawn games; bike and boat rentals nearby

ACCOMMODATIONS

Units 4 guest rooms
All Rooms Shared bath
Some Rooms Bay and/or garden view, fireplace and TV (1)
Bed & Bath Antique beds, sizes vary; 2 full baths, 1 half-bath
Favorites Weston Room—fireplace, king four-poster, views across bay
Comfort & Decor Spacious, bright rooms simply but tastefully furnished. luxurious. Muted colors. Robes for hall passage to bathrooms. Best when not crowded and bathrooms easily available. Good lighting.

RATES, RESERVATIONS, & RESTRICTIONS

Deposit $50; refund w/ 24-hour notice
Discounts None
Credit Cards None; personal or travelers checks, incl. Canadian
Check-in/Out Flexible
Smoking No
Pets No
Kids No
Minimum Stay None
Open All year

Hosts Jett and John Peterson
26 Boynton St.
Eastport, ME 04631
(800) 853-2907 or (207) 853-2907
Fax: (207) 853-0981

www.virtualcities.com/me/
westonhouse
www.bernicechessler.com/
westonhousebnb
westonhouse@prexar.com

WEATHERBY'S, THE FISHERMAN'S RESORT, Grand Lake Stream

OVERALL ★★★½ | ROOM QUALITY ★★★ | VALUE ★★ | PRICE $130–204

Fisherpeople—and those who care about them—can't do much better. Charlene and Ken have operated this rustic inn, one of the country's oldest and best-known fishing lodges, for over 25 years, and grandchildren of original guests are now returning. The Grand Lake area—streams and rivers, and Wabassus, Pocumcus, and Sysladobsis lakes—is filled with lake trout, perch, landlocked salmon, and smallmouth bass. Partially accessible by road, the region is mainly wilderness, and much of it not yet fished extensively. Log cottages, comfy beds, fresh food, fresh air, birds, and woodsy beauty are pleasures for non-anglers as well.

SETTING & FACILITIES

Location Interstate 95 N to Rt. 6 E to Rt. 1 S; or Rt. 9 E to Rt. 1 N; tucked in the St. Croix Valley, on Grand Lake Stream (one of the best salmon rivers in the country)
Near Approximately 2 hrs. from Bangor; more than 32 productive waters surround fishing camp
Building Large turn-of-the-century farmhouse
Grounds Wooded acreage overlooking Grand Lake Stream
Public Space LR, library, closed-in porch, DR
Food & Drink (MAP) Breakfast and dinner; specialties: lobster stew, strawberry-rhubarb pie; will cook catch to order; mealtimes according to individual guests' fishing schedule; lunch on request, cold picnic or hot fishing-site barbecue prepared by guide
Recreation Stream and fly-fishing, boating, hiking, bird watching
Amenities & Services Lawn games, basketball court, tennis court, piano, fishing-tour guides available, boat rentals, fishing licenses, air transportation available, L.L. Bean Introductory Fly-Fishing Schools offered, corp. retreats, daily maid service, ice and wood delivered daily

ACCOMMODATIONS

Units 15 cottages
All Rooms Bath, open brick or Franklin fireplace, screened porch
Bed & Bath Beds vary; baths w/ sep. heaters, some showers only
Favorites Cottages with extra BRs for families
Comfort & Decor Rustic decor, antiques, wood paneled, airy, spacious and comfortable, priv. wooded settings.

RATES, RESERVATIONS, & RESTRICTIONS

Deposit $100/person, refund w/ 21-day notice (Note 15% gratuity added to room rate)
Discounts Family rates, couples, children under 14, singles
Credit Cards V, MC; add 4%
Check-in/Out Flexible, check
Smoking Limited, check
Pets Limited, check
Kids Welcome

Minimum Stay None
Open All year, except winter
Hosts Charlene and Ken Sassi
Box 69
Grand Lake Stream, ME 04637
(800) 639-6353 or (207) 237-2911 or (207) 796-5558
info@weatherbys.com
www.weatherbys.com

LE DOMAINE, Hancock

OVERALL ★★★★ | ROOM QUALITY ★★★★ | VALUE ★½ | PRICE $200–285

You'll feel you're in the French countryside rather than rural Maine. The hostess, trained at the Cordon Bleu and in Switzerland, follows the footsteps of her mother, who opened this restorative restaurant with rooms in 1946, after fleeing France when it was learned she was hiding Jews. The pâté, café au lait, fresh honey and croissants, the copper bowls, French accents, and *joie de vivre* are delightful; and the dinners divine. The house may be unpretentious, but the restaurant is a local favorite, and it's hard to beat indulging on French cuisine and then falling into a bed—awaiting breakfast.

SETTING & FACILITIES

Location On the east side of rural stretch of Rt. 1, about 9 mi. north of Ellsworth.
Near Pierre Monteux Conducting School across street, Hancock/Sullivan "singing" bridge; half-hour to Bar Harbor, Mt. Desert Island, Acadia Nat'l Park, ocean
Building 1950s New England red shingle
Grounds 100 acres; wooded areas, paths, pond, gardens, meadows
Public Space Parlor/entrance hall w/ bar, sitting room, DR, sun porch
Food & Drink (MAP) Cont'l breakfast; 4-course French dinner; specialties: roasted quail w/ Juniper berries, Maine mussels; bread pudding w/ caramel; all-French vintage wine cellar
Recreation Lawn games, rowing on pond; day trips, biking, boat tours, whale watching, beach activities, kayaking
Amenities & Services Badminton, fresh fruit, fax, holiday gourmet gift pkgs. prepared to order

ACCOMMODATIONS

Units 3 guest rooms, 2 suites
All Rooms Bath, writing desk, seating, radio
Some Rooms balcony (4) or priv. porch (4), AC

Bed & Bath Bed sizes vary; some baths, showers only
Favorites Rosemary—cozy, priv., balcony, locally made potter's sink
Comfort & Decor Rooms named after herbs, smallish and hotel-like but comfortable and reliably immaculate. Sparse, some French Provincial touches and antique pieces, hardwood floors, large bright windows

RATES, RESERVATIONS, & RESTRICTIONS

Deposit 1st and last nights; cancellation policy explained at reservation (Note 15% gratuity added to room rate)
Discounts Singles
Credit Cards AE, V, MC, D
Check-in/Out By 5/11
Smoking Outside only, mindful of other guests
Pets By prior arrangement w/ extra charge
Kids Under 5 by prior arrangement
No-No's Unconfirmed dinner reservations
Minimum Stay None
Open June–Oct.
Host Nicole Purslow, proprietor and chef
HC 77, Box 496
Hancock, ME 04640
(800) 554-8498 or (207) 422-3395
Fax: (207) 422-2316
nicole@ledomaine.com
www.ledomaine.com

CROCKER HOUSE COUNTRY INN, Hancock Point

OVERALL ★★★½ | ROOM QUALITY ★★★ | VALUE ★★★½ | PRICE $90–140

Reportedly haunted by the glamorous baroness who once owned it, the Crocker is not filled with glamour today, but a friendly staff makes up for the simple surroundings. The owner/chef serves large portions of good food, and enjoying it seems to be the major activity for many guests. This traditional inn, built during Hancock's shipbuilding era, is not much changed, and that has become a virtue. Though seemingly isolated, it is only three minutes from Frenchman Bay and boat moorings. Americana—the kind that's dying out fast—is its main feature. If you seek an old-fashioned, peaceful, unpretentious inn with a ghost, you've got it.

SETTING & FACILITIES

Location From Ellsworth, 7.9 miles on Rt. 1; look for sign in Hancock; Right turn, 4.8 miles; inn on left, walk to Frenchman Bay
Near Ocean, tennis, golf, horses; Acadia Nat'l Park; 15 miles Bar Harbor
Building Gray–shingle Colonial, opened as inn in 1884
Grounds Lawn w/ horseshoes, croquet
Public Space Parlors, bar/check-in, DR
Food & Drink Full breakfast; à la carte dinner open to public; American cuisine grilled pepper quail, rack of lamb Crocker, Crocker House scallops; liquor license; picnic lunches (fee)

Recreation Clay tennis courts, antiquing, crafts shopping, local events
Amenities & Services Hot tub, bikes, kayak, boat moorings, irons, maps, business retreats, weekend live entertainment

ACCOMMODATIONS

Units 11 guest rooms
All Rooms Bath, out-calling phone
Bed & Bath Varied bed sizes; small baths, showers only
Favorites Room 7—2nd floor, king, alcove

Comfort & Decor Simple, tasteful rooms, upstairs around a stairwell. Decor traditional and neat and welcoming. Floral paper, lace curtains, and furnishings like those grandma had. Adequate lighting, tiny baths

RATES, RESERVATIONS, & RESTRICTIONS

Deposit 1 night; must cancel 10 days in advance
Discounts Off-season
Credit Cards V, AE, MC, D
Check-in/Out 2–7/11; call for later check-in
Smoking Restricted
Pets Restricted
Kids OK
Minimum Stay None

Open Mid-April–Oct. 31, weekends mid-Nov. to New Year's Eve
Hosts Richard and Elizabeth Malaby
HC 77 Box 171
Hancock Point, ME 04640
(207) 422-6806 or (877) 715-6017
Fax: (207) 422-3105
crocker@acadia.net
www.crockerhouse.com

KEEPER'S HOUSE, Isle au Haut

OVERALL ★★★★ | ROOM QUALITY ★★★ | VALUE ★ | PRICE $294–335

The only property in this book with both a lighthouse and an outhouse. Here is an exceptional experience for intrepid travelers and families seeking adventure in a wilderness area that is limited to a few dozen tourists a day. A restored lighthouse-keeper's inn is not for high-maintenance types, but indeed, shunning modern amenities is part of the charm. (If you're prone to seasickness, beware, as the only access is via mailboat.) Guests congregate in the simple kitchen; visit the town (possibly the smallest in America); watch the seals, minks, osprey, and porpoises; and top it off with a candlelight, wholesome dinner and a peaceful sleep. This house is a keeper.

SETTING & FACILITIES

Location Rugged, tiny, appendage of Acadia Nat'l Park; Rt. 1 to Stonington fishing village, 40-min. mailboat cruise through islands to inn's dock on Isle au Haut
Near Stonington, Deer Isle, Blue Hill
Peninsula
Building Turn-of-the-century, gambrel-roofed lighthouse keeper's home, suspended wooden bridge to lighthouse

Grounds On Penobscot Bay, rocky coast; 3 other lighthouses
Public Space LR, Shaker DR, country kitchen
Food & Drink (MAP) Full breakfast; hearty lunch at inn, picnic on trail or shore; candlelight dinner; specialties: egg-plant parmesan soup, chicken and fresh seafood (no red meat), apple charlotte, steamed lobsters on Sundays
Recreation Hiking, biking 17 miles of Acadia trails, swimming pond
Amenities & Services Bikes, links to civilization deliberately disconnected

ACCOMMODATIONS

Units 4 guest rooms in main house, 1 guest room cottage with outhouse
All Rooms Shared bath
Some Rooms Wood stove, sitting area
Bed & Bath Some painted brass double beds, 1 trundle bed; 2 baths in main house; Oil House cottage w/ outhouse, outdoor sink, and shower
Favorites Keeper's Room—wood stove, view of lighthouse; Horizon Room—best water view

Comfort & Decor Minimal, but rugged delights. No phones, no electricity, no priv. baths. Illumination by gaslights, kerosene lanterns, and candles. Airy rooms, handpainted antique furnishings, island crafts, quirky nooks. Ceiling heights vary. Oil House, tiny 10-foot-square, w/ slate roof, double bed, potbellied stove, diminutive painted furniture, tiny deck overlooking water

RATES, RESERVATIONS, & RESTRICTIONS

Deposit $100, full payment 30 days in advance; full refund w/ 14-day notice
Discounts 3rd person
Credit Cards None
Check-in/Out Coincides w/ mailboat schedule, varies seasonally
Smoking No
Pets No

Kids Welcome
Minimum Stay 2 nights July, August
Open May–Oct.
Hosts Judi and Jeff Burke
Box 26
Isle au Haut, ME 04645
(207) 367-2261, leave message
www.keepershouse.com

KINGSLEIGH INN 1904, Southwest Harbor

OVERALL ★★★★ | ROOM QUALITY ★★★★ | VALUE ★★½ | PRICE $75–220

As sparkling as the Champagne in their name, the young hosts make you feel welcome in this comfortable, turn-of-the-century property on a residential street in the heart of Southwest Harbor. The living room has lace curtains at the bay window, but the kitchen is where you enter, chat, and enjoy freshly baked cookies and hot tea or lemonade, and an open refrigerator to store whatever. This informal bed-and-breakfast is an especially good place to interact with others. Think down-home Downeast.

SETTING & FACILITIES

Location Rt. 3 toward Bar Harbor, right on Rt. 102 to Southwest Harbor; in residential area

Near Acadia Nat'l Park, on Mt. Desert Island's quiet side, fishing and boat-building village of Southwest Harbor

Building Pebble-dash and shingles w/ bay windows, turrets, dormers, wraparound porch

Grounds Overlooks harbor, minimal landscaping

Public Space Country kitchen, LR with wood-burning fireplace, DR w/ library, sitting room, porch

Food & Drink Full gourmet breakfast, candlelight; specialties: marscapone-stuffed French toast w/ warm berry sauce, omelets made to order, refreshments, and home-baked "treats"

Recreation Canoeing and kayaking, biking, rock climbing, whale watching, golf, carriage rides, sailing, cruises, XC skiing, snowshoeing, shopping, touring Bar Harbor, fine dining, museums, various seasonal events

Amenities & Services Games, binoculars, reservations; hosts share favorite spots for hiking, biking, kayaking

ACCOMMODATIONS

Units 8 guest rooms, 1 suite

All Rooms Bath, ceiling fan, carpet, flowers, alarm clock, air conditioning

Some Rooms Private balconies overlooking harbor, sitting area

Bed & Bath Antique beds, sizes vary; most shower-only

Favorites Three-room Turret Suite—telescope, LR, TV/VCR, antique king,

wood-burning fireplace, tub; 2nd-floor rear rooms 3 and 5 quiet w/ private balconies overlooking the harbor

Comfort & Decor Comfortable English country feel; Laura Ashley and Waverly fabrics, wallcoverings, and window treatments. Reading lamps at bedsides. Charming.

RATES, RESERVATIONS, & RESTRICTIONS

Deposit 1 night; 50% longer stays

Credit Cards V, MC,

Check-in/Out 3/11

Smoking Non-smoking

Pets No

Kids Over 12

Minimum Stay Two night minimum stay holiday weekends

Open All year

Hosts Cyd and Ken Champagne Collins

373 Main St., Box 1426

Southwest Harbor, ME 04679

(207) 244-5302

Fax: (207) 244-7691

www.kingsleighinn.com

relax@kingsleighinn.com

INN ON THE HARBOR, Stonington

OVERALL ★★★ | ROOM QUALITY ★★★ | VALUE ★★½ | PRICE $105–135

This quirky inn was formerly known as Captain's Quarters. Christina, a New Yorker with family here, renovated the inn in 1997. As common rooms were sacrificed to enlarge the guest rooms, almost total renovation was vital. Now this is a fine romantic waterfront treat. Stonington is a working fishing village with pluses (fresh fish, busy harbor, fog, atmosphere) and minuses (harbor life–and its noises–begins at 4 a.m.). The Inn on the Harbor is not for mall shopping, but from the decks you'll get a close-up glimpse of real rustic Maine.

SETTING & FACILITIES

Location On Stonington Harbor; Rt. 15 SE to Deer Isle bridge, into Little Deer Isle; Stonington at tip; call inn for travel by air or sea

Near Blue Hill, Camden, Isle Au Haut, Penobscot Bay, Haystack School of Crafts in Sunshine

Building Waterfront Victorian, 4 buildings combined

Grounds Decks built right over the 11-foot tide; inn restaurant, Café Atlantic, 2 buildings away

Public Space Reception desk, formal dining room; harbor decks

Food & Drink Cont'l breakfast; espresso bar; informal lunch and dinner served at restaurant

Recreation Walk to quaint village/harbor, biking, tennis, golf, day trips, boat cruises, fishing, ferry to islands, local artisan and crafts shopping, antiquing

Amenities & Services Binoculars in each room; small gift shop, fax

ACCOMMODATIONS

Units 14 guest rooms, including one two-bedroom suite and one efficiency

All Rooms Bath

Some Rooms Priv. or semi-priv. deck, view, fireplace, ceiling fan, phone, TV, disabled access suite w/ sitting room (1), twin bed, large full bath, deck access

Bed & Bath Bed sizes vary, new mattresses; all baths are full

Favorites Victory Chimes—granite fire-place, picture window facing harbor, sitting area, king bed, large bath, deck access

Comfort & Decor Rooms recently renovated, named after Stonington Harbor sailing schooners. Original artwork. Stunning views, large decks, fireplaces. Comfortable, but decor not noteworthy. Overstuffed furnishings, sitting areas in front of bay windows. Harbor often noisy.

RATES, RESERVATIONS, & RESTRICTIONS

Deposit 1 night; refund w/ 14-day notice, subject to $15 service fee

Discounts Off-season, Oct. weekend dinner pkgs., holiday special pkgs.,

Credit Cards V, AE, MC, D

Check-in/Out 3–7/11

Smoking On deck

Pets No; board at nearby kennel

Kids Over 12 welcome

Minimum Stay Holiday weekends

two-day

Open All year;

Host Christina Shipps

Box 69, Main St.

Stonington, ME 04681

(800) 942-2420 or (207) 367-2420

Fax: (207) 367-5165

webmaster@innontheharbor.com

www.innontheharbor.com

ISLAND VIEW INN, Sullivan

OVERALL ★★★½ | ROOM QUALITY ★★★ | VALUE ★★★★ | PRICE $80–120

For travelers who enjoy the isolated beauty of Downeast Maine, this friendly bed-and-breakfast on a private beach offers just that, at half the price of similar Bar Harbor properties, 30 minutes south. The namesake view is superb, encompassing Frenchman Bay and rugged Mt. Desert Island. How can you not take to a place that serves pancakes on Sunday, has a sailboat ready on a private beach, a moose head on the wall, and costs less than a motel?

SETTING & FACILITIES

Location Just off Rt. I in Sullivan, on Frenchman Bay
Near Hancock, Bar Harbor, Ellsworth, Mt. Desert Island, Acadia Nat'l Park, Schoodic Point, Maritime Canada
Building Circa 1900 2-story "summer cottage"
Grounds Lawn with pine trees, priv. beach

Public Space Lodgelike LR, DR
Food & Drink Full breakfast; specialties: French toast w/ berries, pancakes on Sundays
Recreation Golf, tennis, fishing, beach, cruises, mountain biking/climbing
Amenities & Services Canoe, rowboat, paddleboat; 18-foot day sailboat for exp. sailors

ACCOMMODATIONS

Units 7 guest rooms
All Rooms Private bath
Some Rooms Small priv. balcony, water views
Bed & Bath Bed sizes vary
Favorites Waterfront rooms—Bird Room w/ king bed, small balcony; Ships Room w/ twins, small balcony; Lighthouse and Hunt Rooms—queen bed, water

view, balcony
Comfort & Decor Simple, country antiques. Restored original summer home furnishings. TVs/phones deliberately excluded. Modest, clean. B&B interior renovated 1985–86 (on-going improvements). Waterfront rooms have least road noise.

RATES, RESERVATIONS, & RESTRICTIONS

Deposit I night, check w/ B&B for cancellation policy
Discounts Singles, $15 per additional person over double occupancy; children under 5 free
Credit Cards V, MC, D
Check-in/Out 3/11
Smoking Outside only
Pets Yes, if well behaved

Kids 6 and over welcome
Minimum Stay None
Open Late May–Mid-Oct.
Host Evelyn Joost
HCR 32, Box 24
Sullivan, ME 04664
(207) 422-3031
lph@acadia.net
www.maineus.com

GOOSE COVE LODGE, Sunset

OVERALL ★★★★ | ROOM QUALITY ★★★★ | VALUE ★½ | PRICE $124–500

A relaxed waterfront retreat on a pristine bay, this is a great outdoor escape for couples or families. The main lodge features a massive fieldstone fireplace, a mix of Country cottage and Victorian styles, a honey-toned pine ceiling, whole log beams and posts, wide-plank pine floors, and scattered Oriental rugs. Cabins, rooms and suites have similar cozy appeal and comfortable furniture, while two newer architect-designed cottages offer rustic sophistication. Water views surround, activities abound, and this informal spot is considered one of the best dining spots on coastal Maine.

SETTING & FACILITIES

Location Goose Cove, Deer Isle, on sheltered piece of Penobscot Bay; Rt. 1 past Bucksport, right onto Rt. 15 to Deer Isle, right onto Main St. (Sunset Rd.), right at Goose Cove Rd.

Near Haystack Mountain School of Crafts, Stonington, Blue Hill, Camden, Barred Island Nature Preserve, ocean and beaches, mail boat to Isle au Haut, Bar Harbor, Acadia National Park, Island Country Club

Building Log-and-shingle–style main lodge w/ large deck; contemporary and rustic cottages/cabins on wooded hillside, sundecks

Grounds Expansive water views; spruce trees; pink granite ledges, sand beaches; at low tide shore trail leads to Barred Island

Public Space Rustic common room, library, DR, deck café w/ water views; rec. hall, gift shop

Food & Drink Buffet breakfast; pre-dinner cocktails; candlelit dining; innovative regional American fare; specialties: famous local seafood/shellfish and organic meats and vegetables; seasonal Sunday brunch, al fresco lunch and tea on deck, KidCamp children's meals, Monday night lobster feast on the beach, w/ steamed lobsters, grilled steaks, free-range chicken; full liquor license

Recreation Sailing, kayaking, lobster fishing, hiking, biking, galleries, museums, antiquing; bird, seal and porpoise watching, swimming, golf, tennis; high season evening KidCamp, nature walks, star-gazing, nature-related educational activities

Amenities & Services Gift shop and nature center w/ educational activities; bikes, ocean kayaks, canoes, 24-foot sloop; naturalist-guided walks, star-gazing and instruction; evening child program (high season); massage; retreats, reunions, weddings low season); special events pkgs., including Columbus Day weekend Harvest and Wine Dinner

ACCOMMODATIONS

Units 10 guest rooms/suites in main lodge; 7 cabins; 4 duplex cabins; 2 luxury cottages

All Rooms Bath

Some Rooms Fireplace/wood stove, ocean view, private or shared deck, game/dining table, sitting area, kitchenette, 1 handicapped accessible cabin

Bed & Bath Queen/king beds; cabins w/ add'l twin and bunk beds, some sofa beds, cots available; many upgraded full baths, tile floors; some showers only, robes **Favorites** Cottages–Elm and Linnea, closest to water; Bayberry and Thistle fresh, newly built w/ kitchens, French doors to decks, large stone fireplaces in great rooms; Lookout suite in Main Lodge–most spacious suite, ocean views, gas fireplace, full kitchen, living/dining room; king bed in master w/ cathedral ceiling; 2nd bedroom w/ twins, full bath **Comfort & Decor** Rustic rooms chock-full of comfortable furniture. Paneled walls, beamed ceilings, country scatter rugs or Oriental rugs, quilts, framed prints, original artwork, antiques, collectibles, large windows capitalize views. Cabins basic, comfortable, most w/ upgraded baths. More luxurious cottages w/ sleek, country furnishings and design. Fireplaces prepared daily.

RATES, RESERVATIONS, & RESTRICTIONS

Deposit Greater of 1 night or 1/3 of stay; refund (less $25 fee) w/ 30-day notice low season, 60-day high season. **Discounts** Low season midweek pkgs, children, according to age; 3rd person in room **Credit Cards** V, AE, MC, D **Check-in/Out** 3-5/1030 **Smoking** Outside only in designated areas **Pets** No **Kids** Welcome **No No's** Late arrival, early departure (full room charge); deposit will be applied to canceled nights **Minimum Stay** 2 nights all units May–Oct.; week minimum for secluded cabins July and Aug. **Open** Mid-May–mid-Oct. all services; limited winter lodging available without services **Hosts** Joanne & Dom Parisi Box 40 Sunset, Maine 04683 (800) 728-1963 or (207) 348-2508 Fax: (207) 348-2624 goosecove@goosecovelodge.com www.goosecovelodge.com

Midcoast Maine

Relatively flat, the Midcoast region has both sandy and rocky New England beaches, fishing villages, islands, historic sites, resort towns, and a relaxed attitude. While more exotic or more isolated surroundings can certainly be found, you may not find better summering.

Favorable cruising grounds attract private craft and yachts, and harbor watching is an honorable summer activity. **Brunswick** has U.S. naval and arctic explorer history, plus the **Harriet Beecher Stowe House** and historic homes. **Bowdoin College** hosts summer musical theater and festivals and features an art gallery that includes works by **Andrew Wyeth** and **Winslow Homer. Eagle Island**—summer home to **Admiral Robert Edwin Peary,** the first explorer to reach the North Pole—is crammed with arctic explorer accoutrements.

Labor Day sends folk traipsing to **Thomas Point Beach** to celebrate the **Bluegrass Festival,** right on the heels of the August **Topsham Country Fair.**

Wiscasset has been labeled the "prettiest village in Maine," and is home to the landmark **Red's Eats**—the shack at the corner of Route 1 (a line forms before the 11 a.m. opening). **Wiscasset** and **Searsport** are notable even among noted Midcoast antiquing towns. Bath is home to the famous **Chocolate Church** arts center, and the town encourages sun worship at nearby **Reid State Park** and **Popham Beach State Park. Edgecomb** is known for its pottery studios.

The Boothbays offer variety within themselves. **Ocean Point** is a favorite wedding area. Crowded **Boothbay Harbor** sports the **Windjammer Festival** in late June, **Friendship Sloop Days** in late July, the October **Fall Foliage Festival** and early December **Harbor Lights Festival.** (Don't leave Boothbay without a visit to **King Brud's** hot dog cart, a landmark since 1943.) The more peaceful little shipbuilding community of **East**

Boothbay offers sitting on a dock on **Linekin Bay** and a good lobster dock.

Rockland, home to the world's largest fleet of sailing schooners, has the **Farnsworth Art Museum, Andrew Wyeth exhibition,** August **Maine Lobster Festival, The Great Schooner Race** in early July, and more.

Picturesque **Rockport** hosts year-round chamber concerts and the **Maine Photographic Workshop.** Authentic, 200-year-old Union heralds the harvest with the August **Union Fair.** The **Belfast and Moosehead Lake Railroad** takes nostalgic trips through the countryside. **Pemaquid Point lighthouse** and **Fisherman's Museum** at the end of the peninsula near Wicassett are must-sees for maritime buffs. **Camden** is the charming and popular gateway to **Mount Battie** in **Camden Hills State Park** and sponsors numerous winter festivals.

Finally, simple, whale-shaped **Monhegan Island,** with 510 acres of dramatic, natural scenery, is home to rugged lobstermen and inspired artists and is accessible by ferry from Boothbay, Port Clyde, or New Harbor. A limit on construction and a ban on passenger cars help preserve the island.

Small lodgings are plentiful, competitive and excellent; usually homes converted to bed-and-breakfasts or sophisticated small inns. Many close in winter. Book far ahead, as this area fills up fast.

FOR MORE INFORMATION

Boothbay Chamber of Commerce (207) 633-4924 or (207) 633-2353 or (207) 633-4743 email: seamaine@boothbayharbor.com

Camden Bed & Breakfast Association (207) 230-0783 or (800) 813-5015 *www.camdeninns.com*

Camden-Rockport-Lincolnville Chamber of Commerce (207) 236-4404 email: chamber@camdenme.org

Monhegan Island (207) 372-8848 www.monheganboat.com

Rockland-Thomaston Area (207) 596-0376 *www.midcoast.com/~rtacc/*

Searsport Area B&B Association (207) 548-6575 or (800) 691-0150 email: info@mainebedandbreakfast.com *www.mainebedandbreakfast.org*

THE INN AT BATH, Bath

OVERALL ★★★★½ | ROOM QUALITY ★★★★★ | VALUE ★★ | PRICE $85–330

House Beautiful has featured this bed-and-breakfast, and it's easy to see why. Sophistication is evident in the collection of antiques and *objets d'art*. Oriental rugs over plank floors, ornate mantels, and numerous artistic touches add to the decor. Family photos and a local artist's whimsy in startling colors and unexpected detailing warm up the luxury. Host Nick was an investment banker in his previous life and enjoys both the quiet contemplation of books and art and active Maine endeavors, such as fly-fishing. He loves to talk about both.

SETTING & FACILITIES

Location Rt. 1 to Bath, to Washington St., residential area
Near Chocolate Church Arts Center; Bath Iron Works; Maine Maritime Museum; shops and restaurants; wildlife preserves; boat trips, incl. lighthouse tours; Kennebec River; day trips to Acadia Nat'l Park
Building 1810 Greek Revival
Grounds Four gardens; porches; on distinguished street
Public Space Twin parlors, DRs

Food & Drink Full breakfast; specialties: blueberry pancakes, banana French toast; also cont'l breakfast; refreshments, boxed lunches ordered locally
Recreation Golf, tennis, river and deep-sea fishing, boat trips, skiing
Amenities & Services Laundry, irons, bike storage, binoculars, fax, email, Internet access; beach towels, charters booked, trips planned, cots/portacribs, ice and glasses (BYOB), corp. facilities

ACCOMMODATIONS

Units 8 guest rooms, incl. 1 disabled access room; 1 suite
All Rooms Bath, AC, TV/VCR, phone, alarm clock radio/cassette player
Some Rooms 2-BR suites; fireplace w/ wood, desk, dbl. whirlpool, priv. entrance
Bed & Bath Firm/softer mattresses, some four-poster or canopy, sizes vary; dbl. whirlpools in BRs, hairdryers
Favorites River Room—converted hay loft w/ beams, love seat; Lavender Room—antique fishnet-lace canopy double, sofa, bay window
Comfort & Decor Spacious, furnished w/ 18th- and 19th-century antiques, designer fabrics. Elegant, but country touches beams, brick/stone fireplaces, bookcases. Good lighting. Unexpected flair throughout. Immaculate.

RATES, RESERVATIONS, & RESTRICTIONS

Deposit Credit card/check to hold for 1 night; special dep. for graduations, priv. parties; and Jacuzzi/fireplace rooms; refund w/ 14-day notice
Discounts Off-season, including June, longer stays, corp, and per diem, 3rd and 4th person.
Credit Cards All accepted; pref. check or cash
Check-in/Out In anytime (if ready); out by 11 a.m,
Smoking On porch or in garden
Pets Reservation req.
Kids Any age
Minimum Stay 2 nights on weekends, but check for 1 night avail.
Open All year
Hosts Nick Bayard and Barb Wilson
969 Washington St.
Bath, ME 04530
(207) 443-4294 or (800) 423-0964
Fax: (207) 443-4295
innkeeper@innatbath.com
www.innatbath.com

ALDEN HOUSE, Belfast

OVERALL ★★★½ | ROOM QUALITY ★★★★ | VALUE ★★★½ | PRICE $88–125

USA Today rated Belfast "one of the top five culturally cool small towns in America," and this welcoming bed-and-breakfast is warm and pretty cool as well. The former owners, restored the previously neglected mansion, and *The Oprah Winfrey Show* filmed it after renovation. It's not as grand as The White House down the block, but original details include Italian marble mantels and sinks, a handcarved cherry stair rail, tin ceilings, and plaster ceiling medallions. And it's not cluttered up, as many Victorians tend to be.

SETTING & FACILITIES

Location I-95 to Rt. 1 or Rt. 3 to Belfast on residential street near The White House
Near Belfast business and historic district, Penobscot Bay
Building 1840 Greek Revival; renovated 1997
Grounds 1 acre, shade trees
Public Space Double parlors, library, porches, circular staircase in entrance foyer

Food & Drink Multi-course candlelight breakfast; special requests; specialties: homemade fruit strudels, chive & brie soufflé, cranberry-walnut waffles; afternoon refreshments and home baked sweets.
Recreation Water/snow sports, antiquing, local events
Amenities & Services Grand player piano w/ 150 rolls, 100+ videos; disabled access

ACCOMMODATIONS

Units 7 guest rooms, 3 cottages
All Rooms Bath
Some Rooms Water view, priv. deck; all cottages have a fireplace
Bed & Bath Antique beds, king or queen; feather bedding, down comforters, damask sheets; some whirlpool tubs
Favorites Room 7—spacious, full view

of bay, four-poster carved canopy king, whirlpool; Room 10—most priv., queen canopy, view from deck; Cottages—privacy
Comfort & Decor Designer fabrics, antiques in main building; cottages are casual country w/ wicker, very priv.; spacious, charming, immaculate.

RATES, RESERVATIONS, & RESTRICTIONS

Deposit 50%; refund w/ 14-day notice
Discounts Extended stay; specials
Credit Cards V, MC, D
Check-in/Out 4–8/before 11
Smoking Outside only
Pets No; nearby kennel
Kids OK
No-No's Kids under 12 in own room
Minimum Stay None

Open All year
Hosts Bruce and Sue Madara
63 Church St.
Belfast, ME 04915
(207) 338-2151 or (800) 337-8151
Fax same as phone
innkeeper@thealdenhouse.com
www.thealdenhouse.com

THE WHITE HOUSE, Belfast

OVERALL ★★★★½ | ROOM QUALITY ★★★★ | VALUE ★★★½ | PRICE $95–165

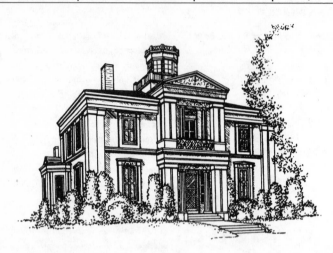

This White House, and original owner James Paterson White, actually hosted a vacationing President Franklin Roosevelt on his way to Campobello Island. It is a much photographed, historic beauty with the largest copper beech tree in Maine, and is wonderful within as well. The rich wallpaper, intricate ceiling medallions, marble mantels, hardwoods, Oriental rugs, crystal chandeliers, polished wood, and antique and reproduction touches are impressive. The owners have worked hard to refurbish this landmark mansion, and offer its presidential-level pleasures at a pleasing bargain rate.

SETTING & FACILITIES

Location At the head of Church St.

Near Penobscot Bay, 6 state parks, Fort Knox, Warren Island, half-hour to Camden, 1 hour to Bar Harbor, walk to village and harbor

Building Striking mid-1800s columned Greek Revival

Grounds Triangular lawn, terrace, gardens, 1800s gazebo, harbor view

Public Space Ornate DR, parlors, library

Food & Drink Early riser coffee/tea; full breakfast, lunch baskets (fee)

Recreation Golf, tennis, horses, antiquing, water/snow sports; day trips (car/boat)

Amenities & Services Bicycle storage, irons, laundry service (fee); corp. facilities, games, celebrations (fee); videos

ACCOMMODATIONS

Units 3 guest rooms, 2 suites; carriage house, spacious w/ priv. entrance, terrace

All Rooms Bath, some hall access; flowers, plush rugs, phone

Some Rooms Water view, TV/VCR

Bed & Bath Some four-posters, sizes vary; robes for hall baths, hairdryers, 1 bath w/ fireplace

Favorites Belfast Bay—king four-poster, fireplace, whirlpool, views

Comfort & Decor Strikes a balance between elegant and country comfort. Sizes vary, but luxury level consistent. Overhead lighting, w/ table lamp augmentation. New, immaculate furnishings.

RATES, RESERVATIONS, & RESTRICTIONS

Deposit 1 night

Discounts 4 nights or more

Credit Cards V, MC, D

Check-in/Out 3–8/before 1030; call for a check-in after 8

Smoking No

Pets No

Kids Over 12

Minimum Stay None

Open All year

Hosts Robert Hansen, Terry Prescott

1 Church St.

Belfast, ME 04915-6206

(888) 290-1901 or (207) 338-1901

Fax: (207) 338-5161

whitehouse@mainebb.com

www.mainebb.com (reservations)

ANCHOR WATCH, Boothbay Harbor

OVERALL ★★★½ | ROOM QUALITY ★★★★ | VALUE ★★★ | PRICE $95–150

Host-driven, this little bed-and-breakfast is warm and welcoming with super breakfasts and views, and appealing with its immaculate cottage-style accommodations. The former English teacher innkeeper and her daughter make guests feel right at home, with the run of the house. Feed the ducks, watch the birds and scudding clouds, or walk to the busy boating center. This inn seems far away from the tourist bustle.

SETTING & FACILITIES

Location Rt. 1 to Edgecomb to Rt. 27, 12 miles to Oak St., to Commercial St., follow to dead end; left to Eames Rd.; residential area

Near Shore in Boothbay Harbor, lighthouses, ferry to Monhegan and other islands; walk to town

Building Late 19th-century sea captain's home

Grounds Lawn down to fishing pier, float; views of islands, sunsets, and boats

Public Space Sun porch, small parlor, open-air porch, kitchen, breakfast nook

Food & Drink Full breakfasts; specialty: egg-and-cheese pie; afternoon tea, microwave popcorn

Recreation Boating, fishing; day trips on excursion boats owned by innkeeper's son

Amenities & Services Discounts for ferry trips to Monhegan Island; laundry and kitchen facilities

ACCOMMODATIONS

Units 5 guest rooms

All Rooms Bath, clock, radio

Some Rooms Ocean view, balcony, TV, whirlpool, fireplace, AC

Bed & Bath Some canopies, bed sizes vary

Favorites Novelty—fireplace and whirlpool under stained-glass window,

3rd-floor balcony; May Archer—2nd-floor ocean view, queen bed, balcony

Comfort & Decor Simple, but sweet. Each room named after a former Monhegan Island ferry. Country style w/ stenciling, old trunks, borders, quilts, skirted tables in small prints, painted dormers.

RATES, RESERVATIONS, & RESTRICTIONS

Deposit 1 night; must cancel 7 days in advance

Discounts Off-season, singles, pkgs., 3rd person

Credit Cards V, MC

Check-in/Out 2–6/before 11; call for later check-in

Smoking No

Pets No; house cat

Kids Over 10

Minimum Stay Holiday weekends

Open 11 months; poss. winter closing

Hosts Diane Campbell and Kathy Reed

3 Eames Rd.

Boothbay Harbor, ME 04538

(207) 633-7565

diane@lincoln.midcoast.com

www.maineguide.com/boothbay/anchorwatch

HARTSTONE INN, Camden

OVERALL ★★★★ | ROOM QUALITY ★★½ | VALUE ★★½ | PRICE $85–190

A charming couple—an award-winning chef and his hotel-manager wife—purchased this neglected inn in 1998 and has worked successfully to upgrade it. This inn glows with Colonial style, but mostly it's a great restaurant with rooms to rest in between meals. Michael cooks one set dinner at night. Sumptuous breakfast may be lobster-and-asparagus quiche, or smoked salmon Benedict. Dinner? Perhaps sweet potato–crusted pheasant breast with a blueberry demi-glacé, ending with chocolate-Amaretto soufflé with an almond anglaise.

SETTING & FACILITIES

Location Rt. 1 becomes Elm St.; inn on left near business district

Near Camden Harbor, state park, Penobscot Bay, lighthouses, outlet shopping

Building 1835 Mansard-style Victorian, carriage house

Grounds Wooded in-town lot, wild-

flower gardens, patio, mountain views

Public Space DR, parlor, library, game room

Food & Drink Gourmet candlelit breakfast; afternoon tea and coffee; 5-course candlelit dinner (reservations); wine, beer; picnic baskets; cooking classes; food festivals

Recreation Schooner tours, antiquing, water sports, golf, day trips to Acadia Nat'l Park, skiing

Amenities & Services Fax, refrigerator, irons, books, maps, special occasions, off-street parking

ACCOMMODATIONS

Units 8 guest rooms, 2 suites
All Rooms Bath, leather duvets, air conditioning, period furnishings
Some Rooms Fireplace, sitting area, priv. entrance
Bed & Bath Beds vary, lace canopy, iron, brass, four-poster; some antique tubs, robes; some original marble sinks; some showers only

Favorites Tea Cup—2nd floor, fireplace, TV, sitting area, quilt; Magnolia Room—fireplace, hardwoods, sitting area, canopy bed
Comfort & Decor Romantic, some antiques, but still a bit underdecorated. Touches such as candlelight and fresh flowers soften edges. Immaculate. Orchid collection

RATES, RESERVATIONS, & RESTRICTIONS

Deposit 1 night; must cancel 14 days in advance
Discounts Seniors, special pkgs.; MAP available
Credit Cards V, MC
Check-in/Out 3/11
Smoking No
Pets No
Kids over 12

Minimum Stay None
Open All year
Hosts Mary Jo and Michael Salmon
41 Elm St.
Camden, ME 04843
(800) 788-4823 or (207) 236-4259
Fax: (207) 236-9575
info@hartstoneinn.com
www.hartstoneinn.com

HAWTHORN INN, Camden

OVERALL ★★★★ | ROOM QUALITY ★★★★ | VALUE ★★½ | PRICE $100–240

Back from the main road, with a distinctive turret, bay windows, and porches, this handsome house is painted in Hawthorn yellow with red trim. The low-key hosts are former bankers he's British, she's Texan. As they put it, they're "not on top of" guests, and they maintain a bed-and-breakfast of bright, comfortable elegance, with sheer white curtains and tall windows. Plans are to close the garden-level rooms and open luxury rooms on the third floor, with harbor views, whirlpools, and fireplaces—the big draws here.

SETTING & FACILITIES

Location Rt. 1 into Camden, north of public library
Near Bar Harbor, Acadia Nat'l Park, islands, Camden Hills State Park,

Penobscot Bay
Building 1894 Queen Anne Victorian mansion

Grounds 1+ wooded acres; lawn slopes toward harbor; deck
Public Space Parlors, DR
Food & Drink Full breakfast, communal or separate; specialties: crème caramel French toast, crab strata; tea or coffee; picnic baskets

Recreation Harbor/water activities, tobogganing, windjammer cruises, antiquing, museums
Amenities & Services Fridge, irons, fax, meetings (up to 12), maps, toothbrush, hairdryer

ACCOMMODATIONS

Units 6 guest rooms in main house; 4 in carriage house
All Rooms Bath, phone, antiques
Some Rooms "Keyhole" harbor view; carriage house fireplace, TV/VCR, some w/ glass walls onto deck or patio, view
Bed & Bath Some four-poster, iron, brass; queen, twin; some hall access, robes; some showers only in main house, some tubs in room, some dbl. whirlpools in carriage house

Favorites Jillian—sitting room, queen four-poster, 5 windows; Rose—2 twins, lots of windows; in carriage house, Broughman—best views, gas fireplace, dbl. whirlpool, deck
Comfort & Decor Casually elegant, pristine. Pine accents, botanical prints, floral wallcoverings, armoires. Good lighting, and lots of natural light. Varies widely from luxury to comfortable.

RATES, RESERVATIONS, & RESTRICTIONS

Deposit 1 night for up to 3 nights stay, 25% on longer stays; refund w/ 10-day notice
Discounts Longer stays, pkgs., 3rd person $35 where available
Credit Cards V, AE, MC
Check-in/Out 3/11; till noon w/ arrangement
Smoking No; violators pay cleaning fee
Pets No
Kids Over 12

No-No's Late check-in, leaving house w/out a key, front door locks at 9 p.m.
Minimum Stay 2 nights on holidays for carriage house only
Open All year
Hosts Patty and Nick Wharton
9 High St.
Camden, ME 04843
(207) 236-8842
Fax: (207) 236-6181
hawthorn@midcoast.com

INN AT SUNRISE POINT, *Camden*

OVERALL ★★★★½ | ROOM QUALITY ★★★★★ | VALUE ★★ | PRICE $175–375

The original owner was a travel writer, who obviously distilled his knowledge into this secluded bed-and-breakfast beauty. Penobscot Bay laps right up to the cottages, and beyond the expanses of glass are blue sky and water, peace and quiet. The afternoon snacks are especially lavish. Both the mood and the look are cool and serene, and this is one of the few New England properties in contemporary style. It's worth getting up at least once for the sunrise that gives the inn its name.

SETTING & FACILITIES

Location 4 miles north of Camden Harbor, off Rt. 1 on Fire Rd. 9
Near Camden Hills State Park, Camden Harbor, shopping, restaurants, galleries; abuts Penobscot Bay
Building 1920s farmhouse, cluster of cottages; award-winning renovation in 1991
Grounds Path from road to water, through 4 acres; priv. little stony beach, water views
Public Space Domed conservatory, library, LR
Food & Drink Full breakfast; specialty: lobster hash; hors d'oeuvres, snacks
Recreation Lake swimming and fishing, hiking, sailing
Amenities & Services Some disabled access, books, videos

ACCOMMODATIONS

Units 3 guest rooms, 4 cottages
All Rooms Bath, near shore, fireplace, heat controls, TV/VCR, phone, view
Some Rooms Deck; cottages mini-refrigerator, wet bar, some w/ coffee maker
Bed & Bath Queen or king, firm mattresses; some oversized tubs; some dbl. whirlpools, sep. showers, robes
Favorites Fitz Hugh Lane Cottage—10 yards from shore, every upgrade, cruise-cabin views
Comfort & Decor Rooms named after Maine artists and writers, featuring their work. Understated, but upscale, w/ light pine furniture, emphasis on comfort, relaxation. Rooms in main house are smallish w/ cathedral ceilings.

RATES, RESERVATIONS, & RESTRICTIONS

Deposit 50%; must cancel 30 days in advance
Discounts June rates
Credit Cards V, AE, MC
Check-in/Out 3/11
Smoking No
Pets No
Kids By prior arrangement
Minimum Stay 2 nights on weekends
Open Memorial Day–Oct. 31
Hosts Bob and Karleen Hathcock
Box 1344
Camden, ME 04843
(800) 435-6278 or (207) 236-7716
Fax: (207) 236-0820
www.sunrisepoint.com
info@sunrisepoint.com

NORUMBEGA, *Camden*

OVERALL ★★★★½ | ROOM QUALITY ★★★★ | VALUE ★½ | PRICE $145–465

"Norumbega" was a legendary sixteenth-century city of riches. The name fits, as guest rooms are not discernably better than those in nearby inns at half the price. Why stay? For the grandeur of this undeniably beautiful little "castle" built by the originator of the Western Union telegram after he toured the castles of Europe. Much photographed and admired, this stone, turreted showplace with hidden passageways, high ceilings, and leaded windows, is a perfect place for romance and intrigue. And if you want a "yes," spring for the penthouse, with wraparound water views.

SETTING & FACILITIES

Location Off Rt. 1 N just past town overlooking the ocean
Near Walk to Camden Harbor; Camden Hills State Park; drive to Acadia Nat'l Park, Bar Harbor, Searsport, Rockport
Building 1886 stone, slate-roofed mansion
Grounds Several landscaped acres, 2 summer gazebos, on Penobscot River

Public Space DR, elegant parlors, billiards room, deck
Food & Drink Full breakfast, tea or wine, evening wine and cheese, snacks
Recreation Grounds games, sailing, antiquing, boat trips, golf, skiing
Amenities & Services Murder Weekend w/ 2-night-stay prize, games, bikes, meeting facilities

ACCOMMODATIONS

Units 9 guest rooms, 3 suites
All Rooms Bath, phone, clock, robe
Some Rooms Priv. or shared deck, view, fireplace, sitting area, TV; priv. entrance (1)
Bed & Bath Some four-posters, all king, some are twins that may be separated; some showers only, 1 dbl. whirlpool

Favorites Penthouse suite—up spiral staircase in turret, fireplace, wet bar, refrigerator, fold-out sofa, skylight
Comfort & Decor Rooms named for English castles and are spacious and understated. Soft colors and a mix of antiques and reproductions. Good lighting.

RATES, RESERVATIONS, & RESTRICTIONS

Deposit 1 night or 50%; refund w/ 21-day notice; $35 charge for extra guest
Discounts Off-season, pkgs.
Credit Cards V, AE, MC, D
Check-in/Out 3–9/11
Smoking No
Pets No
Kids Over 7
Minimum Stay 2 nights on weekends

and holidays
Open All year
Host Kent Keatinge
61 High St.
Camden, ME 04843
(207) 236-4646
Fax: (207) 236-4990
email form on website
www.acadia.net/norumbega

FIVE GABLES INN, *East Boothbay*

OVERALL ★★★★½ | ROOM QUALITY ★★★★ | VALUE ★★★ | PRICE $120–185

The Southern, friendly, outgoing owners—he a trained chef, she an artist—purchased this peaceful, pretty property in 1995 far from the Boothbay tourist throngs after sailing to Polynesia. They describe their romantic, eclectically decorated bed-and-breakfast best "It's not a 'poofy' place with 10,000 pillows, and swags and draperies everywhere. If your family had a summer cottage for several generations, it would look like this."

SETTING & FACILITIES

Location Rt. 96 through east Boothbay; turn right at blinking light on Murray Hill Rd.; a mile or so on right
Near Boothbay Harbor, Pemaquid Point Lighthouse, Ferry to Monhegan Island, Windjammer Schooners
Building Gothic Revival Victorian
Grounds Lawn to water, paths to shore, dock; overlooks Linekin Bay
Public Space Common room, library, porch

Food & Drink Buffet breakfast (in room by request or communal); specialties: grilled tomatoes w/ herbed cornmeal; afternoon refreshments; picnic lunches
Recreation Whale watching; touring harbor, kayaking, golf, swimming
Amenities & Services 2 boat moorings for guests, irons, games, maps, recipes, celebrations; can reserve entire property

ACCOMMODATIONS

Units 15 guest rooms
All Rooms Bath, water view, sitting area, reading lamp
Some Rooms Fireplace, built-in windowseat
Bed & Bath Some, pencil-post or wrought-iron beds, sizes vary; most, showers only
Favorites Room 14—biggest, king, fire-

place; Room 10—four-poster queen, sunrise bay views
Comfort & Decor Traditional furnishings, softened w/ hand-crocheted afghans and artwork by owners. Casually elegant. Sheer curtains let in sun and water views. Good lighting. Immaculate, smallest rooms under gables are good deals.

RATES, RESERVATIONS, & RESTRICTIONS

Deposit 50%; refund w/ 5-day notice
Credit Cards V, MC
Check-in/Out 2–8/11; can use facilities after vacating room
Smoking In garden or on veranda
Pets No
Kids Over 12
Minimum Stay None

Open Mid-May–Oct. 31
Hosts De and Mike Kennedy
Murray Hill Rd., Box 335
East Boothbay, ME 04544
(800) 451-5048 or (207) 633-4551
info@fivegablesinn.com
www.fivegablesinn.com

LINEKIN BAY BED & BREAKFAST, East Boothbay

OVERALL ★★★½ | ROOM QUALITY ★★★ | VALUE ★★½ | PRICE $85–175

The young hosts are really sweet. She is a special-education teacher; he, a retired policeman. They are still learning the ropes, and seasoning will soften the edges and add character to this modest but sparkling new property. His fresh-baked cookies are great with tea or cider, and their philosophy is "no one should leave the table hungry." The downstairs luxury guest room and bath have been completed, as well as a deck off the dining room, for summer pleasure.

SETTING & FACILITIES

Location Rt. 27 toward Boothbay Harbor to Ocean Point Rd. (Rt.96) in East Boothbay, turn left at only traffic light, look for stained-glass sign
Near Shipbuilding center of East Boothbay, Boothbay Harbor, Ocean Point, Railway Village, lighthouses, nature preserve
Building 1850 Gothic Revival farmhouse
Grounds Gardens, porches

Public Space Common room, DR
Food & Drink Full communal breakfast; specialty: baked peach oatmeal; early-riser coffee; afternoon tea, desserts
Recreation Rail tours, day boat trips, antiquing, tours, boat rentals
Amenities & Services Irons, games, maps, paper, recipes, off-street parking

ACCOMMODATIONS

Units 3 guest rooms, 1 suite
All Rooms Bath, reading lamp, crystal wine glasses and corkscrew
Some Rooms Views of Linekin Bay, fireplace(1)
Bed & Bath Sizes vary; hairdryers, 1 shower only; newly renovated
Favorites Honeymoon suite—fireplace,

king, love seat, bay views; Rhapsody in Blue—views, Laura Ashley
Comfort & Decor Comfortable, clean. Underdecorated, as rooms are new, and hosts haven't accumulated objects. Should improve w/ age. Small, but cozy.

RATES, RESERVATIONS, & RESTRICTIONS

Deposit 1 night; refund w/ 14-day notice
Discounts Longer stays
Credit Cards V, MC
Check-in/Out 2–6/11
Smoking On porch and grounds only
Pets No; hosts own 2 miniature collies, not permitted on premises
Kids Over 12

Minimum Stay None
Open All year
Hosts Marti Booth and Larry Brown
531 Ocean Point Rd.
East Boothbay, ME 04544
(207) 633-9900
info@linekinbaybb.com

COD COVE FARM, *Edgecomb*

OVERALL ★★★★½ | ROOM QUALITY ★★★★ | VALUE ★★★★ | PRICE $95–115

Renovated and opened for business in 1997, this sparkling little property doesn't have a weak spot. It offers warm, helpful hosts; lavish, creative breakfasts; themed guest rooms of imaginative crafting; bucolic river views and gardens; and scrupulous attention to detail. Local artisans created everything from handmade soaps to murals, and Don and wife, Charley, fill Cod Cove Farm with true caring. This newcomer is a delightful winner and a real deal.

SETTING & FACILITIES

Location Minutes from Rt 1, on right, on rural road
Near Ocean, Camden, Rockport, Bath. Boothbay Harbor
Building 1800s high-posted Cape, plus modernization
Grounds Rural landscaping, gardens, pond
Public Space DR, parlor, family room
Food & Drink Full elegant breakfast, communal; specialties: scones, fresh jams, omelets
Recreation Antiquing, river cruises, sailing, fishing, golfing, biking, touring, outlet/boutique shopping
Amenities & Services Priv. parties; games, grand piano, CD, VCR; tented weddings in orchard; house rental in Rangeley, ME

ACCOMMODATIONS

Units 4 guest rooms
All Rooms AC, sink
Some Rooms Bath
Bed & Bath Canopy, antique and artisan beds, varied sizes; 2 rooms share hall bath
Favorites Moon and Stars Room—whimsical, willow queen canopy, celestial stencilings, bath mural; Adirondack Room—twig furniture, queen birch bed
Comfort & Decor Handcrafted, hand-painted furniture. Local artwork and crafts. Antiques, stencilings, lace. Smallish rooms, but impeccable and comfortable, with good lighting. All rooms surround hall and staircase.

RATES, RESERVATIONS, & RESTRICTIONS

Deposit 50%; refund w/ 7-day notice
Discounts Extended stay, group, off-season, third person
Credit Cards V, MC, D
Check-in/Out 4/11; Call to check in later than 6 p.m.
Smoking No
Pets No
Kids Over 11
Minimum Stay None
Open "Most of the year"; check
Hosts Charlene and Don Schuman
Box 94
Edgecomb, ME 04556
(207) 882-4299
stay@codcovefarm.com
www.codcovefarm.com

HARBOR HILL, Friendship

OVERALL ★★½ | ROOM QUALITY ★★★ | VALUE ★★½ | PRICE $90–110

This is really informal and down-home (clean, roomy suites, but a bit cluttered). We recommend our favorite room (Terrace Room) for couples and the cottage—basic, but a good deal—for a family. Liga is Latvian and outgoing, Len was a civil engineer who climbed Mt. McKinley. The end-of-the-road location offers sunrises and close-up glimpses of Maine lobstermen at work at the tip of this rural peninsula. The owners are exceptionally friendly, and so is their golden retriever. The price here is friendly, too.

SETTING & FACILITIES

Location Through town center, left at post office to Town Landing Rd., on left overlooking harbor

Near Fishing village of Friendship, fishing sloops, Camden, Camden Hills State Park, Farnsworth Museum

Building Century-old clapboard farm-house

Grounds Hillside lawn slopes to harbor, fieldstone terrace w/ views, gardens draw hummingbirds, butterflies

Public Space Kitchen, common areas, LR/DR, fieldstone terrace

Food & Drink Full Scandinavian or Maine-style breakfast; specialties: black raspberry muffins, lingonberry preserves, Swedish pancakes, smoked sausage or smoked fish; coffee and tea; special diets

Recreation Day trips, sailing, biking, sloop charters, kayaking, fishing

Amenities & Services Lawn games

ACCOMMODATIONS

Units 3 guest rooms; 2-BR cottage apt.

All Rooms Bath, view, sitting area

Some Rooms 2-BR cottage has kitchen, sun deck; priv. entrance (2); antiques, hardwoods

Bed & Bath Down comforters; some showers only

Favorites Terrace Room—spacious, Empire furnishings, priv. entrance, view

Comfort & Decor Basic Americana with a dash of Europe, reflecting the hosts' Latvian heritage; original artwork showcases local artists, nautical touches and country antiques

RATES, RESERVATIONS, & RESTRICTIONS

Deposit 1 night; refund w/ 10-day notice

Discounts Weekly cottage rental

Credit Cards None

Check-in/Out Afternoon/before noon

Smoking On terrace only

Pets W/ prior arrangement; inn has a dog

Kids W/ prior arrangement

No-No's Alcohol

Minimum Stay None, but prefer 2 nights on weekends

Open Three seasons; Winter by arrangement

Hosts Liga and Len Jahnke
Town Landing Rd., Box 35
Friendship, ME 04547
(207) 832-6646

THE FLYING CLOUD, Newcastle

OVERALL ★★★½ | ROOM QUALITY ★★★ | VALUE ★★★ | PRICE $100–140

Named after the clipper ship that still holds the world speed record, set in 1851, this unassuming old house carries the theme throughout. But the pace is decidedly slower here, and the gracious hosts intend just that. Old-fashioned and homey, with a touch of style, this five-room bed-and-breakfast is on the same leafy street as the upscale Newcastle Inn. You can enjoy a fine dinner there, and walk a few steps back here, saving big bucks and getting some exercise. Warmth, charm, simplicity add up to a good deal here.

SETTING & FACILITIES

Location Coastal Rt. 1; after Wiscasset turn right onto River Rd; .7 mile on left
Near Shipyard, Pemaquid Lighthouse and Beach; day trips to Acadia Nat'l Park, Camden, Rockport, Boothbay Harbor, boat trips to Monhegan Island
Building 1840 Greek Revival (added to 1790 Cape)
Grounds Village yard, hammock, garden; overlooks Damariscotta River
Public Space Common room, LR w/ library; sun porch
Food & Drink Hearty communal breakfast; specialty: pecan waffles and flying cloud sausage; refreshments
Recreation Whale/bird watching, boat trips, day trips, antiquing, events, skiing
Amenities & Services Board games, piano; large library; groups can reserve entire property; celebrations

ACCOMMODATIONS

Units 4 guest rooms, 1 suite
All Rooms Bath, theme decor
Some Rooms Water view, floor-to-ceiling windows, skylight; New York Suite add'l beds in 2nd room
Bed & Bath Four-poster king bed, White Victorian style queen, and others; some hall access, robes, all shower, 1 w/ antique tub
Favorites San Francisco— spacious, river view, king four-poster, sitting area, large priv. bath down hall, thick terry robe
Comfort & Decor Rooms quirky w/ touches reminiscent of cities (Hong Kong, New York, London, Melbourne, San Francisco), ports of call for the namesake *Flying Cloud Clipper*. Smallish, warm, and cozy.

RATES, RESERVATIONS, & RESTRICTIONS

Deposit Major credit card to hold; refund w/ 14-day notice
Discounts Longer stays, groups
Credit Cards V, AE, MC
Check-in/Out 3–7/11
Smoking No
Pets No
Kids W/ prior arrangement
Minimum Stay Two nights holiday and peak season
Open All year
Hosts Karen and Dave Bragg
45 River Rd., Box 549,
Newcastle, ME 04553
(207) 563-2484
Fax: (207) 563-7879
stay@theflyingcloud.com
www.theflyingcloud.com

HARBOR VIEW INN AT NEWCASTLE, Newcastle

OVERALL ★★★★ | ROOM QUALITY ★★★★ | VALUE ★★★ | PRICE $115–160

Just a walk from antiques shops galor, this gracious bed-and-breakfast has pumpkin-pine floors, Oriental rugs, antiques, artwork, and fresh flowers. Joe is a former corporate exec and avid chef. His gourmet breakfast menus, featuring guests' names, may be a bit precious, but the desire to please is evident. A sample freshly squeezed orange juice, fresh fruit parfait, little corn pancake, spiral of eggs, riced parsley potato, tomato, baked ham, and almond sour cream coffee cake. That should hold you till evening, when twinkling window candles and lighted trees welcome you back.

SETTING & FACILITIES

Location Take either Rt. 1 S or Rt. 215 S to Business Rt. 1; B&B is first driveway on left, off Bus. Rt. 1

Near Boothbay Harbor, Pemaquid Point, Camden, Rockport, Popham and Reid state parks, Bath, L.L. Bean outlet, lighthouses, Monhegan Island, Rockland

Building Restored 1840s New England Cape

Grounds Terraced lawn, gardens; overlooks Damariscotta/Newcastle Harbor

Public Space LR, deck; DR; reading room; kitchen; common rooms wheelchair accessible

Food & Drink Gourmet breakfast, communal; friends welcome for fee; refreshments, tea

Recreation Fishing, island cruises, golf, beach activities, bocce, croquet

Amenities & Services Off-street parking, fax, irons, lawn games, maps, touring advice, sailing advice

ACCOMMODATIONS

Units 1 guest room, 2 suites

All Rooms Bath, sitting area, ceiling fan, TV, phone

Some Rooms Gas fireplace, priv. deck, view; Garden Suite wheelchair accessible, shower w/ grab bar, not otherwise specially equipped

Bed & Bath Beds vary; shower only (1)

Favorites Damariscotta River Suite—views, beamed cathedral ceiling, fireplace, deck, king; Newcastle Square Room—views, gas fireplace, special antiques

Comfort & Decor Traditional comfort, refined. Detail oriented. Spacious. Good lighting. Original art, antiques and period furnishings, luxurious accessories.

RATES, RESERVATIONS, & RESTRICTIONS

Deposit 1/2 of total stay (min 1 night); refund w/ 10-day notice

Discounts Singles take off $25

Credit Cards V, MC

Check-in/Out 3–7/11

Smoking Grounds only

Pets No; inn has dog (no access to inn except at guests' request)

Kids Over 12

Minimum Stay 2 nights on peak-season weekends

Open Year-round

Hosts Jean Lannon and Joe McEntee

34 Main St., Box 791

Newcastle, ME 04553

(207) 563-2900

Fax same as telephone

joe@theharborview.com

www.theharborview.com

NEWCASTLE INN, Newcastle

OVERALL ★★★★ | ROOM QUALITY ★★★★ | VALUE ★★ | PRICE $150–250

Unpretentious, this property with its colorful lupine flower gardens is a quiet retreat on the river. Come prepared to eat. Previous owners established its reputation for fine food, and the current owner/chefs are maintaining, with a bent now toward classic French, as in mussels in saffron cream; squash, zucchini, and roasted red pepper soup; duck breast with raspberry cassis; or grilled salmon Troisgros. The inn has been steadily upgraded to match the food (and the increased prices), and remains a glorious getaway for gourmands.

SETTING & FACILITIES

Location 7 mi. past Wiscasset, turn right onto River Rd. and look for inn sign
Near Lighthouses, fishing villages, Boothbay Harbor, Camden, Freeport; in residential area
Building 1800s Colonial carriage house
Grounds Lawn, gardens slope to Damariscotta River
Public Space 2 LRs, porch, TV room; 2 DRs, deck; full-service pub
Food & Drink Multi-course breakfast; afternoon coffee, holiday treats; open to public for dinner; lobster bakes; liquor license
Recreation Touring, antiquing
Amenities & Services Games, books, fax, paper, turndown

ACCOMMODATIONS

Units 14 guest rooms (one new suite)
All Rooms Bath
Some Rooms River view, sitting area, fireplace, whirlpool, decks; priv. entrance (2), AC
Bed & Bath Lace-canopy, sleigh or four-poster, sizes vary; some showers only, 2nd vanity sinks; hairdryers, robes
Favorites Pemaquid Point—fireplace, queen canopy, sitting room, dbl. whirlpool; Monhegan Island—king four-poster, fireplace
Comfort & Decor Eclectic country furnishings, Waverly award for decor, renovations, and upgrades. Polished wood furniture, print wallpapers and patterned fabrics. Rooms small, but some being enlarged. Warm lighting and comfortable feel throughout.

RATES, RESERVATIONS, & RESTRICTIONS

Deposit Half of reserved stay; cancel 14 days in advance
Discounts Off-season, excludes holiday weekends and winter festivities
Credit Cards V, AE, MC
Check-in/Out 3–8/11; call if check-in after 8
Smoking No
Pets No
Kids "Older" only

No-No's Dinner w/out reservations;
more than 2 people in room
Minimum Stay None
Open All year
Hosts Rebecca and Howard Levitan

60 River Rd.
Newcastle, ME 04553
(800) 832-8669 or (207) 563-5685
Fax: (207) 563-6877
www.newcastle.com

THE GOSNOLD ARMS, New Harbor

OVERALL ★★★½ | ROOM QUALITY ★★★ | VALUE ★★★ | PRICE $89–150

Want to see whales and puffins? From this comfortable inn you can take a
boat departing daily for Monhegan Island, where they are often spotted. And
you can walk to many lobster pounds nearby for dinner. Since 1925, this
unpretentious inn has been noted for congenial, family-style atmosphere.
The harbor here is one of the prettiest in Maine, and not overrun with
tourists. Laid-back is the mood, and the prices are right.

SETTING & FACILITIES

Location Rt. 95 to Brunswick, Rt. 1 to
Damariscotta, Rt. 130 S to New Harbor,
Rt. 32, 1 mile to inn, across from harbor
Near Islands, Pemaquid Point, lighthouse,
Fort William Henry, archeological digs,
Hog Island Nature Camp
Building Large 1840 clapboard; attached
barn, cottages
Grounds On shores of Pemaquid Penin-
sula; rocky beach

Public Space Lounge, breakfast porch,
wharf
Food & Drink Full breakfast, lobster
pounds nearby
Recreation Day boat tours to Monhegan Island, daily seal and puffin boat
excursions, water activities, tennis,
horses, golf, antiquing
Amenities & Services Priv. wharf, boat
moorings, board games

ACCOMMODATIONS

Units 12 guest rooms; 14 cottages
All Rooms Bath
Some Rooms Water view, fireplace
Bed & Bath Bed sizes vary, firm mat-
tresses; some baths showers only
Favorites Grey Cottage—fireplace, LR,

water view, deck
Comfort & Decor Simple, comfortable,
early American. Rooms in barn above
gathering room, pine walls, pleasant furnishings. Cottages w/ water views, fireplaces

RATES, RESERVATIONS, & RESTRICTIONS

Deposit One night or 25%, whichever
greater; call for cancellation policy
Credit Cards V, MC
Check-in/Out 1–4/10
Smoking Limited, check

Pets No
Kids In cottages, older kids; check
Minimum Stay 1 week in cottages,
summer
Open May–Oct.

Hosts The Phinney Family
146 State Route 32
New Harbor, ME 04554
(207) 677-3727

Fax: (207) 677-2662
www.gosnold.com
info@gosnold.com

CAPTAIN LINDSEY HOUSE, Rockland

OVERALL ★★★★ | ROOM QUALITY ★★★★ | VALUE ★★★ | PRICE $100–170

A solid, mustard-hued beauty with green awnings, a red door, and teal touches within, this B&B is authentic and stylish. Released from its commercial incarnation as a utilities building, it is again filled with art, artifacts, and artful touches. Old photos, antiques, and international curios make it feel as if the captain himself may reappear from a world voyage any minute. The staff is especially helpful. The owners also have the schooner *Stephen Taber* docked in Rockland, so many sailors congregate here.

SETTING & FACILITIES

Location In town, on side street, off main shopping artery; 2 blocks from water
Near Ocean, Penobscot Bay, Rockland Harbor, Camden Harbor; Monhegan Island artists' colony, Farnsworth Museum, craft and antique shopping
Building Solid 1832 brick Federal
Grounds Small English garden, terrace
Public Space Entrance lobby, LR, library, breakfast room, garden deck
Food & Drink Cont'l breakfast; tea or sherry; lunch and dinner at inn's restaurant and communal-seating pub, open daily
Recreation Live entertainment, darts/TV in pub, golf, tennis, XC skiing, day boat trips, lighthouse, sailing
Amenities & Services Guest refrigerator, irons, 2 vessels owned by inn can be reserved, tour itinerary, off-street parking in restaurant lot; computer port, fax, copier; reservations, pickup

ACCOMMODATIONS

Units 7 guest rooms, 2 suites
All Rooms Bath, phone, TV, radio, AC
Some Rooms Wheelchair access (1)
Bed & Bath Some four-posters, sizes vary; full baths, robes, sep. showers, some soaking tubs, hairdryers
Favorites Room 4—art deco–style, spacious
Comfort & Decor Tasteful seafaring theme, striped wallpapers, and colonial colors. Antique desks w/ reading lamps and comfortable seating. TVs in armoires.

RATES, RESERVATIONS, & RESTRICTIONS

Deposit 1 night; must cancel 10 days in advance
Discounts Seniors, longer stays, off-season, 3rd person, pkgs.
Credit Cards V, AE, MC, D
Check-in/Out After 3/before 11; later often OK
Smoking In pub or garden only

Pets No; nearby facilities
Kids Over 10
Minimum Stay None
Open All year
Hosts Captains Ellen and Ken Barnes
5 Lindsey St.

Rockland, ME 04841
Fax: (207) 596-2758
(800) 523-2145 or (207) 596-7950
www.lindseyhouse.com
info@lindseyhouse.com

SCHOONER STEPHEN TABER, Rockland

OVERALL ★★★ | ROOM QUALITY ★★★ | VALUE ★ | PRICE $838/person

The only property in this book that moves, this is the oldest documented sailing vessel in continuous service in the United States. Captains Ellen and Ken Barnes, who also own Captain Lindsey House and Waterworks restaurant in Rockland, keep their inn shipshape, and this schooner as hospitable as an inn. As a bonus, Capt. Ellen's recipes are tasty enough to be published in *A Taste of the Taber* cookbook. BYOB and BYMI(musical instruments) to sing along. The schooner offers an unbeatable combination, especially for families with teenagers who might be bored at a more stationary site. Guests can combine a unique vacation visit to one or both of the Barnes' accommodations to appease landlubbers.

SETTING & FACILITIES

Location Rt. 1 to Rockland, on Wind-jammer Wharf
Near Prior to sailing, Rockland and Camden; after, hidden harbors along coastal Maine; docks at islands and fishing villages
Building 68-ft. restored 1871 sailing ship
Public Space Yacht deck, main cabin, galley w/ dining area, retractable awning

Food & Drink All meals served daily; fresh fare; island lobster bake; BYOB
Recreation Whale watching, swimming, jogging, rowing when anchor drops; evening singalongs
Amenities & Services Enclosed parking, games, books, ice and glasses for drinks, charters, sailing instruction

ACCOMMODATIONS

Units 2 singles, 4 dbls, 6 twin (holds 22 guests)
All Rooms Windows for light and air
Bed & Bath Minimal bed space; sinks and electricity in cabins; heads and showers above deck

Favorites The pilot berths, in fo' c'sle
Comfort & Decor Bright and attractive cabins, but not much bigger than closets at some New England inns. Gleaming decks. Well designed and clean. Relatively comfortable berths.

RATES, RESERVATIONS, & RESTRICTIONS

Deposit $350, balance paid in full prior to cruise; must cancel 5 weeks prior
Discounts Off-season, 3-day cruises at

beginning/end of season, Captain Lindsey House pkgs., 10% discount if reserve prior to February 1

Credit Cards V, AE, MC, D
Check-in/Out Sunday after 4/Saturday 11; Ship departs Monday after breakfast
Smoking No
Pets No
Kids Over 14
No-No's Portable radios, TVs; hard luggage (must be stowable)
Minimum Stay 6 days, 3 days

Open Memorial Day–fall foliage
Hosts Ellen and Ken Barnes
70 Elm St.
Camden, ME 04843
(800) 999-7352 or (207) 236-3520
Fax: (207) 596-2758
kebarnes@midcoast.com
www.stephentaber.com

HOMEPORT INN, Searsport

OVERALL ★★★½ | ROOM QUALITY ★★★ | VALUE ★★★★★ | PRICE $55–85

Searsport is one of Maine's antique centers, and the opulence of The Homeport Inn puts guests in the mood to rummage. Highway traffic roars by, but the building is solid and quiet inside. This house is a beautiful reminder of a time when Searsport was filled with ship captains, their prosperous homes, and their treasures from around the world. Other mansions in the area are in bad shape, but this bed-and-breakfast is a shining example of taste and upkeep.

SETTING & FACILITIES

Location On Rt. 1 in Searsport
Near Penobscot Bay, Penobscot Marine Museum, Fort Knox, Acadia Nat'l Park, Castine, Camden Harbor, Owl's Head Transportation Museum
Building Hilltop 1861 ship captain's mansion w/ cupola, wraparound porch
Grounds Extends to shore of E Penobscot Bay in rear; fronts on Rt. 1

Public Space Front parlor; publike room
Food & Drink Full communal breakfast
Recreation Boat tours, steam-train tours, golf, water/snow sports, shore walks, antiquing
Amenities & Services Bicycle rentals, lawn games

ACCOMMODATIONS

Units 10 guest rooms; 2 cottages
All Rooms Fairly spacious, flowers
Some Rooms Priv. bath, priv. deck, view; cottages have 2 BRs and kitchen.
Bed & Bath Some canopy beds, antique headboards
Favorites 1st floor back rooms sunny,

quiet, decks, views
Comfort & Decor Floor-to-ceiling windows. Fleur-de-lis wallpaper in some rooms, period decor, 19th-century antiques. Two-BR cottages, charming, gingerbread-trimmed mini-Victorians, work well for families.

RATES, RESERVATIONS, & RESTRICTIONS

Deposit $25; non-refundable
Discounts Singles, 3rd person, kids, off-season, weekly; $600 weekly for cottages
Credit Cards V, AE, MC, D
Check-in/Out Flexible, check
Smoking Limited areas only
Pets No; B&B has 1 cat and 1 dog
Kids Over 3 OK in cottages

Minimum Stay None currently; check
Open All year
Hosts Edith and George Johnson
Rt. 1, E. Main St.
Searsport, ME 04974
(800) 742-5814 or (207) 548-2259
Fax: 508-443-6682
www.bnbcity.com/inns/20015

HARPSWELL INN, South Harpswell

OVERALL ★★★★ | ROOM QUALITY ★★★★ | VALUE ★★★ | PRICE $89–190

Harpswell has more coastline than any other town in America, and this handsome bed-and-breakfast has a long history involving the coastal waters. The kitchen and dining room were once the cookhouse for the nearby shipyard, and the bell on top of the three-story house—which you can still ring—called shipworkers to lunch. Within are collectibles, family photos, a warm hearth and windows overlooking the water and lobster boats. Bill's ancestors settled the area in 1659. A comfortable, homey feel is evident throughout.

SETTING & FACILITIES

Location On Lookout Point knoll overlooking Middle Bay lobster boat harbor
Near Admiral Peary's Eagle Island, Freeport outlet, Boothbay Harbor, Portland, Brunswick, colleges, winery, state parks, lighthouses
Building 1761 Federal Georgian columned clapboard, outbuildings; renovated in 1995

Grounds 3 acres, lawns, gardens to water's edge, stone walls
Public Space Great room, DR, porch
Food & Drink Full communal breakfast; refreshments
Recreation Boat/day trips, beach, tennis, golf, trails, hunting, kayaking
Amenities & Services Bikes, dock, irons, guest refrigerator, daily paper

ACCOMMODATIONS

Units 12 guest rooms and suites
All Rooms Antiques
Some Rooms Priv. bath, views, sitting area, desk, fireplace
Bed & Bath Some four-poster, king, queen & twin
Favorites Lilac Room— love seat, desk, views, full bath

Comfort & Decor Warm and inviting. Some handpainted faux murals, toile, decorator fabrics, Oriental rugs. 2 large suites w/ kitchens, dramatic decor, cathedral ceilings, fireplaces, whirlpools; 1 suite, 2-story, window wall, can accommodate 3rd person; 2nd floor antique ceilings

RATES, RESERVATIONS, & RESTRICTIONS

Deposit 1 night, 50% longer stays
Discounts 3rd person, 14+ days
Credit Cards V, MC
Check-in/Out 4/1030
Smoking Porch only
Pets No; B&B has 1 cat
Kids Over 10
Minimum Stay Req. on weekends and

holidays, July–Oct.; check
Open All year
Hosts Susan and Bill Menz
108 Lookout Point Rd.
Harpswell, ME 04079
(800) 843-5509 or (207) 833-5509
Prefer guests to call 800 number
www.gwi.net/~harpswel

EAST WIND INN & MEETING HOUSE, Tenants Harbor

OVERALL ★★★★ | ROOM QUALITY ★★★ | VALUE ★★½ | PRICE $79–299

Sailing and relaxing at an authentic country inn in a pretty fishing village are a true Maine combo you can enjoy here, as a sloop sails regularly from the inn's pier. This main inn, renovated captain's house, and cottage are owned and operated by a Tenants Harbor native, who has put much effort into restoring and maintaining the informal property. The furnishings are a mix of Victorian and whatever, and the food relies on local seafood such as fish chowder and crab cakes. The harbor view from the porch and rooms is peaceful and lovely.

SETTING & FACILITIES

Location Rt. 1 N to Thomaston, right onto Rt. 131, to Rt. 131 S, bear left at post office; inn 200 yards at water's edge
Near Village shops, Rockland, Farnsworth Art Museum, Rockport, Camden, Lincolville, Marshall Point Lighthouse, Monhegan Island Ferry, Montpelier, Owls Head Transportation Museum, Penobscot Bay
Building 1890 New England–style clapboard
Grounds Oceanfront; overlooks islands
Public Space 3 buildings, common

rooms; main house common room
Food & Drink (MAP) Full breakfast, dinners in restaurant; specialties: baked haddock and horseradish mashed potatoes, strawberry-rhubarb pie; open daily, April–Nov., sporadically and by reservation Nov.–March
Recreation Sailing, biking, nature trails, island trips, lighthouse tours, beach activities, touring, canoeing, horses
Amenities & Services Sailing seminars, conference facilities, deepwater anchorage, piano

ACCOMMODATIONS

Units 26 guest rooms 15 in main house, 8 in Meeting House, 3 in cottage
All Rooms Antiques, phone
Some Rooms TV, priv. bath (19), view,

suites/apts., singles
Bed & Bath Some antique, brass; sizes vary

Favorites Front Rooms—2-story apt. in cottage, king, full kitchen, deck
Comfort & Decor Early American–style brass bedsteads and pine chests. Oak and mahogany furnishings. Rooms appealingly plain. Larger rooms in Meeting House (originally captain's mansion). Wheeler Cottage houses 3 apts. w/ full kitchens/kitchenettes, 2 w/ fireplace

RATES, RESERVATIONS, & RESTRICTIONS

Deposit 1 night, credited to last night; refund w/ 14-day notice; 50% refund 3-day notice
Discounts 7 nights or more, 3rd person
Credit Cards AE, DC, MC, D
Check-in/Out 3/noon
Smoking Permitted, except in DR
Pets Permitted, limited
Kids Over 12
No-No's Early departure forfeits deposit

Minimum Stay 2 nights in suites or apts.
Open All year (check)
Host Timothy L. Watts
Box 149
Tenants Harbor, ME 04860
(800) 241-VIEW or (207) 372-6366
Fax: (207) 372-6320
info@eastwindinn.com
www.eastwindinn.com

SQUIRE TARBOX INN, Wiscasset

OVERALL ★★★★½ | ROOM QUALITY ★★★★ | VALUE ★★★ | PRICE $95–185

Observe morning and evening milkings at this stylish, sophisticated working farm, which produces fresh cheese annually from award-winning, scene-stealing Nubian goats. You can also enjoy the company of two donkeys, a horse, and several chickens. A swing hanging from the rafters, an honor bar, a player piano, and a screened porch overlooking pastures are added amenities. Bill is a pilot, Karen a quilter, and both innkeepers worked in the hotel business. They create stylish, gracious touches and proudly share gentlefolk farming and fresh, fine food.

SETTING & FACILITIES

Location Rural Westport Island, 8.5 mi. down Rt. 144, which joins Rt. 1 between Bath and Wiscasset; at end of country road
Near Bath, Wiscasset, 30-min. drive to Reid State Park ocean beaches, harbors, L.L. Bean outlet, shipbuilding, art museums, craft shops, lobster shacks, and boat cruises
Building New England Colonial farmhouse (1763–1825); barn w/ add'l rooms

Grounds Fields, stone walls, woods, path to saltwater marsh
Public Space Parlors, barn room, music room, rustic DR
Food & Drink (MAP) Buffet full breakfast; cookies and beverages, goat cheese in evening; set dinner, by reservation; liquor license
Amenities & Services Rowboats, bikes, beach towels

ACCOMMODATIONS

Units 11 guest rooms
All Rooms Bath, heat control, window fan or AC
Some Rooms Fireplace
Bed & Bath Some four-posters, sizes vary; showers only

Comfort & Decor Antiques, rocking chairs, candles, quilts, books. Main house more spacious than barn rooms w/ formal decor, fireplace. Seven rustic barn rooms have exposed beams, 4 have priv. entrances. Good reading lights.

RATES, RESERVATIONS, & RESTRICTIONS

Deposit $100, 50% longer stay; refund w/ 14-day notice
Discounts 3rd person
Credit Cards V, AE, MC, D
Check-in/Out 2/11
Smoking Only on weather-protected deck
Pets No
Kids Over 12
Minimum Stay 2 nights on some week-

ends; check
Open Mother's Day–Oct.
Hosts Karen and Bill Mitman
1181 Main Rd., Westport Island
Wiscasset, ME 04578
(207) 882-7693
Fax: (207) 882-7107
squiretarbox@ime.net
www.squiretarboxinn.com

Southern Maine Coast and Greater Portland

The southern Maine coast is a day at the beach. **York, Ogunquit, Wells, Kennebunk, Saco,** and **Old Orchard** have white sand not usually associated with New England's rocky shores. Lodgings are often just a block or so away from the beaches, or even directly accessible to them.

Kittery and **Freeport**—home of the famous **L.L. Bean** outlet—have hundreds of discount shops, and quaint Kittery is also famous for shipbuilding. Freeport's havens from the hectic outlets are **Wolf Neck Woods State Park**'s hiking trails, nature sanctuaries, deep-sea fishing charters, bay cruises, and seasonal excursions to **Eagle Island.**

The Yorks offer a historical perspective, and the **York Historic District** features antique buildings still used today. **The Cape Neddick Lighthouse (Nubble Light)** is one of the oldest and most picturesque in the state.

Ogunquit, although it gets crowded, lives up to its Indian name, "beautiful place by the sea," and offers the historic **Marginal Way Footpath** to **Perkins Cove,** a world-famous art colony, complete with New England's only foot drawbridge.

Bustling **Wells** is indeed bustling, blessed with seven miles of wide, white sand beaches. You can escape to **Wells Estuaries Research Reserve** and **Laudholm Farm** sanctuaries and wildlife refuge.

The **Kennebunk** area, with its rocky shoreline, protected harbors and own share of sandy beaches, is more like traditional New England and more crowded. Kennebunk's waterfront **Dock Square** offers an excuse to go shopping, as does the **Brick Store Museum.**

Portland, Maine's largest city (about 62,000 locals) is small enough to be comfortable, and yet has its share of cultural activities. **Old Port Exchange** and the **Arts District** overlook sparkling **Casco Bay.** Touring historic homes, relaxing to the strains of the **Portland Symphony Orchestra,**

strolling through the **Museum of Art** and bringing kids to the **Children's Museum of Maine** can while away entire rainy days and nights.

On fine days, take a ferry trip on **Casco Bay** to various islands, and bring your bike for touring once you arrive. Area state parks have scenic lighthouses and sandy beaches—yes, even in Portland.

Winslow Homer once lived and painted in **Scarborough,** now a 3,000-acre wildlife refuge and marsh area. Just north of Portland is Falmouth, offering special events, classes, and displays at the **Maine Audubon Society**'s headquarters at **Gilsland Farm. Yarmouth** also sponsors several seasonal fairs, including the **Cumberland Fair** and the **United Maine Craftsmen Fair.**

Southern coastal Maine has many small inns and bed-and-breakfasts from basic to ultra-luxurious, including some of New England's most beloved properties. But the season is short, and crowds are heavy, so reservations are a must to avoid disappointment.

FOR MORE INFORMATION

Convention and Visitors Bureau of Greater Portland (207) 772-5800 or (207) 772-4994; Fax: (207) 874-9043

Greater Portland Region (207) 772-2811

Portland's Downtown District (207) 772-6828

BAGLEY HOUSE, Durham

OVERALL ★★★ | ROOM QUALITY ★★★ | VALUE ★★★ | PRICE $75–135

This property has had many lives: church, schoolhouse, store, and public house. Today it is a modest bed-and-breakfast, a quiet option in an area not exactly brimming with accommodations. Antiques and handmade crafts are all around you, and here you are far from the crowds at nearby outlet shopping. The site is still evolving, and the enthusiastic hosts, one of them British, feel their considerable efforts are well received. Guests may prefer the main house to the new Bliss Barn.

SETTING & FACILITIES

Location 6 miles north of I-95, Exit 20 Freeport/Durham, on rural Rt. 136
Near 10 minutes from Freeport, lighthouses, ocean and beaches, state parks, nature trails, Casco Bay Islands, XC ski trails, outlets, Portland, colleges
Building Built in 1772 as inn; 2nd building, Bliss Barn
Grounds Rural, 6 acres of fields and woods

Public Space LR, library, country kitchen; Bliss Barn, common room
Food & Drink Full communal breakfast; specialty: sourdough pancakes
Recreation Beach/water activities; lighthouse, island tours; day trips, trails
Amenities & Services Books, games; portacrib; entire can be booked for events, lobster weekend (min. 5)

ACCOMMODATIONS

Units 5 in main house, 3 in barn; I disabled access
All Rooms Bath, custom pieces; heat controls
Some Rooms Fireplace, reproduction Shaker beds, sitting area, carpet, hardwoods, add'l beds
Bed & Bath Sizes vary; some shower only, some hall access

Favorites The Cozy Nook—at top, sloping ceilings, I trundle and I 3/4 bed, good for families; Emma's Room—woodburning fireplace; Pine Tree Room—in barn, queen, gas fireplace, sitting area, views
Comfort & Decor Handsewn quilts, antique linens, flowers. Smallish rooms. Main house, less privacy.

RATES, RESERVATIONS, & RESTRICTIONS

Deposit Hold credit card number
Discounts 3rd person
Credit Cards V, AE, MC, D, JCB
Check-in/Out 3/11
Smoking No

Pets No; B&B has cat and dog
Kids Welcome
Minimum Stay 2 nights if reserve entire inn
Open All year

Hosts Susan Backhouse and Suzanne
O'Connor
1290 Royalsborough Rd.
Durham, ME 04222

(800) 765-1772; (207) 865-6566 or
(207) 353-6372
Fax: (207) 353-5878
bglyhse@aol.com

BUFFLEHEAD COVE INN, Kennebunkport

OVERALL ★★★★½ | ROOM QUALITY ★★★★ | VALUE ★★ | PRICE $115–310

You're a lucky duck, like the buffleheads who are attracted to this cove, if you get to stay here. The Gott family was raised here before the house recently turned into a bed-and-breakfast, and this special, homey property is becoming word-of-mouth-popular. Tranquil views of the tide's ebb and flow or blue heron in flight are just about everywhere, and it's hard to believe that this romantic little hideaway, a sensual treat, is only five minutes from the hubbub of town.

SETTING & FACILITIES

Location Exit 3 (Kennebunk) from I-95, left onto Rt. 35 S, continue for 3.1 miles, on bank of the Tidal Kennebunk River
Near Ocean, Dock Square, town
Building Turn-of-the-century gambrel-roofed house
Grounds Fields, apple trees, hammocks, decks
Public Space Sunny LR, DR; wrap-around porch; breakfast deck on water
Food & Drink Full breakfast; specialties: ginger poached pears in English custard sauce, apple-stuffed French toast, maple-glazed sausage; early riser coffee; evening wine and cheese; teas
Recreation Summer theatre, local events; fishing, whale watching, birdwatch from dock, antiquing
Amenities & Services Beach permits, priv. dock, turn down, wine/cheese in afternoon

ACCOMMODATIONS

Units 3 guest rooms, 2 suites, 1 cottage rented by week
All Rooms Bath
Some Rooms Water view, gas fireplace, balcony, whirlpool; suites sitting room, priv. entrance (1)
Bed & Bath Bed sizes vary; robes, some dbl. whirlpools
Favorites Balcony Room—mahogany dbl. armoire, large balcony; Hideaway—in cottage, dbl. gas fireplace, BR and LR, king, dbl. whirlpool
Comfort & Decor Rooms sunny, quirky, and cozy-romantic. Americana quilts and artisan pieces, wicker and lace. Warm color and floral treatments.

RATES, RESERVATIONS, & RESTRICTIONS

Deposit 1 night, 50% longer stay; refund w/ 14-day notice
Credit Cards V, AE, MC, D
Check-in/Out 3–8/11
Smoking No
Pets No; 1 cat

Kids Limited, check	Box 499
Minimum Stay 2 nights on weekends	Kennebunkport, ME 04046
June–Sept.	(207) 967-3879
Open April–Dec.; check for winter avail.	Fax same as phone
Hosts Harriet and Jim Gott	bcove@dbanet.com

CAPTAIN JEFFERDS INN, Kennebunkport

OVERALL ★★★★½ | ROOM QUALITY ★★★★★ | VALUE ★★ | PRICE $135–295

The gracious owners lovingly redecorated this grand house, removing the kitsch and emphasizing the elegance, with a sophisticated mix of Americana and decorator touches. The spacious, high-ceilinged dining room, the heart of the house, is especially wonderful. Meticulously maintained, this stately white clapboard with picket fence is an acceptable alternative to its more renowned neighbor, The Captain Lord Mansion.

SETTING & FACILITIES

Location Rt. 9E to Main St; right onto Main, right on Pearl St; residential area
Near Ocean, 2 nature preserves; Mt. Agamenticus; 1 block from Harbor
Building 1804 Federal mansion, carriage house
Grounds Smallish; gardens, fountain, terrace, screened-in sun porch
Public Space Garden room, DR, LR
Food & Drink 3-course candlelight breakfast, communal or separate; early coffee; tea
Recreation Board games, sailing, fishing, dayboat trips, outlets/boutiques
Amenities & Services Refrigerator, irons, recipes, paper, grand piano, holiday festivities, celebratory champagne, beach towels; entire facility may be reserved; fax, maps

ACCOMMODATIONS

Units Main building, 2 jr. suites and 10 guest rooms; Carriage House, 3 suites and 1 guest room

All Rooms Bath, ambiance lighting, AC

Some Rooms Fireplace, porch, skylight, priv. entrance (1), fountain (1)

Bed & Bath Four-poster, canopy, sleigh, varied sizes; some shower only, 1 hall access (robes), some soaking tubs or oversized showers, bath w/ fireplace (1)

Favorites Assisi Suite— king iron bed, fireplace, large bath, indoor garden and fountain, oversize Italian tiled shower; Adare Suite—king sleigh, dbl. fireplace (bed and bath), oversize shower

Comfort & Decor Lower-priced rooms are smallish, but all are pristine and pretty w/ sophisticated touches. New owners refurbished rooms in 1997 to reflect favorite places throughout the world.

RATES, RESERVATIONS, & RESTRICTIONS

Deposit 1 night; refund w/ 14-day notice

Discounts Off-season, New Year's Eve pkg.

Credit Cards V, MC, AE

Check-in/Out After 3/11. Call for check-in after 7 p.m.; noon check-out often OK

Smoking No

Pets Dogs w/ reservation and $20 fee; not permitted alone in rooms.

Kids Over 8

Minimum Stay 2 nights on weekends, in-season (May–Oct.)

Open Except Christmas week

Hosts Pat and Dick Bartholomew
Box 691, 5 Pearl St.
Kennebunkport, ME 04046
(800) 839-6844 or (207) 967-2311
Fax: (207) 967-0721
captjeff@captainjefferdsinn.com
www.captainjefferdsinn.com

THE CAPTAIN LORD MANSION, Kennebunkport

OVERALL ★★★★★ | ROOM QUALITY ★★★★★ | VALUE ★★ | PRICE $130–350

A "memory garden" crammed with inscribed stone blocks citing guests with 10 or more visits attests to the popularity of this imposing landmark close to other neighborhood mansions. Continually fine-tuned according to requests, the stellar site is hard to book in season, and is usually filled to the beams. Still, this quintessential New England captain's house remains a great bed-and-breakfast, with a solid feel and great authentic antique furnishings.

SETTING & FACILITIES

Location 5th left off Ocean Ave., in residential area

Near Kennebunk River, ocean, waterfront, boutique and outlet shopping

Building 1814 Federal clapboard mansion; in Nat'l Register of Historic Places, 1807 Federal-style guesthouse

Grounds Acre+ of lawns, flowers, brick pathways

Public Space Wide front hall, 4-story staircase; gathering/DR; antique country kitchen; 2nd floor common room

Food & Drink Full breakfast; refreshments

Recreation Beach, touring, biking

Amenities & Services Games, books, maps, recipes, inn newsletter, gift shop, beach towels, conf. rooms

ACCOMMODATIONS

Units 16 guest rooms, 4 add'l in "Phoebe's Fantasy" guesthouse

All Rooms Bath, fireplace, room diaries; all but 1, AC

Some Rooms 2nd fireplace in bath, antique dolls/toys

Bed & Bath Four-poster, lace canopy beds; Dana Suite—robes; dbl. vanities, some heated marble fls.; some dbl. whirlpools, bidets

Favorites Ship Oriental and Ship Ophelia—large, lavish and lovely; room diaries explain why.

Comfort & Decor Units named for Captain Lord's ships w/ themes. Federal decor w/ spirit, ambient lighting, sitting areas. Large fireplaces, Oriental rugs, oil paintings, gleaming woodwork, crystal chandeliers. Period colors, bold wallpapers, overstuffed chairs and loveseats, eye-catching draperies, antiques. Handmade pillows and whimsical touches.

RATES, RESERVATIONS, & RESTRICTIONS

Deposit 2 nights, 50% of longer stay; refund w/ 15-day notice

Discounts Off season, seasonal and theme pkgs. (e.g., New Year's, Winterfest, Brew Pub, Antique Lover's)

Credit Cards V, AE, MC, D

Check-in/Out After 3/11

Smoking No, violators will pay cleaning fee

Pets No

Kids Over 12

No-No's Returning after 11 p.m.

Minimum Stay 2 nights on weekends, year round

Open All year

Hosts Rick Litchfield and Bev Davis
Box 800
Kennebunkport, ME 04046
(207) 967-3141
Fax: (207) 967-3172
innkeeper@captainlord.com

MAINE STAY, Kennebunkport

OVERALL ★★★ | ROOM QUALITY ★★★★ | VALUE ★★½ | PRICE $95–225

Once a taffy factory and later used by rum-runners, this white-columned Italianate has lots of gleaming lace-curtained French doors, period wallpapers and carpets, restored stained glass, and antiques to help create a romantic, classic bed-and-breakfast. It is a more informal alternative to nearby grander ones, including The Captain Lord Mansion. The hosts are friendly, and the cottages, are especially appealing for families.

SETTING & FACILITIES

Location Traffic light at Rts. 35 and 9, left onto Rt. 9 to Kennebunkport, turn right at Main St.; in residential historic district
Near Village, harbor
Building 1860 Italiante Victorian w/ cupola
Grounds Lawn, playground

Public Space Entrance hall, parlor, porch
Food & Drink Full breakfast; tea
Recreation Sailing; games
Amenities & Services Covered bike rack, 2 phones in main house, papers, refrigerator, beach passes and towels, maps

ACCOMMODATIONS

Units 6 guest rooms; 11 cottage rooms; 1 w/ 2 BRs, LR, kitchen
All Rooms Bath, TV, clock/radio, AC
Some Rooms Fireplace, deck, sitting area; cottage rooms kitchen, coffeemaker, micro, refrigerator, VCR
Bed & Bath Some antiques, brass, sizes

vary; some whirlpools
Favorites Room 14—deck, gas fireplace
Comfort & Decor Victorian and Colonial colors. Romantic, flowery rooms. Cottages, English country charm. Good lighting. Immaculate.

RATES, RESERVATIONS, & RESTRICTIONS

Deposit 1 night or 50%; refund w/ 14-day notice
Discounts Off-season, midweek,
Credit Cards V, AE, MC.
Check-in/Out After 3/11
Smoking No
Pets No
Kids Welcome in some cottages; over 5, main house

Minimum Stay 2–3 nights, peak; check for 1 night avail.
Open All year
Hosts Carol and Lindsay Copeland
34 Maine St., Box 500A
Kennebunkport, ME 04046
(800) 950-2117 or (207) 967-2117
Fax: (207) 967-8757
www.mainestayinn.com

OLD FORT INN, Kennebunkport

OVERALL ★★★★ | ROOM QUALITY ★★★★ | VALUE ★★ | PRICE $99–350

For those who enjoy recreation, this is the best game in town. You enter through an antiques store, and then into a super-size great room overlooking the pool. The imposing bed-and-breakfast's rustic exterior, with cupola, reflects a proud American heritage; its interior luxury reflects its sophisticated, well-traveled owners—he a former oil exec, she a flight attendant. Rooms at this secluded mini-resort are a mix of reliable comfort, amenities and romance. Christmas prelude activities, during the first week in December, are a big deal.

SETTING & FACILITIES

Location I-95 to exit 3, Rt. 35 to Rt. 9, to Ocean Ave., to Old Fort Ave.; estate area 1 1/4 mile from Dock Square
Near Village, lighthouses, 2 golf courses; 1 block to ocean
Building Colonial main building (converted barn); guest house
Grounds 15 acres; 3 acres gardens, lawns; heated pool, tennis court
Public Space Main lodge room, library, patio
Food & Drink Full buffet breakfast; specialty: sticky buns
Recreation Cruises, tennis, swimming, beach combing, horseshoes, shuffleboard
Amenities & Services Antique/gift shop, laundry, storage, fax, copier, surf board, comp. tennis daily, beach towels, meetings (24); entire can be reserved

ACCOMMODATIONS

Units 15 guest rooms, 1 suite
All Rooms Bath, sitting area, TV, wet bar/mini-refrigerators, drinks, snacks, phone, iron, AC

Favorites Corner deluxe rooms—lace canopy beds, gas fireplaces, best baths
Comfort & Decor Rooms spacious, tastefully and carefully appointed with

Some Rooms Fireplace (gas), canopy bed, dining area
Bed & Bath Beds vary; some heated tile bath floors, some whirlpools

antiques. Period furnishings, armoires. Ample reading lights. Romantic ambiance w/ hotel-like amenities. Rooms in carriage house especially priv.

RATES, RESERVATIONS, & RESTRICTIONS

Deposit 1 night, 2 nights for longer stay; refund w/ 15 day notice
Discounts 10% for 7 night stay
Credit Cards V, AE, DC, MC, D
Check-in/Out 3–8/11
Smoking Outside only
Pets No
Kids Over 12
Minimum Stay 2 nights July–Aug., all
weekends; 3 nights holiday weekends
Open Mid-April–mid-Dec.
Hosts Shelia and David Aldrich
8 Old Fort Ave., Box M-1
Kennebunkport, ME 04046
(800) 828-3678 or (207) 967-5353
Fax: (207) 967-4547
info@oldfortinn.com
www.oldfort.com

THE WHITE BARN INN, Kennebunkport

OVERALL ★★★★★ | ROOM QUALITY ★★★★★ | VALUE ★ | PRICE $230–575

A popular icon, this dramatic, sophisticated inn on a busy Kennebunkport street has all things going for it, except perhaps for the grounds, which are limited. Antiques and country artifacts mix faultlessly with luxury detailing. The dining experience is especially delightful, not just because of creative cuisine, but also because of flawless, choreographed service, classical music, and a window wall on a lighted flower garden. The White Barn is a deserving member of the prestigious Relais & Chateaux.

SETTING & FACILITIES

Location I 95 N to Maine Turnpike, Exit 3, follow Rt. 35 S 7 miles to Kennebunkport, straight to Beach St.; inn is .25 mile on the right
Near Wildlife preserves, Dock Square, ocean
Building Large, created from farmhouse and 170-year-old barn
Grounds Lawns, courtyard, flower gardens
Public Space Gracious parlors; sitting, breakfast, and DRs; Victorian porches, copper bar

Food & Drink Full breakfast; tea; 4-course dinner (w/ res.), dinner menu revised weekly, prix fixe $77/person; specialties: lobster dishes, incl. spring rolls, ravioli; full bar, fine wines
Recreation Golf, coast/water activities, XC skiing, horses, tennis, museums
Amenities & Services Outdoor heated pool, massage therapy and spa treatments, canoe and biking equipment; turn-down, morning-evening valet, same-day laundry, business facil., gift cert.

ACCOMMODATIONS

Units 12 guest rooms, 13 add'l rooms and suites in various contemp. annexes and Victorian cottages
All Rooms Bath, fresh flowers and fruit, CD players, voice mail
Some Rooms Deck, priv. entrance, fireplace, sitting area, pool access, entertainment armoire; TV/VCR on request where not standard
Bed & Bath Four-poster, tapestry, contemp., sleigh, antique, handpainted beds, sizes vary; robes, some marble baths, whirlpools, sep. showers

Favorites The Red Suite—dramatic and spacious, priv. porch; May's Annex—king four-posters, fireplaces, marble baths, whirlpools
Comfort & Decor Formal New England period furnishings and Victorian touches, plush carpets, coordinated fabrics and wallcoverings. Room decor from traditional to whimsical. Rooms in May's Cottage most spacious and exclusive. Pool House, simplest rooms. Excellent lighting.

RATES, RESERVATIONS, & RESTRICTIONS

Deposit Check w/ inn, must refund w/ 14 or 30-day notice, depending on the season; credit card req. to reserve dinner
Discounts Off-season, holiday, various pkgs.
Credit Cards V, AE, MC
Check-in/Out 3/11
Smoking No
Pets No
Kids Limited, check w/ inn
No-No's Not cancelling dinner 24 hrs.

in advance
Minimum Stay Varies seasonally, check
Open All year
Host Laurence Bongiorno
37 Beach Ave., Box 560C
Kennebunkport, ME 04046
(207) 967-2321
Fax: (207) 967-1100
innkeeper@whitebarninn.com
www.whitebarninn.com

INN AT PORTSMOUTH HARBOR, Kittery

OVERALL ★★★ | ROOM QUALITY ★★★ | VALUE ★★ | PRICE $135–175

This largely refurbished bed-and-breakfast was formerly The Gundalow Inn. The location, across from a lobster restaurant and shipyard, is picturesque or commercial, depending on your sensibilities. (The Portsmouth area hypes itself as the "restaurant capital of the world," and you can walk or bike from here to several good eateries.) The bed-and-breakfast has a hidden staircase, but everything else is right out in the open. The kitchen, with its big stoves, open shelves and home-baked smells, is the heart of this bright, homey house.

SETTING & FACILITIES

Location From I-95 to Portsmouth or Kittery exits, to US 1, to Water St.; on Maine side of Memorial Bridge, Portsmouth Harbor
Near Outlet shopping, University of New Hampshire, Phillips Exeter Academy, historic homes, Colonial Portsmouth
Building 1890 brick Federal-style
Grounds Privet hedge, roses, and flowers, patio; views of Portsmouth Naval

Shipyard, Piscataque River
Public Space DR, parlor, sun porch
Food & Drink Full breakfast
Recreation Beach activities, boating, day trips, touring
Amenities & Services Games, pickup from Portsmouth bus or train stations, maps, beach towels, recipes, paper, reservations, meeting facilities for 25

ACCOMMODATIONS

Units 5 guest rooms
All Rooms Bath, ceiling fan, phone, TV, dataport, voice mail, heat control and air conditioning

Some Rooms Water/Portsmouth view, skylights
Bed & Bath Bed sizes vary; some tubs w/ hand-held showers, claw-foot tubs

Favorites Royal George—3rd floor, skylight decor, river view
Comfort & Decor Antiques, Victorian decor. Bright rooms designed to maximize views. Some old-fashioned fixtures in baths. Good lighting. Comfortable, warm feeling throughout.

RATES, RESERVATIONS, & RESTRICTIONS

Deposit 1 night or longer stay; refund w/ 14-day notice
Discounts Mid-week stays Nov.–April
Credit Cards V, MC
Check-in/Out 4–7/11
Smoking No
Pets No; house golden retriever
Kids Over 12
Minimum Stay 2 nights weekends, high season, special events/weekends

Open All year except Thanksgiving, Christmas; check in winter
Hosts Kim and Terry O'Mahoney
6 Water St.
Kittery, ME 03904
(207) 439-4040
Fax: (207) 438-9286
innph@cybertours.com
innatportsmouth.com

HARTWELL HOUSE, Ogunquit

OVERALL ★★★½ | ROOM QUALITY ★★★★ | VALUE ★★★ | PRICE $86–185

For groups, weddings, retreats, and business travelers who want the feel of an inn along with state-of-the-art business facilities, this is a fine choice. Spanning both sides of a busy road, the facade looks like a generic business retreat, but within, style and sophistication mixed with antiques and whimsy add up to surprisingly fetching public areas and accommodations, individually decorated in both country and contemporary decor.

SETTING & FACILITIES

Location I-95 to York/Ogunquit Exit, left on Rt. 1, right onto Pine Hill Rd. to end, left on Shore Rd.
Near Footpath along rocky shore, ocean beaches, Perkins Cove, lighthouses
Building 5,200-sq.-ft. Colonial-style building (new); 2nd Colonial-style 1921 farmhouse
Grounds 1.5 acre of landscaped grounds on 2 sides of road
Public Space LR, DR, glassed-in front porch; conf. area (65)
Food & Drink Full gourmet breakfast, communal or separate; full course dinners by arrangement, clam bakes for groups
Recreation Beach, Windjammer cruises, golf, fishing, horses, XC skiing, Christmas by the Sea celebration (2nd week in Dec.)
Amenities & Services Golf privileges at Cape Neddick Country Club, conf. center and coordinator, papers; taxi and limo services, flowers on request, reservations made, spousal activities (for conf.), disabled access

ACCOMMODATIONS

Units 13 guest rooms, 3 suites
All Rooms Bath, antiques, AC
Some Rooms Terrace/balcony; suites LR/dining area, refrigerator, wet bar
Bed & Bath Custom mattresses; full baths, some w/ 2nd sink

Favorites Winslow Homer—floral tapestries, netted canopied bed, balcony
Comfort & Decor European country style, mixed w/ Americana. Hotel-like comforts and sophistication. Crocheted coverlets. Fresh plants. Spacious, elegant.

RATES, RESERVATIONS, & RESTRICTIONS

Deposit 50%, must cancel 14 days in advance; for meetings/functions, 50%, bal. due w/in 21 days of arrival, must cancel 21 days in advance
Discounts "Inn-house Dining" weekend pkgs., New Year's Eve event, getaways
Credit Cards V, AE, MC, D
Check-in/Out 3–9/11
Smoking Outside only
Pets No
Kids Over 14
No-No's Add'l people in rooms, late

check-out (fee)
Minimum Stay 3 nights July, Aug., holiday weekends
Open All year
Hosts Tracey and Chris Anderson
312 Shore Rd., Box 393
Ogunquit, ME 03907
(800) 235-8883 or (207) 646-7210
Fax: (207) 646-6032
hartwell@cybertours.com
hartwellhouseinn.com

NELLIE LITTLEFIELD HOUSE, Ogunquit

OVERALL ★★★½ | ROOM QUALITY ★★★ | VALUE ★★½ | PRICE $75–210

A hundred years ago this notable village house behind a picket fence was a center of summer social activity. Today, once again, the imposing, white-turreted village landmark sparkles within and without, and it has won 10 architectural awards for its remodeling. Nellie's hospitality continues today, a turn-of-the-century later, with warm hosts, hearty breakfasts, a fine location, and pretty period details.

SETTING & FACILITIES

Location Rt. 1 to Ogunquit, turn onto Shore Rd., 1st Victorian on left
Near Marginal Way Walk, Kittery outlet shops, Perkins Cove, ocean
Building 1889 Victorian
Grounds Minimal lawn, gardens
Public Space LR, library, DR; 3 porches; all disabled access

Food & Drink Full buffet breakfast; refreshments, wine and cheese
Recreation Boating, biking, horses, diving, golf
Amenities & Services Exercise room, refrigerator, irons, maps, celebrations, books, beach towels, recipes, paper; fluent German.

ACCOMMODATIONS

Units 6 guest rooms, 2 suites
All Rooms Bath, TV, phone, AC
Some Rooms Priv. deck; 3rd floor keyhole ocean view; disabled access room
(1)
Bed & Bath Queen, twin beds;
whirlpool (1), some showers only

Favorites J.H.—LR, deck, ocean view,
whirlpool, 2 TVs
Comfort & Decor Comfortable and
bright. Some period and antique touches.
Plants. Framed art. Reading lamps. Feels
like a small hotel.

RATES, RESERVATIONS, & RESTRICTIONS

Deposit 1 night; refund w/ 14-day notice
Discounts Longer stays
Credit Cards V, MC, D
Check-in/Out 3/11
Smoking No
Pets No
Kids Over 12
Minimum Stay 2 nights weekends, 3

nights holiday weekends
Open May–Oct.
Hosts Patty and Joerg Ross
9 Shore Rd., Box 1599
Ogunquit, ME 03907
(207) 646-1692
www.visit-maine.com/
nellielittlefieldhouse

TRELLIS HOUSE, Ogunquit

OVERALL ★★★½ | ROOM QUALITY ★★★★ | VALUE ★★★ | PRICE $85–160

Trellises on the grounds give the name to this unpretentious house with a
welcoming, wraparound wicker-filled screened porch, a mix of comfortable
furnishings throughout, and a homey feel. Close to the action of the main
shopping area, and to The Marginal Way walkway on the rocky shoreline, yet
in an off-street atmosphere, you could almost feel that you are on a country
lane. The carriage house and cottage are private and spacious, and a good deal
for long stays. Pat and Jerry are hands-on hosts who know the area well.

SETTING & FACILITIES

Location Rt. 1 to Ogunquit, on a side
street off Shore Rd.
Near Perkins Cove, Ogunquit Village,
Marginal Way historic trail, ocean
Building 1907 country summer cottage
Grounds Gardens, flower arbors and
trellises
Public Space Common rooms, LR

Food & Drink Full breakfast, communal;
specialty: ginger pancakes; tea
Recreation Trolley, boat tours, harbor
and crafts shops, walking tours, horses,
XC skiing
Amenities & Services Off-street parking

ACCOMMODATIONS

Units 8 guest rooms, carriage house, Barbary Cottage

All Rooms Bath, AC, clock

Some Rooms Fireplace, alcove, deck, sitting area, views

Bed & Bath Antiques beds, sizes vary

Favorites The Main Suite—spacious, sitting alcove, ocean view, queen brass bed

Comfort & Decor Eclectic, early American pieces mingled w/ current collectibles. Comfortable, homey, unpretentious. Barbary Cottage priv., romantic. Carriage house w/ fireplaces, priv. decks.

RATES, RESERVATIONS, & RESTRICTIONS

Deposit 50%; refund w/ 21-day notice, service charge $20

Discounts 3rd person, pkgs., weekly (apt.)

Credit Cards V, MC

Check-in/Out 2/11

Smoking No

Pets No; innkeepers have 1 dog

Kids Over 13

Minimum Stay 2 nights weekends; 2 nights, busy season; 3 nights holidays; check w/ B&B

Open All year

Hosts Pat and Jerry Houlihan

2 Beachmere Place, Box 2229

Ogunquit, ME 03907

(800) 681-7909 or (207) 646-7909

www.trellishouse.com

POMEGRANATE, Portland

OVERALL ★★★★½ | ROOM QUALITY ★★★★★ | VALUE ★★★½ | PRICE $95–175

Artistic, sophisticated and witty, this now-beloved city charmer is imbued with flair and faux fun. Artists were given freedom to interpret throughout, and the combination of classic architecture and modern sensibilities works amazingly. Some favorite touches the Matisse-inspired floral walls, and checkerboard floor of the landing, the marbleized columns separating parlor and dining room, the painted irises in Bathroom No. 5, the painted swags in the dining room, etc. This immaculate postmodern bed-and-breakfast is loved most by those who enjoy the surprising pleasures of the offbeat and unexpected, and the hostess' name is appropriate.

SETTING & FACILITIES

Location Historic Western Promenade area

Near Casco Bay, midtown Art District, downtown Portland

Building Italianate Colonial Revival mansion

Grounds City gardens, patio w/ seating

Public Space Common rooms, DR

Food & Drink Full breakfast; refreshments on arrival

Recreation Museums, bay cruises, events, colleges, shipping, galleries

Amenities & Services Books, games

ACCOMMODATIONS

Units 7 guest rooms, 1 suite
All Rooms Bath, cable TV, phone, clock, radio, air conditioning
Some Rooms Fireplace
Bed & Bath Artisan-crafts beds, sizes vary; tiled, porcelain sinks
Favorites No. 7—carriage house, floral

motif, priv. patio
Comfort & Decor Guest rooms big, uniquely hand-painted walls, brash patterns. Bold colors from eggplant to Matisse red to black and white. Artistically interpreted decor. Luxurious, surprising, unique.

RATES, RESERVATIONS, & RESTRICTIONS

Deposit Check w/ inn
Credit Cards V, MC, AE, D
Check-in/Out 4–6/11
Smoking No
Pets No
Kids Over 16 OK
Minimum Stay 2 nights, busy season and holidays

Open All year
Hosts Isabel Smiles and Chris Monahan
49 Neal St.
Portland, ME 04102
(800) 356-0408 or (207) 772-1006
Fax: (207) 773-4426
www.pomegranateinn.com

EDWARDS' HARBORSIDE INN, York

OVERALL ★★★½ | ROOM QUALITY ★★★★ | VALUE ★★½ | PRICE $60–230

Jay, a certified Coast Guard captain, bought and began renovating the bed-and-breakfast in 1985 and has been working and upgrading it since. Sailboats ply by, lobstermen unload their delectable catch by the dock, and the tiny, sandy beach is good for a (short) walk. Aside from that, check out the salty environs, read a book or chat up your fellow guests. A modern building across the water on one side mars the view a bit, but the pace here remains relaxing. Sunlight streams through the porch windows, and sunsets from the pier are especially nice with sherry.

SETTING & FACILITIES

Location Rt. 1A through York Village into York Harbor, right onto Stage Neck Rd.; on ocean and Harbor
Near Portsmouth, Kennebunkport; beach across street w/ rocky cliff path
Building Gray/white, originally Victorian; completely refurbished
Grounds Lawn slopes to water

Public Space Sunporch, parlors
Food & Drink Breakfast, sherry and cheese in p.m.
Recreation Golf, tennis, boating, fishing, L.L. Bean outlet
Amenities & Services Board games, books, hot tub, refrigerator, books, fax, pickup at Portland airport, groups

ACCOMMODATIONS

Units 7 guest rooms, 3 suites
All Rooms TV, AC, clock, radio, dataport
Some Rooms Bath, priv. deck
Bed & Bath Bed sizes vary; priv. or semi-priv., some whirlpools

Favorites The York Suite—view, four-poster, dbl. whirlpool
Comfort & Decor Victorian-style American country charm. Comfortable. Water views though large windows Rooms vary widely.

RATES, RESERVATIONS, & RESTRICTIONS

Deposit 1 night or 50% of longer stay; refund w/14-day notice; groups full payment at reserv.
Discounts Off-season, 3rd person, pkgs.
Credit Cards V, MC
Check-in/Out 3/11
Smoking Outside porches only
Pets No
Kids No
Minimum Stay 2 nights, weekends; 3 nights, peak season
Open All year
Host Jay Edwards
Stage Neck Rd., Box 866
York Harbor, ME 03911
(800) 273-2686 or (207) 363-3037
Fax: (207) 363-1544
yorkharbor@aol.com
www.edwardsharborside.com

Maine—Inland
and Lakes

This so-called "quiet corner" (louder during snowmobile and hunting seasons) extends west/east from **Fryeburg** to **Houlton** and north/south from **Madawaska** and **Edmunston** to **Bangor** and **New Gloucester**. Although an inland portion of the state, this enormous land of loons, pines and covered bridges is nearly flooded with lakes, large ponds, waterways, streams, and white-water rivers.

Maine's extensive snowmobile **Interconnecting Trail System (ITS)** and the impending **International Lakeland Trail** running from New Brunswick, Canada, may threaten the pristine atmosphere, but the attraction remains simply the "great outdoors." Wildlife is really in the wilds. **Baxter State Park,** a 200,000-acre wilderness, has the state's highest population of moose and deer and quite a few bears.

The peaks of mile-high **Mount Katahdin** in the **Longfellow Range** of mountains are the second in the state to be touched by the morning sun and are the terminus of the **Appalachian Trail.** Bike, hike or drive designated scenic Route 201 past farmlands and forest landscapes. **Skowhegan** has the largest Wooden Indian in the state. Crossing over to **Maritime Canada,** the nineteenth-century local-granite-built railway station in **McAdam** is a worthy visit. Foliage season arrives here in September, perhaps the earliest in New England.

Photography, year-round camping, seasonal hunting, fishing, boating, biking, mountain biking, hiking, dog sledding, snowshoeing, cross-country skiing, golf, tennis, and some downhill skiing are popular pastimes. **Penobscot River, St. Croix,** and **The Forks** offer beginner to extreme white-water rafting complete with falls, and any kind of reasonable water or ice-water sport is possible on huge **Moosehead Lake,** including summer water-skiing. White-water rafting runs from mid-April through October, because of dam-controlled water release, and in the long winter season, salmon and trout are caught through the ice. Heated ice huts are available for rent.

Snowmobiling, however, appears to win the popularity contest. Miles and miles (and miles) of groomed snowmobile trails cross the region and connect to the **ITS,** and there are snowmobiling festivals, balls, fairs, and contests.

And for "extreme" activities, the lakes region has an abundance of state-certified outfitters and guides ranging from those who go with you, cook for you and pitch your tent, to those who provide a map and just leave you alone.

Homespun, colorful celebrations abound in towns such as **Caribou, Moosehead, Fort Kent,** and **Presque Isle,** including the **Maine Potato Blossom Festival, Winter Festival, Northern Maine Festival, Fall Arts & Crafts Festivals, Acadian Festival, Canoe Race & Scarecrow Festival, Dog Sled Races and Festivals,** and **Logging Days.**

The bad news is that small lodgings up here—often rustic, converted lodges or camps usually near a lake or stream—are few and coveted, and drives to and between are long. Often you'll be eating all your meals at the inn, and you'll probably have to book for longer than one night. The prevailing atmosphere is outdoorsy, basic, informal, friendly, family-style and hearty. Unlike at more crowded coastal areas, with loads of choices and hotel options, you'll need a reservation in hand or you may find yourself driving all night back to Bangor.

FOR MORE INFORMATION

Androscoggin County (207) 783-2249

Greater Bangor Chamber of Commerce (207) 947-0307

Greater Farmington Area (207) 778-4215
email: info@farmingtonchamber.org

Greater Lincoln Area Chamber of Commerce (207) 794-8065 or (888) 794-8065

Jackman-Moose River Chamber of Commerce (207) 668-4171

Katahdin Area Chamber of Commerce (Millinocket) (207) 723-4443

Kennebec Valley (207) 623-4559 or (800) 393-8629

Upper Kennebec Valley (The Forks) Bingham (207) 672-4100

Moosehead Lake Region (207) 695-2702, email: moose@moosehead.net

Rangeley Lakes Region (207) 864-5571 or (800) MT-LAKES
email: mtlakes@rangeley.org

Skowhegan (207) 474-3621 email: skowman@skowhegan.org

Sugarloaf Area (207) 235-2100

Windham Chamber of Commerce (207) 892-8265 email: wincc@gwi.net

TELEMARK INN, *Bethel*

OVERALL ★★★★ | ROOM QUALITY ★★★ | VALUE ★ | PRICE $95–825

Like to try new adventures? How 'bout skijoring (skiing while being pulled by a dog), training Alaskan Huskies for sled racing, llama trekking, or sweating in an authentic Indian lodge and then plunging into a snowbank? More traditional adventurers can enjoy mountain hiking trails, swimming hole excursions, canoeing, mountain biking, and exploring lakes, waterfalls, and beaver dams. This rustic eco-educational inn, formerly a millionaire's wilderness estate, creates its own electricity, offers healthy meals, and can be challenging or relaxing. You can just sit on the porch, listen to the birds, and twiddle your thumbs. So what if you have to share a bathroom.

SETTING & FACILITIES

Location 10 miles from Bethel Village, 3 miles up a road in a stand of white birches at base of Caribou Mountain, the eastern fringe of the White Mountains
Near Surrounded by White Mountain Nat'l Forest
Building Turn-of-the-century Adirondack-style lodge
Grounds 5 cleared acres, with 22 acres surrounded by White Mountain National Forest, gardens, meadows, lakes, llama farm
Public Space Restored lodge rooms; LR, DR, comfortable porch
Food & Drink Organic fruit, vegetable and herbs; all meals provided; specialty: rhubarb crêpes
Recreation Pkg. activities, training Alaskan Huskies, hiking w/ gear carried by llamas, swimming holes w/ waterfalls and buffet lunch; skiing, snowshoeing, sleigh rides, skating, sledding, ski and skijoring lessons, horses, camping in teepee
Amenities & Services Outside sauna, campfires, learning pkgs., nature talks, picnics, int'l travel tips

ACCOMMODATIONS

Units 6 guest rooms
All Rooms Handcrafted cabinetry, rustic furnishings
Some Rooms Overlook grazing llamas, nat'l forest, mountains
Bed & Bath Some bunk beds; rooms share 3 baths, sinks in each room
Favorites Bunk-bed room—especially fun for kids
Comfort & Decor All rooms comfortable, none outstanding. Some artisan pieces. TVs and phones deliberately excluded. Clean, basic, attractive.

RATES, RESERVATIONS, & RESTRICTIONS

Deposit Typically 50%, varies according to pkg.; refund w/ 30-60–day notice, according to season and pkg.; prices include. meals, lodging and guided activities
Discounts Children, singles, 3rd person
Credit Cards V, MC
Check-in/Out Varies/4
Smoking No

Pets No
Kids Welcome
Minimum Stay 3-, 5- and 7-day pkgs.
Open All year except April; groups only in Nov.
Host Steve Crone

RFD 2, Box 800
Bethel, ME 04217
(207) 836-2703
www.telemarkinn.com
telemark@nxi.com

ADMIRAL PEARY HOUSE, Fryeburg

OVERALL ★★★ | ROOM QUALITY ★★★★ | VALUE ★★★½ | PRICE $80–148

Once the residence of arctic explorer Admiral Robert E. Peary, discoverer of the North Pole, this bed-and-breakfast lets you discover something too that this is a fine stop, especially for tennis lovers, skiers, and outdoor enthusiasts. Geared toward quiet indoor time as well, the house offers books, paintings, a beautiful fireplace, a constantly hot tea pot in the big, country kitchen, and lots of good conversation in any of the nooks and crannies.

SETTING & FACILITIES

Location Mt. Washington Valley; Rt. 302 W to Fryeburg (oldest village in White Mountains); block from center
Near White Mountains, walk to Saco River, Lake Kezar; 6 miles to New Hampshire outlet shopping; 1 hr. to Maine coastline
Building Sprawling 1865 Colonial, barn
Grounds 10 acres; wooded, lawns, award-winning perennial gardens
Public Space LR; library; screened porch

Food & Drink Full breakfast, communal; specialty: Admiral Peary's Penguin Pie, crustless quiche with homemade breads, sausage, fresh jams, and Nancy's baked beans
Recreation Boating, skiing, golf, Fryeburg Fair, antiquing, hiking, snowshoeing
Amenities & Services Hot tub, snowshoe rentals/trails, billiards; bikes, boat rides on Lake Kezar (fee); red clay tennis, lessons, rackets, ball machine; conf. facilities

ACCOMMODATIONS

Units 6 guest rooms
All Rooms Bath, sitting area, heat controls, AC, carpet, bright
Some Rooms 3rd person
Bed & Bath Queen/king; I king can sep. to twins; four-poster, brass, unique antique; showers only, recently remodeled

Favorites North Pole—spacious, large window, country view, brass bed
Comfort & Decor Spacious, comfortably furnished, formal Colonial decor, antique mahogany, decorator fabrics, wallcoverings, ambient lighting. Soothing, tasteful. Good lighting, workspace.

RATES, RESERVATIONS, & RESTRICTIONS

Deposit I night, 50% longer stays; pkgs. paid in full at res.; refund w/ 14-day notice
Discounts 3rd person, 5+ days, pkgs., winter contracts and pkgs, midweek, business
Credit Cards V, AE, MC
Check-in/Out 4/11
Smoking No
Pets No; inn has border terrier dog, cockatiel

Kids Permitted w/ limitations, check w/ inn
Minimum Stay None
Open All year
Hosts Nancy and Ed Greenberg
9 Elm St.
Fryeburg, ME 04037-1114
(800) 237-8080 or (207) 935-3365
Fax same as telephone
admpeary@nxi.com
www.admiralpearyhouse.com

GREENVILLE INN, Greenville

OVERALL ★★★★½ | ROOM QUALITY ★★★★ | VALUE ★★½ | PRICE $125–235

Built by a logging baron, this grand mansion is set in an equally grand location on a pristine lake in the northern Maine woods. Ship carpenters worked ten years to complete the interior, which has a glorious leaded-glass window painted with a spruce tree. Dining is also grand, with heavy silver. A sample three-course dinner might be smoked rainbow trout with capers, grilled swordfish Provençal, and chocolate truffle tart with pecan crust. This inn would be exceptional anywhere, but up here in the middle of nowhere—along with The Lodge at Moosehead Lake—it's a real surprise.

SETTING & FACILITIES

Location Rt. 15 N to Greenville, 2 blocks after blinking yellow light, turn right; overlooking New England's largest lake
Near Bangor, Penobscot, Kennebec, Dead Rivers; Mt. Kineo, Mt. Katahdin, Rip Gorge, state parks, lake beaches; half hr. drive to Bar Harbor, ocean, Acadia Nat'l Park
Building 1895 hilltop Victorian mansion
Grounds Spacious porch; overlooking lake

Public Space Grand entrance stair
Food & Drink Cont'l buffet breakfast; dinner avail.; specialties: escargot, veal; full bar, wine cellar
Recreation Float plane rides, boat tours, water/snow sports; Moosemania (spring), International Seaplane Festival (Sept.)
Amenities & Services Disabled access

ACCOMMODATIONS

Units 4 guest rooms, 2 suites, 6 cottages
All Rooms Bath
Some Rooms Fireplace, sitting area, TV, lake view
Bed & Bath Bed sizes vary, some antique beds; some shower only
Favorites Spacious Master Suite—sitting room, fireplace, large bath, views
Comfort & Decor Main building rooms romantically Victorian, without fussiness. Airy lace curtains and bed covers, period furnishings, muted wallcoverings, carpet. Cottages in meadow setting, mountain view, wicker, floral fabrics, French doors.

RATES, RESERVATIONS, & RESTRICTIONS

Deposit 1 night, 50% longer stays
Credit Cards V, MC, D
Check-in/Out 3/11
Smoking In limited areas
Pets No
Kids Over 7
Minimum Stay 3 nights, Seaplane Fly-in (Sept.)
Open DR and cottages, May 11–Oct. 20; main building, all year
Hosts The Schnetzer Family
Norris St., Box 1194
Greenville, ME 04441-1194
888-695-6000 or (207) 695-2206
Fax: (207) 695-0335
gvlinn@moosehead.net
www.greenvilleinn.com

LODGE AT MOOSEHEAD LAKE, *Greenville*

OVERALL ★★★★½ | ROOM QUALITY ★★★★★ | VALUE ★½ | PRICE $175–425

Yes, this rustic inn has extensive outdoors activities, luxurious accommodations, endless lake views, and hearty food. But what you'll most remember are the four-poster beds, carved by a local artist. Totem poles, bears, nuzzling mooseheads, fish—you've got to see them to believe them. This decidedly over-the-top and far-north lodge is not for those who insist on refinement. But the enthusiastic hosts, relying on their extensive hospitality backgrounds, run this fantasy environment with a sure hand and a sense of fun. It's worth a detour.

SETTING & FACILITIES

Location Rt. 15 N to Greenville, go
through blinking light, 2.5 miles up steep
hill, 3rd building on left, at top
Near Bangor airport, Penobscot, Kennebec, and Dead rivers; Mt. Kineo, Mt.
Katahdin, Rip Gorge, state parks, lake
beaches, 2 1/2 hours to Bar Harbor,
ocean, Acadia Nat'l Park, 3 hours to Quebec City or White Mtns
Building 1917 Lodge-style building
Grounds Unbroken view, pine-treed
hills, pristine Moosehead Lake, gardens

Public Space Common rooms, library;
DR/restaurant; deck
Food & Drink Full buffet breakfast, main
course served; candlelight dinner, 2
nights/week; specialty: Salmon in a Moose
Suit; full bar
Recreation Beach/water/snow activities,
float plane rides, moose safaris, dogsled
trips; Moosemania (spring), International
Seaplane Festival (Sept.)
Amenities & Services Equip. rentals,
billiards, games, guided activities

ACCOMMODATIONS

Units 5 guest rooms, 3 suites
All Rooms Bath w/ whirlpool, gas fireplace, unique, TV/VCR
Some Rooms Retreat Suites spacious,
whirlpool w/ chandelier, sunken LR, patio
overlooking lake; 2nd fireplace in bath (1)
Bed & Bath Unique four-poster/
canopied, 2 suites w/ suspended beds;
dbl. whirlpools w/ TV/VCR
Favorites Majestic Bear Room—lake
view, four-poster w/ carved bears;

Katahdin Suite—fireplace, , bath, moose
antler canopy bed
Comfort & Decor Artistic, eclectic,
rustic. Beds set theme of room. Comfort
and design prioritized. Rough-hewn or
handcarved bedposts mixed w/ Rustic,
period decor. Dramatic, luxurious,
unique. Some rooms—such as Moose
Room w/ huge, nuzzling mooseheads—
border on gaudy.

RATES, RESERVATIONS, & RESTRICTIONS

Deposit 50%; refund w/ 21-day notice,
less $50 admin. fee
Discounts 3rd person
Credit Cards V, MC, D
Check-in/Out 3–5/11
Smoking No
Pets No; inn has 2 dogs
Kids Over 14 welcome
Minimum Stay 2 nights

Open Late december to mid-March, May
through November; summer/fall is high
season
Hosts Jennifer and Roger Cauchi
Upon Lily Bay Rd. Box 1167
Greenville, ME 04441
(207) 695-4400
innkeeper@lodgeatmooseheadlake.com
www.LodgeatMooseheadLake.com

LAKE HOUSE, Waterford

OVERALL ★★★★ | ROOM QUALITY ★★★ | VALUE ★★ | PRICE $110–185

Once a stagecoach stop, then a hotel where Judy Garland, Mickey Rooney, Claudette Colbert, and other stars frolicked by the lake, today the inn is noted for comfy lodging, outdoor activities, and affordable prices. The host is the chef as well, and gourmet food and wine are as lovingly realized as the historic property itself, in this delightful rural village of nineteenth-century white clapboard houses. Lakeside and mountains beckon from eight windows in the most romantic guest room a 600-square-foot former ballroom, with curved ceilings and a claw-foot tub on a dramatic raised dais.

SETTING & FACILITIES

Location On Rt. 35, 18 miles from Rt. 302, in tiny, pretty town
Near Lakes, Mt. Washington Valley, White Mountains, L.L. Bean outlet, Shaker Village
Building Gracious 1787 Greek Revival
Grounds Gazebo; focus on lake and beach across street
Public Space Sitting room, DR
Food & Drink Full breakfast; romantic dinner, creative menu; specialty: chicken Scala; award-winning wine cellar, wine-tasting events
Recreation Water/snow sports, tennis, golf, hunting, horses, mountain and trail biking
Amenities & Services Books, games, parties, event planning, disabled access

ACCOMMODATIONS

Units 7 guest rooms, 1 single-room cottage
All Rooms Bath, antiques, coffee maker
Some Rooms Sitting area, desk, porch access
Bed & Bath Antique beds, sizes vary; some claw-foot tubs, hairdryers, robes
Favorites Grand Ballroom Suite—spacious and airy, four-poster, tub open to room; Dudley House—cozy, romantic, cathedral ceiling, screened porch

Comfort & Decor Room recently redone. Contemp. or mission furnishings w/ authentic Colonial, gleaming hard- woods, Oriental rugs. Original, spacious, romantic, airy.

RATES, RESERVATIONS, & RESTRICTIONS

Deposit I night; refund w/ 14-day notice
Discounts EP, 3rd, corp., group, longer stay
Credit Cards V, AE, MC
Check-in/Out Flexible/11
Smoking No
Pets No
Kids Over 6

Minimum Stay 3rd weekend in July and foliage weekends
Open All year, except April and Nov.
Host Michael Myers
Box 82, Routes 35 and 37
Waterford, ME 04088
(800) 223-4182 or (207) 583-4182
Fax: (207) 583-2831
www.lakehousemaine.com

New Hampshire

The Granite State's first settlers were the Algonquins, whose ancient names—Sunapee, Winnipesaukee, Ammonnoosuc—remain in many New Hampshire locales, lakes, and lodgings. These enlightened natives later instructed Europeans on basic survival tips to survive the rough winters and wilderness terrain of this ruggedly beautiful, mountainous area. (No guidebooks and no bed-and-breakfasts then.)

In 1775, fledgling independent New Hampshire sent three regiments of "Continentals" to fight with Washington for independence. New Hampshire was the first state to both declare its independence and adopt a state constitution. The 1819 state capitol in **Concord** is still in use. And New Hampshire remains the state with the first presidential primaries, a proud rite of early spring, every four years.

New Hampshire's motto, "Live Free or Die," is reflected not only in its history and tough spirit, but also in its outdoor resources and activities. From the small stretch of seacoast in the south, just above the Boston area, to the **White Mountains,** to the northern wilderness, there is much to help you live free—and easy. Recreation ranges from quiet fishing on a lake on one of the more than 100,000 state-owned acres, to skiing at more than 20 alpine resorts. Opportunities abound as well for hikers, hunters, golfers (80-plus courses!), traditional and off-road cyclists, and cross-country skiers.

Southern New Hampshire encompasses classic New England villages with commons and steepled churches in addition to busy, gritty towns. Here you'll find the still-bustling mid-seventeenth-century settlement of **Portsmouth;** the capital, **Concord;** outlet shopping in Manchester; and pretty **Peterborough,** which was Thornton Wilder's model for *Our Town*.

Heading slightly north to the Central New Hampshire/Lakes region, you'll find esteemed **Dartmouth College** in Hanover, the **Newport**

Opera House, and **Mt. Sunapee State Park,** with noteworthy skiing, hiking, and fishing. The region has more than 270 lakes and ponds for water recreation, and the **Barnstormers,** New Hampshire's oldest summer theater, for evening fun.

The northernmost third of the state is our Northern New Hampshire/ White Mountains zone. As its name suggests, the region is dominated by the 780,000-acre **White Mountain National Forest.** Drive the **Kancamagus Highway,** ski from resort towns like Jackson, and view the turn-of-the-century summer grand hotels. The **Great North Woods,** at the top of the state, is a spectacular wilderness area of fishing, hunting, small-town pleasures, and wildlife watching.

Plenty of small accommodations range from basic lodges in the north to established inns in the mountains and lakes area, and historic properties and farmhouses scattered in villages and rural areas throughout New Hampshire. Costs remain generally low in this no-nonsense state, where the motto makes sense: The scenery is to die for, and although you may not live free, you can live cheap.

Southern New Hampshire

Southern New Hampshire delivers the charms of classic New England, with steepled white churches and village greens, and a short but sweet seacoast that may remind you of Maine's coast.

Start your visit in the east, just above the Massachusetts border, maybe cracking bright red lobster claws on a wooden table by the ocean. You can watch bobbing boats haul in their catch, walk for miles on breezy beaches, and set out into the cold Atlantic for deep-sea fishing. Or take in a bit of history: **Odiorne Point State Park,** in Rye, was the first European settlement in the state (founded in 1623, by Scottish fishermen). While there, leave some time for the **Seacoast Science Center.**

Fort Constitution Historic Site, in New Castle, was built in the 1600s and captured by the Revolutionary colonists in 1774. Nearby **Fort Stark Historic Site** also dates to the mid-eighteenth century. Make sure to save some time for antiquing (check out Route 4), shopping, going to the theater, biking, golfing, hiking, or whale watching.

A bit farther west, you'll find New Hampshire's most populated areas. **Concord**, the state capital, is home to the **Museum of New Hampshire History** and the **State House. Manchester** is the site of the **See Science Center,** the **New Hampshire Philharmonic Orchestra,** and the **New Hampshire Symphony Orchestra.**

In **Derry,** visit the **Robert Frost Homestead** with a romantic poet's path where you may want to stop and read a Frost poem at various spots as you stroll along. The 694-acre **Canterbury Shaker Village** dates to 1792. And this area has opportunities for boating, biking, swimming, fishing, and hiking.

In New Hampshire's southwest corner, you'll find the classic New England of movies and pictorial calendars. Hike up **Mt. Monadnock,** cross-country ski, or go for sleigh rides in the many state parks. Try out the summer theater, visit the children's museum, or spend time in one of the many historical museums. This is quiet, dreamy New England and is especially gorgeous in the fall.

Small lodgings are mainly in bed-and-breakfasts, homey and varied, from town mansions to rural old farmhouses.

FOR MORE INFORMATION

Monadnock Lodging Association www.nhweb.com/monadnocklodging

Monadnock Travel Council (603) 355-8155 or (800) 432-7864
Fax: (603) 357-3529
email: info@monadnocktravel.com
www.virtualnh.com

AMOS A. PARKER HOUSE, Fitzwilliam

OVERALL ★★★★ | ROOM QUALITY ★★★★ | VALUE ★★★★ | PRICE $95–110

The liberty pole out front designates that Revolutionaries once plotted on the site of this gray clapboard that has six wood-burning fireplaces and high-style, low-key decor. But it's the acre of gardens surrounded by marsh and woods that you'll remember most, with stone walls and walks, lily ponds, and hundreds of multi-hued annuals and perennials beckoning everything from butterflies to blue herons. Inside, the handpainted murals by local artists are also lovely. Almost-next-door neighbor Hannah Davis House is a big rival. Amos is more refined, Hannah friendlier, but both represent creative innkeeping.

SETTING & FACILITIES

Location NH 119 to Fitzwilliam, less than .7 mi. from Rt. 12
Near Sharon Arts Center, Fry's Measure Mill, Apple Hill Chamber Players, Mt. Monadnock, Cathedral of Pines
Building 18th-century clapboard Colonial
Grounds Extensive gardens, water lily pond, Oriental/Dutch features, unique plantings
Public Space Parlor, DR, borning room, great room (ca. 1700), library, game room
Food & Drink Full formal breakfast; specialties: soufflés, puff-pancakes w/ caramelized apples, crêpes; snacks cookies, tea sandwiches, cheese, fruit
Recreation Mt. Monadnock hiking, XC skiing, tennis, swimming, water sports
Amenities & Services Beach towels, hairdryers, maps, special requests

ACCOMMODATIONS

Units 2 guest rooms, 2 suites
All Rooms Bath, spec. toiletries (incl. razors)
Some Rooms Fireplace, refrigerator (1), stove (1)
Bed & Bath Beds vary, some four-posters; tubs
Favorites Rear 2nd floor room— stenciled garden wall, brass/iron bed, sitting room, view; 1st floor suite—fireplace, sitting area, Pullman kitchen
Comfort & Decor Bright and immaculate. Designer touches. Elegant, tasteful, comfortable. Good lighting. A sure hand in decor and detailing.

RATES, RESERVATIONS, & RESTRICTIONS

Deposit 1 night w/in 10 days of res.; refund w/ 14-day notice
Discounts None
Credit Cards V, MC
Check-In/Out 3–6/11
Smoking No
Pets No
Kids OK
Minimum Stay 2 nights some fall weekends

Open All year
Host Freda B. Houpt
146 NH Rt. 119 West, Box 202

Fitzwilliam, NH 03447
(603) 585-6540

ASHBURN HOUSE, Fitzwilliam

OVERALL ★★★½ | ROOM QUALITY ★★★ | VALUE ★★★½ | PRICE $80–90

As these enthusiastic new innkeepers put it, in 1996 they "came to New England from Old England." And they brought with them some quirky, unusual collectibles, such as a wall of antique English insurance company firemarks, and a dining room table from the House of Commons. Back in London, Tina was a children's theatrical agent, and David an insurance executive. With the accents, the pub, the breakfasts of porridge, tomatoes, mushrooms, eggs, fried potatoes, toast, and marmalade, and the antiques and furnishings, you may think that you are far from this pretty village across the Atlantic

SETTING & FACILITIES

Location 200 yds. off Rt. 119, in village center
Near Fitzwilliam Inn (Old English-style bar, English beer); Old England Enterprises Antiques, performing arts, state forests, covered bridges, crafts, historic societies
Building 1845 Colonial post-and-beam home
Grounds Half-acre garden; lookout from Upper Troy Rd.

Public Space 2 lounges (1 smoking), DR
Food & Drink Early morning tea, coffee; English breakfast, communal or separate; specialty jams; grilled bacon sausages, eggs; hot drinks and juices
Recreation Mt. Monadnock trails, golf, water sports, fishing, hunting (w/ license), sleigh rides, berry picking
Amenities & Services Fridge, irons, books, phone, fax, maps

ACCOMMODATIONS

Units 3 guest rooms, 1 suite
All Rooms Private or en suite bath
Some Rooms Antiques
Bed & Bath Queen, 2 twin beds; Country Room and Rose Room combine for suite; 2, showers only, 1 tub/shower combo

Favorites Blue Room—English Victorian antique queen bed, en suite bath, fireplace; Rose Room—similar w/ priv. bath
Comfort & Decor English antiques and paintings. 2 baths w/ stenciling. Modest, neat, smallish, cheerful.

RATES, RESERVATIONS, & RESTRICTIONS

Deposit Refund w/ 7-day notice
Discounts Singles
Credit Cards V, MC
Check-In/Out 3:30/11; flexible

Smoking Lounge
Pets Dogs; ask on others; gentle in-house St. Bernard restricted if nec., off-limits in guest rooms

Kids Depends on age and number	20 Upper Troy Rd.
Minimum Stay None	Fitzwilliam, NH 03447
Open Closed Christmas Eve/Day, Boxing	(603) 585-7198
Day	Fax: (603) 585-6919
Hosts Tina and David Ashton	ash@top.monad.net

HANNAH DAVIS HOUSE, *Fitzwilliam*

OVERALL ★★★★ | ROOM QUALITY ★★★★ | VALUE ★★★★ | PRICE $70–140

The lovely little village is filled with renovated historic homes such as this one. Guest rooms surprise with unexpected pleasures, and although public space may be limited, the breakfasts aren't. Solo travelers may especially appreciate the spicy aromas and casual environment in the big kitchen, as warm, helpful Kaye chats with guests while preparing new recipes or old favorites. You might be served sourdough French toast stuffed with peaches and cream or with blueberry-strawberry sauce or perhaps scrambled eggs, country ham, potatoes with Portobello mushrooms and chives, and green beans from the garden. Or perhaps stir-fried chicken in crêpes, or . . .

SETTING & FACILITIES

Location S of Keene on NH 119 W, near town common

Near Antiquing, beach, nature areas, historic district

Building Restored 1820 Federal clapboard

Grounds Smallish; overlooks beaver pond

Public Space Open-kitchen entrance, breakfast area; small parlor; dining area; screened porch

Food & Drink Extravagant breakfast; specialties: stuffed french toast, spanikopitas, homemade granola w/ chunky applesauce, lemon-poppy seed or cinnamon-raisin bread; afternoon treats; spec. diets accom.

Recreation Canoeing, golf, hunting, horses, skiing, swimming

Amenities & Services Some disabled access (visual, hearing impaired), maps, turndown

ACCOMMODATIONS

Units 3 guest rooms, 3 suites (1 in Carriage Barn)

All Rooms Bath, clock, radio

Some Rooms Wood-burning fireplace, sitting room, sofa bed, extra bed, priv. entrance, porch

Bed & Bath Mostly queens, one king, one double bed, antique iron beds, one canopy; all w/ tubs and showers, pedestal sinks, footed tubs; some oversize showers

Favorites Popovers—above garage,

vaulted ceiling, antique cannonball bed, wood-burning fireplace, deck and walkway "pop over" backyard and bog; The Loft— former carriage house, spacious duplex, beams, barn siding, fireplace

Comfort & Decor Room size and decor vary, many w/ antique iron and cannonball beds, high ceilings, pedestal porcelain sinks, footed or iron tubs. Some exposed timbers, Southwest feeling. Airy and bright. Natural woodwork.

RATES, RESERVATIONS, & RESTRICTIONS

Deposit 50% w/in 5 days of res., or credit card; refund w/ 10-day notice
Discounts 3rd person $25, singles
Credit Cards V, MC, D
Check-In/Out 3–6/11; call for late arrival
Smoking Outside porches only
Pets No; in-house cat, 1 dogs
Kids Welcome in 2 suites
No-No's No shows (pay full cost of rooms)
Minimum Stay 2 nights, some college weekends, some holidays
Open All year
Hosts Kaye and Mike Terpstra
106 NH Rt. 119 W
Fitzwilliam, NH 03447
(603) 585-3344

INN AT CROTCHED MOUNTAIN, Francestown

OVERALL ★★★★ | ROOM QUALITY ★★★★ | VALUE ★★★★ | PRICE $75–120

On the north side of Crotched Mountain, 1,300 feet above sea level at the end of a winding path, is this way-out-of-the-way inn, built as a farmhouse in 1822. The builder was an Abolitionist who dug a tunnel from the cellar to the road and sheltered slaves on their escape north. Today, you can escape here (without political consequences) to relax, swim, play tennis, meander, and enjoy the flowers, the Indonesian-influenced food and the panoramic view. Crotched Mountain, by the way, takes its name from the shape of the twin peaks to the south.

SETTING & FACILITIES

Location Rt. 136 to Francestown, 3.5 mi. from center of Francestown, on side of Crotched Mountain.
Near Mt. Monadnock, Sharon Arts Center, Petersborough Players, Franklin Pierce Homestead, antiquing, outlet shopping, summer theater
Building Colonial 1822 private farmhouse estate, rebuilt mid-1930s after fire
Grounds Expansive, walking/XC ski trails; vegetable, herb, flower gardens; 40-mile view of Piscataquog Valley
Public Space 2 sitting rooms, 2 DRs, cocktail lounge; most disabled access.
Food & Drink Full breakfast; specialties: fruit, French toast; hot drinks; cookies; liquor license
Recreation Ice-skating, 2 clay tennis courts, wading and 30′ x 50′ pool on site; downhill skiing, mountain climbing nearby
Amenities & Services Irons, games, wheelchair access, meetings (18), fax, maps

ACCOMMODATIONS

Units 13 guest rooms
All Rooms Radio/alarm clock
Some Rooms Fireplace, wheelchair access (2)
Bed & Bath Queen, double, 2 twin beds; 8 priv. baths, 6 full, 5 shower only, 2 half baths

Favorites Room 9—fireplace, door to backyard w/ pool access, great views
Comfort & Decor Country decor w/ antiques and Colonial reproductions. Worn but comfortable. Many w/ great views. Quiet.

RATES, RESERVATIONS, & RESTRICTIONS

Deposit Full, 1 night; 2–4 nights, 1st and last; 50% other; all w/in 7 days of booking; refund w/ 14-day notice; other w/ re-rental (fee)
Discounts Midweek 3+ nights; May–Aug., 3+; 3rd person, singles
Credit Cards None
Check-In/Out 2/11; call for arrivals after 11
Smoking Nonsmoking
Pets OK w/ $5 fee; in-house English cockers, off-limits in guest rooms

Kids OK
Minimum Stay Prefer 2 nights on weekends, 3 on holiday weekends
Open Closed April
Hosts Rose and John Perry
534 Mountain Rd.
Francestown, NH 03043
(603) 588-6840
Fax: (603) 588-6623
www.innbook.com
perry–inncm@conknet.com

HANCOCK INN, *Hancock*

OVERALL ★★★★½ | ROOM QUALITY ★★★★ | VALUE ★★★ | PRICE $106–172

The oldest inn in the state, it has been in continuous operation since 1789, when George Washington first became president. Back then, guests arrived in Concord coaches and often in sleighing parties. Named the Jefferson Tavern until the late 1800s, the inn enlarged when the railroad came in. TV cozies (like tea cozies), hand-sewn quilts, and superb nineteenth-century wall paintings are authentic charms. The American cuisine is satisfying. Named after founding father John, who once owned much of the land here, both the inn and the whole town (with a steeple bell by Paul Revere) are on the National Register of Historic Places.

SETTING & FACILITIES

Location Across the street from the general store on Main St.
Near Walk to Meeting House w/ Paul Revere bell, orig. schoolhouse, cemetery, Norway Pond; Mt. Monadnock, Pitcher Mountain, shopping, Marionette Theater, MacDowell Artists Colony, antiquing, Harrisville, Audubon Sanctuary, Gibson Pewter, Frye's Measure Mill, crafts, galleries, music, theater
Building 1789 columned clapboard inn
Grounds In-town, small, landscaped
Public Space Parlor, LR, garden room, tavern, DR

Food & Drink Full breakfast; specialties: granola, apple-cheddar breakfast pie, Whispering coffee cake; dinner specialties: Shaker cranberry pot roast, pan served seafood bouillabaisse; pre-/post-dinner drinks in the tavern

Recreation Boating/swimming in pond, beach, skiing, blueberry/apple picking, golf, tennis

Amenities & Services 24-hour entry, map of local attractions, kayak rental nearby, online newsletter, packing picnics

ACCOMMODATIONS

Units 15 guest rooms
All Rooms Bath, AC, TV, phone, cassette player
Some Rooms Wood stove, fireplace, mural, 19th-century stencils
Bed & Bath 1 twin, doubles, queens, kings, some antique, some four-posters, some canopies; soaking tubs, whirlpools, tub/showers

Favorites Rufus Porter Room—full, orig. Rufus Porter mural, queen antique four-poster, gas stove, fireplace, tub, shower
Comfort & Decor Period details like stencils and wall paintings, wood stoves and antique tubs. Size varies from cozy to spacious. Some handmade quilts; all full baths.

RATES, RESERVATIONS, & RESTRICTIONS

Deposit Full payment 1 night, others 50%; refund w/ 15-day notice (30 days, stays of 6+ nights)
Discounts Corporate; check
Credit Cards V, AE, MC, D
Check-In/Out 2/11
Smoking No
Pets No; in-house springer spaniel
Kids 12 and up

Minimum Stay Some weekends
Open All year
Hosts Linda and Joe Johnston
33 Main St.
Hancock, NH 03449
(800) 525-1789 or (603) 525-3318
Fax: (603) 525-9301
innkeeper@hancockinn.com
www.hancockinn.com

HARRISVILLE SQUIRE'S INN, *Harrisville*

OVERALL ★★★½ | ROOM QUALITY ★★★ | VALUE ★★★★ | PRICE $80–100

A working mill town, Harrisville is a National Historic Landmark—one of the few in New Hampshire—and this bed-and-breakfast is a fine example of a nineteenth-century farm complex. You won't need lunch—or maybe even dinner—after the five-course farm breakfast, starting with fresh fruit and ending with a dessert such as apple crisp. Some special features at this comfortable bed-and-breakfast Monadnock Bicycle Touring, which plans bike tours, and a three-story barn that houses a gallery, studio, and gift shop, featuring stained glass works by host Pat, local artists, and former guests. Oh, and Pat is a justice of the peace in case you want to wed.

SETTING & FACILITIES

Location Rt. 101 in Dublin, right at fire station; follow 3 mi.; left at fork; inn .3 mi. on right

Near Antiquing, Appalachian Mt. Trail, Mt. Monadnock, theaters, museums

Building 15-room 1842 farmhouse, barn

Grounds 50 acres gardens, meditation/wedding garden, hot tub, fields, trails, woods

Public Space DR, LR, 2nd floor sitting area

Food & Drink Family-style communal breakfast; specialties: quiche w/ tomato, peach cobbler, pears Rosamonde; refreshments, cheese and crackers

Recreation 10K of groomed XC skiing, hiking on site; winter sports, sleigh rides, golf, beach, nearby

Amenities & Services Hot tub, catering, weddings, special events, custom day and overnight bike tours

ACCOMMODATIONS

Units 5 guest rooms; 2 houses on lake (weekly, summer; 2+ nights spring/fall)

All Rooms Bath, sitting area, heat control, garden view, clock, radio

Some Rooms Bath w/ skylight (2), disabled access (1)

Bed & Bath Beds vary, some antique, iron/brass; 1 dbl. shower, 1 whirlpool; 1 bath outside room

Favorites Room 3—English-style paper/furnishings, skylight, whirlpool, beams; Room 5—queen and twin, large, TV, spacious, bath skylight

Comfort & Decor Like grandma's spacious and uncluttered w/ views of fields, gardens, forest. Comfortable, styles from Colonial to modern. Floral prints, wicker. Modern baths.

RATES, RESERVATIONS, & RESTRICTIONS

Deposit One night or 50% of stay; refund w/ 14-day notice

Discounts Singles, third person

Credit Cards V, MC

Check-In/Out 3/11

Smoking Outdoors

Pets No

Kids 10 and up

Minimum Stay Some weekends

Open dates vary, please call

Hosts Pat and Doug McCarthy

797 Chesham Road

Harrisville, NH 03450

(603) 827-3925

Fax: (603) 827-3622

squiresinnbb@top.monad.net

www.harrisvillesquiresinn.com

COLBY HILL INN, Henniker

OVERALL ★★★½ | ROOM QUALITY ★★★½ | VALUE ★★½ | PRICE $105–195

This family endeavor is a comfortable, informal inn about as far as you can get from a chain motel. The cuisine features lots of fish, seafood, and homemade desserts. Easter and Thanksgiving feasts are offered. The wood-paneled dining room takes on a romantic glow in candlelight, and both the food and the view seem endless at breakfast, with a glass wall overlooking the meadowlike lawn of this former farmhouse and stage coach stop. The gracious innkeepers enjoy gabbing and helping out.

SETTING & FACILITIES

Location 17 mi. W of Concord off Rt. 202/9; .5 mi. from center of town

Near Covered bridge, river, Canterbury Shaker Village, New England College, Pat's Peak and Mt. Sunapee Ski Areas

Building Circa 1800 white country inn, tavern, farmhouse

Grounds 6 acres of barns, fields, gardens, pool, carriage house, gazebo, fountains, statuary

Public Space Spacious parlor, game room, DR

Food & Drink Full country breakfast; specialty: scrambled eggs w/ Boursin cheese in puff pastry. Dinner (extra), American w/ cont'l flair; specialty: chicken Colby Hill w/ lobster; hot drinks, cookies; full beverage service, wine list

Recreation Outdoor pool, lawn games on site; tennis, skiing, kayaking, biking nearby, antiquing, outlet shopping

Amenities & Services Lobby and DR have disabled access, irons; room service; group functions (32); business services fax, overhead, easels

ACCOMMODATIONS

Units 16 guest rooms, 2 suites

All Rooms Bath, AC, phone, dataport, some toiletries

Some Rooms Gas fireplaces

Bed & Bath Queens, kings, twins; some canopies, new mattresses; some tubs

Favorites Room 3—large upstairs corner room, king brass/iron bed, woodburning fireplace, tub/shower combo

Comfort & Decor Rooms indiv. decorated w/ antiques, wallpaper. Decorated as a gentleman's farm. Each room w/ different color linens, down comforters. Comfortable rather than luxurious.

RATES, RESERVATIONS, & RESTRICTIONS

Deposit 50% or one night; 7-day cancel. policy; travel agency booking OK

Discounts Singles, 3rd person

Credit Cards V, AE, DC, MC, D

Check-In/Out 3/11

Smoking Outdoors

Pets No

Kids 7 and up

Minimum Stay Some holiday weekends

Open All year

Hosts Cynthia and Mason Cobb
3 The Oaks, Box 779
Henniker, NH 03242
(603) 428-3281 or (800) 531-0330
Fax: (603) 428-9218
info@colbyhillinn.com
www.colbyhillinn.com

INN AT MAPLEWOOD FARM, Hillsborough

OVERALL ★★★★ | ROOM QUALITY ★★★★ | VALUE ★★★★ | PRICE $75–135

A unique bed-and-breakfast with a collection of old radios—this property has its very own station, Radio Maplewood Farm. Jayme collected cassettes of over 1,000 vintage shows like "The Shadow" and broadcasts them through-out the house on a low-power transmitter. Other specialties? Laura's breakfast fantasies, featured in cookbooks—cantaloupe and strawberry soup, orange-oatmeal flan with maple caramel sauce, goat cheese frittata. Old-fashioned touches, such as milk in glass bottles (the milk perhaps produced from the cows grazing beyond), and stylish faux-painted rugs add more flavor to the inn. There's an antique store on the property, homemade chocolates are pro-vided in suites . . . and so on.

SETTING & FACILITIES

Location 89N to 9W; .5 mi. from His-toric Hillsborough Center; 30 min. from Concord

Near Fox State Forest, historic area, beaches, antiquing, auctions

Building Pretty 1794 early Federal; restored 1998; listed w/ National Historic Register

Grounds 14 acres, forest, fields, organic garden, cows, brook, patio

Public Space Entrance, LR, DR

Food & Drink Basket Big Band Break-fast; specialties: scones, cream-basil shirred eggs; tea; special diets

Recreation Golf, hunting, horseback rid-ing, water sports, horseshoes

Amenities & Services Some disabled access (hearing impaired), fruit basket, stocked refrigerator, Port, tennis rackets, bike rental; fax, copier, small meetings.

ACCOMMODATIONS

Units 4 suites

All Rooms Bath, vintage radio, sitting/writing area, mini-library, phone, amenities basket, robes

Some Rooms Fireplace (all but 1), deck (2), 4-person capacity (2)

Bed & Bath King/queen beds, wrought-iron, canopies; 2 tubs

Favorites Front suite, main house—canopied iron bed, fireplace, skylights;

Upstairs suite, barn—2 BRs, cathedral, spindle bed, views

Comfort & Decor Antiques. Home-made candies, cordials by bed. Environ-mentally green rooms available. Radio Maplewood Farm accessible in rooms. Skylights, views. Barn suites spacious. Thoughtful, stylish, special. Good lighting, seating areas.

RATES, RESERVATIONS, & RESTRICTIONS

Deposit Credit card or 50%; full refund w/ 14-day notice

Discounts 3rd person, corp., longer stays, pkg. weekends incl. free instruction in orienteering and skiing

Credit Cards V, AE, DC, MC, D

Check-In/Out 2–6/11; late arrivals call ahead

Smoking No

Pets No

Kids With advance notice

Minimum Stay Holidays, special week-ends

Open May 1–early Dec.

Hosts Jayme Henriques Simoes and Laura Simoes

447 Center Rd.

Hillsborough, NH 03244

(800) 644-6693 or (603) 464-4242

Fax: (603) 464-4242

jsimoes@conknet.com

www.conknet.com/maplewoodfarm

RAM IN THE THICKET, Milford

OVERALL ★★★ | ROOM QUALITY ★★★ | VALUE ★★★★★ | PRICE $60–75

The inn's name refers to the owners' quest for a substitute to their life in the Midwest; the Old Testament story is that Abraham finds "a ram caught in a thicket" and sacrifices it instead of his son, Isaac. Andrew and Priscilla bought the mansion in 1977, restored and renovated it, adding an indoor pool, and as a nod to their Dutch heritage, Delft tiles in the dining room (where the cuisine is international). Andrew enjoys a quip "We have shared baths, but you don't have to share them at the same time." And as for the decor, "We don't call it Victorian. We think Queen Victoria was quite stuffy."

SETTING & FACILITIES

Location 200 feet off Rt. 101, just W of Milford; 10 mi. from Nashua
Near Flea markets, antiquing, beach, nature areas, Mt. Monadnock, American Stage Festival, film, galleries
Building 1870 Victorian mansion
Grounds 8 acres, gardens
Public Space Lounge, sitting room, 4 DRs, porch, screened porch
Food & Drink Cont'l breakfast; changes frequently; spec. diets accom.; full bar
Recreation Canoeing, golf, hunting, horses, skiing, balloon rides
Amenities & Services Fridge access, irons, hairdryers; heated indoor pool, whirlpool; meetings (30)

ACCOMMODATIONS

Units 9 guest rooms
All Rooms Original detailing, period pieces
Some Rooms Bath (3), fireplace
Bed & Bath Beds vary, most doubles, some canopies, four-posters; some tubs
Favorites Canopy Room—floral paper, canopy bed, claw-foot tub, good sun
Comfort & Decor Some rooms combine for families. Many turn-of-the-century details, antiques. Size varies. Old-world European charm. Basic, old-fashioned.

RATES, RESERVATIONS, & RESTRICTIONS

Deposit 50%; refund w/ 1-day notice, unless full
Discounts Singles, 3rd person
Credit Cards AE; checks preferred
Check-In/Out No specified check-in/12
Smoking Lounge, some rooms
Pets OK; in-house cat and dog
Kids OK
Minimum Stay None
Open All year
Hosts Andrew and Priscilla Tempelman
24 Maple St.
Milford, NH 03055
(603) 654-6440
aretee@jlc.net
www.jlc.net/~aretee/ram

APPLE GATE BED AND BREAKFAST, Peterborough

OVERALL ★★★ | ROOM QUALITY ★★★ | VALUE ★★★★½ | PRICE $65–85

Across from an orchard, with a gated picket fence, this bed-and-breakfast's name was an obvious choice, but another could be "The Little Apple." The theme is carried out sweetly and crisply (sorry) with apple pancakes on apple-patterned plates and room names, including Granny Smith and Cortland. All rooms have apple chips to munch, the dog is named Macintosh, and there are apple games and wooden apples in the window. In the spring the orchards are especially beautiful, and you can pick apples in the fall. But thankfully, the basic, comfortable rooms are decorated in decidedly non-fruity country furnishings and fabrics.

SETTING & FACILITIES

Location 2 mi. from downtown Peterborough, by country road; across from apple orchards
Near Concerts in the Park, theater, country fairs, harvest festivals, antiquing, auctions, Cathedral in the Pines, 6 covered bridges, Peterborough Basket Company, Pickity Place in Mason, Mt. Monadnock State Park, Sharon Arts Center
Building 1832 Colonial farmhouse
Grounds 3 acres, gardens, woods, hammock
Public Space DR, parlor, music/reading room, porch
Food & Drink Full candlelight breakfast; specialties: baked pancakes, French toast w/ sautéed apples; special meals avail.; coffee area
Recreation Fishing, maple sugaring, berry/apple picking, skiing, sleigh rides
Amenities & Services Irons, refrigerator, games, books, maps, bikes, canoe, ski rental nearby

ACCOMMODATIONS

Units 4 guest rooms
All Rooms Bath, sitting area
Some Rooms Stenciling, nonworking fireplace
Bed & Bath 2 twins, queens, ¾ bed; 1 tub, 1 tub/shower, 2 showers, robes
Favorites Granny Smith—large front corner, overlooks orchard, built-in desk, Laura Ashley fabrics
Comfort & Decor Period farmhouse decor. Braided rugs, dried wreaths, ruffled curtains, wide floorboards. Front rooms sunniest. Macintosh, smallest.

RATES, RESERVATIONS, & RESTRICTIONS

Deposit 1 night; refund w/ 7-day notice
Discounts Singles
Credit Cards V, MC
Check-In/Out 3/11
Smoking Porch, outside only
Pets No; in-house dog, cat
Kids Over 12
No-No's More than 2 to a room
Minimum Stay 2 nights summer and fall weekends
Open All year

Hosts Dianne and Ken Legenhausen
199 Upland Farm Rd.
Peterborough, NH 03458

(603) 924-6543
Fax: (603) 924-6543

BIRCHWOOD INN, Temple

OVERALL ★★★ | ROOM QUALITY ★★★ | VALUE ★★★★½ | PRICE $60–79

Thoreau stayed here (escaping the solitude of Walden Pond, perhaps), and
the inn has housed the Temple post office, a general store, the town meeting
hall, and an antique shop. In one form or another it has been the centerpiece
of this pretty village since around the time of the Revolution. Judy and Bill
haven't been innkeepers here quite that long (more like 20 years), but their
touch is reflected in the way things hum and the tales they can tell. .

SETTING & FACILITIES

Location 1.5 mi. off Rt. 101, on Rt. 45,
on Common in center of village
Near Antiquing, Mt. Monadnock, summer
theater, Monadnock Music Series, Cathedral of the Pines
Building 1775 Federal brick inn;
addition
Grounds Porch, woods incl. birches,
lilacs
Public Space DR, 2 sitting areas, TV
room
Food & Drink Full country breakfast;
dinner, blackboard menu, (extra; reservations), BYOB, open to public, country
American cuisine w/ homemade soups,
breads, desserts
Recreation Skiing, horses, hayrides,
antiquing, trout fishing, hunting
Amenities & Services Puzzle table,
games

ACCOMMODATIONS

Units 7 guest rooms
All Rooms TV
Some Rooms Priv. baths (5)
Bed & Bath Twin, queen, double beds;
showers only
Favorites Seashore—overlooks village;
Thoreau—because he reputedly stayed
here
Comfort & Decor Rooms decorated
by theme music, train, editorial, library,
general store, school, seashore, w/ coordinated furnishings. Braided rugs on hardwood floors. TVs a plus for most. One
ground floor, disabled accessible room.
Comfortable, basic, and homey.

RATES, RESERVATIONS, & RESTRICTIONS

Deposit 1 night; refund w/ 14-day notice
Discounts 3rd person (1 room only)
Credit Cards None
Check-In/Out 2/11
Smoking No
Pets No
Kids Over 10
Minimum Stay 2–3 days, weekends
Sept./Oct.

Open All year except 2 weeks in Nov. and April
Hosts Judy and Bill Wolfe
Box 197
Temple, NH 03084

(603) 878-3285
Fax: (603) 878-2159
wolfe@birchwood.mv.com
virtualcities.com

Central New Hampshire and Lakes

Stretching from the Connecticut River to the Maine border, the Central New Hampshire/Lakes region is home to rural retreats, water sports, skiing, and hills. The Dartmouth/Lake Sunapee area, stretching to the west near the Vermont border, is filled with rural villages and farming areas, now often catering to tourists or weekenders. The best-known town around is **Hanover,** home to **Dartmouth College,** with its world-class cultural offerings and seasonal festivities such as **Winter Carnival.**

The area is also known for **Mount Sunapee State Park,** with skiing, and nearby **Lake Sunapee's** fishing and water sports. Northwest of the lake lie **New London** and the **Barn Playhouse,** well known for summer theater. **Enfield** has a Shaker settlement. In **Newbury,** check out the **Fells Historic Site** at the **John Hay National Wildlife Refuge,** or visit **Charlestown's Fort at No. 4** with its reconstructed stockade.

To the east are almost 300 lakes and ponds, providing opportunities for all sorts of water sports. Open vistas of hills reflect in the water; climb up for fabulous views or drive around the lakes for the scenery. Swim, boat, fish, ski, or take a lake cruise. And if you don't mind winter weather, try ice fishing or ice sailing, or if you're really adventurous, ice auto-racing.

But the area isn't all water or winter. **Milton** houses the **New Hampshire Farm Museum,** and there's **Wakefield's Museum of Childhood** where adults as well as children will discover how to uncover some of the mysteries of life. The region also has plenty of craftspeople and galleries with unique gifts.

Lodging is plentiful and unpretentious in this part of the state, with a large proportion of inns. People have been coming here for decades, spending a week or so enjoying the natural assets, eating good food, and getting away from crowds. Bed-and-breakfasts, mostly refurbished Victorians, are clustered near towns, where the proud homeowners once went to work.

You can feel the personal history of these places, no matter how many layers of paint have been applied.

FOR MORE INFORMATION

Lakes Region B&B Association www.virtualcities.com/nh/lakesregion

Sunapee Vacations
Sunapee Lodging Bureau
Box 400
Sunapee, NH 03782
(800) 258-3530
www.sunapeevacations.com
email: chamberinfo@nnvt.net

GLYNN HOUSE INN, Ashland

OVERALL ★★★★ | ROOM QUALITY ★★★★ | VALUE ★★½ | PRICE $99–199

If you like Victoriana, you'll love Glynn House, which is quintessentially so, inside and out, from the top of the turret to the expansive, wraparound porch, and within every cozy nook and cranny. But the hosts are decidedly modern, with experience in the food business and in marketing, and their skills shine through at breakfast and in the little touches that make a place memorable. They love to collect antiques, and the oak-paneled rooms are filled with treasures massive and tiny. Savvy care and attention to detail make a fine transition from this turn-of-the-century to the last.

SETTING & FACILITIES

Location About a mile off I-93 Exit 24, on quiet, tree-lined street on the edge of town
Near Franconia State Park, White Mountains, Squam Lake (*On Golden Pond* lake), Lake Winnepesaukee, Science Center of NH, Lakes Region Summer Theatre, Keepsake Quilting, antiquing, outlets
Building 1896 Queen Anne Victorian
Grounds 1.5 acres, carriage house, garden, flowers
Public Space Sitting room, DR, foyer, porch
Food & Drink Morning coffee/tea; full communal breakfast; specialties: eggs Benedict, apple strudel, Belgian waffles, stuffed French toast, omelets; snacks, wine, sherry avail.
Recreation Board games, canoeing, boating, skiing, snowshoeing
Amenities & Services Video library, microwave, beach towels, fax, dataports; Polish, Russian spoken

ACCOMMODATIONS

Units 4 guest rooms, 7 suites
All Rooms Bath, AC, TV/VCR, clock/radio/tape player, zone heating
Some Rooms Mountaintop views, fireplace, sitting room
Bed & Bath Mostly queen beds, some canopies, four-posters; some tub/shower combos, some dbl. whirlpools
Favorites Room A—2nd floor, half circle, queen canopy, whirlpool; Room H—1st floor, lace-canopied bed, fireplace, dbl. whirlpool; Carriage House suites
Comfort & Decor Rooms indiv. decorated in Victorian style; not too fussy, but not for minimalists. Chocolates, romantic touches. Ornate florals. Immaculate.

RATES, RESERVATIONS, & RESTRICTIONS

Deposit 50%; 14-day cancel. policy
Credit Cards V, MC
Check-In/Out 3–11/11
Smoking Not in bedrooms
Pets No; in-house dog and 2 cats (never in inn)
Kids Quiet, well-behaved, in some rooms
No-No's Check-out after 11 a.m.
Minimum Stay 2 nights most weekends, holidays, foliage

Open All year
Hosts Karol and Betsy Paterman
59 Highland St., Box 719
Ashland, NH 03217

(800) 637-9599 or (603) 968-3775
Fax: (603) 968-9415
glynnhse@lr.net
www.glynnhouse.com

ROSEWOOD COUNTRY INN, Bradford

OVERALL ★★★½ | ROOM QUALITY ★★★★ | VALUE ★★ | PRICE $109–225

Once a summer resort hosting celebs such as Jack London, Gloria Swanson, Mary Pickford, and Charlie Chaplin, it was abandoned for years until Lesley and Dick renovated it into an all-year property with stenciled walls and a country tavern. Special here are the creative packages, holiday, and annual events. For example Mother and Daughter Weekends; The Intimate Escape (champagne, fruit, cheese, and crackers in room on arrival); Weekend Getaway for Gourmet Cooks; and Dickens Christmas Weekend dinner and fireside storytelling with a professional storyteller.

SETTING & FACILITIES

Location Rt. 114 through Bradford, to Pleasant View Rd, on a hill
Near Mt. Sunapee skiing, Lake Sunapee cruise boats, Shaker villages, NH Int'l Speedway, Kearsarge Indian Museum, John Hay Estate, summer theater, concerts, Dartmouth College
Building Country Victorian
Grounds 12 acres meadows, woods, gazebo, pond, award-winning gardens, wild deer and turkeys, organic garden
Public Space Tavern Room BYOB bar; 2 formal LRs, DR; reception room (85); all public rooms and 1 public bath disabled-accessible
Food & Drink "Candlelight and crystal" breakfast; specialties: ham/asparagus quiche, Belgian waffles w/ bananas Foster and praline sauce, plum pudding; wine, hors d'oeuvres; soda, water
Recreation Winter sports, fishing; nearby downhill skiing, golf, swimming, boating, antiquing
Amenities & Services Fridge, irons, picnic baskets, papers, fax, weddings

ACCOMMODATIONS

Units 3 guest rooms, 8 suites
All Rooms Bath, clock, radio, hairdryers
Some Rooms AC, fireplace, TV/VCR, thermostat, sitting area, separate dressing room (1)
Bed & Bath Queens and Kings, some canopies, four-posters, Old Hickory; some tub/shower, some dbl. showers and whirlpools, some dbl. sinks
Favorites Dreamcatcher—3rd floor, Lake Placid Lodge decor; beamed cathedral, fireplace, dbl. whirlpool, AC, TV/VCR; Mary Pickford Suite—2nd floor corner, fireplace, views
Comfort & Decor Emphasis on suites, whirlpools, fireplaces. Upgrading continuous. Views from all rooms; country-Victorian decoration. Comfortable rather than luxurious.

RATES, RESERVATIONS, & RESTRICTIONS

Deposit Full payment 1–2 nights, 50% for 3+ nights; refund w/ 14-day notice
Discounts 3rd person, long stays
Credit Cards V, AE, DC, MC, D
Check-In/Out 3–8/11
Smoking Outside porch and deck only
Pets No; in-house collie (in owners' quarters)
Kids Over 12
Minimum Stay 2 nights weekends, 3

nights holiday weekends
Open All year, closed 2 weeks after Easter
Hosts Lesley and Dick Marquis
67 Pleasant View Rd.
Bradford, NH 03221
(800) 938-5253; (603) 938-5253 or (603) 938-5220
rosewood@conknet.com
www.rosewoodcountryinn.com

RED HILL INN, Centre Harbor

OVERALL ★★★½ | ROOM QUALITY ★★★ | VALUE ★★½ | PRICE $105–175

This comfortable country inn on a hill hosted the Duke of Bavaria in the 1940s, but usually caters to just plain folks who want to relax and play. Rooms are spread among an 1850 farmhouse, the main inn, and adjacent cottages. Decor is a mix, with beams, oak paneling and picture windows—culminating in a bar constructed from half a boat and a wall of license plates. A swimming pool adds to the many water sports already enjoyed at nearby Squam Lake. Chef Stefan Ryll serves what he calls "New England gourmet" cuisine, based on local, seasonal products, and herbs from the garden. Sunday Brunch is lavish, with everything from omelets to duck to lamb chops.

SETTING & FACILITIES

Location 2 hrs. N of Boston on I-93, 5 mi. from Lake Winnipesaukee
Near Canterbury Shaker Village, antique/craft/factory stores, Lake Winnipesaukee, Squam Lake, covered bridges, Mountains and Kancamagus Hwy., Red Hill climbing
Building 100-year-old brick mansion
Grounds 60 acres nature preserve, sports field, pond, 4-person outdoor hot tub, herb garden

Public Space Lounge; spacious LR, DR
Food & Drink Full country breakfast; buffet or à la carte, candlelight dinner; specialties: shrimp scampi, lemon-meringue pie; wine list; lighter dinner in lounge, cocktails
Recreation XC skiing, swimming on site; nearby water sports, downhill skiing
Amenities & Services Maps; weddings/events; XC ski rental

ACCOMMODATIONS

Units 16 guest rooms, 5 suites, in inn, farmhouse, and cottage
All Rooms Bath, phone

Some Rooms AC, fireplace, priv. balcony, sitting area, desk

Bed & Bath Beds vary; some dbl. whirlpools, some tubs
Favorites Fireplace rooms—spacious, views of mountains and lakes, 5 w/ whirlpools

Comfort & Decor Rooms vary in size and decor. Named after mountains. Antiques, wood floors; some high ceilings, exposed beams. Some gorgeous views.

RATES, RESERVATIONS, & RESTRICTIONS

Deposit 50% w/in 10 days; 14-day cancel. policy w/ fee or re-rental
Discounts 3rd person, singles; theme pkgs
Credit Cards V, AE, MC, D
Check-In/Out 3/11
Smoking OK (not in DR)
Pets No
Kids 10 and older
Minimum Stay 2 nights weekends,

some holidays longer
Open All year
Hosts Rick Miller, Don Leavitt
RFD #1, Box 99M
Centre Harbor, NH 03226
(800) 5REDHILL or (603) 279-7001
Fax: (603) 279-7003
info@redhillinn.com
www.redhillinn.com

STAFFORD'S IN THE FIELD INN, Chocorua

OVERALL ★★★★ | ROOM QUALITY ★★★ | VALUE ★★★½ | PRICE $80–160

These devoted innkeepers came from sunny California to cold, rural Yankeeland about 35 years ago, and with hard work and love have kept this special, peaceful place going. Fred has dry wit that not everybody gets (those who do have a ball). Sweet Ramona is a marvelous cook and turns out a different French-based menu each night. Photos of their family and the development of the property are in the parlor. This is a bucolic, isolated, rambling inn—great for a wedding—with rustic charm and well-worn beauty. It's one of the last of its old-fashioned kind, with character and characters, a true original based on two originals.

SETTING & FACILITIES

Location Off Rt. 113, between Chocorua and Tamworth
Near Nature preserves, Lake Winnipesaukee, Squam Lake, rivers, waterfalls, antiquing, summer theaters
Building 1700s Federalist-style main building; red barn for large events
Grounds 36-acre estate w/ view, rolling fields, brook, garden, orchard, sugar house

Public Space Entrance, library, taproom, DR, veranda
Food & Drink Full breakfast; specialties: blueberry pancakes w/ maple syrup, cheddar and salsa omelet; cocktails; candlelight dinner (charge; reservations); specialties: mock turtle soup, pork tenderloin, brandied bread pudding; liquor license, wine list, ice avail.; special diets accom.

Recreation Climbing, swimming, boating, fly fishing, XC skiing
Amenities & Services Welcome fruit/cookies, climbing maps, snowshoes; receptions (250), meetings (30), pickup from bus, picnic (fee), canoe, Steinway grand piano

ACCOMMODATIONS

Units 13 guest rooms, cottages
All Rooms Good view, fan
Some Rooms Fireplace, bath (5), wheelchair accessible (1)
Bed & Bath Double beds in shared-bath rooms; queens/king in rooms w/ priv. baths; some canopies; 2 large clawfoot tubs, 3 shower/tub
Favorites Hearthroom—large fireplace, canopy bed, windows on 3 walls; Orchard room—beam ceiling, wicker and green oak furniture; both w/ 16-inch mattresses
Comfort & Decor Rooms eclectic and individually decorated. Some signs of wear, but acceptable. Sizes vary but all comfortable, w/ useable antiques. Tasteful, some whimsy.

RATES, RESERVATIONS, & RESTRICTIONS

Deposit 50%; refund w/ 14-day notice
Discounts Long stays
Credit Cards V, MC
Check-In/Out 11/3
Smoking No
Pets No
Kids Over 12
Minimum Stay 2 days some weekends

Open All year; usually closed April
Hosts Ramona and Fred Stafford
Box 270
Chocorua, NH 03817
(800) 446-1112 or (603) 323-7766
Fax: (603) 323-7531
staffordsinthefield@acornworld.net
www.staffordsinthefield.com

GODDARD MANSION, *Claremont*

OVERALL ★★★½ | ROOM QUALITY ★★★ | VALUE ★★★½ | PRICE $75–125

Remember Buster Brown shoes and Tige? (If not, your parents or grandparents will.) This turn-of-the-nineteenth-century, 18-room mansion was built by the shoe manufacturer, who obviously profited grandly from shodding our little feet. Debbie has a good sense of humor, sets a low-key tone, and loves to chat about the extensive restorations and the history of the house and town. Interesting elements abound, including a Tiffany lamp in the dining room, a working Wurlitzer organ from the 1930s, a wraparound screened porch and a tea house set among the gardens.

SETTING & FACILITIES

Location 30 min. S of Hanover; 10 min. from VT; 1.5 mi. from town center
Near Dartmouth College, St.-Gaudens Nat'l Hist. Site, The Fort at #4, Simon Pearce Glass Blowing and Ceramics, Catamount Brewery and Tours, antiquing, theater

Building 1905 English Manor Victorian shingled mansion
Grounds Porches, teahouse, gazebo, lawn
Public Space LR, music/sitting room, library, TV room, DR
Food & Drink Full communal breakfast; specialties: muffins, jam from mansion's gardens; tea; spec. diets accom.
Recreation Skiing, golf, horses, tennis, boating, mountain biking
Amenities & Services Baby grand piano; receptions, celebrating spec. occasions

ACCOMMODATIONS

Units 10 guest rooms
Some Rooms Bath, environmentally green rooms, panoramic mountain view, TV, AC
Bed & Bath Beds vary, some canopies, four-posters; tub (2)
Favorites Former MBR—large corner room, airy, mountain view; Cloud Room—papered in whimsical clouds
Comfort & Decor Decor varies; incl. country French, Colonial, Laura Ashley, Victorian. Airy, light-filled, natural woodwork, light papers. Corner room good for families.

RATES, RESERVATIONS, & RESTRICTIONS

Deposit $50 check or credit card, full payment on arrival; refund w/ 7-day notice, less $15 cancellation fee
Discounts Seniors, corp., longer stays, 3rd person
Credit Cards V, AE, MC, D
Check-In/Out 4/11; call for late arrival
Smoking Porches and tea house only
Pets No
Kids Welcome; toy corner, swing, croquet for children
Minimum Stay 2 nights holidays
Open All year
Host Debbie Albee
25 Hillstead Rd.
Claremont, NH 03743-3317
(603) 543-0603 or (800) 736-0603
Fax: (603) 543-0001
deb@goddardmansion.com
www.goddardmansion.com

HIGHLAND LAKE INN, *East Andover*

OVERALL ★★★½ | ROOM QUALITY ★★★★ | VALUE ★★★½ | PRICE $85–125

The winding road leading to this nineteenth-century house is classic rural New Hampshire, with roughly stacked fieldstone and leafy maples bordering green fields, farms and red barns beyond. The porch with its swing is old-fashioned and welcoming. Living room walls are yellow, decorated with old plates and accented with blue and white Delft tiles. The rooms upstairs are similarly charming, done up with antiques, Oriental rugs and quilted coverlets. The atmosphere will make you feel less stressed, one of the great bonuses of a good bed-and-breakfast.

SETTING & FACILITIES

Location I-91 exit Rt. 11 or I-93 Exit 17 to Rt. 11; opposite Andover Congregational Church
Near Canterbury Shaker Village, Ruggles Mine, Proctor Academy, Mt. Sunapee Ski Resort, Ragged Mountain Ski, factory stores, Norsk Cross-Country Skiing, antiquing, auctions, nature preserve
Building Private home, ca.1767
Grounds 12 acres on hill, overlooks lakes, mountains; 2 porches
Public Space Gathering room, DR, porch
Food & Drink Breakfast, communal or separate; specialties: waffles w/ fresh fruit sauces, featherbed eggs; cookies; snacks, sodas, homebaked bread & muffins
Recreation Boating, golf, ice skating, horseback riding, boat cruises, priv. beach
Amenities & Services Books, beach towels, meeting space for 30–40; business services fax, phone, laptop modem; touring advice/maps, making reservations

ACCOMMODATIONS

Units 10 guest rooms
All Rooms Bath/shower, period pieces
Some Rooms Fireplace, wheelchair access (not bathrooms) (2)
Bed & Bath King, queen, 2 twin beds; some four-posters; showers only
Favorites Highland—antiques, fireplace, window seat, lovely view; Andover—fireplace, four-poster
Comfort & Decor Elegant country decor w/ floral shades, wood floors. Immaculate. Refined/feminine but not fussy. Bright and airy.

RATES, RESERVATIONS, & RESTRICTIONS

Deposit Credit card, 1 night or 50% w/in 7 days of booking; refund w/ 14-day notice
Discounts None
Credit Cards V, AE, MC, D; personal & travelers checks accepted
Check-In/Out 3/11
Smoking No
Pets No; call for alternate arrangements
Kids 8 and older
Minimum Stay 2 days some weekends
Open All year
Hosts Mary and Peter Petras
Box 164, 32 Maple St.
East Andover, NH 03231
(603) 735-6426
Fax: (603) 735-5355
www.highlandlakeinn.com

TRUMBULL HOUSE BED AND BREAKFAST, Hanover

OVERALL ★★★★ | ROOM QUALITY ★★★★ | VALUE ★★ | PRICE $125–250

Spacious rooms and luscious breakfasts are features at this Dartmouth-area bed-and-breakfast that obviously caters to college families but is a pleasant stop for any traveler. You can wake up to a cheese omelet with Portobello mushrooms and Brie, French toast made with English muffins, and scrambled eggs with smoked salmon, cream cheese and chives. Colors are vivid. The dining room has red walls and white trim, and guest rooms are aptly named "Green," "White," "Blue" and so on. The helpful innkeeper is colorful, too. She sold her business in Connecticut and renovated a wing of the house for her five kids, in her spare time of course.

SETTING & FACILITIES

Location I-89 Exit 18 or I-93 Exit 13; 4 mi. E of Dartmouth College; 3 mi. from Dartmouth-Hitchcock Medical Center
Near Dartmouth cultural and sports events, Hanover shopping, sightseeing
Building White 1919 Colonial, remodeled 1995
Grounds 16 acres w/ swimming pond, meadow, woods; link to Appalachian Trail
Public Space LR, DR, reading nook, porches
Food & Drink Breakfast; specialties: fresh-baked pastry; tea; fruit; low-fat, veg. meals
Recreation Hiking, XC skiing on site; water/snow sports, golf, horses, tennis
Amenities & Services Cordless phones, iron, paper, CDs, copier, fax, conf. center, internet, celebrating occasions

ACCOMMODATIONS

Units 4 guest rooms, 1 suite
All Rooms Sitting area, TV, desk, clock, radio
Some Rooms Window seat, whirlpool, dataport
Bed & Bath King, queen, four-poster (1), sleigh (1); tubs (4), whirlpool (1), bath in suite (2)
Favorites Yellow room—cheerful, romantic, sleeping alcove, window seat
Comfort & Decor Spacious rooms, wood furniture, some with details like sleeping alcoves, dormers, built-ins. 3rd floor cozy w/ eaves.

RATES, RESERVATIONS, & RESTRICTIONS

Deposit Full payment 1 night or 50%
Discounts 3rd person, corporate. rates avail.
Credit Cards V, AE, MC, CB
Check-In/Out 4–8/11
Smoking No
Pets No; in-house 2 cats, 2 dogs
Kids Welcome; babysitting on-site
Minimum Stay 2 nights weekends, foliage season
Open All year
Host Hilary A. Pridgen
40 Etna Rd.
Hanover, NH 03755
(603) 643-2370 or (800) 651-5141
Fax: (603) 643-2430
bnb@trumbullhouse.com
www.trumbullhouse.com

MANOR ON GOLDEN POND, *Holderness*

OVERALL ★★★★★ | ROOM QUALITY ★★★★★ | VALUE ★½ | PRICE $210–375

As close as you can get to an English country manor in New England, this imposing property was built in 1907 by a wealthy Brit who made a fortune in Florida land deals. In the 1930s it became a photographers' colony. The mansion is nestled among tall pines on rolling lawns and overlooks "Golden Pond," of movie fame. With a pool, tennis court, and rooms with TVs, VCRs, and numerous luxuries, many guests book for a week.

SETTING & FACILITIES

Location On Squam Lake, 4.7 mi. off I-93 Exit 24

Near Squam Lake, White Mountains, Science Center, *On Golden Pond* boat tours, outlets, glassblowing, crafts, quilt shop, gorge at Lost River, beach

Building Large 1907 English country manor-style showplace

Grounds 14 acres on a hill; pool, tennis court, porch; 3 frontage acres on Squam Lake, boathouse

Public Space 2 sitting rooms, registration area, pub, 2 DRs, terrace

Food & Drink Breakfast w/ hot entrée; specialties: waffles, pancakes, omelet of the day; tea; prix fixe dinner New American cuisine nightly mid-May–end Oct. and holidays, other Wed.–Sun. (extra, res. req.); menu changes nightly; award-winning wine list

Recreation Canoeing, fishing on-site; skiing, sleigh rides, ice fishing, golf, boat cruises

Amenities & Services Boathouse, rec. facilities, turndown, transportation to outdoor Sunday services on island

ACCOMMODATIONS

Units 17 guest rooms in main inn, 4 cottages

All Rooms Bath, AC, TV, phone

Some Rooms Wood-burning fireplace, priv. deck, refrigerator, wet bar, CD, VCR

Bed & Bath Mostly king beds, some canopies; lavish baths, some dbl. whirlpools

Favorites Stratford—trapper's lodge motif w/ bearskin rug, barnboard walls,

king canopy, fireplace; Dover-cottage by lake—2 BRs, kitchen, fireplace (rented by week, no breakfast)

Comfort & Decor Spacious rooms and designer fabrics in tasteful, luxury mix. Something for everyone. Many lake view, some w/ decks. Good lighting. Well-appointed, extremely comfortable. Theme rooms are fun.

RATES, RESERVATIONS, & RESTRICTIONS

Deposit Full payment, 1 night; other 50%; refund w/ 14-day notice (30 for holidays)

Discounts 3rd person, pkgs.; check on weekly cottage rentals

Credit Cards V, AE, MC

Check-In/Out 3–6/11; call for early/late check-in

Smoking No

Pets No

Kids 12 and up

No-No's Children in Manor House

Minimum Stay 2 nights holiday/fall foliage weekends

Open All year; some accom. seasonal

Hosts Brian and Mary Ellen Shields
Box T, Route 3
Holderness, NH 03245
(800) 545-2141 or (603) 968-3348
Fax: (603) 968-2116
info@manorongoldenpond.net
www.manorongoldenpond.com

PRESSED PETALS INN, *Holderness*

OVERALL ★★★ | ROOM QUALITY ★★½ | VALUE ★★ | PRICE $95–165

Pretty as a flower, this immaculate, modest bed-and-breakfast across from the renowned Manor on Golden Pond, is a reflection of innkeeper Ellie, who carries out the namesake theme with framed pressed flowers on each guest room door, matching key rings, and a charming gift of a pressed-flower bookmark. The dried florals are her creation, the result of a childhood hobby. Simple, understated guest rooms, including Mock Orange, Forget-Me-Not, Azalea, and Wisteria, are colorfully furnished. For a great deal, you can have a fabulous meal at the luxury neighboring inn, a five-minute walk away, and then fall into bed under an embroidered coverlet at this neat, sweet haven.

SETTING & FACILITIES

Near White Mt. Nat'l. Forest, Franconia Notch, Squam Lake, The Flume, Weir's Beach, Lake Winnipesaukee, Castle Springs, Science Center of NH, covered bridges
Building Century-old farmhouse w/ gingerbread trim
Grounds Wraparound porch, floral highlights
Public Space Entry parlor, upstairs parlor, DR
Food & Drink Candlelight breakfast; specialties: oven-baked French toast w/ apple cider sauce, crab and egg casserole; finger desserts and hot drinks; hors d'oeuvres Sat. nights
Recreation Golf, horses, boating, snowmobiling, skiing
Amenities & Services Refrigerator, irons, disabled access; meetings (20), fax

ACCOMMODATIONS

Units 6 guest rooms, 2 suites
All Rooms Bath, paddle ceiling fan, clock, hairdryer, luxury linens, robes
Some Rooms Disabled access (1)
Bed & Bath Queen, twin, robes; shower/tub (2)
Favorites Blue Hydrangea—Victorian headboard, rocking chair, china cabinet
Comfort & Decor Simple, comfortable rooms, each decorated w/ a floral theme. Smallish. Good lighting.

RATES, RESERVATIONS, & RESTRICTIONS

Deposit 1 night or 50%; refund w/ 14-day notice
Discounts Off-season, 3rd person in suites
Credit Cards V, MC, D
Check-In/Out 3–7:30/11
Smoking Outside porch only
Pets No
Kids Over 10
Minimum Stay 2 days, Oct.; peak weekends; weddings

Open Closed Thanksgiving, Christmas	(800) 839-6205 (outside NH) or
Host Ellie Dewey	(603) 968-4417
Shepard Hill Rd.	Fax: (603) 968-3661
Holderness, NH 03245	www.pressedpetalsinn.com

THE ALDEN COUNTRY INN, Lyme

OVERALL ★★★½ | ROOM QUALITY ★★★ | VALUE ★★★ | PRICE $85–165

Next to the glorious Lyme Congregational Church, with a bell cast by Paul Revere that rings hourly, this former tavern, stagecoach stop, and ballroom has been hosting guests for almost 200 years. In the mid-nineteenth century, tiny Lyme was the most successful sheep-raising village in New England. The only flocks evident today are outdoor enthusiasts, leaf peepers, and antiquers. The old tavern with its fireplace and original tables is especially cozy on a cold night, and the tasty eclectic cuisine is complemented by an extensive wine list.

SETTING & FACILITIES

Near Dartmouth College, shopping in Hanover, Hopkins Center, Connecticut River and Appalachian Trail
Building 1809 inn, 1820 tavern
Grounds Lawn, field, gardens
Public Space Common rooms, tavern, small DRs, library
Food & Drink Full country breakfast; specialty:stuffed French toast w/ maple syrup; Sunday brunch; lunch, dinner nightly (extra); specialties: fresh local ingredients; veg. options, holiday meals; lfull bar, with large selection of single malt Scotches and draft beer
Recreation Skiing, golf, biking, fishing, canoeing, hiking
Amenities & Services Spec. occasions, function rooms, conf., business services, weddings

ACCOMMODATIONS

Units 15 guest rooms
All Rooms Bath, phone, AC, TV
Some Rooms Extra bed, fireplace
Bed & Bath Mostly king/queen, some twins; full baths
Favorites Governor's Quarters—spa-cious suite, TV, refrigerator, king, full bath
Comfort & Decor Country decor, antiques. Views of green, woods. Church bells a distraction to some. Small rooms. Authentic, spare feeling.

RATES, RESERVATIONS, & RESTRICTIONS

Deposit 1 night, refund w/ 14-day notice
Credit Cards V, AE, MC, D
Check-In/Out 3/11
Smoking No
Pets No
Kids OK
Minimum Stay 2 nights foliage, summer weekends

Open All year	(800) 794-2296 or (603) 795-2222
Hosts Mickey and David Dowd	Fax: (603) 795-9436
Box 60, On the Common	info@aldencountryinn.com
Lyme, NH 03768	www.aldencountryinn.com

MEREDITH INN, Meredith

OVERALL ★★★½ | ROOM QUALITY ★★★★ | VALUE ★★★ | PRICE $99–139

This bed-and-breakfast near the center of Meredith has been an integral part of this small town's life for over 100 years. The original owner was a doctor who birthed a lot of the local kids; their grandchildren still come by now and then. The second owner was a popular dentist. The Carpenters, warm and helpful, are the third owners, and they have added private baths and whirlpools in beautifying this kid-friendly, rose-colored "Painted Lady." The Victorian house is not laden and overstuffed; the decor is actually rather light and airy, and a handsome staircase, handcrafted detailing and high ceilings add to the overall effect.

SETTING & FACILITIES

Location 9.5 mi., Exit 23 off I 93, 104 East to Rt. 3 North, left at downtown light onto Main St., at Waukewan St.
Near Lake Winnipesaukee, White Mountains, arts, festivals, theater, craft shows, Science Center, historic district, shopping
Building 104-year-old Gothic Victorian "Painted Lady"; restored 1997
Grounds .5 acre in town, some gardens, small lawn
Public Space LR, dining area, porch

Food & Drink Full breakfast; specialties: French toast w/ Italian bread, frittata w/ ham or tomatoes and Monterey jack, blueberry or apple walnut pancakes
Recreation Water/snow/mountain activities, skating, go-karting, archery, berry/apple picking, beaches, bike/horse/carriage/train rides
Amenities & Services Menus, tour guidance, reservations, bike and boat rentals

ACCOMMODATIONS

Units 8 guest rooms
All Rooms Bath, heat controls, TV, phone, 2 fans in summer
Some Rooms Wheelchair access, sitting area, bay windows, window seats, fireplace, desk
Bed & Bath King (3), queen (3), twin bed (2); whirlpool/shower (6), tiled shower only (2), one spacious

w/ built-in seat
Favorites Room 7—king bed, deep dbl. whirlpool, fireplace, 2nd floor
Comfort & Decor Some turret sitting areas. Special antiques such as oak bureaus, hand-carved Chapman rocker, one spool bed made into a porch bench.

RATES, RESERVATIONS, & RESTRICTIONS

Deposit 1 night w/in 7 days of booking; refund w/ 14-day notice
Discounts Off-season (Nov.–April)
Credit Cards V, MC, D
Check-In/Out 3/11
Smoking No
Pets No
Kids 6 and older
Minimum Stay 2 nights weekends,

most rooms
Open All year
Hosts Janet, Ed, and Fay Carpenter
2 Waukewan St., Box 115
Meredith, NH 03253
(603) 279-0000
Fax: (603) 279-4017
inn1897@meredithinn.com
www.meredithinn.com

OLDE ORCHARD INN, *Moultonborough*

OVERALL ★★★★ | ROOM QUALITY ★★★★ | VALUE ★★★ | PRICE $75–175

This inn comes by its name honestly. The property, acquired by Batchelder Brown for his wife in the late 1700s, is planted with hundreds of apple, cherry, plum and pear trees, so from the first flowerings in May to the last of the apple harvest in November, you can enjoy the beauty and the (literal) fruits of the innkeepers' efforts. Mary and Jim spent 26 years in the Foreign Service, and the old house is filled with international treasures such as Russian dolls, Afghan rugs, and Indian chests, mixed with a beehive oven, antique candlesticks, and other Colonial remnants. And, of course, there are modern luxuries such as whirlpool tubs.

SETTING & FACILITIES

Location Rt. 25 to Old 109 in Moultonborough, .25 mi. to Lee Rd., turn right; in foothills of White Mountains.
Near Castle in the Clouds, Loon Center, Lake Winnipesaukee, Mt. Washington, antiquing; walk to The Old Country Store (opened ca. 1800)
Building 1790 farmhouse; brick addition, 1812; major renovation 1996
Grounds 13 acres; mountain, brook; orchards, pond w/ paddleboat, gazebos
Public Space LR, game room, DR, breakfast room, sun room

Food & Drink Candlelight country breakfast, communal or separate; specialties: apple crisp, scones, cherry-berry coffeecake, frittata; soft drinks; special diets
Recreation Exercise room, sauna, spa, golf, lake sports, antiquing
Amenities & Services Antique shop, hot tub, videos, refrigerator, irons, beach towels, microwave, meeting area (40), fax; weddings, events; bikes, fishing equip., croquet, boat rental

ACCOMMODATIONS

Units 9 guest rooms
All Rooms Bath, AC, TV
Some Rooms Fireplace, coffee maker,
clock, radio
Bed & Bath Queen, double, twin; some
tub/shower, whirlpools, robes
Favorites Upper and Lower pond

rooms—queen, fireplace, whirlpool
Comfort & Decor Antiques and Oriental carpets collected during owners'
diplomatic travels. Varied trunks at foot of
beds. New wing w/ fireplaces and
whirlpools.

RATES, RESERVATIONS, & RESTRICTIONS

Deposit 1 night; refund w/ 14-day notice
Discounts Long stays, off-season, 3rd
person, kids (crib $5)
Credit Cards V, MC, D
Check-In/Out 3/11; call for arrival after
8
Smoking Outside
Pets Kennel space in barn if arranged; in-
house dogs
Kids Welcome
Minimum Stay 2 days on certain sum-

mer/fall foliage weekends
Open All year, may close for week in
winter, spring
Hosts Mary and Jim Senner
RR Box 256
Moultonborough, NH 03254
(800) 598-5845 or (603) 476-5004
Fax: (603) 476-5419
innkeep@oldeorchardinn.com
www.oldeorchardinn.com

MAPLE HILL FARM, New London

OVERALL ★★★ | ROOM QUALITY ★★★ | VALUE ★★★½ | PRICE $75–125

Generations of the same family lived here from 1824–1976, when the farm
produced maple sugar, butter, and eggs. Today you can still sleep in their
stenciled beds, and do gentle farm-related chores that most young children
love. This informal, lakeside inn hasn't changed much, and has tin walls
and ceilings, painted wooden floors, and quilts that Roberta crafted. She
also spins yarn from resident lambs—and yarns of the past. Dennis cooks
hearty breakfasts of blueberry pancakes and biscuits and sausage. From
1880–1950 you could stay here for $11 a week. With all meals. You'll have
to pay a bit more now, but this simple place is still good value, especially for
families and groups. In 2000, they built a large new lakefront house that
can be rented weekly.

SETTING & FACILITIES

Location 1 block off I-89, Exit 12, on
pastures
Near Antiquing, country fairs, theater,
museums

Building 1824 farmhouse
Grounds Little Lake Sunapee .25 mi.
behind barn, farm animals, pasture, sand-
box, playground, beach

Public Space LRs, DR, porches, barn, dance floor, basketball court, BYOB beverage bar

Food & Drink Early bird coffee; breakfast; specialty: wild blueberry pancakes (once voted finest in NH); dinner for groups of 10 or more

Recreation Swimming, snowshoeing on site; XC and downhill skiing, ice skating, golf, tennis, boating, health club, fishing

Amenities & Services 6-person hot tub, canoe and bikes, games, books, CDs; small conf., receptions, dinners, hayrides for groups

ACCOMMODATIONS

Units 10 guest rooms; sep. lake house

All Rooms Good lighting, indiv. decorated

Some Rooms Priv. bath (6), priv. entrance, pull-out loveseat, extra bed

Bed & Bath Beds vary, but firm; sofa beds; basic baths, some vintage fixtures

Favorites Room 1—double, bath, tin ceiling, antique mahogany sleigh bed;

Room 4—double, bath, closet, 2nd floor; Room 6—queen, pull-out loveseat, bath, Chippendale cherry bed

Comfort & Decor Farmhouse decor. Many with indiv. details like 104-year old master bed (owned by orig. farm family), mahogany chests, homemade curtains. Basic, clean, simple.

RATES, RESERVATIONS, & RESTRICTIONS

Deposit Credit card; refund w/ 7-day notice

Discounts Stays of 3+ nights, children, packages w/ hayride for 10 couples or more, incl. meals

Credit Cards V, AE, MC, D

Check-In/Out Flexible

Smoking No

Pets No; 2 in-house dogs

Kids Welcome (extra charge)

Minimum Stay 2 nights Jan.–Mar., July, Aug., Oct., weekends

Open All year

Hosts Roberta and Dennis Aufranc
200 Newport Rd.
New London, NH 03257
(800) 231-8637 or (603) 526-2248
Fax: (603) 526-4170
info@maplehillfarm.com
www.maplehillfarm.com

FOLLANSBEE INN, North Sutton

OVERALL ★★★½ | ROOM QUALITY ★★★ | VALUE ★★½ | PRICE $90–175

By this inn on Kezar Lake there's a pier where you can sun and swim, and an island that you can canoe to and picnic on, with lunch packed by the hosts. You can hike up Mt. Kearsarge, and in winter, there's skiing, ice fishing, and reading by the fire. And this comfy former farmhouse, filled with informal furnishings such as an old school desk and cast-iron stove, is especially good for singles and people-people—you help yourself to breakfast and join the group at the table or hang around the piano. The whole experience is relaxed and unpretentious.

SETTING & FACILITIES

Location About 2 mi. off I-89, Exit 10; lakeside; follow signs
Near Summer stock theater, outdoor band concerts, antiquing, art galleries, beach, farm museum, St. Gaudens Nat'l Hist. Site (sculpture), nature area
Building 1840 New England Cape farmhouse
Grounds Porch w/ views; overlooks Kezar Lake; near pier, priv. beach
Public Space Wide hallways, 2 sitting rooms, bar
Food & Drink Full breakfast; specialties: granola, strawberry blintzes tea, wine/cheese; dinner by special arrangement; beer and wine license
Recreation Tennis, golf, water/snow sports, kayak, horses
Amenities & Services Bikes, boats (rowboat, canoe, paddleboat, kayak) windsurfing gear, maps

ACCOMMODATIONS

Units 20 guest rooms; cottage
All Rooms Indiv. decor
Some Rooms 11 baths, lake views; cottage priv. lake access, kitchen, fireplace, LR/DR
Bed & Bath Beds vary; some shower/tub combos, some showers only
Favorites Ira's Room (#11) and Icha-
bod's Room (#9)—overlook lake, queens, priv. baths
Comfort & Decor Low ceilings, papered walls. Rooms named after town's ancestors. Cottage is intimate, secluded. Some rooms share bath. Good deal. Neat and basic.

RATES, RESERVATIONS, & RESTRICTIONS

Deposit Credit. card; 1 night's rent if canceling and others turned away
Discounts Singles, longer weekday stays; cottage $625/week
Credit Cards V, MC; prefers checks
Check-In/Out 2–10/11; call for other check-in
Smoking No
Pets No; kennel recomm.
Kids Over 8 (not in cottage)
Minimum Stay 2–3 nights, peak weekends
Open Year round.
Hosts Dave and Cathy Bead
Box 92
North Sutton, NH 03260
(603) 927-4221 or (800) 626-4221
follansbeeinn@conk.net
www.follansbeeinn.com

DEXTER'S INN AND TENNIS CLUB, Sunapee

OVERALL ★★★★ | ROOM QUALITY ★★★★ | VALUE ★½ | PRICE $135–400

Do you hanker for a love game? Have it both ways a tennis serve on cushioned courts and eggs Benedict served at 10 a.m. in an antique bed. Guests can enjoy the pool, fly-fishing, lawn games, hiking, or skimming hundreds of books. The inn is family-friendly, and kids will enjoy a recreation room in the barn and good, basic food. Originally the inn was a farmhouse, built in 1801 by a craftsman who carved bowls for ships' compasses from on-site maples. Restored by an advisor to President Herbert Hoover, it was run by Holly's parents from 1969–87, and by the next generation.

SETTING & FACILITIES

Location I-89 Exit 12; left on Rt. 11; 5.5 mi. to Winn Hill Rd.; take a left, 2 mi. to inn, on steep back road
Near Mt. Sunapee State Park, beach, antiquing, historic sites, St. Gaudens Museum, Lake Sunapee, *MV Mt. Sunapee II* cruise boat, dinner cruises, New London barn playhouse, Fells Nature preserve, Hopkins Center for the Arts, outlets, New London indoor tennis, Mt. Kearsarge
Building 1801 clapboard Colonial, barn; remodeled 1998
Grounds Gardens, pool, view of lake, mountains
Public Space DR, LR/library, FR, scr. porch
Food & Drink Full breakfast
Recreation Water sports, golf, billiards, table tennis, basketball, Foosball
Amenities & Services 3 tennis courts (ask about lessons); weddings, family reunions; limited disabled access; conf. rooms, fax, dataport; piano; grill

ACCOMMODATIONS

Units 19 guest rooms 10 in house, 7 in annex, 2 in cottage
All Rooms Bath, AC
Some Rooms LR, kitchen, priv. entrance, antiques
Bed & Bath Antique beds, four-posters; tubs
Favorites Room 12—four-poster, good view, in annex
Comfort & Decor Individually decorated w/ mix of modern and antique furnishings. Large, airy, bright. Fresh fruit, flowers. Some oddly shaped rooms. Cottage w/ LR, fireplace, kitchen, 2 BRs

RATES, RESERVATIONS, & RESTRICTIONS

Deposit 2 nights; refund w/ 14-day notice
Discounts Singles, kids, 3rd person, off-season, groups, longer stays, tennis pkgs., weekly cottage rates
Credit Cards V, MC, D
Check-In/Out 3/11
Smoking No
Pets OK ($10/day) in cottage, annex
Kids Welcome; arrange prior for babysitting
Minimum Stay Usually 2 nights on weekends
Open June 15–Oct 15
Hosts Holly and Michael Durfor
258 Stagecoach Rd.
Sunapee, NH 03782
(603) 763-5571 or (888) 205-5120
dexters@tds.net
www.bbhost.com/dextersinn

Northern New Hampshire and White Mountains

If scenic grandeur interests you, this is your region. Here you will find perhaps the most dramatic vistas in New England. The **Kancamagus Highway** is northern New England's only National Scenic Byway, and its mountain views are worth the trip alone. The scope, height and quiet, granite ridges, rushing waters, and tiny isolated villages are invigorating to mind, body, and spirit.

Before air-conditioning was invented, well-off New England and New York families came here for the entire summer to avoid the city heat, and the grand hotels and vacation homes of that era still remain. Today the area is a year-round, short-stay destination offering abundant recreational opportunities in the 780,000-acre **White Mountain National Forest,** considered New Hampshire's home of outdoor activity.

From cross-country and downhill skiing, fishing, hiking, and mountain climbing to picnicking by a waterfall or just gazing in solitude at the snow-frosted peaks, you won't have to worry about being bored, despite the fact that there is little to do after sundown except in the town of **Jackson** during ski season. The bustling ski town is filled with activities, lodgings and restaurants, and is the hub of nightlife, so to speak, with live music every night during ski season. The village of Jackson features a covered bridge, waterfall, and spectacular cross-country ski trails.

Back indoors, there is plenty of tax-free shopping, including the **North Conway outlets.** In the **Mt. Washington Valley,** drive the eight miles to the summit of the highest peak in the Northeast (6,288 feet), or leave your car behind and try the **Mt. Washington Cog Railway.** There are seven downhill ski areas and six ski touring areas in the Valley alone.

Story Land, near **Glen,** is a pint-size, fairy-tale world for little ones; nearby **Heritage, New Hampshire** tells the story of the past 350 years of the state's history.

Country inns and bed-and-breakfasts center in ski areas and are relatively scarce otherwise. Not surprisingly, the atmosphere of these inns tends to be geared to families and activities, often with ski storage, hearty meals, and basic décor—style-conscious travelers with sophisticated palates be fore-warned. In ski season and on weekends, be sure to reserve well in advance.

FOR MORE INFORMATION

Country Inns in the White Mountains (603) 345-9460
email: stay@white-mountains-inns.com
www.white-mountains-inns.com

New Hampshire's Connecticut Lakes Region (603) 538-7118
www.nhconnlakes.com

North Country Chamber of Commerce (800) 698-8939, ext. 1

The Open Door Bed and Breakfasts
Box 1178
N. Conway, NH 03860
(800) 300-4799
www.mountwashingtonvalley.com/opendoor

White Mountains B&B Association
White Mountains Attractions
Box 10
North Woodstock, NH 03262
(603) 745-8720 or (800) 346-3687
www.visitwhitemountains.com

COVERED BRIDGE HOUSE, Bartlett

OVERALL ★★★½ | ROOM QUALITY ★★★ | VALUE ★★★★½ | PRICE $59–109

This Colonial bed-and-breakfast's name refers to its most unique feature, their very own restored 1850s covered bridge, the only one privately owned in the U.S. The inn has a gift shop at one end offering country crafts and New England souvenirs. So homey that guests have come to breakfast in slippers and pajamas, the country-casual atmosphere has the innkeepers and their offspring much in evidence. With a private beach on the Saco River, and kids under 12 free in their parents' room, this pretty, well-maintained property offers a special environment for families and couples alike.

SETTING & FACILITIES

Location 7 mi. N of North Conway, next to covered bridge
Near Story Land, Heritage New Hampshire, Conway Scenic Railroad, Cog Railway, Covered Bridge Shop (on-site N.E. crafts, antiques), outlet/specialty shops, Kancamagus Highway
Building Circa 1900 Colonial
Grounds 2 acres by Saco River w/ tubing, swimming holes

Public Space LR, DR, outdoor hot tub
Food & Drink Country breakfast; specialties: Belgian waffles w/ berry sauce, eggs any style; snacks hot drinks, cookies
Recreation Mini-golf, golf, canoeing, fishing, tennis, skiing
Amenities & Services Roll-aways, cribs, tubing tubes, irons, kitchen privileges, maps

ACCOMMODATIONS

Units 6 guest rooms
All Rooms Clock/radio
Some Rooms AC, bath (4)
Bed & Bath Some queens; tub (1)
Favorites Crawford Notch—featherbed, afternoon sun, bath; Carter Notch—Victorian, armoire, sofa,

stenciling
Comfort & Decor Antiques, colonial style. Bedside lighting. Some papered, some stenciled. Named for notches in White Mountains. Two rooms sharing bath connect, perfect for family.

RATES, RESERVATIONS, & RESTRICTIONS

Deposit 50%; refund w/ 14-day notice
Discounts Off-season, kids under 12, midweek, singles, 3rd person
Credit Cards V, AE, MC, D
Check-In/Out 3–10/11
Smoking No
Pets No
Kids OK; call ahead
Minimum Stay 2 nights holidays, fall

foliage, some weekends
Open All year
Hosts Nancy and Dan Wanek, Brian and Allison
Route 302
Bartlett, NH 03838
(800) 232-9109 or (603) 383-9109
cbhouse@landmarknet.net
www.coveredbridgehouse.com

ADAIR COUNTRY INN, Bethlehem

OVERALL ★★★★★ | ROOM QUALITY ★★★★★ | VALUE ★★ | PRICE $165–345

The hosts purchased this elegant hilltop inn in 1998. Bill, a former ad exec who enjoys gardening, and Judy, a caterer, apply their talents to this already renowned mansion, with grounds designed by the Olmsteds brothers, who designed Central Park. You are treated as if you are visiting the original owner, Dorothy Adair Hogan, who was given the estate by her father, a famed trial lawyer, in 1927. Guests' names are written at the entry, as a welcome, and the quiet pampering continues. Rooms are named for the White Mountains, which can be seen from many of the luxury guest rooms. And the evolving dinner cuisine can reach lofty peaks as well.

SETTING & FACILITIES

Location I-93 to Exit 40; 3 mi. W of center of Bethlehem
Near Antiquing, museums, White Mountain Nat'l Forest, shopping in Littleton, summer theatre, summer lectures
Building 1927 Georgian Colonial, remodeled 1996
Grounds 200-acres trails, tennis, gardens, patio, gazebo, pond, woods
Public Space Huge LR, DR; activity room, library

Food & Drink Coffee, tea, full breakfast; specialties: well-known for popovers, French toast w/ Vermont cob-smoked bacon; dinner in season, Wed.–Sun. (extra, res. req., no credit. cds); tea, cakes
Recreation Tennis, skiing, golf, walking, boating, fishing, hiking, snowshoeing
Amenities & Services Priv. phone, newspapers, pool table; business retreats, family reunions, large screen TV, video library; offers turndown service

ACCOMMODATIONS

Units 8 guest rooms, I suite; suite in cottage has 2 guest rooms
All Rooms Bath
Some Rooms Fireplace; cottage deck, fireplace, TV
Bed & Bath Queen/king; baths recently renovated; one whirlpool, 2 soaking tubs
Favorites Dalton—extra-large 3rd-floor

room, view of Dalton Mt.; 1,400 sq.ft. cottage w/ modern art, Oriental rugs, quilts, 2-person soaking tub
Comfort & Decor Spacious w/ antiques and reproductions, carpet, views. Feel of privacy in mansion. Good bedside lighting. Whimsical and warming touches. Quietly luxurious.

RATES, RESERVATIONS, & RESTRICTIONS

Deposit I night; refund w/ 15-day cancel.
Discounts 3rd person, groups. Winter, midweek
Credit Cards V, AE, MC, D
Check-In/Out 3–8/before 11

Smoking No
Pets No; in-house cat; boarding nearby
Kids Over 12
Minimum Stay 2 nights weekends, foliage; 3, holidays

Open All year; closed 1 week April or
Nov
Hosts Judy and Bill Whitman
80 Guider Lane
Bethlehem, NH 03574-0359

(603) 444-2600, 888-444-2600
Fax: (603) 444-4823
adair@connriver.net
www.adairinn.com

DARBY FIELD INN, Conway

OVERALL ★★★½ | ROOM QUALITY ★★★★ | VALUE ★½ | PRICE $120–290

Named not after a meadow but after an Irishman named Darby Field, the
first white man to climb Mt. Washington (1642), this comfortable inn is
atop Bald Hill in the wilds of mountainous northern New Hampshire. The
hosts are an interesting combo Marc has traveled the world and especially
enjoys chatting about golf and skiing; Maria is a proponent of natural heal-
ing, massage therapy, Buddhism, and meditation. After a day on the slopes,
in the pool, or hiking by a nearby waterfall, what could be better than a
tasty meal overlooking a valley sunset, and then a special inn nightcap, an
Irish Revolution, by the wood-burning stove in the pub?

SETTING & FACILITIES

Location 2.5 mi. S of Conway; on the
border of White Mountain Nat'l Forest
Near Antiquing, beach, Mt. Washington,
Kancamagus Hwy., Scenic and Cog Rail-
roads, covered bridges
Building 1826 Colonial homestead
Grounds Great views; gardens, forest,
outdoor pool, patio, XC skiing trails, hot
tub; 1,000 feet above valley

Public Space LR, tavern, DR
Food & Drink (MAP) Full breakfast;
candlelight dinner; specialties: roast duck-
ling w/ raspberry Chambord, Darby
cream pie; low-fat/veg. meals
Recreation Golf, horses, skiing, tennis,
rock/ice climbing, river sports
Amenities & Services Access to
XC ski trails, maps; full-service inn

ACCOMMODATIONS

Units 4 basic, 5 traditional, 5 deluxe
All Rooms Bath, garden or mountain
view
Some Rooms Bay window, whirlpool,
TV/VCR, AC, sitting room, fireplace, bal-
cony, steam room
Bed & Bath Beds vary; private bath-

rooms in all
Favorites Suite—AC, queen, bay window w/ views, whirlpool
Comfort & Decor Casual, w/ antiques,
collectibles, reproductions. carpet. Creative use of space to create baths.

RATES, RESERVATIONS, & RESTRICTIONS

Deposit 50%; refund w/ 14-day notice

Discounts Singles, groups, longer stays; call for groups, weddings

Credit Cards V, AE, MC

Check-In/Out 2–6/9–11

Smoking Tavern only

Pets No; in-house dog

Kids Welcome if well-supervised

Minimum Stay Many weekends, fall

foliage, holidays

Open May–March

Hosts Maria and Marc Donaldson

185 Chase Hill Rd.

Albany, NH 03818

(603) 447-2181 or (800) 426-4147

Fax: (603) 447-5726

marc@darbyfield.com

www.darbyfield.com

BUNGAY JAR BED & BREAKFAST, *Franconia*

OVERALL ★★★★½ | ROOM QUALITY ★★★★ | VALUE ★★½ | PRICE $105–225

Benny Goodman's bathtub, a llama herd, a moosehead of vines on a massive stone fireplace, banisters created from lightning rods, salvage decor with old church doors and stained glass—it's whimsical and constantly surprising. Cluttered and off-beat, this converted four-level barn with the hayloft great room is not for traditionalists. But for those who enjoy artistic, hands-on originality, magazine-cover gardens with lily ponds and twig gates, and warm and enthusiastic hosts, it's a delight. Oh, and a Bungay Jar isn't a vessel for "bungays"; it's a folksy term for an unusual spring wind that shakes things up. This place does just that.

SETTING & FACILITIES

Location From NY, Rt. 112, 12 mi. to Rt. 116 N (left); B&B, about 5 mi. on right
Near Robert Frost Museum, Franconia Notch Park, Cannon Mountain, Appalachian Trail, Lost River Echo Lake; Sugar Hill, Franconia
Building Rustic 18th-century barn moved to site in 1967; sep. Plum Cottage in Franconia village
Grounds 12 secluded areas, garden paths, pond, woods, llamas and horses, terraced gardens, pergola
Public Space 2-story living area, DR, decks, small library
Food & Drink Buffet-style country breakfast; specialty: popovers; tea, snacks
Recreation Hiking, skiing, biking, antiquing
Amenities & Services Sauna, garden shop, games, garden workshops (fee)

ACCOMMODATIONS

Units 5 guest rooms, 1 suite, sep. Plum Cottage
All Rooms Bath, ornate bed
Some Rooms Priv. balcony, skylight, fireplace; Plum Cottage—fireplace, TV, whirlpool, kitchen
Bed & Bath Some king, four-poster, canopy, sleigh, antique beds; unique baths, skylight showers, claw-foot tubs, Benny Goodman's 6-foot soaking tub
Favorites Garden Suite—kitchen/dining area, fireplace, dbl. Jacuzzi facing mountains, priv. garden; Stargazer—3rd floor, tiny, skylights, view, twig furniture, telescope, claw-foot tub
Comfort & Decor Eclectic to the max, from small to large, traditional to unique. Rustic wide-plank floors, beams, leaded glass, whimsy, antiques. Mountain views all around.

RATES, RESERVATIONS, & RESTRICTIONS

Deposit Check; refund/cancellation, check w/ host
Discounts Singles; weekly rates for cottage
Credit Cards V, AE, MC
Check-In/Out 3/11
Smoking No
Kids Only in cottage
Pets In cottage only; inn has cats and dogs
Minimum Stay 2 nights foliage, holiday weekends
Open All year except some holidays, check with inn.
Hosts Kate Kerivan and Lee Strimbeck
P. O. Box 15, Easton Valley Rd.
Franconia, NH 03580
(800) 421-0701 or (603) 823-7775
Fax: (603) 823-8044
info@bungayjar.com
www.bungayjar.com

SUGAR HILL INN, *Franconia*

OVERALL ★★★★ | ROOM QUALITY ★★★★ | VALUE ★★ | PRICE $90–335

Sweet as its name, this unpretentious, warm, and welcoming inn doesn't take itself too seriously, and the innkeepers have lavished it with love.

Stone walls, buildings of white clapboard with blue trim, flower borders, simple country furnishings—it's hard not to rest here, especially in the glow of fireplaces crackling away. The mountains loom, all seasons are spectacular, the skiing is grand, and the feeling is old-fashioned pleasure, much as when local Bette Davis used to stay here to relax. But two new suites with whirlpool tubs may be harbingers of things to come.

SETTING & FACILITIES

Location From I-93, right on Rt. 18N, right on Rt. 117W, .5 mi. on right
Near Robert Frost home, New England Ski Museum, Franconia Notch State Park, Mt. Washington, Cog Railway
Building 1789 New England farmhouse, expanded
Grounds 16 acres nestled in hills, woodlands, lawns
Public Space DR, pub, large wraparound porch, two large LR
Food & Drink (MAP) Three-course country breakfast; specialty: Swiss eggs. Dinner specialty: rosemary-crusted rack of lamb; afternoon tea, scones, sweet bread; wine cellar; spec. diets accom.
Recreation Skiing, skating, snowshoeing, golf, tennis, fishing
Amenities & Services Packages, incl. Harvest Your Own Christmas Tree; sleigh rides, concert and lecture series; bottled water, hairdryers, robes

ACCOMMODATIONS

Units 8 guest rooms, 2 suites; 6 cottage rooms
All Rooms Bath, antiques
Some Rooms Fireplace, mountain view
Bed & Bath Varied bed sizes, some canopy four-posters; small baths w/ soaking tubs; whirlpools in suites
Favorites Bette Davis—views on three sides; two new suites w/ whirlpool and fireplace; Cottage rooms—w/ fireplace, more space
Comfort & Decor Small, but cozy. Each room stenciled, w/ reproductions and modest antiques. Immaculate and sweet. Separate cottages w/ fireplaces more private and spacious.

RATES, RESERVATIONS, & RESTRICTIONS

Deposit One night or 50%; two nights fall foliage, holiday weekends; refund w/ 14-day notice
Discounts Packages, extra person;
Credit Cards V, MC, AE
Check-In/Out 3/11
Smoking No
Pets No
Kids Over 12 in main house, OK in cottages (no cribs available)
No-No's Return of fee if arriving late or leaving early
Minimum Stay 2 nights, foliage, holiday weekends
Open Except Christmas week
Hosts Barbara and Jim Quinn
Scenic Route 117
Franconia, NH 03580
(800) 548-4748 or (603) 823-5621
Fax: (603) 823-5639
info@sugarhillinn.com
www.sugarhillinn.com

BERNERHOF INN, Glen

OVERALL ★★★★ | ROOM QUALITY ★★★★ | VALUE ★★★½ | PRICE $79–155

Built in the 1880s as a traveling spot for people on their way to Mt. Washington, the inn was purchased in the 1950s by a Swiss couple, who named it after their native city of Bern. They yodeled, played the Alpine Horn, and loved this area, so similar to the Tyrol. The current hosts have modernized the rooms, but they maintain a bit of European atmosphere. If you would like a taste, so to speak, of cooking school in a mountain setting, "A Taste of the Mountains" includes lodging and wine seminars, instruction, and all meals. And on the fourth morning, you get a champagne breakfast in bed.

SETTING & FACILITIES

Location 1 mi. W of Rt. 302 and Rt. 16 intersection, 1 mi. E of Attitash
Near N Conway village, Mt. Washington, Saco River, Cog Railroad, Attitash Bear Peak, Black Mt., Cranmore Resort, Wildcat and Bretton Woods skiing, theater
Building Large, like small hotel, w/ turrets; ca. 1880
Grounds 10 acres gardens, pool, playground
Public Space Sitting room, restaurant, pub, lounge
Food & Drink Full breakfast; fine dining, creative cont'l cuisine; specialties: Wiener schnitzel, trout w/ almonds, pots de crème; wine list
Recreation Snow/water sports, ice/rock climbing, sleigh rides, horses
Amenities & Services Custom amenities for indiv. rooms (flowers, chocolate truffles)

ACCOMMODATIONS

Units 7 guest rooms, 2 suites
All Rooms Bath, AC, phone, TV
Some Rooms Whirlpool, window alcove
Bed & Bath Rooms disabled access. (baths not wheelchair access.); some kings, some brass; most w/ whirlpool, pedestal sinks
Favorites 2 rooms in turret—angles, queens, spacious; Suite—iris stained-glass window, tear drop shower, whirlpool, sauna, sitting room w/ day bed, TV/VCR; Room 9—3-leaf clover whirlpool, bath w/ shower, 3rd floor, great view
Comfort & Decor Interesting lighting options—many windows, skylights, stained-glass windows, direct lighting, decorative lighting. Individually decorated w/ Victorian flavor.

RATES, RESERVATIONS, & RESTRICTIONS

Deposit Refund w/ 14-day notice, less $25 bookkeeping fee
Discounts Longer midweek (not holidays)
Credit Cards V, AE, MC, D
Check-In/Out 2–10/10–11
Smoking No
Pets No
Kids OK
Minimum Stay 2–3 nights weekends, holidays; flexible

Open All year
Hosts Sharon Wroblewski
and Susan Bagley
Box 240
Glen, NH 03838

(800) 548-8007 or (603) 383-9132
Fax: (603) 383-0809
stay@bernerhofinn.com
www.bernerhofinn.com

NOTCHLAND INN, Hart's Location

OVERALL ★★★★½ | ROOM QUALITY ★★★★★ | VALUE ★½ | PRICE $175–345

Nestled on 100 acres among mountain walls, this English manor house is an artful expression of enthusiastic innkeeping. The inn's front parlor was designed by Gustav Stickley, a founder of the Arts and Crafts movement, and there are tin ceilings, a dozen fireplaces, an outdoor hot tub, a school-house suite annex, and more. Interesting facts: *The Secaucus Seven* was filmed on the property, which is home to llamas, and Bernese Mountain Dogs. Hart's Location is New Hampshire's smallest town, and has the first votes reported in national primary elections. Voting takes place in the Inn's dining room.

SETTING & FACILITIES

Location East of Crawford Notch, on Rt. 302, across from swimming holes and Saco River
Near Mt. Washington, White Mountain Nat'l. Forest, Kankamagus Hwy., covered bridges, antiquing, ski areas, 5 golf courses, Conway Scenic RR, Cog Railway
Building 1860s granite Tudor Revival
Grounds 100 acres, award-winning gardens, wooden hot tub in gazebo, pond, swimming holes; 8,000 ft. of Saco River frontage; at base of Mt. Bemis

Public Space DR , front parlor, music room, sun room, library
Food & Drink Early-bird hot beverages; full country breakfast; 5-course dinner; specialty: coriander and fennel-crusted salmon, chicken Escoffier; spec. diets accom.; liquor license
Recreation Trails, fishing, swimming on-site; snow/water/mountain sports, strawberry picking, brewery tour nearby
Amenities & Services Some disabled access., pkgs., online availability, check

ACCOMMODATIONS

Units 7 guest rooms, 6 suites
All Rooms Bath, wood-burning fireplace, sitting area, quilts, antiques
Some Rooms Whirlpool, mountain view, AC, sitting room, porch/deck
Bed & Bath King/queen, some extra beds, four-poster (2), some Eastlakes; some tub/shower, some whirlpools
Favorites Mad River Premium Suite—

king, queen fold-out sofa, French doors to deck, dbl. whirlpool, views
Comfort & Decor Green and blue hues, designer fabrics. Lots w/ capacities of 2–4 people. Front rooms, more road noise. Good lighting. Airy, sunny, stylish, spacious. Two suites in adjacent former schoolhouse.

RATES, RESERVATIONS, & RESTRICTIONS

Deposit 50% w/in 7-days; refund w/ 14-days notice; less than 14-days, refund only if room rebooked

Discounts Singles, 3rd person, midweek

Credit Cards V, AE, MC, D

Check-In/Out 4/11

Smoking No

Pets No; in-house Bernese mountain dogs

Kids Over 12

No-No's Kids under 3 at dinner

Minimum Stay 2 nights most Saturdays, 3 in-season

Open All year

Hosts Ed Butler and Les Schoof

Route 302

Hart's Location, NH 03812

(603) 374-6131 or (800) 866-6131

Fax: (603) 374-6168

notchland@aol.com

www.notchland.com

GIBSON HOUSE, Haverhill

OVERALL ★★★★½ | ROOM QUALITY ★★★★★ | VALUE ★★½ | PRICE $110–250

On the sleepy green of Haverhill Corners, this traditional house is anything but. Keita, the gracious owner and resident artist, provides an otherworldly feast of texture and color and spirit—yellow and lime in unexpected places in the breakfast room (where the food presentation is just as eye-opening), faux windows, tribal rugs, stained-glass moons that light up the night. An art gallery is in the basement—the former stable of a 1776 stagecoach inn. But the whole of this new bed-and-breakfast is an artwork. And the house pets include a three cats—Gracey, Max, and Osirus—and an American Eskimo dog, Queenie.

SETTING & FACILITIES

Location Village Green, Haverhill,
Near Hanover (Dartmouth Coll.), lakes,
Appalachian Trail, antiquing
Building 1850 Greek Revival
Grounds 1.5 acres walking gardens with
central lily pond, gazebo, sculpture, bird-
bath, wildflower meadow with walking
circle
Public Space Parlors, LR, DRs, two
large balconies w/ view across Valley to
Vermont

Food & Drink Full gourmet breakfast;
specialties: blueberry pancakes, maple
syrup, smokehouse bacon; fresh fruit,
refreshments, afternoon tea, cocktail
Recreation Tennis, skiing, golf, boating,
swimming, cycling, hiking, antiquing
Amenities & Services Gallery, garden
wedding facil., catering, hot-air balloon
and horse/carriage rides, artist and group
retreats

ACCOMMODATIONS

Units 6 guest rooms
All Rooms Bath, phone, ceiling fan
Some Rooms Four-poster bed, fireplace
Bed & Bath Varied bed sizes; some
murals, pedestal sinks, claw-foot tubs
Favorites Avalon Suite—king antique
teak bed, Moravian starlight draped
daybed, fireplace, French doors to priv.

porch, beamed ceiling, whirlpool with
arched stained-glass window
Comfort & Decor Creative theme
rooms, such as Taj North w/ stained-glass
moon and night sky over walnut bed; A
Day at the Beach w/ hanging rope chair.
Hand-stamped walls. Lush whimsy. Dramatic colors. Not designed for comfort,
but very romantic.

RATES, RESERVATIONS, & RESTRICTIONS

Deposit Full refund w/ 7-day notice
Discounts 3rd, groups, long stays,
singles
Credit Cards None
Check-In/Out 3/11
Smoking No
Pets No; cat and parrot at inn
Kids No

Minimum Stay None
Open All year
Host Keita Colton
RR 1 Box 193, Rt. 10
Haverhill, NH 03765
(603) 989-3125
Fax: (603) 989-5749
gibson.house@ConnRiver.net

THE FOREST, Intervale

OVERALL ★★★½ | ROOM QUALITY ★★★★ | VALUE ★★★ | PRICE $80–170

You *can* see The Forest for the trees on these 25 wooded acres. Bikers especially enjoy this Country Victorian lodging, part of a route with other inns
and bed-and-breakfasts. The parlor was a general store from the 1830s,
moved to enlarge the premises in the 1880s, and the stone cottage was the
office of one of New Hampshire's first female lawyers. Hearty breakfasts
feature apple pancakes and eggs with all the trimmings. Guest rooms are
comfortable and old-fashioned, the parlors look lived in, and the feeling

here is kick-your-shoes-off relaxed. Grounds adjoin a cross-country ski trail, and the swimming pool is a big plus.

SETTING & FACILITIES

Location 1.5 mi. from North Conway on Rt. 16A, adjoining XC skiing trails
Near North Conway outlets, jazz festivals, equine festivals, local theater, concerts, White Mountain Nat'l. Forest
Building 3-story Victorian, mansard roof; stone cottage
Grounds 25 acres, woods, stream, gardens, heated outdoor pool, picnic tables, grill, trails
Public Space 2 LRs, TV room, porch

Food & Drink Full breakfast; specialties: blueberry pancakes, spiced Belgian waffles, Amaretto French toast, homemade jam; refreshments
Recreation Swimming, snow/water activities, golf, horses, tennis, sleigh rides
Amenities & Services Picnic area, gas grill, refrigerator, lawn games, after-ski refreshments in winter; celebrating spec. occasions, gatherings, inn-to-inn bike tours

ACCOMMODATIONS

Units 8 guest rooms, 3 cottage rooms
All Rooms Bath, coordinated fabrics, plants
Some Rooms Fireplace, ceiling fan
Bed & Bath Queens, brass, sleigh beds, four-posters in cottage; whirlpool (1)

Favorites Cottle Room—in cottage, fireplace, priv. veranda
Comfort & Decor Quilts and comforters, antiques, country furniture. Flowered wallpapers. Cottages most romantic.

RATES, RESERVATIONS, & RESTRICTIONS

Deposit 50%, refund w/ 14-day notice
Discounts Off-season, 3rd person
Credit Cards V, AE, MC, D
Check-In/Out 2/11
Smoking No
Pets No
Kids Over 6
Minimum Stay 2 nights most weekends, 3 nights holidays

Open May–March
Hosts Lisa and Bill Guppy
Box 37
Intervale, NH 03845
(603) 356-9772 or (800) 448-3534
Fax: (603) 356-5652
forest@ncia.net
www.forest-inn.com

CARTER NOTCH INN, Jackson

OVERALL ★★★½ | ROOM QUALITY ★★★★ | VALUE ★★½ | PRICE $69–189

When last visited a few years ago, this former home of the owners of the old Eagle Mountain House next door (now condos) was a homey, ho-hum little budget bed-and-breakfast with a dumbwaiter elevator. But a later visit shows that innkeepers can make or break a place. Still the kind of lodgings where you can put your feet up, hosts Jim and Lynda stress that guests are considered company, and have upgraded all around. Breakfasts are now lavish, with favorites like whole-wheat blueberry pancakes, guest rooms have been freshened, and the third floor transformed into luxury units. Jackson Falls is still a walk away for picnicking, the golf course across the road is as pretty as ever from the porch, and the dumbwaiter remains.

SETTING & FACILITIES

Location Half mi. from village on country road, across from golf course, near Jackson Falls, cross-country skiing from front door

Near Wildcat River Valley, Jackson Falls, White Mountain Nat'l. Forest, outlets, downhill skiing, golf courses, waterfalls

Building Circa 1909 former inn, annex, and family homestead; renovated 1995

Grounds Wraparound porch; outdoor hot tub w/ view

Public Space Cottage-style LR w/ fireplace, sitting area, orig. weighted elevator

Food & Drink Country breakfast, specialties: pumpkin pancakes, Grand Marnier stuffed French toast, omelets; p.m. snacks hot drinks, Carter Notch Inn cookies; special meals

Recreation XC skiing from the door, hiking; 5 min. to downhill skiing, golf, canoeing, pool, tennis

Amenities & Services AC, hosts' foliage and touring maps, refrigerator, kitchen privileges, rec. facil. next door, celebrating spec. occasions

ACCOMMODATIONS

Units 8 guest rooms

All Rooms Bath, AC, clock, radio

Some Rooms Fireplace, whirlpool (2), Jacuzzis, TV/VCR and deck (5)

Bed & Bath Most queens/doubles, some extra beds; new baths

Favorites Room 5—cozy, double, blue-hued, sun from bay window overlooking

golf course, new sitting area w/ TV

Comfort & Decor Small. Light, airy, lots of white. Painted floors and furniture, dried flowers, straw hats. Simple and elegant. Great views of Wildcat River Valley. Third floor luxury Jacuzzi rooms w/ decks and fireplaces.

RATES, RESERVATIONS, & RESTRICTIONS

Deposit 1 night; 14-day cancel. w/ fee

Discounts Off-season, midweek, singles, 3rd person, frequent stay card

Credit Cards V, AE, MC, D

Check-In/Out After 1/before 11

Smoking No

Pets No; in-house dog (mag.-cover dog—ask) and cat

Kids 6 and up

Minimum Stay 2 nights fall foliage, weekends; 3 nights 3-day weekends

Open All year

Hosts Lynda and Jim Dunwell
Box 269, Carter Notch Rd.
Jackson, NH 03846-0269
(800) 794-9437 or (603) 383-9630
www.carternotchinn.com

CHRISTMAS FARM INN, *Jackson*

OVERALL ★★★★ | ROOM QUALITY ★★★★ | VALUE ★★★★ | PRICE $78–135

If you like talking politics, you can debate with innkeeper Bill, who served in the U.S. House of Representatives. Cutesy Christmas references abound Mistletoe Pub, Sugar Plum Dining Room, and guest rooms named Prancer, Blitzen, et al. But there's much more at this family-oriented inn. The Jackson Ski Touring Federation was founded in their living room, and access to 80 kilometers of trails is easy. Accommodations vary from suites in an up-to-date function center and cozy old-fashioned rooms in the main house, to cottages with two bedrooms and baths. And for those who can't wait, the Christmas-in-July fete has a tree and Santa.

SETTING & FACILITIES

Location .25 mi. from post office on Rt. 16B
Near Antiquing, beach, historic sites, outlets, trails; walk to Jackson Falls
Building 1778 homestead, barn, outbuildings
Grounds 14 acres award-winning gardens; rec. facil., sauna, hot tub
Public Space Pub, LR, library, DR, wheelchair access
Food & Drink (MAP) Full breakfast; specialty: homemade doughnuts; poolside lunch, beverages; candlelight dinner; specialty: medallions of pork w/ brandy; spec. meals avail.; liquor license
Recreation Tennis, guided ski tours, sleigh rides, ice skating, wine tastings in season
Amenities & Services Packing lunch, spec. events coord., banquets (80). Corp. functions conf. center (50), dataports, a/v, VCRs, wide-screen TVs, fax, copier, overnight mail, flip charts

ACCOMMODATIONS

Units 10 guest rooms in inn, 9 in Salt Box; 4 suites in barn, cottages, log cabin, sugar house
All Rooms Bath, phone
Some Rooms Whirlpool, TV, refrigerator, shared sauna, fireplace, mountain views, sundeck, 2 BRs, priv. entrance, LR, loft
Bed & Bath Beds vary, some canopies, four-posters; most tubs; some whirlpools
Favorites 2 Salt Box—2nd floor, alcove, great view
Comfort & Decor Colonial w/ Laura Ashley, but varies by type of lodging. Country feel. Small in main house. Quietest in outbuildings.

RATES, RESERVATIONS, & RESTRICTIONS

Deposit 1 night, 50% for foliage, holidays, school vacations; 14-day cancel. policy
Discounts 3rd person, corp., longer stays, seniors, groups, kids under 12 sharing w/ parents; extra for singles, dbl. occupancy in cottage
Credit Cards V, AE, MC
Check-In/Out 3/11
Smoking Some rooms
Pets No

Kids OK
Minimum Stay 2 nights winter
weekends
Open All year
Hosts Synda and Bill Zeliff
Route 16

Jackson, NH 03846
(603) 383-4313 or (800) 443-5837
Fax: (603) 383-6495
info@christmasfarminn.com
www.christmasfarminn.com

THE INN AT THORN HILL, Jackson

OVERALL ★★★★½ | ROOM QUALITY ★★★★★ | VALUE ★½ | PRICE $90–400

An old Victrola phonograph and grand piano are nostalgic elements of this complete, premier Jackson inn. If you want romance, there's candle-light dining and private cottages with whirlpools and fireplaces. If you're with a group, you can rent out the carriage house with its six guest rooms surrounding a central great room with fireplace. Foodies will savor dishes like lobster pie or seafood sausage with lemon-caper butter. And active types can swim in the pool, or cross-country ski from the doorstep to a 146-kilometer touring trail. Designed by famed architect Stanford White, well-managed and casual, Thorn Hill is much more a rose than a thorn.

SETTING & FACILITIES

Location Just up the hill from town
Near Antiquing, historic sights, galleries, Jackson Falls, Wildcat River, White Mountain Nat'l. Forest, Mt. Washington Valley Theater Company, Mt. Washington Auto Rd., Story Land, Conway Scenic RR, Cog Railway, Attitash Bear Peak and Fields of Attitash
Building Built 1895, designed by Stanford White
Grounds 9 acres fields, stream, pond, flower/herb gardens, pool, views of Mt. Washington
Public Space Porch, pub, common rooms
Food & Drink (MAP) Full breakfast of breads, muffins, entrée choices, eggs; 3-course dinners (res.), specialties: shrimp-and-asparagus open lasagne, grilled cumin chicken breast; wine list; veg. meals avail., over 1,000 wines on list
Recreation Canoeing, golf, tennis, skiing, tennis racket rental, glider flights
Amenities & Services Books, games, hot tub; packed picnics, arranging massages, guided hikes; near canoe, mountain bike rentals; celebrating spec. occasions

ACCOMMODATIONS

Units 3 cottages; Inn and carriage House 12 guest rooms, 4 suites,
All Rooms Bath, AC, hairdryer, robes
Some Rooms Extra bed, LR, gas fireplace, deck, skylight, coffeemaker, phone, wet bar, TV/VCR
Bed & Bath Most queens, some kings, some four-posters; some whirlpools, dbl. whirlpools.

Favorites Katherine's Suite—queen, dbl. whirlpool, LR w/ dbl. gas fireplace, TV **Comfort & Decor** Main inn rooms in Victorian decor, named after nearby mountains. Cottages, French country. Carriage house in Adirondack decor, named after local hills. Some fabulous views.

RATES, RESERVATIONS, & RESTRICTIONS

Deposit Half the stay; refund w/ 14-day notice
Discounts 3 or more nights, off season
Credit Cards V, AE, DC, MC
Check-In/Out 3/11
Smoking No
Pets No
Kids Over 8
Minimum Stay 2–3 nights most week-ends, holidays, some peak
Open All year
Hosts Ibby and Jim Cooper
Thorn Hill Rd, Box A
Jackson, NH 03846
(603) 383-4242 or (800) 289-8990
Fax: (603) 383-8062
thornhll@ncia.net
www.innatthornhill.com

NESTLENOOK FARM, *Jackson*

OVERALL ★★★★ | ROOM QUALITY ★★★★ | VALUE ★½ | PRICE $125–340

The name well describes this picturesque, hyper-romantic bed-and-breakfast with a cage filled with love birds, a little chapel for weddings, and an arched covered bridge, perfect to pop the question. Victoriana is celebrated in guest room decor and details, and each summer the staff dresses in period costume for a day, and leads Victorian games. Horse-drawn sleighs (summer on wheels) whisk you to a forest, where you can feed deer, and around the 65 acres with gardens and paths, a heated lakeside gazebo and farm animals. The Never-Never Land quality works, if you like it and let it.

SETTING & FACILITIES

Location Rt. 16, .5 mi. past covered bridge, 1st right onto Dinsmore Rd.
Near Beach, shopping, antiquing
Building Gingerbread Victorian; parlor ca. 1800
Grounds 65 acres forest, lake, pool, gazebo, Riverside Chapel, Angle Island
Public Space Sitting room, game room, guest kitchen, DR

Food & Drink Full country breakfast; specialties: pumpkin bread, baked omelets; fruit, wine/cheese hour; diet, low-fat meals
Recreation Downhill skiing, water sports, golf, horses, sleigh rides
Amenities & Services Some disabled access for visual, hearing-impaired, refrigerator, turndown, celebrating spec. occasions; banquet facil., weddings

ACCOMMODATIONS

Units 7 guest suites
All Rooms Whirlpool bath, antique radio, clock

Some Rooms 19th-century parlor stove, AC, 1 fireplace

Bed & Bath Queen/king, some four-posters, canopies; dbl. whirlpools in all
Favorites Paskell Room—private, hand-carved king four-poster; Morton Room—oldest, orig. beams, brick hearth, porch access
Comfort & Decor Victorian feel.

Rooms named after local artists, featuring their paintings. Antiques, wallpapers. Hand-painted, patterned radiators. All w/ stove or fireplace. Highly romantic. Most, views of river or lake; 3rd-floor suite, three-way views

RATES, RESERVATIONS, & RESTRICTIONS

Deposit 50%; refund w/ 14-day notice
Discounts AAA, longer stays, 3rd person
Credit Cards V, MC, D
Check-In/Out 3/11
Smoking No
Pets No
Kids Over 12
Minimum Stay 2 nights weekends, 3

holidays
Open All year
Host Linda Wagstaff
Dinsmore Rd.
Jackson, NH 03846
(603) 383-9443 or (800) 659-9443
email through website
www.nestlenook.com

WILDCAT INN AND TAVERN, Jackson

OVERALL ★★★ | ROOM QUALITY ★★★ | VALUE ★½ | PRICE $129–350

This lively, basic inn offers in-town location, a real lunch, nightly entertainment in season, and a great price. The front porch dining room is a people-watching venue where you'll enjoy home-baked pastries at breakfast, bagels and lox for lunch, and for dinner, maybe Wildcat chicken in puffed pastry, and rhubarb-pudding cake or sour-cream apple pie (you can afford the calories after skiing, tennis or golf). Après-ski and live entertainment go on most nights, in-season Tuesday is open-mike night in the tavern; Thursdays, R&B and jazz. This informal inn has roaring fireplaces, funny rules on the tavern wall, commotion, and acceptable rooms. For romantics, or those seeking a bucolic escape, try the cottage—or another inn.

SETTING & FACILITIES

Location Route 16A in center of Jackson Village
Near Jackson Ski Touring Foundation across the street, near other ski centers, outlets in North Conway
Building Blue Colonial house and annex
Grounds Award-winning garden, small-ish lawns

Public Space Sitting, game rooms, tavern, glassed-in porch/DR w/ disabled access
Food & Drink (MAP) Farm breakfast, brunch/lunch; tea, cocoa, cookies; dinner; homemade desserts; taking dinner to room OK, spec. diets accom.

Recreation Snowshoeing, ice skating, golf, tennis, fishing
Amenities & Services Live entertain-

ment, maps, games; catering, celebrating spec. occasions, refrigerator, irons

ACCOMMODATIONS

Units 14 guest rooms, 1 cottage
All Rooms AC, TV/VCR, phone
Some Rooms Pull-out sofa; cottage LR, kitchen, 1.5 baths, 2 BR
Bed & Bath Twin, double, king beds; some tub/shower

Favorites Room 14—relatively large, queen, faces 7 windows, sunny
Comfort & Decor Colonial style w/ antiques, wallpaper, and prints in style of New England farm. Sunny, basic; can be noisy at night.

RATES, RESERVATIONS, & RESTRICTIONS

Deposit 1 night; 14-day cancel. w/ fee
Discounts Off-season, singles, pkgs. (e.g., horse shows); cottage
Credit Cards V, AE, MC
Check-In/Out 12/10:30
Smoking Tavern
Pets No
Kids OK
Minimum Stay 2 nights weekends; 3 on

holiday weekends
Open All year
Hosts Pam and Marty Sweeney
Route 16A, Box T, Main St.,
Jackson, NH 03846
(603) 383-4245 or (800) 228-4245
Fax: (603) 383-6456
wildcat@ncia.net
www.wildcatinnandtavern.com

BUTTONWOOD INN, North Conway

OVERALL ★★★★ | ROOM QUALITY ★★★★ | VALUE ★★½ | PRICE $105–225

Creativity abounds, cute as a button. Sample breakfast entrées "Sunrise Puff," topped with spicy orange sauce, and "To Die for French Toast," baked caramel apple slices and egg-soaked bread topped with spiced apple-sauce. But get serious. An on-site meeting planner takes care of conference details, and candlelight dinners highlight winter Saturdays. Other pluses The pool has a backdrop of old barn foundations. A New England scene borders the walls in the downstairs game room, the upstairs reading room has clouds on the ceiling and a box full of amenities, and the hosts provide day packs for hikers.

SETTING & FACILITIES

Location 16 N to North Conway, 2 mi. from town, on dead-end road
Near Antiquing, beach, museum; 2 1/2 hrs. from Dartmouth, 1.5 from Portland
Building 1820s Cape-style farmhouse

Grounds 17 acres on Mt. Surprise award-winning gardens, pool, trails
Public Space LR, FR, conf. rooms, DR
Food & Drink Full breakfast; hot drinks; spec. diets avail.

Recreation Horses, water/snow sports, tennis, billiards, golf, hiking, canoeing, mountainbiking
Amenities & Services Fridge, day packs, guidebooks, picnic blankets, XC skiing trails, theme weekends; meetings/events (20); fax, dataport, sep. phone line, on-site meeting planner

ACCOMMODATIONS

Units 10 guest rooms
All Rooms Individual decor, quilts, AC
Some Rooms Bath, fireplace, living area, whirlpool
Bed & Bath Queens, many Shaker-style headboards; some claw-foot tubs
Favorites Garden room—tub/shower, garden/pool views, sitting area, AC; Room 9—bright, yellow/white wide-striped paper
Comfort & Decor Country style, wide-pine floors, Shaker furniture, period stenciling, antiques, reading lamps.

RATES, RESERVATIONS, & RESTRICTIONS

Deposit 50%
Discounts Singles, 3rd person, family; packages
Credit Cards V, AE, DC, MC
Check-In/Out 3/11
Smoking No
Pets No
Kids Over 6
Minimum Stay 2 nights winter/holiday weekends
Open All year
Hosts Claudia and Peter Needham
Box 1817, Mt. Surprise Rd.
North Conway, NH 03860-1817
(603) 356-2625 or (800) 258-2625
Fax: (603) 356-3140
innkeeper@buttonwoodinn.com
www.buttonwoodinn.com

FARM BY THE RIVER, North Conway

OVERALL ★★★★ | ROOM QUALITY ★★★★ | VALUE ★★★ | PRICE $75–175

King George III deeded this property on the river to Rick's ancestors in 1771, and it was a dairy farm until 30 years ago. As a kid, Rick helped his grandmother run a boarding house here, so it was a natural for him to create a bed-and-breakfast. The past is evident not just in the beamed barn built in 1772, but in family treasures and old photos, and guest rooms named after ancestors or former guests. Charlene is a landscape architect and artist, and both talents are evident. Today, you can savor Belgian waffles with strawberries and cream by a crackling fire in the dining room, or on the deck overlooking 70 acres and the White Mountains. Then saddle up, or climb up nearby Cathedral Ledge.

SETTING & FACILITIES

Location Rt. 16 to Conway; 2 mi. from village on Saco River, .5 mi. from Echo Lake State Park, on sandy beach
Near Cathedral Ledge, N Conway shopping, Conway Scenic Railroad, Mt. Washington, Story Land, Heritage N.H.

Building White clapboard farmhouse land-granted by King George III; in family since 1771

Grounds 70 acres forest, pasture, gardens w/ pond, barns, deck, maple sugar orchard, 18 horses

Public Space 2 common rooms, DR, deck

Food & Drink Breakfast; specialties: blueberry pancakes, French toast amandine

Recreation Water sports, horseback riding stables, wagon/sleigh rides, XC skiing, snowshoeing onsite; near rock climbing, golf, downhill skiing

Amenities & Services Snowshoes, dinner reservations, maps

ACCOMMODATIONS

Units 10 guest rooms; 5 deluxe rooms; 2 suites

All Rooms Flowers, high ceiling, view, bath, AC

Some Rooms Bath, whirlpool, fireplace

Bed & Bath King/queen, 1 full; 1 bath outside room (sink in room), some tubs

Favorites Mrs. Carrol's—2-person

whirlpool, fireplace, pedestal sink, mountain view

Comfort & Decor Family heirlooms, views of mountains/pastures/horses. Mix of colonial and Victorian. Maple and walnut furniture, Oriental rugs. Good rooms. 2 two-room suites.

RATES, RESERVATIONS, & RESTRICTIONS

Deposit Full payment 1-2 nights; 1st and last nights for 3+; refund w/ 14-day notice

Discounts Singles, 3d person

Credit Cards V, AE, MC

Check-In/Out 4–9/before 10:30

Smoking No

Pets No; in-house dog and horses; kennel 1 mi.

Kids In rooms w/o fireplaces

Minimum Stay Some rooms some

weekends

Open All year

Hosts Charlene and Rick Davis
2555 West Side Rd.
North Conway, NH 03860-5925
(603) 356-2694, 888-414-8353
Fax: (603) 356-2694 (call first)
info@farmbytheriver.com
www.farmbytheriver.com

NERELEDGE INN, North Conway

OVERALL ★★★½ | ROOM QUALITY ★★★ | VALUE ★★★ | PRICE $59–159

Old-fashioned, inexpensive, and informal, this bed-and-breakfast by the river, built in 1787—and an inn for over 100 years—is noted mainly for its hospitality. And then, for its farmhouse breakfasts. The dining room is a cheery cherry-red and white, and you get to choose from a menu including creative omelets—maybe tomato, basil, and ricotta—or chocolate chip pancakes, and definitely dessert: English apple crumble topped with vanilla ice cream. To work this off, rock climbers and fly-fishers take note. Some of the best rock climbing in the East is nearby, and a fishing school is on site on seasonal weekends. The rest of us can bike, hike, canoe, chat with

Valerie and Suzanne by the spinning wheel, or just wait eagerly until the next morning's repast.

SETTING & FACILITIES

Location Rt. 16 into North Conway; 3 min. walk from town, on a quiet road near the Saco River
Near Summer theater, 4 downhill ski resorts, and 1,000-km XC skiing, minutes. away
Building 1787, built by Moses Randall; inn since ca.1922
Grounds 2 acres; lawn; small herb, vegetable, flower gardens
Public Space Entry, breakfast room, old pub room, large sitting room, old DR

Food & Drink Country breakfast; specialties: blueberry pancakes w/ maple syrup, muffins; hot drinks, cookies; spec. diets accom.
Recreation River sports; near rock/ice climbing, golf, tennis, amusement parks, mountain biking
Amenities & Services Grand piano, irons, refrigerator, hairdryer, microwave, XC ski rental nearby; bus pick-up/drop-off; bike/canoe rental; fax, phone, dataport

ACCOMMODATIONS

Units 11 guest rooms
All Rooms Individual country decor, AC
Some Rooms Bath
Bed & Bath Mostly queens, extra beds; firm beds; some half-baths
Favorites 5-dormer, country decor and

floral paper, queen and single beds
Comfort & Decor Simple rooms. Cathedral ledge, mountain views. Informal, but immaculate. Set up especially for groups/families w/ multiple beds in rooms. Reading lights.

RATES, RESERVATIONS, & RESTRICTIONS

Deposit 2 nights; 2-week cancel. policy
Discounts Off-season, midweek, singles, 3rd person, kids ($1 extra for each year)
Credit Cards V, AE, MC, D
Check-In/Out 3/10:30; call for arrival after 10 p.m.
Smoking No
Pets No; will arrange local boarding
Kids Welcome
Minimum Stay Call; generally 2 nights

weekends
Open All year
Hosts Valerie and Suzanne (mother & daughter)
River Rd., Box 547
North Conway, NH 03860-0547
(603) 356-2831
Fax: (603) 356-7085
info@nereledgeinn.com
www.nereledgeinn.com

FOXGLOVE, Sugar Hill

OVERALL ★★★★ | ROOM QUALITY ★★★★ | VALUE ★★★½ | PRICE $85–165

Details, details, details—nine Christmas trees, typed-up day trips, special bedding, extensive lupine gardens—and Janet and Walter are sophisticated and hands-on. Let some of the breakfasts speak for the entire B and B experience: scrambled eggs with chives, corn cob–smoked ham, and fried apples and walnuts; sunflower toast with homemade marmalade; cornmeal pancakes with scallions and corn, sour-cream dill topping, and smoked salmon; lemon-zest popovers; banana-pecan buttermilk pancakes with smoked turkey and mango. Janet is an interior designer with a sensual touch and soft palette, so the look is unusual and eclectic. And, she'll cook dinner.

SETTING & FACILITIES

Location I-93 Exit 38, right on Rt. 18, .25 to Rt. 117 turn left, 2.3 mi. on right, in hilly residential area
Near Franconia Notch, Upper Conn. River, Mt. Washington Valley, cog railway to top of Mt. Washington, summer theater, concerts, museums, covered bridges, Robert Frost's cottage
Building 1898 New England gabled
Grounds 3 acres, lush woodland, quiet glades, terrace, gardens, fountains
Public Space LR, sitting area, DR, 2 glassed-in porches; porch and DR w/ views

Food & Drink Full breakfast; specialties: puffy baked cinnamon-apple pancakes; lunch and dinner by special request (extra); specialties: Belgian carrot soup, grilled salmon fillet, white chocolate tart; spec. diets accom
Recreation Golf, tennis, water/snow sports, balloon/glider/sleigh rides, rock/wall climbing
Amenities & Services Games, 3D puzzles; recipes (cookbook in progress); Internet news daily (European news), meetings (15), fax, dataports; weddings, cycling tours, planned day trips

ACCOMMODATIONS

Units 6 guest rooms
All Rooms Bath
Some Rooms Sitting area
Bed & Bath 1 double, 2 queens, 2 kings, excellent mattresses, some upholstered or antique headboards; some claw-foot tubs, pedestal sinks, glass-enclosed showers
Favorites Mrs. Harmes' Room—turret, 4

lace-curtained windows, maple table from Parisian boudoir; Gingham Room—pastel palette, handpainted beds, antique armoire, "large and creamy" bath
Comfort & Decor Individually decorated, in sophisticated, eclectic style. Attention to detail. Meticulous. New carriage house most private.

RATES, RESERVATIONS, & RESTRICTIONS

Deposit 50%; refund w/10-day notice
Discounts Longer stays, groups, singles
Credit Cards V, MC
Check-In/Out 3/10
Smoking No
Pets No; kennel facilities can be arranged
Kids Over 12
Minimum Stay None

Open All year
Hosts Janet and Walter Boyd
Route 117 at Lovers Lane
Sugar Hill, NH 03585
(603) 823-8840
Fax: (603) 823-5755
foxgloveinn@compuserve.com
www.foxgloveinn.com

SUNSET HILL HOUSE, Sugar Hill

OVERALL ★★★★ | ROOM QUALITY ★★★★ | VALUE ★★★½ | PRICE $85–165

Bought at a foreclosure auction, this once-decrepit inn is a real success story. The family has transformed the old lady, if not again into a grand hotel, at least into a fine inn. Continuous upgrading is turning simple rooms into luxury units, now appealing to romantics as well as to families, golfers, skiers, and conference attendees. The heated pool faces the mountains, where lunch is served in summer. Golf is across the road, and in winter you can cross-country ski or take a horse-drawn sleigh ride over the course. There's lots to do, good food, and comfortable digs—plus, that sunset.

SETTING & FACILITIES

Location Rt. 117 to the top of Sugar Hill, turn on to Sunset Hill Rd.; straddles a 1,700-foot ridge
Near Major downhill ski areas, Franconia Notch State Park (home of NH's Old Man of the Mountains), village center, shopping, antiquing, hiking, golf, XC skiing
Building 1880 three-story 2nd Empire Victorian annex to grand hotel; refurbished 1993, and continuously
Grounds Lawns, gardens, panoramic views
Public Space Three airy fireplace parlors, DRs, tavern, art gallery in hall

Food & Drink Three-course table-side country breakfast; contemporary French-American fine dining; casual meals in the tavern
Recreation Golf, XC skiing, swimming, trails, shopping
Amenities & Services 9-hole course (fees), banquet room (120), heated pool, special packages and events such as wine or cider tastings, Murder Mystery weekends, live entertainment, art and craft workshops; Thanksgiving, Christmas and New Year's celebration

ACCOMMODATIONS

Units 26 guest rooms, 2 suites
All Rooms Bath, view, coordinated fabrics, outgoing phone
Some Rooms Whirlpool, brass bed, fireplace, bay windows, corner tower
Bed & Bath Varied bed sizes; refurbished antique or new fixtures

Favorites Jacuzzi Suite—whirlpool, king/queen; odd-numbered rooms have preferable views
Comfort & Decor Simple, neat. Bay windows, hardwood floors. Refurbished rooms w/ fireplaces, whirlpools. Some rooms spartan, small.

RATES, RESERVATIONS, & RESTRICTIONS

Deposit Last night stay in advance (guaranteed reservation

Discounts Packages, extra person, kids under 12, MAP, military, corporate

Credit Cards V, AE, MC, D

Check-In/Out 3/11

Smoking No

Pets No

Kids OK (prefer not in restaurant under 12)

Minimum Stay 2 nights most

weekends/holidays

Open All year

Hosts Lon and Nancy Henderson, and family

231 Sunset Hill Rd.

Sugar Hill, NH 03585

(800) SUN-HILL or (603) 823-5522

Fax: (603) 823-5738

innkeeper@sunsethillhouse.com

www.sunsethillhouse.com

Vermont

Vermont is classic New England: village greens with white, steepled churches; dirt roads; covered bridges over rushing streams; flaming autumns and winter-wonderland settings; mountains and lakes; rolling farmland punctuated by red barns; maple-sugaring buckets hanging under spigoted trunks; hand-crafted products and fresh local foods. This state is aware that much of its revenue comes from tourism, and it zealously protects its still-undeveloped countryside and rural traditions. After all, neither **Burlington** nor **Montpelier,** its major towns, has even 50,000 residents.

Originally home to the Iroquois and Algonquin Indians, Vermont was settled by Europeans following the explorations of Samuel de Champlain in 1609. The area was a site of the French and Indian War and the American Revolution, where the Green Mountain Boys fought with Ethan Allen and Benedict Arnold. As an independent republic in 1777, the state was the first to prohibit slavery; and, recently, the first to sanction civil rights of gays and lesbians. Presidents Arthur and Coolidge were native Vermonters.

Vermont's mountains, lakes, and winding dirt paths offer bracing outdoor pleasures. The **Green Mountains** became the home of Eastern skiing and the birthplace of the ski tow at pretty **Woodstock** in 1934. With more than 200 inches of annual snowfall, the state caters to the winter sports crowd with vast condo complexes and world-class resorts. Seventeen ski areas include **Killington, Stowe, Mt. Snow, Smuggler's Notch, Jay Peak, Stratton, Sugarbush, Mad River Glen, Okemo, Askutney, Burke,** and **Bromley**. Nine mountains are over 2,000 vertical feet, and there more than 1,000 ski trails.

The state also has 60-plus cross-country centers, with more than 2,000 miles of marked trails over woods and open fields. And there are more than 5,000 miles of marked snowmobile trails. Other winter activities include snowboarding, horse-drawn sleigh rides, ice skating, snowshoeing, and ice fishing. Winter carnivals are popular; check before your visit to see if one is scheduled while you're here.

Lake Champlain, along the state's western border, is another exceptional source of recreation, with fishing, boating, and water activities. Throughout Vermont you'll find more than 400 lakes and ponds and over 5,000 miles of rivers and streams. You can spend a solitary afternoon in a canoe or race in a powerboat. Summer pursuits include camping, golfing, biking, horseback riding, hunting, kayaking, swimming, and tubing.

Artisans have flocked to Vermont for centuries, and the Hitchcock Chair and art glass—still being produced at the **Simon Pearce factory in Quechee**—are just two examples of the high level of craftsmanship. In the same tradition, the **Vermont Teddy Bear Company** has proudly used the state name as a symbol of quality, turning a cozy craft into a world-class business.

Fresh, good foodstuffs made from local products are points of pride, and industries are being developed on coffee, cheddar cheese, maple syrup, and most successfully, **Ben & Jerry's Ice Cream.** But stop at a general stores to sample other local products as well. The **New England Culinary Institute** near Burlington offers elaborate meals prepared by student star-chefs-to-be, who take Vermont cuisine to a new level.

At **Shelburne Farms,** south of Burlington, you can learn about historic farming, dairy farming, and cheesemaking, and visit the bakery. Vermont's official state animal is celebrated here at the **National Museum of the Morgan Horse.** The **UVM Morgan Horse Farm** in **Weybridge** is also worth a trip.

Lodging throughout the state is exceptionally charming and increasingly sophisticated, often set in ski areas or villages that are beauty spots. Many high-powered types dream of retiring to this lovely state and opening the perfect bed-and-breakfast or small inn—and their fulfilled dreams and hard work are yours to enjoy at the end of a glorious drive.

FOR MORE INFORMATION

Vermont Guide
vermontguide.com

Vermont Lodging Directory
vtweb.com/wheretostay/

Southern Vermont

Bucolic, beautiful, old-fashioned, mountain-framed, artsy-craftsy, and relaxing, Southern Vermont stretches from the Massachusetts border in the south to the edge of the Green Mountains/Champlain region to the north. New York forms the western boundary, and New Hampshire lies to the east. I-91, the major thoroughfare, runs near the New Hampshire border and easily connects the Boston area. For Connecticut and New York visitors, Route 7 winds closer to the west, providing a more scenic trip through mountain and river terrain.

Although this southern part of the state is perhaps less revered by expert skiers than northern regions, it offers excellent, family-oriented skiing and snowboarding. **Mt. Snow/Haystack, Magic Mountain, Bromley,** and **Stratton Mountain** are major resorts here, focusing on superb teaching and accessible lifts. During the glorious fall leaf-peeping season, the **Stratton Arts Festival** shows off Vermont arts and crafts, and offers cultural and pops performances.

For invigorating hiking, try **Equinox Mountain, Putney Mountain,** or **Mount Ascutney.** While in **Manchester** you can enjoy the **Manchester Music Festival,** held in July and August, and exceptional, year-round outlet shopping.

Near the **Baltimore Covered Bridge,** the **Eureka Schoolhouse** is an eighteenth-century throwback, complete with old textbooks and antique classroom materials. Throughout Southern Vermont are public libraries and municipal halls, steepled churches, village greens, general stores, small factories, and farmhouses that impart a feeling of a time long gone. Fast-food chains and strip malls are only in a few concentrated areas.

Bennington, with its three covered bridges, fine college, and tradition of arts is an excellent overnight destination. The **Bennington Museum** has an outstanding collection of **Grandma Moses'** paintings as well as regional exhibits, including **Bennington pottery.** The **Bennington Center for the Arts** offers first-rate, year-round exhibits and seasonal plays and musicals.

Nearby in **Wilmington,** you can learn about contemporary Vermont farming at the **Adams Farm.** Further east, visit **Brattleboro,** where Rudyard Kipling wrote the *Just So Stories.* Brattleboro was the first permanent European town in the state, settled in 1724. In **Putney,** a conservative place where summer residents couldn't wear shorts until the 1960s, the kids can check out **Santa's Land,** a Christmas village complete with petting zoo, open seasonally.

Regional foods are a big part of the menus at small restaurants and diners. Indulge at the **Whitingham Sugar Festival** in March, a celebration of maple syrup, or stop in general stores and take some cheese or syrup home.

Lodging in southern Vermont varies from five-star, sophisticated luxury inns to unpretentious family-oriented bed-and-breakfasts. Most lodgings cluster around towns like Manchester or near ski resorts. During ski season and in the fall, lodgings close to the mountains fill up fast.

FOR MORE INFORMATION

Lodging Association of Southern Vermont
www.lodgingvermont.com

INN ON COVERED BRIDGE GREEN, Arlington

OVERALL ★★★★ | ROOM QUALITY ★★★★ | VALUE ★½ | PRICE $140–330

Whether or not you love Norman Rockwell's artistic vision of America, you can't help loving the idea of sleeping in his bedroom, with a view of the covered bridge that gives its name to the property. Rockwell's studio (where his bicycle hangs from the ceiling) also can be rented out as a two-bedroom apartment, and his son's former studio has a loft bedroom with a view. The great illustrator lived here from 1943 to 1954. This centuries-old farmhouse is filled with antiques from world travels. Not surprisingly, Rockwell worked on a series called *The Four Seasons* right here. It just doesn't get more New England.

SETTING & FACILITIES

Location From Rt. 7 or 7A, take Rt. 313 W 5 mi.; left, through covered bridge
Near Village church, Battenkill River, Rockwell Museum, East Arlington, shopping, restaurants
Building 209-year-old farmhouse; two studios
Grounds Over 5 acres, on river; maple trees, apple orchards, gardens, tennis court; 360-degree mountain and meadow views
Public Space Library, DR

Food & Drink Full communal gourmet country breakfast; specialties: baked French toast w/ caramel pecan topping and maple syrup; whole wheat applechunk pancakes; quiches, fritatas, homebaked goods
Recreation Tennis, fishing, canoeing, downhill and XC skiing, ice-skating, snowshoeing, sleigh rides
Amenities & Services Games, books, puzzles, concierge services, requests

ACCOMMODATIONS

Units 4 rooms, 2 studios
All Rooms Private Bath, queen beds antiques, AC
Some Rooms Skylight, gas fireplace
Bed & Bath Four-posters; some whirlpools, some tubs
Favorites Spooners Room—formerly

Norman Rockwell's BR; four-poster rice bed, fireplace, view of bridge, AC
Comfort & Decor Charm and a feel of historic interest. Good views. Fine antiques. Rooms adaptable for suites. Studio: rustic, former grain shed, with beams, ladder to loft.

RATES, RESERVATIONS, & RESTRICTIONS

Deposit Credit card or check for first night; refund (less 10%) w/ 14-day notice
Discounts Long stay
Credit Cards V, MC; personal and

travelers checks, cash
Check-In/Out 3/11
Smoking No
Pets In studios

Kids OK
Minimum Stay 2/3 nights some weekends, holidays (foliage); subject to change
Open All year
Hosts Clint and Julia Dickens
3587 River Rd.

Arlington, VT 05250
(800) 726-9480 or (802) 375-9489
Fax: (802) 375-1208
cbg@sover.net
www.coveredbridgegreen.com

HUGGING BEAR INN, Chester

OVERALL ★★★½ | ROOM QUALITY ★★★ | VALUE ★★★½ | PRICE $90–135

Bears perch on the porch, stare mutely out the windows, poke through the banisters, sit at the piano, grin from fabrics, and wait on every bed. In firefighter costumes, as bride and groom, on the antlers in the entry, propped on shelves and chairs—a veritable plethora of huggable stuffed ones. Over 10,000 bear-related items are in the shop, plus reading matter, and accessories. Georgette is famous for "puppet acting during breakfast" in this relaxed, family-oriented Victorian on the green. Little kids and kids at heart will love this place, but you may just have to grin and bear it.

SETTING & FACILITIES

Location On the green, near a cemetery with Revolutionary War gravestones
Near Summer theater, Vermont Stoneworks, galleries, shops, ski areas
Building 1850 Victorian w/ turret; transformed 1882
Grounds Small, green as front yard
Public Space Entry, turret room, breakfast room, library, LR, front porch

Food & Drink Full breakfast in DR, communal; specialties: blueberry pancakes, French toast, afternoon refreshments
Recreation Golf, fishing, tennis, swimming, biking, skiing, sledding, games, shopping
Amenities & Services Games, puzzles, books, piano, lawn games, gift shop

ACCOMMODATIONS

Units 6
All Rooms Bath, bears
Some Rooms AC, extra bed
Bed & Bath King, queens, doubles, twins; cots if needed
Favorites Tower Room—queen, roundish room, views of Main St. and village green; Pooh Room—furnished with

fabric of Winnie the Pooh characters
Comfort & Decor Teddy bears everywhere. Bears in every bed, bear motifs for rooms. Combination of 19th century and modern decor, original woodwork. Comfortable, child-friendly. Bright, airy.

RATES, RESERVATIONS, & RESTRICTIONS

Deposit Credit card for deposit, refund w/ 14-day notice

Discounts Singles, long stays, gift shop (good for 30 days after departure)

Credit Cards V, AE, MC, D
Check-In/Out 2/11
Smoking No
Pets No; one cat in residence
Kids Welcome
Minimum Stay 2 nights weekends
Open All year except Thanksgiving,
Christmas Day

Host Georgette Thomas
244 Main St.
Chester, VT 05143
(802) 875-2412 or (800) 325-0519
Fax: (802) 875-3823
georgette@huggingbear.com,
inn@huggingbear.com (reservations)
www.huggingbear.com

ROWELL'S INN, Andover

OVERALL ★★★ | ROOM QUALITY ★★★★ | VALUE ★★½ | PRICE $120–205

Built in 1820 as a stagecoach stop called The Simonsville Hotel by Major
Edward Simon (for whom the hamlet also was named), this handsome
brick building was later a general store and post office. When F. A. Rowell
came along 100 years later, he added the tin ceiling and cherry and maple
flooring. Louise. a West Coast transplant, carries on the tradition.

SETTING & FACILITIES

Location 7 mi. west of Chester on
Rt. 11, in tiny hamlet
Near Brook, country road, summer the-
ater, shopping, Weston Priory; Okemo,
Stratton, Magic, and Bromley mountains
Building 1820 brick Greek Revival Fed-
eral stagecoach hotel; 2nd- and 3rd-floor
porch on Nat'l Register of Historic
Places
Grounds Gardens, mature trees, bor-
dered by Lyman Brook, on road
Public Space Sunroom, parlor, DR, full-
service bar, front porch, patio

Food & Drink (MAP) Full country-
breakfast; specialties: Eggnog French
toast, Eggs Benedict, Apricot scones; 4-
course set menu w/ one entrée; beer and
wine list; assortment of tea; specialties:
Cognac glazed game hen, Caramel-Fudge
Pecan pie
Recreation cross country and Alpine
skiing, golf, tennis, fishing, hiking
Amenities & Services Games, fireplaces, full service bar; afternoon cheese
and crackers

ACCOMMODATIONS

Units 7 guest rooms
All Rooms Bath, featherbeds, com-
forters
Some Rooms Fireplace, porch
Bed & Bath Double, queen, king; some
brass, some extra beds; sinks in rooms,
some claw foot tubs
Favorites #1—queen, wood-burning

fireplace, soaking tub, no shower; 3rd
floor room—largest, 2 beds, claw-foot
tub, once part of ballroom
Comfort & Decor Individually decorated w/ antiques in period style. Rooms
in back quietest. Homey, comfortable,
unpretentious. Good lighting. Country
charm.

RATES, RESERVATIONS, & RESTRICTIONS

Deposit 1 night; refund (less 10% admin. fee) w/ 14-day notice; during peak-season, room must be re-rented for refund

Discounts AAA, senior

Credit Cards V, AE, MC, D preferred

Check-In/Out 3/11

Smoking No

Pets No

Kids 12 and up

Minimum Stay 2 or 3 nights weekends, some holidays

Open All year, except part of April and November.

Host Louise Riehl-Haley
1834 Simonsville Rd.
Andover, VT 05143
(802) 875-3658 or (800) 728-0842 for reservations
Fax: (802) 875-3680
innkeep@rowellsinn.com
www.rowellsinn.com

CORNUCOPIA OF DORSET, Dorset

OVERALL ★★★★½ | ROOM QUALITY ★★★★★ | VALUE ★★½ | PRICE $125–225

In a gracious, idyllic village where the sidewalks are made of marble and the former quarry—the country's oldest—is now a swimming hole, this late-nineteenth-century house fits right in. Its patio is made of marble, but more special than its surfaces are its services—a bouquet of thoughtful touches to make guests feel truly pampered. You can have coffee in your room, a cooked-to-order breakfast whenever you want, deluxe baths, and help with touring, finding restaurants for dinner, and other needs. The cottage suite is especially luxurious, but all rooms are lovely, and true to its name, this inn is brimming with good things

SETTING & FACILITIES

Location 6 mi. N of Manchester on Rt. 30, near village church

Near Galleries, shops, antiquing, theater, Robert Todd Lincoln's "Hildene," Hunter Park (Vermont Symphony summer home), Southern Vermont Art Center, outlets

Building 1880 Colonial, white clapboard, plus additions

Grounds 3-season lush gardens, marble patio

Public Space Library, LR, solarium, covered porch

Food & Drink Wake-up tray of tea, coffee, flowers; candlelight breakfast; specialties: pear-almond breakfast pudding, cinnamon-apple puff pancakes; wines, champagnes; sweets/hot drinks; wine, champagne (extra)

Recreation Winter and water sports, hay/sleigh rides, horseback riding

Amenities & Services Champagne welcome; cookies, chocolates, fruit in rooms on arrival; kitchen privileges; video library, iron; daily papers, books, recipes, fax, turndown; pick-up at bus, bike rental nearby

ACCOMMODATIONS

Units 4 guest rooms, 1 cottage suite

All Rooms Bath, AC, sitting area, deluxe toiletries, magnifying mirror, robes, phone, dataport, clock/radio and/or cassette player, hairdryer, area guides

Some Rooms fireplace (4); stereo, cable, desk, loft, skylight, LR, kitchen, patio, French doors, cathedral ceiling

Bed & Bath Queen, king, some four-posters, canopies; full baths

Favorites Green Peak—great garden view, country decor, pencil-post queen, sitting area, corner stove fireplace; Cottage Suite—beamed cathedral, loft BR, skylight, kitchen, patio

Comfort & Decor Spacious, comfortable rooms named after Dorset Mountains. Some built-in bookshelves. Good lighting. Blend of antiques, fine reproductions, and art. Handpainted touches, fresh flowers.

RATES, RESERVATIONS, & RESTRICTIONS

Deposit 50% or 1 night w/in 5 days; refund w/ 14- or 30-day notice

Discounts Off-season, midweek, longer stays

Credit Cards V, AE, MC

Check-In/Out 3–10/11

Smoking No

Pets No; nearby boarding

Kids Over 16

Minimum Stay 2 nights weekends, peak periods; 3 nights holidays

Open All year; closed Christmas Eve/Day, 3 days following Labor Day, part of April

Hosts Linda and Bill Ley
Box 307, Rt. 30
Dorset, VT 05251
(802) 867-5751 or (800) 566-5751
Fax: (802) 867-5753
cornucop@vermontel.com,
innkeeper@cornucopiaofdorset.com
www.cornucopiaofdorset.com

INN AT WOODCHUCK HILL FARM, *Grafton*

OVERALL ★★★★ | ROOM QUALITY ★★★★ | VALUE ★★ | PRICE $89–275

Gabriel family members grew up in this understated hilltop house, built in 1790 for the town's first minister. An antique shop was once in the barn, which is now restored into rustically elegant suites. The main house is a beauty, filled with antiques, books, family belongings, and art pieces. Two other outbuildings offer more private accommodations. The porch overlooks miles of Vermont countryside, and a swimming pond beyond the barn has a dock for sunning. Nearby are a gazebo and a sauna, heated by wood cut from orchards on the 200-acre spread. This is a special retreat in a truly lovely New England village.

SETTING & FACILITIES

Location About 2 mi. up the hill from village, at end of country road, on left
Near Shopping in historic Grafton Village, galleries
Building Restored 1790 Colonial farmhouse
Grounds 200 acres: woods, fields, country lanes, barn, pond, swimming area, gazebo, sauna/steam room, apple orchard

Public Space Open porch, large lounge
Food & Drink Breakfast specialties: French toast, homemade jams; wines, local beers on porch or in lounge; Grafton cheddar cheese, crackers
Recreation Tennis, sledding, ice-skating, snow shoeing, XC skiing
Amenities & Services Bike rental, books, menus, play equipment

ACCOMMODATIONS

Units Main House: 6 guest rooms, 1 studio suite, 1 suite; Barn: 1 suite, 1 guest room, 1 residence (4 person max.); 1 cottage (7 person max.)
All Rooms Sitting area
Some Rooms Bath, fireplace, kitchen (rooms with kitchens, breakfast en suite), corner rooms, priv. entrance, coffee maker, deck, multiple rooms, parking
Bed & Bath Beds vary, some canopies,

extra beds; tiled baths
Favorites Frank Gabriel's room—2nd floor, window walls, twin beds, fireplace, secretary w/ boyhood books
Comfort & Decor Light and airy w/ country antiques, some meadow and mountain views. Barn has original beams. Some skylights. 3rd floor room smaller, under eaves.

RATES, RESERVATIONS, & RESTRICTIONS

Deposit 1 night or 50% (3+ nights); refund w/ 14-day notice
Discounts 1 night free w/ weekly rental
Credit Cards V, AE, MC, D
Check-In/Out 1/11

Smoking No
Pets No
Kids OK
Minimum Stay Varies; call for info

Open All year; dates closed varies
Hosts Marilyn and Mark Gabriel
244 Woodchuck Hill Rd..
Grafton, VT 05146

(802) 843-2398
info@woodchuckhill.com,
mmggabri@sover.net
www.woodchuckhill.com

ANDRIE ROSE INN, Ludlow

OVERALL ★★★½ | ROOM QUALITY ★★★★ | VALUE ★ | PRICE $80–650

You enter through the granite-countered kitchen, which emphasizes the informality of this bed-and-breakfast complex. For groups, there's a conference room; for those in the main house, a full breakfast in the cheerful pink-and-blue dining room. For skiers at Okemo Mountain who want informal atmosphere and an in-town location, this is the best bet, especially for those staying a week or so. You can walk easily to the shops, entertainment, and restaurants of this popular ski town. There is a frequent, free shuttle to the mountain; and hot chocolate and snacks are waiting when you come back from a day on the slopes. The street name is appropriate.

SETTING & FACILITIES

Location Quiet street .25 mile from Okemo Mountain; off Rt. 131, one block N of only stoplight in town
Near Arts and crafts fairs, 5 ski resorts, antique shows, music festivals, shopping and outlets, lakes, waterfalls w/ swimming holes
Building 4 early 1800s buildings at base of Okemo Mountain; Greek Revival, Federal style, Victorian
Grounds Multilevel rose garden, flower boxes; small area
Public Space LR, sunroom, porches, kitchen entrance
Food & Drink Full candlelight breakfast; specialties: buttermilk waffles w/ Ben & Jerry's ice cream, cinnamon-walnut French toast w/ maple syrup; cookies, snacks, hot/cold drinks, cocktail hour w/ local cheese, grapes, bread, crackers; full liquor license
Recreation Golf, tennis, horseback riding, ice-skating, sleigh rides
Amenities & Services Personal welcome notes, chocolate mints, maps, turndown, shuttle to Okemo Mountain

ACCOMMODATIONS

Units 9 guest rooms in main lodge; 2 luxury, 2 family suites in guesthouse; 3 suites in Victorian townhouse; 7 solitude luxury suites
All Rooms Bath, toiletries, local info.
Some Rooms Skylight, library, fireplace, kitchen, AC
Bed & Bath King (suites), hairdryer; some whirlpool/showers, pedestal sinks
Favorites Solitude luxury suites—fireplace, CDs, VCR, whirlpool, refrigerator
Comfort & Decor Antiques, skylights, whirlpools, Main house rooms small but cozy

RATES, RESERVATIONS, & RESTRICTIONS

Deposit 50% w/in 7 days; $200 deposit for family suites; refund w/ 14 day notice
Discounts Midweek, off-season, seniors; family suites $200–430, sleep 4–6; townhouses $200–650, sleep 10–12; breakfast not included for family suites, Victorian suites (w/ kitchens)
Credit Cards V, AE, MC
Check-In/Out 3/11
Smoking No
Pets No

Kids Guest house, Victorian buildings
Minimum Stay 2 nights winter, summer, fall
Open All year
Hosts Michael and Irene Matson
13 Pleasant St.
Ludlow, VT 05149
(802) 228-4846 or (800) 223-4846
Fax: (802) 228-7910
andrie@mail.tds.net
www.bbonline.com/vt/andrierose

THE GOVERNOR'S INN, Ludlow

OVERALL ★★★★ | ROOM QUALITY ★★★★ | VALUE ★★ | PRICE $105–315

Indeed, this award-winning bed-and-breakfast was once the home of Governor Stickney, and a marbleized slate fireplace dominating the parlor harkens to the turn of the century. Today, this small inn is renowned for "Vermont's Best Apple Pie" (often a fruit course at breakfast) and for fabulous food, including gourmet picnics. Both hosts trained in Europe and give cooking classes. The dining area is the epicenter: tables set formally, augmented by classical music, candlelight, crystal, and linen. The six-course dinners have been consumed by residents of the White House, Paul Newman, and Robert Redford, and none have complained.

SETTING & FACILITIES

Location East of town green on Main St., one mi. from Okemo Mountain, east of intersection of Rt. 103 and 1100 south
Near Calvin Coolidge birthplace, antiquing, shopping, theater, Priory
Building 1890 Victorian
Grounds Small yard
Public Space Foyer, parlor, lounge, DR, breakfast room
Food & Drink (B&B and MAP) Full breakfast; specialties: "Cuckoo's Nest" (a personal soufflé) with apple smoked bacon, apple pie stuffed French toast

afternoon; tea; dinner by reservation Thu.–Sun., 6-courses; a specialties: Pepper Crusted Beef, Tenderloin w/ portabello Cabernet sauce, Venison medallions w/ madeira and demi-glace sauce; apricot Victorian dessert; gourmet picnic baskets; full bar
Recreation Canoeing, golf, fishing, horses, skiing, front porch rocking, nearby XC and downhill skiing, cooking seminars held at Inn
Amenities & Services House chocolates, evening turn-down

ACCOMMODATIONS

Units 8 guest rooms, 1 suite
All Rooms Bath, AC, robes, toiletries, butler's basket
Some Rooms Whirlpool, sitting area, Vermont Castings gas stove
Bed & Bath Beds all sizes; some brass; showers, some w/ tubs

Favorites #5—tranquil, garden view, queen w/ large head/footboard, sitting area
Comfort & Decor Individually decorated. Lace curtains, antique armoires, bedside lamps. Smallish, stylish

RATES, RESERVATIONS, & RESTRICTIONS

Deposit First night; full refund w/ 7- to 14-day notice (seasonal)
Discounts Singles, longer stays, seasonal pkgs
Credit Cards V, AE, MC, D
Check-In/Out 2-6/11
Smoking No
Pets No
Kids Over 12

Minimum Stay Winter weekends
Open Closed Dec. 23-26
Hosts Cathy and Jim Kubec
86 Main St.
Ludlow, VT 05149-1113
(802) 228-8830 or (800) GOVERNOR
Fax: (802) 228-2961
kubec@thegovernorsinn.com
www.thegovernorsinn.com

1811 HOUSE, Manchester

OVERALL ★★★★ | ROOM QUALITY ★★★★ | VALUE ★★½ | PRICE $120–230

Except for the 30 years when it was the home of President Lincoln's granddaughter, Mary Lincoln Isham, the main house has been an inn since 1811. It was built in 1770 and retains a dark, low-ceilinged look, with wainscoting, Oriental rugs over hardwood floors, and an outstanding array of Early

American furnishings. The beamed tavern offers a dartboard and a wide selection of Scottish malt whiskies, and you can chat with Marnie and Bruce while they tend bar, or you can pick up cookies in the kitchen. Named after prominent Manchester residents including Charles Orvis of fly-fishing fame, the guest rooms vary widely in size, but all are meticulous and decorated in fine period style. The terraced gardens and the view of golf greens and mountains beyond are also exceptional.

SETTING & FACILITIES

Location Center of village opposite Equinox Hotel; adjacent to church
Near Antiquing, historic sites, museums, nature areas, Southern Vermont Art Center, Fly Fishing Museum
Building 1761 Colonial; Nat'l Historic Register
Grounds 7.5 acres, gardens, terraces, pond, herb garden
Public Space Pub, 2 sitting rooms w/ fireplaces, rec room
Food & Drink Full breakfast; specialty: 1811 House French Toast, full English breakfast; chocolate chip cookies; sherry; special meals
Recreation Water/snow sports, golf, hunting, horseback riding, tennis
Amenities & Services Kitchen privileges, videos, use of Equinox Hotel's spa and facilities

ACCOMMODATIONS

Units 13 guest rooms, 1 suite
All Rooms Bath, AC, period pieces, seating area, reading light
Some Rooms Fireplace; sitting room (1), porch (1), priv. staircase (1)
Bed & Bath Doubles, queens, kings, canopies, four-posters; claw-foot tubs, sep. showers, large showerheads
Favorites Robert Todd Lincoln—canopy four-poster, fireplace, slate mantel; Henry and Ethel Robinson—marble shower, claw-foot tub, porch, great view of gardens/mountains
Comfort & Decor Elegant yet relaxed w/ Oriental rugs, fireplaces, period antiques, paintings. Some original windows, beams. Some mountain views. Can be cramped, but cozy under eaves. Good lighting.

RATES, RESERVATIONS, & RESTRICTIONS

Deposit 1 night; refund w/ 14-day notice
Discounts Corp., off-season
Credit Cards V, AE, MC, D
Check-In/Out 2/11
Smoking No
Pets No; 2 in-house cats
Kids Over 16
Minimum Stay 2 nights weekends
Open All year
Hosts Marnie and Bruce Duff, Cathy and Jorge Veleta
Rt. 7A, Box 39
Manchester, VT 05254
(802) 362-1811 or (800) 432-1811
Fax: (802) 362-2443
stay1811@vermontel.net
www.1811house.com

THE INN AT ORMSBY HILL, *Manchester Center*

OVERALL ★★★★½ | ROOM QUALITY ★★★★★ | VALUE ★½ | PRICE $190–370

History resonates throughout this superb bed-and-breakfast, named after Gideon Ormsby, local Revolutionary War hero. The basement contains one of the earliest jail cells in Manchester, bars intact. Ethan Allen hid in the smoke room during the Revolutionary War, and it may have been a safe house for the Underground Railroad. More? A former owner was in law practice with Lincoln's son, and President Taft stayed here. Today, you can enjoy rare books, classical music, hooked rugs made by Ted's mother, and a gourmet breakfast in the dramatic, sunny conservatory—with dessert from renowned chef Chris. In fact, their cereal recipe has been adapted commercially.

SETTING & FACILITIES

Location Historic Rt. 7A S, 2 mi. W of town center

Near Bromley and Stratton mountains, shopping, barn sales, auctions, Southern Vermont Art Center, antiquing

Building 1764 restored Manor house

Grounds 2.5 acres: gardens, mountain views

Public Space LR, gathering room, conservatory, TV room, porch w/ hammock

Food & Drink Breakfast, either full or buffet, breakfast dessert; specialties: risotto w/ bacon and egg, baked pancakes, scrambled eggs in puffed pastry, basil scrambled eggs on Portobello mushrooms; advance notice for special diets

Recreation Swimming, golf, horseback riding, fly-fishing, all winter sports

Amenities & Services Homemade cookies on arrival, irons, refrigerator, bike/XC ski rental nearby; small conferences, weddings (20) if whole inn reserved

ACCOMMODATIONS

Units 10 guest rooms

All Rooms Bath, fireplace, AC, clock/radio, phone, dataport, hairdryer, robe, guest journal

Some Rooms Priv. entrance, deck, disabled access

Bed & Bath Queens, kings, most canopy; all rooms dbl. whirlpools, some showers w/ seat

Favorites Tower Room—newest, turret, desk, views, sitting area, queen bow-top canopy, tiled bath, dbl. shower, multi-leveled; Taft—largest room, vaulted wooden ceiling, brass chandelier, king canopy, afternoon sun, desk, sitting area, dbl. shower

Comfort & Decor Romantic and comfortable, w/ rubber duckies and candlelight for whirlpools, details like beamed ceiling from 1764. Fireplaces seen from beds, whirlpools. Not much missing.

RATES, RESERVATIONS, & RESTRICTIONS

Deposit 50%; refund w/ 10-day notice
Discounts Midweek, corp.
Credit Cards V, MC, D
Check-In/Out 3–9/11
Smoking No; $100 fee for smoking
Pets No
Kids No
Minimum Stay 2 nights weekends, some holidays

Open All year
Hosts Chris and Ted Sprague
Historic Rt. 7A
Manchester Center, VT 05255
(802) 362-1163 or (800) 670-2841
Fax: (802) 362-5176
stay@ormsbyhill.com
www.ormsbyhill.com

THE RELUCTANT PANTHER, *Manchester Village*

OVERALL ★★★★ | ROOM QUALITY ★★★★ | VALUE ★★ | PRICE $139–339

Upgrading continues at this popular, purple-hued inn, originally home to the village blacksmith. Common rooms are few, but the focus is on dining and guest rooms. Lavish suites with two-way gas fireplaces, terra-cotta and marble floors, and a marble terrace are especially sought-after. Swiss-born Robert was food and beverage director at The Plaza in New York City, and the ambitious restaurant is in a trio of rooms, including a greenhouse. If you're a traditionalist, you'll prefer nearby 1811 House; sybarites who like the feel of a small, luxury hotel will seek this Panther, and with no reluctance.

SETTING & FACILITIES

Location About 1 block from village green
Near Bromley and Stratton mountains, shopping, barn sales, auctions, Southern Vermont Art Center, antiquing

Building 1850s 3-story purple-hued main house
Grounds Annuals/perennials, old maples, marble sidewalks

Public Space Panther bar, restaurant, greenhouse, marble patio
Food & Drink (MAP) 3-course breakfast; specialties: pancakes, cinnamon-amaretto French toast; dinner (reservations) Thurs.–Mon., 7 days foliage/holidays, weekends only in winter; American, Swiss specialties: raclette, osso buco, Wiener schnitzel; wine list
Recreation Swimming, horses, fly-fishing, tennis, golf, XC skiing (extra)
Amenities & Services Welcome gifts (wine), in-room safety deposit boxes, access to Equinox Hotel spa facilities, turn-down, concierge, priv. DR (25)

ACCOMMODATIONS

Units 21 guest rooms, suites
All Rooms Bath, phone, TV, climate controls, soft colors
Some Rooms Fireplace, Jacuzzi for two, AC, Vermont Castings stove, desk
Bed & Bath Kings, queens; luxury baths

Favorites Mark Skinner Suite—fireplaces in bed and bath, 2-pers. whirlpool
Comfort & Decor Antiques, some luxury-papered, size varies. Locally handcrafted furnishings. Reading lamps. Mainly village views. Plush.

RATES, RESERVATIONS, & RESTRICTIONS

Deposit Full payment 1 night; refund w/ 10-day notice
Discounts 20% off regular rates during "quiet season(s)."
Credit Cards V, AE, MC, D
Check-In/Out 3/11; to 6 p.m. (for a fee)
Smoking No
Pets No
Kids Over 14
Minimum Stay 2 nights most weekends, 3 nights holidays
Open All year
Hosts Maye and Robert Bachofen
1 West Rd.
Manchester Village, VT 05254-0678
(802) 362-2568 or (800) 822-2331
Fax: (802) 362-2586
stay@reluctantpanther.com
www.reluctantpanther.com

FOUR COLUMNS INN, Newfane

OVERALL ★★★★½ | ROOM QUALITY ★★★★★ | VALUE ★★ | PRICE $115–340

Washington may not have slept or dined here, but Henry Kissinger, Mick Jagger, Tom Cruise, Michael Douglas, Paul Newman, Nicole Kidman, John Irving, Ron Howard, and John Kenneth Galbraith have, among many others. Star chef Greg Parks is constantly tweaking the renowned menu, which features delectable dishes from venison loin and sweetbreads to Chilean sea bass. Snow tubing, a swimming pool, and a stream beckon guests on breaks from dining in the beamed barn. Not much is newfangled at Newfane. It's just old-fashioned pleasures and surprising warmth in this uncommonly good columned inn on the most photographed village common in Vermont.

SETTING & FACILITIES

Location 12 mi. N of Brattleboro on Rt. 30, behind courthouse, on historic town common

Near Shopping in Newfane, antiquing, beach, museum, outlets, theater

Building 1832 Greek Revival manor; Nat'l Historic Register

Grounds 150 acres, pool, stream, 2 ponds, trails, woods, gardens

Public Space Restaurant; LR; tavern w/ full-service pewter bar, deck; 3 porches

Food & Drink Buffet breakfast, including homebaked breads, hot entrée, oatmeal, fresh OJ; dinner, blend of New American, French, Asian; specialties: Black Angus sirloin w/ portobella mushrooms and sweet & sour dipping sauce, Chilean sea bass marinated in miso, soy and ginger; wine list online; special meals accom

Recreation Winter sports, sleigh rides, golf, mountain biking, hiking, canoeing, swimming, fishing, board games

Amenities & Services Computer, some disabled access, bike rental nearby, weddings, special occasions, fax, secretarial services, conferences, copier

ACCOMMODATIONS

Units 4 standard rooms, 5 deluxe, 6 suites

All Rooms Bath, AC, alarm clock, radio, phone

Some Rooms Fireplace, 2-person whirlpool, sitting room, couch, wide pine floors, vaulted ceiling, fireplace in bath, skylight, ceiling fan

Bed & Bath Queens and kings, canopies, four-posters, irons; bath and a half, dbl. whirlpools, some showers only, dbl. sinks

Favorites Deluxe Suite 3—queen, 2 rooms, Rice four-poster, pink marbled bath, gas fireplace in bath, dbl. whirlpool; #16—Queen brass, tub, in garden wing, sliding glass doors, reading area, gas fireplace

Comfort & Decor Lots of antiques. Plants, bedside lights, lots of natural light. Former parlor turned into huge suite. Top floor suite, 2-person Jacuzzi, overlooking common.

RATES, RESERVATIONS, & RESTRICTIONS

Deposit 1 night or 50%; refund w/ 14-day notice

Discounts Off-season pkgs

Credit Cards V, AE, DC, MC

Check-In/Out 2/11

Smoking No

Pets OK w/ prior approval

Kids Welcome

Minimum Stay 2 nights most week-
ends, 3 nights some holidays
Open All year, except Christmas Day
Hosts Pam and Gorty Baldwin
Box 278, West St.

Newfane, VT 05345
(800) 787-6633 or (802) 365-7713
Fax: (802) 365-0022
innkeeper@fourcolumnsinn.com
www.fourcolumnsinn.com

HICKORY RIDGE HOUSE, Putney

OVERALL ★★★½ | ROOM QUALITY ★★★ | VALUE ★★ | PRICE $95–300

Once a college president's home, this Federal manor looks out over acres of
country lawns through a Palladian window. For music, there's a piano for
guests. Despite many shared baths, it offers quiet pleasures at a good price.
A few minutes' walk away is an old-fashioned swimming hole (more special
than a heated pool). The Connecticut River is a short drive down a country
road, where you can canoe, fish, walk along the shores, or loll in the sun.
Good restaurants are nearby, and you can ski the fields under moonlight.
One of the bedrooms has an original fireplace and a headboard created
from a choir stall.

SETTING & FACILITIES

Location 2 mi. from Putney on country
hillside; 3 mi. off I-91 Exit 4
Near Shopping in Putney and Brattleboro, theater, antiquing, crafts, music festival; 2 mi. from Connecticut River; 45 min.
to Stratton
Building 1808 brick Federal country
manor; Nat'l Register of Historic Places
Grounds 8 acres on hillside: country,
quiet road, meadows, gardens
Public Space Common rooms, upstairs
sitting room, deck
Food & Drink Full breakfast, home-
grown herbs, local products; specialties:
fresh egg dishes (from on-site chickens),
hot applesauce, stollen
Recreation Swimming, canoeing, kayaking, skiing
Amenities & Services TV, refrigerator;
weddings, receptions, small
conferences, business services; disabled
accessible room

ACCOMMODATIONS

Units 6 guest rooms, 1 cottage
All Rooms Individually decorated,
antiques and reproductions
Some Rooms Fireplace (5); cottage w/
2 BRs, LR, deck, kitchen, fireplace
Bed & Bath Queens, kings, sleigh beds,
cribs, comforters, quilts, coverlets, line-
dried sheets; 3 baths
Favorites Federal rooms—4 original
BRs, spacious, Rumford fireplaces,
antiques
Comfort & Decor Individually decorated in period decor. Airy, comfortable,
pretty colors. Rooms in original house
preferred. Families can reserve newer
wing. Lemon room w/ whimsical choir
stall headboard. 1st-floor room disabled
access, w/ fireplace. Well-maintained

RATES, RESERVATIONS, & RESTRICTIONS

Deposit Credit card number; refund w/ 10-day notice

Discounts 3rd person, singles, for long stays

Credit Cards V, AE, MC

Check-In/Out 3–7/11

Smoking No

Pets No

Kids OK

Minimum Stay 2 days cottage; call for

minimums for holidays or peak times

Open All year

Hosts Linda and Jack Bisbee

RR 3, Box 1410

Putney, VT 05346

(800) 380-9218 or (802) 387-5709

Fax: (802) 387-5387

hickory@sover.net

www.hickoryridgehouse.com

THE INN AT WEATHERSFIELD, *Weathersfield*

OVERALL ★★★★ | ROOM QUALITY ★★★★ | VALUE ★★ | PRICE $185–225

Ghosts reside in this columned, country property filled with stenciled walls and family antiques. It was a stagecoach inn and a stop on the Underground Railroad—a hiding place for slaves fleeing to Canada before the Civil War. Today, you may just want to hide away for other reasons: poetry readings at breakfast, a wassail cup in a keeping-room cauldron, guest rooms named Wuthering Heights and Tara, with canopy beds, fireplaces, and mountain views. (Weddings are popular here.) But it's the food that is most notable—fresh, seasonal, and highly original—served by a warm staff, by candlelight flickering in the beamed, low-ceiling dining room.

SETTING & FACILITIES

Location Half-mile S of Perkinsville on Rt. 106, set back on a tree-lined drive, off a hilly country road

Near Conn. River, country stores, covered bridge, cheese and syrup factories, glass blowing; Springfield

Building 1780s farmhouse, since expanded, w/ attached barn

Grounds 21 acres, lawn, old lumber trails, pines, English gardens, pond, amphitheater

Public Space Gathering room, keeping room, parlor, taproom, carriage house DR, game room, front porch, green house

Food & Drink Full breakfast w/ poetry readings; four diamond à la carte dining, menu changes nightly, open to public; specialties: Dijon Rack of Lamb, salmon Wellington, sour cream blueberry pie; award-winning wine list; piano entertainment; tea, popcorn

Recreation Skiing, golf, water sports, berry picking, sleigh/carriage rides

Amenities & Services Pool table, exercise equipment, lawn games, movies; receptions, business events; turn-down, tour guidance, some disabled access, airport pickup

ACCOMMODATIONS

Units 9 guest rooms, 3 suites
All Rooms Bath, desk, Colonial trimmings, phone
Some Rooms Fireplace (8); sitting
room, balcony
Bed & Bath Beds vary, some canopies;
some claw-foot tubs, whirlpool, low ceilings, some tiny
Favorites Tara—large corner room,
main house, wide floorboards, four-

poster; Bridal Suite—3rd floor, highly
romantic and private.
Comfort & Decor Rooms, from
Wuthering Heights to Tara, named and
decorated after love stories. Handmade
quilts, wide plank floors, antiques. Rooms
in new wing smaller, more country style.
Main house, more character, noisier during dinner; new wing, old tubs, fireplaces.

RATES, RESERVATIONS, & RESTRICTIONS

Deposit 1 night; refund w/ 14-day notice
Discounts Off-season, 3rd person, sin-
gles, groups, multiple nights, business,
packages, B&B rates
Credit Cards V, AE, DC, MC, D
Check-In/Out 2/11
Smoking No
Pets No
Kids Over 8

Minimum Stay 2 or 3 nights some
weekends and holidays
Open All year
Hosts Mary and Terry Carter
Rt. 106, Box 164
Weathersfield, VT 05151
(802) 263-9217 or (800) 477-4828
Fax: (802) 263-9219
www.weathersfieldinn.com

INN AT SAW MILL FARM, West Dover

OVERALL ★★★★★ | ROOM QUALITY ★★★★★ | VALUE ★ | PRICE $360–495

On a whim, these famed innkeepers bought the farm, so to speak, in 1967,
and decided to create an inn. Rodney is an architect, Ione a decorator, and
son Brill a chef—so how could they go wrong? The Williamses are pioneers
in establishing the kind of elegant, expensive inn that sophisticated travelers
now demand, such as The Mayflower in Connecticut or The White Barn in
Maine. The atmosphere is mellow, with no TVs or phones in rooms, yet
slightly formal, so that you can show off your casual designer clothes. Copper collections glow in candle and firelight, flowers accent chintz and beams,
wine and food are divine, and Relais & Chateaux can book you.

SETTING & FACILITIES

Location Rt. 100 N to West Dover; first
left after village church, on the left after
bridge
Near Museums, antiquing, galleries,
auctions, summer theatre, symphony,

Mt. Snow
Building Restored cluster of farm buildings, main barn w/ old posts, beams
Grounds Set in woods; lawns, pool, tennis courts, gardens, 2 trout ponds

Public Space Stairs up to common room, loft library, DRs, lounge w/ copper bar, terrace
Food & Drink (MAP) Full breakfast; specialty: fresh tomato juice; dinner, evening attire, cont'l/American cuisine; specialties: fresh sautéed foie gras, breast of pheasant, pork tenderloin; meals open to public; summer cocktails; 36,000–bottle wine list
Recreation Fitness club, horseback riding, golf, winter and water sports, tennis, f
Amenities & Services Baby grand piano, Godiva chocolates, A/V equipment, fishing lessons by Orvis, priv. airport 5 min., massage arrangements

ACCOMMODATIONS

Units 20 guest rooms, suites, cottages
All Rooms Bath, fireplace, carpet, antiques
Some Rooms Balcony, sitting room w/ fireplace, reading area, desk
Bed & Bath Canopied kings, fine linens, extra pillows, down duvets; dressing rooms, luxury baths, thick towels
Favorites Farm house—pastel colors, fireplace, dressing room and bath; Cottage suites—sitting room w/ fireplace, coord. papers and fabrics, canopied beds
Comfort & Decor Lavish. Stylishly country, vivid florals. Antiques and reproductions. Spacious. King beds. Books, good reading lights. Large closets. Some Victorian decor, some English chintz. Decorator touches throughout.

RATES, RESERVATIONS, & RESTRICTIONS

Deposit 1 night; refund w/ 14-day notice (30 for foliage, holidays)
Discounts Corp. packages, off-season
Credit Cards V, AE, MC, D
Check-In/Out 3/12
Smoking No
Pets No
Kids Not recommended
Minimum Stay 2 nights on weekends; 3 on major holidays
Open All year
Hosts Rod, Ione, Brill Williams
Crosstown Rd. and Rt. 100, Box 367
West Dover, VT 05356
(802) 464-8131 or (800) 493-1133
Fax: (802) 464-1130
sawmill@sover.net
www.vermontdirect.com/sawmill

WINDHAM HILL INN, West Townshend

OVERALL ★★★★½ | ROOM QUALITY ★★★★★ | VALUE ★½ | PRICE $200–335

Panoramic views of the West River Valley envelop this hidden, hilltop beauty with all things going for it. Built in the early nineteenth century as a dairy farm, it was in the Lawrence family until the 1950s. Will Ackerman, who founded Windham Hill Records, worked here for a few summers in the 1960s and helped build what is now the music room, with an old Steinway grand and loads of CDs and games. The hayloft of the barn, guarded by a whimsical (fake) cow, has guest rooms with hand-hewn plank floors, skylights, and soaking tubs. Meals are delectably creative.

SETTING & FACILITIES

Location 1.5 mi. off Rt. 30, about 5 mi. S of Windham, at end of hilltop road
Near Shopping, antiquing, outlets, crafts, state parks, Stratton Mountain, Mt. Snow, Bromley Mountain; auctions, Southern Vermont Art Center
Building 1825, 3-story white farmhouse, converted barn
Grounds 160 acres: hillside, forest, fields, pond, gardens, pool, tennis, trails, views
Public Space Bar, check-in desk; music room, deck; parlor; pub room; DR
Food & Drink Full country breakfast; specialties: Belgian waffles, German soufflé pancake w/ warm apple compote, cinnamon-raisin brioche; hors d'ouevres;

4-course candlelight dinner (reservations, $40 for Inn guests, $45 for dinner guests tax/tip included), seasonal menu; specialties: lamb w/ mustard-seed crust, strawberry-rhubarb soufflé; wine list, full bar; lunch for groups by arrangement
Recreation Winter and water sports, mountain biking, golf, horseback riding, carriage/sleigh rides nearby
Amenities & Services XC skis, snowshoes, and toboggan; 1888 Steinway grand piano; weddings, conf. center (50+), executive retreats, customized dining (corp.), full business equipment, computer access, tour guidance; floor plans of rooms on Web site

ACCOMMODATIONS

Units 13 guest rooms in main house, 5 guest rooms and 3 loft rooms in White Barn
All Rooms Bath, phone, sitting area, AC, writing table, great views
Some Rooms Fireplace, Vermont Castings stove, priv. deck (10), daybed, window seat, porch, skylight
Bed & Bath Most queens/kings, canopies/reproductions; some whirlpools, 2-person tubs, tub/showers, soaking tub
Favorites Jesse Lawrence—king, bath,

soaking tub near fireplace, window seat, stove, 3rd floor; Forget-Me-Not—porchside, king, fireplace, soaking tub
Comfort & Decor Antiques, locally made furniture. English country decor. Wallpapered. Good windows and reading lights. Stuffed animals on bed, but not kitschy. Barn rooms, rustically elegant, w/ skylights, tartan fabrics. Main house, country comfort. Baths smallish. One barn room wheelchair accessible.

RATES, RESERVATIONS, & RESTRICTIONS

Deposit 1 night; refund (less $25 fee) w/ 14-day notice
Discounts Off-season, B&B rates, singles, 3rd person, midweek/seasonal packages, corp.
Credit Cards V, AE, MC, D
Check-In/Out 2/11
Smoking No
Pets No; in-house pets
Kids 12 and up
Minimum Stay 2 nights most weekends, foliage; 3 nights some holidays; for

weddings, must be rented in entirety, 2 nights
Open All year except week of Christmas; check on April
Hosts Pat and Grigs Markham
311 Lawrence Drive
West Townshend, VT 05359
(800) 944-4080 or (802) 874-4080
Fax: (802) 874-4702
windham@sover.net
www.windhamhill.com

JUNIPER HILL INN, Windsor

OVERALL ★★★★½ | ROOM QUALITY ★★★★ | VALUE ★★★½ | PRICE $95–175

This elegant 1902 mansion was built for Maxwell Evarts, CFO for Union Pacific Railroad and son of the U.S. Attorney General who defended Andrew Johnson from impeachment. Former Presidents Rutherford Hayes, and Teddy Roosevelt visited here. Views of Mt. Ascutney loom from rooms and pool. After biking in the valley, or paddling downriver to the covered bridge at Cornish, you'll return to a four-course candlelight dinner by the hearth. The hosts pamper with classical music, chocolates, and sherry.

SETTING & FACILITIES

Location On small mountaintop overlooking Lake Runnemede; from Rt. 5 S about 3 mi.; right onto Juniper Hill; halfmile, another right; left at junction
Near Vermont State Crafts Center, Old Constitution House, covered bridge, brewery, Dartmouth, Raptor Center, antiquing, galleries, village shops
Building 14,500-sq.-ft. Georgian-style mansion, built 1902; Nat'l Historic Reg.
Grounds 14 acres, pines, gardens, lake, mountain view, pool
Public Space Great hall, floor-to-ceiling

fireplace, gentleman's sitting parlor; DR
Food & Drink Full country breakfast; homemade pastries; 4-course dinner Tues.–Sat. ($34, reservations), candlelight; specialties: rack of lamb, poached salmon; vegetarian w/ prior notice; fully licensed
Recreation Skiing, golf, horseback riding, sleigh rides, skating
Amenities & Services Irons, breakfast in bed, bike rentals; weddings, functions, business services, meetings (24; priv. conf. room), dinner parties; pickup from station, fax, bike routes

ACCOMMODATIONS

Units 16 guest rooms
All Rooms Bath, sherry, hairdryer, flashlight, AC, CDs and player
Some Rooms Desk; lake or mountain view; fireplaces (11, 2 gas), balconies (2)
Bed & Bath Four-poster, canopy, sleigh beds; some claw-foot tubs, marble sinks

Favorites Corner queen deluxes—canopies, seating areas, fireplaces
Comfort & Decor Period wallpapers, art, antiques, and reproductions. Small details: corkscrews, crystal glasses, fresh flowers and chocolates.

RATES, RESERVATIONS, & RESTRICTIONS

Deposit 1 night; refund w/ 14-day notice
Discounts Midweek, returning guests
Credit Cards V, AE, MC, D
Check-In/Out 3/11
Smoking No
Pets No; 2 in-house Welsh Corgis
Kids No
Minimum Stay 2 nights, call for details

Open Closed first 3 weeks of April
Hosts Susanne and Rob Pearl
153 Pembroke Rd.
Windsor, VT 05089
(800) 359-2541 or (802) 674-5273
Fax: (802) 674-2041
innkeeper@juniperhillinn.com
www.juniperhillinn.com

Midstate Vermont/ Champlain

Vermont's Green Mountains/Champlain region starts at **Lake Champlain,** at the western border with New York, and is bordered on the north by Canada, on the east by the Upper Valley/Northeast Kingdom, and in the south by Vermont towns such as **Ascutney** and **Ludlow.**

The Lake Champlain area is highlighted by **Burlington,** Vermont's largest city, with a whopping 39,000 people. Burlington overlooks the lake and offers sailing, sea kayaking, and biking as well as ferries to the Adirondacks, across the water in New York. The **Ethan Allen homestead,** just north of town, commemorates the local revolutionary.

Downtown, the **Church Street Marketplace** is brimming with lively sidewalk cafés and shops. The discount-hungry can visit the **South Burlington Outlet Center** to fill up on bargains. Summer is when Burlington's cultural life shines: in June, at the **Discover Jazz Festival;** in July and August at the **Champlain Shakespeare Festival** and the **Vermont Mozart Festival.** And the **New England Culinary Institute** offers a chance to dine with future star chefs.

Shelburne Museum, south of Burlington, is a repository of Americana and fine arts. **Shelburne Farms** gives visitors a taste of early farming, cheese making, and baking (pre-microwave life; we're talking churns). Educational programs, featuring chores with barn animals, will especially delight children.

The **Middlebury** area is surrounded by farms and orchards and is highlighted by the handsome New England college town. Revolutionary War buffs can visit historical sites of **Fort Ticonderoga, Mount Independence,** and the **Hubbarton Battlefield.** Along uncrowded winding roads are antique finds as well as local crafts and foods.

The **Green Mountains** are a renowned ski and snowboard destination, with an annual snowfall of 250 inches. **Killington,** farther south in the region, is the largest of the resorts, and in addition to snow-related activities—which can run as late as June—it hosts a music festival in July and August and is a hiking draw for those seeking challenging terrain. **Smuggler's Notch,** another well-equipped ski resort, is farther north.

The **Long Trail** runs 270 miles from the Massachusetts border to Canada. Begun in 1910, it is part of the **Appalachian Trail** system in the south; in this region, it's maintained by the **Green Mountain Club.**

Along with maple syrup and cheddar cheese, Vermont is known for **Ben & Jerry's Ice Cream,** and a visit to the factory in **Waterbury** is a delicious experience; tours—and samples—are provided. At **St. Albans,** in northern Vermont by the lake, check out the **Vermont Maple Festival** in April.

Jedediah Hyde's log cabin in **Grand Isle** is one of the oldest log cabins in the country. The round white church in **Richmond** and the **New England Mountain Biking Festival** in **Randolph** are good stops. In **Plymouth Notch,** history buffs can visit **Calvin Coolidge's birthplace;** it's nicely maintained and more interesting than you'd expect, with "Silent Cal's" quiet reputation.

Lodging in this region caters to both romantics and families, skiers and active types, and ranges from small bed-and-breakfasts to larger inns, intimate to rustic. Many are clustered around Burlington, the Middlebury/Vergennes area, and the ski resorts, but there are plenty of worthy places in less-traveled areas. Summer, fall, and winter can be crowded on weekends, and many places close during early spring—aptly known as mud season.

THOMAS MOTT HOMESTEAD, Alburg

OVERALL ★★★★ | ROOM QUALITY ★★★★ | VALUE ★★★ | PRICE $85–175

One of a kind, and an incredible deal, this 1838 farmhouse on Lake Champlain is filled with delights. Raspberries are planted for guests to "steal." The freezer is always stocked with Ben & Jerry's. Birds, including baby quails, abound. In mid-summer the famed Lipizzaner horses from Austria perform in a meadow down the road. Photos are snapped of all guests: a copy for you, one for the album in the family room—27,000 so far. The property also houses a pin collection representing hometowns in 90 countries and 50 states. No planes, no highway noise, just canoeing on a lake framed by mountains, frozen lake cross-country skiing in winter, and soaking in the pleasure.

SETTING & FACILITIES

Location Follow signs off Hwy. 78
Near Alburg Auction (Sat.), Mississquoi Wildlife Refuge, Shrine of St. Anne, Lake Champlain Islands; 1 hour, Montreal
Building 1838 black-and-white farmhouse, barn
Grounds 2.5 acres, 325 feet of lake frontage, dock, gazebo
Public Space Original beams, floors; outdoor decks, cable TV, breakfast room

Food & Drink Full breakfast in breakfast room or on deck, includes entrée, pastries, fruit, yogurt, coffee and juice
Recreation Water activities, paragliding, golf, feeding quail, sky diving
Amenities & Services Canoes, XC ski trails, nearby ski rental, kitchen privileges with 5 room rental, refrigerator access, shop on premises, tour guidance/maps, weddings, nearby catering

ACCOMMODATIONS

Units 3 guest rooms; 1 suite
All Rooms Bath, lake view, quilts, antiques, ceiling fans
Some Rooms Fireplace, balcony, daybed, sitting area, priv. entry
Bed & Bath Queen shaker, some extra beds, 1 king; 2 full baths, 3¾ baths
Favorites Honeymoon suite—fireplace,

balcony overlooks lake; Corner Suite—downstairs, larger, wraparound lake view, queen, daybed
Comfort & Decor Built around quilts, individually collected. Papered. Some cathedral ceilings. Bedside lamps, reading chairs. Great lake views. Peaceful feeling. Bright decor.

RATES, RESERVATIONS, & RESTRICTIONS

Deposit 50%; refund w/ 7-day notice
Discounts 3rd person, rental of entire property
Credit Cards V, MC
Check-In/Out 2/11

Smoking No
Pets No
Kids Over 12
Minimum Stay None, but $25 surcharge for single night

Open All year
Hosts Lee and Linda Mickey
Blue Rock Rd. on Lake Champlain
Alburg, VT 05440-9620

(802) 796-4402 or (800) 348-0843
tmott@together.net
lmickey164@aol.com
www.thomas-mott-bb.com

LILAC INN, Brandon

OVERALL ★★★★ | ROOM QUALITY ★★★★ | VALUE ★★ | PRICE $120–260

Albert Farr made a fortune in the Midwest, then built this huge Georgian Revival summer cottage in 1909. As Michael puts it, "We want it to seem you are visiting Farr at this vacation house, indulging in fine food and drink, relaxing on the grounds or in your room, and enjoying Vermont's attractions." They succeed. The coach entrance, grand staircase (with a time capsule from 1991 in the newel post), a putting green, tavern, library, and environs are at your disposal. But book weekdays in season: They have hosted 200 weddings, and counting.

SETTING & FACILITIES

Location .25 mi. E of Rt. 7 and center of Brandon, near village green
Near Historical sites, gardens, covered bridges, arts and crafts, outlets, concerts, Middlebury College, brewery, Teddy Bear factory, museums, Shelburne Farms, Wilson Castle, UVM Morgan Horse Farm, waterfalls
Building 1909 Greek Revival 10,000-sq.-ft. mansion, 5-arch facade; Nat'l. Historic Register
Grounds Gardens, 2 ponds, waterfall, gazebo, courtyard: flower-lined cobblestone
Public Space Grand ballroom, library

(2,500 books), tavern, garden conservatory
Food & Drink Breakfast, Sun. brunch; specialties: baked apple turnovers, grilled maple-glazed grapefruit, eggs Benedict w/ smoked ham, chocolate soufflés
Recreation Lake Champlain boat tours, XC skiing (rentals), golf, mountain biking
Amenities & Services Irons, historic walking tour maps, turn-down; weddings, receptions (300); wedding specialists, cakes; cultural arts events: readings, concerts, art shows, cooking classes; conferences (75)

ACCOMMODATIONS

Units 9 guest rooms
All Rooms Bath, TV, iron, heat and AC controls
Some Rooms Fireplace (3), breakfast area, bridal suite
Bed & Bath 8 queens, two w/ 2 twins,

four-posters, canopies; tile baths, whirlpools, some original 1909 tubs, pedestal sinks
Favorites Albert's #7—step-up pine canopy bed, fireplace, wingback chairs, footboard

Comfort & Decor Period decor, Ralph Lauren prints, Laura Ashley, American folk. TVs in armoires. Art collection and collectibles. Desks and wingback chairs in most rooms. Some rooms connect.

RATES, RESERVATIONS, & RESTRICTIONS

Deposit Gift certificate w/ less than 30-day notice
Discounts Frequent guests, tell-a-friend coupons, gov't, singles, multiple night stays, 3rd person
Credit Cards V, MC, D
Check-In/Out 3/11
Smoking Outside only
Pets No
Kids Welcome

Minimum Stay 2 nights holidays and foliage
Open All year
Host Michael Shane
53 Park St.
Brandon, VT 05733
(802) 247-5463 or (800) 221-0720
Fax: (802) 247-5499
lilacinn@sover.net
www.lilacinn.com

OCTOBER COUNTRY INN, *Bridgewater Corners*

OVERALL ★★★★ | ROOM QUALITY ★★★★ | VALUE ★★ | PRICE $129–245

Glorious red-and-gold October may be the namesake, but the rest of the year around here isn't exactly mud. June brings the nearby Quechee Hot Air Balloon Festival; August, the Scottish Festival; winter has top skiing and Dartmouth's Winter Festival; spring, biking and maple sugaring. An outdoor summer deck nestles in the hillside, and the swimming pool is a sapphire in a meadow with a mountain view. This open, airy farmhouse with cozy hearths offers varying international cuisine, even Hungarian and African. Patrick and Richard love to talk theatre, and are exceptionally helpful—arranging just about anything your heart may desire.

SETTING & FACILITIES

Location Near intersection of Rt. 100A and Rt. 4; up a back road, across from general store
Near Summer theater; 8 mi. to Woodstock, Dartmouth College, Coolidge Homestead, 5 mi. to Killington, antiquing, shopping, museums
Building Deep red 19th-century farmhouse
Grounds 5 acres, pool, gardens, terraced hillside, meadows, apple trees; view of valleys and mountains

Public Space Open LR, library; 2 DRs; deck
Food & Drink (MAP) Early bird coffee; breakfast; specialty: blueberry pancakes; dinner; ethnic cuisine varying nightly; family-style, home-grown vegetables; special meals avail.; liquor license; tea and cookies
Recreation Skiing, fishing, golf, beach, horse shows, ballooning
Amenities & Services Hot tub, boat rental nearby, irons, beer/wine refrigerator

ACCOMMODATIONS

Units 10 guest rooms
All Rooms Fan, antiques
Some Rooms Bath (8), AC, extra bed, skylight
Bed & Bath 6 queens, others vary; firm mattresses; some tubs, some showers only, some multiple sprayers

Favorites Skylight rooms—light and well decorated
Comfort & Decor Eclectic and individual. Good lighting. Some stenciling, some flowering, nothing like Laura Ashley. Views of gardens, hillside, trees. Well-maintained, airy.

RATES, RESERVATIONS, & RESTRICTIONS

Deposit Check w/ inn; refund w/ 10-day notice
Discounts 3rd person, singles, families, longer stays, weekends
Credit Cards V, AE, MC
Check-In/Out 2/11:30
Smoking No
Pets No; 2 in-house cats
Kids Welcome

Minimum Stay None
Open Nov. 21–April 1, May 1–Oct. 31
Hosts Patrick Runkel and Richard Sims
Upper Rd., Box 66
Bridgewater Corners, VT 05035
(802) 672-3412 or (800) 648-8421
for reservations
oci@vermontel.com
www.octobercountryinn.com

WILLARD STREET INN, *Burlington*

OVERALL ★★★★½ | ROOM QUALITY ★★★★ | VALUE ★★½ | PRICE $120–225

This cultural and all-around capital of Vermont prospered from lumbering fortunes in the late-nineteenth century, when this redbrick, gabled mansion was built. You'll adore the glorious solarium with its green-and-white flooring, three walls of paned windows overlooking the lake, and comfortable seating by a gas stove. Stay in the room named Martha's Memoirs to encounter the resident lady ghost.

SETTING & FACILITIES

Location I-89 Exit 14W, Left to Rt. 7S; 2 blocks, on right corner of Cliff St. in residential area, next to Champlain College
Near Shelburne Farms, Shelburne Museum, Ben & Jerry's, Vermont Teddy Bear Co., Church Street Marketplace
Building 1800s brick w/ slate roof, exterior marble staircase; Queen Anne, Colonial–Georgian Revival style
Grounds Elaborate English gardens, fountain, summer lake view
Public Space Large foyer, parlor, solarium
Food & Drink Full breakfast in solarium; specialties: eggs Benedict, waffles, homemade granola; tea and coffee avail. all day
Recreation Burlington bike path, skiing, bocce, croquet
Amenities & Services Irons, hairdryers, cable TV, piano; nearby banquet/meeting facility (100), culinary workshops; reservations at innkeepers' restaurants

ACCOMMODATIONS

Units 15 guest rooms
All Rooms Bath, AC, cable TV, Phone, cookies at night, clock, radio
Some Rooms Sitting area, lake and mountain views
Bed & Bath Kings, queens, canopies, iron beds, extra beds; some whirlpools
Favorites Tower Room—cozy, priv. bath, queen, white wicker sitting area, enclosed widow's walk, best views

Comfort & Decor Individually decorated, coordinated fabrics. Period antiques and reproductions, Victorian-style papers, armoires. Room colors vivid—creams, dark greens, blues, periwinkle. Varied sizes (some, previous servants' quarters). Third-floor rooms best deal, w/ best views of Lake Champlain, Adirondack Mountains.

RATES, RESERVATIONS, & RESTRICTIONS

Deposit 1 night; refund w/ 7-day notice
Discounts Corp., AAA
Credit Cards V, AE, DC, MC, D, CB
Check-In/Out 3/11
Smoking No
Pets No; in-house 3 cats, 1 dog
Kids OK
Minimum Stay 2 nights summer/fall weekends

Open All year
Hosts Beverly and Gordon Watson
319 S. Willard St.
Burlington, VT 05401
(802) 651-8710 or (800) 577-8712
Fax: (802) 651-8714
info@willardstreet.com
www.willardstreetinn.com

FOX CREEK INN, Chittenden

OVERALL ★★★★ | ROOM QUALITY ★★★★ | VALUE ★½ | PRICE $129–409

Formerly the Tulip Tree Inn, Thomas Edison's sidekick built this sprawling hilltop home to retire to, and you can see why. Private and peaceful, in woods by a babbling brook, it seems miles from anything, but you're on cross-country trails, near downhill skiing at Killington, and close to canoeing, swimming, and fishing in the nearby reservoir. Geared for quiet and romance, you'll find no phones or TVs. You will find an award-winning wine list, a glowing pub, a four-course, candlelight dinner and rustically elegant rooms with whirlpools and fireplaces.

SETTING & FACILITIES

Location From Rutland, N on Rt. 7; at Y in road (at country store), go right for 6 mi.; at fire station, half-mile more to inn, on left
Near Shopping, antiquing, museums, galleries, Killington

Building 1830s home of William Barstow, Thomas Edison's collaborator
Grounds Lawns, flowers, surrounded by woods
Public Space 2 common rooms, pub, library, large porch

Food & Drink (MAP) Full breakfast buffet: apple, cheese, or blueberry pancakes; candlelight dinner; specialties: curried carrot soup, beef w/ Béarnaise sauce; menu changes nightly, vegetarian possible; wine list

Recreation Golf, horses, tennis, plane flying, mountain biking, train rides
Amenities & Services Refrigerator, irons, maps; small weddings, tour guidance/maps

ACCOMMODATIONS

Units 9 guest rooms
All Rooms Bath, antiques
Some Rooms Whirlpool (6), fireplace (3), bay window
Bed & Bath Mostly queens, some four-posters; all full baths
Favorites Room 9—spacious, fireplace,

dressing room, dbl. whirlpool, dbl. shower, 2 vanities, fireplace in bath
Comfort & Decor Antiques, reproductions, collectibles. Colors vary, in whites, creams, greens, blues. Some stenciling. 9th room new in 1999.

RATES, RESERVATIONS, & RESTRICTIONS

Deposit 50%; refund w/ 21-day notice
Discounts Midweek, off-season
Credit Cards V, MC
Check-In/Out 3/11
Smoking No
Pets negotiable
Kids Ok
Minimum Stay 2 nights weekends

Open Closed early April, early Nov.
Hosts Ann and Alex Volz
49 Dam Rd.
Chittenden, VT 05737
(800) 707-0017 or (802) 483-6213
Fax: (802) 483-2623
ttin@sover.net
www.foxcreekinn.com

TEN BENDS ON THE RIVER, *Hyde Park*

OVERALL ★★★★ | ROOM QUALITY ★★★★ | VALUE ★★★★ | PRICE $95–115

What a find. You don't have to be a trout angler to love this refined, sophisticated little hideaway with knockout views of the river and mountains from the grounds, porch, and many of the rooms. (A great place for a small wedding!) The living room is awash in light, with white walls and furnishings, throw rugs, pillows, *objets d'art,* wide plank floors, and pretty rugs. Fishing lodges and drop-dead gorgeous don't often mix, but, happily, they do here. And Oatis and Madie, the two friendly labs, make you feel so much at home, you may never want to leave.

SETTING & FACILITIES

Location 2 mi. N of Stowe on Rt. 100, left on Stagecoach Rd., left on Cady's Falls Rd., left on Main St. Bear left at Lute's Sales & Service to farmhouse on the riverbend
Near Stowe, Snuggler's Notch, Jay Peak Ski areas
Building 1859 New England farmhouse
Grounds Rural, on banks of Lamoille River w/ mountain views

Public Space LR, DR, library, porch, open kitchen
Food & Drink Gourmet communal breakfast; specialties: granola, scones, blueberry pancakes
Recreation Skiing, snowboarding, snowshoeing, river sports
Amenities & Services Refrigerator w/ drinks; weddings

ACCOMMODATIONS

Units 3 guest rooms
All Rooms Antiques, down comforter
Some Rooms Bath
Bed & Bath Queen or double iron beds
Favorites Violet Room—river view from

bath, watercolors, old quilts
Comfort & Decor Artwork, eclectic mix of furnishings, artful use of color. Exceptionally tasteful, peaceful, lovely. Good lighting. Good everything.

RATES, RESERVATIONS, & RESTRICTIONS

Deposit Credit card holds reservation
Discounts None
Credit Cards V, MC
Check-In/Out 3/11; flexible
Smoking No
Pets No; two dogs at inn
Kids OK
Minimum Stay None

Open All year
Host Aimee B. Stearns
454 Black Farm Rd.
Hyde Park, VT 05655
(802) 888-2827
rahboo@pop.state.vt.us
www.mt-mansfield.com/tenbends

CORNWALL ORCHARDS, Middlebury

OVERALL ★★★½ | ROOM QUALITY ★★★ | VALUE ★★★½ | PRICE $95

Sparkling, homey, breezy, this understated property on a country road has a long history; the sons of the second owner, Elisha Hurlbutt, were in the

War of 1812. Juliet was an assistant to a musician and composer; Bob is a lawyer. Both are warm and helpful innkeepers. In the hills near a fine college town offering crafts and cultural attractions, this uncluttered, pleasurable bed-and-breakfast prepares healthy and bountiful breakfasts, using multigrain flour for pancakes, seasonal fruits, and free-range eggs. As it's minutes from cross-country trails and right off a famed hiking trail, you at least can work off the breakfast.

SETTING & FACILITIES

Location 2 mi. from Middlebury College on Rt. 30, next to and across from orchards

Near Vermont State Craft Center, state parks, Fort Ticonderoga, Mount Independence, Hubbarton Battlefield, Lake Champlain, antiquing, trails, public golf course; 45 min. to Burlington or Sugarbush

Building 1783 Vermont farmhouse, expanded Cape; barn; restored, 1994

Grounds 14 acres, on ridge w/ mountain views

Public Space Kitchen entry, LR w/ fire-places, DR, porch

Food & Drink Full breakfast, all organic; specialties: granola, multigrain blueberry pancakes, strawberry-rhubarb compote, free-range eggs, Vermont bacon and sausage; refreshments

Recreation Biking, skiing, golf, tennis, fishing, canoeing, hiking

Amenities & Services Discount to Shelburne Museum, flowers, basketball equipment, lawn games, public rooms all disabled accessible

ACCOMMODATIONS

Units 5 guest rooms

All Rooms Bath, country pieces

Some Rooms Disabled access

Bed & Bath Queens, twins, firm mattresses; tub/shower (3), showers (2); 2nd floor, tiled, wainscoted baths

Favorites Gov—first-floor corner, off LR, quiet, largest, view of Adirondacks

Comfort & Decor Mountain views. Simple, clean, tasteful, country look. Wide board floors, ruffled white curtains, lots of light, breezy. Baths updated. Immaculate.

RATES, RESERVATIONS, & RESTRICTIONS

Deposit 1 night; refund if room re-rented, or w/ 14 days notice

Discounts 3rd person (2 rooms)

Credit Cards None

Check-In/Out Flexible/noon

Smoking No

Pets No

Kids Welcome; crib avail.

Minimum Stay 2 days summer, foliage, holiday weekends

Open All year

Hosts Juliet and Bob Gerlin
1363 Route 30
Cornwall, VT 05753
(802) 462-2272
cornorch@together.net
www.cornwallorchards.com

BLACK LANTERN INN, Montgomery Village

OVERALL ★★★H | ROOM QUALITY ★★★★ | VALUE ★★★½ | PRICE $75–145

Almost touching the Canadian border, this 1803 former stagecoach stop once catered to salesmen purveying to local mill workers—and the pub bar, recycled from an Ohio hotel, was the center of activities. Not today. You can travel internationally—skiing Canadian mountains—or ski nearby Jay peak, and swim, canoe, and fish in the nearby reservoir. Rooms are simply decorated but offer luxury amenities. Four-course dinners by candlelight are surprisingly sophisticated. Bob and Deb live in the converted barn in back.

SETTING & FACILITIES

Location On Rt. 118, center of village, near Trout River
Near Jay Peak, covered bridges, auctions, antiquing, shopping in Canada, Hazen's Notch
Building 1803 white-pillared former stagecoach stop; Nat'l. Historic Register
Grounds Backyard; gazebo w/ hot tub
Public Space Sitting room, TV room, bar, DR
Food & Drink (MAP) Full breakfast; candlelight dinner nightly (reservations); specialties: spinach stuffed mushrooms, shrimp w/ salmon mousse, filet mignon
Recreation Skiing, snowmobiling, fishing, golf, tennis
Amenities & Services Hot tub for 6–7, games, bike route advice/maps

ACCOMMODATIONS

Units 10 guest rooms, 6 suites
All Rooms Bath, individual heat, fans
Some Rooms Fireplace, whirlpool
Bed & Bath Beds vary; some whirlpools
Favorites Room 10—queen, gas fireplace, dbl. whirlpool, deck w/ mountain view; Suite 12—3 BRs, LR w/ wood stove, TV/VCR, whirlpool
Comfort & Decor Individual decorated w/ Vermont antique furniture. Continually renovated. Main house rooms small.

RATES, RESERVATIONS, & RESTRICTIONS

Deposit Daily rate, refund w/ 15-day notice
Discounts Off-season, groups, singles, kids (half price), 3rd person, 5-night stay
Credit Cards V, AE, MC
Check-In/Out Any time in afternoon/11; check-out flexible
Smoking None inside inner suites
Pets No; in-house chocolate lab on grounds
Kids OK
Minimum Stay None
Open All year
Hosts Deb and Bob Winders
Rt. 118
Montgomery Village, VT 05470
(802) 326-4507 or (800) 255-8661
Fax: (802) 326-4024
blantern@together.net
www.blacklantern.com

NORTHFIELD INN, Northfield

OVERALL ★★★½ | ROOM QUALITY ★★★ | VALUE ★★★ | PRICE $85–159

Once occupied by a princess, this pretty, pristine turn-of-the-century mansion, set on a mountain-side, is now owned by another formidable lady, of Greek origin. Host Aglaia is an independent, interesting woman who loves to suggest outings or talk by the fire. She hosts many business travelers. Cookies, fruits, and drinks are always available on the sideboard by the open kitchen; the dining room table is elaborately set with a lace cloth and crystal; and breakfasts are decadent, with courses such as warm, apple bread pudding. Charming, immaculate rooms are small, some of them with sinks by the bed, and showers and toilets in separate (literal) water closets. Resourceful, but not great for privacy.

SETTING & FACILITIES

Location Exit 5 off Rt. 89, past Norwich University
Near State capital, granite quarries, Ben & Jerry's, Shelburne Farms & Museum, Norwich University, Stowe, Sugarbush, five covered bridges
Building 1901 Colonial 4-story mansion
Grounds 2 acres of gardens, apple orchards, meadows, woods, pond; gazebo, hammock in the woods; views
Public Space Parlors, sitting room, library, porches, TV/video lounges

Food & Drink Full, formal breakfast, communal; specialties: French toast, German apple pancakes, crêpes, omelettes, eggs Florentine; evening wine; fruit, snacks, beverages
Recreation Winter sports, lawn/board games, videos
Amenities & Services Picnic baskets, binoculars, fitness room; group dinners and special events by arrangement; fax, overhead projectors, computer ports, Greek spoken

ACCOMMODATIONS

Units 12 guest rooms, 2 suites
All Rooms Victorian decor, antique mahogany beds, bath
Some Rooms Private bath, brass or carved-wood bed
Bed & Bath Bath within rooms; two rooms share bath, mostly showers
Favorites 2nd floor corner rooms—

deluxe furnishings, more space and privacy
Comfort & Decor Victorian charm w/ lace, antiques, oriental rugs, art collections, but not overdone. Pristine. Smallish rooms, w/ little storage. Some rooms a bit cool in winter

RATES, RESERVATIONS, & RESTRICTIONS

Deposit First and last day; request 14-day notice; handling fee may apply w/ less than 3-day notice

Discounts AAA, AARP, extended stays, groups; 7th night comp.
Credit Cards V, AE, MC, D

Check-In/Out 3–6/11

Smoking No

Pets No

Kids Over 15

Minimum Stay 2 nights Sept. 15–Nov.1;
4 nights for special events

Open All year

Host Aglaia Stalb

228 Highland Ave.

Northfield, VT 05663

(802) 485-8558

www.pbpub.com/inn/northfieldinn

NORTH HERO HOUSE COUNTRY INN, North Hero

OVERALL ★★★★½ | ROOM QUALITY ★★★★★ | VALUE ★★★ | PRICE $95–225

A recent million-dollar-plus renovation turned this flagging island property around, big time. The illusion of old-fashioned Americana almost hides the elegance and comfort (so unpretentious it is almost pretentious). Lake Champlain practically laps against the nineteenth-century buildings and stretches to the horizon like an ocean; guests used to arrive by steamship, but today often drive between the Vermont and New York sides of the lake. The town is a New England gem, general store and all, and is summer home of the white Lipizzaner stallions of Austria. Dining is in a reworked greenhouse with water views, of course, and creative American cuisine. Some say Champ, cousin of the Loch Ness monster, resides in the lake.

SETTING & FACILITIES

Location On Grand Isle, in Lake Champlain: Take I-89 N to Exit 17, to Rt. 2 W to North Hero Island; connected to mainland by bridges, on Rt. 2 or take ferry from Plattsburgh

Near Ski areas, Grand Isle Ferry, Platts-burgh, Burlington, Univ. of Vermont, St. Michael's College Playhouse, Shelburne Museum, St. Anne's Shrine, Ausable Chasm; state parks; working waterside farms, Revolutionary War villages; Montreal

Building 1891 Colonial, fieldstone/clap-board; verandas on 2 floors; 3 other buildings; restored, 1997

Grounds Big trees, trails, pier, sandy Lake Champlain beach, swim platform, lakeside sauna, large spa tub; boat rentals nearby, mountain views

Public Space Main common room, library, sitting room

Food & Drink (MAP) Buffet breakfast w/ hot entrée selection; specialties: almond-crusted salmon, pesto-crusted rack of lamb; breast of duck. The Pub, specialties: Black Angus burgers and sir-loin, baby back ribs, grilled pizza; weekend buffets; closed Mon. and Tues. in winter

Recreation Water and winter sports, tennis, golf, duck hunting, fishing, bird-watching vineyards

Amenities & Services French spoken; massage, boat slips, live entertainment, moonlight snowshoeing, sleigh rides, ten-nis privileges nearby, disabled access (check w/ inn); irons, hairdryers; cribs, cots; weddings, conferences; movies in room

ACCOMMODATIONS

Units 26, 3 lakeside annexes/ only 12 open in winter

All Rooms Bath, phone/dataport, TV

Some Rooms Priv. deck/porch, fire-place, lake view, sitting area, window seat

Bed & Bath Four-poster, antique, canopy, half-canopy, or handcrafted arti-san beds; all sizes, deep mattresses, add'l beds; some marble baths, some whirlpools; 1 w/ claw-foot soaking tub under moon window overlooks lake

Favorites Main House Room 203—arti-san-crafted wrought iron canopy under transom window, muslin side curtains, sit-ting room, fireplace, priv. porch, green marble bath, large whirlpool; Cove House Cobbler's Room—lakeside suite, rustic, 3-foot interior stone walls, sitting room, stone fireplace, sleeper sofa, BR w/ hand-hewn pine bed, screened patio

Comfort & Decor Unusual, special, extremely attractive. Many w/ fantastic views, luxury touches. Carpet. 2 attic rooms rather small. Striped wallpapers pretty, old-fashioned, or almost contem-porary. Homestead building notably newer, summer-cottage style. 1800s Cove House: some suites, exposed brick walls, sliding doors to lakeside porches, best for water lovers.

RATES, RESERVATIONS, & RESTRICTIONS

Deposit Credit card; no charge w/ 14-day notice

Discounts B&B meal plan; kids, midweek rates; specials and packages: Murder Mys-tery, ice fishing, cooking classes, pair skat-ing, more (check w/ inn)

Credit Cards V, AE, MC

Check-In/Out After 2/11

Smoking No

Pets No

Kids Welcome under 12, w/ $10 charge

Minimum Stay 2 nights summer week-ends, 3 nights Summer holidays

Open All year
Host Derek Roberts
P.O. Box 207
North Hero, VT 05474

(888) 525-3644 or (802) 372-4732
Fax: (802) 372-3218
nhhlake@aol.com
www.northherohouse.com

THE INN AT SHELBURNE FARMS, Shelburne

OVERALL ★★★★★ | ROOM QUALITY ★★★★ | VALUE ★★ | PRICE $95–365

Though this grand mansion on the lake is magnificent enough for a Vanderbilt, the property was always a working dairy farm. The on-site plant is where award-winning cheddar is made by hand from the raw milk of Brown Swiss cows. Children can milk the cows, gather eggs, groom sheep, and do chores. The focus is public education and promotion of conservation ethics, and programs include field trips, summer camps, and professional development workshops. Spare, spacious rooms seem frozen in time: Check out the attic dollhouses. You feel like a socialite farmer here. The unique experience and many weddings and groups means high occupancy.

SETTING & FACILITIES

Location On Lake Champlain; from Burlington Rt. 89 to Exit 13, travel S on Rt. 7 approximately 5 mi., turn left at stop light in center of Shelburne, drive 1.6 mi. to entrance of farm, past gate house, follow signs along 2 mile driveway to hilltop
Near Shelburne Museum, state parks; 8 mi. to Burlington; 30 mi. to Stowe
Building 1887 mansion, eclectic w/ Tudor, Queen Anne, Gothic Revival features
Grounds 1,400 lakeside acres, working dairy farm and nonprofit environmental education center; castlelike stone barn, gardens by Olmsted, paths, pastures, view of mountains
Public Space Tea room, main hall, billiards room, library; porches (2)

Food & Drink Cont'l breakfast and afternoon tea; dinner avail. in 2 elegant, orig. DRs; full breakfast (add'l charge) served in marble DR, specialties: bread from on-site bakery, fresh eggs, pancakes w/ homemade syrup; picnic lunches avail.; Sun. brunch; dinners, regional fare, homegrown produce, extensive wine list
Recreation Special events, museum, tennis, croquet, boating
Amenities & Services Priv. rocky lake beaches; farm tours and special events comp. to overnight guests incl. July Mozart Festival, Sept./Oct. art exhibition, July draft-horse field day, Sept. Harvest Festival; other farm special events, house tours; turn-down, maps, forgotten necessities, refrigerator storage; cribs, cots

ACCOMMODATIONS

Units 24 guest rooms, 2 cottages
All Rooms Decorative tiled fireplace (not functional), seating, phone, clock
Some Rooms Priv. bath (17), 7 rooms share 5 baths; cottages w/ kitchenettes
Bed & Bath Four-poster, canopy, antique beds; many baths w/ orig. soaking tubs, marble fixtures, tile floors
Favorites Overlook Room—Lila Vanderbilt-Webb's BR, large corner room w/ window wall, views, king bed, orig.

writing desk
Comfort & Decor Huge rooms, spare luxury. Elegant, elaborate Vanderbilt pieces original to mansion. Carpet. Rich color schemes. Rustic cottage bungalows are honeymoon favorites, 1 w/ working fireplace. Can be warm in summer, cool in fall. Former servant's rooms Spartan but best deal. Public rooms spacious, w/ furnishings original to Webbs and Vanderbilts.

RATES, RESERVATIONS, & RESTRICTIONS

Deposit 1 night; refund (less $25 fee) w/ 15-day notice
Credit Cards V, AE, MC, D
Check-In/Out 3/11
Smoking No
Pets No
Kids Welcome; under 2, free
Minimum Stay 2 nights weekends

Open Mid-May to mid-Oct.
Host Karen Polihronakis
1611 Harbor Rd.
Shelburne, VT 05482
(802) 985-8686
Fax: (802) 985-8123
www.shelburnefarms.org

EDSON HILL MANOR, Stowe

OVERALL ★★★★ | ROOM QUALITY ★★★★ | VALUE ★★★ | PRICE $139–179

A former gentleman's estate, Edson Hill Manor remains horsy, woodsy, and romantic—and surprisingly family-friendly. The pool is striking, and the public areas quietly elegant, with pine paneling, beams hewn from Ethan Allen's barn, Delft tiles around the fireplace, needlepoint-covered chairs, and fine paintings. You can catch a trout in the stocked ponds and have it for breakfast or dinner, ride guided trails, and cross-country ski practically from the door. (No wonder Alan Alda filmed the winter scenes here for *The Four Seasons*.) Food and wine are tops, views are panoramic.

SETTING & FACILITIES

Location Halfway between Stowe and Mt. Mansfield, 1,500 feet up, off Rt. 108
Near Mt. Mansfield and village, Ben & Jerry's, Camel's Hump
Building Brick/wood manor house, completed in 1940, enlarged to present

size in 1954
Grounds Rolling countryside, 225 forested acres; free-form pool, stocked ponds, red barn stable, trails, mountain views
Public Space LR, DR, lounge

Food & Drink Full country breakfast, buffet style; candlelight dinner, open to public; American cuisine with French and Italian influences; specialties: chilled melon soup w/ honey and lime, grilled Vermont rabbit; tea/coffee
Recreation Snowshoeing, sleigh/carriage rides, skiing, canoeing, tennis, horseback riding
Amenities & Services Stables, pool, stocked fishing ponds, trails, games XC ski rental, fax, catering, French spoken, some disabled access

ACCOMMODATIONS

Units 9 guest rooms in manor, 16 in carriage house
All Rooms Bath, phone, artwork
Some Rooms Fireplace, TV, sitting area, canopy bed
Bed & Bath Pencil-post canopy beds, varied sizes; most tubs, some showers only

Favorites Manor house rooms—special fabrics, charming accents
Comfort & Decor Antiques throughout. Carriage house rooms larger, more subdued, w/ fireplaces, pine paneling, and beams. Manor house rooms more romantic w/ coordinated fabrics and wallcoverings.

RATES, RESERVATIONS, & RESTRICTIONS

Deposit 1 night; refund w/ 15-day notice
Discounts 3rd party in room, groups, off-season, extended stays, kids under 4 free
Credit Cards V, MC, D
Check-In/Out 2/11
Smoking No
Pets Yes
Kids Yes

Minimum Stay 1 night; 5 nights, holidays
Open All year
Hosts William and Juliet O'Neil
1500 Edson Hill Rd.
Stowe, VT 05672
(800) 621-0284 or (802) 253-7371
Fax: (802) 253-4036
www.stowevt.com

SIEBENESS, Stowe

OVERALL ★★★½ | ROOM QUALITY ★★★ | VALUE ★★½ | PRICE $79–225

The German name of this cozy, cheery bed-and-breakfast mystifies many guests—it means "seven S's" for the seven S-curves on a nearby Stowe ski trail. This world-class resort town gives this bed-and-breakfast a mix of sophisticated, international clientele and informal sports enthusiasts. Big pluses are access to cross-country trails right from the property, and the outdoor pool, which keeps summer guests happy.

SETTING & FACILITIES

Location 3.5 mi. from village, 2 mi. from Mt. Mansfield; in heart of Stowe, turn toward mountain on Rt. 108; B&B on left
Near Ski resorts, Mt. Mansfield—Vermont's highest peak, Stowe and Craftsburg villages, Ben & Jerry's, Cabot Cheese Creamery, Shelbourne Museum, sugarhouses

Building 1952 Colonial, bay windows, front porch

Grounds Adjacent to Stowe's recreation path; XC ski or snowshoe to major trail systems or into village

Public Space DR, LR w/ Grand Field-stone fireplace

Food & Drink Breakfast; specialty: Belgian Waffles w/ fruit; BYOB bar w/ hot cider, afternoon tea

Recreation Winter and water sports, sleigh rides, horseback riding, golf, antiquing, spa visits

Amenities & Services Outdoor hot tub, village-mountain shuttle stop at inn, pool w/ mountain views; snow reports, maps, fax, dataport

ACCOMMODATIONS

Units 12 guest rooms

All Rooms Bath, AC

Some Rooms Gas fireplace, deck, 2-person Jacuzzi, TV, refrigerator

Bed & Bath Some canopy, four-poster, antique, feather beds, sizes vary; some shower-only, some 2-person whirlpools

Favorites Mountain View Studios—gas fireplaces, decks, queen featherbeds, 2-person Jacuzzi, TVs, refrigerators, private

Comfort & Decor Country pine furnishings, quilts, hand stenciling. Some awkwardly designed rooms, some more spacious. Light and bright. Phones and TVs deliberately excluded.

RATES, RESERVATIONS, & RESTRICTIONS

Deposit 50%; refund w/ 14-day notice; 1 month notice for holidays/special weekends

Discounts Singles, holiday packages, ski packages, many others (10% gratuity and Vermont taxes)

Credit Cards V, AE, MC

Check-In/Out 3/10

Smoking No

Pets No

Kids No

No-No's Early departure

Minimum Stay 2 nights weekends; 3-5 holidays

Open Except April and November

Host William Ruffing
3681 Mountain Rd.
Stowe, VT 05672
(800) 426-9001 or (802) 253-8942
Fax: (802) 253-9232

TEN ACRES LODGE, Stowe

OVERALL ★★★★ | ROOM QUALITY ★★★★ | VALUE ★★★ | PRICE $75–220

This Stowe favorite, well known for its fine food and wines, was bought by the owners of nearby Edson Hill Manor in 1993. It offers a more traditional, less rarified atmosphere of comfortable Americana, with paneled walls, slate floors, and paintings by Walt Whitman's brother-in-law, Charles Heyde. Hill House units here are preferable to the Edson Hill Manor carriage house units, but the main house rooms don't measure up to those in the main house at EHM. Guests can use both facilities, and eat at both excellent restaurants, so budget-conscious travelers can stay here and enjoy the grounds and facilities at its lovely sibling up the mountain road.

SETTING & FACILITIES

Location 2 mi. N of Stowe on Rt. 108 to Barrows Rd. Left for half-mile.
Near Mt. Mansfield, Ben & Jerry's, Trapp Family Lodge
Building 1835 farmhouse; recent addition
Grounds 10 acres, pastures, mountain views
Public Space LR, DR, library, lounge

Food & Drink Full country breakfast; dinner w/ New American cuisine, open to public; tea/snacks; extensive wine list
Recreation Horseback riding, snowshoeing, canoeing, skiing
Amenities & Services Outdoor hot tub, tennis, pool (unheated), XC ski trails, massage, trail/sleigh rides, fax, French-speaking host

ACCOMMODATIONS

Units 16 guest rooms, 2 cottages
All Rooms Bath, phone, AC
Some Rooms TV, four-poster, fireplace, sitting area, kitchenette, balcony
Bed & Bath Queen/king, some four-poster, brass; most baths with tub
Favorites Hill House—fireside seating

area, balcony, AC, TV
Comfort & Decor Rooms in main lodge more traditional, smaller, w/ country antiques. Hill House, fireplaces, balconies. Cottages w/ kitchenettes, 2 BRs. All comfortable.

RATES, RESERVATIONS, & RESTRICTIONS

Deposit 1 night; 2 during foliage, Christmas, and Presidents' week
Discounts Extended stay, groups, kids, 3rd person, off-season
Credit Cards V, AE, MC, D; prefer final bill paid in cash or check
Check-In/Out 2/11
Smoking Only in Hill House units
Pets Check
Kids OK

No-No's "Staying longer than a week without settling bill"
Minimum Stay None
Open All year
Host Eric Lande
14 Barrows Rd.
Stowe, VT 05672
(800) 327-7357 or (802) 253-7638
Fax: (802) 253-4036

STRONG HOUSE INN, Vergennes

OVERALL ★★★★½ | ROOM QUALITY ★★★★ | VALUE ★★½ | PRICE $75–270

A banking bigwig named Strong created this distinguished home in the nineteenth century, and its appeal is stronger than ever. His portrait looms over the living room, but the house has been enhanced with Mary's award-winning innkeeping talents. If you're peckish, you can raid the guest refrigerator in the kitchen, and dinner baskets, prepared by a local French restaurant, can be in your room on arrival. (Why don't more bed-and-breakfasts offer this option?) Activities include winter quilting seminars, with a quilt teacher on-site ("sewing and eating," as Mary puts it). The luxury country house addition, opened in 1999, is loaded with amenities.

SETTING & FACILITIES

Location Rt. 22A, 1 mi. S of Vergennes Center
Near Antiquing, covered bridges, crafts, historic sites, Middlebury College, Yale
Building 1834 Federal, cottage; Nat'l. Historic Registry; country house addition, 1999
Grounds 6 sloping acres; meadow, forest, trails, gazebo, gardens; mountain views
Public Space Freestanding stairway in entry, LR, DR, library
Food & Drink Full breakfast; specialties: Grand Marnier French toast, eggs Benedict, apple dumplings, crêpes; 4-course tea monthly, open to public, Nov.–May (reservations); appetizers, desserts; dinner baskets, picnic baskets, sandwiches and salads for late-arrivals (prearranged, extra); liquor license
Recreation Snowshoeing, sledding, ice-skating on site, skiing
Amenities & Services New conference center (full liquor license), AC, refrigerator, irons, daily paper, boutique, turn-down (suites), packing picnics, wedding arrangements; quilting and wellness pkgs

ACCOMMODATIONS

Units 12 guest rooms (6 in country house), 2 suites
All Rooms Bath, AC, thermostat, TV, phone
Some Rooms Fireplace, library, whirlpool (1), balconies (2), porches (2), garden (1); coffee niche, coffeemaker; breakfast option: delivered or in main house for country house rooms
Bed & Bath Doubles, queens, kings, some canopies; tubs and showers
Favorites Adirondack—twig furniture, king canopy, stone fireplace, breakfast area, wet bar, refrigerator, dbl. whirlpool, dbl. vanity; Plantation—Southern style, 2nd floor, king four-poster, fireplace, balcony; Vermont room—French doors, views, pine queen four-poster
Comfort & Decor Mountain views and wonderful sunsets. Green Mountains in front, Adirondacks in back. Names match decor. Rooms individually decorated, from coastal theme to 18th-century English to Provence. Luxury and creative style. Country house, w/ coffee niches, breakfast areas, doors out to garden.

RATES, RESERVATIONS, & RESTRICTIONS

Deposit 1 night; refund w/ 14-day notice
Discounts Off-season, 3rd person, corp.
Credit Cards V, AE, MC
Check-In/Out 3/11
Smoking No
Pets No; in-house cat
Kids Well-behaved over 8
Minimum Stay 2 nights summer weekends, holidays

Open All year
Hosts Mary and Hugh Bargiel
82 West Main St.
Vergennes, VT 05491-9531
(802) 877-3337
Fax: (802) 877-2599
innkeeper@stronghouseinn.com
www.stronghouseinn.com

WHITFORD HOUSE INN, Vergennes

OVERALL ★★★★½ | ROOM QUALITY ★★★★ | VALUE ★★½ | PRICE $110–225

On a little-traveled road by Dead Creek sits a sophisticated country home in the midst of meadows, cornfields, and mountains. Slate, wool, wood, glass, multi-paned and picture windows, a stone hearth, Morris chairs, wideboard floors, Southwest touches, and artwork from daughter Amy create a casually elegant ambiance. Breakfasts are comparable to the understated, striking style of the property. Bruce estimates that almost half of their guests are references or returns, and they "get lots of notes saying thanks." This open, informal house is contemporary country—and the former California hosts are a big part of things without being intrusive.

SETTING & FACILITIES

Location 25 mi. from Adirondack High Peaks, 2 mi. E of Lake Champlain, on a dirt road with meadows and fields; hosts consider themselves in Addison, in spite of Vergennes address

Near Adirondack Mountains, Middlebury College, Revolutionary War sites, antiquing, Shelburne American Folk Art Museum, wildlife preserves, Lake Champlain

Building 1790s post-and-beam Cape Cod farmhouse; modernized without changing its look; cottage

Grounds 37 acres: fields, woods, organic garden, recycling; views of mountains

Public Space Dramatic LR, library, DR, veranda, decks

Food & Drink Full breakfast; specialties: homemade bread, eggs Florentine, frittatas, stewed apples; wine/cheese, hors d'oeuvres; dinner w/ prior reservation; special meals accom.
special meals accom.

Recreation Boating, skiing, golf, kayaking, horseshoes, swimming, tennis, horseback riding, fishing, lawn games, flying kites

Amenities & Services Games, books, baby grand piano, canoes, bikes; limited disabled access; weddings, receptions, conferences

ACCOMMODATIONS

Units 3 guest rooms in main building, 1 suite, cottage

All Rooms Bath, alarm clock, antiques

Some Rooms Sitting room, wet bar

Bed & Bath 2 twins, doubles, king; tubs, glass showers; radiant heat slate floors

Favorites Suite—spacious, king, sitting

room, bath, pull-out bed, large windows

Comfort & Decor Great mountain views. Dramatic mix of country and contemporary. Old windows, few curtains or drapes. Oriental rugs, mostly antique, many collected on travels. Fresh flowers. Cottage separated by brick path.

RATES, RESERVATIONS, & RESTRICTIONS

Deposit 1 night; refund w/ 14-day notice; surcharges peak season (9/20-10/20) and special weekends

Credit Cards V, MC

Check-In/Out 1/11; flexible

Smoking Outside only

Pets OK, arrange prior; in-house cat, 2 beagles

Kids Welcome

Minimum Stay Special weekends only

Open All year

Hosts Barbara and Bruce Carson
912 Grandey Rd.
Vergennes, VT 05491-8851
(802) 758-2704 or (800) 746-2704
Fax: (802) 758-2089
whitford@together.net
www.whitfordhouseinn.com

THE INN AT THE ROUND BARN FARM, Waitsfield

OVERALL ★★★★★ | ROOM QUALITY ★★★★★ | VALUE ★★½ | PRICE $135–250

The nineteenth-century farmhouse and attached barns were part of a dairy farm until the 1960s, and the idyllic setting remains. Resident ducks such as Huey, Dewey, and Lucy waddle from the pond; black-and-white cows look like they are painted on the green hills by the cartoon artist at Ben & Jerry's. You also get classical music, farm breakfasts, swimming into a greenhouse filled with hibiscus, acres of trails, maybe an apple tart and sherry by the fire, and similar delights. The big, rare barn is extremely popular for weddings and conferences, and skiers are only a few minutes from great slopes. This bed-and-breakfast is deluxe yet friendly, truly elegant and original—a deserved classic.

SETTING & FACILITIES

Location From Rt. 100 in Waitsfield, turn onto Bridge St., through covered bridge, bear right at fork onto East Warren Rd; 1 mi. to B&B, in heart of farm country

Near Pastures with cows, covered bridge, Sugarbush, Mad River Glen

Building 1910 former farm buildings; newer wing attached to huge round barn, used for functions

Grounds 85 acres of hills, gardens, lily ponds, terraces, mountain views

Public Space Eat-in breakfast area off kitchen, traditional parlors, library, barn

Food & Drink Lavish full breakfasts; specialty: French toast w/ sautéed fruits; afternoon goodies, sherry; some weekend dinners in winter

Recreation Swimming, bird watching, skiing, golf

Amenities & Services 60-foot lap pool; rentals and instructions; snowshoe rentals and tours

ACCOMMODATIONS

Units 12 guest rooms

All Rooms Bath, fresh flowers, heat controls, reading lamp, lighted makeup mirror, clock

Some Rooms Fireplace, cathedral ceiling, steam shower, oversized whirlpool tub

Bed & Bath Varied bed sizes, canopied beds and four-posters; inviting baths with views, skylights, robes

Favorites Sterling Room—1st floor, stenciled walls, handpainted headboard, skylight, fireplace; window wall vistas make up for small size; all rooms have special appeal

Comfort & Decor House rooms more traditional, w/ antiques, some fireplaces and enlarged baths. New wing in former barn, canopied beds, cathedral ceilings, beams, gas fireplaces, steam showers, whirlpools. Sumptuous

RATES, RESERVATIONS, & RESTRICTIONS

Deposit 1 night, full; 2 or more, 50%

Discounts Singles, 3rd person, midweek packages

Credit Cards V, AE, DC, MC, D

Check-In/Out 3/11, call if arriving after 7 p.m.

Smoking No

Pets No

Kids Over 16

Minimum Stay Varies

Open All year

Host AnneMarie DeFreest

RR1 Box 247, E. Warren Rd.

Waitsfield, VT 05673

(802) 496-2276

Fax: (802) 496-8832

roundbarn@madriver.com

www.innattheroundbarn.com

THE PITCHER INN, *Warren*

OVERALL ★★★★★ | ROOM QUALITY ★★★★★ | VALUE ★ | PRICE $300–600

Fantasy lovers and fast-trackers, you ain't seen nothing till you see the revolving fowl in the Mallard Room. Or the whimsical, luxurious details throughout. Ask to see other units, if humanly possible, or peek in while the maid is cleaning. (My evil twin must have said that!) Completely rebuilt on the site of a burned-down landmark, this beauty has become another, and each unique habitat is astoundingly designed with a Vermont theme, by a different top architect. The dining is divine, the baths, to die for. Cool-ish atmosphere can't compete with the decor, but who cares? This inn is now a member of Relais & Chateaux.

SETTING & FACILITIES

Location North of Rutland on Rt. 100, along the Mad River; one hour South of Burlington Airport in hamlet across from general store and antique stores

Near River, antiques-filled villages, spa, Mad River Glen, Sugarbush Ski Resort

Building 1997 replica of 19th-century inn

Grounds Minimal, with gardens, grape arbor, decks overlooking waterfall; mountain views

Public Space Porch, reception area, common room, library dedicated to Robert Frost, lounges, basement game room, 4,000-bottle wine cellar,

DRs, decks

Food & Drink Full breakfast; creative American cuisine from renowned chef; dinner, breakfast open to public, dining in wine cellar; tea/pastries

Recreation Snowboarding, nordic and Alpine skiing, skating, sleigh rides, golf, tennis, horseback riding, shuffleboard, fly-fishing

Amenities & Services Spa package avail., locker/storage rooms, ski boot and glove warmer, gift shop, 19th-century billiards table, elevator; preferences noted, business facilities, disabled access

ACCOMMODATIONS

Units 9 guest rooms in main building, 2 suites in barn

All Rooms Bath, concealed TV/VCR, phone, dataport, AC, whirlpool

Some Rooms Fireplace, steam shower, balcony

Bed & Bath Mix of styles, mostly kings; huge, lavish baths, some w/ dbl. whirlpools and showers, radiant heat floors

Favorites Lodge Room—unique four-poster, star-studded ceiling, slate fireplace, TV in lecturn; all rooms qualify for favorite

Comfort & Decor Incredible detailing, luxury and wit. Many artifacts. Over-the-top themes include locals Calvin Coolidge (quiet, w/ two-wall handpainted mural), Chester Arthur (disabled access), a schoolroom (blackboard behind the bed, w/ chalk), trout fishing (tie your own flies), etc.

RATES, RESERVATIONS, & RESTRICTIONS

Deposit 50%; refund w/ 30-day notice

Discounts Midweek package, single occupancy less $75

Credit Cards V, AE, MC

Check-In/Out 3/11

Smoking No; on porches only

Pets No

Kids OK

Minimum Stay 2 nights weekends, 5 nights Christmas week

Open All year

Hosts Heather and John Carino

P.O. Box 347

Warren, VT 05674

(888) TO-PITCHER or (802) 496-6350

Fax: (802) 496-6354

pitcher@madriver.com

www.pitcherinn.com

WEST HILL HOUSE, Warren

OVERALL ★★★★ | ROOM QUALITY ★★★★ | VALUE ★★★ | PRICE $115–180

Dotty and Eric are exceptionally warm and thoughtful innkeepers, and their presence permeates every aspect of this outstanding little bed-and-breakfast. Built in the 1850s, and once a ski lodge, its "great room" addition was recently built by Eric, who was in the construction business. In winter, guests occasionally gather around the brick bake oven and build individual pizzas for informal group dinners, and Dotty may cook a special Saturday night dinner or prepare a birthday cake. Close to Sugarbush resort, the mood here is personal and unassuming. This is a haven for solo travelers, and those who want to feel like part of a family

SETTING & FACILITIES

Location 1.5 mi. up from Rt. 100, on quiet road adjacent to championship golf course
Near 1 mile to Sugarbush, Mad River Glen Ski, Ben & Jerry's, Cabot Cheese Creamery, Cold Hollow Cider Mill, Montpelier, Rock of Ages Granite Quarry
Building 1850s farmhouse; recent addition
Grounds 9 acres: woods, apple trees, meadows, gardens, 3 ponds, mountain views; terraced rear yard w/ deck, gazebo
Public Space Library, great room, DR, sunroom
Food & Drink 3-course communal breakfast, specialties: sticky buns, streusel, ginger-lemon muffins, soufflés; après-ski tea and refreshments; cocktail hour treats; wet bar and refrigerator in great room stocked w/ set-ups, soft drinks, spirits, beer and wine for purchase (please no BYOB); family-style candlelight dinners served to minimum 6 guests Sat. nights in season or by reservation (add'l per-person charge), 4-course menu agreed on by guests at breakfast; holiday dinners/celebrations, birthday/wedding cakes; comp. champagne for honeymooners and anniversary couples
Recreation Soaring, summer theatre/concerts, sleigh rides; Vermont Icelandic Horse Farm Trekking, hiking, river swimming holes
Amenities & Services Snowshoes, sleds, binoculars, beach towels; irons, guest phone line and number, daily paper, maps, refrigerator; videos; meetings, full wedding services, fitness center nearby

ACCOMMODATIONS

Units 6 guest rooms, 1 suite
All Rooms Bath, good reading lights, thermostat, AC or ceiling fans, fireplace, TV/VCR
Some Rooms Sitting room, on request, 3rd person beds
Bed & Bath Comfortable beds, queen or king/twin; some 2-person steam showers, whirlpools; hairdryers, some robes, new fixtures and tile
Favorites Stetson Suite—ground floor, gas woodstove in sitting room w/ sofa bed, TV/VCR, tub, 2-person steam shower; Secluded Fireplace Room—priv. spiral staircase, fireplace, queen, beamed ceiling, lots of windows, large bath
Comfort & Decor Room sizes vary, but all comfortable. Original artwork, sloped ceilings, handmade quilts, stenciling, sponge-painted walls. Good lighting. Carpet or original wide plank floors w/ handmade rugs, exposed beams, barn siding walls. Wreaths, candles, ambiance lighting, antiques.

RATES, RESERVATIONS, & RESTRICTIONS

Deposit 1 night; refund w/ 21-day notice
Discounts 3rd person; custom
packages, ski, golf
Credit Cards V, AE, MC, D
Check-In/Out 3/11; flexible
Smoking No
Pets No
Kids Over 12
Minimum Stay 2 nights, weekends; 3

nights, holidays/foliage
Open All year
Hosts Dotty Kyle and Eric Brattstrom
1496 West Hill Rd.
Warren, VT 05674
(800) 898-1427 or (802) 496-7162
Fax: (802) 496-6443
westhill@madriver.com
www.westhillhouse.com

INN AT BLUSH HILL, Waterbury

OVERALL ★★★★ | ROOM QUALITY ★★★★ | VALUE ★★★½ | PRICE $79–150

Originally a stagecoach stopover, and the oldest lodgings in Waterbury, this pristine bed-and-breakfast is up a steep hill off a busy road where horse-drawn carriages once clanked along, and yet it seems isolated. Window walls highlight sunrise over the mountaintops, and warm woodwork and greetings add to the sunshiny feel. Dieters will face a dilemma with breakfast temptations served in the rustic kitchen. How about cornmeal waffles with warm applesauce and bacon, or four-berry pancakes topped with maple syrup and ice cream from neighbor Ben & Jerry's? Pam was in the hospitality business in Washington, D.C., and boy, does it show. You'll feel pampered.

SETTING & FACILITIES

Location I-89 to Exit 10 N, left onto Blush Hill Rd., B&B is on right at top of hill; alternately, site is just off Rt. 100
Near Stowe, Sugarbush Ski Resorts, Ben & Jerry's Ice Cream Factory, Cabot Cheese Creamery, Cold Hollow Cider Mill, Montpelier, Burlington, Lake Champlain, state parks, shopping, quaint villages and antiques, covered bridges, Art Vermont, Maritime Museum, Shelburne Museum, Vermont Teddy Bear Co.
Building Circa 1790 Cape; 1840 addition, broad veranda
Grounds 5 rolling acres, gardens, Green

Mountain views
Public Space Parlor, DR, country kitchen
Food & Drink Full country breakfast; specialties: dishes featuring Ben & Jerry's products: breakfast parfait, melon w/ sorbet; cont'l breakfast for late risers; refreshments
Recreation Winter and water sports, soaring, summer theatre/concerts, guided snowmobile tours
Amenities & Services Refrigerator, binoculars, irons, videos, discount ski lift tickets, maps, recipes

ACCOMMODATIONS

Units 5 guest rooms

All Rooms Bath, clock/radio

Some Rooms Mountain views; fireplace (1), sitting area (1); accommodate 3rd person

Bed & Bath Some antique brass, oak, canopy beds, queen or double; some shower only, whirlpool (1),hall access bath w/ robes (1)

Favorites Sunflower—largest room, full canopy queen, 15-foot-wide window views

Comfort & Decor Mixed styles, some colonial antiques. Each room includes special amenity or antique: fireplace, romantic bed, love seat, whirlpool, Laura Ashley prints. Some head-banging slanted ceilings. Adjoining rooms work for families, companions.

RATES, RESERVATIONS, & RESTRICTIONS

Deposit 50%, min. 1 night; refund w/ 14-day notice

Discounts Packages, 3rd person, family, long stays

Credit Cards V, AE, MC, D

Check-In/Out 3/11

Smoking No

Pets No

Kids Over 6

No-No's Changing length of stay

Minimum Stay No Saturday-only stays

Summer and some holidays

Open All year, except Thanksgiving, Christmas Eve, Christmas Day

Host Pam Gosselin

784 Blush Hill Rd.

Waterbury, VT 05676

(800) 736-7522 or (802) 244-7529

Fax: (802) 244-7314

blushhill@aol.com

www.blushhill.com

Vermont—Upper Valley/ Northeast Kingdom

The Northeast Kingdom ranges from the **Green Mountains** in the west to the **Connecticut River** on the east. Quebec is north. This is Vermont's wildest, quietest side, where you can hunt, trap, bike, fish, canoe, hike, and gaze at a sky full of stars.

The great outdoors here offers 50 public boat launch sites, remote lakes, and over a million forested acres. Cross-country and downhill ski trips at **Jay Peak** and **Burke** offer quieter, less-crowded venues than at more popular resorts. **Stowe** is one of the oldest and finest ski destinations in the country. **Lake Willoughby** has beaches, swimming, and fishing, with pretty lake views. With more dirt roads than paved ones, the northern corner is great for hiking and biking. And keep an eye out for moose—in some areas you're more likely to meet up with the formidable bearded beasts than with tourists (bearded or not).

Although truly rural, this northeast corner of Vermont is not without culture and family-centered activities. **Craftsbury** features the **Craftsbury Chamber Players.** You can enjoy a civilized, traditional tea at **Perennial Pleasures** in **East Hardwick.** The **Caledonia County Fair** in **Lyndonville** and the **Orleans County Fair** in **Barton** (both in August) are among the best in New England. Stop by church suppers, auctions, or fiddling contests. For kids, **The Bread & Puppet Circus** is based in **Glover,** and **Circus Smirkus** is in **Greensboro.**

The region is the birthplace of **Ethan Allen** furniture, and fine craftsmakers still choose to live and work here. Local galleries and workshops show blown glass, wood carvings, quilts, pottery, and photographs. And there's plenty of antiquing at good prices.

Noteworthy architecture is another plus. After admiring the 1878 church and 1856 courthouse in the old railroad town of **St. Johnsbury,** stop by the **Fairbanks Museum and Planetarium,** which has enough stuffed animals to keep tots happy. Covered bridges and barns also abound. In **Burke,** the **Inn at Mountain View Farm** (one of our profiled lodgings), has outstanding old barns.

Agriculture is a cornerstone of Vermont, and the **Billings Farm & Museum** in **Woodstock** provides a history. Cabot Cheese, produced in the area, is good enough for star chefs to demand; the plant offers tours and samples. Restaurants serve mainly fresh, local fare, and country stores and general stores are a charming remnant of classic New England, with local crafts and foodstuffs crammed among the canned goods and mops.

Lodging in the Northeast Kingdom ranges from famed romantic inns to simple, inexpensive places. Crowds aren't a problem, but the farther north you go, the fewer accommodations you'll find. To be sure, reserve ahead.

MAPLE LEAF INN, Barnard

OVERALL ★★★★ | ROOM QUALITY ★★★★ | VALUE ★★ | PRICE $150–230

Built around 1990, this gabled bed-and-breakfast was created by Gary and
Janet with romance in mind, and it seems in many ways 100 years older
than it really is. Old-fashioned octagonal bath tiles cover heated floors. Vin-
tage-looking pedestal sinks and wainscoting contrast with soaking tubs for
two. King-size beds face fireplaces salvaged from an old Boston house. A
maple leaf welcome card waits at arrival, and chocolates are placed by your
turned-down bed. Breakfast is at tables for two, surrounded by "Love"
postage stamp samplers cross-stitched by Janet. As for the videos for the in-
room VCRs, forget Stallone—chick-flicks reign.

SETTING & FACILITIES

Location Rt. 12, 9 mi. N of Woodstock;
.25 mile S of Barnard General Store
Near Woodstock, arts/crafts galleries, Sil-
ver Lake, Billings Farm & Museum, Ver-
mont Institute of Natural Science, Raptor
Center, Pentangle Council on the Arts,
Quechee Gorge, Calvin Coolidge birth-
place, glassblowing, Appalachian Trail, Long
Trail, covered bridges
Building Victorian-style farmhouse; built
1990s
Grounds 16 acres, mountain/lake views,
gazebo
Public Space Parlor; library, Middle East

artifacts; DR; wraparound porch, gazebo
Food & Drink Gourmet breakfast, 3
courses; specialties: apple fritters, ricotta
pancakes, buttermilk scones, sautéed
bananas w/ ice cream, stuffed French
toast w/ maple sausage; dinner by
arrangement, food allergies/special diets
accomm.; tea
Recreation Skiing, biking, golf, tennis,
fishing, horseback riding, games, puzzles
Amenities & Services Refrigerator,
irons, bike rental nearby, romantic
movies; small weddings, maps, dinner
reservations

ACCOMMODATIONS

Units 7 guest rooms
All Rooms Bath, sitting area, TV/VCR, phone
Some Rooms Wood-burning fireplace, disabled access
Bed & Bath Kings, 1 iron bed, most oak, some Victorian, 1 four-poster; most whirlpools, dbl. whirlpools, soaking tubs, heated floors
Favorites Winter Haven—2nd floor, oak

Victorian rolltop panel bed, dbl. whirlpool, fireplace; Country Garden—picket fence–style headboard, mini-garden on mantel, fresh flowers
Comfort & Decor Bright lace curtains. Maple and birch views. Victorian Country look. Handmade quilts, room themes, stenciled walls. Lots of cross-stitching, needlework by host. Excellent reading lights.

RATES, RESERVATIONS, & RESTRICTIONS

Deposit 50%; refund w/ 14-day notice, longer notice for multiple reservations
Discounts Midweek off-season
Credit Cards V, AE, DC, MC, D
Check-In/Out 3–6/11; prior arrangement for late arrival
Smoking No
Pets No
Kids No

No-No's 3rd person in room
Minimum Stay 2 nights weekends, holidays, foliage
Open All year
Hosts Janet and Gary Robison
Box 273
Barnard, VT 05031
(802) 234-5342 or (800) 51-MAPLE
www.mapleleafinn.com

TWIN FARMS, *Barnard*

OVERALL ★★★★★ | ROOM QUALITY ★★★★★ | VALUE ½ | PRICE $900–1,600

In a class by itself, Twin Farms is worth what it costs. Novelist Sinclair Lewis built it for his bride, journalist Dorothy Thompson, in 1928. Today, it's one of the world's greatest small properties, with sumptuous, themed rooms and cottages and incredibly pampering yet casual luxury. Service, beauty within and without, food, recreation—all are close to perfection. Acres of wildflowers, private ski runs (with perhaps a mountaintop picnic lunch), Hockney and Avery paintings, a jukebox, a Japanese furo tub, a private covered bridge, mountain bike rides (pick-ups for uphill, with champagne, if desired)—anything goes, and you should, too. Bill Gates stayed here, but if it's more of a stretch for you, rooms in the main house are the best deal, almost as sublime as the "cottages."

SETTING & FACILITIES

Location 1.5 mi. E of the general store on Rt. 12, in rural area overlooking mountain vista

Near Covered bridges; 10 mi. to Woodstock

Building Two 18th-century farmhouses renovated into main house; 9 widely scattered, large cottages and lodge, varied styles; game house/pub, furo tub building

Grounds 235 acres: woods, meadows, gardens, orchards, lake, ski runs, covered bridge

Public Space Main house: great room, wine cellar, rustic DR, parlor; porch; furo Japanese bathhouse; pub and game building, jukebox

Food & Drink All meals and drinks included; breakfast, lunch, dinner, snacks served anywhere on property; star-chef Neil Wigglesworth, creative American cuisine; cocktails at 7; wine cellar

Recreation Water sports, fly fishing, tennis, biking, downhill and XC skiing, tennis, croquet, ice-skating; golf nearby

Amenities & Services Fitness center, skates, toboggans, bikes, spa treatment rooms, Steinway piano; massage (fee), turn-down, food delivered anywhere, shuttles; business/group support; 2:1 staff/guest ratio

ACCOMMODATIONS

Units 4 suites, 8 cottages, 2 suites in lodge

All Rooms Bath, fireplace, phone, TV/VCR, CD, AC, mini-refrigerator, antiques, sitting area, custom furnishings

Some Rooms Porch, loft, skylight, collections

Bed & Bath King beds, four-posters, antique; huge, lavish baths w/ soaking tubs, whirlpools, steam showers, antique fixtures, stone/natural materials, skylights

Favorites Cottages are all remarkable; Treehouse—beams, four-poster, stone fireplace, heated slate floor in bath,

screened porch; Studio—largest, loft BR, splatter-paint floor, orig. art (incl. Stella, Hockney)

Comfort & Decor Breathtaking beauty, space, style, luxury. Whimsical. Fantasy themes, w/ no expense spared, include 19th-century Log Cabin, Moroccan tented palace, Scandinavian farmhouse, Tuscan cottage in woods. Disabled access in main house, Washington Room. House rooms huge, lavish, more traditional, best deal for budget-conscious. $26+ million spent. Decor by Jed Johnson, designer who died in TWA 800 crash

RATES, RESERVATIONS, & RESTRICTIONS

Deposit Paid in full, 30 days in advance, 90 days foliage and holidays; *Note:* Rates are all-inclusive.

Discounts None; entire property, $20,000/night

Credit Cards V, AE, MC, D

Check-In/Out 4/12

Smoking No

Pets No

Kids Over 18, unless renting entire property

No-No's Daytrippers

Minimum Stay 2 nights weekends, 3 nights holidays

Open All year except April
Hosts Beverley and Shaun Matthews
P.O. Box 115
Barnard, VT 05031

(800) TWIN-FARMS or (802) 234-9999
Fax: (802) 234-9990
www.twinfarms.com

GREEN TRAILS INN, *Brookfield*

OVERALL ★★★★½ | ROOM QUALITY ★★★★ | VALUE ★★★ | PRICE $90–170

Overlooking the longest floating bridge east of the Mississippi, this oddly shaped bed-and-breakfast was home to one of Rutgers University's first women professors, a botanist who invited friends and students to join her horseback riding on the namesake trails (now used for cross country skiing, snowshoeing and hiking). The 1790 Guest House has a corner room with floor-to-ceiling stencils from those days—and now, a two-person whirlpool tub. Brookfield's few white clapboard houses haven't changed much, and the entire village is on The National Historic Register. But time passes, as Mark, an avid clockmaker, is well aware. The house is filled with about 50 working timepieces, some of them 175 years old (most for sale), and a shop on the property sells, repairs, and restores antique clocks.

SETTING & FACILITIES

Location Center of village, across the road from Sunset Lake, by former riding trails
Near Floating bridge, Ariel's Restaurant, Chandler Music Hall, New England Culinary Institute restaurants, Ben & Jerry's
Building Marcus Peck House (ca.1840); 18th-century guest house
Grounds 17 acres behind inn, on Sunset Lake by floating bridge, trails; front of inn faces village and town park on Lake
Public Space Common rooms, sitting area, dining area, formal DR, parlor; parlor in guest house

Food & Drink Early bird coffee; full breakfast 8–9, cont'l after 9; specialties: homemade muffins, baked omelets, buttermilk waffles; hot drinks; MAP plan w/ restaurant across street; wine and beer
Recreation Fishing, canoeing, swimming, 35km XC skiing trails, snowshoeing, downhill skiing nearby
Amenities & Services Weddings/functions (175), maps, brochures, refrigerator use, iron, forgotten toiletries, music collection, books, magazines, games, canoe, XC skis, snowshoes; concierge service, mountain bike deliveries

ACCOMMODATIONS

Units 9 guest rooms, 4 suites
All Rooms Individually decorated
Some Rooms Bath (9 priv.), fireplace, Jacuzzi; some rooms can join
Bed & Bath Doubles, queens, twins;

some whirlpools, some tubs; 1, tub only w/ hand-held shower
Favorites Stencil suite—wingback chairs, dbl. whirlpool, 1830s stenciling.

Comfort & Decor Comfortable. Mix of antiques, reproductions, Oriental rugs. Excellent lighting. Most with reading chairs. Constantly being updated. Guest House most luxurious.

RATES, RESERVATIONS, & RESTRICTIONS

Deposit 1 night; refund w/ 14-day notice
Discounts Package discounts
Credit Cards V, MC, D
Check-In/Out 3/11; call for late check-in
Smoking Outdoors only
Pets No; boarding nearby
Kids Over 10
Minimum Stay 2 nights holidays, some weekends
Open All year
Hosts Sue and Mark Erwin
By the Floating Bridge
Brookfield, VT 05036
(802) 276-3412 or (800) 243-3412
greentrails@quest-net.com
www.greentrailsinn.com

SHIRE INN, Chelsea

OVERALL ★★★★ | ROOM QUALITY ★★★★ | VALUE ★★½ | PRICE $115–225

Set between the Connecticut Valley and Stowe, this out-of-the-way village is untouched by ski developers, factory outlets, or colleges. This inn of understated charms and pleasures fits perfectly into this environment of commons, Federal-era buildings, and not much else. Karen is an award-winning chef, and her multicourse candlelight dinners, punctuated with a sorbet intermezzo, are romantic and delicious. Attention to small details is evident; even the sheets are ironed. The innkeepers also rent out a separate two-bedroom cottage on ten acres of woods, with a wood-burning stove, gas heat, and antiques. And check out the antique in the inn's backyard: a five-hole privy.

SETTING & FACILITIES

Location Near center of village from VT 110, on White River
Near 2 town commons, dairy farms, covered bridges, Rock of Ages, Woodstock, Cold Hollow Cider Mill, Montpelier, Ben & Jerry's, Dartmouth College
Building 1832 brick Federal Davis House mansion; Nat'l Historic Register
Grounds 23 hilly acres: stream, apple trees, wildflowers, gardens, river w/ farm bridge
Public Space Circular stairway, parlor, porch, DR

Food & Drink (MAP) Full breakfast; specialties: waffles, pancakes, asparagus omelets; tea; 6-course dinner, candlelight, inn guests only; 3 entrées, specialties: rainbow trout, chicken Boursin, eggplant ravioli, apple-cranberry crumble w/ vanilla ice cream; wine cellar: 1,000 bottles, many by glass
Recreation Fishing, biking, XC skiing, boating, ice skating
Amenities & Services Tour books, games, hiking maps, bikes, XC skis, Vintage Vermont tours

ACCOMMODATIONS

Units 6 guest rooms, 1 cottage
All Rooms Bath, antiques
Some Rooms Wood-burning fireplaces
(4)
Bed & Bath 3 queens, 1 king, 2 doubles,
some canopies, hand-ironed cotton
sheets, antique quilts, some extra beds.
Favorites Windsor—former master BR,

canopy bed; Essex—yellow and green
decor, canopy bed
Comfort & Decor Rooms named after
Vermont shires. 10-foot ceilings and large
windows, wide-planked floors, super-soft
sheets. Quilts, period antiques. High ceilings. Immaculate.

RATES, RESERVATIONS, & RESTRICTIONS

Deposit Refund w/ 14-day notice
Discounts Call for avail. discounts,
weekly and monthly rates
Credit Cards V, MC, D
Check-In/Out 3/11
Smoking Covered porch only
Pets No
Kids Over 6
Minimum Stay 2 nights most
weekends

Open Except April, Nov., winter weekdays
Hosts Karen and Jay Keller
Main St.
Chelsea, VT 05038
(802) 685-3031 or (800) 441-6908
Fax: (802) 685-3871
info@shireinn.com
www.shireinn.com

HEERMANSMITH FARM INN, Coventry

OVERALL ★★★½ | ROOM QUALITY ★★★ | VALUE ★★★★★ | PRICE $60–75

This unassuming, truly rural farmhouse is not for neatnicks. It is far north,
hard to find, and so low-key that you might wonder, why bother? Maybe
because it's about the closest you can come to life in these parts 50 years
ago. And the delicious, reasonably priced, surprisingly sophisticated meals
have earned a whopping reputation from locals. Home to generations of
the same family, this rumpled inn offers a true value and a country escape
with soft-spoken Vermont hosts. And it is worth the trip just to see the little covered bridge and the hidden waterfall down the road, and the bril-
liance of stars when you're miles from anything.

SETTING & FACILITIES

Location Vermont 5 to Coventry; left at Martha's Diner, right at beginning of Common, right at Stop, up hill (Heermanville Rd), 4th house on right

Near Black River, Canadian border; Jay Peak, Burke Mountain ski areas, Craftsbury Village, Stowe

Building 1850 farmhouse; outbuildings (sugar shack, barn)

Grounds Nonworking farm, in quiet valley; pond, flower garden; rear deck

Public Space Entry hall, bar; library; spacious DR

Food & Drink Full breakfast; specialties: strawberry French toast, blueberry pancakes, eggs Florentine; 4-course dinners, candlelight table settings; specialties: pan-seared scallops with a whiskey and leak cream sauce, duck w/ strawberry Chambord sauce; wine list, full bar; vegetarian avail.

Recreation Hidden waterfall, covered bridge, snowmobile trails (also used for XC skiing), Alpine skiing, wooded nature walks, canoeing, bike trails

Amenities & Services Bike storage, cots (no cribs), games

ACCOMMODATIONS

Units 6 guest rooms

All Rooms Private bath, reading light, sitting area

Bed & Bath Some antique beds; most shower-only

Favorites Room 1—largest; orig. pine flooring, high-post double bed, handmade quilt, meadow views, only room w/ full bath

Comfort & Decor Rooms small and modest. Homey comfort, not elegant or elaborate. Simple, clean charm.

RATES, RESERVATIONS, & RESTRICTIONS

Deposit None, but credit card number; half of reservation charged w/ less than 7-days notice

Discounts Kids, 3rd person; cottage $500 weekly; $5 add'l per person/breakfast, cottage

Credit Cards V, AE, MC

Check-In/Out 2/11

Smoking No

Pets Welcome

Kids Welcome

Minimum Stay None

Open All year

Hosts Jon and Mariah Fletcher and Jack Smith

Heermanville Rd.

Coventry, VT 05825

(802) 754-8866

hersmith@sovernet.com

www.scenesofvermont.com/heermansmith

INN ON THE COMMON, *Craftsbury Common*

OVERALL ★★★★★ | ROOM QUALITY ★★★★★ | VALUE ★½ | PRICE $250–300

The Inn on the Common is anything but. After chocolates and coffee in the library, just before retiring to your canopied, quilt-covered bed by a flickering fireplace, you'll probably surmise that life really is grand. This inn complex with a white rose and wisteria-entwined pergola by the clay tennis courts welcomes families seeking great cuisine and wine. It offers elegant communal dining for singles, and even gives a conditional OK for pets. There's just no excuse not to splurge here, even though it is a bit of a drive, close to the Quebec border. The sleepy hamlet is the perfect setting to walk off a meal and dream of the next—perhaps designing your own omelet.

SETTING & FACILITIES

Location Off Rt. 14 N, on left of village common

Near Craftsbury Nordic Center, Big Hosmer Lake

Building Three Federal-style buildings: large white 18th-century main house, south annex, north annex

Grounds 10 acres: maple and cedar trees, extensive perennial gardens, views

Public Space Elegant DR, parlors, library/lounge

Food & Drink (MAP) Full breakfast; hors d'oeuvres; candlelight gourmet dining; specialties: parmesan corn cakes, chilled lobster salad, garlic soup, lamb, venison; extensive wine list

Recreation XC skiing, swimming, croquet, boating, golf

Amenities & Services Pool, clay tennis courts, connected to Craftsbury Nordic Center, common TV/VCR w/ 250 movies, guest kitchen in south annex, refrigerator; baby-sitting, catering, bike/canoe rentals; fitness facility, meetings

ACCOMMODATIONS

Units 14 guest rooms, 2 suites in 3 buildings

All Rooms Bath, sitting area, clock

Some Rooms Fireplace, canopy bed

Bed & Bath Some canopies, brass and iron; varied tubs, showers

Favorites Room 10, south annex—fishnet canopy, couch facing fireplace; Room 7—2-BR suite with easy chairs, fireplace

Comfort & Decor Elegantly appointed. Wallcoverings and fabrics blend. Each room different, from airy and simple to lavishly traditional. Good lighting. Lovely views.

RATES, RESERVATIONS, & RESTRICTIONS

Deposit 1 night; snow guarantee or deposit returned

Discounts Kids under 3 free; packages

Credit Cards V, AE, MC

Check-In/Out 1(earlier by arrangement)/11

Smoking Limited

Pets With notice and $15

Kids OK

Minimum Stay 2 nights during peak

Open All year

Hosts Penny and Michael Schmitt
North Main St.
Craftsbury Common, VT 05827
(802) 586-9619 or (800) 521-2233
Fax: (800) 521-2233 or (802) 586-2249
info@innonthecommon.com
www.innonthecommon.com

BIRCHWOOD BED AND BREAKFAST, Derby Line

OVERALL ★★★½ | ROOM QUALITY ★★★ | VALUE ★★★★ | PRICE $85

You are so close to Canada that in the nearby opera house the border runs down the middle of the hall. The audience sits in one country, the players in other! Other delightful spots in the area include The Old Stone House Museum, designed and built by Rev. Alexander Twilight, thought to be the United States' first black college graduate and first black legislator. Dick, an avid golfer, loves talking about music; Elizabeth is an antiques dealer and enjoys gardening in the pretty yard. For those traveling to Montreal, this neat little bed-and-breakfast is a pleasant stop.

SETTING & FACILITIES

Location I-91 to Exit 29 (last U.S. exit), turn left, .75 mi. to Main St., turn left, B&B is half-mile on right, on quiet residential road in village

Near Canadian border, lakes, mountain views, historic opera house, park, antiquing, outdoor concerts, museums; 90 min. to Montreal

Building 1920 Colonial Revival; restored 1993

Grounds Gardens behind house; panoramic view

Public Space DR, LR, porch

Food & Drink Full candlelight breakfast; specialties: homemade muesli, fruit-filled crêpes; afternoon tea
Recreation Water sports, golf, tennis, sleigh rides, maple sugaring
Amenities & Services Flowers, chocolates, maps of Canada

ACCOMMODATIONS

Units 3 guest rooms
All Rooms Private baths, individually decorated, fresh flowers, antiques
Bed & Bath Twins, double, queen, firm mattresses; showers
Favorites Double room—former maid's quarters, antique pineapple bed, marble dresser, Waverly fabrics, hooked area rugs
Comfort & Decor Individually decorated w/ antiques. Wonderful views. Rooms small to large. Immaculate. Basic. Attention to detail.

RATES, RESERVATIONS, & RESTRICTIONS

Deposit 1 night; refund w/ 5-day notice
Credit Cards None
Check-In/Out 3/11
Smoking No
Pets No
Kids No
Minimum Stay 2 nights on weekends
Open All year

Hosts Elizabeth and Dick Fletcher
502 Main St., Box 550
Derby Line, VT 05830
(802) 873-9104
Fax: (802) 873-9121
birchwd@together.net
www.homepages.together.net/~birchwd

INN AT MOUNTAIN VIEW FARM, *East Burke*

OVERALL ★★★★ | ROOM QUALITY ★★★★ | VALUE ★★½ | PRICE $145–210

A century ago this farm provided meat and dairy products to a New York City hotel. Now it serves them only to happy guests, along with organically grown vegetables and beer from a local microbrewery. John is a cardiologist, and Marilyn is an avid skier who emphasizes that they "love children!" The views are great, and the colors, memorable: deep-red barns, green-and-white-striped umbrellas on the patio, raspberry and apple-green interiors. It's good for families, conferences, and weddings. With an adjoining restaurant open to the public, the complex is surprisingly elegant despite the farm atmosphere, which includes a pet Holstein cow named Clover as well as an enormous oak icebox used to store cheese.

SETTING & FACILITIES

Location Exit 23 off I-91, above the valley on a rural road
Near Burke Mountain, Lake Willoughby
Building 1890 redbrick Georgian Colonial creamery, butter churn cupola; restored/modernized in 1989

Grounds 440 acres of hills, meadows, gardens; impressive barns, stable; mountain views

Public Space Large hall, parlors, DR

Food & Drink Full breakfast, communal or in-room; specialties: blueberry-lemon pancakes, breakfast polenta; dining on weekends, open to public; well-selected wine and beer; light lunches, picnic baskets; tea, punch, après-ski wine

Recreation Trout/ice fishing, skiing, table tennis, lawn bowling, croquet

Amenities & Services Function room, VCR, videos, farm animals; catering, sleigh/hay rides, bike/canoe rentals

ACCOMMODAT...

Units 8 guest rooms, 1 suite, 1 cottage

All Rooms Bath, alarm clock, coordinated fabrics

Some Rooms Sitting area; cottage w/ fireplace, whirlpool

Bed & Bath Antique beds; tiled baths, coordinated w/ BR

Favorites The Westmore—corner room w/ green sleigh bed, cranberry florals

Comfort & Decor Authentic and special, with a spare, country feel. Rooms smallish, but comfortable and pretty with botanicals and chintz. Reading lamps, skirted tables, artwork. Small windows. Unique sense of farmhouse living.

RATES, RESERVATIONS, & RESTRICTIONS

Deposit One night on credit card

Discounts Packages, singles, more than 2 nights

Credit Cards V, AE, MC

Check-In/Out 3/11

Smoking No

Pets No

Kids OK

Minimum Stay Appreciate 2 days on weekends

Open All year; restaurant on weekends, winter and summer

Hosts Marilyn and John Pastore

Box 355, Darling Hill Rd.

East Burke, VT 05832

(800) 572-4509

Fax: (802) 626-3625

innmtnview@kingcon.com

www.innmtnview.com

LAKEVIEW INN, Greensboro

OVERALL ★★★½ | ROOM QUALITY ★★★ | VALUE ★★ | PRICE $125–250

Like fine wine and cheese, a good bed-and-breakfast grows more interesting and wonderful with age. And this new one, set in a carefully refurbished historic inn in this tiny, white-clapboard village, will undoubtedly ripen well. The young hosts are locals who lovingly care about historical detailing, and intend to carefully grow this into a more evocative property. It will take time, and cash, but the heart is already there. The "excellent fishing, repose, delightful scenery, healthful food, bracing air," extolled in a publication from 1885, still apply.

SETTING & FACILITIES

Location From south, on the right, on Greensboro's main street

Near Lake Caspian, Stowe, Burke Mountain, Morgan Horse Farm, Vermont Historical Society Museum

Building 1872 former boarding house, National Register of Historic Places

Grounds 2 acres, bird sanctuary, gardens, mountain views

Public Space Common rooms, beamed DR, porch

Food & Drink Full breakfast; specialties: vanilla-almond French toast, mango pancakes; light meals until 7 p.m., baked goods and takeout

Recreation Skiing, boating, fishing, golf, tennis, antiquing, snowshoeing, snowmobiling

Amenities & Services Café/bakery, gift shop; big-screen TV, puzzles, maps, irons; disabled access, catering, packed lunch

ACCOMMODATIONS

Units 9 guest rooms, 1 suite

All Rooms Bath, antiques, heat

Some Rooms AC

Bed & Bath Varied sizes, queens and twins; small baths

Favorites Rooms on the backside—expansive views

Comfort & Decor Some antiques, mainly reproductions. Rooms in historic colors, underdecorated in keeping with boarding house theme. Comfortable, good lighting. Size varies. Needs seasoning, more sense of place.

RATES, RESERVATIONS, & RESTRICTIONS

Deposit One night or 50%; refund w/ 14-day notice

Discounts Long stays, singles, groups

Credit Cards V, MC, D

Check-In/Out 4/11

Smoking No

Pets No

Kids Well-behaved

No-No's Check-in after 6:30

Minimum Stay 2 nights, weekends in

season

Open All year

Hosts Kathryn Unser and John Hunt

Box 180, Main St.

Greensboro, VT 05841

(802) 533-2291

Fax same as phone

lakeview@hcr.net

www.hcr.net/lakeview

SOMERSET HOUSE, Hardwick

OVERALL ★★★½ | ROOM QUALITY ★★★ | VALUE ★★★★½ | PRICE $65–99

Walkways through a hedged "secret garden" are a special treat at this economical bed-and-breakfast far from crowds and the stress of daily life. The house incorporates an English country-house atmosphere in Vermont-style lodgings. This politically-correct operation won an environmental award, and upgrading continues, creating private baths for all rooms. Hardwick has population of a mere 1,800, and the innkeepers put it best: "We're an old-fashioned small town in Vermont's remote Northeast Kingdom, with friendly people and beautiful surroundings." The village has a good bookstore, so you can find a nook and read in peace.

SETTING & FACILITIES

Location 1 block from intersection of Vermont Rts. 14 and 15, in a quiet, residential neighborhood, 1 block from the Lamoille River

Near Village, hiking trails, lakes, XC ski areas, Stowe, Montpelier, Canadian border, VAST trail 14

Building 1894 unusual plantation style/Queen-Anne Victorian

Grounds Village lawn, porches, secret garden, perennial plantings, butternut trees

Public Space Sitting room w/ working fireplace, formal DR, writing alcove

Food & Drink Full breakfast; free-range or floor-range eggs, B&B garden or local co-op fresh produce (often organic), tea and coffee at all times; specialties: homemade breads, soups (on request)

Recreation Mountain/trail biking, canoeing, fishing, sailing, swimming, kayaking, hiking, XC skiing, snowshoeing, golf, arts, reading

Amenities & Services Fans in rooms, irons, bike storage; small group meetings, retreats

ACCOMMODATIONS

Units 4 guest rooms

All Rooms Fresh flowers, carpet, seating

Some Rooms Bath, balcony, robes, cots for 3rd person (20)

Bed & Bath Iron, brass beds; firm bedding, queen and twin sizes; some shower only; some hall access, robes

Favorites Room 4—Light, airy room w/

bay window and balcony

Comfort & Decor Rooms vary: large, cozy, bright. All w/ fresh flowers, pretty wallpaper, antique furnishings, artwork. Large round tower room, queen bed, connects w/ cozy twin bed room. Bay windows, collectibles.

RATES, RESERVATIONS, & RESTRICTIONS

Deposit 1 night; refund w/ 5-day notice

Discounts 5+ days or book all four rooms

Credit Cards V, MC

Check-In/Out By arrangement

Smoking No

Pets No

Kids Check

Minimum Stay None

Open All year

Hosts Judy and Roger Waible
130 Highland Ave., Box 1098
Hardwick, VT 05843-1098
(800) 838-8074 or (802) 472-5484
www.somersethousebb.com

RABBIT HILL INN, Lower Waterford

OVERALL ★★★★★ | ROOM QUALITY ★★★★★ | VALUE ★½ | PRICE $220–380

For groups, weddings, retreats, and business travelers who want the feel of Gentle, warm, exquisite, welcoming, pampering, luxurious, and romantic don't begin to define this inn. Hosts Leslie and Brian, the Ginger and Fred of innkeeping, make it look easy. They rightly call it "a paradise for the senses, vacation for the soul." Whatever the magic "it" is, the award-winning hospitality, refined cuisine, and perfectionism established by the former owners continue, unabated. Sweet and sophisticated, lively and peaceful, carefully orchestrated with appreciative management and skillful care, this is truly an award-winning, 24-carrot inn experience. Can the "it" be love?

SETTING & FACILITIES

Location Edge of tiny historic white village, off Rt. 18

Near Franconia Notch State Park, Fairbank's Museum, Cabot Cheese Creamery, antiques, art galleries

Building Restored 1795 white-columned Greek Revival inn

Grounds 15 acres, gardens, spring-fed swimming pond, waterfall, gazebo, shuffleboard, horseshoes; mountain views

Public Space Common rooms, library, pub, video and TV room, DRs, oil lamp–lit porches, phone rooms, all in period, w/ antiques, art

Food & Drink (MAP) Lavish, candlelit multi-course breakfast; 5-course dinner, open to public, harpist on Sat.; specialty: warmed sweet potato and red cabbage salad w/ toasted walnuts and spiced apple cider vinaigrette; tea/snacks; drinks in pub

Recreation Sledding, snowshoeing, XC skiing, golf, swimming, stave puzzles, games

Amenities & Services VCR library, full concierge services, gift popcorn with videos; candle, soft music at turn-down; 1:1 staff to guest ratio, preferences noted; disabled accessible room

ACCOMMODATIONS

Units 9 guest rooms, 12 suites

All Rooms Bath, seating, hairdryer, coffee maker, climate controls, CD and radio, robes

Some Rooms AC, gas fireplace, sundeck, porch, enlarged sitting area, skylight

Bed & Bath Mostly kings, canopies, four-posters; some whirlpools in BR

Favorites Jonathan Cummings Suite—queen canopy, 2nd fireplace in sitting room, whirlpool for 2, porch, mountain views

Comfort & Decor Rooms vary in size, decor, and luxury. All w/ romantic touches and attention to smallest detail, each w/ a theme, a room diary to record thoughts, and romantic lighting. Rugs, antiques, murals and stenciling, photos. Rooms in inn less private.

RATES, RESERVATIONS, & RESTRICTIONS

Deposit 1 night, more for extended stay; refund w/ 14-day notice (30 days, holidays and foliage)

Discounts Single, 3rd person, packages

Credit Cards V, AE, MC

Check-In/Out 2/11

Smoking No

Pets No

Kids Over 12

No-No's Jeans at dinner, tipping

Minimum Stay 2 nights on weekends, holidays

Open Except first two weeks of April
and Nov.
Hosts Leslie and Brian Mulcahy
Box 55
Lower Waterford, VT 05848

(800) 76-BUNNY or (802) 748-5168
Fax: (802) 748-8342
info@rabbithillinn.com
www.rabbithillinn.com

WILDFLOWER INN, Lyndonville

OVERALL ★★★½ | ROOM QUALITY ★★★ | VALUE ★★½ | PRICE $85–220

Children are pampered at this sprawling 1796 farmhouse complex on 500 acres, once part of an estate. Kiddie amenities include a playroom with dress-up clothes, bumper pool, a separate swimming pool, nightly games and movies, baby-sitting, a children's theater, a petting farm, pony rides, early family-style meals, a teen rec center, and more. Families have the run of the place except during school, when couples and conferences reign. Lovers can retreat to the former one-room schoolhouse suite with a two-person whirlpool, and enjoy the sunset view along the ridge, in peace.

SETTING & FACILITIES

Location 4 mi. from I-91, same road as Mountain View Creamery, on Darling Hill
Near Burke Mountain Ski Resort, over 50 lakes and ponds, 4 golf courses, covered bridges, museums, dairy farms, maple sugar houses, antiquing, Cabot Cheese Creamery; 2 hrs. to Montreal
Building Large farm (settled in 1796); several farmhouse-style buildings, barns, and outbuildings
Grounds 500+ farm acres, gardens, trails
Public Space Sitting rooms
Food & Drink Full breakfast; specialties: eggs, bacon or sausage, pancakes, blueberry muffins; p.m. snack; simple dinner avail. in public restaurant, open all year/days vary, reservations recommended; breads, soups, children's menu
Recreation Golf, winter and water sports, horseback riding, fall foliage tours
Amenities & Services Gift shop, art gallery; sauna, hot tub; indoor/outdoor play areas, petting barn, pool; tennis, basketball, batting cage, soccer, skating, XC/snowshoe trails, summer children's programs/theater, add'l cots/cribs, guests may use grounds after check-out

ACCOMMODATIONS

Units 15 guest rooms, 8 suites in main farmhouse, carriage house, 1 cottage
All Rooms Bath, endless country view
Some Rooms Priv. deck/balcony/patio, priv. stairway, dining/sitting area, bunk bed, sofa bed, kitchenette, washer/dryer; disabled access (1)
Bed & Bath Some canopy, four-posters; some shower-only, some 1- and 2-person whirlpools
Favorites Yellow Room—upstairs, main farmhouse, twin and double beds in 1 room, double canopy in 2nd, full bath; School House Cottage—private, queen, dbl. whirlpool, deck, kitchenette, dining/sitting area.

Comfort & Decor Vary from family units to secluded cottage. Touches including stenciling, antique or reproduction beds, country quilts. Simple but comfortable. Can be noisy when school not in session.

RATES, RESERVATIONS, & RESTRICTIONS

Deposit 1 night; refunds w/ 14-day notice (check for holiday rate increases; add 10% gratuity, Vermont taxes)
Discounts Various packages, midweek, longer stays, singles, 3rd person, kids (under 3 free), seniors 10% (midweek nonholiday)
Credit Cards V, MC
Check-In/Out 3/11
Smoking Outdoors only
Pets No

Kids Welcome
Minimum Stay 2 nights, weekends
Open All year
Hosts Mary and Jim O'Reilly
Darling Hill Rd.
Lyndonville, VT 05851
(800) 627-8310 or (802) 626-8310
Fax: (802) 626-3039
wldflwrinn@aol.com
www.wildflowerinn.com

COUNTRY GARDEN INN, Quechee

OVERALL ★★★★½ | ROOM QUALITY ★★★★ | VALUE ★★★ | PRICE $110–180

Have you ever waded in a nineteenth-century, waterfall-fed rock pool? That is only one of many special parts adding up an extra-special whole at this sophisticated, ever-delightful bed-and-breakfast. Other examples: bathrooms with nineteenth-century chamber-pot seats and modern massaging shower heads; breakfast and afternoon tea in a brick-floored, plant-filled greenhouse; and a den with hundreds of videos and an old safe recycled into a complimentary minibar. Amid the decor you'll find Russian decorated eggs, musical instruments, stained glass, stenciling, Oriental rugs and sleigh beds. Shelly decorates with objects from her travels, but even better, knows how to please and surprise.

SETTING & FACILITIES

Location Left after covered bridge; 1st driveway past church
Near Theaters, brewery, glassblowing, museums, antiquing, art galleries, Dartmouth College
Building Circa 1819, w/ original beams, ceilings; Victorian (and later) additions
Grounds Garden, 1840 wading pool w/ waterfall, BBQ, picnic tables
Public Space Greenhouse, common rooms, lounge, parlor, DR
Food & Drink 3-course country breakfast; specialty: French toast w/ walnuts; tea by appt.; hot and soft drinks; evening cocktails
Recreation Games, exercise equipment, fly-fishing, sleigh/hay rides
Amenities & Services Breakfast concerts some summer Sundays; fire, security system; turn-down, pick-ups from airport; privileges at Quechee Club: golf, pool, tennis, skiing, boating, fishing, health club, seasonal polo (Sat.), bike/canoe rentals nearby

ACCOMMODATIONS

Units 4 guest rooms
All Rooms Bath, AC, robes, clock/radio,
phone on request
Some Rooms Extra bed, unusual artifacts
Bed & Bath Beds vary, some canopy,
sleigh; massage shower heads, curling
irons, hairdryers
Favorites Rose room—queen brass

bed, Tiffany-style lamps, window seat,
chandelier, huge bath
Comfort & Decor Details, details.
Embroidered pillow cases, handmade
quilts. Flower themes, Oriental rugs.
Sophisticated touches. Thoughtful amenities. I family-oriented w/ daybed and priv.
entrance.

RATES, RESERVATIONS, & RESTRICTIONS

Deposit I night; refund w/ 14-day notice
(30 days, multiple rooms)
Discounts Off-season
Credit Cards V, MC
Check-In/Out 3–7/10
Smoking No
Pets No
Kids 12 and up
No-No's Check-in after 11 p.m.
Minimum Stay 2 nights weekends, all
nights Sept. 15–Oct. 31, some holidays,

events; 3 nights holiday weekends, Dartmouth graduation
Open May 15–October 30
Host Shelly Gardner
37 Main St.
Quechee, VT 05059
(802) 295-3023
Fax: (802) 295-3121
innkeeper@country-garden-inn.com
www.vtcountryinn.com

WILLOUGH VALE INN, Westmore

OVERALL ★★★½ | ROOM QUALITY ★★★ | VALUE ★★ | PRICE $89–245

Location, location, location. This isolated area has been designated a regis-
tered national landmark by the National Park Service. If you can't get to
Norway, a fjord-like lake high up in Vermont will suffice quite nicely. After
staying at the inn in 1909, Robert Frost wrote about it in his poem "A Servant to Servants." More prosaically, if you enjoy large Victorians, front
porches, hanging baskets, and breathtaking views, this spacious, informal
property will appeal. Cottages are more private than rooms in the main
house, and the atmosphere is casual throughout.

SETTING & FACILITIES

Location Rt. 5A, facing Lake Willoughby
Near Burke Mountain, Jay Peak
Building Circa 1900 Victorian farmhouse
Grounds Lawn to shore of lake; views of
granite cliffs beyond lake; gazebo
Public Space Common room, DR, tap-
room, porch, cozy DR

Food & Drink Cont'l breakfast for Inn
guests; creative American cuisine at dinner (limited public seating)
Recreation Swimming, (ice) fishing,
boating, skiing
Amenities & Services Books, puzzles,
games; snowmobile/snowshoe rentals

ACCOMMODATIONS

Units 7 guest rooms, 2 suites; 4 lakefront cottages (heated)

All Rooms Private bath, TV, handcrafted furnishings, heat

Some Rooms Queen four-poster, large Jacuzzi, fireplace; cottages: kitchen, LR, fireplace, deck/porch, private docks(Summer)

Bed & Bath Vermont furnishings, queen beds; cottages, 1- or 2-BR; some whirlpools

Favorites The Angler—lakefront cottage for 2 w/ French doors on water, sunken LR, fireplace, kitchen

Comfort & Decor Casual furnishings, spare, almost hotel-like feel. Bright, clean, contemporary. Wall sconces and table lamps. Heated cottages have fireplaces, priv. docks, decks, screened porches. Good lake views.

RATES, RESERVATIONS, & RESTRICTIONS

Deposit Check or credit card w/in 10 days; refund w/ 14-day cancellation

Discounts Packages, extra person, singles, kids under 12, free; half off Green Mountain Inn, Stowe

Credit Cards V, AE, MC

Check-In/Out 2/11

Smoking No

Pets Negotiable, $20/night

Kids OK

Minimum Stay Two nights July, August, and foliage

Open All year

Hosts Katherine and Randall Johnson
RR 2 Box 403
Westmore, VT 05860
(800) 594-9102 or (802) 525-4123
Fax: (802) 525-4514
info@willoughvale.com
www.willoughvale.com

ARDMORE INN, Woodstock

OVERALL ★★★★ | ROOM QUALITY ★★★★ | VALUE ★★★½ | PRICE $85–150

International influence defines this Greek Revival bed-and-breakfast with a red slate roof. The Tullys from Ireland, the original owners, gave the guest rooms their family names, and Ardmore means "Great House" in Gaelic. Current host Giorgio, born in Peru, creates healthy breakfasts such as multigrain pancakes, but his specialty is "Woodstock Sunrise," a baked concoction of Vermont flatbread filled with eggs, peppers, mushrooms, and cheddar. Furnished with Oriental rugs, an antique sideboard with service in the Governor Winthrop design, and local artwork, the house is known for its great architecture.

SETTING & FACILITIES

Location On Woodstock's main street in historic district

Near Galleries, arts/crafts shops, covered bridges, glassblowers, potters, Dartmouth College, antiquing, theater, Killington

Building 1850 Victorian Greek Revival; renovated 1994

Grounds Back lawn, garden, maple trees

Public Space Parlor, DR, screened veranda

Food & Drink Full breakfast; specialties: berries in maple wine sauce, sautéed eggs, truffle butter and veggies on flat Vermont bread w/ cheddar, asparagus, or Hollandaise sauce; p.m. tea, espresso; wine/cheese, fruit; special diets accom.

Recreation Sleigh/carriage rides, skiing, biking

Amenities & Services Chocolates, fresh flowers; concierge, tour guidance/maps, limited disabled access (vision, hearing)

ACCOMMODATIONS

Units 5 guest rooms

All Rooms Bath, fireplace, clock, radio

Some Rooms Sitting area

Bed & Bath Queens, king, double; 1 four-poster, cannonball; whirlpools, marble baths

Favorites Sheridan—1st floor, hand-carved French walnut queen, marble shower, whirlpool; Maggie's Room—2nd floor, smallest, morning sun, antique carved oak double, Victorian feel

Comfort & Decor Rooms named for owner's family members. Spacious, graceful, comfortable. Vary widely in size and style from Colonial to Victorian. Tarma, former billiard room in back, quietest.

RATES, RESERVATIONS, & RESTRICTIONS

Deposit 1 night; refund w/ 14-day notice

Discounts Off-season

Credit Cards V, AE, MC

Check-In/Out 3–7/11

Smoking No

Pets No

Kids No

Minimum Stay During Sept. 20–Oct. 20

Open All year

Host Giorgio Ortiz

23 Pleasant St.

Woodstock, VT 05091-0466

(802) 457-3887 or (800) 497-9652

Fax: (802) 457-9006

ardmoreinn@aol.com

www.ardmoreinn.com

CHARLESTON HOUSE, Woodstock

OVERALL ★★★½ | ROOM QUALITY ★★★★ | VALUE ★★½ | PRICE $110–195

Hosts Willa and Dixi have been married 34 years and counting and seem to love innkeeping—and having as much fun as their guests. This in-town bed-and-breakfast is less pricey and stylish than other Woodstock properties noted in the book, yet offers a warm, traditional, and comfortable stay. After a candlelight breakfast of Swiss soufflé you can easily stroll to most shops and restaurants in this classic town, then hole up in your room by the fire or soak in a whirlpool tub. Nearby restaurants are numerous, and the hosts are happy to give recommendations. The third-floor room is especially large and suitable for families.

SETTING & FACILITIES

Location 10 mi. W of I-89 and I-91, at edge of village
Near Nature area, galleries, museums, Woodstock Village Green, auctions
Building 1835 brick Greek Revival townhouse; Nat'l Register of Historic Places
Grounds Small, landscaped lawn
Public Space LR, porch

Food & Drink Full candlelight breakfast, communal or in room; specialties: Charleston French toast, Swiss soufflé
Recreation Canoeing, golf, horseback riding, skiing, swimming, sleigh rides
Amenities & Services Irons, access to kitchen refrigerator, limited disabled access (visual, hearing)

ACCOMMODATIONS

Units 9 guest rooms
All Rooms Bath
Some Rooms TV, fireplace, sitting area, porch, adjoining rooms
Bed & Bath Queens, some twins, some headboards, 4 four-posters, canopies; some claw-foot tubs, whirlpools

Favorites Summer Kitchen—queen bed, whirlpool, fireplace
Comfort & Decor Colonial decor or more formal. Drapes, carpet, coordinated bedspreads. Village views, great reading lights. Each room decorated differently, from country to traditional.

RATES, RESERVATIONS, & RESTRICTIONS

Deposit 1 night; refund w/ 14-day notice
Discounts Longer stays, off-season
Credit Cards V, AE, MC, D
Check-In/Out 2:30/11
Smoking No
Pets No; 1 in-house cat
Kids Depends; check w/ B&B
No-No's Cots or 3rd person in room
Minimum Stay 2 nights in season

weekends
Open All year
Hosts Willa and Dieter (Dixi) Nohl
21 Pleasant St.
Woodstock, VT 05091
(802) 457-3843 or (888) 475-3800
Fax: (802) 457-2512
nohl@together.net
www.charlestonhouse.com

JACKSON HOUSE INN, Woodstock

OVERALL ★★★★½ | ROOM QUALITY ★★★★½ | VALUE ★½ | PRICE $195–340

Have you ever seen a pond with a tiny beach of ground marble? Expect the unexpected. The bed-and-breakfast is gleaming with Chef Andrew Turner, formerly of Le Louis X in France and Fleur de Lys in San Francisco, turning out meals to match the surroundings: elegant, superb, sensual, refined, memorable. If you're not about to spring for nearby Twin Farms, you won't be exactly slumming at this 1890 clapboard with great gardens, fine antiques, themed guest rooms, and basement spa. Enjoy evening hors d'oeuvres served by hosts Carl and Linda, and on the weekend, the library piano as well. Viva!

SETTING & FACILITIES

Location 1.5 mi. W of Woodstock on Rt. 4, in semi-residential area at edge of village

Near Art and craft galleries, antiquing, theater

Building 1890 Victorian clapboard, copper roof; Nat'l Register of Historic Places

Grounds 5-acre garden, huge trees, meadow, pond, arched bridge, brook

Public Space Parlor, library, DR, front veranda; wheelchair access

Food & Drink Full breakfast; specialties: fresh smoked salmon and shallots in scrambled eggs, fruit compote w/ peach schnapps; evening cocktails and hors d'oeuvres; dinner; specialties: grilled venison tenderloin w/ chestnut spaetzle, Maine lobster, Maine scallops; pastry chef; open to public

Recreation Horseback riding, canoeing, swimming, golf, tennis, skiing, sleigh rides, hot-air ballooning

Amenities & Services Refrigerator, irons, on-site spa w/ exercise equipment, big-screen satellite TV; weddings, business services, nearby bike and ski rentals

ACCOMMODATIONS

Units 9 guest rooms, 6 suites

All Rooms Bath, AC, hairdryer

Some Rooms Desk, chair, French doors, balcony, fireplace, wheelchair access, skylight

Bed & Bath Kings and queens; four-posters, some brass, iron, spool, cannonball, sleigh, antique; marble, whirlpools, massage tubs for 2

Favorites Half-a-Six Pence—New England country, queen, desk, French doors, balcony, small and cozy; Wales Johnson—queen cherry sleigh bed, antique English desk, gas fireplace, French doors to patio/gardens, whirlpool

Comfort & Decor Themed decor, w/ period antiques, detailing. Styles from Napoleonic to Victorian to New England country. Oriental rugs, ceiling fans, wide plank floors, art. New suites: especially luxurious baths. French doors to views of gardens.

RATES, RESERVATIONS, & RESTRICTIONS

Deposit 100%; refund w/ 15-day notice, rebooking fee

Discounts Midweek seasonally

Credit Cards V, AE, MC

Check-In/Out 3/11

Smoking No

Pets No

Kids 14 and up

No-No's 3rd person in room

Minimum Stay 2 nights weekends

Open All year

Hosts Carl and Linda Delnegro
114-3 Senior Lane
Woodstock, VT 05091
(802) 457-2065 or (800) 448-1890
Fax: (802) 457-9290
innkeeper@jacksonhouse.com
www.jacksonhouse.com

WOODSTOCKER, Woodstock

OVERALL ★★★½ | ROOM QUALITY ★★★ | VALUE ★★★ | PRICE $85–155

With a low-key atmosphere, cheery rooms, and a convenient location at the edge of the village, this former farmhouse and attached barn (with suites) is a good choice for budget travelers and families. Like so many bed-and-breakfast owners, sociable Nancy and Tom left their former lives, seeking togetherness and a chance to stay home and raise their family. They moved from Cleveland in 1996, and have been tweaking the property since. Tom, an accountant, does the maintenance; Nancy, a former English teacher, sets out a bountiful buffet breakfast in the comfortable family room filled with country furnishings, warmth, cookies, and a big-screen TV.

SETTING & FACILITIES

Location Just over Rt. 4 (River St.) bridge, at western edge of Woodstock
Near Covered bridge, galleries, crafts, shopping, Marsh-Billings Nat'l Park, Historical Society Museum
Building 1830s 2-story Cape-style farmhouse, attached barn
Grounds Small lawn, picket fence
Public Space Common room
Food & Drink Buffet breakfast; special-ties: puffed pancakes w/ banana-walnut topping, eggs w/ Vermont cheeses, appleberry crisp w/ raspberries from garden; tea; fresh-ground coffee
Recreation Skiing, fishing, maple sugaring, ice-skating, sleigh rides
Amenities & Services 5-person whirlpool (winters), local bike rental, pick-up from train/bus

ACCOMMODATIONS

Units 7 guest rooms, 2 suites
All Rooms Bath, individual heat
Some Rooms Kitchen, TV (1), extra bed, AC, sitting room, balcony (1)
Bed & Bath 2 doubles, queens, 1 canopy; tub/showers; cribs/roll-aways
Favorites Canopy room—roses, cherry floors, antique Victorian chairs; Room 6—wicker, Shaker-style furnishings, sunflower print fabrics
Comfort & Decor Individually decorated. Spacious suites w/ TV, kitchen, great for families. Antiques and reproductions, floral coordinates, braided rugs, skirted tables. Comfortable and casual. Rooms in back, quietest. Well-maintained.

RATES, RESERVATIONS, & RESTRICTIONS

Deposit Full payment 1 night; others 50%; refund w/ 14-day notice
Discounts Off-season
Credit Cards V, AE, MC
Check-In/Out 3–6/11; call for late arrival
Smoking No
Pets No; in-house dog (lab/greyhound mix) Chelsea
Kids OK
Minimum Stay Some weekends and holidays; check
Open All year
Hosts Nancy and Tom Blackford
61 River St., Rt. 4
Woodstock, VT 05091
(802) 457-3896
Fax: (802) 457-3897
woodstocker@valley.net
www.scenesofvermont.com/woodstocker

Massachusetts

Every school kid knows that Massachusetts's history goes back to the Pilgrims who landed at **Plymouth** on the *Mayflower*, sharing Thanksgiving with the Native Americans who accepted them. The state was home to the opening skirmishes of the American Revolution, from the Boston Tea Party to Lexington and Concord, and it was a major manufacturing center during the Industrial Revolution, 100 years later.

With a third technological revolution now upon us, Massachusetts is again a major player, which makes historical buildings and sites fascinating places to visit—the real deal, not virtual—and the state's great universities, arts groups, and museums offer world-class cultural opportunities.

Martha's Vineyard's beaches, Fenway Park, Sturbridge Village, cranberry bogs, the **Berkshires Hills** scenery. Massachusetts' varied pleasures include beaches and whale watching in the east, historic villages with classic commons and hilly terrain for skiing in the west. And fairs, festivals, exhibits, and just about everything in between keep visitors busy throughout the year. This is an all-season state in all ways.

Massachusetts reveals much of its history in its architecture, including red brick townhouses in **Boston** and rows of eighteenth-century homes in historic **Deerfield,** on the other side of the state. Foliage season runs from mid-September to late October throughout the varied landscapes—figure on peak color around Columbus Day.

In the Boston area, spend a day walking the **Freedom Trail** through the city, visiting **Old North Church** and **Faneuil Hall** (once a planning spot for the Revolution, it's now a shopping mecca). Take in a **Red Sox** game. Check out the new exhibits at the **Museum of Fine Arts.** Listen to the **Boston Pops,** or tour **Harvard University.**

When you are ready to escape, head just north to Marblehead's rocky beaches or to **Salem's witch sites.** Or head to the quiet area south of

Boston and take a trip to the **New Bedford Whaling Museum** or to **Plimoth Plantation,** a re-creation of the 1627 community.

About an hour's drive from the southern Boston area is **Cape Cod,** with its dune-backed, sandy ribbon of beaches and the art scene in **Provincetown** at the tip. **The Cape** is also home to the **John F. Kennedy Memorial and Museum** in **Hyannis, the Woods Hole Oceanographic Institute,** and the **National Marine Fisheries Aquarium** in **Woods Hole,** and to summer theater and antiquing.

Ferries can take you to **Martha's Vineyard** or **Nantucket Island.** The Vineyard is home to several communities: **Edgartown** is among the most bustling, while **Gay Head** provides a serene preserve among colorful cliffs. **Nantucket Island** is a National Historic District for its 800 buildings built before 1850. After walking or biking around the island, visit the specialty shops or the **Whaling Museum** in **Nantucket Town.**

Central/Western Massachusetts may not have beaches, but its delights include **Old Sturbridge Village,** which re-creates life in 1830s New England; the **Worcester Art Museum** in the state's second-largest city; and colleges including **Smith, Mt. Holyoke, University of Massachusetts at Amherst,** and **Hampshire** near the western border south of the **Berkshires.**

Bordered by Connecticut to the south, Vermont to the north, and New York to the west, the glorious **Berkshire Hills** are home to **Tanglewood Music Festival** and **Williamstown,** with its great college and museums. This refined area of arts, villages with grand mansions, and camps and farms with rural vistas seems far from the bustle of Boston but offers similar cultural delights in a setting of much-photographed New England beauty.

Small lodging is plentiful throughout Massachusetts, from Berkshire mansions to Cape Cod sea captains' homes, many beautifully restored. The tradition of wayside inns is another part of this state's pleasures, and continues in fine form.

FOR MORE INFORMATION

Bed and Breakfast Associates, Bay Colony, Ltd.
(781) 449-5302 or (888) 486-6018
email: info@bnbboston.com
www.bnbboston.com

Massachusetts B&B Association
Box 352
Chesterfield, MA 01012

Massachusetts Lodging Association
(617) 720-1776
Fax: (617) 720-1305
email: info@masslodging.com
www.massachusettslodging.com

Boston Region

From **Plymouth Rock** and **Plimoth Plantation** (a re-creation of the 1627 Plymouth settlement), to the **New Bedford Whaling Museum, Boston Harbor,** and the fishing villages of **Rockport, Gloucester,** and **Newburyport,** the history of the Boston region seems defined by the Atlantic Ocean it borders.

South of Boston, visit the **Buzzards Bay villages** and **Horseneck State Reservation,** plus more recent historical sites with **Battleship Cove,** home to U.S. Navy ships. Try whale watching, visit a vineyard or a park, or attend a concert at the **Great Woods Center for the Performing Arts** in **Mansfield.** There are plenty of period homes to visit, as well as museums that highlight the shipbuilding, sea-captain, and early settlement histories of the region.

Boston is New England's great city and one of the finest concentrations of our history and culture. The **Freedom Trail,** with 16 textbook-familiar sites, includes **Paul Revere's House, Old North Church,** and **Faneuil Hall**—with its shops, entertainment, and restaurants. The USS *Constitution* (the navy's oldest ship), the **New England Aquarium, Museum of Science, Museum of Fine Arts, Isabella Stewart Gardner Museum, Kennedy Library and Museum,** and **Boston Tea Party Ship and Museum** are just a few more worthy stops.

You can stroll through **Harvard Square** in **Cambridge,** glide on a swan boat in the **Public Garden,** listen to the **Boston Symphony Orchestra,** or catch the **Red Sox** in action. And the **Black Heritage Trail** highlights Boston's nineteenth-century black community on **Beacon Hill.**

North of the city, eighteenth- and nineteenth-century fishing, sailing, and whaling towns have become suburbs with character. **Salem,** site of the 1692 witch-hunting trials, now has museums and a village dedicated to the pointy-hatted, broom-flying ladies in black.

Rockport, Marblehead, and **Gloucester**—working ports and artists' colonies, blue collar and artsy—are full of homes and bed-and-breakfasts with notable architecture. **Newburyport** is an undiscovered gem of nineteenth-century architecture. On the north edge of the Atlantic coast, **Salisbury** and **Plum Island** are worthy beach destinations, where you can sea kayak, canoe, and whale watch.

Lexington and **Concord,** in the **Merrimack Valley** just to the west, are where the first shots of the Revolution rang out in 1775. **Louisa May Alcott** and **Ralph Waldo Emerson,** among others, had homes here that are now open to visitors. **Buckman Tavern,** where the Minute Men once met, is also open seasonally, as is the **Hancock-Clarke House,** to which Paul Revere rode, warning of the British. The **Concord Museums,** housing treasures like Revere's signal lantern, is open year-round in **Concord.**

Check out nearby **Lowell's Sports Museum of New England,** and relive the city's mill history at the **Lowell National Historic Park. Lowell,** a center of the industrial revolution, has canal footpaths by many of the brick mills.

The city of **Boston** has few small lodgings—hotels and motels naturally dominate. But many old homes in surrounding areas, especially to the north, have become bed-and-breakfasts, and to the west are a few inns dating back 200 years. If you want to stay in the Boston region, book early and be prepared to commute to the city, and check out Amtrak's high-speed run, which connects Washington, D.C., with Boston.

FOR MORE INFORMATION

A Bed & Breakfast Agency of Boston
(617) 720-3540 or (800) 248-9262
Fax: (617) 523-5761

Citywide Reservation Services, Inc.
(617) 267-7424 or (800) 468-3593
Fax: (617) 267-9408
email: crsinc@cityres.com
www.cityres.com

Just Right Reservations
(617) 423-3550
www.ziplink.net/~jimwells

MORINS VICTORIAN HIDEAWAY, Blackstone

OVERALL ★★★ | ROOM QUALITY ★★★ | VALUE ★★★★½ | PRICE $65–75

This big pale yellow clapboard, built in 1844, is on the midpoint of a 27-mile canoe tour on the Blackstone River. Canoeists paddle along, then stop here, maybe take in a movie and a meal in nearby Providence, spend the night in a comfortable room, and enjoy breakfast before paddling away. The bed-and-breakfast is also near a major bike trail. The inn is in an area on the Rhode Island border not exactly known for tourism. A billiards room and swimming pool await, walls are stenciled or rag-painted, and a fireplace is marbleized in mid-nineteenth-century style.

SETTING & FACILITIES

Location Off Rt. 122 (Main St.)
Near Walk to Blackstone River and Gorge; zoo, historic Quaker Meeting House, boat tours, state park, Providence, restaurants, outlets; hour to Newport, commuter rail to Boston
Building 1844 19-room Victorian
Grounds 3.5 acres, woods, lawn, pool
Public Space Entrance foyer, sunny gathering room, library area, billiards

room, guest kitchenette
Food & Drink Cont'l breakfast buffet; guest refrigerator; kitchen always stocked w/ refreshments, snacks
Recreation Providence activities, antiquing, day trips, extensive trails
Amenities & Services Exercise room, TV, cordless phone, iron, roll-away bed, train schedule, maps

ACCOMMODATIONS

Units 3 guest rooms
All Rooms Spacious, bright
Some Rooms Priv. bath, decorative mantel
Bed & Bath Some antique beds; double, queen, twin; add'l bath on 3rd floor, some orig. fixtures
Favorites Rose Room—romantic, hand-

painted furnishings, priv. tile bath, large shower
Comfort & Decor Almost Heaven Room w/ cherubs, 3 beds, mantel. Shares old-fashioned bath w/ Lilac Room. Bay window w/ river, sunset views; queen bed, original in-room sink. Comfortable, basic.

RATES, RESERVATIONS, & RESTRICTIONS

Deposit 1 night; refund w/ 7-day notice
Discounts 7+ day stays
Credit Cards None
Check-in/Out 2/11
Smoking No
Pets No

Kids Limited, check w/ B&B
Open All year
Hosts Lynn and Chip Morin
48 Mendon St.
Blackstone, MA 01504
(508) 883-7045

MARY PRENTISS INN, *Cambridge*

OVERALL ★★★★ | ROOM QUALITY ★★★★ | VALUE ★★ | PRICE $99–229

There were no traffic jams in 1843 when Mary Prentiss' father-in-law built this Greek Revival home as a country house outside of Boston for the newly-weds. Mary's ancestors were among Cambridge's founding families in the 1600s, and their graves are in the nearby Historic Old Burying Ground. The innkeepers have preserved the essence of the old and added artful touches while bridging to a new wing of rooms and updating with phones, air-conditioning, and other high-tech conveniences. It's no longer rural here, so breakfast on the sunny deck among the flowers is about as close as you'll get to a country getaway.

SETTING & FACILITIES

Location Off Massachusetts Ave. between Harvard Square and Porter Square, on a residential street
Near Harvard Univ., Lesley College, Christ Church, museums, subway, bus line to Boston
Building 1843 Greek Revival; Nat'l Register of Historic Places
Grounds Side yard, pear trees, front planters, deck
Public Space Entry, curved stairway; DR; conservatory; 1,000-sq.-ft. deck
Food & Drink Full breakfast; special-ties: quiche and potatoes, raisin scones, apple pancakes; tea and cookies; summer lunch, outdoor café; weekend dinners (extra); specialties: cream of broccoli soup, chicken or fish; comp. wine
Recreation Tennis, gym, pool, golf, rowing, rollerblading, sports fields nearby
Amenities & Services Hot tub, refrigerator, irons, books, daily paper, fax, limited underground parking, flowers/chocolates in rooms (extra); meetings (4–5), weddings (20–25)

ACCOMMODATIONS

Units 15 guest rooms, 5 suites
All Rooms Bath, phone, cable, dataport, individual heat/AC
Some Rooms Wheelchair access, fireplace, wet bar, refrigerator
Bed & Bath Varied sizes, four-posters, cannonballs; tiled, tubs, dbl. whirlpools, makeup mirrors, hairdryers
Favorites Garden Room—priv. deck, fireplace, whirlpool
Comfort & Decor Oversized armoires, antique wingchairs and desks. Oriental rugs, vaulted ceilings, original moldings, 1800s wood floors, exposed beams. Some rooms dark. Twin beds for parents and kids sharing room.

RATES, RESERVATIONS, & RESTRICTIONS

Deposit 1 night when making reservation; refund w/ 14-day notice
Discounts Seniors, longer stays, singles, off-season, 3rd person
Credit Cards V, AE, MC
Check-in/Out 3–9/11; bags OK until 4; arrange late check-in
Smoking No

Pets No
Kids Welcome
Minimum Stay 2 nights holidays, weekends; 3 nights graduation, events
Open All year
Hosts Jennifer and Nicholas Fandetti

6 Prentiss St.
Cambridge, MA 02140
(617) 661-2929
Fax: (617) 661-5989
www.maryprentissinn.com

HAWTHORNE INN, Concord

OVERALL ★★★½ | ROOM QUALITY ★★★ | VALUE ★★ | PRICE $150–285

History drifts all around this traditional, comfortable property off the Battle Road of 1775, on land where Emerson, the Alcotts, and Hawthorne once lived. Popular yet not really commercial, it caters midweek to conferences, weekends to families. Gregory, whose ancestors settled here in 1637, paints and sculpts. Marilyn quilts and is a hospice volunteer. These helpful and informative hosts donate money to Habitat for Humanity every time they rent a room. The spiritual nature of the nineteenth-century literary greats and the American Revolution remain.

SETTING & FACILITIES

Location Near Exit 30B (Rt. 2A W) off Rt. 128-95, across from Hawthorne's home (The Wayside)
Near Sleepy Hollow Cemetery, Old North Bridge; homes of Emerson, Alcott, Hawthorne, Thoreau; 30 min. from Boston, 20 min. from Cambridge
Building Built 1870 as priv. home
Grounds 1.5 acres of maples, pines, ornamental trees, eclectic perennials bordered by Mill Brook; seating nooks throughout yard; tree house, swing for children; view of Wayside, home of Alcotts and Hawthornes; large parking lot

Public Space Common room, DR
Food & Drink Cont'l breakfast, communal; specialty: honey-molasses bread; tea, coffee, snacks at check-in by request
Recreation Swimming at Walden Pond, bike rentals, birding, museums, antiquing
Amenities & Services Daily paper, books, piano, irons; meetings off-season (10), fax, early breakfast; pick-up at train; whole property rental

ACCOMMODATIONS

Units 7 guest rooms
All Rooms Bath, AC, toiletries, snacks, hairdryer, iron/board, books, clock/radio, telephone w/ modem jack
Some Rooms Skylight
Bed & Bath 3 queens, 3 doubles, 1 queen with fold-out; 2 cots; tubs in 4

Favorites Bay window—overlooking gardens; Wayside—lace canopy queen w/ fireplace, antique artwork
Comfort & Decor Eclectic, antique furnishings; extensive artwork: African, Asian, island masks, paintings, sculpture; Oriental rugs, handmade quilts, wood floors

RATES, RESERVATIONS, & RESTRICTIONS

Deposit 1 night, 1–2 nights; other 50%; refund w/ 2-week notice; can book through travel agency
Discounts Long stays
Credit Cards V, AE, MC, D
Check-in/Out After 3/11
Smoking No
Pets No; 3 in-house dogs and 4 cats
Kids OK
Minimum Stay 2 nights, Sept–Oct.

Open All year
Hosts Gregory Burch and Marilyn Mudry
462 Lexington Rd.
Concord, MA 01742
(978) 369-5610
Fax: (978) 287-4949
hawthorneinn@concordmass.com
www.concordmass.com

GEORGE FULLER HOUSE, Essex

OVERALL ★★★ | ROOM QUALITY ★★★ | VALUE ★★ | PRICE $115–225

If you like water views, you have them here. The salt marsh reaches the border of the lawn during high tide. Most of the time though, this modest bed-and-breakfast in this historic shipbuilding town by the river is high and dry. George Fuller was a shipbuilder (what else?). An easygoing, family feel pervades.

SETTING & FACILITIES

Location 30 mi. N of Boston near I-95
Near Salem, Gloucester, Rockport, Boston, ship-building museum, fine restaurants
Building 1830 Federal home
Grounds 3 porches, balcony, small lawn
Public Space LR, DR, porch
Food & Drink Full breakfast; specialties: gingerbread pancakes, French toast with brandied lemon butter; afternoon coffee, tea, cold drinks
Recreation Sailing, river cruise, kayaking, whale-watching, antiquing, tennis, golf, beach nearby
Amenities & Services Gift certificates, fax

ACCOMMODATIONS

Units 3 guest rooms, 3 suites
All Rooms AC, TV, phone
Some Rooms View, fireplace, priv. entrance, reading room, French doors, seating area, priv. bath, futon, sofa bed, murals
Bed & Bath Beds vary; robes for shared baths
Favorites Magnolia Studio—blue decor, queen, futons, priv. bath; view of water and on clear days, Boston
Comfort & Decor Room size varies. Country-style decor, floral paper in most. Modest, but tasteful, well-coordinated. Good lighting. TVs and phones a plus for many. Rooms in back, quietest.

RATES, RESERVATIONS, & RESTRICTIONS

Deposit None
Discounts Off-season, senior citizens, business travelers
Credit Cards V, AE, MC, D
Check-in/Out 3/11
Smoking No
Pets Check
Kids Over 12

Open All year
Hosts Marie and John Orlando
Stacy Blvd., 71 Western Ave.
Gloucester, MA 01930
(800) 299-6696 or (978) 283-2277
info@harborviewinn.com
www.harborviewinn.com

HARBORVIEW INN, Gloucester

OVERALL ★★★½ | ROOM QUALITY ★★★ | VALUE ★★★ | PRICE $79–159

Once a guest house owned by descendants of the Gortons (famed for fish sticks), this comfortable, unassuming little bed-and-breakfast near the famous Gloucester Fisherman Memorial statue reemerged if not as a swan, then at least as pretty ducky after a 1994 *Better Homes and Gardens* makeover. Its main attractions are the location—facing the sea and a walk to America's oldest fishing harbor—and a cozy, shipshape feel, with nautical paintings and other original trinkets interspersed among the coordinated fabrics and wallcoverings.

SETTING & FACILITIES

Location Near Exit 14 off Rt. 128 by fisherman statue, in residential neighborhood across the road from water
Near Galleries, shops, restaurants, beaches, harbor, art colony, Salem witchcraft exhibits, Rockport
Building 1839 3-story clapboard
Grounds Small yard, porch, patio

Public Space Small entrance area, LR, DR
Food & Drink Cont'l buffet breakfast until 11
Recreation Whale watching, sailing, sight-seeing, museum
Amenities & Services Books, games

ACCOMMODATIONS

Units 8 guest rooms, 9 suites
All Rooms Bath, antiques, lace curtain
Some Rooms Garden view, fireplace, sitting area, AC. Chauffeur's cottage priv. entrance, fireplace, wet bar, sitting room, refrigerators. Garden cottages priv.,

fireplace, sitting area, porch, TV, whirlpool tubs
Bed & Bath Bed sizes vary, some elaborate antique beds; some hall access, some showers only

Favorites Room 5—largest, sitting area, charming, Oriental rug, fireplace

Comfort & Decor Period wallcoverings, lighting fixtures. Victorian nooks and corners. Chauffeur's cottage w/ stained glass and skylights. Cottages w/ porches, small, BR/sitting area in one. Beamed cathedral ceilings, commercial grade carpet, wicker furnishings, minimal decoration.

RATES, RESERVATIONS, & RESTRICTIONS

Deposit 2 nights; refund w/ 14-day notice.

Discounts 3rd person

Credit Cards V, AE, MC, D

Check-in/Out 3–9/1030; can stay till 1130 w/ arrangement

Smoking No

Pets No; inn has dog, Sheltie, not permitted in guest rooms

Kids Over 12

Minimum Stay 2 nights

Open April 15–Nov. 15

Host Malcolm "Mac" Noyes
106 West St.
Bar Harbor, ME 04609
(800) 437-0088 or (207) 288-3759
Fax: (207) 288-2974
manor@acadia.net
www.barharbormanorhouse.com

MILES RIVER COUNTRY INN, Hamilton

OVERALL ★★★★½ | ROOM QUALITY ★★★★ | VALUE ★★★ | PRICE $80–210

Ever want to stay over at a sophisticated friend's gorgeous country estate set among acres of landscaped lawns and flower beds, rare birds and wildlife? Sleep in a room with a fireplace and windows overlooking marshlands and river? Walk in a secret garden with a two-story iron gate, then enjoy a breakfast of fresh-laid eggs, homemade preserves, and honey from the estate's bees? You can, at this sprawling home, which the hosts didn't leave when their kids grew up. It's yours for the taking (and you don't have to bring a gift—just some cash). A cottage on the property can be rented weekly during the summer, monthly during winter, like a private country estate. Gretel speaks French, Spanish, and some German. The rooms are named after the hosts' children.

SETTING & FACILITIES

Location 2.5 mi. N of center of Hamilton off Rt. 1A, halfway between Hamilton and Ipswich; in estate and horse country

Near Beaches, Cape Ann, shopping in Newburyport, galleries in Rockport, Gloucester, Salem, Manchester-by-the-Sea; historical sights in Salem, Ipswich, Gloucester, Essex

Building 200-year-old Colonial farmhouse estate; 24 rooms, 12 fireplaces

Grounds 30+ acres: terraces, woodland walkways, 10 gardens, fountain, 2 ponds; Miles River on property

Public Space Garden terraces, glassed-in porch, common rooms, study

Food & Drink Full buffet breakfast; specialties: estate-produced fresh fruit, honey, eggs; early riser coffee; afternoon tea
Recreation Sailing, XC skiing, whale watching, horse competitions
Amenities & Services Hiking trail maps, bike maps, birder's reference book

ACCOMMODATIONS

Units 8 guest rooms; 1 apartment; 1 cottage
All Rooms Elegantly furnished, books, artwork
Some Rooms Priv. bath (6), fireplace (4), four-poster, desk, sitting room; apartment and cottage: kitchen, LR, DR
Bed & Bath Beds vary; some claw-foot tubs, tub/shower
Favorites Liesl's room—garden view, fireplace, four-poster, claw-foot tub
Comfort & Decor Colonial, much authentic, inherited from host's family. Wooden bedsteads, study are 19th century French Some views of garden, river, waterways.

RATES, RESERVATIONS, & RESTRICTIONS

Deposit Credit card; refund w/ 14-day notice, otherwise re-rental and $15 fee
Discounts Weekly rates, off-season
Credit Cards V, MC
Check-in/Out After 3/11; call with arrival time
Smoking No
Pets Yes
Kids OK
Open All year
Hosts Gretel and Peter Clark
823 Bay Rd.
Hamilton, MA 01936
(978) 468-7206
Fax: (978) 468-3999
milesriver@mediaone.net
milesriver.com

DIAMOND DISTRICT BREAKFAST INN, Lynn

OVERALL ★★★★ | ROOM QUALITY ★★★★ | VALUE ★★ | PRICE $145–265

The once-fashionable neighborhood on the North Shore was designed by the same architect who built the Schubert Theater in Boston, and the homes have the dramatic flair of turn-of-the-century prosperity. This elegant bed-and-breakfast was built for a worldly shoe manufacturer who had factories in Paris and Moscow—hence the guest rooms' whimsical footwear names. The friendly and easygoing hosts, who once lived in another house on the block, now reside in the huge basement floor. And when it comes to attention to details, they are anything but easygoing.

SETTING & FACILITIES

Location Just N of Boston in Diamond District, 300 feet to 3-mi. beach, in residential neighborhood
Near Beach, shops, restaurants, Boston, Salem, Marblehead, 2,000-acre nature area; bus to Boston
Building 21-room 1911 Georgian-style estate

Grounds Manicured lawn, gardens, gazebo, 36-foot veranda w/ ocean views

Public Space Banquet-size DR, formal parlor

Food & Drink Candlelight breakfast; specialties: lobster quiche, eggs Caron, apple puff pancakes, breads and muffins; early-morning coffee; special diets accom.; chips and soda

Recreation Whale watching, jogging, croquet, heated outdoor spa

Amenities & Services Fax, maps, videos, refrigerators, iron, beach towels and umbrellas; theater

ACCOMMODATIONS

Units 9 guest rooms, 2 suites

All Rooms AC, TV, phone w/ voicemail, dataport

Some Rooms Bath, fireplace, whirlpool, deck, VCR, CD player

Bed & Bath Bed and room size varies; some canopies; 2 orig. claw-foot tubs/shower, 2 shower/whirlpool, 4 tub/showers, 1 orig. built-in tub/shower, 1 shower

Favorites Gaiter—2nd floor, fireplace; Slipper—1st floor, antique English four-poster canopy, gel fireplace, VCR

Comfort & Decor Formally decorated w/ antiques, collections, Oriental rugs. Good reading lights. Some ocean views. Highly individualized rooms. Feel of grand house, w/ quirky corners, personality.

RATES, RESERVATIONS, & RESTRICTIONS

Deposit Credit card or deposit; refund w/ 14-day notice

Discounts Off-season

Credit Cards V, DC, MC, D

Check-in/Out After 3/11

Smoking No

Pets No

Kids Well-behaved (they're "not child-proof")

No-No's Leaving w/ keys ($25 fee)

Minimum Stay 2 nights, summer–Nov.

Open All year

Hosts Sandra and Jerry Caron

142 Ocean St.

Lynn, MA 01902

(781) 599-4470 or (800) 666-3076

Fax: (781) 599-5122

diamonddistrict@msn.com

THE BISHOPS BED AND BREAKFAST, *Marblehead*

OVERALL ★★★ | ROOM QUALITY ★★★ | VALUE ★★½ | PRICE $85–145

Stay here because it is quiet, and has the feel of a real house sitting on the water, and indeed it has been the home of the innkeepers' family for three generations. For those who like to feel like a local rather than a visitor, this house by the sea off a quiet residential street makes you feel just that. You can walk to the center of Marblehead, or just hang out in your pleasant room, with two things to view: the in-room TV or the boats and waves and birds of Little Harbor. It's especially good for families or friends, who could rent out all three guest rooms.

SETTING & FACILITIES

Location Peach's Point and Little Harbor, in Historic District, residential area 5 min. from center
Near Shops, restaurants; 25 mi. north of Boston
Building Mid-1800s cottage, renovated 1997
Grounds Seawall just outside inn, large yard

Public Space Minimal; entry area, kitchen, sitting room
Food & Drink Cont'l breakfast of fresh, seasonal fruit, tea, coffee, juice, baked goods
Recreation Walk to Brown's Island for swimming, walk to Marblehead's historic old town, beach access
Amenities & Services Ample parking

ACCOMMODATIONS

Units 2 guest rooms, 1 suite
All Rooms TV, views
Some Rooms Large priv. bath w/ dressing room, priv. entrance, sitting area
Bed & Bath 1 king, 1 queen and 1 double; suite has priv. bath
Favorites Landfall Suite—1st floor, priv.

entrance through greenhouse, sitting area, dressing room/full bath, king and twin beds
Comfort & Decor All rooms close enough to hear waves on the shore. Rooms pleasant, smallish on 2nd floor. Sunny, immaculate.

RATES, RESERVATIONS, & RESTRICTIONS

Deposit 1 night w/in 1 week of reserving; refund (less 10% fee) w/ 7-day notice
Credit Cards V, MC
Check-in/Out 2–5/10:30; flexible if necessary
Smoking No
Pets No; 2 resident cats
Kids 12 and up
Minimum Stay 2 nights weekends

May–Oct. and holidays
Open Most of year; check
Hosts Hugh and Judy Bishop
10 Harding Lane
Marblehead, MA 01945
(781) 631-4954
Fax: (731) 631-2102
jbishop@shore.net
www.bishopsbb.com

HARBOR LIGHT INN, *Marblehead*

OVERALL ★★★★½ | ROOM QUALITY ★★★★★ | VALUE ★★½ | PRICE $125–275

Luxurious and stately, this twin-Federal building on a narrow street in the historic district retains a formal hush of the past. Deep red and Wedgwood blue walls, old paintings, softly chiming mantel clocks, brass touches, and arched doorways create an elegant ambiance. The innkeeper is a sailor, as are many of the residents and visitors to this historic seaport town whose harbor is filled with bobbing sail masts, as it was in Washington's time. If you climb up to the roof walk, you can see the Marblehead Light for which the bed-and-breakfast was named and much the same view as when the house was built.

SETTING & FACILITIES

Location On narrow street in historic harbor district, 15 mi. N of Boston, Logan; 15 mi. from I-95 and Rt. 128
Near Marblehead's historic district, downtown Boston; walking distance to harbor, antiques, galleries; zoo, aquarium, nature area, winery
Building 1720 Colonial, 19th-century wing, annex next door
Grounds Rooftop walk; heated pool

Public Space Formal sitting rooms, DR, conf. room
Food & Drink Cont'l buffet breakfast; specialty: smoked salmon; tea, cookies, wine and cheese or cordials
Recreation Canoeing, golf, hunting, table tennis, swimming
Amenities & Services AC, fax, seminar/retreat meetings to corp. groups

ACCOMMODATIONS

Units 21 guest rooms
All Rooms Private bath
Some Rooms Fireplace (11), whirlpool (5), skylight
Bed & Bath Pencil-post or carved mahogany canopy beds; spacious, modern baths, some whirlpools

Favorites Poolside room—2nd floor, priv. deck
Comfort & Decor Rooms individually decorated. Fireplace rooms special. Oriental carpets, pine floors, chandeliers, carvings, small-paned windows. High ceilings, spacious and luxurious. Good baths.

RATES, RESERVATIONS, & RESTRICTIONS

Deposit 1 night or 50% for 2+ nights, w/in 7 days; refund w/ 14-day notice; early departures treated as partial cancellations
Credit Cards V, AE, MC
Check-in/Out After 1/10. Call for check-in after 10 p.m.
Smoking No
Pets No
Kids Over 10; others by special

arrangement
Minimum Stay 2 nights, weekends; 3 nights, holiday weekends
Open All year
Host Peter C. Conway
58 Washington St.
Marblehead, MA 01945
(781) 631-2186
Fax: (781) 631-2216
www.harborlightinn.com

SEAGULL INN, *Marblehead*

OVERALL ★★★ | ROOM QUALITY ★★★★ | VALUE ★★ | PRICE $125–250

The "host with the most"(according to *Boston* magazine) has turned his family's rambling house on the water, long ago a small hotel, back into a welcoming respite for travelers. Skip is a former corporate guy who worked on the furniture and painted murals, and has a great sense of humor and gift of gab. (His reported description of the sitting room: "a blend of handcrafted furniture and antiques, including the owner.") While the rooms and breakfast are fine, this is a prime example of innkeepers' impact at small properties such as bed-and-breakfasts and inns. They can and do make or break them.

SETTING & FACILITIES

Location Marblehead Neck, a residential peninsula, 18 mi. N of Boston
Near Beach, lighthouse, fishing fleets, sailboat races
Building Restored, shingled century-old summer hotel
Grounds Gardens, decks, water views
Public Space Sitting room

Food & Drink Cont'l breakfast; specialties: smoked salmon, homemade granola, freshly ground coffee
Recreation Water sports, golf, antiquing, kayaking
Amenities & Services Local info in rooms, books, videos, games; meeting space, fax, computer

ACCOMMODATIONS

Units 3 suites

All Rooms Bath, TV/VCR, phone, coffee maker, AC

Some Rooms Kitchen, deck, ocean views, artifacts

Bed & Bath Queen beds, four-posters; hairdryers

Favorites Lighthouse Suite—duplex apt. w/ priv. entrance, grill, hammock, kitchen, bath and roof deck w/ views, sofa bed and daybed in LR, 4-poster queen in upstairs BR

Comfort & Decor Rooms sunny and individually decorated w/ cherry floors, Shaker furniture, and original paintings. Two multiple rooms. Tasteful. Much of furniture crafted by innkeeper.

RATES, RESERVATIONS, & RESTRICTIONS

Deposit Refund w/ 14-day notice

Discounts 7th day free

Credit Cards V, MC

Check-in/Out Check-in 2 p.m. or arranged

Smoking No

Pets Yes

Kids Yes

Minimum Stay 2 night min. some

weekends and holidays

Open All year

Host Ruth Sigler

106 Harbor Ave.

Marblehead, MA 01945

(781) 631-1893

Fax: (781) 631-3535

www.seagullinn.com

SPRAYCLIFF, *Marblehead*

OVERALL ★★★★ | ROOM QUALITY ★★★★ | VALUE ★★½ | PRICE $175–200

The name fits, as this bright and breezy Tudor is set within the salty spritz of the Atlantic, the only oceanfront bed-and-breakfast in Marblehead. Color accents are knockout aspects within. Wicker in red, blue, and yellow, and bright pottery and art, all painted by talented interior designer Sally, are set against vivid white walls, and the pretty guest rooms are filled with bold hues as well. This romantic property is popular with gay and lesbian travelers, among others.

SETTING & FACILITIES

Location 15 mi. N of Boston on the ocean (B&B)
Near Old Town Marblehead, beach, Logan International Airport, shopping
Building Large 1910 Tudor, redecorated 1995
Grounds Oceanfront atop a seawall, courtyard and gardens

Public Space Patio on the water; Gathering Room
Food & Drink Cont'l breakfast; afternoon libations
Recreation Hiking, biking, antiquing
Amenities & Services Daily papers, library, beach towels, bikes, fresh flowers, special requests

ACCOMMODATIONS

Units 7 suites
All Rooms Bath, sitting area
Some Rooms Fireplace, ocean view, bay window
Bed & Bath Queen or king, some full; some tubs
Favorites Winnetka—king, fireplace,

priv. oceanfront patio,
Comfort & Decor Antique and hand-painted furnishing. Styles vary, and evoke locations where hosts resided (Athens, Winnetka, Little Rock, etc.). Fresh flowers. Windows and water views. Immaculate and refreshing.

RATES, RESERVATIONS, & RESTRICTIONS

Deposit 1 night's stay; cancellations w/ 7-day notice and $25 fee
Discounts Off-season (Nov.–April)
Credit Cards AE, V, MC
Check-in/Out 3–7/11
Smoking No
Pets No; 2 in-house schnauzers
Kids No
Minimum Stay 2 nights most week-

ends, 3 nights some holiday weekends
Open All year
Hosts Sally and Roger Plauche
25 Spray Ave.
Marblehead, MA 01945
(800) 626-1530 or (781) 631-6789
Fax: (617) 639-4563
spraycliff@aol.com
www.marbleheadchamber.org/spraycliff

CLARK CURRIER INN, Newburyport

OVERALL ★★★★ | ROOM QUALITY ★★★★ | VALUE ★★★ | PRICE $95–155

This elegant three-story bed-and-breakfast reflects the classic grace and beauty of this still-wonderful port town—which was the country's fourth-largest city in 1803, when the house was built. Today it is filled with world treasures from that era. Pretty and well-maintained, with decorative moldings and classical music, it has an informal sitting room and a charming little garden to lighten the formality

SETTING & FACILITIES

Location 2 mi. off I-95, Exit 57, in historic downtown district
Near Market Square historic district, performing and visual arts, museums, Historical Society of Old Newbury, waterfront park, shopping, nature areas, beach
Building 1803 Federal 3-story; remodeled 1994; Nat'l Historical Register
Grounds Restored garden w/ gazebo, roses, tiny pond
Public Space Wide entrance hall, parlor,

library, garden room w/ TV
Food & Drink Cont'l breakfast; can take tray to room; afternoon tea in garden room, sherry in library
Recreation Deep-sea fishing, whale/bird watching, harbor cruises, hay rides, ice-skating, XC skiing, beaches, parks, nature trails
Amenities & Services Small weddings, seminars, other engagements during off-season only

ACCOMMODATIONS

Units 8 guest rooms
All Rooms Bath, AC
Some Rooms Enclosed porch, deck, priv. entry
Bed & Bath Queen, double, twin, 2 canopy; tub/shower (1), most shower only

Favorites Currier—pencil-post bed, enclosed porch
Comfort & Decor Rooms named for prominent locals, such as John P. Marquand, Pulitzer Prize–winning author; individually decorated w/ antiques and reproductions, period furnishings.

RATES, RESERVATIONS, & RESTRICTIONS

Deposit 1 night; refund w/ 5-day notice
Discounts Corp. rates
Credit Cards V, AE, MC, D
Check-in/Out 3–9/11
Smoking Outside
Pets No; in-house cat
Kids Over 10
No-No's Arriving after 9 p.m. without special arrangement

Minimum Stay 2 nights weekends, in-season, 3 nights some holidays
Open All year
Hosts Bob Nolan and daughter Melissa
45 Green St.
Newburyport, MA 01950
(978) 465-8363
www.clarkcurrierinn.com

THE WINDSOR HOUSE, Newburyport

OVERALL ★★★ | ROOM QUALITY ★★★ | VALUE ★★½ | PRICE $110–145

As English as its name, this bed-and-breakfast has the feel of a modest English country house and was built in the eighteenth century—before the house of Windsor came to be. Host John was in the Royal Navy and lived in a cottage by King Arthur's castle in Tintagel; Judith writes about Neolithic Britain, and it's not surprising that they run a tour company specializing in Great Britain. Check out the details of the guest room dedicated to Princess Di.

SETTING & FACILITIES

Location 45 min. N of Logan Airport off I-95, on quiet residential street across from a church, 2 blocks from center
Near Plum Island, Parker River Wildlife Refuge, Custom House Maritime Museum, Historical Society, state park
Building 1786 3-story brick Federal mansion, remodeled 1998
Grounds Across from brick church, courtyard, garden

Public Space Common room, DR, meeting space (10), eat-in kitchen
Food & Drink Full two-course English breakfast; afternoon tea; special diets accom.
Recreation River cruises, whale watching, deep-sea fishing, antiquing; local events, architecture
Amenities & Services Fax, copier, washer/dryer, some disabled access

ACCOMMODATIONS

Units 4 guest rooms
All Rooms Priv. bath, AC, alarm clock, phone, tea/coffee maker
Some Rooms Priv. entrance, library, sleigh or four-poster bed, fireplace
Bed & Bath Beds vary, king or queen
Favorites English Rose—in memory of

Princess Diana, rose wallpaper, photos, mementos, king bed
Comfort & Decor Rooms restored to memory of original use w/ some original features. Old-fashioned, pluses and minuses of English style. A bit fussy.

RATES, RESERVATIONS, & RESTRICTIONS

Deposit 1 night or credit card
Discounts Singles, corp., 3rd person $35
Credit Cards V, AE, MC, D
Check-in/Out 4/11
Smoking No
Pets By arrangement; in-house cat
Kids Over 6
Minimum Stay 2 nights weekends, 3 on holidays

Open All year
Hosts Judith and John Harris
38 Federal St.
Newburyport, MA 01950
(888) TRELAWNY or (978) 462-3778
Fax: (978) 465-3443
windsorinn@earthlink.net
www.bbhost.com/windsorhouse

ADDISON CHOATE INN, Rockport

OVERALL ★★★½ | ROOM QUALITY ★★★ | VALUE ★★½ | PRICE $105–150

Without luxury touches, but with a pleasant old-fashioned atmosphere, this is a throwback to a time before whirlpools and fireplaces and themes became popular. The look is summery and eclectic, and the perennial borders and outdoor pool are especially inviting. Knox is a landscape architect and architectural designer who enjoys birding and photography; Shirley is an interior designer, weaver, and gardener. Both are friendly and helpful. Waking to the smell of freshly baked muffins and brewed coffee in the morning is one of this bed-and-breakfast's simple but comforting pleasures.

SETTING & FACILITIES

Location Hour N of Boston, tip of Cape Ann; on main residential street
Near Town center, state park, ocean, walking trails
Building 1851 late Greek Revival
Grounds Wraparound porch w/ seating overlooking garden
Public Space Living room, DRs, TV room

Food & Drink Buffet breakfast: baked goods, granola, fresh fruit; in-room possible; tea; restaurants 5 min. walk
Recreation Outdoor pool; nearby bird/whale watching, sea kayaking
Amenities & Services Binoculars, irons, maps, recipes, daily papers, phone, fax, copier; pick up from train

ACCOMMODATIONS

Units 5 guest rooms; 3 suites
All Rooms Bath, reading lamp, hairdryer, sitting area, toiletries
Some Rooms TV; refrigerators in suites, AC (all but one), kitchen, dining area, loft, skylight, ceiling fan
Bed & Bath King, queen, twin, tub/shower combo
Favorites Chimney Room—sunny, chimney through it, queen canopy, antique

bureau, tub/shower. Celebration Suite—BR, sitting room, view of Rockport and ocean, pine queen canopy
Comfort & Decor Rooms mix antique and reproduction furniture in homey style. Suites in the Stable House include loft bedrooms, kitchen, and dining areas. Individually and tastefully decorated with attention to detail.

RATES, RESERVATIONS, & RESTRICTIONS

Deposit One night, refund w/ 10-day notice or re-rental; can book through travel agency
Discounts Singles, 3rd person (suites); Stable House suites $800 weekly, not incl. breakfast
Credit Cards V, MC, D; cash or check preferred
Check-in/Out 3–7/11
Smoking No
Pets No; 2 in-house cats

Kids 12 and older
Minimum Stay 2 nights mid-June–mid-Sept., most holidays, 3 nights July 4 weekend
Open All year, except 2 weeks in Nov.
Hosts Shirley and Knox Johnson
49 Broadway
Rockport, MA 01966
(978) 546-7543 or (800) 245-7543
Fax: (978) 546-7638
www.cape-ann.com/addison-choate

EDEN PINES INN, Rockport

OVERALL ★★★★½ | ROOM QUALITY ★★★★ | VALUE ★★★ | PRICE $150–175

The house is decorated in casually elegant style, and the breathtaking view from the deck and most rooms is mesmerizing day and night: ocean and rocky cove, Thatcher island with twin lighthouses, lobstermen tending traps, seagulls hovering over boats, sea cormorants surface diving, sunrise and moonrise. And you can hear the waves lapping. The charming innkeeper agrees with Emerson: "Make acquaintance with the sea." And this is the place.

SETTING & FACILITIES

Location 1.5 mi. from downtown Rockport, in residential area overlooking water
Near Beaches, Rockport tourist attractions
Building 1900 Federal-style home
Grounds Rock garden, croquet, porch, brick sun deck

Public Space LR, DR
Food & Drink Continental breakfast; specialty: homemade cake; tea and cookies, snack
Recreation Swimming, golf, tennis, whale watching, fishing trips
Amenities & Services Daily papers, refrigerator, irons, maps

ACCOMMODATIONS

Units 6 guest rooms
All Rooms Bath, AC, sitting area
Some Rooms Marble or tile bath, sep. showers and tubs, priv. deck (6)
Bed & Bath Queen, king, or 2 double beds, most canopy; robes for long stays
Favorites #2—blue/yellow decor, decks

w/ view, soaking tub, marble bath; #6—canopy queen, pink/green florals; 3rd floor penthouse—king canopy, balcony, large wicker sitting area
Comfort & Decor Priv. decks overlook the sea, California colors and styles, especially blues and yellows. Casually elegant.

RATES, RESERVATIONS, & RESTRICTIONS

Deposit 1 night; refund w/ 14-day notice; booking through travel agent OK (in-house preferred)
Discounts 3rd person
Credit Cards V, MC; personal checks
Check-in/Out 2/11
Smoking Outside and porches only
Pets No
Kids Teenagers
Minimum Stay 2 days, 3 on holiday

weekends—paid in full
Open Mid-May–Oct.
Host Inge Sullivan
48 Eden Rd.
Rockport, MA 01966
(978) 546-2505; winter (978) 546-2490
Fax: (978) 546-1157, mid-May–Oct. only
www.rockportusa.com/edenpinesinn

SEACREST MANOR, *Rockport*

OVERALL ★★★★½ | ROOM QUALITY ★★★★ | VALUE ★★★½ | PRICE $98–158

"Decidedly small, intentionally quiet" is the way the Seacrest Manor describes itself, and that seems true. There's only one phone line—in the office—and this is not a place for Frisbee throws on the lawn. Gentility, propriety, elegance come to mind, in the style of an English country house. The spacious living room features a gilt mirror from the old Philadelphia Opera House. A red oak tree out front dates from the nineteenth century, and the mood does, too. Leighton is a retired NBC exec; Dwight is a retired college professor who looks like an older cousin of movie star Matt Damon. He is.

SETTING & FACILITIES

Location Less than 5 mi. from northern end of Rt. 128, 1 mi. from center of Rockport, in residential area
Near Beach; across the street from 9-acre John Kiernan Nature Preserve
Building 1911 brick structure, pedestaled portico
Grounds 2 acre corner lot: gardens, statues, fountain; 2nd story deck w/ ocean view
Public Space DR, library, spacious LR
Food & Drink Full, formal breakfast; specialties: spiced Irish oatmeal w/ chopped dates, corn fritters w/ hot syrup; early bird coffee and tea; afternoon tea, snacks
Recreation Golf, deep-sea fishing, boat trips, tennis, whale watching nearby
Amenities & Services Safe, stationery, daily papers, Sun. papers (fee), notecards (fee), beach towels, gift cert., bike rental, turn-down, men's shoe polishing, BYOB set-up (dry town)

ACCOMMODATIONS

Units 6 guest rooms, I suite
All Rooms TV, radio, fan, fresh flowers
Some Rooms Priv. bath (6), priv. entrance, nonworking fireplace
Bed & Bath Most queen or king, some double; suite shares bath

Comfort & Decor Rooms 7, 8—open directly on deck, ocean views
Favorites Carpeted rooms. Shakespeare quotes on pillows w/ mints. Elegant.

RATES, RESERVATIONS, & RESTRICTIONS

Deposit I night; 2 nights for weekends, 7+ days; refund w/ 14-day notice
Discounts Singles less $10, 2-week or longer stay less 5%
Credit Cards None
Check-in/Out 2/11
Smoking Outside only
Pets No
Kids Over 12
No-No's Groups; check-in after 9 p.m.; 3 people in a room; incoming calls after 9

p.m.; bare feet in public rooms
Minimum Stay 2 nights mid-May–Oct., 3 nights holiday weekends
Open April–Nov.
Hosts Dwight B. MacCormick Jr. and Leighton T. Saville
99 Marmion Way
Rockport, MA 01966
(978) 546-2211
seacrestmanor@rockportusa.com
wwwseacrestmanor.com

AMELIA PAYSON HOUSE, Salem

OVERALL ★★★½ | ROOM QUALITY ★★★ | VALUE ★★★ | PRICE $85–150

Witches are welcome (as well as non-witches) in this little homestead located north of Boston near the site of the Witch Trial and other historic happenings. The blue-painted, columned facade is a prelude to a formal but friendly in-town bed-and-breakfast, which allows you to easily visit the museums in this historic town without having to get in a car. Pink and mauve and other pastels are the colors of choice, and the atmosphere is delicate, with swag drapes and marble mantels. Halloween is when the town gets crowded, and the town is jumping with people wearing black.

SETTING & FACILITIES

Location Half-hour N of Boston on IA N
Near Boston; walk to Salem shopping, restaurants, Salem Witch Museum, House of the Seven Gables, Peabody Essex Museum, Nat'l Maritime Site, ferry,

Amtrak station
Building 1845 Greek Revival
Grounds City backyard garden, deck area
Public Space Parlor, DR

Food & Drink Cont'l-plus, family-style breakfast with baked goods
Recreation Tennis, swimming, sailing, whale watching, dinner and music cruises nearby

Amenities & Services Fridge, baby grand piano, microwave, beach towels, irons, books; pickup from train and ferry

ACCOMMODATIONS

Units 4 guest rooms
All Rooms Bath, AC, hairdryer, TV, clock/radio
Some Rooms Tub, canopy bed
Bed & Bath Queens, some twins in addition, antique frames; full baths except one shower only
Favorites The Canopy—canopied four-poster, antiques, Oriental rugs
Comfort & Decor Sunlit spacious rooms, floral paper with soft rose and blue accessories, lace and antiques.

RATES, RESERVATIONS, & RESTRICTIONS

Deposit 1 night; refund w/ 7-day notice; 30 days for Halloween. Travel agent booking OK (prefer in-house).
Discounts None
Credit Cards V, AE, MC, D
Check-in/Out 4/11
Smoking Outdoors
Pets No
Kids Over 14
Minimum Stay 2–3 days for weekends/holidays; 6 days during Halloween
Open Late March–Nov.
Hosts Ada and Donald Roberts
16 Winter St.
Salem, MA 01970
(978) 744-8304
bbamelia@aol.com
www.ameliapaysonhouse.com

AMERSCOT HOUSE, Stow

OVERALL ★★★★ | ROOM QUALITY ★★★★ | VALUE ★★★ | PRICE $120–145

If you enjoy rural life and dream of owning a farm or just spending some time on one, you'll especially enjoy this authentic, charming farmhouse with a dollop of Scottish influence. The fields stretch out beyond this warm house, and the hearth, rustic parlor, and open kitchen are comforting and restful. You can retire to the luxury of a suite with a whirlpool or a combined room and loft. Apple picking in nearby orchards or an evening of Scottish Country dancing are charming diversions, and business travelers are well-supported with services. As Doreen and Jerry would say it, *cead mille fialte:* a hundred thousand welcomes.

SETTING & FACILITIES

Location Rural, 5 mi. from Rt. 495 and
Rt. 2, near Concord
Near Shopping in Boston and Concord,
Mayard, Sturbridge; 4 golf courses
Building Early American (ca. 1734) farm-
house
Grounds 2.5 acres: gardens, greenhouse,
side porch
Public Space Colonial DR, FR; function

room (25–30)
Food & Drink Full breakfast; specialty:
homemade granola; tea and scones,
sherry.
Recreation Canoeing, trails, apple picking; Scottish country dancing with hosts
Amenities & Services Copy, fax, dataports; secretarial services for business
travelers

ACCOMMODATIONS

Units 2 guest rooms, 1 suite
All Rooms Bath, fireplace, phone, cable
TV
Some Rooms Sitting room, adjoining
lofts with twin beds, whirlpool, desk
Bed & Bath 2 queens, 1 king with twin

option
Favorites The Lindsay Suite—Queen
canopy bed, sitting room, whirlpool
Comfort & Decor Rooms decorated
with antiques, handmade quilts, and fresh
flowers. Paned windows, bedside lighting.

RATES, RESERVATIONS, & RESTRICTIONS

Deposit 1 night; 7-day cancellation
policy
Discounts Singles, corp. rates, 3rd
person
Credit Cards V, AE, MC, D
Check-in/Out 4–9/11
Smoking No
Pets No
Kids OK

Open All year
Hosts Doreen and Jerry Gibson
61 West Acton Rd., P.O. Box 351
Stow, MA 01775
(978) 897-0666
Fax: (978) 897-6914
doreen@amerscot.com
www.amerscot.com

Central/Western Massachusetts

Central Massachusetts, with meadows, ponds, farms, and low mountains, is highlighted by Worcester, the second-largest city in the state and home to the **Worcester Art Museum** and the **New England Science Center.**

Old Sturbridge Village, which re-creates 1830s New England, is south of the city and has two covered bridges, staff in period costumes farming with ox teams, and crafting products you can buy. **Hardwick** also has a covered bridge. In **Sutton, Purgatory Chasm** runs 70 feet deep and makes for wonderful sightseeing.

Shoppers can load up in outlet malls in both **Worcester** and **Gardner** ("Chair City of the World"), as well as at roadside stands for corn and tomatoes in summer, pumpkins and apples in fall. This region is the home of **Johnny Appleseed,** and the trail named after this legendary planter starts in **Lancaster** and winds through 25 communities in the north-central area, with orchards, galleries, antique centers, wineries, microbreweries, and furniture outlets. Nearby **Wachusett Mountain** offers skiing and panoramic views.

Hoop fans will want to stop at the **Naismith Memorial Basketball Hall of Fame** in the city of **Springfield,** where the game began. The first U.S. armory is here as well. The colleges of **Smith, Mt. Holyoke, Hampshire,** and the **University of Massachusetts at Amherst** are nearby. In summer you can waterslide 400 feet down **Mount Tom's Pipe Dream,** where you can also ski or snowboard in winter.

Fans of history won't want to miss the town of **Deerfield,** complete with period architecture and decor and 14 museum-houses open to the public. Horses clippity-clopping by, pulling carriages along the cobblestones, carry you back two centuries. Check out **Yankee Candle** to watch how beeswax tapers were traditionally made.

Western Massachusetts may be best known for the **Berkshire region,** at the far end of the state, bordered by New York. It's a bucolic area of low-mountain landscape and art-filled villages. This was an area where artists, writers, and many of New England's wealthiest families created an alternative to **Newport** in the late-nineteenth century. Mansions remain, some converted to bed-and-breakfasts or museums, their facades highlighting pretty village greens and backroads.

In addition to strolling through gardens and estates, and biking, hiking, and skiing the mountains, there's an array of summer cultural events—music, dance, theater, and more. Popular sites are the **Norman Rockwell Museum** in **Stockbridge; Tanglewood** (summer home to the Boston Symphony Orchestra) near **Lenox;** the **Hancock Shaker Village; Williams College** in charming, museum-filled **Williamstown;** and the evocative **Massachusetts Museum of Contemporary Art (Mass MoCA)** in a restored mill complex in **North Adams.**

Bed-and-breakfasts and country inns in this area are sophisticated and choice, often in old famous taverns and coach stops, former mansions, or historic homes. Many are clustered in the western end of the state.

FOR MORE INFORMATION

Southern Berkshire Chamber of Commerce
(413) 528-4006
email: info@berkshirelodging.com
www.berkshirelodging.com

ALLEN HOUSE VICTORIAN INN, Amherst

OVERALL ★★★★ | ROOM QUALITY ★★★★ | VALUE ★★★½ | PRICE $75–175

Even if you're not a fan of ornate Victoriana, a mélange of peacock feathers, Eastlake furnishings, and William Morris prints, you can't help admire the dramatic effect of this award-winning bed-and-breakfast, re-creating the "Aesthetic period" of the 1880s, when Emily Dickinson still lived in town. Both hosts love to create romantic touches when requested, such as roses on pillows, chocolates, and champagne, and they serve special dishes on holidays and special occasions. Alan stayed here first as a student and was thrilled to own this Painted Lady. Today, he and Amanda are renovating barns and expanding gardens to include a Japanese tea house and a bicycle cottage. Continual improvement is a sign of a really fine property.

SETTING & FACILITIES

Location About 6 mi. from Exit 19 off I-91
Near Walk to Emily Dickinson Homestead, Amherst, Hampshire College, UMass, Nat'l Yiddish Bookcenter, Yankee Candle, Historic Deerfield, Old Sturbridge Village, Hancock Shaker Village, Norman Rockwell Museum, galleries, theaters, shopping
Building 1886 Queen Anne Stick–style Victorian
Grounds 3.5 landscaped acres, shade trees, gardens, meadow
Public Space DR, LR
Food & Drink Full formal, 5-course Victorian breakfast in room, communal or separate tables; specialties: eggs Benedict, soufflés, quiche, Belgian waffles; can be in-room; afternoon and evening tea, pastries, cookies, lemonade in summer, hot cider in fall. Special diets accom. Nearest restaurant, 5-min. walk.
Recreation Concerts, tennis, golf, XC skiing, Hampshire Fitness (fee); bike rental nearby
Amenities & Services Daily papers, fax, refrigerator, irons; shuttle to town, to and from local colleges, pick-up from train/bus; storage, concierge service

ACCOMMODATIONS

Units 15 guest rooms
All Rooms Bath, AC, ceiling fan, antique-style radio, clock, phone, dataport, fine Swiss chocolates, English toiletries
Some Rooms Larger, space for add'l guests
Bed & Bath 6 full and 9 queen beds, some add'l twin beds; tile baths, some deep claw-foot tubs
Favorites The front rooms, such as Louis Comfort Tiffany—large, filled w/ Victoriana, silk-screened wallpapers, extra bed
Comfort & Decor Rooms spacious in front, smaller in former maids' rooms in back. Individually decorated w/ antiques, period art. Museum-quality restorations. Feels like 1880s, but dataports and modern comforts. Meticulous attention to detail.

RATES, RESERVATIONS, & RESTRICTIONS

Deposit Within 7 days of reserving; refund w/ 14-day notice
Discounts Off-season, long stays, extra person

Credit Cards V, MC, D
Check-in/Out 3/11
Smoking Outside verandas only
Pets No
Kids 10 and older
Minimum Stay Holiday, graduation, and
Oct. weekends: 3 nights; high season
weekends: 2 nights

Open All year
Hosts Alan and Amanda Zieminski
599 Main St.
Amherst, MA 01002
(413) 253-5000
allenhouse@webtv.net
www.allenhouse.com

DEERFIELD INN, Deerfield

OVERALL ★★★★½ | ROOM QUALITY ★★★½ | VALUE ★★ | PRICE $188–255

Bonafide ghosts Cora and Herschel haunt this award-winning inn on "The Street," filled with a dozen historic clapboard and brick eighteenth- and nineteenth-century houses. This fine house is one of the original New England inns and is well aware of that history, abounding in antiques, decorative arts fabrics, and wallcoverings. Popular with the public, it can get busy during dining hours but is a complete, traditional New England experience. It's especially lovely to retire for the evening with the clip-clop of horse-drawn carriages outside the window.

SETTING & FACILITIES

Location Exit 24 off I-91 N, Exit 25, S on "The Street"
Near Museum houses, Memorial Hall Museum, historical sights, Williamstown
Building 1884 Federal-style inn; large double porch with pillars
Grounds Fronts old Main St.; flower beds, small lawns; village view, on-street parking and behind inn
Public Space LRs, DRs, refurbished tavern, coffee shop, porches, terrace

Food & Drink Full country breakfast; dinner open to public; specialty: mussels steamed with chorizo sausage, coconut milk, and lime; light fare in Terrace Café; tea/snack
Recreation 3-mi. loop walk, boating, XC skiing, whitewater rafting, tennis
Amenities & Services Elevator, refrigerator, wheelchair access, catering, business support

ACCOMMODATIONS

Units 23 rooms
All Rooms Bath, climate controls, phone, TV with cozy, quilts, hairdryer, lighted mirrors, robes
Some Rooms Queen, four-poster, cannonball beds
Bed & Bath High beds with steps; tub and shower

Favorites Room 143—ultra-traditional w/ charming details
Comfort & Decor Antique and reproduction mix. Rich draperies and furnishings. Authentic period patterns. Historic, comfortable.

RATES, RESERVATIONS, & RESTRICTIONS

Deposit One night; refund w/ 7-day notice
Discounts AAA seniors, off-season, groups, extended stays, midweek
Credit Cards V, AE, MC, D
Check-in/Out 2/noon
Smoking Porch or terrace only
Pets No
Kids "Well-behaved" welcome
No-No' Late check-out, $50 charge; entry after 11 p.m (permitted, but no greeting), inappropriate attire in DR
Minimum Stay 2 nights, busy weekends
Open All year except Dec. 23–26
Hosts Jane and Karl Sabo
81 Old Main St.
Deerfield, MA 01342-0305
(800) 926-3865 or (413) 774-5587
Fax: (413) 773-8712
frontdesk@deerfield inn.com
www.deerfieldinn.com

BALDWIN HILL FARM, *Great Barrington*

OVERALL ★★★★½ | ROOM QUALITY ★★★ | VALUE ★★★½ | PRICE $89–130

Once a working dairy farm, this truly bed-and-breakfast retains almost 500 acres of its original farmland; another 190 acres across the way has been purchased and will remain undeveloped. The quiet Berkshire Hills countryside seems to stretch forever in a 360-degree panorama so striking it was featured in *Travel & Leisure*. At "retirement" in 1989, Dick and Priscilla added a swimming pool and turned the unpretentious, comfortable house into a bed-and-breakfast. As a kid, Dick slept in the same simple rooms and ate at the same breakfast table guests now enjoy.

SETTING & FACILITIES

Location Rt. 71 to Baldwin Hill Rd. E/W, left for 1 mi.; turn left at crossroad, B&B is 200 yards further on the right, on rural town road
Near Tanglewood, Berkshire School Choral Festival, Berkshire Summer Theatre Festival, Shakespearean Theatre, Jacob's Pillow, Norman Rockwell Museum, Egremont Country Club, French Park, Prospect Lake, Appalachian Trail, Mount Everett (highest Berkshire peak), Monument Mountain, ski areas
Building Civil War–era country hilltop Victorian farmhouse, Gothic overtones; barn and outbuildings
Grounds Hundreds of acres: Catalpa trees, gardens, wildlife, 3-state views; ungroomed XC skiing trails, heated pool
Public Space Twin parlors, DR, screened porch
Food & Drink Full breakfast; choose from menu for next morning; specialty snacks
Recreation Picnics, antiquing, golf, tennis, trails, lake boating
Amenities & Services Outdoor pool, refrigerator, heat adjusted according to guests' preferences, maps for biking, hiking etc., restaurant menus

ACCOMMODATIONS

Units 4 guest rooms

All Rooms Seating, reading lighting, alarm clock, rural view, quilts

Some Rooms Priv. bath (2), some heirloom Victorian pieces

Bed & Bath Queen, king/twin beds, new mattresses every 2 years; 2 rooms share 1.5 baths, robes, 2 w/ sink/vanity in room

Favorites Bay Window Room—sitting area in window, extensive views

Comfort & Decor Marble-topped dressers, antique mirrors—at least 1 piece per room. Country floral wallpapers, soothing color schemes. Quilts. Small, authentic, old-fashioned feel, well-maintained.

RATES, RESERVATIONS, & RESTRICTIONS

Deposit 1 night; refund w/ 10-day notice

Discounts 4+ night stays w/ $10 rate reduction on-season(no breakfast Monday–Thursday)

Credit Cards V, AE, MC, D

Check-in/Out 3–6/ 11

Smoking No

Pets No, nearby facilities

Kids Over 10

Minimum Stay 2 nights high-season

weekends, 3 nights holidays

Open All year

Hosts Priscilla and Richard Burdsall 121 Baldwin Hill Rd. North & South Egremont, MA 01230 (888) 528-4092 or (413) 528-4092 Fax: (413) 528-6365 rpburds@bcn.net www.baldwinhillfarm.com

WINDFLOWER, Great Barrington

OVERALL ★★★½ | ROOM QUALITY ★★★★ | VALUE ★★ | PRICE $120–200

A kid-friendly, people-friendly environment awaits in this comfortable, established bed-and-breakfast. Over two decades ago Barbara and Gerry opened the Tulip Tree Inn in Vermont. Five years later daughter Claudia, an experienced chef, and husband, John, with a degree in arbor culture and lots of handyman experience, came to co-innkeep here in the Berkshires. Accommodating is the word, in every way: For an allergic guest, they removed carpeting and used special supplies—he stayed three months. A Polish visitor with dietary problems was given special foods, and Barbara shopped with him before he left. A party of 80 paid to have all furnishings removed and replaced (the party went fine).

SETTING & FACILITIES

Location Across road from Egremont Country Club; to Rt. 23 & 41 to Egremont for 3 mi., follow signs to Country Club and B&B

Near Berkshires mountains, Tanglewood, Jacob's Pillow, theatre festivals,

Shaker Village, Clark Art Institute, Norman Rockwell Museum, Edith Wharton's home, 400-acre John Drummond Kennedy park, ski areas, Egremont dining and shops

Building 1850 Colonial, columned front porch

Grounds 10 acres: perennial gardens, organic berry, vegetable, and herb gardens

Public Space LR, reading room

Food & Drink Full breakfast; specialty: cottage cheese soufflé pancakes; tea, cookies; B&B chef caters for groups, events

Recreation Antiquing, tennis, golf, boating, horseback riding

Amenities & Services Pool, discounted ski tickets; cribs, roll-aways; ltd. disabled access, BYOB set-ups, refrigerator, iron; fly-fishing; bike storage, weddings, meetings, etc. (150), catered, planned; recipes

ACCOMMODATIONS

Units 13 guest rooms

All Rooms Bath, good lighting, radio alarm clock, TV, AC

Some Rooms Fireplace, seating, access to common porch, add'l bed, window seat, bay window

Bed & Bath Some four-poster, canopy, elaborately carved beds, sizes vary; baths vary: modern, claw-foot tub/shower, shower only; extra-large tile showers(1), pedestal sinks

Favorites Room 12—fieldstone

fireplace, Laura Ashley, stocked bookshelves, door to common porch; Room 1—MBR—fireplace, queen and twin bed, dressing room

Comfort & Decor Rooms 4 and 5, sunny, four-poster canopies, but some traffic noise. Fairly spacious rooms, constant maintenance and upgrades. Carpet or hardwood floors. Some small, Dura-log-only fireplaces. Some bold pattern combinations.

RATES, RESERVATIONS, & RESTRICTIONS

Deposit 1 night, applied to last night stay; refund w/ 21-day notice

Discounts Seasonal packages; 3rd person/children, infants, corp. and midweek

Credit Cards AE

Check-in/Out 2/11

Smoking No (Great Barrington non-smoking)

Pets No

Kids Welcome

Minimum Stay 2 nights weekends; 3 nights weekends July, August, holidays

Open All year

Hosts Barbara and Gerry Liebert; Claudia and John Ryan

684 South Egremont Rd.

Great Barrington, MA 01230

(800) 992-1993 or (413) 528-2720

Fax: (413) 528-5147

wndflowr@windflowerinn.com

www.windflowerinn.com

CLARK TAVERN INN, Hadley

OVERALL ★★★★ | ROOM QUALITY ★★★★ | VALUE ★★★ | PRICE $95–155

Minutemen stayed here en route to the Battle of Concord, and one of the many Early American antiques is a chair from poet Emily Dickinson's estate. The swimming pool is set among flowers, birdsong, and a placid water garden. Hearty breakfasts (optionally in your room), evolve from a local organic farm. This bed-and-breakfast is authentic Americana, moved and saved from demolition when the I-91 expressway was built—and lovingly, meticulously restored. The young innkeepers are a big plus: gentle, helpful former health caregivers who not only dote on guests, but on animals wild and domesticated.

SETTING & FACILITIES

Location I-91 Exit 19, Rt. 9 E 25 mi. to Bay Rd., 1.1 mi. on left
Near Live music and performances, antiquing, historic Deerfield, Univ. of Mass., 4 colleges
Building 1742 New England Colonial inn
Grounds 1+ acres, gardens, priv. garden nooks, hammock, water garden w/ goldfish, pool
Public Space Keeping room, common room, circular screened patio
Food & Drink Full breakfast, make choices night before; early breakfast OK; specialties: hot spiced apples, orange French toast, hash browns and ham; vegetarian sausage avail.; beverages all day
Recreation Bird watching, trails, Conn. River marinas, hot-air balloon or glider rides
Amenities & Services Binoculars, videos, refrigerator, irons, books, beach towels, recipes, daily papers, (lawn) games, fax

ACCOMMODATIONS

Units 3 guest rooms
All Rooms Bath, TV/VCR, table/chairs, phone, dataport
Some Rooms Fireplace (2), vaulted ceiling w/ chandelier (1)
Bed & Bath Queens, 2 canopies, high-grade mattresses, roll-aways; baths new, large; showers, tubs, handheld shower, antique sink vanities; hairdryer, forgotten toiletries
Favorites Gardenview Room—vaulted ceiling, back of inn, large bath; Fireplace Room—fireplace, canopy bed, 4 windows, front of inn, large bath
Comfort & Decor Colonial decor, yet comfortable and relaxed with modern conveniences. Upholstered chairs. Attractive comforters. Simple, authentic feel. TV nice option. Most queens.

RATES, RESERVATIONS, & RESTRICTIONS

Deposit 50%; refund w/ 14-day notice
Discounts Longer stays, singles, off-season
Credit Cards V, AE, DC, MC, D
Check-in/Out 3–8/11; call for late arrival
Smoking Outdoors
Pets OK w/ prior approval; in-house cats
Kids Over 12
Open All Year
Hosts Ruth and Mike Callahan
98 Bay Rd.
Hadley, MA 01035-9688
(418) 586-1900
Fax: (413) 587-9788
mrcallhn@aol.com
members.aol.com/mrcallhn

APPLEGATE, Lee

OVERALL ★★★★ | ROOM QUALITY ★★★★ | VALUE ★★ | PRICE $95–295

In 1929 this was the summer home of a New York surgeon. Indeed, it feels as if you are a guest at a gracious house that hasn't changed much at all—still comfortable, tasteful, and serene, with lots of space, classical music in the air, and a double-size, lived-in living room with built-in bookshelves, and family and guest photos. The screened porch overlooks a swimming pool, and golf is across the street—a rarity at a bed-and-breakfast. Godiva chocolates and brandy awaiting in your room, a game room and a grand piano are other pleasures, and Len and Gloria pamper ceaselessly. The pillared portico seems grand, but the unpretentious beauty within is grander.

SETTING & FACILITIES

Location .5 m from center of town; take I-90 to Exit 2, bear right on Rt. 20 into town, pass 1st stop sign to inn on left, across from golf course
Near Albany Berkshire Ballet; homes of Herman Melville and Edith Wharton; Contemporary Artists Center, Bidwell House, ski area, Mass MoCa Modern Art Museum, Marionette Theatre; unique Santerella in Tyringham, Sculpture House and Museum; Pittsfield Players, other performing arts, quaint villages, parks, antiquing
Building 1920s pillared Jeffersonian-style Colonial

Grounds 6 acres: pines, gardens, rose arbors, old apple trees, croquet
Public Space Entryway, carved staircase; spacious LR, TV room, large screened porch
Food & Drink Full candlelight breakfast; specialty: sour-cream walnut muffins; evening wine and cheese
Recreation Tennis, golf, boating, horseback riding
Amenities & Services Pool, baby grand piano, refrigerator, bike storage, telephone, dataports, bikes, whirlpool tubs, fireplaces

ACCOMMODATIONS

Units 8 main house guest rooms; 2 new suites; 1 carriage house apt. (services/rates vary from B&B)
All Rooms Bath, seating, luggage rack, closet, AC
Some Rooms Fireplace, garden views, King beds, TV/VCR, dataport, wet bar, whirlpool tubs, patios, refrig., coffeemaker, microwave, sleeper sofa
Bed & Bath Four-poster, canopy, iron

and brass, sleigh beds; some shower only, extra-large steam shower (1), pedestal sinks
Favorites Room 1—largest, most expensive, huge sitting area, steam shower for 2, king four-poster bed, fireplace; Room 6—may be best value, smallest, carved Russian Victorian double bed; Room 5—sunny corner, illusion canopy draped over four-poster bed, garden view

Comfort & Decor Guest rooms small/average to almost enormous. Stylish elegance, pretty Victorian or romantic touches. Antiques. Some wallpapers detract from otherwise lovely rooms. Fresh flowers, guest journals, brandy and chocolates in room. Two-bedroom carriage suite: living room, TV/VCR, kitchen facilities, priv. deck, whirlpool. Check for minimum stay

RATES, RESERVATIONS, & RESTRICTIONS

Deposit 1 night, 50% 2+ nights; refund w/ 14-day notice, 30 days July/August
Discounts Pkgs., 3rd person, midweek, weekly; carriage house $1,550 weekly
Credit Cards V, AE, MC; personal checks
Check-in/Out 2/11
Smoking No
Pets No
Kids Over 12
Minimum Stay 2 nights weekends June,
Sept., Oct.; 3 nights weekends July, Aug., holidays
Open All year
Hosts Gloria and Len Friedman
279 West Park St.
Lee, MA 01238
(800) 691-9012 or (413) 243-4451
Fax: (413) 243-9832
lenandgloria@applegateinn.com
www.applegateinn.com

AMADEUS HOUSE, Lenox

OVERALL ★★★½ | ROOM QUALITY ★★★★ | VALUE ★★½ | PRICE $80–225

Books line the walls floor to ceiling, there's a large CD collection, and guests are encouraged to "pick up a baton and conduct a symphony in the living room." Mary and John opened this comfortable, refined turn-of-the-last-century site in 1993. John was a deputy foreign editor for National Public Radio, and Mary is a freelance editor. Like Walker House, rooms are named after composers, and you can sleep in a bird's-eye maple four-poster in namesake Mozart, with his bust staring back at you. Guests rave about the cleanliness and personal service, and the feeling is indeed more like a Mozart concerto here than at the village's other music-oriented bed-and-breakfast (more Brahmsian, perhaps).

SETTING & FACILITIES

Location At edge of village, near Cliff-side B&B; residential side road off village main street
Near Near center of Lenox Village; Berkshire mountains, Tanglewood, Jacob's Pillow, Theatre Festivals, Hancock Shaker Village, Clark Art Institute, Norman
Rockwell Museum, 400-acre John Drummond Kennedy park, ski areas, wildlife sanctuary
Building Rustic 1820 Colonial farmhouse, Victorian touches
Grounds .5 acre, lawns
Public Space Parlor, library, DR

Food & Drink Full breakfast; specialties: orange waffles, "no-cal" yogurt pancakes; tea

Recreation Edith Wharton's home, antiquing, boating, horseback riding

Amenities & Services Extensive recording and book collections, background music, refrigerator, phone, lawn games, chocolate violins, fax

ACCOMMODATIONS

Units 7 guest rooms, 1 suite

All Rooms Antiques, clock/radio, fan

Some Rooms Priv. bath, sitting area, space for add'l guests, priv. porch (1); suite: phone, desk, refrigerator, AC

Bed & Bath Some antique or four-poster beds; robes for shared bath and suite

Favorites Sibelius—hostess' favorite, most cozy, shared bath

Comfort & Decor Sparsely yet richly furnished w/ antique wicker, Shaker and Colonial pieces. Muted wall colors, floral and pastel fabrics. Wreaths, quilts, artwork. 4 room types: small, shared bath; medium, priv. bath; larger, priv. bath; suite, 2 BRs, small living room, kitchen, bath.

RATES, RESERVATIONS, & RESTRICTIONS

Deposit Full payment summer and fall, weekends and holidays; 1 night midweek off-season; refund w/ 14-day notice

Discounts 3rd person, midweek rates, weekly rates, special pkgs., off-season dinner pkgs.; spa services

Credit Cards V, AE, MC, D

Check-in/Out 2/11:30

Smoking Not inside or on porches

Pets No

Kids Over 10

Minimum Stay 2 nights weekends and holidays; 3-4 nights weekends late June–Labor Day and some holidays, 2 nights some midweek stays

Open All year

Hosts Mary Gottron and John Felton
15 Cliffwood St.
Lenox, MA 01240
(800) 205-4770 or (413) 637-4770
Fax: (413) 637-4484
info@amadeushouse.com
www.amadeushouse.com

BLANTYRE, Lenox

OVERALL ★★★★★ | ROOM QUALITY ★★★★★ | VALUE ★ | PRICE $315–850

Baronial halls, velvet chairs, antelope heads, rocking horses, turrets, tapestries, whites for tennis, gargoyles, grilled loin of lamb with lemon-thyme-braised turnips, a harpist, fragrant flowers, gentility, friendliness: Blantyre. This estate sanctuary is a cross between a country inn and a luxury hotel, but the level of personal attention here tips it toward inn. A deserving member of Relais & Chateaux, this ever-better property does not have the icy attitude of some wannabes. And that, in the end, is why guests feel they get their money's worth. The Fitzpatricks also own the Red Lion Inn in Stockbridge, a classic country hotel.

SETTING & FACILITIES

Location From Stockbridge, take Rt. 7 N to 2nd light (5 mi.), right onto Rt. 20, .5 m to Blantyre; from Lee, take Exit 2 off Mass. Pike, take Rt. 20 W to inn on right
Near Botanical gardens, mountains, Tanglewood, Jacob's Pillow, theatre festivals, Hancock Shaker Village, Clark Art Institute, Norman Rockwell Museum, 400-acre John Drummond Kennedy park, ski areas
Building 1901 mansion reminiscent of Edwardian "castle" w/ Tudor features
Grounds Nearly 100 acres: lawns, lightly wooded areas, meadows, gardens, trails
Public Space Museum-quality common rooms, huge hearthed fireplaces; music room; terrace

Food & Drink Cont'l breakfast; full breakfast, add'l fee; hors d'ouevres in main hall, prix-fixe 3-course dinner; maitre d', over 600 wines, candlelight, harpist; seasonal menu; specialties: grilled squab, pan-roasted black sea bass, warm plum-almond tarts with plum compote and crème fraiche ice cream.
Recreation Skeet shooting, Lenox fitness center, arts centers and events, museums, historical home tours
Amenities & Services Tennis, pool, whirlpool, sauna, croquet, newspapers; tennis instruction, ltd. wheelchair access; comp. beverage/snack baskets in rooms, turn-down; corp. and priv. events

ACCOMMODATIONS

Units 24 total; 3 suites and 5 guest rooms in main house; others in carriage house, cottage suites; 2 secluded 2-BR cottage
All Rooms Antiques, sitting area, phone, TV, AC
Some Rooms Fireplace, dressing room, sitting room, 2 baths, 2 double beds, refrigerator, sliding doors to patio, balcony
Bed & Bath Antique brass, canopy, four-poster beds, sizes vary; robes, towel warmers
Favorites Main House rooms—high ceilings, 5 w/ working fireplaces; Windyside Carriage House Suite—loft ceiling w/ mural, balcony, spiral staircase to king bed
Comfort & Decor Large, grandly elegant rooms. Carriage House located poolside. Grandfather clocks, secretaries, armoires, leather-covered desks. Finely upholstered furnishings. Antique beds, some in bay window alcoves. Large, comfortable conversation areas. Rooms vary from masculine mahogany, to summery wicker, to feminine, romantic. Paterson Suite fit for royalty.

RATES, RESERVATIONS, & RESTRICTIONS

Deposit 50%; refund w/ 28-day notice; 10% gratuity added to price
Discounts 3rd person, special packages
Credit Cards V, AE, MC, D
Check-in/Out 3/noon
Smoking Restricted
Pets No
Kids Over 12
Minimum Stay 2 nights weekends, Sept.

24–Oct. 17
Open May 4–Nov. 4
Hosts Senator John Fitzpatrick and family
16 Blantyre Rd.
Lenox, MA 01240
(413) 637-3556
Fax: (413) 637-4282
hide@blantyre.com
www.blantyre.com

BROOK FARM INN, Lenox

OVERALL ★★★★ | ROOM QUALITY ★★★★ | VALUE ★★½ | PRICE $90–215

Named for a nearby literary commune, "There is poetry here," is the credo of this artsy, Victorian bed-and-breakfast. The seasonal newsletter, "Brook Farm Bard," always includes a new poem. Anne and Joe present informal poetry readings at Saturday tea (guests can join in), and offer a daily poem on a podium in a library of 1,500 books. There's music, too. A piano, light opera, show tunes, and classical music on CD, and live chamber music at Sunday breakfasts during Tanglewood season. You can even hear festival practice sessions from the pool area. Oh, and maestro Leonard Bernstein stayed here, when it was a boarding house.

SETTING & FACILITIES

Location Massachusetts Turnpike to Exit 2 (Lee), turn onto Rt. 183, towards Lenox, bear left at monument in Lenox, left onto Old Stockbridge Rd., right onto Hawthorne St., residential road, walk to village

Near Dining and shops; walk to Tanglewood, near Berkshires, Jacob's Pillow, theatre festivals, Hancock Shaker Village, Clark Art Institute, Norman Rockwell Museum, 400-acre John Drummond Kennedy park, ski areas

Building 100-year-old Colonial farmhouse, Victorian touches

Grounds 1 acre: lawn, garden, hammock

Public Space Large entry hall, library, DR

Food & Drink Full buffet breakfast; specialties: egg strata, bread pudding; English tea; 2nd floor guest pantry always open, boiling water faucet, icemaker, beverages

Recreation Edith Wharton's home, antiquing, tennis, golf, boating, horseback riding

Amenities & Services Pool, ongoing library puzzle; large collection of poetry, fiction, and history; add'l 70+ poets on tape; guest refrigerator; hall basket of practical toiletries; writing desk in guest pantry; gift cert., recipes

ACCOMMODATIONS

Units 12 guest rooms

All Rooms Bath, reading lighting, phone, ceiling fan, AC, carpet

Some Rooms Fireplace, seating, dormer, stained glass window

Bed & Bath Some brass, canopy, four-poster beds; some shower only, some tiny baths, all newly tiled

Favorites Room 1—Spacious, queen canopy, sitting area, fireplace, heart-shaped checkers; Room 9—real attic space, skylights, beamed slanted ceilings, 1 queen

and 2 twin beds; Bridal suite, Room 2—mahogany canopy bed, fireplace, hand-painted antique hope chest, balcony

Comfort & Decor Cozy, warm, casually romantic. Quilts, stenciled walls, artwork. Wicker, oak. Lovely mantels, special antiques, rocking chairs. Pastel color schemes. Country, but not rustic. Five rooms remodeled 1998–99. Room sizes vary. Smaller Rooms A, C, 8, and tiny room 7 best values—most attractive, comfortable.

RATES, RESERVATIONS, & RESTRICTIONS

Deposit 50%, full payment Tanglewood, foliage season; refund w/ 15-day notice
Discounts Specials include dinner, spa, sports, art, New Year's pkgs., 3rd person, 7+ night stays, midweek
Credit Cards V, MC
Check-in/Out 3–7/noon
Smoking Outside only
Pets No
Kids Over 15
No-No's Facilities and meals for guests only—guests may not bring guests

Minimum Stay 2 nights most weekends; 3 nights holidays, Tanglewood, foliage season
Open All year
Hosts Anne and Joe Miller
15 Hawthorne St.
Lenox, MA 01240
(800) 285-POET or (413) 637-3013
Fax: (413) 637-4751
innkeeper@brookfarm.com
www.brookfarm.com

CLIFFWOOD INN, Lenox

OVERALL ★★★★ | ROOM QUALITY ★★★★ | VALUE ★★½ | PRICE $90–240

Well-traveled Joy and Scottie lived in France, Belgium, Italy, and Canada and bring international flair to this former summer home built for McEvers Livingston, one-time U.S. diplomat to France. With 12-foot ceilings, inlaid floors, and a veranda overlooking the pool, it was built during the "Gilded Age," from 1880–1920 when Lenox became "inland Newport," as Vanderbilts, Morgans, and Carnegies grew bored with their Rhode Island favorite. The hosts are dealers for quality Eldred Wheeler Colonial reproduction furniture, and the atmosphere is stylish, but not standoffish; in fact, to get to the indoor lap pool and spa you have to go through the basement.

SETTING & FACILITIES

Location I-90 E to Lee exit, take Rt. 20 to Rt. 7A N to Lenox, look for signs to B&B, on quiet, residential street
Near 2 blocks from center of Lenox Village; Berkshire mountains, Tanglewood, Jacob's Pillow, theatre festivals, Hancock Shaker Village, Clark Art Institute, Edith Wharton's home, Norman Rockwell Museum, 400-acre John Drummond Kennedy park, ski areas, walk to dining and shops
Building 1890s Stanford White–style Colonial Revival mansion, Belle-Epoque flourishes
Grounds 1.5 acres: gardens, picnic gazebo, deck, pool
Public Space Entry foyer; LR, music room; DR; common rooms
Food & Drink Cont'l breakfast; p.m. wine and cheese; breakfast served most seasons; otherwise, coupon for breakfast locally
Recreation Boating, golf, horseback riding, winter sports
Amenities & Services Outdoor pool; indoor counter-current pool, whirlpool, winter robes for pool; refrigerator, BYOB set-ups; activities guidebook computer created by hosts, seat cushions/beach chairs for Tanglewood

ACCOMMODATIONS

Units 6 guest rooms, 1 suite
All Rooms Bath, seating, ceiling fan, AC
Some Rooms Fireplace (6), small writing desk, small TV (4)
Bed & Bath Some canopy, four-poster beds, antique double (1), queen (1), king/twin sizes; some shower only, hall access bath w/ robes (1); whirlpool (1), skylight; fireplace (1)
Favorites Jacob Grosse Jr. Room—fireplace, seating, canopy king, full bath, balcony; Walker/Linton suite—king

four-poster canopy, curtained partition sitting room w/ fireplace, hidden TV, shower bath
Comfort & Decor Strong European influence. Contemporary art pieces, personal, period antiques. Corner fireplace in most expensive Helen Walker room w/whirlpool bath. Best value: Karl Stimm room, hall access priv. bath, fireplace, four-poster double bed. Cozy Catherine White room on 3rd floor w/ king bed, fireplace in bath, visible from bed.

RATES, RESERVATIONS, & RESTRICTIONS

Deposit Full payment at reservation; refund w/ 14-day notice
Discounts Midweek rates, except high season; 3rd person
Credit Cards None
Check-in/Out 2–10/11
Smoking Gazebo only
Pets No
Kids Over 11
No-No's Guests' guests using premises; personal food on-premises except gazebo or lower deck
Minimum Stay 2 nights (some rooms

3) weekends foliage season; 3 nights (some rooms 4) all week Tanglewood season; 3 nights (some rooms 4) some weekends other seasons
Open All year
Hosts Joy and Scottie Farrelly
25 Cliffwood St.
Lenox, MA 01240
(800) 789-3331 or (413) 637-3330
Fax: (413) 637-0221
joy@cliffwood.com
www.cliffwood.com

THE GABLES INN, Lenox

OVERALL ★★★★ | ROOM QUALITY ★★★★★ | VALUE ★★½ | PRICE $90–250

Edith Wharton, author of *The Age of Innocence* among many other fine nineteenth-century novels, spent two productive years writing in the eight-sided library—while waiting for her nearby mansion, The Mount, to be completed. The Gables was then known as Pine Acre and was home to her mother-in-law. With its red damask paper, portrait of Edith above the parlor mantel, and florid furnishings, the bed-and-breakfast seems much as it must have in its glamorous heyday. Frank is a stage producer and knows and hosts many celebs, so the glamour continues. Warmth isn't the draw here; dramatic decor, luxury suites, history, and the tennis court and swimming pool are what sells.

SETTING & FACILITIES

Location From south, follow Rt. 7 N through Stockbridge, bear left onto Rt. 7A to Lenox, look for signs to inn

Near Berkshire mountains, Tanglewood, Jacob's Pillow, theatre festivals, Hancock Shaker Village, Clark Art Institute, Norman Rockwell Museum, 400-acre John Drummond Kennedy park, Edith Wharton's home, ski areas, walk to dining and shops

Building Circa 1885 Queen Anne "cottage"

Grounds Gardens, waterfall, patio, pool, tennis court

Public Space Entrance hall, library, staircase, breakfast room

Food & Drink Full breakfast; specialties: French toast, breads and pastries

Recreation Shopping, antiquing, tennis, golf, boating, horseback riding, some bike rentals, skiing, music

Amenities & Services Summer indoor pool, summer tennis court, grand piano, rare document/book collection, recorded music library features pre-Sondheim Broadway themes, BYOB set-ups; 1st floor rooms disabled accessible

ACCOMMODATIONS

Units 12 guest rooms, 4 suites

All Rooms Bath, seating, antiques, clock/radio, phone, AC, TV

Some Rooms Fireplace, sitting area, desk, balcony, TV/VCR, refrigerator

Bed & Bath Antique beds, incl. quilted headboards, elaborately carved Edwardian-style headboards, canopy and four-poster beds; some shower-only

Favorites Edith Wharton suite—fireplace, plush carpet, four-poster w/ charm-

ing quilt, seating area, artwork feminine and romantic; Teddy Wharton suite—most popular, masculine counterpart, boldly striped wallcoverings, leather sofa, carved bed

Comfort & Decor Rooms smallish. Suites are 1 large room. TVs small, not hidden. High ceilings, carpet-on-carpet. Lushly decorated according to themes. Rose

RATES, RESERVATIONS, & RESTRICTIONS

Deposit 1 night, full payment Tanglewood season; refund w/ 14-day notice

Discounts 3rd person

Credit Cards V, MC, D

Check-in/Out 2/noon

Smoking Restricted, and no cigars	some holidays
Pets No	**Open** All year
Kids Over 12	**Hosts** Mary and Frank Newton
No-No's Others besides guests using	81 Walker St., Route 183
facilities	Lenox, MA 01240
Minimum Stay 2 nights, Oct., all holiday	(800) 382-9401 or (413) 637-3416
weekends; 3 nights, Tanglewood season,	www.gableslenox.com

WALKER HOUSE, Lenox

OVERALL ★★★★ | ROOM QUALITY ★★★ | VALUE ★★½ | PRICE $80–220

This bed-and-breakfast has a doorbell that plays Beethoven's "Ode to Joy." Peggy was editor of *Performing Arts* magazine, and Richard was a music critic and arts administrator, so the conversation at this comfortable, cluttered, Federal-era house is lively and artsy. The library has hundreds of videos and a 12-foot movie-mogul-like screen. A third plus, depending on your preferences, is the pet-friendly environment. Four-legged guests may especially enjoy the giant stuffed animal "tea party" around an antique oak table and the animal-shaped doorstop collection on the stairs. And as for the rooms, Handel is airy, Verdi has lime-green wallpaper, and Puccini has a porch.

SETTING & FACILITIES

Location Near center of Lenox and down the street from Gables Inn
Near Berkshires mountains, Tanglewood, Jacob's Pillow, theatre festivals, Shaker Village, Clark Art Institute, Norman Rockwell Museum, Edith Wharton's home, 400-acre John Drummond Kennedy park, ski areas, walk to dining and shops
Building 1804 Federal Clapboard, Greek Revival touches
Grounds 3 landscaped and natural, wooded, acres; picnics encouraged
Public Space Parlor, library, DR,
screened porch
Food & Drink Generous cont'l breakfast, communal; homemade muffins; afternoon tea
Recreation Golf, boating, horseback riding
Amenities & Services Comp. summer tennis at Lenox Tennis Club, games, grand piano, extra beds avail., large-screen TV, refrigerator, bike storage; radio/tape recorders, old-time radio show tapes, quarterly B&B newsletter; weddings, reunions

ACCOMMODATIONS

Units 8 guest rooms
All Rooms Bath, clock/radio, AC
Some Rooms Fireplace, sitting area, priv. small porch (1)
Bed & Bath Antique, four-poster, canopy beds, sizes vary; some claw-foot soaking tubs, some shower only

Favorites Mozart—Mahogany furnishings, antique loveseat, queen fishnet canopy bed, antique harpsichord, fireplace

Comfort & Decor Fairly spacious

rooms w/ 1 exception, named for composers. Period furnishings, wallcoverings, artwork. Little touches of added comfort, wine, bubble bath. Not high style, but comfy.

RATES, RESERVATIONS, & RESTRICTIONS

Deposit 1 night; 3 nights July, August, holidays; refund w/ 14-day notice

Discounts 3rd person, weekly, midweek, packages

Credit Cards None

Check-in/Out 2/noon

Smoking No

Pets Well-behaved dogs by prior arrangement, dog sitting avail.

Kids Over 12

Minimum Stay 3 nights in July, August, holidays

Open All year

Hosts Peggy and Richard Houdek
64 Walker St.
Lenox, MA 01240
(800) 235-3098 or (413) 637-1271
Fax: (413) 637-2387
phoudek@vgernet.net
www.walkerhouse.com

THE SALTBOX, Northampton

OVERALL ★★★★ | ROOM QUALITY ★★★★ | VALUE ★★★ | PRICE $115–136

College town inns and bed-and-breakfasts don't always have the incentive to sparkle because they can count on group- and student-related business much of the year. But this little property, right across from the Smith College campus, sparkles away. Craig is the president of a local hospital. Carol's background includes teaching, travel, entertaining, and design, and her decorating flair is evident throughout. Rooms are refurbished to bring out history of this eighteenth-century house (named for its architectural style) with a light, welcoming touch. Unassuming, tasteful, comfortable, welcoming.

SETTING & FACILITIES

Location Exit 18 from 91N (20 min. from Mass. Turnpike and Rt. 2); across the street from Smith College, Botanical Gardens, Paradise Pond, and Mill River

Near UMass, Hampshire, Amherst, Mt. Holyoke, Deerfield, Williston, Conn. River, Berkshires, arts venues and outdoor recreation, ample dining

Building 1784–86 home; converted 1997

Grounds Priv. backyard, flower gardens,

seating areas

Public Space Entry hall, small guest parlor and breakfast room; disabled access

Food & Drink Breakfast w/ fresh, seasonal ingredients served in room; specialties: coffee from local roaster, poached pears, crisps, baked apples; wine glasses, corkscrew, welcome snacks; special items avail. with advance notice; dozens of restaurants in walking distance

Recreation XC skiing, tennis, picnicking, hiking biking; walking distance to YMCA

Amenities & Services Maps/books, irons

ACCOMMODATIONS

Units 3 suites

All Rooms Bath, priv. entrance, heat controls, AC, TV, coffee pot, refrig.

Some Rooms Efficiency kitchen, disabled access, daybed, priv. patio, sitting area, fireplace, Jacuzzi

Bed & Bath 2 queens (one w/ add'l, quilted daybed in alcove), 1 double; excellent mattresses; heated towel racks; whirlpools for 2, oversized showers

(w/seats), tub/showers

Favorites Hester's Retreat—queen four-poster, seating/sleeping alcove, dbl. whirlpool; The Sabbatical—queen four-poster, wicker seating area, efficiency kitchen

Comfort & Decor Upstairs rooms overlooking Holyoke Mountain Range, best in winter. Creative style. Comfortable and cheery. Ground-floor room, separate entrance and patio

RATES, RESERVATIONS, & RESTRICTIONS

Deposit 50%, refund w/ 14-day notice; can book through travel agency

Discounts Long stays, 3rd person

Credit Cards V, AE, MC, D

Check-in/Out 2–6/11

Smoking No

Pets No; in-house cat and schnauzer

Kids Older children OK

Minimum Stay 2/3 night when short

stays avail.

Open All year

Hosts Carol and Craig Melin
153 Elm St.
Northampton, MA 01060
(413) 584-1790
www.javanet.com/~saltbox

HISTORIC MERRELL INN, *South Lee*

OVERALL ★★★½ | ROOM QUALITY ★★★ | VALUE ★★½ | PRICE $85–225

Built in 1794 for a general in the Massachusetts militia, this columned building was turned into a stagecoach stop, and the framed visages of the original innkeepers stare out in the tavern room. The circular birdcage bar is the last extant example of its kind in this country. The sliding bars protected the liquor, the cash, and the bartender from sometimes rowdy highwaymen.

Today's guests may not be as disorderly, but they do enjoy the same river views, beehive oven, candlebeam lighting, and seconds at breakfast. And the country guest rooms, while small and simple, are undoubtedly more romantic than when the Merrells presided.

SETTING & FACILITIES

Location On Housatonic River; 1 mi. E of Stockbridge Village
Near Quaint Stockbridge Village, Norman Rockwell Museum, Tanglewood, theater festivals, Jacob's Pillow Modern Dance Festival, outlets; Lee and Lenox Villages, ski areas
Building 200 year-old plantation-style Federal
Grounds 2 riverfront acres, parklike lawns, gazebo, hammocks

Public Space Parlor; tavern room, rare birdcage bar; keeping room; TV room
Food & Drink Full breakfast, choice of entrées; specialties: basil/cheese omelets, blueberry pancakes, sausage
Recreation Picnics, mountain swimming, scenic drives, antiquing
Amenities & Services Refrigerator, BYOB set-ups

ACCOMMODATIONS

Units 9 guest rooms, 1 suite
All Rooms Bath, phone, TV, AC
Some Rooms Fireplace, desk, seating or sitting area
Bed & Bath Some canopy, half-canopy beds; queen, king/twin sizes; most shower only
Favorites Room 1—Emerald-green walls, paisley fabrics, canopy queen, fireplace, wood floors, sofa; Room 3—river

view, country decor, fireplace; Riverview Suite—sep. wing, fireplace, bookshelves, dining table, balcony overlooking river
Comfort & Decor Rather small rooms, well furnished. Decor from Early American to country. Walls painted Federal colors or papered w/ romantic or country prints. Window swags, Oriental carpets. VCR. Some rooms dark. B&B is close to road, back rooms quietest.

RATES, RESERVATIONS, & RESTRICTIONS

Deposit 1 night, refund w/ 14-day notice
Discounts Off-season, corp. rates
Credit Cards V, MC
Check-in/Out 2–10/11
Smoking No
Pets No
Kids Check w/ B&B, no cribs; no kids in summer season
Minimum Stay 2 nights weekends; 3

nights July, August
Open All year, except Christmas week
Hosts Faith and Charles Reynolds
1565 Pleasant St., Rt. 102
South Lee, MA 01260
(800) 243-1794 or (413) 243-1794
Fax: (413) 243-2669
info@merrell-inn.com
www.merrell-inn.com

FIELD FARM GUEST HOUSE, Williamstown

OVERALL ★★★★½ | ROOM QUALITY ★★★★★ | VALUE ★★★½ | PRICE $125

Here's a chance to stay in a modern art museum set in almost 300 acres of unspoiled nature. Actually, it's the former house of art patron Lawrence

Bloedel, and although much of his collection is now in museums, including the nearby Williams College Museum of Art, many of the sculptures and handmade furniture from this American modern 1948 cedar building do remain. The views of the countryside and mountains beyond are as beautiful as the artwork. Enjoy the pool, tennis, and the on-site Folly House, opened only for tours. This unique haven for modernists and nature-lovers is managed by a Massachusetts land conservation trust, started in 1891.

SETTING & FACILITIES

Location At the foot of the Taconic mountain range in North Berkshire County; Rt. 7 S from Williamstown to Rt. 43 S, right onto Sloan Rd., 1.2 mi. farther on right

Near Williamstown Theatre Festival, Clark Art Institute, Williams College, Mountain Meadow Preserve, Jiminy Peak ski area, Pittsfield Players

Building 1948 American modern-style contemporary 16-room main house; unique circular structure; 2nd building, Folly House, built as guest house, 1966

Grounds 296 acres: mountain views, sculptures, gardens, beaver pond, corn fields, meadows, woods; 4 mi. of trails

Public Space Large LR, DR, common terrace, kitchen and pantry

Food & Drink Full breakfast, communal; specialties: Friendship bread, egg pie, granola, peach French toast

Recreation Picnicking, bird watching, photography, fishing, swimming

Amenities & Services Heated summer pool, tennis court, pantry and refrigerator, phone, books, small nature center

ACCOMMODATIONS

Units 5 guest rooms

All Rooms Bath, reading lamps, alarm clock, fresh flowers, picture window

Some Rooms Priv. deck, fireplace, writing desk

Bed & Bath Some w/ Scandinavian-style bookshelf headboards, queen, twin sizes; some shower only, range from quite small to fairly spacious, 1940s vintage baths

Favorites Master Room—most spa-

cious, fireplace, large deck, views, large bath; North Room—queen, fireplace w/ butterfly tiles, mirrored dressing table, coziest

Comfort & Decor Sparsely furnished, in keeping w/ museum-style contemporary theme. Top-quality 1950s spare furnishings. Graceful table light fixtures. Tile-bordered fireplaces. Original artwork. TVs, phones deliberately excluded.

RATES, RESERVATIONS, & RESTRICTIONS

Deposit 100%; refund w/ 14-day notice or rebook

Discounts 3rd person, singles

Credit Cards V, MC, D

Check-in/Out 2–10/11

Smoking Outside only

Pets Not inside house, welcome on grounds

Kids Welcome—no cots or cribs

Open All year

Hosts The Trustees of Reservations
554 Sloan Rd.
Williamstown, MA 01267
(413) 458-3135
Fax same as phone, call first

RIVER BEND FARM, Williamstown

OVERALL ★★★½ | ROOM QUALITY ★★★ | VALUE ★★★★ | PRICE $90

This truly historic, truly authentic Colonial house was built by one of Williamstown's original founders and commander of the victorious Massachusetts forces at the Revolutionary Battle of Bennington, which was planned in the Tap Room. Ethan Allen, Seth Warner, and Benedict Arnold all walked these wavy floors, in spare rooms with the same details today. The chimney provides five fireplaces, two bake-ovens, an attic smoking chamber, and a cellar ash pit. Restoration is total throughout the house; there's no plastic anywhere, bread is fresh-baked, as it was for Revolutionary soldiers, and you feel transported 200 years back. Yes, bathrooms are shared, but the chamber pots are for decoration only.

SETTING & FACILITIES

Location On Rt. 7, "intown" country setting

Near 1 mi. from village and Williams College; Hoosic River adjacent to property, Appalachian Trail, Mount Graylock, ski areas, museum, Clark Art Institute, Mass MoCA, Williamstown Theater Festival, Tanglewood, Jacob's Pillow, Shaker Village, Berkshire attractions; 15 mi. to Pittsfield; day trip to Saratoga and historic Deerfield Village

Building Col. Benjamin Simonds House, ca. 1770, river valley restored Georgian Colonial; on Historic Register, certified Historic Structure

Grounds 5 acres, picnic area, gardens, patio, mountain views

Public Space LR; orig. tap room, "funeral" or "casket" side door; keeping room, originally borning room w/ open hearth fireplace and bake oven

Food & Drink Cont'l breakfast, communal; homemade granola, muffins, jam, honey; p.m. tea on request; fresh fruit

Recreation Golf, tennis, horseback riding, bikes avail. for rent in town, sleigh/carriage rides

Amenities & Services Refrigerator, phone, picnic area, canoe

ACCOMMODATIONS

Units 4 guest rooms

All Rooms Authentic Colonial furnishings

Some Rooms Decorative mantel, wainscoting

Bed & Bath Double, twin, four-posters, rope beds, feather mattresses; 1 room and shower bath on 1st floor; 3 rooms and bath w/ claw-foot tub on 2nd floor

Favorites Parlor Room—decorative

open hearth fireplace, double antique rope four-poster, Oriental rugs

Comfort & Decor Rooms large. Not cozy or romantic in 20th-century sense. Early American simplicity, modernized. Wing-backed chairs, braided or Oriental rugs on wide-plank flooring, dried flowers, Colonial light fixtures, spinning wheel. Federal colors.

RATES, RESERVATIONS, & RESTRICTIONS

Deposit 50%; refund w/ 14-day notice

Discounts Add'l person, group rental

Credit Cards None

Check-in/Out Upon request

Smoking Outside only

Pets No

Kids Welcome

Minimum Stay 2 nights some weekends in summer

Open April–Oct.

Hosts Judy and Dave Loomis

643 Simonds Rd., Route 7

Williamstown, MA 01267

(413) 458-3121

Cape Cod

Cape Cod—that flat, narrow, breezy peninsula that looks on a map like a flexed bicep—is an hour southeast of Boston, and a great place to relax. If you want to veg out on a ribbon of sandy beach, backed by undulating sand dunes (once substituted as the Sahara in silent movies), the Cape is still the perfect spot. But it isn't just a beach destination or the place to catch the **Martha's Vineyard** or **Nantucket** ferries.

When the sun is too intense, or for an off-season visit, there's still plenty to keep you occupied. You can drive, bike, or walk the 300-mile shoreline. The **Cape Cod Rail Trail** is 25 miles of former train tracks, and another path from the **Salt Pond Visitor's Center** passes dunes, sea grasses, and wooden bridges. Kite flying, whale watching, antiquing, shopping, golfing, theater-going, and slurping clam chowder are other pleasures.

The 27,000-acre **Cape Cod National Seashore** is the best place to explore wild flora and fauna. **Woods Hole** is home to the **National Marine Fisheries Aquarium** and the **Woods Hole Oceanographic Institute.** Lighthouses, as traditional as boats hauling catches on wooden wharves, dot the shoreline. The **Highland Light,** built in 1795, is in **North Truro,** and the **Scargo Hill Observation Tower** in **Dennis** has a view across **Cape Cod Bay.**

History, recent and not-so, is here, from the **John F. Kennedy Museum** in **Hyannis** to the **1797 Grist Mill** in **Chatham,** at the "elbow" of this peninsula. **Eastham** has a one-room schoolhouse, and **Brewster** has the **Cape Cod Museum of Natural History and Expedition.** Pretty, old **Sandwich,** established in 1637, sparkles with a glass museum and restored homes at **Heritage Plantation. Whydah Sea Lab** in **Provincetown** is the home of pirate treasure (in fact, the only such authentic place in the world).

Colors seem brighter in the sun of the Cape. Crimson sunsets, scarlet cranberry bogs, cherry-red lobsters and, burgundy chrysanthemums—

these hues, and blue, yellow, and green as well seem to come into focus in the clear air. And the night, pierced by silver sprinkles, seems black velvet.

Gabled, gray-shingled homes—many of them built by sea captains—are scattered along Route 6A, the **Old King's Highway** and still Cape Cod's main road, which can get mighty congested in summer. Many homes have been turned into alluring bed-and-breakfasts and small inns. Some stay open throughout the year, though most close in the dead of winter. Summer weekends need to be booked way ahead, but in September, still warm here but delightfully uncrowded, rooms are often available last minute, especially midweek.

FOR MORE INFORMATION

Bed & Breakfast Cape Cod
Nantucket: (800) 686-5252
Fax: (508) 775-2884
email: bedandb@capecod.net

Harwich Accommodations Association (HAA)
(508) 432-7166 or (800) 321-3155
email: lionhead@capecod.net

Orleans Bed & Breakfast Associates
Bed & Breakfast Cape Cod: (508) 225-3824 or (800) 541-6226
Fax: (508) 240-0599
email: info@bedandbreakfastcapecod.com
www.capecod.net/bb

THE CAPTAIN FREEMAN INN, Brewster

OVERALL ★★★★ | ROOM QUALITY ★★★★ | VALUE ★★½ | PRICE $100–220

Carol is a gourmet chef with her own cooking classes and Tom raises orchids and creates stained glass. Their talents are put to obvious use in this award-winning bed-and-breakfast. Breakfasts and snacks are lavish and fresh, in good weather served on the screened porch or by the herb and perennial gardens surrounding the pool. The careful restoration of this captain's mansion is recorded in photos, fun to study by the fireplace. The feeling of romance is evident, perhaps because the innkeepers themselves were married here.

SETTING & FACILITIES

Location Exit 10 off Rt. 6, faces "Currier and Ives" town green
Near Cape Cod Nat'l Seashore, theater, Museum of Natural History and Exhibition, Cape Cod Bay, antiquing, galleries
Building 1866 Victorian
Grounds 1.5 acres: woods, gardens, pool
Public Space Parlor, screened dining porch, DR, sitting room
Food & Drink Full breakfast, freshly squeezed juice, fruit; specialties: French sausage pastry, eggs Benedict, lemon— wild rice pancakes; tea, lemonade, mulled cider, baked goods, fruit
Recreation Whale/bird watching, golf, tennis, biking, all water sports, horseback riding
Amenities & Services Badminton, croquet, bikes, binoculars, videos, refrigerator, beach towels, recipes, daily papers; meetings (25–30), fax, email, flipchart, overhead; laundry, ironing, pick-up from plane/train; winter cooking school, weekends

ACCOMMODATIONS

Units 6 guest rooms, 6 luxury rooms
All Rooms Bath, sitting area, hairdryer, antique desk, large closet or armoire, dresser, AC
Some Rooms Refrigerator, TV/VCR, phone w/ answering system, fireplace, dbl. whirlpool
Bed & Bath Queen canopies; 2-person whirlpools or tub/shower combo
Favorites The Eastham Room—2nd floor, fireplace, large sitting area, sunset view from balcony whirlpool
Comfort & Decor Antique Victorian furnishings, wood floors, period decorating. Baths: marble and tile or original wood floors with plaster detail. Wicker, lace canopies. Two rooms disabled accessible. Luxury rooms just that.

RATES, RESERVATIONS, & RESTRICTIONS

Deposit Full payment, 1–3 nights; 50% others; for stays of 4+ nights, balance due 14 days before arrival; cancellations within 14 days refunded only if room re-rented
Discounts Add-on pkgs. for special occasions: champagne and two 45-min. massages in-room by masseuse, 3rd person

Credit Cards V, AE, MC	**Hosts** Carol and Tom Edmondson
Check-in/Out 2–8/11	15 Breakwater Rd.
Smoking No	Brewster, MA 02631
Kids Over 10	(508) 896-7481 or (800) 843-4664
Minimum Stay 2 nights	Fax: (508) 896-5618
Open All year	www.captainfreemaninn.com

FERNBROOK INN, Centerville

OVERALL ★★★ | ROOM QUALITY ★★★★ | VALUE ★★★½ | PRICE $110–148

Built in 1881 by a hotelier from Boston's Parker House, this gabled Queen Anne has landscaping and a heart-shaped rose garden designed by F.L. Olmsted of Central Park fame. The next owner co-invented Technicolor, and hosted Disney, DeMille, and other Hollywood types. Left to the Catholic church, the grand house became a retreat, and later a summer home for Boston's Cardinal Francis Spellman, whose guests included John Kennedy Sr. and Richard Nixon. Recent guests have been Bill Murray and Alec Baldwin, visiting the nearby Kennedy Compound. Friendly owner Mary Anne is a European-trained art historian. You can stay in the former chapel, amid stained glass and real cathedral ceilings.

SETTING & FACILITIES

Location Exit 5 Mid-Cape Highway, cross Route 149; first right on Old Stage Rd.; continue to lights at Route 28, continue straight; road turns into Main St., B&B on left

Near Antiquing, beaches, boat/ferry trips, Kennedy compound in Hyannis, JFK Museum

Building 1881 Queen Anne Victorian; Nat'l Register of Hist. Places

Grounds Landscaping by Frederic Law Olmsted in 1881; heart-shaped sweetheart—1 acre (out of orig. 18), rose garden, ponds, unusual trees and plantings

Public Space Ballroom, LR, DR all formal; sitting room/orig. library; 2 large covered porches

Food & Drink Full breakfast; specialty: crabmeat/cheese quiche; afternoon tea, cakes

Recreation Skeet shooting, whale watching; Fourth of July parade watching; Christmas stroll on Main St., Centerville Old Home Week in August

Amenities & Services Refrigerator, irons, books, beach towels; meetings (80), weddings

ACCOMMODATIONS

Units 7 guest rooms, 1 cottage

All Rooms Bath, individual furnishings

Some Rooms Fireplace, refrigerator, priv. entrance, TV, sitting room

Bed & Bath Twins, queens, kings, some canopies, four-posters; full baths, new baths

Favorites The Cardinal Room—formerly chapel, cathedral ceiling, stained glass, TV, exquisite antiques, sweetheart garden view; Cottage—cathedral ceiling, living area, TV, cooking facil., balcony, flowers

Comfort & Decor Rooms named after events in the inn's history. Oriental rugs. Hardwood floors. Antiques, sitting rooms, sundeck, suite in turret.

RATES, RESERVATIONS, & RESTRICTIONS

Deposit 50%; refund w/ 14-day notice

Credit Cards None

Check-in/Out 1/11; flexible

Smoking Porches only

Pets No

Kids Over 12

No-No's More than 2 to a room

Open All year

Host Mary Anne Wuthrich

481 Main St.

Centerville, MA 02632

(508) 775-4999

CYRUS KENT HOUSE INN, Chatham

OVERALL ★★★★ | ROOM QUALITY ★★★★ | VALUE ★★ | PRICE $95–290

The previous owner, a bright and elegant innkeeper and long-time local with a career in fashion, created, not unexpectedly, a bright and elegant inn. Current owners Steve and Sandra Goldman purchased the inn in 1999 and have since renovated the front porch and extensive gardens. Seek out the luscious rooms in the Carriage House, especially the romantic second-floor area.

SETTING & FACILITIES

Location Close to downtown Chatham, in residential neighborhood, 1 block from Main St.

Near Galleries, dining, shopping, beach; whale watching, Cape Cod Nat'l Seashore

Building White Victorian Clapboard, carriage house

Grounds Landscaped yard, parking area

Public Space LR, DR, deck, porch overlook gardens

Food & Drink Homebaked cont'l breakfast; specialties: hot fruit compote, granola; afternoon tea and coffee

Recreation Fishing, whale watching, beach, bike trails

Amenities & Services Beach towels, recipes, daily paper, baby grand piano, refrigerator, irons, kitchen privileges; meetings (12), weddings/groups (20)

ACCOMMODATIONS

Units 10 guest rooms, including 4 suites

All Rooms Bath, phone, TV, AC

Some Rooms Priv. entrance

Bed & Bath Queen and full beds, canopies, four-posters; baths w/ showers only (4)

Favorites Room 10—large BR w/ fireplace and canopy bed; Room 8, in Car-

riage House—2nd floor, canopy bed, fireplace, cathedral ceiling, sitting area

Comfort & Decor Each room unique. Many antiques. Bedrooms restored to preserve original character. 4 w/ parlor beds. Deluxe rooms in Carriage House, sitting rooms and fireplaces. Real flair.

RATES, RESERVATIONS, & RESTRICTIONS

Deposit One night; refund w/ 10-day notice or charge 1 night as future stay credit; can book through travel agency

Discounts Long stays, seniors; groups can reserve entire, 3rd person

Credit Cards V, AE, MC

Check-in/Out 2/11

Smoking No

Pets No

Kids Over 6

Minimum Stay 2 nights

Open All year

Hosts Steve and Sandra Goldman

63 Cross St.

Chatham, MA 02633

(800) 338-5368 or (508) 945-9104

Fax: (508) 945-9104

cyrus@cape.com

www.capecodtravel.com/cyrusken

MARY ROCKWELL STUART HOUSE, Chatham

OVERALL ★★★½ | ROOM QUALITY ★★★ | VALUE ★★ | PRICE $110-275

It's fun to watch an emerging property ripen. Opened in 1998, this former private mansion is still a work in progress, and the enthusiastic owners have wallpapered, replaced windows, and upgraded patios, outdoor furniture, and landscaping. They are delighted that people stop to admire their efforts, and hope to add function and warmth with history and romance in mind. "The porch, with its pillars and railings, seems to define the house," says Deborah, who met hubby, Ron, at an inn, and knows the power of romantic ambiance. As for local color, the three-hour Fourth of July parade passes in front, and band concerts are nearby.

SETTING & FACILITIES

Location Rotary through town to 314
Main St., at end
Near Lighthouse Beach, shopping, Nantucket/Martha's Vineyard ferries, fishing
pier, Monomoy Island wildlife refuge
Building Prestigious-looking Victorian
Cape, 1823–1901
Grounds 1 acre set off from Main St.,
ocean views, mill pond across street;
porches, patio
Public Space Large LR, breakfast room,
wraparound porch

Food & Drink Full breakfast; specialties:
Stuart Scrambler w/ ham and cheese,
sourdough French toast, blueberry pancakes, baked goods, fresh fruit; hors
d'oeuvres w/ hosts Sat. evenings; afternoon tea
Recreation Fishing, whale watching,
boating, tennis, antiquing
Amenities & Services Irons, books,
daily papers, disabled access, meetings
(12), picnic lunches (extra)

ACCOMMODATIONS

Units 4 guest rooms, 2 suites
All Rooms Bath, gas fireplace, ceiling
fan, phone, hairdryer, toiletries
Some Rooms Deck, disabled access
Bed & Bath Queens, some four-posters,
iron, brass, cherry spindle; new, large
baths, spacious counters, Corian sinks,
tile floors, tub (1)
Favorites Large 3rd floor room—won-

derful views, deck, fireplace; 1st floor
suite—spacious, priv. porch, priv. entrance
Comfort & Decor Individually decorated. Spacious rooms with antiques,
comfortable chairs, pine floors, quilts.
Light and airy w/ big windows. Four
rooms on second floor. Fireplaces nice
touch.

RATES, RESERVATIONS, & RESTRICTIONS

Deposit 1 night by check or credit card;
refund w/ 7-day notice
Discounts Off-season
Credit Cards V, AE, MC
Check-in/Out 3/11
Smoking No
Pets No; in-house indoor white Persian
cat
Kids Over 14
No-No's More than 2 people in a room

Minimum Stay 2 nights holidays, season
weekends
Open All year
Hosts Deborah and Ron McClelland
314 Main St.
Chatham, MA 02633
(508) 945-4634
Fax: (508) 945-8012
www.axs.com/mrshouse

ACWORTH INN, Cummaquid

OVERALL ★★★★ | ROOM QUALITY ★★★★ | VALUE ★★★ | PRICE $85–185

This small, typical Cape house displays flowers within and without, and its
all-white look is fresh and pretty. But the warmth and cheerfulness of the

innkeeper is the real strength. She loves to recommend jazz clubs and bird-watching spots, and greets guests as if they were forever friends. Classical music, a crackling fire, ribbons and greenery on breakfast tables, heart-shaped waffles—no charming detail is overlooked. (Even embossed toilet paper!) Guest journals reflect the appreciation of happy visitors in this relaxed, comfortable Inn.

SETTING & FACILITIES

Location 4.6 mi. E of Rt. 6A off Rt. 132N; N side of Mid-Cape
Near Cape Cod Nat'l Seashore, Hyannis Airport, antiquing, galleries, historic landmarks, beaches, ferries to Nantucket and Martha's Vineyard, summer theatre
Building Secluded 1860 Cape Cod farmhouse
Grounds .3-acre flower and herb garden
Public Space Sitting room, library, dining area, deck, hammock

Food & Drink Buffet breakfast; specialties: low-fat granola, seasonal fruit w/ edible flowers, fresh pastries, hot entrées; cranberry spritzers on arrival; afternoon tea; nearest restaurant 2 min.
Recreation Whale watching, golf, tennis, boating, horseback riding
Amenities & Services Daily papers, recipes, beach towels, bikes, irons, fax, books

ACCOMMODATIONS

Units 4 guest rooms, 1 suite
All Rooms Bath, triple sheeting, fresh flowers, toiletries
Some Rooms AC, fireplace, tub and shower, sitting area; suite: whirlpool, gas fireplace, mini-refrigerator
Bed & Bath Queens, some canopy; some tubs, robes
Favorites Cummaquid Room—1st floor,

fireplace, French doors, full bath; Yarmouth Port Room—2nd floor, TV, full bath, sitting area
Comfort & Decor Light, airy rooms with a romantic feel accentuated by painted floors and furniture, lace and decorator fabrics. Fresh flowers and turn-down service.

RATES, RESERVATIONS, & RESTRICTIONS

Deposit 50% or one night's stay
Credit Cards V, AE, MC, D
Check-in/Out 3–7/11
Smoking No
Pets No; dog on property
Kids Over 12
No-No's Canceling w/out 15-day notice; $20 cancellation fee
Minimum Stay 2 nights weekends and

holidays
Open All year, except Christmas week
Host Joan Tognacci
Box 256
Cummaquid, MA 02637
(508) 362-3330 or (800) 362-6363
Fax: (508) 375-0304
www.acworthinn.com

SCARGO MANOR BED AND BREAKFAST, Dennis

OVERALL ★★★ | ROOM QUALITY ★★★ | VALUE ★★½ | PRICE $90–195

You can relax on the 55-foot dock on freshwater Scargo Lake, attend a play at The Cape Playhouse, or go in just about any direction from here, the center of the peninsula. Summer festivals and Christmas holiday tours are popular. This peak-roofed nineteenth-century captain's house, is relatively new and unheralded in the press, yet a nice place to unwind. It's one of the many mid-level, mid-range bed-and-breakfasts in New England that line main roads and byways, edge lakes and woods. No high style, no whirlpools, just comfortable king or queen canopy beds, private baths, ample breakfasts and afternoon refreshments, and warm atmosphere.

SETTING & FACILITIES

Location Near Sagamore Bridge on Rt. 6A, overlooking Scargo Lake.
Near Summer theater, Cape Cinema, Scargo Pottery, Dennis Antique Center, museums, fine restaurants
Building 1895 Victorian
Grounds 3 manicured acres, gazebo, 30′ of sand beach and 55′ dock on the lake; paths, gardens
Public Space Enclosed porch, large sitting room, LR, DR; 3rd floor sitting room
Food & Drink Full breakfast; specialty: stuffed French toast; coffee/tea self-service
Recreation Public golf course, Cape Cod bike trail (Dennis-Provincetown), 25-mi. ocean beach, whale watching, deep-sea fishing, sunset/sightseeing cruises, tennis courts, swimming in fresh and ocean water, small gallery and lawn games on site
Amenities & Services Beach towels/chairs, recipes, daily papers, irons, refrigerators; complimentary bikes and small boats

ACCOMMODATIONS

Units 4 guest rooms; 2 suites
All Rooms Bath, AC, hairdryer
Some Rooms TV, iron; large suite: working fireplace, tub, shower
Bed & Bath king (1) and queen canopy (2), queen spool beds (2), queen four-poster; tub/shower (1), glass showers (5)
Favorites Hydrangea—at the back of 3rd floor, vaulted ceilings, ceiling fan and skylight; overlooks Scargo Lake; Sarah Hewes-windows on three sides
Comfort & Decor Designer bedding, down pillows and comforters, Amish quilts, crochet canopies. Individually designed rooms w/ period furniture, sitting areas, extra bed in suites, painted wide floorboards, wing-back chairs. Ceramic tile floors in bathrooms.

RATES, RESERVATIONS, & RESTRICTIONS

Deposit 1–2 nights: full payment, 3–4
nights: 2 nights payment, 5+ nights: 50%
payment. Refund w/ 14-day notice
Discounts 3rd person (suites)
Credit Cards V, AE, DC, MC, D
Check-in/Out 2–9/11
Smoking No
Pets No; inn has golden retriever

Kids Welcome
Minimum Stay 2 nights on in-season
weekends
Open April–Dec.
Hosts Lin and Rich Foa
909 Main St., Route 6A
Dennis, MA 02638
(800) 595-0034 or (508) 385-5534

OVER LOOK INN, Eastham

OVERALL ★★★½ | ROOM QUALITY ★★★ | VALUE ★★★ | PRICE **$95–175**

This popular nineteenth-century house is a family-run operation. The
warm internationally influenced hosts are Scottish and fluent in Portuguese, French, and Spanish. Nan is President of the Eastham Chamber of
Commerce; Ian is a chartered surveyor who takes guests out in his vintage
London taxicab and plays bagpipes at afternoon teatime. The sons have
lived in the Amazon region and Canada. At holiday time you can ring in
the New Year with a Scottish traditional dinner package, and Scottish
woolens are always on sale at the shop onsite. Then there's the Hemingway
billiard room, the Churchill library, and lots of comfortable fun.

SETTING & FACILITIES

Location Heart of the Outer Cape
between Chatham and Provincetown
Near Cape Cod Nat'l Seashore, Salt
Pond Visitor's Center, Wellfleet Audubon
Sanctuary
Building 1869 Queen Anne Victorian
Grounds 3 well-treed acres w/ garden,
porch
Public Space Parlor, tea room, library,
billiard room, DR
Food & Drink Full Scottish breakfast;

specialties: kedgeree-smoked cod, rice,
raisins, porridge; scones for afternoon;
walk to nearest restaurant
Recreation Bike trails; kayaking, horseback riding, windsurfing, antiquing
Amenities & Services Daily papers,
refrigerator, irons, beach towels, recipes,
Scottish woolens shop; meetings (20),
weddings (50); fax, easel and flipcharts;
reserving entire property

ACCOMMODATIONS

Units 14 guest rooms, 4 BR lodge, cottage

All Rooms Bath, AC, hairdryer, alarm clock, sitting area

Some Rooms Cathedral ceiling, clawfoot bathtub, fireplace

Bed & Bath Twin, double, queen brass beds; baths w/ pedestal sinks, robes

Favorites The Garden Room—priv. porch, log fireplace

Comfort & Decor Rooms decorated w/ Victorian antiques, original artwork by hosts' artist-son. Cottage w/ kitchenette. Comfortable, not elegant.

RATES, RESERVATIONS, & RESTRICTIONS

Deposit Full payment for 3 nights or less, other 50%; refund w/ 10-day notice

Discounts 3rd person, packages

Credit Cards MC, V AE, D, DC

Check-in/Out 2–5/11

Smoking Library only

Pets No

Kids Welcome

Open All year

Hosts Ian and Nan Aitchison, Mark and Clive

PO Box 771

Eastham, MA 02642

(508) 255-1886

Fax: (508) 240-0345

stay@overlookinn.com

www.overlookinn.com

WHALEWALK INN, Eastham

OVERALL ★★★★½ | ROOM QUALITY ★★★★★ | VALUE ★★ | PRICE $170–300

The Kents of tobacco fortune lived here in the 1920s as gentleman farmers (the luxury saltbox cottage was once a chicken coop). But originally, like so many others in this region, this was a whaling captain's house. The friendly hosts, both former advertising executives, keep working hard to maintain this exceptional, airy, elegant retreat. Its reputation is formidable, but in reality it is a warm and fuzzy bed-and-breakfast in sophisticate's trappings. Dick creates tempting breakfasts—how about granola pancake pizza topped with fresh fruit?—and Carolyn wins awards for decorating. But we're the real winners.

SETTING & FACILITIES

Location Rock Harbor Rd. exit off
Orleans Rotary; left on Rock Harbor,
right on Bridge Rd.; in residential
neighborhood
Near Hyannis ferries, Wellfleet Wildlife
Sanctuary
Building Enormous 1830 Federal; outbuildings
Grounds 3 acres: lawns, meadows, gardens
Public Space 2 parlors: 1 formal, 1
informal; formal DR; guest pantry; sun-
porch; garden patio

Food & Drink Full imaginative breakfast,
in-room by request; specialties: cran-
berry/blueberry Cape-Cod pancakes,
corn pancakes with smoked salmon, Belgian waffles; refreshments, cookies;
evening hors d'oeuvres
Recreation Cape Cod Nat'l Seashore,
bike to Cape Cod Rail Trail Bike Path,
whale watching
Amenities & Services Refrigerator,
irons, books, beach towels, bikes; meetings (8–10), fax, email, bike storage

ACCOMMODATIONS

Units 11 guest rooms, 5 suites; rooms in
the inn, barn, guest house, carriage house,
saltbox
All Rooms Bath, AC, iron, clock/radio,
hairdryer
Some Rooms Fireplace, wet bar,
TV/VCR, coffee/tea service
Bed & Bath 2 twins, queens, kings, most
antiques; whirlpools, some tubs, some
sep. showers
Favorites Room w/ king antique four-

poster, sitting area w/ fireplace, priv.
entrance off patio; room w/ queen four-
poster, large sitting area w/ fireplace, tub
for 2, garden view
Comfort & Decor Soft colors, contemporary, spacious. Mix of country antiques
and reproductions, some country cottage. Bed skirts, coverlets, and decorative
pillows. Light-filled, airy, fresh flowers.
Suites exceptionally spacious, w/ kitchens;
Cape saltbox: priv. patio.

RATES, RESERVATIONS, & RESTRICTIONS

Deposit 50%; refund(less $25 fee) w/
14-day notice
Discounts Off season
Credit Cards V, AE, MC
Check-in/Out 2/11
Smoking No
Pets No
Kids Over 12
Minimum Stay 2 nights in-season,
weekends; 3 nights holiday weekends

Open April 1–Dec 12 (winter weekends)
Hosts Carolyn and Dick Smith
220 Bridge Rd.
Eastham, MA 02642
(508) 255-0617
Fax: (508) 240-0017
information@whalewalkinn
www.whalewalkinn.com

MOSTLY HALL, *Falmouth*

OVERALL ★★★★ | ROOM QUALITY ★★★★ | VALUE ★★ | PRICE $185–225

The name comes from a child who visited over 100 years ago; he walked in, looked at the 35-foot foyer, and exclaimed, "Why Mama, it's mostly hall!" Halls or not, it feels like a home, and a distinctive one. Built by a sea captain for his New Orleans bride, this plantation-style "raised cottage" is the oldest summer house in Falmouth. The 13-foot windows and wraparound porch seem more Bayou than Back Bay. Convenient to the historic district, it is nonetheless private, set back from the busy road on sweeping lawns. Christina and Bogdan are warm hosts, breakfasts are creative, the enclosed widow's walk den is special. So, mostly, it's delightful.

SETTING & FACILITIES

Location Just off Falmouth Village Green
Near Beaches, trails, harbors, Woods Hole (marine science), Cape Cod Nat'l Seashore, train rides, galleries, ferries, theaters
Building 1849 plantation-style house; Nat'l Hist. Register
Grounds 130 ft. from road, gardens, 1.3 acres; lush, secluded setting; gazebo
Public Space Enclosed Widow's Walk, den sitting space; wraparound porch; LR; LR/DR; library wall 2nd floor

Food & Drink Full gourmet European breakfast w/wide variety of cheeses; octopus and seafood salads, fresh pastries
Recreation Golf, whale watching, canal cruises, Shining Sea bikeway, antiquing
Amenities & Services Bikes and helmets, AC, inn cookbook, irons, hairdryers, use of host refrigerator, beach towels/passes, daily papers, rides to ferry or shuttle bus

ACCOMMODATIONS

Units 6 guest rooms

All Rooms Bath, AC, ceiling fan, reading chairs, antiques

Bed & Bath Queen four-poster canopies; showers only, some small, some marble-topped sink outside bath

Favorites Downstairs—13-foot ceilings, floor-to-ceiling windows

Comfort & Decor Floral papers, Oriental rugs. Reading chairs. Antique and traditional furniture. All corner rooms w/ garden views. Bright and airy, big, shuttered windows. Rooms in back, second floor most private.

RATES, RESERVATIONS, & RESTRICTIONS

Deposit Full payment 1 night, other 50%; refund w/ 14-day notice

Discounts Off-season, honeymoon package (ferry tickets w/ 3 nights)

Credit Cards V, AE, MC, D

Check-in/Out 3–7/11

Smoking No

Pets No; kennel nearby

Kids Over 16

Minimum Stay 2 nights May–Oct.,

weekends; 3 nights holidays, Falmouth Road Race Weekend

Open Mid-Mar.–Mid-Dec.

Hosts Christina and Bogdan Simcic
27 Main St.
Falmouth, MA 02540
(800) 682-0565 or (508) 548-3786
Fax: (508) 457-1572
mostlyhall@aol.com
www.mostlyhall.com

WILDFLOWER INN, Falmouth

OVERALL ★★★★ | ROOM QUALITY ★★★★ | VALUE ★★★ | PRICE $95–225

Lavender poached pears, lemon-flower pancakes, rose-petal morning cakes, sunflower crêpes, pansy butter, ten-fruit compote sprinkled with chopped marigolds—sound yummy? Not for you? Never fear, the edible flowers grown at this homey bed-and-breakfast are an optional part of your five-course breakfast. Phil is a barber, Donna a former social worker and quilting teacher, and between them they have 8 children and 12 grandchildren, who probably prefer pizza to candied violets.

SETTING & FACILITIES

Location .5 mi. from 1st set of lights after divided highway ends on Rt. 28; in Falmouth's historic district

Near Martha's Vineyard ferry, aquarium, nature area, Woods Hole, Plimoth Plantation, beaches, winery, shining sea bikeway, downtown village

Building Pre-1898 Victorian, wraparound porch

Grounds Award-winning; herbs and edi-

ble flower gardens, sitting area, fish pond, gazebo

Public Space Gathering room, 3rd floor TV room

Food & Drink Breakfast in-room or in gathering room; specialties: cooked w/ edible flowers: frozen fruit smoothies, fresh fruit w/ herbs; hot drinks, wine, snacks avail. 24 hours; afternoon tea; dessert; special diets accom.

Recreation Water sports, sports center, antiquing, billiards, bicycling
Amenities & Services Grill, laundry service, phone, games, bikes, computer, fax; comp. champagne for special occasions

ACCOMMODATIONS

Units 5 guest rooms, 1 cottage
All Rooms Bath, AC, ceiling fan, dataport, alarm clock, radio, shower, robes
Some Rooms Skylight, window seat, priv. entrance, sitting area
Bed & Bath Queens, some four-posters, sleigh, iron, canopies, featherbed (1); some tub/showers, dual shower heads, claw tubs, whirlpools

Favorites Third-floor room—bed w/ skylight, whirlpool, 2-head shower
Comfort & Decor Unique decors are comfortable and elegant: antiques, floral, garden effect furniture, wicker, tailored. Tasteful. Good light. Cottage: queen and pull-out sofa, kitchen, spiral staircase, LR, loft bedroom

RATES, RESERVATIONS, & RESTRICTIONS

Deposit 50%; refund w/ 30-day notice
Discounts 3rd person, gov't, 5-day stay (10%), theme packages: quilting, Christmas, antiques, lighthouse, etc.; cottage rented weekly, monthly
Credit Cards V, AE, MC
Check-in/Out 3/11
Smoking No
Pets No
Kids No

Minimum Stay 2/3 nights May 1–Oct. 31, weekends
Open March 1- Dec 30
Hosts Donna and Phil Stone
167 Palmer Ave.
Falmouth, MA 02540
(508) 548-9524 or (800) 294-5459
Fax: (508) 548-9524
wldflr167@aol.com
www.wildflower-inn.com

AUGUSTUS SNOW HOUSE, Harwich Port

OVERALL ★★★★ | ROOM QUALITY ★★★★ | VALUE ★★½ | PRICE $105–190

Gables, dormers, a screened gazebo, turrets, leaded windows, organs that don't work, pianos that do—this imposing Queen Anne mansion is filled with charms. The atmosphere has a decidedly feminine slant—from a cabinet brimming with Cabbage Patch dolls to the pretty guest rooms, named after Joyce and Steve's daughters. The romantic inn is a fine spot for a small wedding, as the landscaped lawn and patio with its white furniture are a lovely setting for ceremonies and cocktails. The Garden Room can hold 60 guests, with fine catering and all services, and that working piano is ready for the wedding march or swing music.

SETTING & FACILITIES

Location Exit 10 off Rt. 6, S on 124/39;
near Main St., Harwich Center
Near Martha's Vineyard ferry, shopping in
Chatham, downtown Harwich; 1 block
from priv. beach on Nantucket Sound;
Nantucket ferry, 1 mi.
Building Large 1901 Queen Anne Victo-
rian estate
Grounds 1+ acre; gazebo, porch, views,
patio

Public Space Entry, LR, porch, wraparound veranda
Food & Drink Breakfast; specialties:
baked pears w/ raspberries and cream,
cinnamon-pecan bread pudding w/
brandy-caramel sauce; refreshments
Recreation Swimming, golf, tennis, boating, whale watching, lawn games
Amenities & Services Gift cert.,
books, games, fax; weddings

ACCOMMODATIONS

Units 5 guest room; new carriage house
suite
All Rooms Bath, AC, fireplace, TV,
phone, ceiling fan
Some Rooms Whirlpool, refrigerator,
sitting area, orig. bathroom, bay window
Bed & Bath Queen or king beds; full
tubs and showers, whirlpools

Favorites Melissa's Room—4-poster
canopy, sitting area, bay windows, bath w/
ornate marble sink, dramatic wallcovering
Comfort & Decor Rooms large. Victorian decor and modern amenities. Individually decorated. Baths in period style
with imported European fixtures.

RATES, RESERVATIONS, & RESTRICTIONS

Deposit 50%. Check deposits w/in 5
days of reserving. Refunded w/ 15-day
notice
Discounts Off-season, packages, 3rd
person
Credit Cards V, AE, MC, D
Check-in/Out 2/11
Smoking Outdoors
Pets No
Kids Over 12
Minimum Stay 3 nights July/August

weekends, 2 nights other weekends and
July/August midweek
Open All year except 3–4 weeks in Jan.
Hosts Joyce and Steve Roth
528 Main St.
Harwich Port, MA 02646
(800) 320-0528 or (508) 430-0528
Fax: (508) 432-6638
info@augustsnow.com
www.augustsnow.com

DUNSCROFT-BY-THE-SEA, Harwich Port

OVERALL ★★★½ | ROOM QUALITY ★★★ | VALUE ★★ | PRICE $95–295

Hearts and flowers are all around you at this weathered shingle Colonial—
especially the former: heart-shaped pillows, picture frames, boxes, shells
and rocks, a book called *Hearts*. At Valentine's Day, mimosas for breakfast,
treats in your room. Cupids, "love letter" info letters in each guest room

addressed to Scott and Zelda and other lovers, roses, Hershey's Kisses—get the point? Alyce, the romantic-minded host, insists "it's not overdone." But be forewarned, it may be intoxicating: she and Wally were married here.

SETTING & FACILITIES

Location Rt. 10 mi. E of Hyannis, on quiet tree-lined street between beach and village

Near Cape Cod Nat'l Seashore, JFK Museum, Pilgrim Monument, Nantucket, Martha's Vineyard, Plymouth Rock and Plantation, shopping, galleries

Building 1920 Beachside Colonial Revival

Grounds Priv. mile-long beach on Nantucket Sound; sun and shade; patio, porch, water views; croquet

Public Space LR, library, porch; DR

Food & Drink Full country buffet breakfast, communal or separate; specialties: fried apples, blueberry buckle, cottage pudding, Caribbean French toast; juice and hot drinks, cookies avail.

Recreation Whale watching, horseback riding, golf, scuba; boat rental nearby

Amenities & Services Baby grand piano, refrigerator, irons, beach chairs/towels, recipes, daily papers, picnic baskets; fax, copier; meetings (10–15), weddings off-season (30)

ACCOMMODATIONS

Units 8 guest rooms, 1 cottage

All Rooms Bath, robes, hairdryer, phone, toiletries

Some Rooms AC, whirlpool, fireplace, TV/VCR, kitchenette, priv. entrance; disabled access (1)

Bed & Bath King and queen, four-posters, canopies, sleigh beds; shower-

only baths (3), tub/shower (2), whirlpool/shower (3)

Favorites King suite, cottage, and Room 6—romantic beds, whirlpools

Comfort & Decor Decidedly romantic, with heart pillows, lace window treatments. Feminine

RATES, RESERVATIONS, & RESTRICTIONS

Deposit Full payment 1–4 nights; refund w/ 21-day notice; reservations w/in 21 days of arrival require full nonrefundable payment

Discounts Off-season, 3rd person

Credit Cards AE, V, MC

Check-in/Out 2/11; ask for late departures

Smoking No

Pets No

Kids 14 and up

Minimum Stay 3 nights July–Labor Day, 2 nights other in-season weekends, holidays

Open All year

Hosts Alyce and Wally Cunningham
24 Pilgrim Rd.
Harwich Port, MA 02646
(800) 432-4345 or (508) 432-0810
Fax: (508) 432-5134
dunscroft@capecod.net
www.dunscroftbythesea.com

BED AND BREAKFAST OF SAGAMORE BEACH,
Sagamore Beach

OVERALL ★★★½ | ROOM QUALITY ★★★ | VALUE ★★★½ | PRICE **$95**

A big painting of Carmen Miranda hanging in the living room? Grandma's bedspread brought from Italy? Omelets on tortillas with salsa, and cinnamon coffee? If these original, offbeat touches appeal, then you won't mind sharing a bath at this beach house on a hill, overlooking Cape Cod Bay. You can sit on the decks and porches and enjoy the serenity, then come in and enjoy John's eclectic talents. He is a well-known food stylist, chef, author, and former art director, and his cooking classes are renowned. So the food presentation is fabulous, accentuated by bright colors, and he may test out recipes with you. This bed-and-breakfast by the sea may be over-the-top for many, but for others, it's just tops.

SETTING & FACILITIES

Location On a hill overlooking Cape Cod Bay, near Sagamore Rotary
Near Beach, shops, restaurants, Sandwich, Cape activities; Boston
Building Large 1900 Cape Cod beach house
Grounds Large, outdoor enclosed shower; lawns, vegetable, herb, and flower gardens; hammock
Public Space LR, large porches
and decks
Food & Drink Healthy breakfast, communal; specialties: theme breakfasts, such as all blueberry dishes or dairy-free
Recreation Tennis courts, semi-priv. beach a short walk
Amenities & Services Large porches for meetings; beach towels; cooking/decorating discussions

ACCOMMODATIONS

Units 3 guest rooms
All Rooms Fresh flowers, robes, on 2nd floor
Some Rooms Water views
Bed & Bath Double antique beds; 1 shared bath
Favorites Four-poster room—white
coverlet, blue walls, orig. paintings, two breezy window exposures
Comfort & Decor Exciting use of fabric and color w/ eclectic furnishings and antiques. All beds different, antique. Original, quirky. Fresh flowers, plants. Ceiling fans. Smallish rooms.

RATES, RESERVATIONS, & RESTRICTIONS

Deposit None
Discounts Weekend packages, incl. cooking class
Credit Cards Cash only
Check-in/Out After 5/11
Smoking No
Pets No
Kids No

Minimum Stay I night
Open All year
Host John F. Carafoli
Box 205
Sagamore Beach, MA 02562

(508) 888-1559
Fax: (508) 888-1859
carafoli@cape.com
bbchannel.com

BAY BEACH BED AND BREAKFAST, Sandwich

OVERALL ★★★★½ | ROOM QUALITY ★★★★★ | VALUE ★½ | PRICE $200–345

Less is more here, in the style of Japan or Sweden, but warmth is not the strong point at this award-winning beauty on a private beach. The hosts spent almost 30 years in the business, are well-traveled, and love good restaurants. They stay in the background, and the emphasis is on seclusion, understated luxury, and low-key elegance. Fresh flowers are everywhere inside and out, the water views are gentle through window walls, cookies are on the kitchen counter, a telescope looks out to the bay, and there is a sense of beauty and peace throughout. The closest cousin to fine inns such as The Inn at Sunrise Point in Camden, Maine, or The Inn at Canoe Point near Bar Harbor, Maine, this is a place for those who appreciate water views, privacy—and the pristine perfection of carpets vacuumed in concentric circles.

SETTING & FACILITIES

Location Near Rt. 6A-E off the Sagamore bridge; residential area overlooking water on private road
Near Plimoth Plantation, Plymouth Rock, Kennedy compound, Glass Museum, Heritage Plantation, other historical sites, waterfront, marina
Building Contemporary inn, opened 1987
Grounds Secluded priv. waterfront property, lots of flowers, gardens, boardwalk to priv. beach, view of Cape Cod Bay and Canal
Public Space Boardwalk, deck
Food & Drink Wine, fruit, cheese, crackers in room on arrival; nearest restaurant 5 min.
Recreation Boating, golf, inline skating, whale watching
Amenities & Services Irons, daily papers, fresh flowers, daily faxing, books

ACCOMMODATIONS

Units 3 suites
All Rooms Bath, priv. deck, phone, TV, cable, CD player, refrigerator, AC, ceiling fan, hairdryer, toiletries, whirlpool, fireplace
Bed & Bath King beds; full baths
Favorites Dune Caper and Canal Caper—oceanfront suites w/ marsh view, whirlpools, fireplaces
Comfort & Decor Rooms are spacious and contemporary w/ wicker furniture, fresh flowers, mirrored walls, and views of ocean or marsh.

RATES, RESERVATIONS, & RESTRICTIONS

Deposit Varies by length of stay; refund
w/ 30-day notice
Credit Cards V, MC
Check-in/Out 2–6/12
Smoking Outdoors only
Pets No
Kids 16 and older
No-No's Sand on the carpets
Minimum Stay 2 nights midweek, 3 on

weekends, holidays
Open May 1–Oct. 1
Hosts Emily and Reale Lemieux
3 Bay Beach Lane
Sandwich, MA 02563
(508) 888-8813 or (800) 475-6398
Fax: (508) 888-5416
www.baybeach.com

HONEYSUCKLE HILL BED AND BREAKFAST,
West Barnstable

OVERALL ★★★½ | ROOM QUALITY ★★★★ | VALUE ★★½ | PRICE $100–200

Mary and Bill know their business—they were innkeepers in Vermont for a
dozen years and lectured at seminars for prospective innkeepers. They cook
together—parceling out parts of the original, lavish breakfasts in a kitchen
built for two—and the results are delicious. Their bed-and-breakfast, furnished comfortably with antiques and family pieces, is on a former stagecoach path, and is fresh and pretty and unassuming, with a wicker-filled
screen porch. The beds are fluffy featherbeds, the linens are ironed, and the
new baths, gleaming marble.

SETTING & FACILITIES

Location About 2 mi. from Exit 5 off Rt.
6 E, on former stagecoach path
Near Beach, Cape Cod Nat'l Seashore,
Sandwich Glass Museum, JFK Museum,
Heritage Plantation, Cape Cod Rail Trail
Building 1810 Queen Anne–style home;
Nat'l Register of Hist. Places
Grounds 1+ acre; lawns, gardens, water-
fall, fish pond, view
Public Space LR, DR, screened porch

Food & Drink Full breakfast, communal
or separate; specialties: "Dutch babies,"
Grand Marnier French toast, granola;
early-riser coffee and papers; snacks,
sherry, soda, coffee/tea; nearby restaurant
Recreation Whale watching, golf, tennis,
swimming, fishing, bird watching
Amenities & Services Refrigerator,
irons, books, beach towels/chairs/umbrel-
las, recipes, daily papers

ACCOMMODATIONS

Units 4 guest rooms; 1 suite
All Rooms Priv. bath, AC, clock/radio,
drink set-up, English toiletries
Some Rooms Writing desk, dressing

tables, TV/VCR, priv. entrance (1)
Bed & Bath Double and queen featherbeds; marble and brass baths, seats in
oversize showers

Favorites Magnolia—1st floor, queen four-poster, sitting area, dressing table **Comfort & Decor** Sunny, comfortable. Recently redecorated with antiques, white wicker, Battenburg lace. All rooms named after flowers, and all pretty.

RATES, RESERVATIONS, & RESTRICTIONS

Deposit 1 night; 50% for longer stays; refund w/ 14-day notice
Discounts Off-season
Credit Cards V, AE, MC, D
Check-in/Out 3–9/11
Smoking Garden only
Pets No
Kids 12 and over
Minimum Stay 2 nights on weekends

Open All year
Hosts Mary and Bill Kilburn
591 Old King's Hwy., Historic Rt. 6A
West Barnstable, MA 02668
(866) 444-5522 or (508) 362-8418
stay@honeysucklehill.com
www.honeysucklehill.com

INN AT LEWIS BAY, West Yarmouth

OVERALL ★★★½ | ROOM QUALITY ★★★ | VALUE ★★★ | PRICE $98–138

How can you not enjoy sleeping in a room named "Picket Fence," "Cranberry Bog," "Birdsong," or "Howling Coyote"? The young innkeepers at this informal, friendly mid-Cape bed-and-breakfast enjoy the quiet residential neighborhood in close proximity to activities. A major landscaping project is part of general upgrading. The senses are teased and pleased, with salty breezes from nearby Lewis Bay, flickering candles, fresh flowers, classical music, and the feel of handcrafted quilts. This Dutch Colonial house is highly decorated for Thanksgiving and Christmas, quiet times on the Cape.

SETTING & FACILITIES

Location Near Route 6, Exit 7; in seaside neighborhood near the beach
Near JFK Museum and Memorial, beach, whale watching, Nantucket/Martha's Vineyard ferries
Building 1920 Dutch Colonial
Grounds Small grounds, flowers, view
Public Space Large DR, LR, book nook

Food & Drink Full candlelight breakfast, communal; specialties: cranberry-orange juice w/ raspberry sherbet, crab casserole; afternoon tea and cookies
Recreation Bocce, trails, sailing, horseback riding, mini/regular golf
Amenities & Services Daily papers, beach towels/chairs, irons, info

ACCOMMODATIONS

Units 7 guest rooms
All Rooms Bath, AC
Bed & Bath queen, double, and twin

beds, some canopies; some showers only, modern tub/shower (1); antique tubs and showers

Favorites Secret Garden—2nd floor, queen four-poster, sunny, partial view
Comfort & Decor Country decor, scattered antiques, braided rugs. Modest, clean, comfortable accommodations, w/ armchairs, space for personal objects. Rooms named after Cape Cod area.

RATES, RESERVATIONS, & RESTRICTIONS

Deposit Full payment for 1 night; other, 50%; 14-day notice or re-rental for refund
Discounts Holiday packages; seniors, 3rd person, long stays, singles, off-season, AAA
Credit Cards V, AE, MC
Check-in/Out 3–8/11
Smoking No
Pets No

Kids 12 and over
Minimum Stay 2 nights in-season
Open All year, except Christmas Day
Hosts Rick and Liz Latshaw
57 Maine Ave.
West Yarmouth, MA 02673
(508) 771-3433 or (800) 962-6679
Fax: (508) 790-1186
stay@innatlewisbay.com
www.innatlewisbay.com

WEDGEWOOD INN, *Yarmouth Port*

OVERALL ★★★ | ROOM QUALITY ★★★★ | VALUE ★★½ | PRICE $115–205

Lots of interesting talk here: Gerrie was a professional dancer, Milt played pro football with the New England Patriots and was an FBI agent assigned to the notorious Bronfman kidnapping. Set among 200-year-old trees and extensive gardens, this was the first architect-designed house in classic Early Americana, built for a maritime attorney (fees were apparently huge in 1812, too). Public rooms in the main house are small, furnished formally with nineteenth-century antiques and interesting pieces like a blacksmith's bellows table. The rustic carriage barn is great for groups, with its beamed common room and suites with soaking tubs, fireplaces, dataports, and private decks.

SETTING & FACILITIES

Location Rt. 6, Exit 7, turn right on Willow St. to Rt. 6A; turn right, inn on right, 100 yards from corner, on knoll
Near Beaches, antiquing, galleries, boutiques
Building 1812 Greek Revival/Federal inn
Grounds 2 acres, lawns, gardens, patios, gazebo, huge trees
Public Space Entryway, common room, DR, carriage barn; wheelchair access
Food & Drink Tea trays in rooms, early

bird coffee, full breakfast, in room if requested; specialties: Belgian waffles w/ strawberries, pecan pancakes; special diets accom. w/ prior notice; afternoon tea
Recreation Whale watching, golf, tennis, fishing, sailing, harbor cruises
Amenities & Services Refrigerator, irons, beach towels, daily papers; pick-up from plane; 2 meeting rooms (15–20 each), fax

ACCOMMODATIONS

Units 4 guest rooms, 5 suites (3 in Carriage House)
All Rooms Bath, fresh fruit, wood for fireplace, hairdryer, evening tea tray, AC
Some Rooms Working fireplace (7), screened porch(2), deck (2), phone (3), TV
Bed & Bath Kings in carriage house, queen canopies in main house suites, oth-

ers queens, pencil posts; some claw-foot tubs, 3 oversized tubs, large baths
Favorites Wedgwood Blue Room—spacious, canopy bed, porch w/ wicker
Comfort & Decor Period design and detailing, stencils. Wide-board floors, Oriental carpets. Wing-back chairs, spacious sitting areas. Comfortable and truly Colonial. Antiques but not restrictive.

RATES, RESERVATIONS, & RESTRICTIONS

Deposit Full payment, 1 night; others 50%; refund w/ 15-day notice
Discounts Off-season
Credit Cards V, AE, DC, MC
Check-in/Out 2/11
Smoking No
Pets No
Kids Over 10

Minimum Stay None
Open All year
Hosts Gerrie and Milt Graham
83 Main St.
Yarmouth Port, MA 02675
(508) 362-5157 or (508) 362-9178
Fax: (508) 362-5851
www.wedgewood–inn.com

Martha's Vineyard/ Nantucket

Nobody seems to be quite sure just who Martha was (for sure, not Stewart), but the Vineyard is named for the wild grapes that were abundant here in 1602, when explorer Bartholomew Gosnald discovered the little island (and did not, for sure, stay in a bed-and-breakfast or small inn!).

Most commonly accessed by ferry or boat from Cape Cod or Nantucket, **Martha's Vineyard** is an ever-popular beach destination and an increasingly stylish haven for the rich and famous, who for centuries have built huge summer mansions along the water. Presidents, moguls, heads of state, and celebs relax here in season, and you are likely to see a tanned and rested famous face at a local restaurant or hardware store.

The main towns have distinct personalities, and all have many shops and restaurants. Edgartown was a nineteenth-century whaling port; the 1843 **Old Whaling Church** is now a performing arts center. **Vineyard Haven** is the ferry port and retains vestiges of a turn-of-the-last-century community. For seafaring buffs, the **Seaman's Bethel** houses whaling artifacts.

Oak Bluffs, a mid-nineteenth-century Methodist campground, offers an enchanting photo opportunity: teeny gingerbread cottages adorned in a rainbow of brightly colored facades that long ago replaced the original campground tents. Also in Oak Bluffs, **Flying Horses** is supposedly—like one in Rhode Island—the oldest working carousel in the country.

"Up island" **West Tisbury** and **Chilmark** are quieter destinations, with rolling farmland. **Gay Head,** at the tip of the Vineyard, has a secluded beach backed by multicolored clay cliffs, a wildlife preserve, and lighthouse. Check out the seasonal tours at **Chicama Vineyards** in **West Tisbury,** or the **Cedar Tree Neck Wildlife Sanctuary,** containing 300 acres on the northern part of the island.

Many small lodgings, most of them reconverted seamen's homes or established inns in or near the towns, will arrange transfers to the ferry. Make ferry reservations far ahead in summer season, when the island gets crowded, especially if you plan to bring your car. Martha's Vineyard is a haven for bicyclists, and a car is unnecessary for many parts of the island.

A bit farther out, 30 miles from Cape Cod, is crescent-shaped **Nantucket Island,** which still looks like a whaling-ship port from 1850. More quaint and low-key than the larger, trendy **Vineyard, Nantucket** is one entire National Historic District. In town you'll find cobblestone streets, shops and restaurants, as well as many captains' houses renovated into bed-and-breakfasts, showing off the widow's walk roofs and architectural detailing of centuries past. The decor and feel are traditional and period, simple and engaging.

Nantucket Town houses the **Whaling Museum,** and there are whale watching and fishing trips from the wharf. For the ecologically minded, **Nantucket** has a natural history museum, observatory, aquarium, the **Maria Mitchell Science Center,** and the **Marine and Shellfish Laboratory,** as well as the **Nantucket Vineyard,** open seasonally.

FOR MORE INFORMATION

Most sources for Cape Cod can also help with reservations and information for Martha's Vineyard and Nantucket (see page 290).

SHIVERICK INN, Edgartown

OVERALL ★★★½ | ROOM QUALITY ★★★★ | VALUE ★½ | PRICE $145–360

Dr. Clement Shiverick was the town physician in 1840 when this gracious home with a mansard roof was built near the center of a thriving whaling center. Today, Edgartown is still thriving, and still a whale center, but the huge mammals attract people to watch them rather than catch them. Shiverick's house has been hosting visitors as a comfortable, refined bed-and-breakfast since 1981. The emphasis is romance, and this three-story, white clapboard Victorian retreat is one of several fine properties here geared toward couples. The chandelier in the cupola casts a soft glow that has become a landmark on summer evenings.

SETTING & FACILITIES

Location 1 block from Main St., in heart of Edgartown
Near Antiquing, dining, cinema, harbor, museums, summer events

Building 1840 Victorian three-story mansion with Mansard roof
Grounds Small English garden w/ fountain, wrought-iron furniture

Public Space Garden, garden room, terrace; library, drawing room
Food & Drink Warm gourmet breakfast; specialties: island preserves, coffee cake, homemade granola and breads, fresh fruits and juices; afternoon tea with refreshments

Recreation Biking, nature trails, beaches, sailing, fishing, swimming, tennis, golf, historical museums
Amenities & Services Refrigerator, irons, hairdryers, alarm clocks, French milled soaps, beach towels and chairs, island and public phones

ACCOMMODATIONS

Units 10 guest rooms
All Rooms Bath, AC
Some Rooms Fireplace (9)
Bed & Bath Kings, queens; canopies and four-posters; tubs and showers
Favorites 2 front rooms—1 canopy, fireplace, 1 on south side of house (bright)

Comfort & Decor 18th–19th-century early American, English and French antiques, Oriental rugs, wood floors. Lighting varies. Romantic style. Stylish, tasteful, refined. down comforters, freshly pressed linens

RATES, RESERVATIONS, & RESTRICTIONS

Deposit Full payment at booking; refund (less 10% fee) w/ 14-day notice
Discounts Off-season, packages
Credit Cards V, AE, MC, D
Check-in/Out 2+/11
Smoking No; only in cottage garden
Pets No
Kids Over 12
Minimum Stay 2 nights June 1–14; 3 nights June 15–Oct. 8

Open Year round
Hosts Paul I. Weiss, Bryan D. Freehling, and Kristin Allen
5 Pease's Point Way, Box 640
Edgartown, MA 02539
(800) 723-4292 (reservations only) or
(508) 627-3797
Fax: (508) 627-8441
shiverickinn@vineyard.net
www.mvweb.com

TUSCANY INN, *Edgartown*

OVERALL ★★★★ | ROOM QUALITY ★★★★ | VALUE ★½ | PRICE $100–395

Italian is not the most typical influence for an inn on the Vineyard, but this former sea captain's mansion in the heart of town evokes a hilltop farm in Tuscany—at least within. Laura is Tuscan and has decorated the house with stylish flair and sunny colors. The feel is sophisticated and sensual, a far cry from the New England/nautical atmosphere of many properties on the islands and Cape. She offers Northern Italian cooking classes weekends off-season, and in season, the restaurant serves filet mignon with Gorgonzola ravioli on the patio. *Tutto bene.*

SETTING & FACILITIES

Location Downtown Edgartown

Near Block from harbor, ferries, restaurants, shops; 2 blocks from beach, museums, galleries, public transportation

Building Grand, newly remodeled Victorian

Grounds Pond, herb/flower gardens, hammock

Public Space LR, library, common room, breakfast area off kitchen

Food & Drink Breakfast; specialties: fresh bread, blueberry pancakes; afternoon biscotti, cappuccino; family-owned La Cucina restaurant, North Italian dinner seasonally

Recreation Biking, nature trails, golf, tennis, fishing, sailing

Amenities & Services Refrigerator, flowers

ACCOMMODATIONS

Units 8 guest rooms

All Rooms Bath

Some Rooms Harbor view, whirlpool

Bed & Bath Beds vary, some canopies; robes, some tubs

Favorites Room 5—King bed under eaves, whirlpool, view

Comfort & Decor Antique furniture, toile prints, sponge-painted walls. High style. Some rooms small, all attractive. Airy, fresh, sophisticated decor.

RATES, RESERVATIONS, & RESTRICTIONS

Deposit Full payment 1–3 nights; others 50%; refund w/ 15-day notice

Discounts Off season

Credit Cards V, AE, MC

Check-in/Out 2/11

Smoking No

Pets No

Kids Over 8

Minimum Stay 3 nights for summer weekends

Open Except part of winter

Host Laura Sbrana
22 North Water St.
Edgartown, MA 02539
(508) 627-5999
Fax: (508) 627-6605
tuscany@vineyard.net
www.tuscanyinn.com

THE VICTORIAN INN, Edgartown

OVERALL ★★★★ | ROOM QUALITY ★★★★ | VALUE ★½ | PRICE $100–385

Across from the town's famous "Pagoda Tree" brought in a bucket from China in the nineteenth century, this award-winning bed-and-breakfast of the same era was a whaling captain's home. Like other fine properties in this book (not always noted as such) it is listed in the National Register of Historic Places. Karyn and Stephen are personable innkeepers and seem to enjoy polishing the hardwood floors and brass; in the half-dozen years since they bought the three-story, white-clapboard house, they have been constantly renovating. Breakfasts are exceptional, served in the wainscoted dining room or enclosed garden patio.

SETTING & FACILITIES

Location Hist. Edgartown, 1 block from town dock, Main St., harbor

Near Restaurants, museums, galleries, summer theater, wildlife sanctuaries, beaches

Building Restored whaling captain's home

Grounds English garden, walk to town

Public Space Entry, common rooms, DR

Food & Drink Award-winning 4-course breakfast; specialties: scrambled eggs w/ basil and feta cheese, banana-rum pancakes; afternoon tea in garden

Recreation Tennis, golf, horseback riding, sailing, fishing, swimming

Amenities & Services Games, books, advice

ACCOMMODATIONS

Units 14 guest rooms

All Rooms Bath, flowers, sherry, AC, ceiling fan

Some Rooms Priv. balcony (6), deck, balcony, sundeck, porch, harbor view, bay window

Bed & Bath Beds vary, four-posters, canopies, pencil-posts; some baths small,

papered, laminate surfaces

Favorites Third floor rooms—French doors to balconies, best views

Comfort & Decor Individually decorated w/ family furniture, antiques, flowers. Bedside lighting. Floral papers and fabrics.

RATES, RESERVATIONS, & RESTRICTIONS

Deposit Full payment 1–3 nights; other 50% w/ full payment 14 days before arrival; refund w/ 15-day notice

Discounts Off-season, singles

Credit Cards V, MC

Check-in/Out 2–6/11

Smoking Balconies and porches only

Pets Dogs from Nov.–March: $20 fee

Kids Over 8

Minimum Stay 2 nights April–Oct.

Open Valentine's Day–New Year's Day

Hosts Karyn and Stephen Caliri

24 South Water St.

Edgartown, MA 02539

(508) 627-4784

victorianinn@vineyard.net

www.thevic.com

OUTERMOST INN, *Gay Head*

OVERALL ★★★★½ | ROOM QUALITY ★★★★ | VALUE ★½ | PRICE $210–340

Streaking sunsets over multicolored cliffs, a private beach, a flashing beacon, catamaran sails, and dunes filled with birds, rabbits and deer are among the natural delights just outside your door. The land by the lighthouse at the tip of the island was in Jeanne's family, and no other house can be built here. Surrounded by water and bluffs of bayberry and scrub oaks, this unique, understated house is understandably hard to book. Only drawback is the distance from restaurants, as dinner here isn't nightly. Hugh is

brother to James and Livingston Taylor (you'll spot the resemblance imme-
diately), and he's musical too.

SETTING & FACILITIES

Location Western tip of Martha's Vineyard, on Gay Head Cliffs
Near Beaches; 18 mi. from down-island
towns
Building Built 1971; gabled, wraparound
porch; recently renovated
Grounds 6 acres: lawn, lounge chairs,
hammocks; 20-plus acres: open land,
wildlife; priv. beach; views of ocean, dunes,
islands
Public Space DR, 2 LRs, large porch,
dining area, self-serve bar
Food & Drink Early-bird coffee and
tea; full breakfast; specialties: Belgian
waffles, omelets, French toast; afternoon
drinks on porch; prix fixe dinner option
spring–fall (reservations needed); specialties: smoked bass chowder, grilled
swordfish, stuffed free-range chicken
breast; special diets accom.
Recreation Sportfishing, windsurfing,
sailing on hosts' catamaran, bike rental
nearby, horseback riding
Amenities & Services Daily papers,
BYOB orders and delivery

ACCOMMODATIONS

Units 7 guest rooms
All Rooms Bath, phone, TV, water views
Some Rooms Suite: LR, sep. BR; extra
bed/sofa bed, hot tub (1)
Bed & Bath Queens, 1 king; most
shower/tub
Favorites Oak Room—king, best space,
large sun-porch; Lighthouse Suite—own
entry, deck; Beech Room—hot tub
Comfort & Decor Wood flooring. No
curtains at picture windows. No frills,
lace, or clutter. Light, white, airy, casually
elegant. Wildflowers.

RATES, RESERVATIONS, & RESTRICTIONS

Deposit Full payment 1–3 nights by
credit card; 50% other; refund w/ 15-day
notice
Credit Cards V, AE, MC, D
Check-in/Out 2/11
Smoking In some areas, not in rooms
Pets No; local kennels
Kids Over 12
Minimum Stay Usually 2 nights
Open May–Oct.
Hosts Jeanne and Hugh Taylor
RR1, Box 171, Lighthouse Rd.
Gay Head, MA 02535
(508) 645-3511
Fax: (508) 645-3514
inquiries@outermostinn.com
www.outermostinn.com

CORNER HOUSE, Nantucket

OVERALL ★★★½ | ROOM QUALITY ★★★ | VALUE ★★ | PRICE $75–275

Comfortable and authentic are adjectives that come to mind about this
roomy eighteenth-century bed-and-breakfast complex. It's really a trio of

houses on the corner of a residential block, an easy walk to the cobble-stoned center of Nantucket. British-born John is an actor, appearing in local productions; Sandy has run these relaxed lodgings since 1981, and both know the best of the many nearby shops and restaurants. History buffs will especially appreciate the original details of the main house, with its keeping room, hearths, uneven planked floors and Colonial colors. A full afternoon tea with scones and sandwiches by the fireplace is a real treat, and so is breakfast on the flower-rimmed patio.

SETTING & FACILITIES

Location Across from Congregational Church on Centre St.
Near Ferries, shops, museums, theaters, beaches
Building Colonial, c. 1790
Grounds Screened porch w/wicker furniture, garden terrace
Public Space Cozy sitting rooms, patio
Food & Drink Cont'l breakfast buffet; afternoon tea w/ sandwiches, cakes, scones, fruit breads, mulled cider (seasonal)
Recreation Tennis, beach, shopping, antiquing, walking, sailing, theater
Amenities & Services Beach towels, games, concierge service w/ international staff, bike racks

ACCOMMODATIONS

Units 16 guest rooms, suites in 3 buildings
All Rooms Bath, AC, reading lamps, antiques
Some Rooms Kitchenette (1), sitting area, fireplace, TV, refrigerator, patio
Bed & Bath Queens, doubles, some canopies, some high-post; large towels; some shower only
Favorites Elderberry—1st floor, main house, canopy bed, TV, decorative fireplace; Lily—3rd floor, cozy, beams, harbor view
Comfort & Decor Romantic w/ English and American antiques. Rich colors. Rooms range widely—tiny to spacious to suites. Main house most authentic, 3rd floor most private. Swan's nest—larger, same style and decor. Two rooms on floors above innkeepers' quarters.

RATES, RESERVATIONS, & RESTRICTIONS

Deposit 50% or 3 nights; refund (less 10%) w/ 15-day notice
Discounts Off-season, midweek
Credit Cards V, AE, MC
Check-in/Out 1/10:30
Smoking Outdoor sitting rooms only
Pets No
Kids Over 6, one per family
Minimum Stay Usually 4 nights weekends, 3 nights midweek; call for shorter stays
Open Mid-April–mid-Dec.
Hosts Sandy and John Knox-Johnston
49 Centre St., Box 1828
Nantucket, MA 02554
(508) 228-1530
info@cornerhousenantucket.com
www.cornerhousenantucket.com

MARTIN HOUSE INN, Nantucket

OVERALL ★★★½ | ROOM QUALITY ★★★ | VALUE ★★ | PRICE $75–310

Debbie is especially helpful and gracious and keeps this nearly 200-year-old mariner's home a warm and cozy house even in the windiest, wettest of Nor'easter storms. The open-plan living/dining area is inviting, with fireplace, piano, TV, and windowseats. Families will appreciate accommodations that can sleep four guests—hard to find on this pretty island. The convenient location by the cobblestoned streets of the village center by the ferry landing means more noise from crowds, but more convenience.

SETTING & FACILITIES

Location Walk from ferry, 400 yards; historic district, near center
Near Beaches, shopping, center
Building Columned 1803 mariner's home; refurbished 1991
Grounds Large yard w/ seating, hammock
Public Space Large LR, opens to DR; side porch

Food & Drink Communal cont'l breakfast; specialties: cranberry muffins, granola
Recreation Swimming, boating, other water activities
Amenities & Services Piano, 2 guest refrigerators, irons, books, daily papers, flowers; bike rental nearby

ACCOMMODATIONS

Units 12 guest rooms; 1 suite
All Rooms Sherry; individual, traditional decor; large
Some Rooms Fireplace, bath, refrigerator
Bed & Bath Most queens, some doubles, twins; canopies, four-posters, extra beds; baths tiled, some shared, some full, shower only (4)

Favorites Room 21—priv. porch, canopy bed, wood-burning fireplace, sofa, refrigerator, huge but cozy
Comfort & Decor Antique period pieces. Some rooms papered, some sponge-painted. Lots of old windows, so breezy. Large, bright. Rooms in back quietest.

RATES, RESERVATIONS, & RESTRICTIONS

Deposit 1–3 nights full payment, 50% longer; refund w/ 14-day notice
Discounts Singles, off-season (Nov.–May), extra person
Credit Cards V, AE, MC
Check-in/Out 3/11

Smoking No
Pets No
Kids 9 and up
Minimum Stay 2 nights off-season weekends, 3 nights in-season, 4 nights July/August weekend

Open All year, closed 2nd week of
Jan.–1st week Feb.
Host Debbie Wasil
61 Centre St., Box 743
Nantucket, MA 02554

(508) 228-0678
Fax: (508) 325-4798
martinn@nantucket.net
nantucket.net/lodging/martinn

THE PINEAPPLE INN, Nantucket

OVERALL ★★★★½ | ROOM QUALITY ★★★★ | VALUE ★★ | PRICE $125–325

In the colonies, sharing a hard-to-acquire pineapple was the height of hospitality, so the name well fits this luxurious bed-and-breakfast acquired by the former owners of Island Quaker House Inn and Restaurant. A total, architecturally sensitive renovation—reportedly for $1 million—has transformed Captain Uriah Russell's Greek Revival house into the island's most luxurious bed-and-breakfast. No hot breakfasts are allowed at Nantucket small properties (complicated tourist-board reasoning), but Bob and Caroline manage nicely: spinach and cheese tart with pecan pesto, nectarine and blueberry clafouti (custard tart), and other delectables.

SETTING & FACILITIES

Location Steamship Authority or Hy-Line Cruises from Hyannis; ferry 3–4 blocks from B&B; heart of hist. district
Near Hist. waterfront, ferry, restaurants, galleries, theaters, museums
Building Classic Clapboard, ca. 1838, Federal Colonial, Greek Revival touches
Grounds Brick garden patio, small pineapple-topped fountain, privacy fencing
Public Space Parlor, formal DR
Food & Drink Cont'l breakfasts, communal inside, individual tables on patio, staff-served; espresso, cappuccino; specialties: pecan sticky buns, currant scones w/ nutmeg cream, fruit tarts
Recreation Golf, tennis, shopping, cultural events, Christmas Stroll events
Amenities & Services Classical music in DR, parlor; bike racks, 1 wheelchair equipped room, daytime concierge, DR/conf. room; fax, copier; recipes

ACCOMMODATIONS

Units 12 guest rooms
All Rooms Bath, good reading lights, desk, phone/voice mail/dataport, AC, alarm clock, temperature controls
Some Rooms Ornamental fireplace, seating, French doors, priv. patio (1)
Bed & Bath Hand-crafted Eldred Wheeler beds, mostly four-poster w/ fishnet canopies, queen/king sizes; white marble baths, some shower only
Favorites Captain George Pollard Room—King canopy, priv. garden patio
Comfort & Decor Most windows overlooking rear gardens. Victorian light fixtures. Oriental carpets. Quality reproductions and 19th-century antiques. TVs in highboys. Rooms named after Nantucket whaling captains. Comfort and quiet romance. Queen bed rooms, smallish; king rooms spacious.

RATES, RESERVATIONS, & RESTRICTIONS

Deposit Full payment 1–3 night stays; 50% 4+ nights; refund w/ 15-day notice, earlier notice for holidays
Discounts None
Credit Cards V, AE, MC
Check-in/Out 3/11
Smoking No
Pets No
Kids No
No-No's 3rd person in room
Minimum Stay 2–3 nights

weekends/holidays
Open last weekend in April–Dec., after Christmas Stroll
Hosts Caroline and Bob Taylor
10 Hussey St.
Nantucket, MA 02554
(508) 228-9992
Fax: (508) 325-6051
info@pineappleinn.com
www.pineappleinn.com

MARTHA'S PLACE, Vineyard Haven

OVERALL ★★★★ | ROOM QUALITY ★★★★★ | VALUE ★½ | PRICE $100–425

This romantic new bed-and-breakfast with more than a harbor breeze of history and sophistication was built by Nathaniel Mayhew, descendent of a Martha's Vineyard founder who also built Seaman's Bethel and Sail Martha's Vineyard next door, which were originally The Tisbury School, and later a Congregational Church. A white Liberty Pole nearby commemorates the three teenage girls who blew up the town's pole in 1776 so that the British couldn't use it as a mast. Richard and Martin are engaging innkeepers, yet know to respect your privacy. With antique fainting couches, crystal chandeliers, tasseled knobs, brass wall sconces and lush, detailed decor, this is, as Martha Stewart would say, "a good thing."

SETTING & FACILITIES

Location Across from Owen Park, overlooking Vineyard Haven Harbor, next door to sailing school
Near Ferry and town, beaches
Building 1840s Greek Revival
Grounds Small yard, surrounded by roses
Public Space Large entry, LR, DR, reading room, porch, patio

Food & Drink Expanded cont'l breakfast; in room or in bed on request
Recreation Tennis, biking, sailing, beach
Amenities & Services Beach towels/chairs, coolers, tennis racquets/balls, bikes, power boat to charter, daily papers, refrigerator, irons, turndown, limited disabled access

ACCOMMODATIONS

Units 6 guest rooms
All Rooms Bath, antiques
Some Rooms Chandelier, harbor view, most fireplace, AC, sep. sitting room (1)

Bed & Bath Full and queen; top-quality fixtures, tile and granite; many whirlpools, shower/tub (1), others showers only; hairdryer, robes

Favorites Empire Room—whirlpool, bath fireplace, antique brass bed w/ half tester in blue velvet, Oriental rug
Comfort & Decor Individually deco-rated in romantic style. Period antiques, custom window dressings, hardwood floors, Oriental rugs. Spacious and sunny.

RATES, RESERVATIONS, & RESTRICTIONS

Deposit Full payment 1–6 nights, 50% other; refund w/ 30-day notice
Discounts Off-season, longer stays during off-season, 3rd person (1 room only)
Credit Cards V, MC, D
Check-in/Out 1/10; call a day ahead with arrival time
Smoking Outside
Pets No
Kids OK, 1 room best
No-No's More than 2 to a room; no cots, roll-aways, or cribs

Minimum Stay 2 nights weekends, 3 nights July/Sept. weekends, 3 nights August
Open All year
Hosts Richard Alcott and Martin Hicks
114 Main St., Box 1182
Vineyard Haven, MA 02568
(508) 693-0253
Fax: (508) 693-1890
info@marthasplace.com
www.marthasplace.com

THORNCROFT INN, *Vineyard Haven*

OVERALL ★★★★ | ROOM QUALITY ★★★★ | VALUE ★½ | PRICE $180–475

Romance is emphasized at this shingled cottage on what was once the Thorncroft estate. You choose your breakfast menu the previous evening and can opt for a private breakfast in your room. Thoughtful room touches include earphones for TVs (so others don't have to listen to Leno if they have other ideas), lots of stacked wood for the fireplace, wine glasses and corkscrews, and a chocolate on the pillow. The super-organized hosts live nearby. If you're laid-back and don't need everything laid out, opt for the private cottage. And if you like soaking, book the room with a hot tub big enough for a dozen, but just for two.

SETTING & FACILITIES

Location From ferry dock take right to Main St.; 1 mi. on left in residential area, 1 block from ocean
Near Ferry dock, Main St.
Building Craftsman bungalow, 2 add'l buildings; built 1908-1918 as estate's guest house
Grounds 3.5 landscaped acres
Public Space 2 DRs, sunroom, LR

Food & Drink Full country breakfast; specialties: buttermilk pancakes w/ blueberry honey sauce, almond French toast, burritos, quiche; afternoon tea, pastries
Recreation Shopping, beaches
Amenities & Services Bike storage, daily paper delivered, wood for fires year-round; meetings (10), preparing fireplaces, evening turn-down

ACCOMMODATIONS

Units 14 guest rooms, 1 guest cottage
All Rooms Bath, AC, phone, TV/VCR, hairdryer, robes, iron/board
Some Rooms Wood-burning fireplace, furnished balcony/porch, priv. entrance, skylight, refrigerator
Bed & Bath Most canopies, high-back Victorian, four-posters; brass faucets, claw-foot tub, 2-person whirlpools, 300-gallon hot tub

Favorites The Cottage—king-size canopy, porch w/ hammock, dbl. whirlpool in mirrored alcove, fireplace; Room 1—carved Victorian headboard, woodburning fireplace, 300-gallon hot tub
Comfort & Decor Individually decorated, some 1900-style w/ antiques. Big windows, bedside lights. Carriage house in Colonial style, most spacious.

RATES, RESERVATIONS, & RESTRICTIONS

Deposit Full payment 1–3 nights, 50% for 4+ nights; deposit by credit card only; refund w/ 30-day cancellation notice
Discounts Off-season, on local car rental (call for info)
Credit Cards V, AE, DC, MC, D
Check-in/Out 3–9/11; arrange for check-in after 9 p.m.
Smoking No, extra-tough smoking policy
Pets No
Kids No

No-No's Roll-aways or cots, cash, TVs in main house without earphones
Minimum Stay 3 nights in-season
Open All year
Hosts Lynn and Karl Buder
460 Main St., Box 1022
Vineyard Haven, MA 02568
(508) 693-3333 or (800) 332-1236
Fax: (508) 693-5419
innkeeper@thorncroft.com
www.thorncroft.com

Rhode Island

It may be tiny, but a state whose flag's motto is "Hope," and which was founded by Roger Williams in 1636 on the principles of religious and political freedom, is indeed impressive. Rhode Island was the first colony to declare independence from British rule; the first to denounce its own profits and prohibit the importation of slaves; and the last to sign the Constitution—on May 4, 1776—holding out until the Bill of Rights was incorporated.

Merely 37 miles wide by 48 miles long (you could cover it in less than an hour), Rhode Island still packs a punch, with art museums, **Brown University** in booming **Providence,** historic sites, and performing arts centers. And this Ocean State has 100 miles of sandy beaches and 400 miles of ocean coastline.

The gem is **Newport,** a prominent New World shipping port that thrived on farming and sea trade. In the Gilded Age of the late nineteenth century, it provided the ultimate lifestyle for the rich and famous. It retains elaborate mansion "cottages," **Ocean Cliff Walk,** music festivals, shopping, fine dining, beaches—and some of the most authentic and luxurious bed-and-breakfasts in America.

In addition to **Providence** and **Newport,** down-to-earth **Pawtucket** is credited as the "Birthplace of American Industry," **Bristol** is known for shipbuilding, **Blackstone** offers river activities, **Block Island** is a fresh breath of the past, and **Watch Hill** has one of the oldest carousels in America.

Squeezed into the southeastern corner of New England, Rhode Island is 60 miles from Boston and 180 miles from New York City, so weekenders abound. Veer across Massachusetts or Connecticut and dip into its choice pleasures at wildly luxurious or basic small inns and bed-and-breakfasts— some among the best bargains in New England. Look for Victorian retreats on **Block Island,** reconverted mansions in **Newport,** the academic and quirky little houses in **Providence,** and industrialists' former homes in seaside town and river valley bed-and-breakfasts.

FOR MORE INFORMATION

Anna's Victorian Connection
(401) 849-2469 or (800) 884-4288
email: annas@wsii.com

RI State Tourism Bureau
(888) 746-6835 or (800) 556-2484
email: visitrhodeisland@riedc.com

Rhode Island Tourism
www.visitrhodeisland.com
(links to area weather, tourism)

Newport and Little Compton, Rhode Island

A foremost shipping port in the 1700s, **Newport** became a synonym for luxury and ostentatious living as a summer resort in the late 1800s, catering to Vanderbilts, Carnegies, and hundreds of their nearest and dearest. Later, Jacqueline and John F. Kennedy were married in **St. Mary's Church** here in town, hosting a wedding reception at Jackie's home, **Hammersmith Farm,** the "summer White House" from 1961–1963.

Today the "City-by-the-Sea" is less elitist but still cultivates and glories in its image. Numerous grand cottages are open for tours. Some favorites: **The Breakers** residence, stables, and carriage house, a 70-room, ocean view, Italianate complex featuring Vanderbilt memorabilia and furnishings; **Belcourt Castle,** Louis XIII–style down to its full-size gold coronation coach; the **Astors' Beechwood,** with costumed actors; and **Chateau-Sur-Mer,** lavishly, dreamily Victorian.

Newport's historic trappings back up the mansions. **Touro Synagogue,** the oldest temple in America, was built in 1763; **Pelham Street** was the first in the country to install gas-illuminated streetlights. **The White Horse Tavern,** ca. 1673, the oldest tavern building in the country, still dispenses suds.

You can sail or cruise, visit the **International Tennis Hall of Fame** or the yachting or doll museums, enjoy jai alai, a day spa, or even an aquarium. Summer theater is popular, and Newport hosts fairs, shows, and tournaments including music festivals in July and August, a boat show in September, and a 10-day **Winter Festival** in dreary February. A brisk walk along Newport's three-and-a-half mile **Ocean Cliff Walk** may put this bounty in perspective.

Easton's Beach is the beach, and **Fort Adams State Park** is the nature retreat among all this activity. The information center in the historical district operates as a transportation/activity/information hub. At Christmas, the town sponsors prizes for best seasonal decorations, right down to the symbolic luminaria candle lights.

Not surprisingly, the mansion bed-and-breakfasts in town maintain high standards and cut-above service. Many properties offer the option of packages that include dinner at a local restaurant and mansion-tour tickets.

The nearby, isolated island of **Little Compton** is far from the bustling crowds; it is rural and small townish with farms and vineyards and some simple bed-and-breakfasts. It couldn't be more of a contrast with Newport.

FOR MORE INFORMATION

Bed & Breakfast Newport
(800) 800-8765
Newport County Commerce & Visitors Bureau
(800) 976-5122
Fax: (401) 849-0291
www.gonewport.com

Newport Inns Association
(401) 847-1355
email: nibbs@newport1.com

THE ROOST, Little Compton

OVERALL ★★★★★ | ROOM QUALITY ★★★ | VALUE ★★★★ | PRICE $100

A really kid-friendly site, this informal bed-and-breakfast allows guests, young and old, to play with the wooly llamas and even take the them for walks. Here you are far from the crowds with water views, easy access to nature, and peace and quiet. The original owners raised six children in New Hampshire and then traveled north, cleared this land, and built a comfortable, free-flowing house for themselves, family, and guests. The hosts enjoy chatting about farming, canoeing, music, birding, gardening and, of course, their llamas.

SETTING & FACILITIES

Location Rt.77 S, through traffic light at Tiverton Four Corners; Sakonnet Vineyards is on left, 3 mi. after the light
Near Ocean; 30 min. to Newport, Providence; 1 hour to Boston
Building: Orig. rustic farmhouse, natural shingles, porches
Grounds Over 50 acres of vineyards, founded in 1975
Public Space Cozy common room, small dining area

Food & Drink Communal cont'l breakfast; specialties: scones, muffins
Recreation Antiquing, beach activities, tours, comp. winery tours/tastings
Amenities & Services Phone avail.; monthly fall–spring Sakonnet Chefs program, cooking classes, dinner, appropriate wines served; Sakonnet House facil. avail. for business meetings, priv. dinners, weddings; rooms freshened daily

ACCOMMODATIONS

Units 3 guest rooms
All Rooms Bath, seating, reading light
Some Rooms Skylight
Bed & Bath 1 queen canopy bed, 1 double, 2 twins, trundle; 2 full, 1 shower bath
Favorites Blue Room—queen canopy,

largest room, pickled floor, shutters, tiled shower
Comfort & Decor Guest rooms on 2nd floor. Recently renovated and decorated. Gray room quietest, back of house. Two twins can be fitted together. Cozy, small rooms.

RATES, RESERVATIONS, & RESTRICTIONS

Deposit 1 night or 50% if longer; refund w/ 14-day notice; otherwise, credit
Discounts Events packages
Credit Cards V, AE, MC
Check-in/Out 4/11
Smoking No

Pets No
Kids Over 12
Minimum Stay 2 nights weekends, Memorial Day–Columbus Day; 3 nights holiday weekends

Open All year
Hosts Susan and Earl Samson
162 West Main Rd.
Little Compton, RI 02837

(800) 91-WINES or (401) 635-8486
Fax: (401) 635-2101
sakonnetri.@aol.com
www.sakonnetwine.com

1855 MARSHALL SLOCUM GUEST HOUSE, Newport

OVERALL ★★★½ | ROOM QUALITY ★★★★ | VALUE ★★½ | PRICE $99–199

Delightful Joan states that she has a large family of guests who make this pretty bed-and-breakfast their home away from home. "I love what I do, it truly is a wonderful life." And it's a family affair. Daughter Julie lends a hand with summer lobster dinners on the deck on Wednesdays, a real New England treat. Few owners have tampered with this nineteenth-century, gingerbread-trimmed structure, so there has been little modernization and loads of enhanced charm and comforts remain for you to enjoy, along with the lobster and the handcrafted antique beds.

SETTING & FACILITIES

Location Kay-Catherine area of Newport; Victorian residential neighborhood
Near Easton's Beach, ocean, historic mansions, Tennis Hall of Fame, Bowen's Wharf, cobblestone Marine District, Brick Market Place, Cliff Walk, state park, museums, aquarium, summer theater, White Horse Tavern
Building 1855 Victorian
Grounds Spacious rear yard, back deck, barbecue
Public Space Traditional LR, lived-in parlor, DR
Food & Drink Yankee-style 3-course breakfast, communal, separate or in room; specialty: crêpes w/ asparagus and ham in cheddar sauce; refreshments, hors d'oeuvres: homemade Boursin with Chardonnay; lobster dinner Wed. nights, comp. w/ 3-night midweek stay, summer only; beach picnics avail.; gourmet menu for priv. functions
Recreation Shopping; harbor cruises, golf; summer classical music festival, jazz festival, and folk festival
Amenities & Services Beach towels, irons, daily paper; fax, computer services; maps, recipes; catering, weddings, functions, groups

ACCOMMODATIONS

Units 6 guest rooms
All Rooms Bath, reading lights, clock/radio, AC
Some Rooms Ceiling fan, skylight, 3rd person, quilts, fireplace
Bed & Bath Antique, handcarved, brass beds, queen and twin sizes; some showers only, 1 claw-foot tub, robes
Favorites Brass Room—brass queen, hunter green walls, white wicker, mirrored French doors
Comfort & Decor Cozy and inviting. Under-the-eaves warmth, skylights. Comforting fabrics, wallpapers, rugs. Antique furnishings and period touches.

RATES, RESERVATIONS, & RESTRICTIONS

Deposit Credit card; one night charged if cancellation with less than 14 days notice
Discounts 3rd person
Credit Cards V, AE, MC
Check-in/Out 2/noon
Smoking No
Pets No
Kids Over 12
Minimum Stay 2 nights weekends, 3

nights holidays
Open All year
Host Joan Wilson
29 Kay St.
Newport, RI 02840
(800) 372-5120 or (401) 841-5120
Fax: (401) 846-3787
info@marshallslocuminn.com
www.marshallslocuminn.com

CLARKSTON, *Newport*

OVERALL ★★★★ | ROOM QUALITY ★★★★ | VALUE ★★½ | PRICE $95–245

On one of Newport's first streets, this is one of the oldest inns anywhere in the states; the current dining room was the entire original one-story, one-room structure. History is much appreciated and venerated by Tamara and Rick, who named and decorated guest rooms after famous or infamous locals. This bed-and-breakfast wins the Newport town prize for holiday decorations every year, a reflection of their efforts throughout. The enthusiastic hosts love their antique home—renovated in the 1990s and decorated to provide updated comfort while retaining authentic Colonial charm

SETTING & FACILITIES

Location On America's Cup Ave. in Newport, turn left at the Marriott onto Marlboro St., right onto Thames, left onto Touro St., second right to Clarke St.; B&B is on left
Near Tennis Hall of Fame, Yachting Museum; Bowen's Wharf, cobblestone Marine District, Brick Market Place, state park, museums, aquarium, summer theater, Hammersmith Farm, ocean, Cliff Walk, mansions; walk to harbor, restaurants
Building 1705 Village Colonial; addition in late 1800s; renovated under auspices

of Parks Commission in 1993
Grounds Minimal; parking lot
Public Space Entry parlor, DR
Food & Drink Full breakfast; comp. tea/coffee/soft drinks
Recreation Tennis, golf, boating, harbor cruises, beach activities; Music Festival (July), Jazz and Folk Festivals (Aug.), Int'l Boat Show (Sept.) Christmas in Newport (Dec.), and Winter Festival (Feb.)
Amenities & Services Refrigerator w/ refreshments, irons, phone, daily paper, maps, fax, dataport

ACCOMMODATIONS

Units 9 guest rooms

All Rooms Bath, fireplace or whirlpool, AC

Some Rooms Orig. wide-plank or hardwood floors, Oriental rugs; sound/media system (1), sitting area (2), 3rd person (1)

Bed & Bath Some four-poster, sleigh, canopy beds, queen or king, all featherbeds; luxury baths, marble, some dbl. sinks, tiled oversized showers, some 2-person whirlpools

Favorites Joseph Burrill—fireplace, king four-poster, blue/white decor, corner w/ 4 windows, dbl. shower; Harry Belmont Room—dbl. whirlpool, king sleigh bed, hunter green walls, dbl. marble vanity

Comfort & Decor 3rd-floor rooms smaller but lots of Colonial character, antique wide-plank floors. Mrs. Oelrich Room, casual white-and-green–striped fabrics, wicker, summery decor, w/ all amenities: fireplace, 1-person whirlpool, sitting area

RATES, RESERVATIONS, & RESTRICTIONS

Deposit 100%

Discounts Midweek, AAA, corp./groups, longer stays

Credit Cards V, AE, MC

Check-in/Out 3/11

Smoking No

Pets No

Kids Welcome in certain rooms only

Minimum Stay 2 nights weekends, 3 nights holidays/festivals

Open All year

Hosts Tamara and Rick Farrick

28 Clarke St.

Newport, RI 02840

(800) 524-1386 or (401) 849-7397

Fax: (401) 847-7630

clarkeston@travelbase.com

www.innsofnewport.com

CLIFFSIDE INN, Newport

OVERALL ★★★★★ | ROOM QUALITY ★★★★★ | VALUE ★½ | PRICE $245–500

Originally built for Maryland Governor Thomas Swann, Cliffside was purchased by American painter and eccentric recluse, Beatrice Turner, who dressed exclusively in Victorian garb, painted her house black and even painted her embalmed father. She created 3,000 paintings—over 1,000 self-portraits. Short-sighted executors burned most of her works in 1948, and in 1980 passersby rescued the rest from piles tossed on a rainy sidewalk. In 1996, savvy businessman Winthrop Baker—original producer of the *Oprah Winfrey Show*—spent over $1 million to restore Cliffside. Today, he offers a reward for Turner paintings, and continues to enhance this lush, evocative, dramatic property.

SETTING & FACILITIES

Location Quiet residential neighborhood, 1 mi. from downtown Newport, on Seaview Ave.

Near 1 block to ocean Cliff Walk, 5 min. walk to ocean beach, walk to Gilded Age mansions, Tennis Hall of Fame, shopping and restaurants, cobblestone Marine District, Brick Market Place, state park, museums, aquarium, summer theater

Building 1880 Second-Empire Victorian summer mansion; Cliffside Cottage, purchased and renovated in 1996

Grounds Garden, veranda; Seaview Cottage: semi-priv. patio, seating; 1 acre total

Public Space Front hall, spacious parlor; breakfast alcove

Food & Drink Gourmet breakfast communal or separate; specialties: red pepper cornbread, farmhouse eggs Benedict w/ rosemary Hollandaise, chocolate tart; wake-up coffee/tea delivered to rooms; Victorian afternoon tea; after-dinner treats

Recreation Tennis, harbor cruises, golf, biking, summer music festivals

Amenities & Services Hot tub, laundry, refrigerator, irons, bicycle storage, turndown, maps, daily paper, videos, fax, beach towels; small meetings

ACCOMMODATIONS

Units Main building: 6 guest rooms, 10 suites; Cliffside Cottage: 3 suites

All Rooms Bath, antiques, TV/VCR, phone, heat/AC controls, alarm/radio, fireplace, whirlpool

Some Rooms Ceiling fan, hardwood floors, dramatic architectural features, skylight, window seat, dataport, priv. entrance, priv. or semi-priv. outdoor space, ocean view (1)

Bed & Bath Antique or handcrafted beds, queen or king; robes, hairdryers, some dbl. whirlpools, separate showers, some fireplaces, some showers only, some hand-held showers, 1 steam bath, 1 antique Victorian birdcage shower, 1 heated bath floor, fresh flowers

Favorites Seaview Cottage Cliff Suite— study, LR, BR, obscured water views, king plantation bed, 3 fireplaces, stereo/media systems, bath skylight, large whirlpool, dataport, pine-paneled cathedral ceilings

Comfort & Decor Oak and mahogany trim, antiques, stenciled walls, Laura Ashley florals. Victorian Tower Suite: 18-foot paneled cupola ceiling. Garden Suite: 2 levels. Beatrice's room: floral murals, preserved over 90 years.

RATES, RESERVATIONS, & RESTRICTIONS

Deposit 50%; nonrefundable, 1 year credit for future stay w/ 15-day notice

Discounts Packages Nov.–April, check; extra $25 charge high-season weekends, holidays/festivals

Credit Cards V, AE, MC, D

Check-in/Out 3–9/11; till noon by arrangement

Smoking No

Pets No

Kids Over 13

Minimum Stay 2 nights over Sat., 3 nights holidays/festivals

Open All year

Hosts Stephan Nicolas, innkeeper; Winthrop P. Baker, owner
2 Seaview Ave.
Newport, RI 02840
(800) 845-1811 or (401) 847-1811
Fax: (401) 848-5850
cliff@wsii.com
www.cliffside.com

ELM TREE COTTAGE, Newport

OVERALL ★★★★★ | ROOM QUALITY ★★★★★ | VALUE ★½ | PRICE $195–450

Perfect hosts Priscilla and Tom, both trained artists and artisans, established a bed-and-breakfast evocative of the "casual ritziness" of Newport's gilded age—a time when local mansions were honestly called summer cottages. Tom's stained glass and Priscilla's watercolors are showcased, and they work in the basement producing magnificent windows, many for guests. The hosts continue to add glamour and glitz to rooms once owned by a railroad heiress. Cheeky touches includes a pub interior with portholes, and a bar inlaid with silver dollars. Luxury, romance, warmth, unexpected pleasures, and lavish comfort describe this wonderful bed-and-breakfast experience.

SETTING & FACILITIES

Location In estate neighborhood; Rt. 138 to Newport Bridge, take Scenic Newport Exit, turn right onto Farewall St., right onto America's Cup Ave., the road becomes Memorial Blvd., left onto Gibbs Ave., B&B is 3rd house on right after stop sign
Near Overlooks Easton Pond and First Beach; Cliff Walk, Easton's Beach, mansions, Tennis Hall of Fame, Bowen's Wharf, cobblestone Marine District, Brick Market Place, state park, museums, aquarium, summer theater
Building 1882 Shingle-style summer mansion, 8,000 square feet

Grounds 1 acre, landscaped lawns
Public Space Sunroom; spacious LR, pub room, DR
Food & Drink Cold buffet, hot entrée breakfast; specialties: French toast soufflé w/ whipped maple cream, Chateau potatoes topped w/ poached egg and parmesan cheese sauce, Quiche Lorraine in crêpe cups w/ broiled tomato; coffee always avail.; BYOB bar
Recreation Tennis, golf, boating, harbor cruises, biking, summer music festivals
Amenities & Services Grand piano, books, games, turn-down, gift cert.

ACCOMMODATIONS

Units 6 guest rooms
All Rooms Bath; French, English, and Newport estate antiques
Some Rooms Fireplace, sitting area, AC, TV
Bed & Bath Carved queen or Louis XV king beds, crown or half canopies; luxury appointments in baths, some showers only
Favorites The Windsor—nearly 1,000 square feet; winter water views, crown

canopy king bed, 2 sitting areas, fireplace, stained glass, Victorian decor; sink w/ crystal legs, two-person whirlpool, TV, refrig.
Comfort & Decor Creatively coordinated fabrics/wallcoverings. Elaborately elegant pieces toned down by casual/country appointments. Original carved mantels. Dramatic, romantic beds. Playful props carry room themes. Abundance and comfort.

RATES, RESERVATIONS, & RESTRICTIONS

Deposit 1 night or 50% with longer stay, by check or money order; refund (less 10% of reservation) w/ 30-day notice; multiple room reservations nonrefundable

Discounts Off-season

Credit Cards AE, V, MC

Check-in/Out 2/11; will hold luggage for early arrival

Smoking No

Pets No

Kids Over 14

Minimum Stay 2 nights weekends; 3 nights weekends June–Oct./holidays/ festivals

Open Feb. and March weekends only; April–early Dec.

Hosts Priscilla and Tom Malone
336 Gibbs Ave.
Newport, RI 02840
(888) ELM TREE or (401) 849-1610
Fax: (401) 849-2084
elmtree@home.com
www.elm–tree.com

FRANCIS MALBONE HOUSE, Newport

OVERALL ★★★★½ | ROOM QUALITY ★★★★★ | VALUE ★½ | PRICE $155–425

This house is attributed to America's first famed architect, Peter Harrison, who also designed Newport's Truro Synagogue. Legend is that Colonel Malbone, a wealthy shipping merchant, built an underground tunnel to the nearby waterfront to smuggle rum and avoid taxes. The house was later seized by the British Army to store gold, and in the 1800s was returned to the colonel's son, a U.S. senator. Today this historic bed-and-breakfast, now near shops and trendy restaurants, is little changed from when its forebears dined by the open hearth or slept in the high-ceilinged bedrooms (except maybe for the whirlpools and skylights—and the raspberry cream-cheese French toast).

SETTING & FACILITIES

Location Downtown harborfront, Rt. 138 E into Newport; Scenic Newport Exit to downtown, to Thames St.

Near Ocean, Tennis Hall of Fame, museums, Bowen's Wharf, cobblestone Marine District, Brick Market Place, Cliff Walk, state park, aquarium, summer theater, White Horse Tavern

Building 1760 Colonial mansion; Mediterranean-style rear building exterior; 1996 addition

Grounds Flagstone patio, gardens, fountain; French doors to 2nd secluded courtyard.

Public Space Formal entrance foyer, 3 guest parlors, library, shaded courtyard

Food & Drink Gourmet breakfast, early riser coffee/tea, afternoon treats; specialties: Dutch pancakes, Greek fritattas, eggs Florentine, stuffed French toast

Recreation Tennis, golf, harbor cruises, biking; summer music festivals, incl. Jazz Festival

Amenities & Services Concierge service, nightly turndown, postcards/ postage, corp. meeting space

ACCOMMODATIONS

Units 16 guest rooms, 4 suites
All Rooms Bath, antiques, hardwood
floors, phone, AC, TV, CD player, robes,
irons w/ boards
Some Rooms Sitting area, desk/table,
Jacuzzi, VCR, French doors to semi-priv.
courtyard, 3rd-person bed, wet bar (1),
mini-refrigerator (1), priv. entrance (1)
Bed & Bath Queen Anne four-poster
king and queen beds; plush towels, 9 double Jacuzzis
Favorites Courtyard Suite—fireplace,

spacious sitting area, wet bar, French
doors to courtyard, king four-poster,
whirlpool, TV; Counting House Suite—all
amenities plus dbl. whirlpool, refrigerator, priv. entrance; rooms in addition are
desirable for courtyard access
Comfort & Decor Guest rooms in traditional Colonial style. High ceilings, spacious, hardwood floors, Oriental rugs,
traditional mahogany furnishings. Window
seats, period art prints, federal colors.

RATES, RESERVATIONS, & RESTRICTIONS

Deposit 1 night or 50% with longer stay;
refunds (less 10%) w/ 14-day notice
Discounts Midweek corp. retreats,
meeting planners, travel agents
Credit Cards V, AE, MC
Check-in/Out 2/11; will hold luggage
Smoking Courtyard only
Pets No
Kids Over 12
Minimum Stay 3 nights weekends,
July–Oct.; 2 nights weekends, Nov.–June;

check for holidays
Open All year
Hosts Will Dewey, Mark and Jasminka
Eads
392 Thames St.
Newport, RI 02840
(800) 846-0392 or (401) 846-0392
Fax: (401) 848-5956
innkeeper@malbone.com
www.malbone.com

HYDRANGEA HOUSE INN, Newport

OVERALL ★★★★ | ROOM QUALITY ★★★★ | VALUE ★★ | PRICE $145–280

This blooming beauty on top of Newport's historic hill is aptly named after the flowering plant beyond the veranda. (According to legend, mansion gardeners took cuttings from summer Gilded Age gardens, thereby spreading the luxury.) The owners are former antiques dealers, and the on-site art gallery showcases an extensive fine-art collection from all over the world. Breakfasting here amid the paintings is a real treat, and the magnificent suite is darkly, lushly romantic.

SETTING & FACILITIES

Location Center of Newport's historic walking district
Near Ocean, Tennis Hall of Fame, Yachting Museum; shopping and restaurants, cobblestone marine district; Brick Market Place, state park, museums, aquarium, summer theater, White Horse Tavern
Building 1876 Victorian cottage-style; art gallery storefront; renovated, 1994
Grounds Roof sun deck, verandah perennial gardens, hydrangeas, onsite parking
Public Space Formal DR; faux marble entrance, drawing room
Food & Drink Full buffet breakfast; specialties: raspberry pancakes, seasoned eggs, home-baked breads and granola; English tea
Recreation Tennis, harbor cruises, 3.2 mi. Cliff Walk, musical festivals
Amenities & Services Refrigerator access, beach towels, maps, fax

ACCOMMODATIONS

Units 8 guest rooms, including 5 suites
All Rooms Bath, antiques, orig. artwork, AC, crystal glasses, plush carpet, fresh flowers
Some Rooms Suites: Jacuzzi, fireplace, TV/VCR
Bed & Bath Some four-posters, sizes vary; some showers only; Jacuzzis
Favorites The Hydrangea Suite—fireplace, elegant king bed, sitting area, dbl. whirlpool in room, steam bath in marble bath, TV/VCR, phone, turn-down service
Comfort & Decor Fresh flowers, plush carpet, and Oriental rugs, ambiance lighting, Federal colors, gleaming woodwork, rich fabrics. Formal romance—possibly too dramatic for some. Street-front rooms can be noisy. Suite is super-deluxe.

RATES, RESERVATIONS, & RESTRICTIONS

Deposit Greater of 1 night or 50%; refund (less fee) w/ 14-day notice
Discounts Midweek 2nd night free Nov.–April (exclusions); internet specials updated daily
Credit Cards V, AE, MC, D
Check-in/Out 2–8/11
Smoking No
Pets No
Kids No
No-No's 3rd person in room
Minimum Stay 2 nights high-season weekends, 3 nights all holidays and all event weekends; but check for 1 night availability
Open All year
Hosts Dennis Blair and Grant Edmondson
16 Bellevue Ave.
Newport, RI 02840
(800) 945-4667 or (401) 846-4435
Fax: (401) 846-6602
hydrangeahouse@home.com
www.hydrangeahouse.com

IVY LODGE, Newport

OVERALL ★★★★½ | ROOM QUALITY ★★★★★ | VALUE ★★½ | PRICE $125–225

Considered one of Newport's most exciting bed-and-breakfasts, the property's original, remarkable paneled entry hall soars with a triple staircase and balconies with enough spindle balusters for every day of the year. The rest, designed by famed Stanford White, is decidedly anticlimactic, but still lovely. The dining room has a 20-foot table seating 16, and an antique sideboard is laden at breakfast with goodies such as popovers with peaches and Romanoff sauce. Maggie was a social worker, and her caring ways can be seen throughout. All the guest rooms are charming, but the turret room is, well, tops.

SETTING & FACILITIES

Location Rt. 138 across Newport Bridge, Memorial to Bellevue to Narragansett, turn left at 1st light and left again onto Clay St., B&B is 1st large house on right, near the cottages
Near Ocean Cliff Walk, Easton's Beach, Gilded Age mansions, Tennis Hall of Fame, Bowen's Wharf, cobblestone Marine District, Brick Market Place, state park, museums, aquarium, summer theater
Building Large 1886 Shingle Victorian designed by Stanford White
Grounds 1 acre: privacy hedge, lawn games, English-style specimen gardens

Public Space 3-story entry hall; airy LR, floor-to-ceiling windows/arched doors to veranda; small sitting room; DR
Food & Drink Communal buffet breakfast; specialties: smoked fish, bananas flambé, bread pudding; afternoon refreshments
Recreation Tennis, boating, harbor cruises, biking, golf, summer music festivals
Amenities & Services Baby grand piano, irons, beach towels, maps, recipes, small/medium meetings, small weddings

ACCOMMODATIONS

Units 8 guest rooms
All Rooms Bath, fresh flowers, carpet, AC
Some Rooms Fireplace, whirlpool, balcony
Bed & Bath Antique, four-poster beds, sizes vary; some showers only
Favorites The Library—mahogany sleigh

bed, fireplace, whirlpool; The Turret—great view, connecting room
Comfort & Decor Striking Victorian feel, Laura Ashley fabrics/papers. Pretty decorative touches such as wicker birdcage, open parasol, bedside topiary. Configurations good for family or friends.

RATES, RESERVATIONS, & RESTRICTIONS

Deposit 50%
Discounts Singles, longer stays
Credit Cards V, AE, MC, D
Check-in/Out 2/11, later by

arrangement
Smoking On veranda only
Pets No
Kids Welcome

Minimum Stay 2 nights weekends
Open All year, except Thanksgiving Eve,
Christmas Eve, and Christmas Day
Hosts Maggie and Terry Moy

12 Clay St.
Newport, RI 02840
(800) 834-6865 or (401) 849-6865

JAILHOUSE INN, *Newport*

OVERALL ★★★ | ROOM QUALITY ★★★ | VALUE ★½ | PRICE $45–385

For those who relish the idea of a night in the pokey, this former jail will have to do. (An unnamed source mentioned handcuffs found in guest rooms over the years, presumably voluntary.) A reception area behind bars, cell doors leading to the breakfast room, and hallways created from the original cell blocks are a few of the fun touches, but a bit more decorative imagination would be a bonus. Kids might especially enjoy the idea of spending "time," here, near the wharf and shops, and it beats being incarcerated.

SETTING & FACILITIES

Location Historic downtown Newport
Near 1 block to Visitor's Center, shops and wharf, ocean, museums, aquarium, summer theater, historic White Horse Tavern
Building 1772 white brick, columns, Colonial facade; restored jailhouse
Grounds Front porch
Public Space Reception area behind bars; orig. cell doors lead to breakfast room; cell blocks are now inn's hallways; breakfast room and airy lobby
Food & Drink Cont'l breakfast; tea; MAP avail. (area restaurants)
Recreation Tennis, boating, harbor cruises; music festivals, eating
Amenities & Services Irons; hairdryers, sewing kits, masseuse avail.

ACCOMMODATIONS

Units 23 guest rooms, 5 suites
All Rooms Bath, TV, compact refrigerator, phone, AC
Some Rooms Sitting area or 2nd BR, skylight, wheelchair access (1)
Bed & Bath Queen or king beds; full baths
Favorites 3rd floor walk-ups—sitting area, skylight; L-shaped corner room—partly obstructed harbor view
Comfort & Decor Contemporary ambiance, austere, small rooms. Not romantic. Comfortable bedding, striped bedsheets, prints of Elvis in Jailhouse Rock on walls.

RATES, RESERVATIONS, & RESTRICTIONS

Deposit 1 night; refund w/ 5-day notice
Discounts Off-season corp., military and longer stay; children free; MAP packages incl. 2 tickets to Newport Mansions Tour
Credit Cards V, AE, MC
Check-in/Out 3/11
Smoking Front porch only
Pets No

Kids Welcome
Minimum Stay 2 nights weekends; 3 nights holidays and festivals
Open All year
Host Bob Briskin

13 Marlborough
Newport, RI 02840
(800) 427-9444 or 201-847-4638
Fax: (401) 849-0605

OLD BEACH INN, Newport

OVERALL ★★★★ | ROOM QUALITY ★★★★ | VALUE ★★ | PRICE $95–295

Originally a commodore's home, named The Anchorage, the 1879 property indeed has an anchor carved in the wood at the top of the house. The guest room names are more evocative, such as Ivy, with its dark green accents and cozy, masculine feel, and Forget-me-not, in blues and yellow, with a fireplace. But today, the name Old Beach Inn, after the road it's on, most reflects the interests of Newport's bed-and-breakfast guests: water pleasures, tradition, cottage architecture, and good times.

SETTING & FACILITIES

Location Newport's Top of the Hill area of Historic Hill
Near Tennis Hall of Fame, Yachting Museum; Bowen's Wharf, cobblestone Marine District; Brick Market Place, state park, museums, aquarium, summer theater, Hammersmith Farm; walk to ocean beach, Cliff Walk, Gilded Age mansions, restaurants
Building 1879 Gothic Victorian, renovated in 1991
Grounds Village yard: flower gardens, Japanese fish pond, gazebo, brick patio
Public Space Entrance foyer, parlors, breakfast room
Food & Drink Cont'l buffet breakfast, full breakfast on Sun.; guest pantry
Recreation Harbor cruises, music festivals, Int'l Boat Show (Sept.) Christmas in Newport (Dec.), and Winter Festival (Feb.)
Amenities & Services Refrigerator, irons, maps, beach towels, daily paper, small meetings, Dec. decorations

ACCOMMODATIONS

Units 5 main house guest rooms, 2 carriage house rooms
All Rooms Bath, carpet, AC
Some Rooms Fireplace, TV, skylight, antique English wood stove (1)
Bed & Bath Some handpainted antique beds, full and queen sizes; some showers only
Favorites Romantic Rose Room—most spacious, creative queen canopy bed, fireplace, oak armoire, wicker
Comfort & Decor Main house guest rooms: high ceilings, original moldings, nooks and alcoves. Carriage house rooms more private, separate entrances. Whimsy in creative use of laces, wreaths, flowers, artwork, stenciling, collectibles, coordinated fabrics.

RATES, RESERVATIONS, & RESTRICTIONS

Deposit 1st 3 nights or 50%; refund w/ 15-day notice (30 for multi-room bookings); cancellations w/ less notice receive future-stay credit if room is re-rented
Discounts Longer stays, midweek off-season
Credit Cards V, AE, MC, D
Check-in/Out 2–8/11
Smoking Outside only
Pets No
Kids Over 12

Minimum Stay 3 nights holiday/festival weekends
Open All year
Hosts Cynthia and Luke Murray
19 Old Beach Rd.
Newport, RI 02840
(888) 303-5033 or (401) 849-3479
Fax: (401) 847-1236
info@oldbeachinn.com
www.oldbeachinn.com

BALDWIN PLACE INN, Newport

OVERALL ★★★★½ | ROOM QUALITY ★★★★ | VALUE ★★ | PRICE $135–300

Formerly Savanas' Inn, this bed-and-breakfast arrived in 1998, after perfectionists Ande and Phil had delayed the opening for two years to complete the restoration to their satisfaction. The Savanas are only the third owners of this historic property, filled with parquet and hardwood floors, bold Oriental rugs, Victorian mantels and woodwork, period wallpapers, and gilded finishes. Family photos and other warm touches remind guests that this elegant bed-and-breakfast is also a home, and guests are encouraged to chat in the kitchen. Still evolving in a city filled with other wonderful properties, this diminutive one rises up to the formidable challenge.

SETTING & FACILITIES

Location Historic Hill District; on Pelham St.
Near Bowen's Wharf, Antique Row, Cliff Walk, Easton's Beach, Gilded Age mansions, Tennis Hall of Fame, cobblestone Marine District, Brick Market Place, state park, museums, aquarium, summer theater
Building 1865 Second-Empire Victorian
Grounds English gardens, fountains, walking paths, sitting areas, pergola, secluded stone-encased hot tub
Public Space Foyer, parlor, "Men's club"

library, DR
Food & Drink Gourmet breakfast, communal; specialties: puffed pancakes w/ fruit garnish, vegetable frittatas, salmon corn cakes; refreshments on arrival; evening cordials and treats
Recreation Tennis, golf, boating, harbor cruises, biking, summer music festivals
Amenities & Services Hot tub, irons, hairdryers, fax, shuttle to town, maps, turn-down; videos; small/medium meetings, weddings and adjunct services, groups

ACCOMMODATIONS

Units 3 guest rooms, 1 suite
All Rooms Bath, TV/VCR, phone, voice
mail, AC, heat controls
Some Rooms Fireplace (1), keyhole
harbor view (2)
Bed & Bath Antique beds, sizes vary;
showers only, heat fans, robes
Favorites Louis XV Suite—quietly lavish,

tapestry rugs, sitting room w/ keyhole
harbor view, queen leather sleigh bed
Comfort & Decor Restored theme
rooms. Casino Room: brass bed, tartan
wallpaper, tennis, yachting, and golf prints.
English country garden Cottage Room:
elaborate iron bed, lush tea-stained wallpaper. Special, immaculate.

RATES, RESERVATIONS, & RESTRICTIONS

Deposit 50%; refund w/ 15-day notice;
gift cert. for future stay, valid for one year,
issued
thereafter
Discounts Various packages w/ dinners,
mansion tours
Credit Cards V, AE, DC, MC, D
Check-in/Out 3/11; will hold luggage,
may use common rooms for late departure
Smoking On porch or in gardens
Pets No

Kids Not encouraged, but check
Minimum Stay 2 nights weekends high
season, 3 nights holidays/festivals
Open All year
Hosts Andrea (Ande) and Phil Savana
41 Pelham St.
Newport, RI 02840
(888) 880-3764 or (401) 847-3801
Fax: (401) 841-0992
inquiries@savanas.com
www.savanasinn.com

THE VICTORIAN LADIES INN, Newport

OVERALL ★★★★ | ROOM QUALITY ★★★★ | VALUE ★★½ | PRICE $125–225

These Painted Ladies on a busy road are not just another pretty facade. The eclectic, richly decorated guest rooms have been featured on the home-improvement show *Room by Room,* the gardens win annual awards, and local magazine readers named it "Favorite B&B" for three consecutive years. Helene and Donald opened the property after being struck by the lifestyle while at a California bed-and-breakfast, and have been going strong for 20-something years. Elaborate seasonal decorations and a New Year's Eve cocktail party are some of the holiday festivities at this decidedly stylish, somewhat feminine Victorian.

SETTING & FACILITIES

Location On Memorial Blvd.; Rt. 138
to Newport; look for "Area Beaches"
sign; left on Rt. 138A, left at second light
Near Museums; Bowen's Wharf, Marine
District; Brick Market Place, state park,

aquarium, summer theater; Easton's
Beach, Cliff Walk, Gilded Age mansions
Building 1851 Painted Lady Victorian; 2
carriage houses

Grounds 3 award-winning garden/ courtyard areas; storybook brick walking paths to courtyards, Japanese garden; 2 goldfish ponds, 1 koi fishpond; foot bridge, patio, seating

Public Space LR, adjoining DR

Food & Drink Full breakfast, communal, separate or in room; choice of 2 entrées;

specialty: Portuguese bread w/ marinated ham, poached eggs and Hollandaise sauce

Recreation Tennis, golf, boating, harbor cruises; music festivals

Amenities & Services 1 car per room comp.; irons, fax, maps, beach towels, board games, recipes; small meetings

ACCOMMODATIONS

Units 11 guest rooms

All Rooms Bath, chairs or love seat, radio/alarm clock, TV, AC

Some Rooms Sitting room, desk/table, phone, hardwood floors, carpet

Bed & Bath Some antique, four-poster or sleigh beds, 9 queen beds, 2 king beds; full baths

Favorites Burgundy Canopy Room— Romantic large room, second level main house, w/ small sitting room, queen-size

canopy bed, burgundy wallpaper, coordinated bedding, telephone

Comfort & Decor Eclectic combination of antiques and modern accent pieces, formal Victorian furnishings, English cottage-style floral fabrics. Romantic beds, artwork. All pretty, some frilly. Colorful walls, coordinated patterns. Many rooms overlook gardens. Carriage house and rear rooms most quiet, spacious.

RATES, RESERVATIONS, & RESTRICTIONS

Deposit 1 night, 50% longer stays, add on tax; refund w/ 15-day notice

Discounts Longer stays, groups, midweek stays

Credit Cards V, MC

Check-in/Out 2–8/11

Smoking No

Pets No

Kids Over 10, only in certain rooms

Minimum Stay 3 nights July/August/hol-

iday weekends

Open Feb. 11–Jan. 1

Hosts Helene and Donald O'Neill

63 Memorial Blvd.

Newport, RI 02840

(401) 849-9960

Fax same as telephone

info@victorianladies.com

www.victorianladies.com

WYNSTONE, Newport

OVERALL ★★★★½ | ROOM QUALITY ★★★★★ | VALUE ★★ | PRICE $195–325

This lavish, romantic getaway calls to mind the gilded age in this evocative city. Luxury details are loaded into the property, including one bed so large it had to be built in the room. The bathrooms are especially notable, clad in colored marbles and swagged window treatments, with tapestries and sconces— sybaritic retreats where the towels are plush and the private sound systems can play Luther Vandross or Vivaldi while you soak, solo or duo.

SETTING & FACILITIES

Location Newport's Historic Hill
Near Antique row, ocean, Tennis Hall of
Fame, Yachting Museum; shopping and
restaurants, cobblestone Marine District;
Brick Market Place, Cliff Walk, state park,
museums, aquarium, summer theater,
White Horse Tavern
Building 1850 Greek Revival

Grounds Small garden area w/ seating
Public Space DR, halls
Food & Drink Full breakfast
Recreation Tennis, boating, harbor
cruises, beach activities; music festivals
Amenities & Services 2 small guest
refrigerators, irons, large video library

ACCOMMODATIONS

Units 5 guest rooms
All Rooms Bath, fireplace, plush carpet
or hardwoods, Oriental or tapestry rugs,
stereo/CD system, TV/VCR
Some Rooms Sitting area
Bed & Bath Featherbeds; luxury marble
baths, dbl. whirlpools, sep. showers, robes
Favorites The Belcourt—enormous

carved California pine king bed, hunter
green walls.
Comfort & Decor Custom fabrics and
wallcoverings, antiques. Polished cherry,
mahogany furnishings. Rich colors. Pampering baths. Elaborate ornamentation
without clutter. Large beds, lots of pillows.

RATES, RESERVATIONS, & RESTRICTIONS

Deposit Payment in full
Credit Cards V, AE, MC
Check-in/Out 3/11
Smoking No
Pets No
Kids No
No-No's 3rd person in room
Minimum Stay 2 nights weekends; 3 or
4 nights holidays and festivals

Open All year
Host Cathy Darigan
232 Spring St.
Newport, RI 02840
(800) 524-1386 or (401) 849-7397
Fax: (401) 847-6071
wynstone@travelbase.com
www.innsofnewport.com

Block Island

The Native-American name for Block Island is Manisses, or "God's Little Island." Travel by private boat, ferry, or air to Block Island and you may agree—or not—with the Indians.

The "Little Island" part is accurate: only 11 square miles, with scenery often compared to Ireland—rolling hills, dramatic bluffs, but with panoramic water vistas. This island—seven miles long by three miles wide—comprises long stretches of sandy ocean beaches and 365 ponds—including the vast **Great Salt Pond.** Mopeds and bikes can be rented right at the ferry docks, and slips for private boats are available.

Shopping, dining, and people watching are respected and expected activities in restored **Old Harbor.** The **Block Island Club** sponsors sailing, windsurfing, tennis, swimming, and social activities for the entire family, and accepts memberships for a week or the entire season.

More isolated activities include a trek to **Mohegan Bluffs,** a stratospheric 200 feet above sea level, and **Beacon Hill** with a 360-degree view of the island and surrounding water. Tour the island cemetery, or glimpse rare birds protected in the island's **Nature Conservancy.** Walking and hiking nature trails will lead you across the shoreline and through meadows and woods.

During the 1800s Block Island was called the stumbling block of the New England coast, as ships floundered attempting to navigate its treacherous waters. Modern technology has solved this problem, and today the old lighthouses built to warn of the fog and rocky shoals are historical beauties. Poetic **Southeast Light,** built in 1875, perches at the pinnacle of **Mohegan Bluffs;** at the other end of the island, granite-and-iron **North Light,** from 1867, stands guard at **Sandy Point.**

Block Island was originally a Victorian retreat, and bed-and-breakfasts here reflect every creative variation of that era's accommodations—formal, summery, romantic, or a combination. June to Labor Day is the island season, but if you're willing to brave blustery winds and weather, some places remain open, and the ferry runs all year. For ferry information call Interstate Navigation, (401) 783-4613. For air service call New England Airlines, (800) 243-2460

FOR MORE INFORMATION

Block Island Chamber of Commerce
(401) 466-2982
Fax: (401) 466-5286
email: Bichamber@BIRI.com

Block Island Tourism Council
(401) 466-5200 or (800) 383-BIRI
www.blockisland.com

Ferry Information
Interstate Navigation from Point Judith: (401) 783-4613
Viking Fleet from Montauk, Long Island: (516) 668-5700

1661 INN, Block Island

OVERALL ★★★★ | ROOM QUALITY ★★★★ | VALUE ★★ | PRICE $50–370

The Abrams family operates many of the best properties on the island, and one, the Hotel Manisses across the street, can provide dinner to all. Nearby, The Dodge Cottage, a pretty ca. 1900 farmhouse, has nine rooms, all with private baths, some with kitchenettes, and breakfast is at the 1661 Inn. The Dewey Cottage, a 1906 home renovated in 1994, has six rooms with modern furnishings. Continental breakfast is available at the cottage, or you can have a buffet breakfast at the 1661 Inn. Within this complex you can find luxury to budget accommodations.

SETTING & FACILITIES

Location From the ferry, Water St. S, up hill on Spring St.
Near Rest of the 1,500-acre island
Building White clapboard 1870 mansion and outbuildings, incl. replica of church destroyed by hurricane in 1938
Grounds Colorful gardens, big decks, ocean views
Public Space Parlor w/ reception desk, DR, screened porch overlooking ocean
Food & Drink Lavish buffet breakfast; specialties: whole baked bluefish, corned beef hash; afternoon wine and nibbles; dinner avail. w/ reservations in the Hotel Manisses; opt. champagne or cheese platter in room, boxed picnic lunches; refreshments/honor bar in each room
Recreation Beach activities, horseback riding, harbor cruises; touring lighthouse, bluffs, Old Harbor
Amenities & Services Access to farm animals, games, dinner at Hotel Manisses; comp. hour-long island tour, luggage storage for early arrivals/late departures

ACCOMMODATIONS

Units 9 in main house, 9 in Guest House; 3 in Nicolas Ball Cottage
All Rooms Antique furniture
Some Rooms Priv. bath, loft, porch, stained-glass window, add'l/sofa bed; kitchenette (1)
Bed & Bath Antique four-poster and canopy beds, sizes vary; some whirlpools, stained glass, showers for 2
Favorites Edwards—spacious, king-size canopy bed, full ocean view, priv. deck and loft w/ spa tub; Staples—every upgrade and best view
Comfort & Decor In main house, fantastic ocean views. Units vary widely. Rooms named after early settlers; Guest House rooms modest, minimal views. Cottage rooms romantic. Multiple levels.

RATES, RESERVATIONS, & RESTRICTIONS

Deposit 50%; refund w/ 15-day notice
Discounts Various packages
Credit Cards V, MC
Check-in/Out 1–2/11
Smoking Most rooms nonsmoking; can request smoking, but will limit room choices
Pets No

Kids Welcome
Minimum Stay 3 nights, weekends in July/August, holidays
Open Hotel Manisses: all year; check specifically for availability in the 1661 Inn
Hosts Joan and Justin Abrams

1 Spring St.
Block Island, RI 0280
(800) 626-4773 or (401) 466-2421
Fax: (401) 466-3162
biresorts@riconnect.com
www.blockisland.com

BLUE DORY INN, Block Island

OVERALL ★★★½ | ROOM QUALITY ★★★★ | VALUE ★½ | PRICE $155–425

Blue accents. A carousel horse and a flag snapping in the breeze, a blue paint job, and a back deck overlooking the (blue) sea. Dynamic owner Ann, a former New York legislator, purchased the bed-and-breakfast in 1989 after staying here for over 20 years, and has opened several others. The Adrianna Inn is close to the old harbor. Waverly Cottage is the most luxurious with private decks, ocean views, whirlpools, and one apartment. Both have Blue Dory beach rights. The Sherman Cottage is a three-bedroom Victorian-contemporary home, and Harmony Cottage has four bedrooms, a stone fireplace, a view of the lighthouse and ocean from the upper deck, and two baths. All units are romantic, tasteful, casual.

SETTING & FACILITIES

Location From ferry, up Dodge St., 3rd building on right
Near Oceanfront, in historic/business district; backs onto ocean, fronts onto active village street; stroll to Crescent Beach
Building Shingle, century-old Victorian
Grounds Patio and garden, front door opens on island's main street
Public Space Victorian parlor, basement breakfast room
Food & Drink Cont'l breakfast; specialty: frittata; coffee, juice, tea, fresh fruit always avail.; afternoon wine and cheese; evening cookies; Thanksgiving and Christmas dinners
Recreation Boating, beachcombing, tennis, surfing, touring by moped
Amenities & Services Grill for guest use, chess; tours, rentals arranged; extra persons in rooms, chef-prepared Thanksgiving dinner; Christmas decorations and dinner w/ guest participation

ACCOMMODATIONS

Units 11 guest rooms and 3 suites; 4 cottages
All Rooms Bath
Some Rooms Ocean view, TV/VCR, AC, kitchenette
Bed & Bath Sizes vary; some period brass or wooden, many w/out headboards or w/ wispy wicker backs; some whirlpools; newly renovated

Favorites The Dodge Suite—Victorian sitting area, sleeps up to 4 comfortably, w/ refrigerator, TV/VCR, AC; The Doll House and The Tea House—aptly named 1-room cottages, cozy for couples
Comfort & Decor Victorian touches

and colors, lots of pillows. Summery lie-about ambiance. Reproduction wicker; a few more substantial, genuine pieces. Back rooms quieter. Flowery borders, feminine feeling.

RATES, RESERVATIONS, & RESTRICTIONS

Deposit 50%, full payment due at check-in
Discounts Off-season (3 seasons), mid-week
Credit Cards V, AE, MC, D
Check-in/Out 11/3; can stay later if room not needed right away
Smoking Tolerated
Pets Check for approval, limited to cottages and suites
Kids Welcome in cottages and suites

No-No's Not reserving ahead
Minimum Stay June–Sept. 2 nights, 3 nights for holidays; 2 nights weekends rest of year
Open All year
Host Ann Law
Box 488, Dodge St.
Block Island, RI 02807
(800) 992-7290 or (401) 466-5891
Fax: (401) 466-9910
rundezvous@aol.com

HOTEL MANISSES, *Block Island*

OVERALL ★★★★ | ROOM QUALITY ★★★★ | VALUE ★★ | PRICE $50–370

This beautifully refurbished landmark hotel may not reflect the earliest settlers here, but instead the genteel pace of more than 100 years of tourism. It is the hub for the complex of five restored properties including the 1661 Inn and Cottages, all within a short walk, and it sparkles throughout as colorfully as its stained-glass windows. Attention to detail is apparent, from brandy glass decanters by the beds, to sun-filled, immaculate rooms. Dining is sophisticated and features fresh local ingredients.

SETTING & FACILITIES

Location Spring St. across from 1661 Inn
Near Rest of the 1,500-acre island
Building 1872 Victorian summer hotel, refurbished exterior
Grounds Deck in back, animal petting zoo, small garden, no special views
Public Space Hotel parlor, bar; sun-filled DR, open to public; library/sitting room
Food & Drink Full buffet breakfast in the 1661 Inn's breakfast room/porch; can be in room; afternoon wine and nibbles

for guests; dinner avail. w/ reservations; can order champagne or cheese platter in room, boxed picnic lunches; refreshments and honor bar in each room
Recreation Beach activities, harbor cruises; touring lighthouse, Bluffs, Old Harbor, beach horseback riding, hiking, kayaking
Amenities & Services Games, comp. hour-long island tour; library can be reserved for meetings

ACCOMMODATIONS

Units 17 guest rooms
All Rooms Bath, antique furniture, phone
Some Rooms Priv. porch, add'l bed, whirlpool, TV, small refrig.
Bed & Bath Bed sizes vary, some whirlpools, 1 whirlpool in room

Favorites Princess Augusta—in-room dbl. whirlpool, king bed
Comfort & Decor Victorian, Victorian, Victorian. Wallpapers, carpets, and antique furnishing. Dark, understated, Old World elegant. Some rooms small. Immaculate.

RATES, RESERVATIONS, & RESTRICTIONS

Deposit 50%; refund (less %25 fee) w/ 15-day notice
Credit Cards V, MC
Check-in/Out 1–2/11; will hold luggage
Smoking Guest house only
Pets No
Kids 10 and older; all ages in other buildings
Minimum Stay 3 nights, weekends in

July/August, holidays
Open All year
Hosts Joan and Justin Abrams
1 Spring St., PO Box 1
Block Island, RI 02807
(800) 626-4773 or (401) 466-2421
Fax: (401) 466-3162
biresorts@riconnect.com
www.blockisland.com/biresorts

SEA BREEZE INN, Block Island

OVERALL ★★★½ | ROOM QUALITY ★★★ | VALUE ★★½ | PRICE $90–240

With its swan pond and fields of roses and wildflowers, this serene little complex of cottages, is wonderful for weddings or for when you want to get away with a significant other. You can have breakfast on a porch in your room and not see anyone but your love and the ocean. Hosts are transplanted from Manhattan: she's an artist, he's a doctor, both are avid gardeners. They worked hard to restore these once-tired properties, and the resultant bed-and-breakfast now has a freshness, like salt-air.

SETTING & FACILITIES

Location Crest of Spring St. hill
Near Ferry, shops, Old Harbor
Building 4 shingle cottages in a compound
Grounds Hilltop ocean, coastline view, 2 acres of wildflower meadows, perennial gardens w/ over 100 varieties, swan pond

Public Space Sitting room, writing/sitting area, library
Food & Drink Cont'l breakfast; specialty: Viennese coffee, homemade preserves; served in sitting room or brought to room in basket (this option only for rooms w/ priv. bath)

Recreation Beach/water activities, harbor cruises; touring lighthouse, Bluffs, Old Harbor, Nature Conservancy programs
Amenities & Services Kayak for use in pond, guest refrigerator, sink for guest kitchen use, beach towels, maps, bike rental, nature workshops

ACCOMMODATIONS

Units 10, some suites
Some Rooms Cathedral ceiling, water view (6), small priv. porch (4)
Bed & Bath Double and twin beds; 5 priv. baths, 5 shared baths, all showers only

Favorites Room 10—fabulous view
Comfort & Decor Cottages low-key, befitting summer boarding-house origins. Eclectic decor mix of country, artsy, and summer seaside. Relaxing, understated.

RATES, RESERVATIONS, & RESTRICTIONS

Deposit 50%; refund w/ 14-day notice
Discounts Weekly rates, off-season rates
Credit Cards V, MC
Check-in/Out 2/11; will hold luggage
Smoking No
Pets No
Kids Over 5

Minimum Stay 2 nights; 3 nights over holidays
Open All year
Hosts The Newhouse Family
Spring St., Box 141
Block Island, RI 02807
(800) 786-2276 or (401) 466-2275

SHEFFIELD HOUSE, Block Island

OVERALL ★★★½ | ROOM QUALITY ★★★ | VALUE ★★★ | PRICE $50–185

Breakfast or evening cocktails in a small garden filled with golden daffodils is typical of the quiet delights at this homey, casual bed-and-breakfast near the beach. Former owners, the McQueeny family lovingly passed their summer home from generation to generation, and personal heirlooms and mature flowerbeds are among the happy results. Now hosted by Nancy Sarah, rock on the front porch swing, watch the sunrise from the tower sitting room, or just relax with a book and gaze at the water. Here the outside is vintage, the interior modernized, and the welcome sincere.

SETTING & FACILITIES

Location In historic district, near beach, ferry
Near Old Harbor, ocean
Building 1888 Queen Anne Victorian cottage
Grounds Privacy, small yard, award-winning gardens
Public Space Porch, sitting room; country-style kitchen
Food & Drink Full breakfast, afternoon snacks, cookies always out

Recreation Swimming, hiking, windsurfing, kayaking, boating, fishing, bicycling
Amenities & Services Guest refrigera-

tor, games, grill, bike rack, beach towels,
books, island tour, on-island transportation when possible

ACCOMMODATIONS

Units 6 guest rooms
All Rooms Queen beds, Full-length mirror, ceiling fan
Some Rooms 4 rooms have private
bath, 2 rooms share a bath
Bed & Bath New queen beds, 1 w/ add'l
twin bed; 5 priv. baths, 2 shared

Favorites 2nd floor rooms—water
views and priv. baths
Comfort & Decor Room sizes vary.
Irish lace curtains, quilts, and hand-
hooked rugs. Some heirloom and antique
pieces. Airy and summery. Casually comfortable. Some water views.

RATES, RESERVATIONS, & RESTRICTIONS

Deposit Full payment for 1 night, 50%
for longer stays; refund w/ 14-day notice
Discounts Off-season, midweek
Credit Cards V, AE, MC, D
Check-in/Out 2/11; will hold luggage
Smoking No
Pets No
Kids No
No-No's Mopeds on property
Minimum Stay 3 nights for high-season

weekends, 4 nights holiday weekends
Open All year; reservations required for
summer stays
Host Nancy Sarah
351 High St., P.O. Box 1387
Block Island, RI 02807
(866) 466-2494 or (401) 466-2494
Fax: (401) 466-7745
sheffieldhouse@aol.com
www.blockisland.com/sheffieldhouse

WEATHER BUREAU INN, Block Island

OVERALL ★★★★ | ROOM QUALITY ★★★★ | VALUE ★½ | PRICE $169–349

If you watch the Weather Channel, then you might especially enjoy this little bed-and-breakfast which, as its name denotes, was a weather bureau for
most of its almost-100 years. In the early 1900s forecasts were provided by
banners on the flagpole atop the pretty rooftop deck, seen by all on the
island (just as you can see all of the island). Later, weather info was broad-
cast from here until the 1950s. Within are cozy rooms with great views and
antique weather forecasting equipment, including an original barometer.
The lawn slopes to New Harbor, where you can kayak. Breakfast or afternoon wine and cheese are on the back deck, overlooking the sound, and
sunset is clearly "cool."

SETTING & FACILITIES

Location Center of the island, on hilltop
Near Ferry, shops, Old Harbor
Building Former U.S. weather station, built 1903; 2 story, widow's-walk rooftop deck, railing; Nat'l Register of Historic Places
Grounds Lawns to harbor edge
Public Space Common rooms, front and back porches

Food & Drink Full breakfast; specialties: raspberries and cream granola w/ strawberries/blueberries, Portobello mushroom quiche, berry-filled biscuits, cinnamon buns; wine and cheese; chocolate-chip cookies
Recreation Beach/water activities, harbor cruises, biking, croquet
Amenities & Services Games, beach chairs/towels, bikes, kayaks

ACCOMMODATIONS

Units 4 guest rooms
All Rooms Bath, water view
Some Rooms Woodburning fireplace, seating area
Bed & Bath Queen and king beds, some brass; small, standard baths

Favorites White Cap—fireplace, seating area, queen four-poster, most spacious
Comfort & Decor Attractive, water views. Beds positioned for views. Bright, airy. Rooms in back quietest. Antiques, wood floors, some damask wallcoverings.

RATES, RESERVATIONS, & RESTRICTIONS

Deposit Credit card number
Discounts 5th day free, midweek
Credit Cards V, AE, MC, D
Check-in/Out 1/11
Smoking No
Pets No
Kids Over 14

Open All year
Host Brian Wright
Beach Ave.
Block Island, RI 02807
(401) 466-9977 or (800) 633-8624
Fax: (401) 466-8899
www.weatherbureauinn.com

Mainland Rhode Island/ Providence

With civic improvements and a brighter image, **Providence** now sparkles as Rhode Island's capital and primary metropolis. *There's Something About Mary* was filmed here, and the TV drama titled (what else?) *Providence* has filmed at outdoor cafés on **Wickenden Street,** in restored Colonial shops on **South Main,** and in boutiques and eateries on hip **Thayer Street.** Also featured on film are the arch leading to **Little Italy at Federal Hill, Kennedy Plaza**—the town square—complete with sculpture fountain, and a Bruins hockey game at the **Civic Center.**

Providence's other treasures include **Brown University;** the restored **Mile of History** on eighteenth-century **Benefit Street,** with shipping-magnate mansions next to modest sailor homes; the **Rhode Island School of Design;** and the **Museum of Art.**

Other options? **William Rodgers Park, the zoo,** the **Museum of Natural History and Planetarium, Waterplace Park** with its water taxis, gondolas, and fire/water shows, Rockefeller-Center–modeled **Fleet Skating Center,** the **Performing Arts Center, India Point Park,** the **Children's Museum,** or downtown itself—locals call it downcity.

Mainland attractions focus on the water. **Watch Hill,** famous for antiquing, has a good beach, an 1858 lighthouse and museum, and one of the nation's oldest carousels. **Jamestown** has both a lighthouse and a windmill. **Bristol** is noted for shipbuilding and **Blithewold Mansion,** 33 acres with gardens overlooking **Narragansett Bay** and **Bristol Harbor.** The **Swamp Meadow Covered Bridge** in **Foster** is worthwhile, as is the **Butterfly Zoo** in **Middletown.**

Narragansett Bay has **Point Judith Lighthouse** and The Towers beach, and icy **New Year's Day Polar Bear and Penguin plunges**—fun to watch, if not to join. **Woonsocket** and **Wakefield** have notable performing arts and summer theater. And **Wilcox Park** at **Westerly Town Hall,** an 18-acre

1898 Victorian park, features twentieth-century sculpture in trees and ponds along its walking trails, **Colonial Theater's Shakespeare in the Park,** and summer pops concerts.

Inland Pawtucket's **Blackstone River State Park** and **Lincoln Woods State Park** offer greenery as well as canoe portage, historic walking trails, and Colonial homesteads. The **Blackstone River Bikeway,** opened in October 1998, will ultimately provide a 17.1-mile, 12-foot-wide bikeway linked to both the **East Coast Greenway**—running from Florida to Maine—and the **East Bay Bike Path.**

Bed-and-breakfasts are not as numerous here as in Newport or on Block Island, but new ones are opening each year, many in nineteenth-century homes with fine detailing. Inns are few. **Providence** offers a few quirky bed-and-breakfasts. Coastal Rhode Island offers beachy New England complete with antiques and charm. Inland spots tend to be homey, with personal atmosphere and service.

FOR MORE INFORMATION

Bed-and-Breakfast Referrals of South Coast Rhode Island
(800) 853-7479

Blackstone Area Web
www.tourblackstone.com

Bristol County Chamber of Commerce
(888) 278-9948
email: bristolcountychamber@wsii.com
www.bristolcountychamber.org (for East Bay)

Providence Web
www.providenceri.com/home

Providence/Warwick Convention and Visitors Center
(401) 751-1177 or (800) 233-1636

South Country Web
email: kathleen@southcounty.com
www.southcounty.com

The Greater Westerly-Pawtucket Chamber of Commerce
(401) 596-7761 or (800) 732-7636

Warwick
(401) 738-2000 or (401) 739-9150
Fax: (401) 738-6639
www.warwickri.com

BRADFORD-DIMOND-NORRIS HOUSE, Bristol

OVERALL ★★★½ | ROOM QUALITY ★★★ | VALUE ★★★½ | PRICE $95–120

When Governor William Bradford's house was destroyed by British fire during a 1778 raid, the torched structure was replaced by this stately home. The third-floor exterior filigree balustrade added after the Civil War earned it the nickname "Wedding Cake House," and later additions gave it an even more distinctive appearance. You sense layers of history within as well, with Victorian marble mantels and furnishings such as camelback couches and bonnet-topped highboys. It is on the route of the oldest Fourth of July parade in American history and a real piece of America itself.

SETTING & FACILITIES

Location In historic waterfront district; Hope St. in Bristol
Near Roger Williams University, Providence, Newport, state park; 1 hour to Mystic; walk to bike trail, waterfront antiques shops, restaurants, museums, historical home tours, $6 movie theater
Building 1792 Federal-style mansion; restored 1995
Grounds Rear veranda overlooks gardens and huge purple beech tree

Public Space Entrance foyer, sitting room, DR
Food & Drink Expanded cont'l breakfast in DR, at Duncan-Fyfe communal table or on veranda
Recreation Museums, shopping, antiquing, historic tours, performing arts, 15-mi. bike trail, walking trails, water sports, day trips
Amenities & Services Bike storage, irons, hairdryers

ACCOMMODATIONS

Units 4, all can be opened to suites for 3rd person
All Rooms Bath, seating, reading lamps, TV, central AC
Some Rooms Decorative orig. mantel
Bed & Bath Queen lace-canopy beds; white tile shower baths, glass showers

Favorites Pink Room—mantel, canopy bed, highboy, love seat, dressing table, soft colors
Comfort & Decor Custom window treatments, hardwood floors w/ Oriental rugs. Comfortably formal decor. Antiques and reproductions

RATES, RESERVATIONS, & RESTRICTIONS

Deposit Credit card holds room; no charge w/ 10-day notice
Discounts 3rd person
Credit Cards V, AE, MC
Check-in/Out Flexible

Smoking No
Pets No
Kids Over 14
Minimum Stay 2 nights weekends; 3 nights holidays

Open All year	(888) 329-6338 or (401) 253-6338
Hosts Suzanne and Lloyd Adams	Fax: (401) 253-4023
474 Hope St.	bdnhouse@edgenet.net
Bristol, RI 02809	www.edgenet.net/bdnhouse

ONE WILLOW BY THE SEA, Charlestown

OVERALL ★★★ | ROOM QUALITY ★★★ | VALUE ★★★★ | PRICE $75–90

Take a shower on a warm summer night under starry skies and sea breezes at the bed-and-breakfast's outside facility. This is a simple, peaceful retreat with an interesting, feminist host who was once president of NYC National Organization for Women (NOW); the fascinating political photos scattered about the house tell the tale. Guaranteed stimulating conversation is yours for the asking, and bird watchers can watch the seasonal migrations. And the big breakfasts are outstanding (not so always in Rhode Island, where bed-and-breakfast continental breakfasts can be as small as the state).

SETTING & FACILITIES

Location Residential area, bordered by nature area
Near Bird migration flyways, ocean, restaurants; 25 min. to Newport, Mystic
Building Split-level house
Grounds Rural, peaceful; sun decks, gardens; outdoor shower
Public Space LR, sun deck
Food & Drink Full breakfast; specialties: French crêpes, English scrambled eggs w/ ham, cheese and asparagus tips
Recreation Beachcombing, whale watching, sailing, local cultural/crafts events, kayaking, bird-watching, golf. theater
Amenities & Services Outside shower for beach; grill, refrigerator; parking for boat trailers, storage for kayaks, bicycles, beach gear; will meet trains

ACCOMMODATIONS

Units 3 guest rooms
All Rooms Bedside radio, ceiling and floor fans, reading lamps
Some Rooms Priv. bath
Bed & Bath Queen beds, cots; sun-dried sheets and towels
Favorites Suite—sitting room, TV/VCR
Comfort & Decor Ordinary, but bright and clean.

RATES, RESERVATIONS, & RESTRICTIONS

Deposit 1 night; 2 nights longer stay; refund w/ 6-day notice
Discounts Off-season, 3rd person, after 4-day midweek stay
Check-in/Out 11/12
Credit Cards None
Smoking No
Pets No; cat on premises
Kids Children welcome weekdays; 3 and under free; cots, playpens supplied

No-No's Teenagers
Open All year
Host Denise Dillon Fuge
1 Willow Rd.

Charlestown, RI 02813-4162
(401) 354-0802
josyrealty@aol.com
www.virtualcities.com/ri/onewillow

EDGEWOOD MANOR, Cranston

OVERALL ★★★★½ | ROOM QUALITY ★★★★★ | VALUE ★★½ | PRICE $110–225

Like the idea of sleeping in a former convent? You can here, but anyone would savor the luxury of this finest Rhode Island bed-and-breakfast outside of Newport. Five years of restoration have paid off handsomely. The turn-of-the-century, 18-room mansion is laden with showcase details such as a foyer staircase with three spindle types, handcarved oak paneling, silk tapestry wallcoverings, and original leaded and stained glass. The charming and enthusiastic hosts are justifiably proud of their considerable accomplishment, and word of this elegant newcomer near the capital should spread quickly.

SETTING & FACILITIES

Location I-95 to Exit 18, right on to Allen's Ave.; look for Norwood Ave., right turn
Near Walk to Roger Williams Park and Zoo, antiques stores, Narragansett Bay; 3 mi. from downtown Providence; 30 min. to Newport; 1 hour to Foxwoods Casino, Boston
Building 1905 Greek Revival mansion, Rococo overtones
Grounds .5 acre rear yard, sculptured lawns, fountain, patio, statuary
Public Space Grand foyer, salon, DR; each common room presents a varied theme
Food & Drink Full breakfast; afternoon tea
Recreation Activities in 430-acre park, museum, boathouse, zoos
Amenities & Services Bike storage, priv. parking, daily paper

ACCOMMODATIONS

Units 11 guest rooms, 3 suites
All Rooms Bath, TV, antique furnishings
Some Rooms Fireplace, seating, whirlpools, priv. porch (1)
Bed & Bath Antique four-poster, canopy beds; king/queen sizes; marble baths, 2 w/ shower only, 4 w/ whirlpools/sep. shower, 1 full bath
Favorites Scarlett's Retreat—king rice four-poster, carved fireplace inset w/ Grueby tile, priv. porch, marble bath w/ whirlpool
Comfort & Decor Victorian and Empire furnishings. Rooms elegant and romantic, although not enormous. Uncluttered. 18th- and 19th-century antique furnishings, fine art pieces throughout.

RATES, RESERVATIONS, & RESTRICTIONS

Deposit 50%; refund w/ 7-day notice
Discounts Seniors
Credit Cards V, AE, MC
Check-in/Out After 3/11
Smoking Restricted
Pets No
Kids Limited; check w/ B&B
Minimum Stay 2 nights weekends; 3

nights holidays; check
Open All year
Host Andrew Lombardi
232 Norwood Ave.
Cranston, RI 02905
(800) 882-3285 or (401) 781-0099
www.travelguides.com/inns

1900 HOUSE, Narragansett

OVERALL ★★★½ | ROOM QUALITY ★★★★ | VALUE ★★★★½ | PRICE $65–95

Relaxed and approachable describe the hosts—and the feel—of this cozy bed-and-breakfast, where the window boxes, birdfeeders, gingerbread trim, flower gardens, and collectibles match their charming personalities. Touch the quilts and the dress from 1911, read the old postcards, open the boxes, pick up the 3-D stereoptic camera, and swap books: this is a hands-on bed-and-breakfast with personality. The strawberries, from Bill's garden, are served on Lusterware and Depression glass, and you can enjoy unlimited refills of freshly baked muffins and other goodies.

SETTING & FACILITIES

Location Rt. 1 to Narragansett Exit, right at exit, left onto Rt. 108 N; enter rotary, exit to Narragansett; next light, right onto Kingstown Rd., residential street
Near Ocean, village; short drive to fishing port, 11 golf courses, wildlife conservatories, horseback riding, Watch Hill, Wickford, Narragansett Towers, Newport; 1 hour to Foxwoods Casino
Building Circa 1900 Victorian
Grounds .5 acre yard, vegetable and flower gardens, shed

Public Space Sitting room, DR, screened porch
Food & Drink 3-course breakfast; specialties: French-dipped filled croissants, tarragon eggs and bacon, stuffed baked apple
Recreation Boating, kayaking, fishing, surfing; local events, whale-watching cruises
Amenities & Services Guest refrigerator, beach towels, outdoor post-beach shower and sep. changing room; pick-up from train

ACCOMMODATIONS

Units 2 guest rooms, 1 suite
All Rooms Bath, TV
Some Rooms Canopy bed

Bed & Bath Antique full-size beds; old-fashioned tubs.

Favorites Blue Room—canopy bed, claw-foot tub; Gable Room—new bath **Comfort & Decor** Laura Ashley fittings and comforters. Not luxurious, but interesting artifacts, rugs, antiques. TVs a plus. Good lighting.

RATES, RESERVATIONS, & RESTRICTIONS

Deposit 1 night; refund w/ 14-day notice
Discounts Off-season, 7th night free, 3rd person
Check-in/Out 3/11; may use shower and changing room after check-out
Smoking Porch only
Pets No; 2 resident cats
Kids OK

Minimum Stay 2 nights, but check for 1 night availability
Open All year
Hosts Sandra and Bill Panzeri
59 Kingstown Rd.
Narragansett Pier, RI 02882
(401) 789-7971

FOUR GABLES, *Narragansett*

OVERALL ★★★ | ROOM QUALITY ★★★ | VALUE ★★★★ | PRICE $65–105

Narragansett has much of the charm and appeal of Newport, without the crowds, and this little bed-and-breakfast reflects that mood. Barbara is a landscape designer and has put her talent to obvious use in the perennial and herb borders. Savoring homemade preserves and cranberry-nut bread on the veranda, or in the dining room overlooking a breathtaking view of Narragansett Bay is the greatest delight here. Otherwise, full of nooks and crannies and great woodwork, it feels like a home away from home.

SETTING & FACILITIES

Location Rt. 1 to Narragansett, right at ramp, straight to inn, in residential neighborhood
Near Narragansett Pier; walk to ocean beaches, incl. historic Tower Beach; Newport, Mystic, Foxwoods Casino, Providence
Building Small ca. 1900 Shingle-style summer cottage
Grounds 1 acre; small perennial gardens, quaint paths; brick patio
Public Space LR; parlor; DR, opens to veranda
Food & Drink Hearty communal breakfast; specialty: cheese crêpes w/ blueberry-ginger sauce; p.m. refreshments
Recreation Seawall walks, boat trips, biking, kayaking, fishing, summer theater
Amenities & Services Fax, computer, gym equipment, irons, common TV, board games, videos, binoculars; pick-up from train, turn-down, small meetings; Spanish spoken

ACCOMMODATIONS

Units 2 guest rooms
All Rooms Shared bath, antiques, ceiling fans
Some Rooms TV on request
Bed & Bath Antique four-posters, 1 queen, king converts to twins; robes, hairdryer
Favorites King room—bay views
Comfort & Decor Inviting, charming wallpapers and decorative pieces, arts and crafts. Ceiling fans. Good lighting. Quiet.

RATES, RESERVATIONS, & RESTRICTIONS

Deposit 50%, refund w/ 7-day notice
Discounts Midweek 3-night stay, longer stays, reserve both rooms
Credit Cards V, AE, MC
Check-in/Out 3–7/11, later OK
Smoking On veranda/patio only
Pets On approval; house dogs and cats
Kids Over 12
Minimum Stay 2 nights summer weekends, 3 nights holidays
Open All year, except Christmas
Hosts Barbara and Terry Higgins
12 South Pier Rd.
Narragansett, RI 02882
(401) 789-6948
Fax same as phone
tjhiggins@ids.com

MURPHY'S, Narragansett

OVERALL ★★★½ | ROOM QUALITY ★★★ | VALUE ★★★★ | PRICE $80–100

Morning sun on Irish-linen tablecloths; antique silver table settings; warm, fragrant yeast bread and cinnamon rolls; thick preserves from the bed-and-breakfast's own berries—get the picture? In this small property, a walk from restaurants and a fishing pier, you will feel as pampered as a private guest. Martha wrote the book on breakfasts—literally *(The Bed & Breakfast Cookbook)*. Kevin is a commercial fisherman, and carves scrimshaw on swordfish swords, some displayed. They do nice things like finding theater tickets and placing them on your pillow.

SETTING & FACILITIES

Location Block from ocean, set back from street
Near Narragansett Pier; Wickford antiques shops, drive to Newport, Mystic, Block Island Ferry, Foxwoods Casino, vineyards
Building 1894 Victorian cottage
Grounds Front porch, café tables
Public Space Entrance hall, LR, upstairs reading nook, DR, large, renovated kitchen
Food & Drink Lavish communal breakfast; seasonal menu, early riser coffee; specialties: peaches-and-cream French toast, eggs Benedict
Recreation Seawall walks, beach activities, boat trips, kayaking, fishing, summer theater
Amenities & Services Refrigerator, special occasion celebrations

ACCOMMODATIONS

Units 2 guest rooms
All Rooms Bath, fresh flowers, TV, AC, privacy (no common walls)
Bed & Bath Queen or king/2 twins; robes, ocean views
Favorites Queen room—good ocean view, chaise

Comfort & Decor Under-the-eaves. Simple, handcrafted headboards, Laura Ashley wallpapers, traditional furnishings. Original honey-colored wide-pine floors. Bright, fresh. Good lighting. Comfortable and inviting.

RATES, RESERVATIONS, & RESTRICTIONS

Deposit 50%; refund w/ 14-day notice
Discounts Longer stays, various off-season specials including workshops on operating a B&B and baking at home
Credit Cards None
Check-in/Out 1/11
Smoking On porch only
Pets No
Kids Over 8

Minimum Stay 2 nights; 3 nights, holidays
Open May–Oct.; Nov.–April weekends
Hosts Martha and Kevin Murphy
43 South Pier Rd.
Narragansett, RI 02882
(401) 789-1824
Fax: (401) 788-0778

STONE LEA, *Narragansett*

OVERALL ★★★★ | ROOM QUALITY ★★★ | VALUE ★★★ | PRICE $125–175

The name of this grand "cottage" by famed architects McKim, Mead, and White derives from its stone construction, and the lea, or green meadow by-the-sea, on which it's built. Owner Guy is a surgeon, and his helpful parents help him run this breeze-filled place with the magnificent stairway and huge living room (and supposed ghost room). Peaceful, romantic, dramatic, and right on the lapping water, you'll feel like a nineteenth-century millionaire—when a million was a million

SETTING & FACILITIES

Location From South Pier Rd., south on Ocean Rd., towards ocean on Newton Ave., last house on left; in area formerly known as Millionaire's Row
Near Oceanfront; 20 min. to Newport; 45 min. to Mystic; 10 min. to Block Island Ferry
Building Imposing 1884 Victorian mansion w/ Tudor overtones
Grounds 2 sprawling acres, 9,000 square feet of oceanfront
Public Space Stunning entrance foyer w/ dramatic "Grand Piano" staircase and balcony, spacious LR, elegant DR, sitting room, breakfast room

Food & Drink Full, chef-prepared breakfast; specialty: ham and potato omelet

Recreation Fishing, tennis, golf, summer theater, evening entertainment, jai alai

Amenities & Services Guest refrigerator, irons, beach towels, gift cert., meetings (20)

ACCOMMODATIONS

Units 5 guest rooms, 3 suites

All Rooms Priv. bath, antiques, hardwood floors, ocean view, named after nearby islands

Some Rooms Oceanfront, add'l bed; 1 suite w/ sitting room, sleeper sofa

Bed & Bath Beds vary, all new, all-natural fibers; some hall access baths, 1 shower only

Favorites The Block Island Room—blue decor, in-room bath, queen and double beds, 2-way ocean view

Comfort & Decor Sizeable rooms, many hall baths. Comfortable, pleasant. Fresh flowers. Good lighting.

RATES, RESERVATIONS, & RESTRICTIONS

Deposit 1 night; 50% longer stay; refund w/ 14-day notice

Discounts Off-season, holidays and special event weekends excluded; extra person

Credit Cards None; V, MC only to hold reservations

Check-in/Out 3/11; may extend stay to 1 p.m.

Smoking No

Pets No

Kids Over 10

No-No's Check-in after 10 p.m.

Minimum Stay 2 nights all weekends; 3 nights all holiday weekends

Open April–end of Nov.

Hosts Guy and Stephanie Lancellotti
40 Newton Ave.
Narragansett, RI 02882
(401) 783-9546

C C LEDBETTER, Providence

OVERALL ★★★ | ROOM QUALITY ★★★ | VALUE ★★★½ | PRICE $75–125

Slightly down-at-the-heels but in the best area for college kids' parents, this bed-and-breakfast is funkily stylish, and the innkeeper keeps it fresh. She speaks French and Italian, loves to chat about literature, art, cartography, and gardening—and growing David Austin English Roses—and corresponds with repeat guests between bed-and-breakfast visits to exchange books. Make reservations a few years in advance (seriously). The site, on historic Benefit Street, across from the John Brown house in the charming Colonial area near Brown University is very popular and can be booked for graduation weekends up to two years in advance.

SETTING & FACILITIES

Location Benefit St. between Charlesfield and Power, directly across from the John Brown House; no sign, look for building

Near Museum, Supreme Court; 1 block to Brown University, Rhode Island School of Design, downtown Providence

Building 1768 Colonial, Victorian-style mansard roof; renovated in 1997

Grounds Double lot, extensive gardens, hammocks

Public Space LR, DR

Food & Drink "Cont'l Plus" communal breakfast, gourmet coffees/teas, fresh fruit; specialty: coffee cake; afternoon tea, refreshments

Recreation Waterfront gondolas, rent canoes, river walks, park activities, galleries

Amenities & Services Lots of reading material

ACCOMMODATIONS

Units 5 guest rooms

All Rooms Good reading lights, TV, AC

Some Rooms Priv. bath, decorative mantel

Bed & Bath Bed sizes vary, 1 extra-long king; full baths

Favorites The Twin Bed Room—coziest, prettiest artwork, sunny

Comfort & Decor Dhurrie rugs, Delft tiles, plants, quilts. Added-on 3rd floor, high ceilings. King-bed room, rowing machine, can have private bath. Host continually freshens interior and exterior. Modest, interesting.

RATES, RESERVATIONS, & RESTRICTIONS

Deposit 1 night; refund w/ 7-day notice

Discounts Singles, 3rd person

Credit Cards V, AE, MC, D

Check-in/Out 1/11

Smoking Restricted; 1 dog at the inn

Pets Restricted

Kids Check w/ B&B, will consider

Minimum Stay During local college

events

Open All year

Host Ms. C.C. Ledbetter
326 Benefit St.
Providence, RI 02903
(401) 351-4699
Fax same as phone

HISTORIC JACOB HILL INN, Providence

OVERALL ★★★★½ | ROOM QUALITY ★★★★★ | VALUE ★★ | PRICE $129–359

City lights with country views. Exposed corner posts date from 1722. The original servant's call box and antique wainscoting date from the Hunt Club period, 1920–1943, when the site hosted Vanderbilts, Firestones, and Grosvenors; the living room was once the men's smoking room. Because of few owners and careful use, modernizations haven't marred the expansive property. The young, enthusiastic hosts are renovating this exciting hilltop bed-and-breakfast room by room, and Bill's collection of antique toys and glass is displayed throughout. Beyond-the-call services sometimes include spontaneous tours to Newport, Boston, or Cape Cod.

SETTING & FACILITIES

Location Rt. 114A, travel approximately 1 mi., bear right at blinking light (Old Grist Mill Tavern), follow Arcade Ave., right at Rt. 44, left on Jacob St., B&B on left at top of hill (look for black antique carriage)

Near Antique shops, Providence; Brown University; Fall River outlets; Newport; Boston, Cape Cod

Building Large Colonial, orig. structure from 1722; renovated in 1997

Grounds Hilltop location oversees 40 acres; arbor, lawn games, gazebo (frequent weddings here), barn, paddock (horses boarded), hay fields, woods

Public Space Enormous LR, den; DR; outdoor deck

Food & Drink Full breakfast; specialties: blueberry pancakes, stuffed French toast, omelets; welcoming refreshments; afternoon cheese platters

Recreation Seasonal berry picking, pumpkin patches, selecting Christmas trees; horseback riding, hot-air balloon rides

Amenities & Services Kidney-shaped lighted pool, tennis court; use of gas grill, picnic table; bicycle storage, Providence shuttle, horseback riding lessons

ACCOMMODATIONS

Units 8 guest rooms, 2 suites

All Rooms Private bath, fireplace, TV, phone, AC

Some Rooms Priv. porch, French doors, double whirlpool; combine rooms to form suite

Bed & Bath Some antique, canopy, four-posters, illusion lace canopies, sizes vary; some renovated tile baths w/ marble floors, 2-person whirlpools, bidets; some rooms will share baths if not taken as suites

Favorites Mansion Suite—mural of farm, Gothic king bed/dresser, lace canopy, French doors to whirlpool; Vanderbilt Suite—French country, woodstove, hand-painted furnishings, deck overlooking pool

Comfort & Decor Farmhouse decor softened w/ imaginative and romantic touches. Rich pieces, period wallpapers. Third-floor rooms, round-topped windows, slanted ceilings. Some rooms on small side. Aptly named country cottage w/ kitchen, accommodates 2–6, for long-term stays.

RATES, RESERVATIONS, & RESTRICTIONS

Deposit Determined at time of reservation; refund w/ 14-day notice

Discounts 3rd person, singles, various 2-night packages, corp. weekday, extended stay (3+ days), AAA

Credit Cards V, AE, MC, D; checks up to 10 days prior to arrival

Check-in/Out 2/11

Smoking Not inside; violators will be asked to leave, resp. for reserv. plus cleaning fees of $150 and future lost revenues

Pets No

Kids Over 12 w/ notice

No-No's Candles or large coolers in guest rooms

Minimum Stay 2 nights weekends; 3 nights holidays

Open All year

Hosts Bill and Eleonora Rezek
Box 41326
Providence, RI 02940-1326
(888) 336-9165 or (508) 336-9165
Fax: (508) 336-0951
host@inn-providence-ri.com
www.inn-providence-ri.com

ADMIRAL DEWEY INN, *South Kingston*

OVERALL ★★★½ | ROOM QUALITY ★★★★ | VALUE ★★★½ | PRICE $90–140

Named for the hero of the Spanish-American War, The Admiral Dewey celebrated its centennial year as a guesthouse in 1998. In a fascinating photo album, you can chart the property's progress from neglected white elephant without adequate plumbing to the current pretty Victorian filled with touches of past and present. Joan spent two years restoring the creaky, airy house—literally picking it up and moving all 137 tons to a new foundation. The big plus here is the fine beach nearby. The hosts, who also operate an antiques trade and real estate office, are heroes themselves in this impressive venture.

SETTING & FACILITIES

Location In residential area, ocean across street
Near Matunuck Beach across road, Point Judith, Galilee fishing village, Snug Harbor, wildlife preserves, Newport, Mystic, Block Island Ferry, Foxwoods Casino
Building Stately 1898 Victorian, always a beach hotel
Grounds Corner lot, veranda
Public Space Parlor, large DR

Food & Drink Self-serve communal cont'l breakfast; specialty: coffee cake; kitchen open for juice, teas, snacks
Recreation Boat charters/cruises, golf, tennis, summer theater/festivals, events and county fair
Amenities & Services Gas grill, common TV, guest refrigerator, irons, outside shower, maps, beach towels, daily paper; small meetings/weddings

ACCOMMODATIONS

Units 10 guest rooms
All Rooms Antiques, hardwood floors
Some Rooms Bath, Block Island Sound views
Bed & Bath Antique beds; queen, full, twin; priv. baths (8), shared (2), all showers only; some claw-foot tubs
Favorites Honeymoon Room—3rd floor, pastel walls and bedding; Rooms 7,

8—water views
Comfort & Decor French silk navy/rose wallpapers. Poster trundle beds, country pines, brass fixtures, inlaid oak dressers, marble-topped washstands and dressers. Ornate Gothic carved pieces, faux-painted oak. Dormers/eaves. Clean and comfy.

RATES, RESERVATIONS, & RESTRICTIONS

Deposit 50%, refund w/ 7-day notice
Discounts Groups, check w/ B&B for packages
Credit Cards V, MC
Check-in/Out 3–7/11
Smoking On veranda only
Pets No
Kids Over 10

Minimum Stay 2 nights weekends, 3 nights holidays
Open All year
Host Joan LeBel
668 Matunuck Beach Rd.
South Kingston, RI 02879
(800) 457-2090; (401) 783-2090 or
(401) 783-8298

GREEN SHADOWS, *Wakefield*

OVERALL ★★★ | ROOM QUALITY ★★★ | VALUE ★★★ | PRICE $75–120

The friendly, well-traveled hosts literally built this little bed-and-breakfast in 1995, by completely reconstructing and redesigning their home from the ground up. Says Don, "all that was left was the foundation," and the former ranch-style residence is now a homey and attractive contemporary. All guest facilities are on the first floor; Don and Mercedes stay on the second. A half-mile from the ocean, with full breakfasts such as crunchy French toast and homebaked bread, this is a popular choice in an area with relatively few bed-and-breakfasts; the hosts recommend reserving months in advance for summer.

SETTING & FACILITIES

Location Rt. I to Green Hill Beach exit, left onto Green Hill Beach Rd., in residential area; on right;
Near Walk to Green Hill Ocean Beach, Point Judith Pond, wildlife preserves, Block Island Ferry, Newport, Old Mystic Seaport and Aquarium, Foxwoods Casino
Building Cape Cod–style 2-story contemporary
Grounds Landscaped and wooded priv. acre; large, priv. screened back porch overlooks pond
Public Space Entry hall, artwork (some nude studies); library/TV room; all guests on Ist floor; porch
Food & Drink Early riser coffee/tea; full breakfast; specialties: English tea scones, ginger pancakes, soufflé apple pancakes; refreshments
Recreation Fishing, flea markets, summer season at Theater-By-The-Sea, Big Apple Circus, Charlestown Seafood Festival, Wickford Art Fair
Amenities & Services Outdoor beach hot/cold shower, guest refrigerator, recipes, beach towels/supplies, pick-up from train; small priv. affairs/meetings

ACCOMMODATIONS

Units 2 guest rooms
All Rooms Bath, carpet
Some Rooms Antiques
Bed & Bath King beds, antique bed (1); hall access w/ robes (1)
Favorites Room w/ in-room bath
Comfort & Decor Comfortable-sized rooms w/ attractive wallpaper, mix of contemporary and antique pieces, artwork. Comfort rather than style. Low key, informal. Good lighting.

RATES, RESERVATIONS, & RESTRICTIONS

Deposit I night; refund w/ 6-day notice
Discounts 7 days or longer; off-season specials
Credit Cards None
Check-in/Out 2/11
Smoking No
Pets No
Kids Over 10
Minimum Stay 2 nights June–Sept., all
weekends
Open April–Nov.
Hosts Mercedes and Don Kratz
803 Green Hill Beach Rd.
Wakefield, RI 02879-6228
(401) 783-9752
Fax: (401) 783-0802, call first
www.green-shadows.com

WATCH HILL INN, *Watch Hill*

OVERALL ★★★ | ROOM QUALITY ★★★ | VALUE ★★ | PRICE $85–285

Incredible bay sunsets, a casual atmosphere, and a breezy waterfront location are pluses here, along with the fact that there are few other good bed-and-breakfast properties in this part of the state. This modest inn could use a face-lift, but its relaxed, waterfront atmosphere somehow fits the salty environment. A deck seaside restaurant serves seafood, steak dinners, and outstanding clam chowder in an informal setting that has most people in shorts and tees. Old salts and families with young kids—allowed free—will be especially satisfied.

SETTING & FACILITIES

Location Southwest tip of Rhode Island; take Scenic Rt. 1A to Watch Hill, or take Rt. 78 to Watch Hill, look for signs
Near On Bay, Marina; views of Stonington (Conn.), Block Island; short drive to casinos; walk to ocean beaches; Newport, Mystic
Building 1845 New England-style architecture, expanded
Grounds Bay and docked boats, decks, windows showcase views
Public Space Seasonal porch; DR
Food & Drink Cont'l breakfast; lunch and dinner daily in summer and holiday weekends through Sept.; specialty: grilled pizza ("Grizza"); specialties: seafood, steak, award-winning clam chowder; late-night menu till midnight; full service bar and grill; banquets
Recreation Touring historic Watch Hill, residential "summer cottage" mansions, antique shops and art galleries, Flying Horse carousel; inn hosts local bands weekends
Amenities & Services Beach towels; meeting, seminar, wedding and priv. party facilities

ACCOMMODATIONS

Units 12 guest rooms, 4 junior suites
All Rooms Private bath, phone, TV, AC/heat controls, water or village views
Some Rooms Junior suites larger: sitting area w/ pull-out sofa
Bed & Bath Some antique, four-poster beds; some showers only, some claw-foot tubs w/ showers, not luxury baths
Favorites Room 13—more spacious, pretty room w/ keyhole water view, Rooms 9 and 10—most requested, direct water views
Comfort & Decor Low-key Colonial decor. Muted, pretty floral wallcoverings. Traditional mahogany pieces, some Queen Anne–style. Some pieces could be improved w/ refinishing. Americana decor, wreaths, ceramic water pitchers. Carpet.

RATES, RESERVATIONS, & RESTRICTIONS

Deposit 50%; refund w/ 14-day notice, full reservation payment due w/ shorter notice
Discounts 3rd person, various packages include midweek, weekend (exclusions), full week, golf/fishing, seminars/retreats

Credit Cards MC, V, AE
Check-in/Out 3/11; late check-out charged extra day
Smoking On porches and grounds; in restaurant/lounge
Pets No
Kids Welcome, no cots or cribs; young children free
Minimum Stay 2 nights weekends; 3 nights holidays

Open All year
Hosts Mary Farago, Mark Szaro, Marlene Salaun, and Bridgette Hollanderski
38 Bay St.
Watch Hill, RI 02891
(800) 356-9314 or (401) 348-8912
Fax: (401) 348-6301
stay@watchhillinn.com
www.watchhillinn.com

KISMET ON THE PARK, Westerly

OVERALL ★★★ | ROOM QUALITY ★★★ | VALUE ★★★ | PRICE $85–150

If you ever wanted to enjoy cultural events right from your own porch, you can here, including band concerts and Shakespeare plays. Wilcox Park, behind this pleasant downtowner, was modeled after Central Park. A mother-daughter team has worked long and hard to bring this once dilapidated grand house up to speed. Breakfast is light, but a short walk away are restaurants, shops, movies, and the train. The combo of urbanity and greenery is appealing.

SETTING & FACILITIES

Location From south, I-95 to Rt. 78, Exit 3, right to fork, bear right onto High St., property on left
Near Entrance to Wilcox Park, downtown, 2 casinos, Watch Hill, Block Island Ferry
Building 1845 Federal-style townhouse
Grounds Minimal in front, but backs onto large park
Public Space Porch/balcony, public room, DR

Food & Drink Cont'l breakfast; always open for refreshments
Recreation Park activities and cultural events, touring Westerly, golf, tennis, beachcombing, boating
Amenities & Services Hot tub, off-street parking for 4 cars, TV in public room, guest refrigerator, irons, kitchen privileges; meetings (20), priv. parties

ACCOMMODATIONS

Units 4 guest rooms, 1 suite, 1 longer-stay one-bdrm apartment
All Rooms Bath, ceiling fan, antiques
Some Rooms Park view
Bed & Bath Double, queen, king beds, Early American quilts; showers only, 1 w/

whirlpool
Favorites Romance Room—ruffles, whirlpool; The Apartment—full BR and 2nd BR w/ daybed and trundle, living/dining area, Americana

Comfort & Decor Rooms bright w/ sun, white walls, and splashes of heritage colors. Lace, quilts, wicker, and early Colonial pieces. Basic but pretty. Clean and comfortable.

RATES, RESERVATIONS, & RESTRICTIONS

Deposit I night
Check-in/Out 2–4/11
Smoking On porches only
Pets In designated rooms
Kids Over 12; apartment OK for families
Minimum Stay 2 nights

Open April–Dec.
Hosts Cindy Slay & Courtney Slay
I High St.
Westerly, RI 02891
(401) 596-3237
kismetbandb@webtv.net
www.kismetbandb.com

SHELTER HARBOR INN, Westerly

OVERALL ★★★½ | ROOM QUALITY ★★★ | VALUE ★★½ | PRICE $96–172

Situated on busy Route 1 (with neither sea nor harbor in sight), this casual old inn is nonetheless peaceful, buffered from the highway. The low-key host, a self-described Wall Street exile, does not occupy the property, but is around if needed, often mowing the lawn. Antiques run from Stickley-craftsman to Early American, and include an enormous Hoosier hutch and a Simplex wall clock. The nearby salt pond is fun for kids, the three-mile beach is a joy to walk, and the food is tops.

SETTING & FACILITIES

Location I-95 N to Exit 92, turn right onto Rt. 2, I mi. to Rt. 78, to end stoplight, Rt. I, turn left, inn is 4 mi. on right
Near Short drive to private-to-community barrier ocean beach, Watch Hill, Mystic, Newport, ferry to Block Island
Building Rambling 2-story white farmhouse (built 1800–1810), some c. 1900 additions; orig. coach house and barn
Grounds Rolling lawns, patios, gardens; paddle tennis courts, croquet
Public Space Antique Colonial library; year-round sun porch, deck; 3 restaurant DRs

Food & Drink Full breakfast; specialty: ginger-blueberry pancakes; restaurant open to public, 3 meals every day all year; lighter fare in veranda bar; specialties: smoked finnan haddie, other fresh seafood; full liquor license; special holiday dinners
Recreation Ocean activities, trails, antiquing in Watch Hill, theater in Matunuck
Amenities & Services Lawn games, roof deck, hot tub, barbecue, bike storage, cots and cribs, irons

ACCOMMODATIONS

Units 24 guest rooms
All Rooms Bath, seating, reading lamp, TV, phone, AC
Some Rooms Fireplace, deck
Bed & Bath Some four-poster beds, 1 queen or 2 doubles in rooms; most full baths, some shower only
Favorites #9—Corner room, fireplace, priv. deck
Comfort & Decor Comfortable, mix of authentic Victorian antiques, reproduction Colonial pieces. Muted floral bedding, window treatments. Some worn furnishings should be updated. Some Block Island views.

RATES, RESERVATIONS, & RESTRICTIONS

Deposit 1 night; refund w/ 48-hour notice
Discounts Children, singles, business midweek
Credit Cards V, AE, MC, D
Check-in/Out 2/11
Smoking Permitted in guest rooms, bar, outside
Pets No
Kids Welcome
Minimum Stay 2 nights weekends, Thanksgiving; 3 nights other holidays
Open All year
Host Jim Dey
10 Wagner Rd.
Westerly, RI 02891
(800) 468-8883 or (401) 322-8883
Fax: (401) 322-7907

THE VILLA, Westerly

OVERALL ★★★★ | ROOM QUALITY ★★★★ | VALUE ★★½ | PRICE $95–225

"Land of Amore" is the way the owners aptly describes this sensual bed-and-breakfast, and its primary purpose is romantic getaways. Nearby New England neighbors stay here, so the place is usually full on weekends. The pool, whirlpool, and lushly landscaped patio are the focus, but flowers from the cutting garden, in-room whirlpools, soft textures, candlelit breakfast, and soft lighting all speak the "L" word. The romantic theme, accompanied by Italian-inspired room names—La Sala del Cielo, The Blue Grotto, La Sala di Verona— may indeed make you feel like Juliet, or Romeo, or both!

SETTING & FACILITIES

Location Rt. 1 to Rt. 1A (Shore Rd.); cross Airport Rd.
Near Watch Hill, ocean, bay, Mystic Seaport and Aquarium, Westerly, Foxwoods Casino, Newport, ferry to Block Island, ocean view golf course adjacent to property
Building Stucco Dutch Colonial w/ Mediterranean exteriors, styled as villa
Grounds 1.3 acres, gardens, pool and hot tub; decorated seasonally

Public Space Sitting room, dining area, patio

Food & Drink Buffet cont'l breakfast weekdays, full weekends; specialties: homebaked muffins and sweetbreads, Belgian waffles with fresh fruit

Recreation Golf, local events, deep-sea fishing, boating

Amenities & Services Pool

ACCOMMODATIONS

Units 6; 3 in main house, 1 attached, 2 in carriage house

All Rooms Bath, carpet, compact refrigerator, TV, coffee maker, AC

Some Rooms Skylight, fireplace, terrace/balcony; sitting area, love seat/sofa; microwave, dining tables; carriage house rooms: priv. entrances

Bed & Bath Special decor beds (four-poster), sizes vary; dbl. Jacuzzi (4)

Favorites Blue Grotto—stone wall, ceiling fans, fireplace, dbl. whirlpool, king bed, glass doors to pool; Rosa Maiorano—four-poster, brick fireplace, dbl. Jacuzzi, and separate shower; Verona—LR, cathedral ceilings in sleeping area, king bed, skylight above dbl. whirlpool

Comfort & Decor Rooms vary widely. Most good size. Highly romantic and sensual

RATES, RESERVATIONS, & RESTRICTIONS

Deposit 1 night or 50%; balance paid in full at check-in; must cancel 15 days in advance

Discounts Off-season, midweek

Credit Cards V, AE, MC, D

Check-in/Out 3–6/11

Smoking No

Pets No

Kids No

Open All year

Hosts Angela and Peter Gagnon
190 Shore Rd.
Westerly, RI 02891
(800) 722-9240 or (401) 596-1054
Fax: (401) 596-6268
villa@riconnect.com
www.thevillaatwesterly.com

WOODY HILL, Westerly

OVERALL ★★★½ | ROOM QUALITY ★★★★ | VALUE ★★★ | PRICE $85–165

Like to talk about Walt Whitman, Nathaniel Hawthorne, and Edgar Allan Poe along with your sightseeing? Ellen has a Ph.D in nineteenth-century American literature and is happy to chat, so here's your chance. Her family has resided in Westerly since the 1600s, and the Early American ambiance and library full of books reflect her heritage and interests. Pretty and private, bucolic and quiet, Woody Hill is aptly named, nestled in the woods, and has a pool with a lovely view. Here's a great place to bring a book—and then discuss it.

SETTING & FACILITIES

Location Rural setting, off busy highway
Near Ocean, Foxwoods Casino, Mystic, Watch Hill, Newport, Ferry to Block Island, walking trails
Building Recently constructed, authentic-looking shingle Dutch Colonial; separate pool house
Grounds On a hilltop in the woods; 20 acres w/ gardens, pool, pool house
Public Space Porch, front room, library; LR; keeping room

Food & Drink Full breakfast, communal or separate; specialty: apple crisp w/ whipped cream; wintertime hearth-cooked dinner by request
Recreation Local crafts, workshops, cultural events, antiquing, swimming, kayaking, sailing, hiking
Amenities & Services Irons, guest refrigerator, beach towels, recipes, board games; facilities for parties, weddings, functions, meetings

ACCOMMODATIONS

Units 4 guest rooms, 1 suite
All Rooms Fresh flowers; Americana fabrics, appointments, bath, TV
Some Rooms Antique mahogany or cherry furnishings, VCR, priv. entrance, AC, priv. roof deck; phone on request
Bed & Bath Some canopy or bed-curtain beds; all priv. baths, 1 hall access, mostly showers only, 1 dbl. shower, 1 tub
Favorites Room #3—large, windows,

pretty decor, French doors, walkway to pool, can be reserved as 2-room suite; room #1—suitable for families
Comfort & Decor Spacious rooms w/ antiques, wide-plank floors, handmade quilts. Rustic, real Early American. Suite: queen sofa bed in 2nd room. Good lighting.

RATES, RESERVATIONS, & RESTRICTIONS

Deposit 1 night; refund w/ 7-day notice
Discounts Off-season, longer stays, , school nights; add'l person $10
Credits Cards No
Check-in/Out 2/11; guests may use facil. for day after check out
Smoking Outside only
Pets No; 2 cats, not allowed in guest rooms
Kids OK; $10 charge for extra person in room

No-No's Unsupervised kids at pool
Minimum Stay 2 nights on weekends; check for 1-night availability
Open All year
Host Ellen Madison
149 South Woody Hill Rd.
Westerly, RI 02891
(401) 322-0452 or (401) 322-4003
woodyhill@riconnect.com
www.woodyhill.com

Connecticut

Close enough to New York to prioritize sophistication but deeply rooted in New England, the compact Nutmeg State—fewer than 60 miles from north to south and 100 miles across—features 850 lake-and-stream–filled square miles in the **Quinebaug and Shetucket Rivers Valley National Heritage Corridor,** as well as 250 miles of active **Long Island Sound** coastline.

Hartford and **New Haven** are centers of entertainment and cultural opportunities and famed college campuses, hilly terrain, and unspoiled Colonial villages are part of the scene. The state is still two-thirds open land, and even the busy **Merritt Parkway** leading to New York is a designated scenic byway, ideal for foliage splendor.

Other routes make for equally pretty drives. Route 7 runs from Litchfield County's covered **Bull's Bridge** north to the covered bridge in **West Cornwall,** near the **Housatonic River, Kent, Kent Falls,** and several state parks. Route 41 (in the northwest corner of the state) connects **Sharon, Lakeville, Salisbury,** and **Bear Mountain.** Route 77 from Guilford to Durham starts at the shore and runs through real countryside, passing working **Dudley Farm.** Route 146 passes through **Branford** and **Guilford. Route 169** follows from Yankee farm areas near **Woodstock** to **Lisbon** and has been voted one of the top ten scenic roads in the country. Route 202 passes **Nepaug State Park. Route 234** is also known as the **Pequot Trail** and runs through **Stonington.**

Filled with antiques and boutiques, museums and performing arts, **Litchfield, Haddam, Kent, Essex, Putnam, Norwich, Stonington,** and **New London** are quaint, quiet areas along scenic Route 169 and much of the river valley. These towns provide ideal meandering getaways for couples, and for more excitement the nearby **Foxwoods** and **Mohegan Sun Casinos** liven up the night.

**Mystic, Norwalk, Lake Compounce Theme Park, Bristol, Farming-
ton River, Bridgeport, South Norwalk,** and other Connecticut towns
offer steam trains, riverboat cruises, zoos and nature centers, hands-on
experiments, a puppet theater, beach activities, lighthouses, professional
sports, festivals, and fairs.

You can enjoy just about any activity in Connecticut except really good
downhill skiing. You'll find hot-air balloon tours, swimming, boating, parasailing, diving, whitewater kayaking, skiing, fly-fishing and charter fishing,
horseback riding, historical touring, antiques and outlet shopping, theater,
music, dance, hiking, walking, biking, carriage rides, scenic tours, museums, and just-for-kids activities.

Bed-and-breakfasts and inns in this state tend to be romantic and historical, and many are housed in antique farmhouses. Those close to New York
City, in posh **Greenwich** or **New Canaan** areas, cater to business travelers
and harried weekenders, but some are just comfortable and welcome kids.

The state is also noted for dining, from the homey to the five-star sublime, with an adventurous mix of cuisines and cultures. After all, America
was first introduced to pizza in Connecticut.

FOR MORE INFORMATION

Bed & Breakfast Ltd. (203) 469-3260

Bed & Breakfast/Inns of New England
Reservation Service (800) 582-0853

Bed & Breakfsts of Mystic Coast
(860) 892-5006

Covered Bridge B&B Reservation Service
(860) 542-5944

Destinations New England
(800) 333-INNS (all of New England)

Four Seasons International Bed &
Breakfast Reservation Service
(860) 658-2181

Mystic Country Inns (800) 598-7116

Mystic Lodgings (860) 536-0509 or
(800) 536-6709

Nutmeg Bed & Breakfast Agency
(860) 236-6698 or (800) 727-7592
www.bnb-link.com

Connecticut Lodgings & Attractions
Association (860) 657-2259

Connecticut Tourism
(860) 270-8080 or (800) CT-BOUND
www.state.ct.us/tourism/;
www.visitconnecticut.com

Litchfield Hills Travel Council
(860) 567-4506
Fax: (860) 567-5214
www.litchfieldhills.com

Ferry Information

New London to Block Island (seasonal):
(860) 442-9553 or (860) 442-7891

New London to Fishers Island
(year-round): (860) 442-0165 or
(516) 788-7463

New London to Montauk (seasonal):
(516) 668-5700

New London to Orient Point:
(860) 443-5281

Western Connecticut

Postcard-perfect Western Connecticut is filled with steepled churches, picket fences, American flags, Colonial stone walls, and rustic barns, but has some urban areas as well. This zone starts in the northwest foothills of the **Berkshires,** runs south to coastal **Fairfield County** bordering New York, laps into **Long Island Sound,** and west to **New Haven.**

The **Litchfield Hills** area has been a summer retreat for more than 100 years and offers an abundance of recreational activities—antiquing, boating and lake activities, historic home tours, horseback riding, golf, tennis, hiking, snow sports, rafting, and car racing. It also is home to artistic and cultural pursuits—the hills are literally alive with music, dance, and drama.

Near the **Berkshires,** the town of **Washington** is named after the man who indeed slept here and perhaps at a property where we can too. Litchfield is a classic treasure, with a clutch of white-clapboard, black-shuttered mansions. Antique hunters and gallerygoers should stop at quaint Kent, and after scouring for bargains, enjoy the waterfalls. For authentic Americana, nearby are the **Carousel Museum of New England** in **Bristol,** and the 1841 barn-red covered bridge in **West Cornwall.**

Some lodgings are restored mansions with splendid period trappings. More modest accommodations may be creatively built around literary or artistic themes, and still others offer simple and cozy accommodations.

Fairfield County, the western coastal area of the state, is closest to New York and operates partially as an upscale suburb. It offers historic homes and sites, nature centers, museums, shopping, excellent dining, and performing and fine arts in a sophisticated locale. In addition, the calm **Sound beaches** are popular.

Westport is a creative and shopping center, with a sophisticated New York edge and prices to match. **Bridgeport,** a no-nonsense town with some urban ills, is home to the **Beardsley Zoo** and the interactive **Discovery**

Museum. Historic **Norwalk** has a renowned maritime aquarium and **IMAX Theatre.** A ferry ride away is the **1868 Sheffield Island Lighthouse.**

The best bed-and-breakfasts and inns offer a quiet hideaway from New York for weekend R&R, or, conversely, a country base from which to visit the Big Apple. Business travelers are well-received, and lodgings here can be stopovers to or from an extended tour of New England.

Fishing and boating are pleasures of the **Housatonic River,** and low-key accommodations are nearby. The valley was the site of the second-largest Revolutionary War encampment—only Valley Forge was larger.

You can hike through American history on trails in the 183-acre **Putnam Memorial State Park** and gaze at contemporary works at the **Aldrich Museum of Contemporary Art** in **Ridgefield** and the **Brookfield Craft Center** near **Candlewood Lake.** Or enjoy a costumed tour of Colonial history at the **Keeler Tavern Museum** in **Ridgefield,** a center for dining, antiquing and traditional New England charm an hour's drive from NYC.

Although parts of **New Haven** cry out for rejuvenation, **Yale**'s architecturally fascinating campus and renowned art museum are worth a visit. The **Waterbury** region has an amusement park, museums, an opera house, a railroad tour in **Thomaston,** and a new 10,000-square-foot, restored turn-of-the-century antiques district in **Seymour.** Central Connecticut features numerous pick-your-own fruit, vegetable, and pumpkin patches, Colonial walking tours, and more museums and performing arts.

FOR MORE INFORMATION

Central Connecticut Tourism District
(860) 225-3901
Fax: (860) 225-0218
www.centralct.org

Coastal Fairfield County Convention & Visitor Bureau
(203) 899-2799 or (800) 866-7925
www.visitfairfieldco.org

Fairfield Chamber of Commerce
(203) 255-1011

Greater New Haven Convention and Visitors Bureau
(203) 777-8550 or (800) 332-STAY
www.newhavencvb.org

Housatonic Valley Tourism District
(203) 743-0546 or (800) 841-4488
www.housatonic.org

Kent Chamber of Commerce
(860) 927-1463
www.kentct.com

Litchfield Hills Visitors Bureau
(860) 567-4506
www.litchfieldhills.com

Waterbury Region Convention & Visitors Bureau
(203) 597-9527
Fax: (203) 597-8452

HOMESTEAD INN, *Greenwich*

OVERALL ★★★★½ | ROOM QUALITY ★★★★ | VALUE ★½ | PRICE $250–359

Warm, bright owners—he a renowned chef—took over this well-regarded country French and English inn in 1997. *Esquire* has named the inn's restaurant one of the best in the country. The folks at the next table are probably movers and shakers on weekend R&R or local moguls dining out at their round-the-corner neighborhood favorite. Not much to do here but eat and relax in the casually elegant rooms, but for many that's quite enough, thank you. In fact, author William Inge wrote *Picnic* while staying here in the 1950s. Is it a coincidence he wrote about a meal on a lawn, just as you can enjoy on premises?

SETTING & FACILITIES

Location I-95 to Exit 3, left at ramp end; left onto Horse Neck Ln.; left onto Field Point Rd.; inn on right, approx. .5 mi. S of I-95; I mi. from town center, in upscale Victorian-era Belle Haven residential area
Near Historic Greenwich, museums, Pepsico sculpture gardens, Stamford Center for the Arts, Cavalier Art Gallery, commuter rail to Manhattan (45 min.)
Building 1799 Colonial farmhouse w/ Gothic Victorian, Italianate touches
Grounds 3 acres, gardens, stone walls
Public Space Backgammon parlor, LR,

DR, main DR, sun porch, bar, veranda
Food & Drink Early riser coffee; breakfast, lunch, and dinner served in French style; full breakfast menu; lunch specialties: striped bass, grilled veal; dinner specialties: Dover sole, herb-crust rack of lamb; extensive wine list
Recreation Golf, tennis, sound-side beach, historic home tours, antiquing
Amenities & Services Limited disabled access; beach passes; turn-down, wake-up calls; meetings, office capabilities

ACCOMMODATIONS

Units 19 guest rooms and suites in orig. home, the Inn Between and the Cottage
All Rooms Bath, phone/dataport, voice mail, clock/radio, TV, access to veranda, AC
Some Rooms Desk, priv. veranda, sitting rooms
Bed & Bath Antique beds; new baths w/ elaborate fixtures, extra-large showers

Favorites Rooms with king 4-poster beds, stunning fabrics, and backgammon tables
Comfort & Decor Superior attention to guest comfort. Rooms in orig. building, historic feel. High-end, authentic-style furnishings. High-tech. Good lighting. Rooms have all been upgraded.

RATES, RESERVATIONS, & RESTRICTIONS

Deposit Credit card reservation; no charge w/ 48-hour notice for midweek, 7 days for weekends
Credit Cards V, AE, MC
Check-In/Out 3/noon
Smoking Allowed in rooms
Pets No
Kids Over 14
Minimum Stay 2 nights

Thanksgiving/Christmas weekends
Open All year
Hosts Theresa Carroll and Thomas Henkelmann
420 Field Point Rd.
Greenwich, CT 06830
(203) 869-7500
Fax: (203) 869-7502
www.johansens.com

SOUND REACH, Guilford

OVERALL ★★★½ | ROOM QUALITY ★★★★ | VALUE ★★★★ | PRICE $90–110

The name Sound Reach has a double meaning, referring to the view and the music floating across the night air. Lawrence is a professional musician, and executive director of the neighborhood Music School, so the house is filled with instruments, and guests are encouraged to join in for impromptu recitals. Pam lived in Denmark for six years, and her love of Scandinavian culture and aesthetics is evident. A former art editor, she currently free-lances and is passionate about gardening and cooking, useful talents at this rustic, chalet-style log bed-and-breakfast. The inn is on a wooded hill, where you can catch the breeze and sometimes spot a wild turkey.

SETTING & FACILITIES

Location 10 min. from Guilford Green; I-95 to Exit 58; take Rt. 77 N to left turn onto Rt. 80; take next right onto Long Hill; left onto Country Rd.; B&B is 1st right onto Christmas Hill

Near Yale, downtown New Haven, Lake Quonnipaug, Hammonasset Beach State Park, Water Authority property, lake, outlet mall, working colonial farm

Building 1968 hilltop Swiss-style, rustic cedar log cabin; outbuildings
Grounds 3.5 parklike, secluded acres, wooded areas; perennial and herb gardens, trails, clear-day views from Stony Creek to Long Island
Public Space LR, loft rooms, interior balconies; DR
Food & Drink Cont'l breakfast (full breakfast on request); specialty: home-baked breads w/ fresh fruits
Recreation Historic touring, summer farmers' market, antiquing, lake and beach activities, XC skiing, bird watching
Amenities & Services Water Authority passes, refrigerator, gas grill, phone, daily *New York Times*; fax/computer services

ACCOMMODATIONS

Units 3 guest rooms
All Rooms Flowers, 2-phone line, candle lantern
Some Rooms Priv. bath (1), view, writing desk
Bed & Bath 2 rooms share 1 bath
Favorites Double-bed room—charming, priv. bath
Comfort & Decor Dhurrie rugs, painted furniture, Swedish rocker. Original artworks. Romantic candle lanterns in each room. Queen and twin rooms share bath, work well as suite. Rooms at separate end of house, priv.

RATES, RESERVATIONS, & RESTRICTIONS

Deposit 1 night; refund w/ reasonable notice
Discounts Winter packages
Credit Cards V, MC, D
Check-In/Out By arrangement/by 10:30
Smoking No
Pets Check for availability
Kids Check for availability
Minimum Stay 2 nights weekends
Open All year
Hosts Pam Carley and Lawrence Zukof
Christmas Hill Rd.
Guilford, CT 06437
(203) 457-0415
Fax: (203) 457-0225
lzucchini@aol.com

CHAUCER HOUSE, Kent

OVERALL ★★★ | ROOM QUALITY ★★★★ | VALUE ★★★ | PRICE $100–150

The innkeeper, realized a longtime dream when she took over this already pleasant white clapboard. She has added new guest rooms and decorated all in markedly different styles, with more flair than in years previous. Breakfasts are especially original, with delectables such as eggnog French toast. Kent is a center of shopping for art and antiques, an easy walk from here, yet the bed-and-breakfast is just far enough away from the weekend crowds to allow for peaceful sleep. Inquire far in advance; the site is often booked two years in advance for events at the Kent School—a pilgrimage, so to speak.

SETTING & FACILITIES

Location Follow Rt. 7 into Kent; B&B on main street
Near Walk to antiquing, Housatonic River, historic sites, Kent Falls State Park, Mohawk Mountain ski area, priv./boarding schools, winery, 35 mi. to Danbury
Building 1948 clapboard Colonial; recently remodeled
Grounds 3 acres, Summer gardens, old maples
Public Space Entry, formal DR, library

Food & Drink Full formal breakfast; specialties: eggnog French toast, corn pancakes with crème fraîche and smoked salmon; refreshments, wine and cheese
Recreation Antiquing, waterfall, golf, tennis, water sports, horseback riding, skiing
Amenities & Services Phone, voicemail, dataports, snowshoes, bicycles, car rental

ACCOMMODATIONS

Units 5 guest rooms
All Rooms Bath, fresh flowers, alarm clock, TV, AC
Some Rooms Antiques
Bed & Bath 1 high four-poster, bed sizes vary; robes provided

Favorites Garden Room—Rose wallpaper, white wicker
Comfort & Decor Rooms currently redecorating American country, English hunt classic, and Federal

RATES, RESERVATIONS, & RESTRICTIONS

Deposit Credit card holds reservation; refund w/ 7-day notice, 10-day notice for holiday weekends, 30-day for groups and grad./school event weekends
Discounts 3rd person, subject to availability; singles
Credit Cards V, AE, DC, MC, D
Check-In/Out 4/10:30
Smoking No
Pets No

Kids Over 10
Minimum Stay Subject to availability—check
Open All year
Hosts Mary and James Redrupp
88 North Main St.
Kent, CT 06757-0826
(860) 927-4858
Fax: (860) 927-5399
www.home.att.net/~chaucerbb

ROSEWOOD MEADOW, Kent

OVERALL ★★★ | ROOM QUALITY ★★★ | VALUE ★★★½ | PRICE $85–105

Accommodations are minimal in this popular town, and while a modest place like this may not be outstanding in a town like Camden, Maine, or Woodstock, Vermont—filled with good properties—here it can be noted. You can picnic over at Kent Falls State Park, visit the dozens of antiques shops and galleries, and peruse the collection of Early American tools at the Sloane-Stanley Museum. Sit by the stream on the grass and have afternoon tea. All civilized and pleasurable. And can you guess what Rosenbaum, the innkeepers' surname, means in German?

SETTING & FACILITIES

Location Rt. 7 to Kent, B&B is 2.5 mi. north of the center of Kent
Near Kent Falls State Park, quaint Kent Village
Building 1860 white clapboard home Colonial with Greek Revival touches
Grounds 2 acres, stream, barn, terrace, rose and perennial gardens
Public Space Den, LR, FR, DR
Food & Drink Full breakfast until 11; tea
Recreation Hiking/walking trails, waterfalls, antiquing, restaurants
Amenities & Services Gift shop

ACCOMMODATIONS

Units 2 guest rooms, cottage apt.
All Rooms Bath, sitting room, decorative fireplace
Some Rooms Cottage suite dining area and kitchen facilities, priv. entrance, breezeway porch, TV
Bed & Bath Double sizes, add'l beds avail., firm mattresses
Favorites Rose Room—curved priv. staircase to pretty room w/ fireplace, priv. bath, sitting room
Comfort & Decor Guest rooms feature hand-stenciling, Colonial painted trim. Nicely restored original floors softened w/ country needlepoint-style area rugs. Pretty artwork, some nice antiques. Some country-homey kitsch. Decorative fireplaces. One-BR cottage attached to main house; easy access for breakfast, amenities.

RATES, RESERVATIONS, & RESTRICTIONS

Deposit 50%
Discounts Long-term stays, seniors, AAA, groups
Credit Cards V, AE, MC; traveler check, cash
Check-In/Out 2/11
Smoking No
Pets No
Kids 10 and up
Minimum Stay 2 nights weekends
Open All year
Hosts Pat and Karl Rosenbaum
230 Kent Cornwall Rd.
Kent, CT 06757
(800) 600-4334 or (860) 927-4334
rosewoodmeadowb.b@snet,net
www.rosewoodmeadow.com

TOLL GATE HILL, Litchfield

OVERALL ★★★★ | ROOM QUALITY ★★★★ | VALUE ★★½ | PRICE $100–200

History, history. This famed inn, three barn-red buildings, is on the National Register of Historic Places. It originally welcomed wayfarers as a stagecoach way station, hence its name. The house moved to its present site in 1923. The Tapping Reeve House and Law School and Oliver Wolcott Library, one of the first law schools in the colonies, are a part of the picture-perfect scene. The two-story ballroom with beamed ceilings has a tiny fiddler's loft, which houses dinner musicians; there's jazz on Sundays. Fireplaces glow, floorboards creak, and the food is fusion.

SETTING & FACILITIES

Location Rt. 202, 2.5 mi. W of Litchfield Village

Near Conservation center, Bantam Lake, art galleries, museums, crafts shops and boutiques, performing arts, Bantam art films cinema, state parks, Housatonic River

Grounds 10 acres, lawns, patios, trails, woods

Public Space Lobby; restaurant incl. formal DRs

Food & Drink Cont'l breakfast; lunch and dinner daily in restaurant; bar/lounge, tavern-style; new American cuisine; Fri. dinner and Sun. brunch buffets (kids

Building Gambrel-roofed Colonial; converted schoolhouse; The Captain William Bull Tavern (ca. 1745)

under 6 eat free); restaurant closed in winter, Tues., Wed.

Recreation Antiquing, lake and river activities, picnicking, bird watching, skiing

Amenities & Services Cribs, cots, baby-sitting; meetings, weddings, etc. (125)

ACCOMMODATIONS

Units 15 guest rooms, 5 suites, long-term apt. avail.

All Rooms Bath, phone, TV, AC

Some Rooms Fireplace, deck, sitting area, VCR, mini-bar, refrigerator

Bed & Bath Some canopy beds; queen, double, twin; 2 shower-only baths

Favorites Room 2—mid-priced room in

1745 building, sitting area, fireplace, double canopy

Comfort & Decor Family style. Warm colors. Lots of lighting, ottomans, comfy seating. Mid-to-quality reproduction furnishings, sturdy, attractive. Dressed up w/ fresh, contemporary/country fabrics.

RATES, RESERVATIONS, & RESTRICTIONS

Deposit 1 night; restaurant/lodging credit w/ 10-day notice

Discounts Corp., 3rd person, kids

Credit Cards V, AE, DC, MC, D

Check-In/Out 1/11

Smoking Restricted, notice to inn

Pets Welcome, $10 add'l charge

Kids Welcome

Minimum Stay 2 nights weekends,

holidays

Open All year

Host Fritz Zivic

Box 1339, Route 202 & Tollgate Rd.

Litchfield, CT 06759

(800) 445-3903 or (860) 567-4545

Fax: (860) 567-8397

www.litchfieldct.com/dng/tollgate

ROGER SHERMAN INN, New Canaan

OVERALL ★★★½ | ROOM QUALITY ★★★★ | VALUE ★½ | PRICE $100–350

Roger Sherman, this 18th-century home's namesake, was a Connecticut delegate to the Continental Congress, and the only person to sign all four documents: The Association (1774), Declaration of Independence (1776), Articles of Confederation (1777), and the Constitution (1787). Continental breakfast (no Congress) is amidst salmon-colored walls, ivy stenciling, and Tiffany "ivy" glass. Groups and the public can overrun the house at later meals, but the inn's most formal dining space out of five choices has a few candlelit tables. Alsatian handpainted wallpaper depicts American war scenes; the only similar example is in Washington, D.C.—in the White House.

SETTING & FACILITIES

Location From I-684 take Rt. 35 E to Rt. 124 S; Inn approximately 12 mi. farther on right; 10 min. walk to village
Near Nature center, Norwalk, aquarium, quaint shopping, IMAX Theatre, Stamford, 1 hour to NYC
Building 1783 gabled white Colonial
Grounds Gardens, mature trees
Public Space Bar/lounge, 5 dining areas
Food & Drink Cont'l breakfast; lunch, dinner, Sun. brunch, wine cellar, liquor license, contemp./cont'l menu, Swiss specialties; open 7 days except Mon. lunch; Terrace Room—most formal DR; Hunt Room; summer cocktails on porch, seasonal outdoor dining
Recreation Maple sugar shack, 40 mi. of hiking trails; lounge piano entertainment weekend evenings; lake boating in Norwalk
Amenities & Services Irons, hairdryers, crib. Guest laundry and dry cleaning; functions (175), in 6 connected banquet rooms

ACCOMMODATIONS

Units 16 guest rooms, 1 2-BR suite; main house and carriage house
All Rooms Bath, mini-bar, phone/dataport, seating, TV
Some Rooms Balcony, decorative fireplace, sitting area, writing desk, VCR
Bed & Bath Some sleigh, brass beds; bath sizes vary
Favorites Room 24 (Fruit Room)— open, airy, light; Bridal Suite—queen carved bed, shutters
Comfort & Decor Classifications standard (smallest), superior, deluxe, junior suites, 2-BR suite. Reliable hotel-style furnishings and comfort. Early American ambiance. Quieter carriage house rooms w/ Hitchcock reproduction Colonial pieces. Some TVs in armoires. Attractive, individually styled rooms w/ themes. Junior suites w/ balconies.

RATES, RESERVATIONS, & RESTRICTIONS

Deposit Credit card holds reservation; refund w/ 48-hour notice
Discounts Singles, 3rd person, some corp., infants free
Credit Cards V, AE, MC, DC
Check-In/Out 2/11
Smoking Restricted to smoking lounge, outdoors
Pets No
Kids Welcome

Open All year except for some major holidays, Christmas Day; check
Hosts Thomas and Kay Weilenmann
195 Oenoke Ridge, Route 124
New Canaan, CT 06840
(203) 966-4541
Fax: (203) 966-0503
info@rogershermaninn.com
www.rogershermaninn.com

THREE CHIMNEYS INN, New Haven

OVERALL ★★★½ | ROOM QUALITY ★★★★ | VALUE ★★ | PRICE $190

Yale is a five-minute walk away from this Victorian bed-and-breakfast, nicknamed "The Lady" for its ornate, painted facade. Sitting somewhat timidly behind an iron fence, it languished until the innkeepers (who own a sister Three Chimneys Inn in Durham, New Hampshire) took over in 1996, refurbishing the spacious guest rooms, adding air conditioning, dataports, desks, TVs, and conference rooms. Now it is popular with Yalies, small groups, and those who prefer mounted hunt trophies and oak millwork dating from the Tall Ships era. It is the best, and one of the only, bed-and-breakfasts around this cultural mecca. Chain accommodations are your other options if you go astray.

SETTING & FACILITIES

Location From I-95 E to downtown New Haven Exit 47, proceed to N Frontage Rd., corner of Yale St.; turn right onto York, left at 3rd traffic light onto Chapel St.; B&B 1.5 blocks on right
Near 1 block from Yale, theater, shopping district; 1 hour to casinos, 30 mi. to Hartford
Building 1870 Painted Lady Victorian
Grounds Small landscaped property w/ brick carriage house

Public Space Entry hall, dbl. parlor
Food & Drink Full breakfast, communal or separate; refreshments; catering avail. for functions
Recreation Local special events, school functions, dining, performing arts, day trips
Amenities & Services Extra beds/cots, honor bar, disabled access; concierge, laundry/dry cleaning, fax/copy services, 2 conf. facil.

ACCOMMODATIONS

Units 10 guest rooms

All Rooms Bath, dataport, 2-line phone, desk, TV, AC

Some Rooms Ornamental mantel, sofa bed

Bed & Bath Four-poster and canopy beds, queen and king; heaters

Favorites Room 22—Dramatic teal walls, celebrity photos, full 1920s outfits

decorating walls, king four-poster

Comfort & Decor Rooms tend toward masculine, club-room decor. Decorated around different themes. Elegant fabrics, Oriental rugs, Edwardian bed drapes. Rich Federal wall colors. Special pieces, handcrafted armoires, club or reading chairs, rockers, Georgian furnishings.

RATES, RESERVATIONS, & RESTRICTIONS

Deposit 1 night; refund w/ 7-day notice; payment in full for holidays, local special events, and graduations; extended cancellation policies apply

Discounts Corp., 3rd person

Credit Cards V, AE, MC, D

Check-In/Out 3/11

Smoking No

Pets No; staff will assist in alternate pet accommodations

Kids Over 6

No-No's B&B will not guarantee specific room or bed type

Minimum Stay 2 nights, holidays, local special or school events; 3 nights for graduations

Open All year except Christmas

Hosts Jane and Ron Peterson; Michael A. Marra, Innkeeper

1201 Chapel St.

New Haven, CT 06511

(800) 443-1554 or (203) 789-1201

Fax: (203) 776-7363

chimneysnh@aol.com

www.threechimneysinn.com

HOMESTEAD INN, New Milford

OVERALL ★★★ | ROOM QUALITY ★★ | VALUE ★★★ | PRICE $85–128

Don't confuse this basic, economical bed-and-breakfast with the luxurious same-named inn in Greenwich. Low rates in an otherwise pricey area are the major plus here. Desks and good lighting in each room are a boon to laptop toters, and phones and air-conditioning are other nononsense bonuses. Skip the motel-like rooms in the Treadwell House section, a former restaurant space that is undistinguished. Stick to the main house, where you can play the piano by the fireplace and retire upstairs to get to work.

SETTING & FACILITIES

Location Rt. 7 to New Milford, Rt. 202, turn left at 3rd traffic light onto Village Green (Main St.), 3 blocks to end of Green, right onto Elm St., B&B on left

Near Village Green, shops, restaurants; state parks, New Preston, Lake Waramaug

Building 1850 Victorian farmhouse; Treadwell House, former restaurant
Grounds Small, perennial gardens, historic area
Public Space Lobby, large LR
Food & Drink Cont'l breakfast buffet; refreshments
Recreation Golf, skiing; theater, concerts; antiquing, craft/specialty shops
Amenities & Services Fridge, hairdryers; roll-aways, cribs

ACCOMMODATIONS

Units 8 guest rooms in main house; 6 in Treadwell House
All Rooms Bath, TV, phone and dataport, desk, AC
Some Rooms Add'l bed, bay window, tin ceiling (1)
Bed & Bath Some four-posters, bed sizes vary; some shower-only; non-allergenic bedding
Favorites Rooms 24 and 25—Bay window
Comfort & Decor Comfortable but basic, Country antiques and reproductions. Waverly/Schumacher coordinates. Good setup for business travelers.

RATES, RESERVATIONS, & RESTRICTIONS

Deposit 1 night, credited to last night's stay; refund w/ 48-hour notice
Discounts Kids under 12, singles
Credit Cards V, AE, DC, MC, D
Check-In/Out 2/11
Smoking No
Pets No
Kids Welcome over 12, w/ $6 charge
Minimum Stay 2 nights holidays, May–Oct. weekends
Open All year
Hosts Rolf and Peggy Hammer
5 Elm St.
New Milford, CT 06776
(860) 354-4080
Fax: (860) 354-7046
www.homesteadct.com

THE BOULDERS INN, New Preston

OVERALL ★★★★½ | ROOM QUALITY ★★★★★ | VALUE ★½ | PRICE $210–380

Named for the boulders incorporated into the building, the inn makes the most of nature, with lake views shimmering through expanses of glass. The best all-around active getaway closest to the Big Apple, this casually elegant inn deserves its stellar reputation for stylish comfort, with Northern California laid-back outdoorsy decor and European flair. It feels like a high-end camp for groups, sophisticates, and romantics who frolic lakeside, climb the mountain, maybe snap up an eighteenth-century vase or two in the pretty village, and feast on sesame-crusted sushi-grade tuna with wasabi whipped potatoes in the octagonal dining room, before climbing into the four-poster beds. Beats bunks and Kool-aid.

SETTING & FACILITIES

Location Rt. 202 to New Preston; Rt. 45 towards lake to Inn; at foot of Berkshire Hills Pinnacle Mountain overlooking Lake Waramaug

Near State parks, shopping, public golf course, 18th-century villages

Building 1895 gambrel-roofed Victorian summer cottage; stone porch and chimney

Grounds Waterfront and boathouse, barn, guest cottages

Public Space LR; TV room, game room; octagonal DR

Food & Drink Full breakfast; creative New American dinners (add'l cost); award-winning wine list; full bar

Recreation Bird watching, golf, horses, restaurants, water/winter sports

Amenities & Services Priv. lake beach, sailboats, canoes, paddleboats, rowboats for guest use; trail, bicycles; special requests, gift cert.; weddings, conferences, retreats

ACCOMMODATIONS

Units 3 guest rooms, 3 suites in main house; 3 guest rooms in carriage house; 8 duplex cottage suites

All Rooms Bath, antiques

Some Rooms Fireplace/wood stove, view, sitting area, deck/balcony, whirlpool, refrigerator, coffee maker, AC

Bed & Bath Four-poster, canopy, sleigh beds; cottage baths slightly more luxurious, larger; 1 single whirlpool, 4 dbl. whirlpools; some shower-only

Favorites Main House, Northwest

Suite—lake views, sitting area, king poster bed, full bath; Fieldstone Cottage—spacious, great views, priv. deck, fireplace, dbl. whirlpool; Carriage House Room C2—cozy, double sleigh bed, comfy sitting area, stone fireplace

Comfort & Decor Main house antiques and finer country pieces. Charming guest cottages country decor. Quilts, fireplaces. Cozy carriage house rooms French and period pieces. Cobble Cottage suites add'l beds/rooms.

RATES, RESERVATIONS, & RESTRICTIONS

Deposit 1 night; 50% longer stay; full payment holiday weekends; refund w/ 14-day notice (surcharge added to price holiday weekends in high season; 15% gratuity added w/ taxes)

Discounts Singles

Credit Cards V, AE, MC

Check-In/Out 3/12

Smoking None in main inn; restricted elsewhere

Pets No

Kids By special arrangement

Minimum Stay 2 nights weekends; 3 nights holidays; check w/ inn for availability

Open May 1–Nov., and weekends all year

Hosts Kees and Ulla Adema
East Shore Rd. (Route 45), Box 2575
New Preston, CT 06777-0565
(800) 55-BOULD or (860) 868-0541
Fax: (860) 868-1925
boulders@bouldersinn.com
www.bouldersinn.com

LAKEVIEW INN, New Preston

OVERALL ★★★½ | ROOM QUALITY ★★★★ | VALUE ★½ | PRICE $175–350

Lakeview Inn was the original name of the summer lodgings on this site over 100 years ago; the hip, young owners found the original sign during renovation. Most of the tasteful public space goes to the contemporary, lakeview restaurant, complete with a star chef—and a bit of attitude brought from NYC. Fine dining and hubbub last until late evening. This largely reconstructed inn is still evolving, with plans for major expansion. For now, best to enjoy the warmth and activities at The Boulders across the lake, and come here for a lunch. *Note:* There is a possibility that this inn will become a private residence.

SETTING & FACILITIES

Location From center of New Preston, take Rt. 45 to stop sign (lake on left), straight to 1st left, North Shore Rd., look for inn signs
Near Lake Waramaug, beach, winery, ski area, Kent Falls State Park, XC skiing
Building Turn-of-the-century clapboard, previously Inn at Lake Waramaug
Grounds Veranda; cocktail terrace; mahogany deck; ongoing projects incl. French gardens, apple orchard, herb gardens
Public Space Foyer, library, garden room, main dining area, small priv. DR,

smoking room, bar/lounge
Food & Drink Cont'l breakfast buffet, communal or separate; lunch, dinner avail. 5–6 days/week; open most of year; American cuisine; specialties: free-range chicken, organic salads, Maine lobster, smoked salmon
Recreation Antiquing, moderate and advanced climbing and biking, state park boating, fly-fishing, skiing
Amenities & Services Child play area visible from DR; games in smoking room; videos; some office support

ACCOMMODATIONS

Units 3 guest rooms, 2 suites
All Rooms Bath, sitting area, TVs/VCR
Some Rooms View, kitchen, honor bar
Bed & Bath Antique beds; full baths, some soaking tubs
Favorites Scandinavian suite—king country pine, sitting room, wet bar w/

kitchen amenities
Comfort & Decor Muted, stylish, rich colors in Burgundian Suite. Country themes. Reproduction furnishings. Smallish. Front rooms have noise from popular DR.

RATES, RESERVATIONS, & RESTRICTIONS

Deposit 1 night or 50%; refund w/ 14-day notice
Discounts 3rd person; check w/ inn
Credit Cards V, AE, MC, DC

Check-In/Out 3/11:30; flexible w/ notice
Smoking Restricted
Pets No

Kids Over 12; check for younger kids	107 North Shore Rd.
Minimum Stay 2 nights weekends; 3 nights holiday weekends	New Preston, CT 06777
	(860) 868-1000
Open All year	Fax: (860) 868-2595
Hosts Dorothy and Douglas Hamilton	www.thelakeviewinn.com

ANGEL HILL, Norfolk

OVERALL ★★★★ | ROOM QUALITY ★★★★★ | VALUE ★★½ | PRICE $150–185

Feminine, gentle, caring: Mozart and mimosas, white drapes wrapped in flowers, tented ceilings, a periwinkle clapboard carriage house with a plum front door. Valentine's Day is the all-year favorite here, and no wonder. These giving innkeepers delight in surprising guests with breakfast in their room, sweets, or sweet things. And spontaneously, Donna says, "Guests leave little angels all the time." Beds and breakfasts are dreamy, and although cherubs and florals and purple tones won't appeal to all, true romantics just might find this delicate environment touched by an angel.

SETTING & FACILITIES

Location On Rt. 44, just up the hill from town green, on right side of road in historic residential neighborhood
Near Norfolk Chamber Music Festival, Yale Summer School of Music, state parks; Hillside Gardens, 5 acres of display gardens; Campbell waterfalls, Haystack Mountain Towers, antiquing villages, Berkshires, Lime Rock, rivers
Building 1880 Colonial/Victorian; carriage house
Grounds 3 acres lawns, gazebo; 8 acres gardens, woodlands, brook
Public Space Foyer, LR, DR, library, breakfast sun porch, lounging porch
Food & Drink Full breakfast; specialties: gingerbread waffles w/ Chantilly cream, glazed apples and sausage, edible flowers and herbs; refreshments; carriage house guests invited weekends

Recreation Touring, shopping, summer festivals, covered bridges, vineyards, water sports, golf, Grand Prix racing, XC skiing
Amenities & Services Lawn games, refrigerator, garage space for show cars; arrangements for carriage rides, massage therapy, gift baskets, flowers; beach towels, picnic baskets, breakfast in bed

ACCOMMODATIONS

Units 2 rooms, 2 suites, I carriage house apt.
All Rooms Bath, stereo, breakfast table
Some Rooms Fireplace, desk, TV/VCR, reading chair/daybed; whirlpool, AC, thermostat; carriage house kitchen w/ gas stove
Bed & Bath Queen, king/twin canopies; robes, full baths, I hall access
Favorites Orchard View Room—fireplace, wrought-iron four-poster; Carriage House—treehouse retreat, queen canopy, handpainted clouds, vines, flowers
Comfort & Decor Dramatic beds, decor. Suites with sitting room/dressing room. Victorian Cottage Suite dbl. whirlpool, hall access bath. Some baths could be updated.

RATES, RESERVATIONS, & RESTRICTIONS

Deposit 50%; refund with 10-day notice
Discounts Weekdays, 2+ nights; 3rd person, off-season, weekly (Carr. House)
Check-In/Out 3–8/noon
Smoking No
Pets No
Kids Depends; check
Minimum Stay 2 nights weekends, 3 holidays. Carr. House 2 nights
Open All year
Host Donna Beryle Bierbower
54 Greenwoods Rd. East, Box 504
Norfolk, CT 06058
(860) 542-5920
Fax: (860) 542-5055
dgritman@snet.net
www.angelhill.com

MANOR HOUSE, Norfolk

OVERALL ★★★★ | ROOM QUALITY ★★★★★ | VALUE ★★½ | PRICE $125–250

Staying at this Tudor mansion feels like being in Olde England, perhaps because the original owner was the American who designed Spofford Line of the London subway system. The huge entrance gleams with cherry wood, and the 6-foot stone fireplace with flag-bearing herald reinforces the British atmosphere. Tiffany windows, high ceilings, carved arches, decorative Victorian clothing, and extensive flower gardens add interest. Beekeeper/gardener/chef Hank gives cooking demonstrations, and Diane radiates enthusiasm. The outdoor music festival in this pretty town is sublime. So is returning, perhaps by horse and carriage, to a late-night whirlpool bath under a starry skylight.

SETTING & FACILITIES

Location Rt. 44 onto Maple Ave.; B&B between Terrace View and Laurel Way, before Maple Ave. becomes Lover's Lane
Near Walk to Village, Yale chamber music concerts, Hillside Garden consultants, state parks, ski trails, Housatonic River, 20 mi. to Tanglewood
Building 1898 Victorian Tudor estate mansion; renovated 1997
Grounds 5.5 acres; gardens, walking paths, gazebo
Public Space Entrance hall, LR, sun porch, library
Food & Drink Full communal breakfast; specialties: orange waffles, poached eggs w/ lemon-butter-chive sauce, honey from B&B hives; refreshments avail.; BYOB; microwave
Recreation Lime Rock car racing, water sports, vineyards, Christmas sleigh rides, carriage tours, antiquing, cultural events
Amenities & Services Refrigerator; lake passes, books, massage therapist avail.; wedding, priv. party, corp. facil.

ACCOMMODATIONS

Units 9 standard guest rooms, 1 single
All Rooms Bath, antiques, seating, good lighting, ceiling fans
Some Rooms Fireplace, balcony, whirlpool/soaking tub
Bed & Bath Antique, brass, or illusion canopy beds, queen, king/twin, some daybeds; most, showers only; some dbl. whirlpools and soaking tubs
Favorites Victorian—dbl. whirlpool, gas fireplace, king
Comfort & Decor Rooms vary from ultra-luxurious to standard. Unusual artwork. Period wallcoverings. Sumptuous.

RATES, RESERVATIONS, & RESTRICTIONS

Deposit 50%; refund w/ 10-day notice
Discounts Promos/packages, singles, 3rd person, midweek AAA/gov't./corp.
Credit Cards V, AE, MC
Check-In/Out 3/11:30
Smoking No
Pets No
Kids Over 12
No-No's Kids on weekends
Minimum Stay 2 days weekends; 3 days holidays
Open All year
Hosts Diane and Henry Tremblay
69 Maple Avenue
Norfolk, CT 06058
(860) 542-5690
Fax: (860) 542-5690
tremblay@esslink.com
www.manorhouse-norfolk.com

SILVERMINE TAVERN, Norwalk

OVERALL ★★★½ | ROOM QUALITY ★★★ | VALUE ★★½ | PRICE $110–180

Originally, women in this old crossroads town were not allowed near the bar, and the humorous host has Abigail positioned within the danger zone: a period-dressed mannequin, sporting a red cloak in winter and a print frock in warmer weather, with glass in hand. A river runs by the door and branches into a tavern mill pond, which has ducks, a waterfall, and a spacious deck above, with trees growing through it. Traditional New England cuisine is served in a dining room crammed with over 1,000 old tools and gadgets and an 1887 jukebox. A country-store annex offers old oil paintings and gadgets.

SETTING & FACILITIES

Location I-95N/S to Exit 15, follow Rt. 7N to Exit 2, right at ramp end, 2nd light turn right, right again onto Silvermine, 2nd stop sign bear right, 1.5 mi. to tavern; on mill pond/waterfall
Near Silvermine Art Guild and Gallery, Silvermine River, Norwalk shopping, aquarium; 5 mi. to NYC commuter, nature center; 30 min. to Danbury
Building 1785 many-chimneyed Colonial, Jeffersonian pillared portico; restored 1998
Grounds Summer gardens, water, brick walkway

Public Space 2 spacious parlors
Food & Drink Cont'l breakfast; specialty: famous honey buns; bar/lounge; DR w/ fireplace, serving lunch and dinner, seasonal outdoor dining overlooking Mill Pond; specialties: osso bucco, Seafood Capellini, New England chicken pot pie
Recreation Boating, fishing, antiquing, day trips to Manhattan, live jazz on weekends
Amenities & Services Express checkout, phone, roll-aways; gift shop, collectibles, closed in winter; weddings, meetings, parties

ACCOMMODATIONS

Units 10 guest rooms, 1 suite
All Rooms Bath, seating, desk, reading lighting, clock radio, AC
Some Rooms Sitting area, porch
Bed & Bath Some bow-top Colonial canopy, antique beds, 2 queen rooms, 2 twin rooms, 7 double bed rooms; some antique soaking tubs

Favorites Room T-2—Fairly spacious, double canopy bed, priv. porch, full bath
Comfort & Decor Old-fashioned floral wallcoverings and fabrics, some quilts. Country colonial style. Antique and quality reproduction furnishings. Hardwood floors w/ country area rugs. Suite sitting room, kitchenette, priv. deck on river

RATES, RESERVATIONS, & RESTRICTIONS

Deposit 1 night; refund w/ 24-hour notice weekdays, 72-hour notice on weekends

Discounts Corp. midweek, singles
Credit Cards V, AE, DC, MC, CB
Check-In/Out 4/11

Smoking Restricted
Pets In annex w/ prior arrangement
Kids Welcome
Open All year, except Tuesdays
Hosts Frank and Marsha Whitman, Jr.
194 Perry Avenue

Norwalk, CT 06850-1100
(203) 847-4558
(888) 693-9967
Fax: (203) 847-9171
www.hotel-intl.com

THE ELMS INN, Ridgefield

OVERALL ★★★½ | ROOM QUALITY ★★★★ | VALUE ★★ | PRICE $150–210

Built by master cabinetmaker Amos Seymour on the site of the Colonial
Battle of Ridgefield, this former farmhouse became an inn in 1799. Today,
highwaymen no longer come by horse or coach; weekenders from New
York City arrive on Amtrak or by BMW, in casual-Friday dress, lured by the
reputation of the restaurant. Dishes such as braised rabbit ravioli are typical
of the original takes on standard items, served charmingly in a stenciled
dining room. Guest rooms have also been refurbished, with some canopied
beds and four-posters, but the lodgings take a second to the food.

SETTING & FACILITIES

Location Rt. 35 to center of Ridgefield;
inn on main street in center of quaint village
Near Norwalk, aquarium, museums,
historic homes, nature center, golf
course, 45 min. to Stamford, IMAX
Theatre
Building 1760 Colonial farmhouse
Grounds Village yard, flower gardens,
patio
Public Space Entry hall, sitting room
Food & Drink Cont'l breakfast; separate restaurant serving lunch, dinner;
informal tavern menu after 11:30 a.m.;

specialties: clam and corn chowder,
grilled tenderloin, bangers and mash.
Formal DRs open for lunch and dinner;
creative American cuisine; specialties:
seafood stew, venison, pheasant; need
reservations, closed Mon., Tues., and
Christmas
Recreation Hiking, touring, antiquing,
shopping
Amenities & Services Cribs, roll-
aways; long-term/corp. guest services;
meetings, functions; special bridal
packages

ACCOMMODATIONS

Units 16 guest rooms, 4 suites
All Rooms Bath, phone/dataport, TV, AC
Some Rooms Writing desk, sitting area
Bed & Bath Some four-poster, canopy,

brass; queen or 2 doubles; 1 shower-only,
recently remodeled
Favorites Hostess' Favorite Four-Poster
Room—Corner, quiet, sunny

Comfort & Decor Colonial decor. Some antiques; a few restored pieces date to orig. construction of house. Some rooms, add'l beds. Rooms over restaurant, noisiest; orig., older feeling w/ hardwood floors and area rugs, others carpet. Some TVs hidden in armoires.

RATES, RESERVATIONS, & RESTRICTIONS

Deposit 1 night incl. state tax; refund w/ 48-hour notice
Discounts Singles, long stays w/ advance full payment, 3rd person
Credit Cards V, AE, DC, MC, CB
Check-In/Out 3/noon
Smoking No
Pets No
Kids Welcome
Minimum Stay 2 nights weekends

Open All year
Hosts The Scala Family
500 Main St.
Ridgefield, CT 06877
(203) 438-2541; (203) 438-9206 restaurant
Fax same as phone, call first
innkeeper@elmsinn.com
www.elmsinn.com

UNDER MOUNTAIN INN, Salisbury

OVERALL ★★★★ | ROOM QUALITY ★★★★ | VALUE ★★ | PRICE $180–235

This established inn is on bucolic Route 41, across from a horse farm, and the British innkeepers offer a close-as-you-can-get British experience: Dickens, *The Manchester Guardian,* travel guides, British versions of Monopoly, 220 British videos, English ales, bangers and mash or Scottish salmon, and a real English tea service. The inn, shaded by huge old trees, is historic and handsome—the bar is paneled in antique king's wood and the entrance doors were solicited by the Metropolitan Museum of Art (but they remain as portals for you to enjoy).

SETTING & FACILITIES

Location From Salisbury town, 4 mi. N on Rt. 41; look for sign
Near Berkshire Theatre, choral/music festivals, Norman Rockwell Museum; ski resorts
Building 18th-century Colonial farmhouse
Grounds 3 acres, terrace, wild turkeys, front porch overlooks horse farm activities
Public Space Library, chess/checker

parlor, video lounge, pub DR
Food & Drink (MAP) Full English breakfast; tea and shortbread; dinner; specialty: steak & kidney pie; picnics, wine and spirits
Recreation Lake activities, golf, tennis, antiquing, sleigh rides, white-water rafting
Amenities & Services Refrigerator, mini-kitchen, limited disabled access, conferences (15)

ACCOMMODATIONS

Units 7 guest rooms

All Rooms Bath, seating, reading lighting, sherry decanters, AC

Some Rooms Mountain, horse farm, or lake views

Bed & Bath Canopy, brass, four-poster beds; 1 w/ dbl. soaking tub

Favorites Covent Garden—huge bath, soaking tub; Buckingham Gate—king canopy; Drury Lane—view of mountains from bed

Comfort & Decor Fabrics and wallcoverings coordinate. Wicker, antique rockers. Wide-plank floors w/ braided or Oriental rugs.

RATES, RESERVATIONS, & RESTRICTIONS

Deposit 1 night; refund w/ 14-day notice

Discounts Multiple night stays

Credit Cards V, MC

Check-In/Out 2/11

Smoking No

Pets No

Kids Over 6

No-No's BYOBs in common areas; early check-in

Minimum Stay 2 nights weekends; 3 nights holidays

Open All year

Hosts Marged and Peter Higginson
482 Undermountain Rd., Rt. 41
Salisbury, CT 06068
(860) 435-0242
Fax: (860) 435-2379
www.innbook.com

THE WHITE HART INN, *Salisbury*

OVERALL ★★★½ | ROOM QUALITY ★★★ | VALUE ★★ | PRICE $109–249

Edsel Ford (Henry Ford's son, who had a car named after him in the 1950s), bought this eighteenth-century inn when his son attended nearby Hotchkiss prep school. The inn hung on far longer than the car, but was in need of tune-up of its own. And happily, it's looking polished now, with a major detailing and overhaul. Car racers, including Paul Newman, flock to the area, and the pretty town has the oldest free public library in the country, so you'll have plenty to read. The staff is courteous, the new wing preferable, and although breakfast isn't included and the furnishings are reproductions, this place has the feel of a smaller property.

SETTING & FACILITIES

Location In the center of historic Salisbury, at the junction of Routes 41 and 44; N from the Merritt (Rt. 15), to Rt. 7

Near Appalachian Trail, lakes, mountains; golf courses, XC, downhill ski areas; historic homes; Lime Rock Race Track, Skip-Barber Advanced Driving School

Building 19th-century rambling white clapboard; inn since 1810

Grounds Lawn situated on village green, border gardens

Public Space Lobby, front porch, DRs, banquet room
Food & Drink No meals included in room rates; breakfast, lunch, and dinner served in 3 dining rooms—the Tap Room w/ fireplace, wainscoting paneling, old-style pub decor; Riga Room and the Garden Room, award-winning wine selection, American menu

Recreation Tap Room entertainment on Wed. evening; driving, racing and car club events/lessons; water sports; horseback riding; historic sites, art galleries, and museums; covered bridges; streams, waterfalls, trails; skiing
Amenities & Services Cribs, cots, refrigerators, VCRs, 24-hour front desk service; meetings, weddings, banquets

ACCOMMODATIONS

Units 23 guest rooms, 3 suites
All Rooms Bath, TV, phone, luggage rack, AC
Some Rooms Decorative fireplace, priv. porch, separate sitting area, add'l bed
Bed & Bath Some canopy, carved or four-poster; 1 hall access bath w/ robes
Favorite Ford Room decorative fire-

place, bow-top canopy bed
Comfort & Decor Waverly chintz floral fabrics and wallcoverings. Thomasville mahogany or Lane country-pine reproduction furnishings. Hotel-style reliability and comfort. Some smaller rooms, or rooms above restaurant may be less satisfactory.

RATES, RESERVATIONS, & RESTRICTIONS

Deposit 1 night; refund w/ 7-day notice
Discounts Senior midweek rates; child's cot, crib; corp. rates
Credit Cards V, AE, MC, D, CB
Check-in/Out 3/noon
Smoking Restricted
Pets Restricted, nominal fee
Kids Welcome
Minimum Stay 2 nights weekends April–Dec.; 3 nights holidays

Open All year
Host Scott Bok, General Manager Debra Erickson
The Village Green
Salisbury, CT 06068
(800) 832-0041 or (860) 435-0030
Fax: (860) 435-0040
the.whitehart@snet.net
www.whitehartinn.com

MAYFLOWER INN, Washington

OVERALL ★★★★★ | ROOM QUALITY ★★★★★ | VALUE ½ | PRICE $400–1300

Eleanor Roosevelt stayed here in 1933, and celebs still do. One of the Connecticut members of Relais & Chateaux, this sophisticated—if self-conscious—luxury inn, is really a small country hotel. Adriana and Robert are among the top art collectors in America and own a modern-art gallery in Manhattan. The pricey inn showcases their traditional pieces, flower arrangements feature orchids, everything is placed just-so, and food is described as "Asian-Californian-meets-New England." If you enjoy close-to-perfect atmosphere, you'll enjoy this Mayflower.

SETTING & FACILITIES

Location From Hartford take Rt. 84 W to Exit 15, Southbury; right onto Rt. 6 N, Woodbury; travel 5 mi., left onto Rt. 47 (Woodbury Rd.); Inn 8 mi. farther

Near New Preston, Kent, Woodbury, Sharon, Housatonic River

Building 1894 gambrel-roofed luxury mansion; outbuildings

Grounds 28 acres, streams, trails, Shakespearean and rose gardens, statuary

Public Space Entry hall, LR, library, game room, DR

Food & Drink À la carte breakfast only for guests (charge); lunch and dinner open to public; Tap Room, weekend piano entertainment, outdoor dining, gourmet American/Cont'l menu; excellent wine list, casual dress

Recreation Fly-fishing, golf, horseback riding, river boating, antiquing

Amenities & Services Omni tennis court, summer heated pool, gift shop; concierges, turn-down, 24-hour room service; spa facil. (massages, facials, paraffin treat., trainers, exercise classes and equip.); weddings; meetings in Tea House; new office/presentation equip.

ACCOMMODATIONS

Units 21 guest rooms, 8 suites in 3 buildings

All Rooms Bath, AC, desk, 2-line phone/dataport, voice mail, TV/VCR, mini-safe, mini honor bar/refrigerator, DMX satellite music, AC; fresh flowers, orchids

Some Rooms Fireplace, balcony; suites w/ sitting room w/ fireplace

Bed & Bath Canopy, carved, half-canopy beds, queen/king; spacious, luxury marble baths; dbl. vanity sinks, English deep-soak tubs, walk-in showers

Favorites Winslow Suite—most spacious; romantic fabrics, colors; king canopy bed, fireplace, balcony, 1.5 baths

Comfort & Decor Indiv. decorated, often redecorated. 18th- and 19th-century antiques, or quality reproductions. Collectibles from hosts' int'l travels. English, handcrafted beds. Tabriz rugs over plush carpet, Regency stripe wallcoverings. TVs, VCRs, and mini-bars hidden in armoires.

RATES, RESERVATIONS, & RESTRICTIONS

Deposit Credit card holds reservation; no charge w/ 21-day notice

Credit Cards V, AE, MC; cash, personal and company checks

Check-In/Out 3/1

Smoking Only in Tap Room; no pipe or cigar smoking

Pets No

Kids 12 and up

Minimum Stay 2 nights weekends; 3 nights holiday weekends

Open All year

Hosts Adriana and Robert Mnuchin
118 Woodbury Rd., Rt. 47
Washington, CT 06793
(860) 868-9466
Fax: (860) 868-1497
inn@mayflowerinn.com
www.mayflowerinn.com

HILLTOP HAVEN, West Cornwall

OVERALL ★★★½ | ROOM QUALITY ★★★ | VALUE ★★½ | PRICE $145

From the tree-rimmed terrace at this unique little bed-and-breakfast atop Dibble Hill you can see, on a clear day, if not forever at least the Housatonic River below to the Catskills in New York, some 75 miles away. Guest rooms are basic, the stone library, cluttered and terrific. Since quarters are small, it's ideal for couples or families to reserve both main guest rooms. Everett lives on the property in a separate cabin and is known for his charming eccentricities and off-beat breakfasts. Character is rare, so this unusual lodging by the Appalachian Trail, perched above a picture-book village, is a special joy. As Everett remarks, "Everyone seems to want to come here."

SETTING & FACILITIES

Location Berkshire foothills; Rt. 7 to Rt. 128 (W. Cornwall), turn right to covered bridge into commercial district, call innkeeper
Near Kent, Bantam, Hillside Garden Center, Appalachian Trail, state parks, Hill-Stead Museum, covered bridge, Oct. Scottish Festival, Mohawk Ski Area; Cooking School—The Silo
Building 1930 hilltop retreat, cottage-style
Grounds 63 mountainous, forested acres 800 feet above Housatonic River; terrace, great views
Public Space Stone library, veranda, reading room, music room
Food & Drink Full or cont'l breakfast, as requested; breakfast specialties: Grand Marnier French toast, Strata with crème brûlée; evening sherry
Recreation Sharon Audubon Center, gift shop; river activities (outfitters/guides avail.); clay court tennis, horses, golf, biking (rentals avail.)
Amenities & Services Access to lake beach for guests, breakfast requests

ACCOMMODATIONS

Units 2 guest rooms, main house; 1 cabin suite (3 mi. away)
All Rooms Bath, phone/ans. machine, AC, views
Bed & Bath Sleigh, brass doubles; small full baths
Favorites Sleigh Room—sleigh bed, woods view; Secluded Cabin—modest log cabin in midst of nature, hot tub, woodstove, double sofa bed
Comfort & Decor 2 main-house guest rooms, cozy. Warm, soft lighting. Eclectic furnishings, artwork. Seating and desks. Overall tone rustic, basic. Cottage truly secluded.

RATES, RESERVATIONS, & RESTRICTIONS

Deposit Full payment by personal check
Discounts Winter packages
Credit Cards None
Check-In/Out 430/noon

Smoking On terrace and screened-in porch only	**Hosts** Everett Van Dorn and Victoria Marks (Chef)
Pets No	175 Dibble Hill Rd.
Kids Over 14	West Cornwall, CT 06796
No-No's No walk-ins—reserv. required	(860) 672-6871
Minimum Stay 2 nights; 3 nights some summer holidays	Fax same as telephone, call first
	hilltophaven@hilltopbb.com
Open All year	www.hilltopbb.com

INN AT NATIONAL HALL, Westport

OVERALL ★★★★★ | ROOM QUALITY ★★★★★ | VALUE ★ | PRICE $285–850

The chilly looking, statuesque building was in previous incarnations a bank, shirt shop, newspaper office, and furniture store. After a total reconstruction, it reopened on its 100th birthday as one of New England's most luxurious inns, and a member of Relais & Chateaux. Fashioned after Europe's old, elite manor houses, it includes tromp l'oeil paintings on guest room walls and in the elevator, a second-floor lobby where you're greeted by name, and a charming formal staff with authentic European accents. Rooms are sumptuous, filled with fine antiques and artworks, and some have loft bedrooms. In March of 2001, the inn unveiled its Seville Suite. The restaurant is renowned. Prices are high, and there's not a stuffed animal around (even though one suite is named "Henny Penny").

SETTING & FACILITIES

Location West bank, Saugatuck River, only large red brick structure in downtown Westport; visible from Post Rd.
Near Local business district, commuter train to NYC, shops, local events, cultural activities, beach
Building Enormous riverfront 1873 building; restored cast-iron and red-brick facade
Grounds Small restaurant patio on river boardwalk, fountain
Public Space Reception area, board room, elevator, downstairs classic snooker table from England
Food & Drink Classic European Continental breakfast; a.m. room-service delivery; (Mediterranean cuisine, fine wine list); tea
Recreation River boardwalk, beach activities, antiquing, touring
Amenities & Services Soft drinks in room; cribs, roll-aways, list of baby-sitters, honor bar, videos/movie channels, nearby exercise facil, turn-down, meeting facil., dry cleaning; full concierge, room service

ACCOMMODATIONS

Units 8 guest rooms, 8 suites .

All Rooms Bath, refrigerator, TV/VCR, stereo, 2-line phone/dataport, mini-vault in closet, AC, soundproofing

Some Rooms Sitting area, desk, gas fireplace (1), hardwood floors, armoire custom-built kitchenette (1)

Bed & Bath Canopy or four-posters, mostly king, 3 queens, king/twin split; all full baths, most w/ sep. showers, 1 w/ whirlpool

Favorites Saugatuck River Suite—king canopy, river views, sep. sitting area; Turkistan Lost Suite— (once President Clinton's quarters) ornate four-poster, downstairs library w/ 2-story-high bookcases, enormous windows

Comfort & Decor All rooms spacious, decorated with rich silks, heavy cottons, gilded materials. Hand-painted murals. Imported English antiques, 19th-century quality reproductions. Many 18–20′ ceilings, 12′ windows. Elegant baths; four two-level suites. Equestrian Suite has fireplace, whirlpool, and kitchenette.

RATES, RESERVATIONS, & RESTRICTIONS

Deposit 1 night; refund w/ 7-day notice

Discounts Cribs free, roll-aways reduced, corp. rates

Credit Cards Euro-V, AE, DC, MC

Check-In/Out 3/11:30

Smoking No

Pets No

Kids Welcome

Minimum Stay 2 nights, high season weekends

Open All year

Hosts Greenfield Partners, Gen. Mgr.
Gary Bedell
Two Post Rd. West
Westport, CT 06880
(800) NAT-HALL or (203) 221-1351
Fax: (203) 221-0276
www.innatnationalhall.com

THE FRENCH BULLDOG BED & BREAKFAST AND ANTIQUES, Winstead

OVERALL ★★★½ | ROOM QUALITY ★★★ | VALUE ★★★½ | PRICE $75–150

The bad news: for now, you may have to share a bathroom. Lots of good news, though. This new bed-and-breakfast, and the village of Winstead—which received a $5.8 million grant—are both refurbishing. Tom, an actor on the soap "All My Children," travels for shoots and brings back collectibles. Talk TV, antiques, or travel with the hosts or just maintain your privacy. Victoriana abounds, with one of the oldest square pianos in the world, silk wallpaper, leaded-glass windows, flute background music, Ionic columns, a French Victorian etched-glass and gilt chandelier, period French phones, high teas and tea-leaf readings, and breakfast in the master suite by the piano. Good news wins.

SETTING & FACILITIES

Location Rt. 84 to Rt. 8 N at Waterbury; travel to Winstead, when road
becomes 2-lane, right onto Rt. 44; B&B is
3 blocks on left, across from Jessie's
Restaurant
Near Norfolk, Yale Summer Chamber
Music School, Jacob's Pillow, Tanglewood,
Hillside Garden consultants, state parks,
hiking/ski trails
Building 1895 Queen Anne Victorian,
26-room mansion; French Normandy carriage house; restoration in progress
Grounds English gardens on the banks
of Mad River, porches, summer cottage
seating

Public Space Entrance foyer, formal DR,
parlor
Food & Drink Full formal breakfast;
honeymooners in master suite, breakfast
in suite; refreshments
Recreation Lime Rock car racing, vineyards, Christmas sleigh rides, historic carriage tours, cultural activities, fishing,
boating, golf, shopping
Amenities & Services Period French
phones; guest kitchen, in-room refrigerator on req., antique/gift shop, historic
home tours in Norfolk. Setups for BYOB;
parties, meetings, fax, copier

ACCOMMODATIONS

Units 4 guest rooms, 1 suite; carriage
house luxury suite
All Rooms Antiques
Some Rooms Suite large, priv. bath; 2
add'l priv. baths coming soon, fireplace
Bed & Bath Four-poster, cannonball
beds, queen/full; 4 rooms now share 1 full
smallish bath and half bath, robes provided

Favorites Master Suite—fireplace, large
priv. bath w/dbl. whirlpool, priv. entrance
Comfort & Decor Chandeliers, original
maple flooring. Silk wallpapers, rich fabrics. Spacious rooms full of large antiques.
Antique or quality reproduction reading
lighting. Suite for families, business meetings.

RATES, RESERVATIONS, & RESTRICTIONS

Deposit 50%; refund w/ 2-day notice
Discounts Corp. midweek
Credit Cards None
Check-In/Out After 2/11 (or by
arrangement)
Smoking Porches
Pets No

Kids Check for availability
Minimum Stay Open All year
Hosts Celia and Tom McGowan
151 Main St.
Winstead, CT 06098
(860) 738-9335
Fax same as telephone

Eastern Connecticut

Beginning quietly in the state's northeastern corner next to Massachusetts, running south along the Rhode Island line to the bustling coastal areas surrounding historic **Mystic,** and west through **Connecticut's River Valley** and **National Heritage Corridor,** the eastern half of the state remains largely undeveloped, despite elaborate highway systems and some business and tourist congestion.

Southeastern Connecticut is a major draw. Tiny, charming **Stonington,** jutting into **Long Island Sound,** is one of the nation's oldest authentic fishing villages. **New London** with its submarine shipyards is activity packed, and the southeastern corner has two of the state's three major beaches—**Rocky Neck State Park** and **Ocean Beach Park.**

But **Mystic** is the tourist mecca, with its enormous aquarium, **Olde Mystic Village,** and the **Seaport,** which has the largest collection of old boats and ships in the world, including a replica of the famous 1839 *Amistad,* a 77-foot schooner used to transport kidnapped slaves from Africa. Nightlife and nearby casinos add to evening excitement.

A bit farther west to the midcoastline and inland river valley are the 365 **"Thimble Islands,"** the "beautiful sea rocks" to the Mattabec Indians. **Essex,** originally a ship-building center, has been ranked first in *The 100 Best Small Towns in America* guide. **Old Saybrook** is home to more than 400 antique dealers. Historic and quiet **Guilford,** with its sparkling lakes, is within commuter distance to downtown **New Haven** and is home to the popular **Guilford Handcraft Center.** Tiny **Madison** maintains a traditional New England village green and is near **Hammonasset Beach,** two miles of white sand on the sound. Quietly sophisticated **East Haddam** on the river, **Chester,** and **Ivoryton** are known for musical theatre, opera, and other performing arts, and have deserved reputations for fine dining.

The entire midcoast river section is dotted with nature centers and parks. Small and homey bed-and-breakfasts in this area are typically Victorian or early-American style, many showcasing restorations. There are some notable rustic exceptions worth a stay and several destination inns featuring restaurants and lodgings. A few larger facilities feature Colonial decor.

Not surprisingly, **Hartford** and its surrounding areas primarily serve the business traveler. But there's more: the **Wadsworth Atheneum** in **Hartford** (the first public art museum in America), the oldest statehouse in the nation, and the homes of **Harriet Beecher Stowe** and **Mark Twain.**

Simsbury, a short drive from Hartford's business district, has **The International Skating Center of Connecticut,** which sponsors Olympic-level exhibitions and is open for skating and lessons. The 165-foot, blue basalt tower in **Simsbury's Talcott Mountain State Park** affords a view of four states and the **Farmington River.** The mile hike to the tower is popular for hang gliders seeking a good launch. Also popular are performing and fine arts, children's activities, historic touring, shopping, and antiquing.

The northern central and corner areas of Connecticut's eastern zone are more rural. Newly opened in **Windsor** is a trail that follows the **Farmington River.** The **Lt. Walter Fyler House,** ca. 1640, is one of the oldest frame houses in America. Stop by **Woodstock** to visit **Roseland Cottage,** a former summer retreat for many presidents and still a Gothic-Victorian charmer.

The **New England Air Museum,** early homesteads and historic districts replete with restored antique New England residences, natural history museums, car racing and a Colonial prison are all here in Eastern Connecticut. Herb farms flourish, and the 3,000-acre agricultural and horticultural **University of Connecticut** is open to the public. Don't be dismayed by the small mill sites. The quiet corner blends rural development, deliberately cultivated nature preservation, and quiet industrial work.

FOR MORE INFORMATION

Connecticut River Valley & Shoreline
Visitors Council
(860) 347-0028 or (800) 486-3346
email: mail@cttourism.com
www.cttourism.org

Essex Village Tourism
email: essexinfo@aol.com
www.essexct.com

Farmington Valley Visitors Association
(800) 4-WELCOME
www.farmingtonvalleyvisit.com

Norwich Tourism (888) 4-NORWICH

New London Attractions & Tourism
(800) 510-SAND

North Central Tourism Bureau
(860) 763-2573 or (800) 248-8283
www.cnctb.org

Northeast Connecticut Visitors District
(860) 928-1228 or (888) 628-1228
email: quietcorner@snet.net
www.webtravels.com/quietcorner

Greater Hartford Tourism District
(860) 244-8181 or (800) 793-4480
www.enjoyhartford.com

Southeastern Tourism District
(860) 444-2206 or (800) TO-ENJOY
www.mysticmore.com

HEARTHSIDE FARM, Bozrah

OVERALL ★★★½ | ROOM QUALITY ★★★ | VALUE ★★★ | PRICE $100–150

The original farmhouse and outbuildings here are authentic American, plain and simple, with pewter pieces, tin candle lanterns, butter churns, and a spinning wheel. Reportedly the first electrified farm in New England, it lured amazed locals, as it glowed by means of a coal-driven generator. The Gagers arrived on *The Arbells,* sister ship to *The Mayflower,* and obtained the property by a 1600s land grant. John Gager helped start New London, Olde Saybrook, and Norwich. Look for the original hidden feature in the farmhouse great room, which made Mrs. Gager the envy of her 18th-century neighbors. Luise and Michael are the first non-Gager occupants in over 200 years, but as third-generation innkeepers they have a proud heritage of their own. *Note:* This inn may revert to a private residence.

SETTING & FACILITIES

Location Rural suburb of Norwich; easy access to farm, Rt. 2 E to Exit 23; straight from ramp for .4 mile, left onto Gager Rd.; B&B 1st driveway on right (look for gates).

Near Mystic, Thames River, baseball stadium, galleries, museums, outlets, flea market, covered bridge, historic homes, antiquing, casinos; New London Garde Art Center; Hartford

Building Circa 1793 Georgian Colonial farmhouse

Grounds 120 acres, state trout-stocked stream, wooded areas, patio overlooking horse paddock, outbuildings; trails connect to wildlife management area, protected state property

Public Space Keeping room, library/orig. buttery, great room

Food & Drink Early-riser beverages; weekday cont'l breakfast; full breakfast weekends; homemade breads

Recreation Fishing Weekend; winery tour weekends, planting and harvesting weekends, bird dog training weekends, hay rides; carriage/sleigh rides; touring, incl. old burial grounds

Amenities & Services Gift/antique shop, picnic table, gas grill, refrigerator stocked, in-room and portable guest phones; email/message pickup; fax, dry cleaning; small weddings

ACCOMMODATIONS

Units 3 guest rooms

All Rooms Alarm radio, window AC

Some Rooms Priv. baths, fireplace, wing-chair recliners

Bed & Bath Some four-poster beds, 2 queens, 1 room w/ 2 double beds; 2 w/

priv. hall-access baths, 1 room shares hall bath w/ innkeepers, robes

Favorites The Gager Room—Rumford fireplace, pencil-post bed, priv. hall-access bath

Comfort & Decor Rustic romance. Austere American antiques softened by rich woods, wreaths, local original folk art, flower garlands. New Concord Room, floral comforter and German antique collectibles, table for 2. Fairly spacious rooms.

RATES, RESERVATIONS, & RESTRICTIONS

Deposit Credit card holds reservation; no charge w/ 7-day notice
Discounts Midweek, corp., multiple nights; special events packages, incl. living Colonial history, open-hearth cooking, and beehive-oven baking workshops
Credit Cards V, MC, D
Check-In/Out 3/11
Smoking Outdoors only
Pets Outdoor lodgings avail. for dogs, horses w/ prior notice

Kids Over 8
Minimum Stay 2 nights holiday weekends
Open All year
Hosts Luise and Michael Ernest
15 Gager Rd.
Bozrah, CT 06334
(860) 887-4260
Fax same as phone
info@hearthsidefarm.com
www.hearthsidefarm.com

FRIENDSHIP VALLEY INN, Brooklyn

OVERALL ★★★½ | ROOM QUALITY ★★★★ | VALUE ★★½ | PRICE $120–150

Many trees grow in this Brooklyn area, named by Prudence Crandall, an 1830s Canterbury educator run out of town for teaching women of color in her academy. Abolitionist William Lloyd Garrison, the movement's founder, was married here, and a hidden basement entrance may be part of the Underground Railroad. The inn dates from 1708, the flag out front has 15 stars and stripes, and a dining room mantel is from the home of the founder of Cleveland, Ohio. The charming, Southern Beverly fills the historic house with music and books and indicates she would be pleased to be a guest in any of her understated, antique-filled rooms. So are we.

SETTING & FACILITIES

Location I-395 to Exit 91, travel 4 mi. on Rt. 6 W, right at intersection of 169, travel .25 mile to B&B on right, red oval sign; faces Rt. 169, recently designated 1 of only 14 national scenic byways.
Near Hist. center of hamlet; Putnam antique village, art galleries, fine dining, state parks; Providence, Mystic; Newport,

Hartford
Building 1740–1795 Georgian-style Colonial
Grounds 12 wooded, wetland acres, stone walls
Public Space Entry hall, parlors, library, colonial kitchen, formal DR, screened porch, terrace

Food & Drink Full breakfast; tea (a reservation-only tearoom in town, operated by publisher of *Tea, A Magazine*) **Recreation** Trails; vineyard, herbery, historic sites; boating, fishing, 4-star dining, day trips **Amenities & Services** Refrigerator, guest phone, antique books, maps; very corp. friendly

ACCOMMODATIONS

Units 4 guest rooms, suites
All Rooms Bath, antique furnishings, reading lamps, fans avail.
Some Rooms Ornamental fireplace, capacity to convert to suites
Bed & Bath Antique or reproduction beds include 1 cherry step-up four-poster, antique French oak twins; 1 hall access bath w/ robes
Favorites Prince Suite— vaulted ceiling, queen four-poster, whirlpool, priv. entrance (limited disabled access); Kingsley Room—cozy, iron and brass double bed
Comfort & Decor Guest rooms named for 5 previous owners of house. Original wide flooring, Oriental rugs, Colonial painted trim. Seating varies—wing-back, Victorian rockers. Relatively spacious and not overstuffed.

RATES, RESERVATIONS, & RESTRICTIONS

Deposit 1st and last nights; refund w/ 14-day notice
Discounts Valentine's, other packages; 3rd night 50%; check for corp., midweek
Credit Cards V, AE, MC
Check-In/Out After 2/11
Smoking No
Pets No
Kids Over 7
Minimum Stay No firm policy, but check during high season
Open All year
Hosts Beverly and Charles "Rusty" Yates
60 Pomfret Rd.
Brooklyn, CT 06234-0845
(860) 779-9696
Fax: (860) 779-9844
friendshipvalley@snet.net
www.friendshipvalleyinn.com

RIVERWIND, *Deep River*

OVERALL ★★★★ | ROOM QUALITY ★★★★ | VALUE ★★★ | PRICE $100–185

Pigs and romance are two notable elements of this delightful, folksy house. Decorative piggies are lined on mantels and climbing stairs and shaped into biscuits and served up at breakfast with Smithfield Ham, from America's Ham Capital, where Barbara came from. (You'll be tempted to pig out at breakfast.) The romance refers to carpenter Bob, who helped Barbara remodel the abandoned estate and then married her. It's a fine, fun, sumptuous bed-and-breakfast with a mounted moose head, Mae West quotes, a garden rake handle holding a hanging mantel, and carpenters' tools for towel racks. And as a Justice of the Peace, Barbara can perform weddings.

SETTING & FACILITIES

Location Adjacent to village green; Rt. 9 to Exit 4, left onto Rt. 154 to B&B, 1.4 mi. on right
Near Conn. River, Canfield Woods Preserve (360 acres of trails), Essex Steam Train/Riverboat, Chester, Goodspeed Opera House, Ivoryton Playhouse, state parks; Mystic Seaport, New Haven
Building 1750 Colonial farmhouse w/ Victorian elements
Grounds 1 acre, small gardens, patio
Public Space DRs, parlor, large study, keeping room, games room, small library
Food & Drink Early-riser coffee; Southern-style breakfast, communal or separate; specialties: Smithfield ham, biscuits, hot casseroles; refreshments
Recreation Riverboat cruises, theatre, 4-star dining, antiquing, beach activities
Amenities & Services 2 refrigerators, bike storage, hairdryers, special Christmas decorations, pick-up from train station

ACCOMMODATIONS

Units 8 guest rooms
All Rooms Bath, reading lighting, clock/radio, AC, bottled water
Some Rooms Balcony/deck, ceiling fan
Bed & Bath Canopy, four-poster; queen/double; robes, 1 shower-only, 1 hand-held shower w/ claw-foot soaking tub, 1 hall access bath
Favorites Hearts and Flowers Room—French country furnishings, queen white iron and brass bed; Champagne and Roses Room—Mahogany queen half-canopy bed, Japanese steeping tub, sep. shower, balcony.
Comfort & Decor Rustic Americana, country and period antique furnishings, hand-artisan touches. Color schemes mirror quilts. Beautiful area rugs. Stylish, fun.

RATES, RESERVATIONS, & RESTRICTIONS

Deposit 1 night or credit card; refund w/ 10-day notice
Discounts 3rd person, 50% of room rate
Credit Cards V, MC
Check-In/Out 3–6/11
Smoking Restricted
Pets No
Kids Over 12
Minimum Stay 2 nights, April 2–Jan. 2
Open All year
Hosts Barbara Barlow and Bob Bucknall
209 Main St.
Deep River, CT 06417
(860) 526-2014
Fax: (860) 526-0875
www.riverwindinn.com

GELSTON INN, East Haddam

OVERALL ★★★★ | ROOM QUALITY ★★★★ | VALUE ★★½ | PRICE $100–225

When this cupola-topped Victorian inn opened in 1853 next door to the Goodspeed Opera House, it charged $2.50. Of course, that included a meal. Today you'll pay about 100 times that for a suite (about the same value, and with a breakfast). The owners have completely refurbished this landmark, and it sparkles again like the light on the river behind it. Seasonal menus feature appetizers like clams tempura and entrées including grilled salmon on fennel puree with orange reduction. You can watch the river through window walls as you sup by candlelight, or opt for a Samuel Adams and a hamburger on the terrace. A plus is the theatre a few steps away; a minus is the theatre crowds, and late-night noise, a few steps away.

SETTING & FACILITIES

Location I-91 to Rt. 9 to Exit 7, left at end of ramp; right at 1st traffic light, cross iron bridge, 2nd building on right after bridge, next to the Goodspeed Opera House on Conn. River
Near Gillette Castle, Camelot River Cruises, incl. murder mystery theatre on river
Building 1853 Victorian
Grounds Rear patio w/ pavilion
Public Space Entry, main DR, smaller DR, pub
Food & Drink Cont'l breakfast, lunch, candlelight dinner; cont'l-style w/ Italian influences, new tavern prix-fixe menu, Pepito crusted salmon, stuffed gulf shrimp, veal roulade; pre-theatre dinners; Sun. brunch; full liquor license
Recreation Summer performing arts, musicals; canoeing, sailing, antiquing
Amenities & Services Entertainment on weekends, grand piano; conf. facil.

ACCOMMODATIONS

Units 3 guest rooms, 3 suites
All Rooms Bath, seating, alarm clock, AC, thermostat, TV
Some Rooms Suites w/ LR, river view
Bed & Bath Carved headboards, all queens, roll-away beds; full baths
Favorites Nathan Hale room—suite w/ best river view; Swan room—overlooks gardens and river
Comfort & Decor Traditional Colonial, antique furnishings, carpet. Fresh, pretty look. Can be noisy at dinner, theatre times, late-night. Back rooms quietest.

RATES, RESERVATIONS, & RESTRICTIONS

Deposit Credit card holds room; reasonable notice to cancel
Discounts 3rd person
Credit Cards V, AE, MC
Check-In/Out 2/11
Smoking Tavern only
Pets No
Kids Welcome
Open Mid-Feb. to Jan. 2
Hosts The Carbone Family
8 Main St.
East Haddam, CT 06423
(860) 873-1411
Fax: (860) 873-9300

GUILFORD CORNERS, *Guilford*

OVERALL ★★★½ | ROOM QUALITY ★★★★ | VALUE ★★½ | PRICE $110–170

Suzie and Gary exclaim that Guilford Corners is the quintessential New England experience—the house harks back to the time when the colonies were still under sovereign rule, and the history of the house and town tell the story of New England and America. Guests love to poke into the attic and cellar, with unique architecture rarely seen outside of museum homes. The enthusiastic hosts enjoy explaining their antique historical maps and framed art pieces, including a favorite Lincoln lithograph. For fun, books and games are stocked in a rare built-in Guilford cupboard, and you can borrow a bicycle and pedal to the quaint village.

SETTING & FACILITIES

Location In Guilford village, corner of State St. and Boston Post Rd.; I-95 to Exit 58, proceed south from exit ramp, left onto Rt. 1, B&B entrance 1 block further on left
Near Green shops, restaurants, tennis; sound-side beach; Yale, New Haven, Lake Quonnipaug, Hammonasset Beach State Park, Water Authority property, lake, outlet mall
Building 1732 white clapboard Georgian Colonial, wraparound veranda
Grounds Village lawns, herb and flower gardens; 1.5 blocks from Green

Public Space Guest parlor, informal parlor, sun deck
Food & Drink Cont'l breakfast, home-baked specialties
Recreation Summer farmer's market, antiquing, boating, XC skiing
Amenities & Services Phone, refrigerator, dataport/fax hook-ups, hot tub, bikes, bike storage, lawn/board games, TVs on request, *New York Times* and *Hartford Courant,* travel services, transport to/from Guilford train station; short/long-term relocation stays; meetings, weddings, etc.; BYOB set-ups

ACCOMMODATIONS

Units 2 guest rooms, 1 2-BR suite
All Rooms Bath, sitting area, dining area, clock radio, hot beverage kettles and set-ups
Some Rooms Working fireplace (1), decorative fireplace (1)
Bed & Bath Queen four-posters, suite 2nd BR w/ 2 twins; 2 shower-only baths

Favorites Gentleman's Room—decorative fireplace, large wood-paneled full bathroom
Comfort & Decor Rooms large (20′ x 24′) w/ high ceilings. Muted painted walls, artwork. Antique Georgian-style furnishings, fabrics and carpets. 12-over-12 windows. Original random plank flooring.

RATES, RESERVATIONS, & RESTRICTIONS

Deposit 1 night; nonrefundable, credit w/ reasonable notice

Discounts Weekly and long-term stays, 3rd person

Credit Cards None

Check-In/Out 4–7/11 or by arrangement

Smoking Restricted

Pets OK w/ prior arrangement

Kids "Children w/ well-behaved parents welcome"

Minimum Stay 2 nights May–Sept. weekends

Open All year

Hosts Suzie Balestracci and Gary Parrington

133 State St.

Guilford, CT 066437

(203) 453-4129

Fax: (203) 458-8915

COPPER BEECH INN, Ivoryton

OVERALL ★★★★ | ROOM QUALITY ★★★★ | VALUE ★★½ | PRICE $115–185

The town is named after the early ivory trade, and this handsome clapboard inn, named after its huge copper beech tree, was originally home to an ivory comb and keyboard manufacturer. Carriage house rooms in the back are the quietest; noise levels can rise in rooms too near the street and popular, much-lauded dining rooms. The seasonal menu may include seared fresh duck foie gras with grilled pear, roasted loin of fresh venison with lingonberries and Grand Marnier, and white peach and champagne sorbet with cassis sauce. The conservatory is grand for after-dinner Cognac and coffee. Warning: If you don't plan to dine here, the aromas will drive you mad.

SETTING & FACILITIES

Location 3 blocks from center; I-95 to Exit 69 to Rt. 9 N; approx. 3 mi. to Exit 3; left (W) at ramp end; inn on left; from Hartford, I-91 S to Exit 22; Rt. 9 S to Exit 3

Near Goodspeed Opera House, Ivoryton Playhouse; Gillette Castle, Rocky Neck, and Hammonasset State Parks; sound-side beaches, Mystic, outlet malls, casinos

Building 1880s Victorian cottage

Grounds 7 wooded acres, English gardens w/ thousands of spring-blooming bulbs

Public Space Parlor, Victorian-style conservatory, 4 DRs

Food & Drink Cont'l buffet breakfast; seasonally changing menu, French country dining; comprehensive wine list; à la carte menu, 3-course meal ($45–60); comp. soup, early evening dinner, Tues.–Fri.

Recreation Summer theatre, antiquing, touring, museums, tennis, fishing, boating

Amenities & Services Restaurant disabled access.; priv. affairs, meetings (up to 70)

ACCOMMODATIONS

Units 4 guest rooms in main house, 9 in carriage house

All Rooms Bath, phone/dataport, good reading lights, AC

Some Rooms Bay window, radio in main house; Carriage House rooms French doors to common deck, whirlpool, TV; 2 largest carriage house rooms priv. deck

Bed & Bath Some canopy or four-poster beds. Main house baths antique fixtures, pedestal sinks, some claw-foot soaking tubs, one bath w/ smaller tub only—no shower. Carriage house baths whirlpools

Favorites Room 1, main house—spacious, canopy, bay window; Room 219, carriage house—cathedral ceiling, canopy bed, French doors to deck

Comfort & Decor Most rooms, spacious w/ seating areas. Main house furnishings antique pieces, country-style fabrics, casual contemporary accessories. Pretty floral wallpapers. Carpet w/ area rugs. Converted turn-of-century carriage barn, formal-style reproduction furnishings, Chippendale, Queen Anne. Second floor carriage house rooms cathedral ceilings, exposed beams. DR noise a factor in some main house rooms

RATES, RESERVATIONS, & RESTRICTIONS

Deposit 1 night, 2 nights weekends; refund w/ 5-day notice

Discounts Midweek specials, winter packages, 3rd person

Credit Cards V, AE, MC, D

Check-In/Out 2/11

Smoking Outdoors only

Pets No

Kids Over 10

No-No's TVs in main house rooms

Minimum Stay 2 nights weekends, holidays

Open All year, except Christmas and 1st week of Jan.

Hosts Sally and Eldon Senner
46 Main St.
Ivoryton, CT 06442
(888) 809-2056 or (860) 767-0330
Fax: (860) 767-7840
www.copperbeechinn.com

STONECROFT, Ledyard

OVERALL ★★★★ | ROOM QUALITY ★★★★ | VALUE ★★ | PRICE $140–250

Boating and inns are a rare combo, but here you have it. You can room in a teak yacht docked on the river and enjoy a good breakfast and dinner, too, on Villeroy and Boch china. The inn features Euro-American country ambiance, with hand-painted murals by the same artist who worked at the Inn at National Hall in Westport. The hosts seek to provide serenity, and they certainly score with aromatherapy bath salts, soft background music, and hundreds of surrounding acres of protected land, perfect for strolls and contemplation as well as horseback riding. The Grange addition in the restored barn is rustic and elegant, with candlelight meals, guest rooms with barn flooring and angled fireplaces.

SETTING & FACILITIES

Location I-95 to Exit 89 (Allyn St.), becomes Cow Hill Rd., then Pumpkin Hill Rd.; next to 300-acre woodland conservancy

Near Mystic, Stonington, Rocky Neck State Park, Old Lyme, R.I. ocean beaches, Pequot Research Center and Museum, Garde Art Theatre in New London, Eugene O'Neill playwright workshop, casinos

Building Restored 1807 Georgian Colonial; renovated barn

Grounds 6 rural acres; gardens, terrace, meadows, trails; equestrian center next door

Public Space Great room, Red Room, library, terrace, pergola, grange addition, lounge

Food & Drink (MAP) Early-riser coffee/tea; candlelight cont'l breakfast; full breakfast menu, boat guests also; refreshments; breakfasts, dinners open to public

Recreation Antiquing, fishing charters, tall ship tours, parasailing, beach

Amenities & Services Lawn games, darts, exercise track, phone, multimedia center; transport from/to marina, Amtrak, airport; weddings, conferences

ACCOMMODATIONS

Units 4 guest rooms, house; 4 rooms, 2 suites, The Grange; 1 unit "Boat and Breakfast" aboard docked yacht

All Rooms Bath, sitting area, alarm clock, AC

Some Rooms Fireplace, whirlpool; Grange rooms dataport, terrace/deck

Bed & Bath Some antique beds, queen, king; Grange rooms dbl. whirlpools, walk-in showers

Favorites The Buttery—oldest room (1704), priv. entrance/patio, white iron

and brass queen, wheelchair access. Boat—restored 40′ 1949 wooden motor yacht, teak/mahogany interior, refrigerator, coffeemaker, microwave, 2 single berths

Comfort & Decor Some country, some romantic, Victorian. Murals, wainscoting, love seats, artist's mural, reproduction tiger maple furnishings. Grange rooms, tongue-in-groove ship-lapped ceilings. Wide range of styles, comfort. Boat not for seasick-prone (even though docked).

RATES, RESERVATIONS, & RESTRICTIONS

Deposit 50% refund w/ 14-day notice

Discounts B&B rates, midweek stays; off-season packages, incl. cooking classes, holistic workshops; longer stays; 3rd person

Credit Cards V, AE, MC, D; personal checks by prior arrangement

Check-In/Out 3–6/11

Smoking No

Pets No

Kids Over 10

No-No's Heeled shoes

Minimum Stay 2 nights weekends; check for holiday minimums

Open All year

Host Joan Egy

515 Pumpkin Hill Rd.

Ledyard, CT 06339-1637

(860) 572-0771

Fax: (860) 572-9161

stoncrft@concentric.net

www.stonecroft.com

INN AT LAFAYETTE, Madison

OVERALL ★★★★ | ROOM QUALITY ★★★★ | VALUE ★★½ | PRICE $125–175

This reopened inn was the Madison Methodist Church, built of local wood by local craftsmen in 1837. Forty years later the minister was tried for murder of a parishioner, and was acquitted, but his petulant ghost reportedly lingers about the attic. The church mode is still discernable under the added portico, balcony and side awning. This old Yankee-style shoreline town has one of the country's favorite private booksellers, but still has few tourists. The inn centers on dining and has restructured its namesake restaurant and lightened the cuisine. It has also revamped the stylish guest rooms to support business travelers.

SETTING & FACILITIES

Location In the center of quaint, historic Madison; I-95 to Exit 61, from west take a right onto Rt. 79 S, left onto Rt. 1, inn is on left; from east take left at ramp end
Near Long Island Sound, Hammonassett State Park and Beach; New Haven, Shubert Theatre, Yale; Mystic, casinos
Building Landmark 1840s frame church, columned portico; inn since the 1920s
Grounds Border landscaping, parking lot
Public Space 2nd-floor breakfast nook/sitting area, 4 dining rooms
Food & Drink Continental breakfast in guest rooms or breakfast nook; restaurant (Café Allegre) serves lunch and dinner, artful presentation of classically influenced European and American cuisine, specialties: risotto w/ garden vegetables and garlic herb broth, garlic chicken w/ artichoke hearts, calamata olives, sundried tomatoes; restaurant closed Mondays
Recreation Historical tours, shopping, boating, hiking trails, biking, beach activities, performing arts and cultural activities
Amenities & Services Off-street parking, irons; guest room phones w/ private lines, conference, voice mail, dataport, corp. meeting and dining facilities; copying, printing and fax services

ACCOMMODATIONS

Units 5 guest rooms
All Rooms Private bath, 2 phone lines, TV, dataport, robes
Some Rooms Writing desk, sitting area
Bed & Bath King and queen four-poster beds, Egyptian cotton linens, down comforters; full marble baths, phones in baths, robes, whirlpool (1)
Favorites Room #1 Droney Room— Most spacious room, queen, comfortable seating
Comfort & Decor Wall-to-wall carpet. Muted color schemes. French Colonial furnishings, antiques and quality reproductions. Small-hotel feel. Good lighting, work space. Geared well for business travelers.

RATES, RESERVATIONS, & RESTRICTIONS

Deposit Credit card holds reservation; no charge w/ 7-day notice

Discounts 3rd person, older children in same room, corp. rates

Credit Cards V, AE, DC, MC

Check-in/Out 4/noon, or by prior arrangement

Smoking Restricted, no smoking in guestrooms

Pets No

Kids Over 12; check w/ inn for availability; $25 for extra cot

Minimum Stay None, but check w/ inn on holidays

Open All year

Hosts MRS Madison Corporation
725 Boston Post Rd. Main St.
Madison, CT 06443
(203) 245-7773
Fax: (203) 245-6256
www.allegrecafe.com

APPLEWOOD FARMS INN, Mystic

OVERALL ★★★½ | ROOM QUALITY ★★★½ | VALUE ★½ | PRICE $140–290

It may not be Pebble Beach, but here you can putt on the little green in the yard, and play a bit on the chipping fairway. Clubs are available. Five generations of one family grew up in this farmhouse, and with photos and Early American objects casually placed around, it seems they are still here. The best part of this unpretentious property is the space around it. On a 33-acre former horse farm, you can gaze at the neighboring herd of equines. Or just sit in the gazebo by the pond and watch the birds fly by, or relax in the hot tub—in the former corn crib. Oh, and you can bring your own horse.

SETTING & FACILITIES

Location I-95 to Exit 89, North on Cow Hill Rd. to 2nd traffic light; left on Rt. 184 (Goldstar Hwy), right on Col. Ledyard, B&B 2 1/2 mi. on right; borders nature conservancy acreage

Near Arabian stables, Mystic, Stonington Fishing Village; U.S. submarine base, museum; sound-side, ocean beaches, Up-Down Sawmill, Sturbridge Village; Eugene O'Neill Playwrite Workshop and events; Guard Theatre, casinos

Building The Gallup Homestead, ca. 1826, center-chimney Colonial

Grounds 33 acres, gazebo, walking trails, bird feeders, pond, horse facilities

Public Space Parlor, keeping room, quiet sitting room

Food & Drink Full communal breakfast in keeping room

Recreation Fishing charters, windjammer day trips, whale watching, Newport mansions

Amenities & Services Corn-crib spa/hot tub, USGA chipping/putting green, games

ACCOMMODATIONS

Units 4 guest rooms, 1 small suite w/
priv. entrance
All Rooms Bath, AC window units
Some Rooms Fireplaces (4)
Bed & Bath Some canopy, four-poster
beds, some featherbeds; 1 king, others
queen or double, cot avail.
Favorites Russell Room—fireplace,
queen featherbed, Victorian furniture

Comfort & Decor Fairly spacious
rooms. Walls finished w/ old-fashioned
papers, hand-stenciling, white-wash. Pretty
bedding, Ruffled or lace window treatments. Casual furnishings, some wicker,
some antique country-style or painted
pieces. Slanted ceilings and add'l bed in 2-
room suite. No overhead lighting.

RATES, RESERVATIONS, & RESTRICTIONS

Deposit Reservations paid in full in
advance; refund or 8-month credit w/ 2
weeks' notice, processing fee charged per
night per room
Discounts 4+ day stay
Credit Cards V, AE, MC, D
Check-In/Out 3–9 p.m./11
Smoking Restricted
Pets Polite ones welcome, by arrange-
ment (incl. horses!)
Kids Over 8; by arrangement midweek,

not on weekends
Minimum Stay 2 nights weekends; 3
nights holiday weekends
Open All year
Hosts Frankie and Tom Betz
528 Colonel Ledyard
Mystic, CT 06339
(800) 717-4262 or (860) 536-2022
Fax: (860) 536-6015
applewoodfarmsinn@worldnet.att.net
www.visitmystic.com/applewoodfarmsinn

BRIGADOON, Mystic

OVERALL ★★★ | ROOM QUALITY ★★★ | VALUE ★★½ | PRICE $85–170

Scottish-born Kay imparts her own brand of traditional Scottish-style hospitality at this 15-room Victorian with an attached barn. Scones are often
served for breakfast, and a Scottish flag flutters outside. The front hall has a
house deed signed in the 1800s by Hancock—not John of Declaration-of-
Independence fame, but Charles, possibly a relative. (Kay and Ted are
researching that one.) Of the properties listed here from the Mystic area,
this is the least imposing and the least expensive, and for budget travelers
and families with young children, this informal bed-and-breakfast will be
just fine. Just don't expect luxury or high-style.

SETTING & FACILITIES

Location I-95 to Exit 89 (Allyn St.), left onto Allyn St. if coming from New York, right if coming from Boston; right onto Cow Hill Rd.; 4th house on left, .5 mile from highway

Near 1 mi. to downtown Mystic, Seaport; 2 mi. to aquarium; beaches in Connecticut and Rhode Island 20 min. away.

Building Rambling 15-room farmhouse (ca. 1740) w/ attached blue barn

Grounds Over an acre, stone walls, fruit trees, summer gardens, seating under dogwood tree

Public Space Common room, DR

Food & Drink Full breakfast; specialties: strawberry-walnut pancakes, crêpes; tea; evening wine

Recreation Swimming, sailing, biking, hiking, whale watching, schooner tours, casinos, museums, live theater.

Amenities & Services AFternoon tea, evening beverage (bottled water and soft drinks), fresh flowers, refrigerator, bike storage, games, maps; Victorian teas, bridal showers, family reunions

ACCOMMODATIONS

Units 8 guest rooms

All Rooms Bath, AC

Some Rooms Fireplace (6), priv. deck (1)

Bed & Bath Some iron, four-poster beds, queen/king sizes; some shower-only

Favorites Honeymoon Suite—fireplace,

king bed, priv. entrance/deck, TV

Comfort & Decor Rooms sizes vary— small, medium, larger. Some feature orig. wide-plank or narrow white oak flooring, carpet. Furnishings mix of early-American antiques and reproductions

RATES, RESERVATIONS, & RESTRICTIONS

Deposit $25; refund w/ 7-day notice

Discounts Winter packages, midweek corp., 3rd person, kids under 14 free

Credit Cards V, AE, MC

Check-In/Out 3–5/11

Smoking No

Pets No

Kids Welcome

Minimum Stay 2 nights May–Oct., all

holiday weekends

Open All year

Hosts Kay and Ted Lucas

180 Cow Hill Rd.

Mystic, CT 06355

(860) 536-3033

Fax: (860) 536-1628

brigofdoon@aol.com

www.brigadoonofmystic.com

HOUSE OF 1833, Mystic

OVERALL ★★★★½ | ROOM QUALITY ★★★★★ | VALUE ★★★ | PRICE $95–225

Carol and Matt selected this columned Greek Revival house with pool and tennis court after reviewing 150 other potentials in 1993, and the same care continues at one of the nicest bed-and-breakfasts in Connecticut. Charming murals grace the public rooms, and guest rooms are dramatically romantic with gauzy canopies, striking color combinations, including black and mauve, and a doorway to a rooftop cupola. Matt plays piano during sumptuous, candlelight breakfasts, and sometimes in the evenings too. Not surprisingly, Winter Romance packages are popular.

SETTING & FACILITIES

Location I-95 to Exit 90, Rt. 27 N to Old Mystic Country Store; bear right at stop, B&B approximately .5 mile on right across from steam-powered cider mill
Near 2 mi. from Mystic Seaport, aquarium, historic sites, museums; 5 mi. to casinos; 9 mi. to Watch Hill, ocean beaches, antique shops
Building 1833 Greek Revival mansion
Grounds 3 country acres, gardens, pool, tennis court
Public Space Foyer, front parlor, music room
Food & Drink Communal breakfast; breakfast basket option; specialties: artistic fruit plate, eggs Florentine in puff pastry, honey-mustard ham, cookies and brownies
Recreation Day trips, boat tours, sailing, whale watching tours; trails
Amenities & Services Winter tennis avail., bikes, helmets; refrigerator, phone, bike/kayak storage; popular pkgs., gift cert.

ACCOMMODATIONS

Units 5 guest rooms

All Rooms Bath, fireplace/woodstove, seating, AC, antiques and reproductions

Some Rooms Sitting area, porch/balcony, soaking or whirlpool tubs

Bed & Bath Queen brass, carved, four-poster or canopy; sinks in antique bureaus, full baths, some oversized sep. showers, whirlpools

Favorites Peach Room—11-foot ceilings, illusion queen canopy, 2-person

shower, 2-person whirlpool.

Comfort & Decor Spacious, w/ romantic flair. Bold wallcoverings—black and deep rose tapestry fainting couch in large Oak Room. Veranda Room, antique soaking tub in front of fire. Battenburg lace in Ivy Room. Cupola Room w/ stairway to cupola sitting room. Wide pine flooring, Oriental rugs. TVs and phones deliberately excluded.

RATES, RESERVATIONS, & RESTRICTIONS

Deposit 1 night; refund w/ 7-day notice

Discounts Special packages and promos

Credit Cards V, MC

Check-In/Out 3/11

Smoking No

Pets No

Kids Not on weekends

Minimum Stay 2 nights weekends

Open All year

Hosts Carol and Matt Nolan

72 North Stonington Rd.

Mystic, CT 06355-0341

(800) 367-1833 or (860) 536-6325

www.visitmystic.com/1833

OLD MYSTIC INN, Mystic

OVERALL ★★★★ | ROOM QUALITY ★★★★ | VALUE ★★½ | PRICE $115–175

In a prior life this red Colonial, built in 1794, was a rare-book and map store. The bed-and-breakfast replaced over 20,000 volumes, but retained many of the antique maps. Each guest room, named after a New England author, includes books by that writer, so you can choose based on literary inclinations. Also displayed is an ever-growing collection of stuffed bears. Candlelight breakfasts are served by Michael, your host and chef, by the bay window with a roaring fireplace in the winter and on the porch in the summer. Michael is a graduate of The Culinary Institute of America and also has a degree in Hotel and Restaurant Management.

SETTING & FACILITIES

Location Eastern shore; I-95 to Exit 90 onto Rt. 27 N, approximately 2 mi. to B&B on right

Near Downtown Mystic, Olde Mystic, Mystic Seaport and Aquarium, Stonington, casinos, Newport

Building 1794 Colonial w/ turret, veranda; restored, 1986; carriage house added 1988
Grounds .75 acre; lawn games, swingset, gazebo, old stone walls, rose gardens, perennials, picnic tables
Public Space DR, keeping room, 2nd floor library, 3 porches
Food & Drink Full breakfast; specialty: scrambled eggs w/fine herbs served in a pastry shell topped with sauce mornay and fresh asparagus, Banana Stuffed French Toast with maple walnut syrup, fresh baked cookies and brownies, afternoon refreshments, wine and cheese Sat. nights
Recreation Trails, nature center, beaches; sailing and schooner tours
Amenities & Services Roll-away, refrigerator, phone, chocolates. Staff member always avail.; catered weddings (up to 125); small conf., fax, copy service, gift cert., pkg weekends

ACCOMMODATIONS

Units 8 guest rooms
All Rooms Bath, small sitting area, dataport, thermostat, AC
Some Rooms Fireplace; carriage house rooms outdoor seating, priv. ground floor entrances; love seat sleeper sofas, 1 main house room w/ priv. porch and side entry
Bed & Bath 3 four-poster, 5 canopy beds, queen sizes; full baths, some whirlpools
Favorites The Herman Melville room—largest room, canopy bed, priv. porch w/ stairs to lawn; Dickinson Room—fireplace, four-poster, bay window
Comfort & Decor Rooms named after New England authors. Telephones and TVs deliberately excluded. Carpeted rooms furnished, mix of old and reproduction Colonial. Summery wicker. Simple, country feel.

RATES, RESERVATIONS, & RESTRICTIONS

Deposit Credit card holds reservation; no charge w/ 2-day notice
Discounts Kids under 12 yrs; corp., long stay; AAA
Credit Cards V, AE, MC
Check-In/Out After 2/11 or as arranged
Smoking No
Pets No
Kids Over 8 in main house; all ages in carriage house
Minimum Stay 2 nights weekends in-season
Open All year
Host Michael S. Cardillo Jr.
58 Main St., P.O. Box 634
Old Mystic, CT 06372
(860) 572-9422
Fax: (860) 572-9954
omysticinn@aol.com
www.visitmystic.com/oldmysticinn/

RED BROOK INN, Mystic

OVERALL ★★★★ | ROOM QUALITY ★★★ | VALUE ★★★ | PRICE $100–190

This inn offers a Colonial experience, with whale-oil lamps and iron candle stands, as well as modern comforts, including whirlpool baths. Architecture and decor are meticulously authentic, with much of the painting and renovating done by Ruth herself. On some weekends she even dresses eighteenth-century-style and cooks hearty soup in a kettle and spit-roasted meat on the open-hearth. Moving and restoring Haley's Tavern required photographing, numbering, and coding each piece, and reconstructing literally stone by stone. Ruth earned joint 1986 Transportation and President's Historic Preservation Council award, the only one bestowed on an individual that year.

SETTING & FACILITIES

Location I-95 to Exit 89 (Allyn St.), north from ramp end, 1.5 mi. to traffic light, right (E) at Rt. 184 (Goldstar Highway), left into B&B driveway at next corner, follow arrow up hill to Haley Tavern; B&B not visible from road
Near Mystic, Dennison Nature Center, New London, Stonington, casinos
Building Restored ca. 1740 Haley Tavern and ca. 1770 Crary Homestead
Grounds 7 acres with gardens, lawn games

Public Space Keeping room; ladies' parlor; gentlemen's parlor; tavern
Food & Drink Full breakfast; specialties: walnut waffles w/ sausage, pumpkin pancakes; refreshments mulled cider, iced tea; open-hearth Colonial cooking on Thanksgiving or by arrangement
Recreation Schooner tours, water sports, antiquing, nature trails
Amenities & Services Fridge, phone; crib, highchair; games, TV, maps; transport to/from Mystic train station; recipes

ACCOMMODATIONS

Units 10 guest rooms
All Rooms Bath, antique blanket chest, candle stands, seating, AC
Some Rooms Fireplace (6), add'l bed, writing desk
Bed & Bath Four-poster/canopy beds, queen/double, extra beds are twins; some baths w/ large shower-only, 1-person whirlpools (2)
Favorites Mary Virginia—fireplace, quiet

corner room, 1790 carved bed; Nancy Crary—whirlpool, hand-stenciled flooring, pencil post bed
Comfort & Decor Romantic Colonial. Country rugs over wide board flooring. Lace canopies over Early American four-posters. Pretty handmade coverlets. Needlepoint pillows. Armoires, rare desks, tall chests. Traditional Colonial furnishings. Restored orig. woodwork.

RATES, RESERVATIONS, & RESTRICTIONS

Deposit 1 night; refund w/ 7-day notice
Discounts Singles, 3rd person, whole
week stay, kids in same room free
Credit Cards V, AE, MC, D
Check-In/Out Noon/by 11
Smoking No
Pets No
Kids "Kids who appreciate antiques"
welcome
Minimum Stay 2–3 nights weekends,

holidays
Open All year
Host Ruth Keyes
Route 184 & Wells Rd., P.O. Box 237
Mystic, CT 06372
(800) 290-5619 or (860) 572-0349
Fax: Call first
redbrookin@aol.com
www.virtualcities.com

STEAMBOAT INN, Mystic

OVERALL ★★★★ | ROOM QUALITY ★★★★★ | VALUE ★★ | PRICE $110–285

This turn-of-the-last-century warehouse is the most interesting lodging in Mystic and the only waterfront bed-and-breakfast. The location allows you to walk to shops, restaurants and galleries, avoiding parking problems and traffic, which can be terrible during summer months. The rooms, named after local schooners, are delightfully tasteful and creative, with romantic features such as whirlpools for two, wood-burning fireplaces and views of passing boats and gulls along the Mystic River. You would enjoy staying at this bed-and-breakfast even if it weren't in this historic sea town.

SETTING & FACILITIES

Location On the Mystic River; Rt. 1 and over drawbridge, look for B&B sign
Near Walk to Mystic Seaport Museum, restaurants, docks; seaport, aquarium, shopping village, historic sites, museums, casinos, Fort Griswold, Stonington Village, vineyards
Building Built 1907; B&B opened 1989
Grounds Backyard marina, priv. dock for

guest walks
Public Space Bright common room
Food & Drink Early riser coffee; cont'l-plus breakfast; tea and sherry avail. in the afternoon
Recreation Day trips to ocean, boat tours from B&B dock, sailing, whale watching tours
Amenities & Services irons, books

ACCOMMODATIONS

Units 10 guest rooms
All Rooms Bath, sitting area, phone, data-port, hidden TV, thermostat, whirlpool
Some Rooms Fireplace, views, sofa

sleeper; dock-level rooms have wet bar w/ refrigerator, micro; French doors to small 2nd room (1)

Bed & Bath Some canopy, four-poster beds; hairdryers, five 2-person whirlpools **Favorites** Ariadne, Room 1— most romantic, fireplace, water view, canopy bed, 2-person whirlpool. Summer Girl, Room 5—cheery favorite, fireplace, window wall overlooks drawbridge and water

Comfort & Decor Rooms named after famous Mystic schooners. Romantic period touches, esp. in high-end rooms. Comfortable contemporary-style seating. Antique color schemes and decorative touches, carpet. Dock-level rooms largest.

RATES, RESERVATIONS, & RESTRICTIONS

Deposit 1 night, refund w/ 5-day notice
Discounts Midweek corp., 3rd person, kids under 16 free
Credit Cards V, AE, MC, D
Check-In/Out 2/11
Smoking No
Pets No
Kids In dock-level rooms only
Minimum Stay 2 nights on weekends

Open All year
Host Diana Stadtmiller
73 Steamboat Wharf
Mystic, CT 06355-2551
(860) 536-8300
Fax: (860) 536-9528
sbwharf@aol.com
www.visitmystic.com/steamboat

PALMER INN, Noank

OVERALL ★★★½ | ROOM QUALITY ★★★★ | VALUE ★★ | PRICE $165–230

As the views and foghorns attest, Noank is the Native-American term for "surrounded by water." One hundred years ago, this little village was a major ship-building area, and the imposing 7,600-square-foot mansion with 30-foot entry columns and 13-foot ceilings was home to owner of the eastern seaboard's major boatyard owner. Palmers lived in the house till the 1960s, but today, despite its grandeur, its mood is mellow and the decor is fuzzy Victoriana with local artwork, family portraits, and artisans' ongoing restorations. Pat was a clinical psychologist and is an accomplished sailor, so you can talk neuroses or mainsails. She also won an apple pie contest.

SETTING & FACILITIES

Location In quiet fishing village; at 25 Church, turn left onto Cedar Lane for parking in rear
Near In historic fishing village; 2 mi. to Mystic, 1 block to Long Island Sound, art galleries; Watch Hill antiquing and

beaches, Coast Guard Academy, casinos
Building Circa 1900 Southern Colonial
Grounds 1/2 acre on Peninsula Village, flower and herb gardens
Public Space Main hall; library; large parlor (the "Grand Salon")

Food & Drink Early-riser coffee, cont'l communal breakfast; specialty: granola
Recreation Beach activities, golf, tennis

Amenities & Services Sailing classes nearby; special occasions, holiday theme weekends (large Christmas tree-trimming party)

ACCOMMODATIONS

Units 6 guest rooms
All Rooms Bath, sitting/reading area, AC
Some Rooms Fireplace (1), balcony (1), writing desk, water views, ceiling fan
Bed & Bath Carved mahogany, brass, antique wicker; bed sizes vary; all full baths except 1 tub-only bath (claw-foot tub), hairdryers, herbal toiletries
Favorites Balcony Room—smallest, summer favorite, antique carved bed, har-bor view; Master Suite—spacious corner, balcony, harbor view, fireplace, major headboard
Comfort & Decor 2nd and 3rd floor spacious rooms—some huge. Well-appointed. Restored original light fixtures. Hardwood flooring w/ rugs, some Oriental, hand-hooked.

RATES, RESERVATIONS, & RESTRICTIONS

Deposit 50%; refund w/ 14-day notice
Discounts Midweek sailing lesson packages, midweek corp. rate
Credit Cards V, MC, AE, D
Check-In/Out 2–6/11
Smoking No
Pets No
Kids 16 and up in their own room
No-No's No add'l people in rooms—dbl. occupancy only
Minimum Stay 2 nights, weekends summer and foliage seasons
Open All year
Host Patricia Ann White
25 Church St.
Noank, CT 06340-5777
(860) 572-9000
www.visitmystic.com/palmerinn

ANTIQUES & ACCOMMODATIONS, North Stonington

OVERALL ★★★★ | ROOM QUALITY ★★★★ | VALUE ★★½ | PRICE $100–230

As in the name, the emphasis is on antiques, and as former dealers, Ann and Tom have a knack for finding marvelous furnishings and collectibles, mainly from trips to England. The kick is that you can buy many of the items, and the hosts are delighted to replace them. Change is constant, as needlepoint or Oriental rugs vary according to the host's mood, and romantic guest rooms are updated annually. This striking Victorian, with its 1820 House in the Garden connected by gravel paths, is also known for its seasonal gardens, with 3,000 bulbs blooming in springtime. At breakfast, with flickering candlelight and classical music, you may find a pansy on your pancakes.

SETTING & FACILITIES

Location I-95 to Exit 92, head to W 2.3 mi., bear right onto Main St., large sign announces North Stonington Village, B&B is .2 mile on right (do not go to Stonington)

Near Groton, Stonington, hiking trails, Pawcapuck River/tributaries; 8 mi. to Mystic, 11 mi. to Watch Hill antiquing/beaches, casinos

Building 1861 Victorian farmhouse; 1820 garden cottage

Grounds Village yard w/ English-style gardens, patios, various seating areas

Public Space Sitting room, formal DR

Food & Drink Four-course, communal, candlelight breakfast, served on dazzling silver and crystal; specialties: pear compote with raspberry liqueur, banana-walnut pancake, salmon omelet; sherry, refreshments

Recreation Stonington Village Walk, historic home tours, canoeing, Mystic attractions

Amenities & Services Canoe for experienced guests, refrigerator, cribs, roll-aways; baby-sitting arranged, fax

ACCOMMODATIONS

Units 3 guest rooms in main house, 2 family suites in 1820 House in the Garden

All Rooms Bath, TV, alarm radio, seating, AC

Some Rooms Fireplace, sitting area; large suite in 1820 House has LR, porch, kitchen, 3 BRs; second suite 1-BR rooms w/ baths (2) or 2-BR suite w/ 2 baths (1), common sitting room w/ fireplace and library

Bed & Bath Canopy, four-poster queen beds; 1 small bath, others full

Favorites Jenny's Room—antique chandelier, post mahogany queen, fireplace, antique book library; Susan's Room— all-white double canopy bed, bridal theme

Comfort & Decor Airy rooms in Victorian main house, bright, spacious. Traditional American w/ touch of class. Timothy's Room—1810 Sheraton four-poster queen, antiques, small shower-only bath. 1820 annex house tends towards country American. Creative and elegant touches. During holidays Christmas bed four-posters w/ ribbons, greens.

RATES, RESERVATIONS, & RESTRICTIONS

Deposit Credit card holds reservation; no charge w/ 14-day notice

Discounts Corp., long stays, midweek, kids free

Credit Cards V, MC

Check-In/Out 3/11 or by arrangement until noon

Smoking No

Pets No

Kids Children "w/ appreciation of

antiques" welcome in 1820 house

Minimum Stay 2 nights weekends, check for availability

Open All year

Hosts Ann and Tom Gray
32 Main St.
North Stonington, CT 06359
(860) 535-1736 or (800) 554-7829
Fax: (860) 535-2613
www.visitmystic.com/antiques

BEE AND THISTLE INN, Old Lyme

OVERALL ★★★★ | ROOM QUALITY ★★★★ | VALUE ★★★★ | PRICE $95–110

Years ago when we first stayed here, the owner sang madrigals and played the guitar in the parlor, and we had peach muffins and fresh orange juice on a tray in bed. Today, you can still have breakfast in bed (alas, for a fee), and music is in the air on weekends, but the inn has become increasingly popular with the public for lunch and dinner. The cottage with its decks, dock, and kitchen offers peace and privacy, and the river seems to be yours alone. And the American Impressionism paintings at The Griswold Museum are still only a few steps away.

SETTING & FACILITIES

Location I-95 S to Exit 70, right at ramp's end; inn, 3rd house on left, in historic district
Near Florence Griswold Museum, Goodspeed Opera House, Gillette Castle, Lyme Academy of Fine Arts, art galleries and antique shops, Essex Steam Train and Boat-Ride, state parks, Rocky Neck beaches, Mystic attractions, casinos
Building 1756 Colonial; building moved, various additions
Grounds 5.5 acres along Lieutenant River, broad lawns, perennial gardens, herb garden

Public Space 2 parlors, DR, sun porches
Food & Drink Breakfast (fee); lounge w/ fireplace; breakfast specialties: raspberry crêpes, beef-and-bacon hash; lunch crab cakes; candlelight dinner specialties: contemp. American cuisine, venison pie, wild mushroom lasagna; tea; wine list; Sun. brunch
Recreation Boating, tennis, golf; biking trails
Amenities & Services Weekend entertainment; breakfast in bed option (fee)

ACCOMMODATIONS

Units 11 guest rooms, 1 cottage
All Rooms Bath, antiques, phone, alarm clock, AC, fan
Some Rooms Sitting area, desk
Bed & Bath Antique, canopy, and four-poster beds, sizes vary; some showers only
Favorites Room 1—largest, queen fish-

net lace canopy, overlooks gardens; Cottage—TV room, fireplace, brick floor, kitchen, deck and priv. dock
Comfort & Decor Even small rooms romantic, from Colonial to Victorian. Rich fabrics and wallcoverings. Dark woods, carved antique furnishings. Possible kitchen noise in some rooms.

RATES, RESERVATIONS, & RESTRICTIONS

Deposit 1 night or 50%; refund w/ 10-day notice

Discounts 3rd person in cottage

Credit Cards V, AE, DC, MC, D

Check-In/Out 2/11

Smoking No

Pets No

Kids Over 12

No-No's Add'l people in rooms other than in cottage

Open All year

Hosts Phillip and Marie Abraham
100 Lyme St.
Old Lyme, CT 06371
(800) 622-4946 or (860) 434-1667
Fax: (860) 434-3402
beeandthistleinn@msn.com
www.beeandthistleinn.com

OLD LYME INN, Old Lyme

OVERALL ★★★½ | ROOM QUALITY ★★★ | VALUE ★★½ | PRICE $110–150

A Winslow Homer mural graces one dining room; another, with mounted fish and wall holes from darts that missed their mark, was one of the oldest taverns in Pittsburgh. During the 1920s the property was a riding academy where young Jacqueline Bouvier reputedly took lessons. Even earlier, Old Lyme School Impressionist painters sat in the inn's fields and struggled with their craft. Some old-timers recall square dancing in the old barn that burned down (it stood about 300 yards behind the one still remaining). Quirkier than neighbor Bee and Thistle, it offers bottles of witch hazel in rooms and can feel like a small hotel when groups descend.

SETTING & FACILITIES

Location I-95 S to Exit 70, right (left if traveling north) at ramp end, travel to 1st intersection, right following Rt. 1; travel to 2nd light, inn on left; check inn website for scenic drive and ferry directions

Near Village of Old Lyme, Lyme, Hamburg, Hadlyme, Essex, Conn. River, Mystic; museums, casinos

Building Circa 1850 Colonial farmhouse

Grounds In-village yard (over 1 acre), gardens, outbuildings

Public Space Entry hall, sitting room, Victorian Bar, Empire Room DR

Food & Drink Cont'l breakfast; restaurant open 7 days; Sun. brunch, Grill Room light suppers, Italian Night Wed.; specialties: dilled carrot soup w/bay shrimp, crab cakes; Conn. rabbit; award-winning desserts and wine list; full liquor license

Recreation River boating, nature preserves, antique shops, gallery hopping, croquet

Amenities & Services Weekend entertainment, peppermints; meetings, special occasions (2–70) w/ all support

ACCOMMODATIONS

Units 5 guest rooms in main house; 8 north wing rooms

All Rooms Bath, reading lights, TV, radio/alarm, phone, AC

Some Rooms Writing desk (2)

Bed & Bath Cannonball queens in main house; fishnet lace-canopy queens (7) and king/twin four-poster in north wing, some twins; shower-only bath (1); small main house baths

Favorites Rooms 7, 11-large corner

rooms, garden view, canopied queens

Comfort & Decor North wing rooms larger, more up-to-date, w/ chenille spreads. Main house rooms smaller, not tiny. Muted color schemes, floral wallpapers, carpet. Original art from past-turn-of-century Old Lyme School of artists. Good reproductions and genuine antiques. Two rooms w/ sleeper sofas; kids may bunk on floors in bags or portable facilities.

RATES, RESERVATIONS, & RESTRICTIONS

Deposit $55 main house, $75 north wing per-night deposit; refund w/ 2-day notice; check for special events

Discounts Midweek, corp., 3rd person; kids free

Credit Cards V, AE, DC, MC, D

Check-In/Out 3/noon

Smoking Restricted

Pets Restricted

Kids Welcome (no cots or cribs)

Minimum Stay 2 nights at Christmas

Open All year, check at Christmas

Hosts Diana Atwood Johnson
85 Lyme St.
Old Lyme, CT 06371
(800) 434-5352 or (860) 434-2600
Fax: (860) 434-5352
innkeeper@oldlymeinn.com
www.oldlymeinn.com

COBBSCROFT, Pomfret

OVERALL ★★★½ | ROOM QUALITY ★★★★ | VALUE ★★★½ | PRICE $85–110

Art lover, artful, or just artful at love? In any case, you'll love it here, the results of host Janet and daughter who have painted the walls, furniture and accessories, and watercolorist husband Tom, who sometimes gives workshops and offers artworks for sale. Typical atypical touches include metal outdoor sculptures and a well-worn needlepoint "lolling chair" (Janet can't bear to update the fabric). Antique dealers and parents visiting kids at the nearby prep school like to stay here, perhaps lunching at the nearby vineyard, and viewing the Tiffany windows in the local church.

SETTING & FACILITIES

Location I-395 to Exit 93, left from ramp end onto Rt. 101, travel 6.5 mi. or so to traffic light at Rt. 169, right onto

169 N; B&B approximately 3 mi. on right, across from school

Near Private schools, winery, Sturbridge Village, Worcester outlets and colleges; Providence, R.I. School of Design

Building Circa 1780 farmhouse; rooms added in 1830, 1893

Grounds Old barn w/ furniture shop, art gallery, framing shop; front-yard perennial garden w/ sculptures

Public Space Library, living room

Food & Drink Full communal breakfast; specialties: apple crisp, seasonal cobblers, quiche

Recreation Trails, bird watching, bottle collecting, antiquing; day trips

Amenities & Services On-site gift, furniture shop, art gallery; phone in library, books, games, cots, bike rentals nearby

ACCOMMODATIONS

Units 1 guest room, 2 suites

All Rooms Bath, orig. hardwood floors

Some Rooms Fireplace, dressing room

Bed & Bath Twin/king, queen, king; all full baths, 1 w/ hall access (robes)

Favorites Bridal Suite—largest, most private, fireplace, claw-foot soaking tub; Stencil Room—hand-painted barn-door

headboard, hall access bath, robes

Comfort & Decor Airy, bright rooms. Downstairs suite good for families. Painted furniture pieces, artwork; nicely restored, small antique pieces. Oriental or hand-hooked rugs. Rather plain bedding, accessories, wallcoverings in some rooms.

RATES, RESERVATIONS, & RESTRICTIONS

Deposit Credit card holds reservation; no charge w/ 7-day notice

Discounts Artist's workshop packages, singles, seniors, 3rd person

Credit Cards V, AE, MC

Check-In/Out 2/11

Smoking No

Pets No

Kids 6 and up

Open All year

Host Janet McCobb

349 Pomfret St., Route 169

Pomfret, CT 06258

(800) 928-5560 or (860) 928-5560

Fax: (860) 928-3608

info@cobbscroft.com

www.cobbscroft.com

LINDEN HOUSE, Simsbury

OVERALL ★★★½ | ROOM QUALITY ★★★★ | VALUE ★★ | PRICE $120–230

Opened in October 1998, after a meticulous four-year restoration, this turreted Victorian bed-and-breakfast topped by a weathervane is close to the road, and passersby sometimes stop and ask about it. (Even before it was listed as a business it was booked through word-of-mouth.) Decorated as a cherished, tasteful, private residence rather than commercial lodgings, it soon will have two more working fireplaces so that all units offer the coziness of a bedside hearth. Julia and Myles are retired and are putting in the elbow grease and amenities to upgrade already lovely rooms. Growing pains are inevitable, but check this baby out.

SETTING & FACILITIES

Location Rt. 84 E to Exit 39 onto Rt. 4, travel .25 mile to Rt. 10 N (Hopmeadow St.); approximately 11 mi. to B&B, about 2 mi. from Entering Simsbury sign
Near Downtown Hartford, skating, recreation and nature facilities, Farmington River
Building Circa 1860 Victorian
Grounds 2.5 lawn acres to Farmington River, gardens, apple trees

Public Space Entrance foyer, large sitting room
Food & Drink Full breakfast; tea on weekends
Recreation 8-mi. hiking trail, horses, golf, tennis, antiquing, XC skiing
Amenities & Services Bike storage, telephones avail., BYOB set-ups; occasions recognized

ACCOMMODATIONS

Units 5 guest rooms
All Rooms Bath; 3 working, 2 ornamental fireplaces; seating, AC
Some Rooms Small dressing areas, TV
Bed & Bath Four-poster, sleigh, carved; king, queen, 1 room w/ twins; large baths, all full, claw-foot soaking tubs, 1 w/ whirlpool
Favorites Hostess' favorite—smallest room, Chinese Chippendale furnishings, fireplace; Guests' favorite—romantic four-poster king room, warm yellow walls, antique chaise
Comfort & Decor Antique mahogany pieces, handpainted furnishings. Oriental rugs. Collectibles, artwork. Pale color schemes. Handmade quilts, bedspreads. Ornate, carved Victorian mantels. Twin room, prettiest.

RATES, RESERVATIONS, & RESTRICTIONS

Deposit 20%; refund w/ 24-hour notice
Discounts 3rd person, corp. midweek, corp. long-term
Credit Cards V, AE, MC
Check-In/Out 2–4/11 (will hold luggage)
Smoking No
Pets No
Kids Over 12
Minimum Stay 2 nights weekends
Open All year except Christmas and New Year
Hosts Julia and Myles McCabe
290 Hopmeadow St.
Simsbury, CT 06089
(860) 408-1321

MERRYWOOD, *Simsbury*

OVERALL ★★★★ | ROOM QUALITY ★★★★ | VALUE ★★½ | PRICE $140–230

Gerlinde was an antiques dealer, and textiles and collections from around the world are draped, tossed, placed, hung, set, and framed throughout the premises. Kilims, wooden shoes, Far Eastern hats, Indian robes, and more are thoughtfully labeled, and even the place settings at breakfast are antique and ever changing. In keeping with the creativity, you can select an original dish like the Sea-legs Omelet, filled with crab, onion, tomato, and wine. Eastern philosophical influence and laid-back comfort pervade this brick Colonial Revival, and piped-in classical music emphasizes the serenity. So do six acres of gardens and lawns, and well-equipped guest rooms.

SETTING & FACILITIES

Location Rt. 185 in Simsbury, on Rt. 10 N, right at Chart House Restaurant, travel on 185 approximately 1 mi., start up the hill, small sign on left marks B&B
Near Farmington, downtown Hartford, priv. schools, recreation and nature facil., mountain hiking, antiquing, International World Skating
Building Graceful Colonial Revival
Grounds 6 landscaped, pine-treed acres; carvings, lawns, gardens, patio, walking paths
Public Space LR, glassed-in porch, formal DR, library
Food & Drink Full communal breakfast, guests select night before from cont'l, standard, and gourmet offerings; mimosas, espresso; specialties: German pancakes, Eierroesti (Swiss egg dish)

Recreation Farmington River activities; horses, golf, tennis, touring, skiing, hot-air ballooning, hiking

Amenities & Services AC, room refrigerators w/ soft drinks, beer. Special occasions recognized

ACCOMMODATIONS

Units 2 guest rooms, 1 suite
All Rooms Bath, small refrigerator, TV/VCR, dataport, sherry decanter
Some Rooms Suite w/ kitchenette; priv. sound system
Bed & Bath Queen, king/twin sizes; robes, slippers, hairdryers; 2 smallish baths—1 hall access, small sauna in suite bath
Favorites Victorian Room—lace-canopied queen bed, antique love seat, cut-glass collection, desk
Comfort & Decor Well-used Empire and Victorian antique furnishings. Comfortably cluttered rooms. Original artwork. Oriental influence. Suite small BR, spacious sitting room. Refrigerators unobtrusive. Simple but creative window treatments. Soothing.

RATES, RESERVATIONS, & RESTRICTIONS

Deposit 50%; refund w/ 14-day notice
Discounts Singles, corp.
Credit Cards V, AE, DC, MC, D
Check-In/Out 2/11
Smoking No
Pets No
Kids No

Open All year
Hosts Gerlinde and Michael Marti
100 Hartford Rd.
Simsbury, CT 06070
(860) 651-1785
Fax: (860) 651-8273
mfmarti@aol.com

SIMSBURY 1820 HOUSE, Simsbury

OVERALL ★★★½ | ROOM QUALITY ★★★★ | VALUE ★★★ | PRICE $145–205

Formerly the Elisha Phelps House, this white-brick, many-chimneyed mansion is a mix of Georgian, Adamesque, and antebellum influences. It sits on town-owned land and is the older, smaller sibling of the nearby Simsbury Inn, a luxury 97-room resort. Meeting and recreational facilities of that modern property are available, but guests at this original property have the bonus of country ambiance, close to the capital. For groups, weddings, retreats, and those seeking a longer stay, this is an attractive combination of facilities, space, and charm. Those who seek privacy can escape to the secluded carriage house, or may want to choose another smaller inn or bed-and-breakfast.

SETTING & FACILITIES

Location On Rt. 202 in Simsbury, hilltop site

Near Downtown Hartford, International World Skating

Building Built in 1822; 1890 Beaux Arts renovations; renovated 1999

Grounds Spacious lawns, gardens

Public Space Entry, lobby, dining room

Food & Drink Cont'l breakfast; refreshments; Café open Mon–Thurs only.

Recreation Horseback riding, golf, tennis, hiking trails, XC skiing, antiquing

Amenities & Services Use of nearby Simsbury Inn exercise and spa facil.; party and corp. functions ballroom (125), smaller meeting rooms

ACCOMMODATIONS

Units 20 guest rooms in main house; 12 in carriage house

All Rooms Bath, desk, AC, alarm clock, down pillow w/ comforter

Some Rooms Decorative fireplace, sitting area, sofabed, hidden TV, whirlpool

Bed & Bath Some four-posters, queen/king; 1 room w/ 2 doubles

Favorites Four-poster king—raised sit-

ting area w/ sofabed, whirlpool, priv. entrance

Comfort & Decor Hunt-country classic. Simple but elegantly furnished w/ reproductions and English period pieces. Coordinated fabrics. Luxury touches. Room sizes vary from small to quite large. Feel of smaller property in carriage house.

RATES, RESERVATIONS, & RESTRICTIONS

Deposit 1 night

Discounts AAA, longer stays, corp., government

Credit Cards V, AE, MC

Check-In/Out 3/11

Smoking Restricted

Pets No

Kids Yes

Minimum Stay Check with inn

Open All year

Hosts The Brighenti Family

731 Hopemeadow St.

Simsbury, CT 06070

(800) TRY-1820 or (860) 658-7658

Fax: (860) 651-0724

www.simsbury1820house.com

LORD THOMPSON MANOR, *Thompson*

OVERALL ★★★½ | ROOM QUALITY ★★★★ | VALUE ★★½ | PRICE $110–180

Wedding bells and laptops are frequently seen and heard here, as weekend weddings and weekday meetings are popular throughout the year. This 30-room stucco estate, built in 1917, was given up to the Catholic church after the Depression, and returned to its grand state in 1989, when Jackie and Andrew took over. The upstairs suites, named for horses, are choice, and one includes a rare English needle shower. A billiards room is off the imposing living room, and the breakfast area is warmed with shades of burgundy and grape. Today, much of the Frederick Law Olmsted landscaping remains on dozens of bucolic acres, perfect for strolls to close a deal (or trysts to close a deal, for that matter).

SETTING & FACILITIES

Location From New York take I-95 to Rt. 395 N to Exit 99, right onto Rt. 200 E, B&B is 1st drive on left, watch for sign, cannot see property from road, .5 mi. driveway
Near Antique shopping district, Sturbridge Village, casinos, Mystic
Building 1917 Symmetrical Georgian 30-room manor, Gladding Estate
Grounds 36 acres, old pine trees, walking paths, formal gardens designed by Frederick Law Olmsted, seating
Public Space Entrance hall, drawing room, fully licensed wet bar, billiards room
Food & Drink Full country breakfast; specialties: waffles, ham, Finnish pancakes; in 1998 B&B acquired nearby White Horse Inn restaurant, serving lunch, dinner, Sunday brunch
Recreation Hiking, biking, antiquing, touring, day trips
Amenities & Services Guest refrigerators, cots available, limited disabled access, maps, weddings; corp. meeting facilities

ACCOMMODATIONS

Units 2 guest rooms, 4 suites
All Rooms Writing desk, antiques, AC
Some Rooms Priv. bath, fireplace, sitting area, phone
Bed & Bath Sleigh, canopy, four-poster, wicker beds, down comforters, extra bedding; full original 1917 priv. baths (3); shared large shower bath (3); additional half bath (1)
Favorites Thoroughbred Suite I—Master Suite, 1 large room, fireplace, sitting area, original paneling, ambiance lighting, rich fabrics, queen four-poster bed, antique, English "needle shower" (only 2 or 3 in U.S.), cast iron soaking tub
Comfort & Decor Spacious suites named for horses. Heavy mahogany furnishings, rich wood floors and carpet, fabrics. Elegant, dark tones. All original brass hardware, lighting fixtures retained and restored. Lots of romantic candles. TVs deliberately excluded from romantic rooms. Hosts set-up candlelight bubble baths, champagne, light fires for arrival.

RATES, RESERVATIONS, & RESTRICTIONS

Deposit Credit card holds reservation; no charge w/ 7-day notice
Discounts "Big Chill Weekend" packages, dinner packages, children, 3rd person, midweek corp. rates
Credit Cards V, AE, MC, D
Check-in/Out 3/11
Smoking No
Pets No
Kids Welcome
No-No's Guests may not bring their own alcohol

Open All year
Hosts Jackie and Andrew Silverston
Rt. 200, P.O. Box 428
Thompson, CT 06277

(860) 923-3886
Fax: (860) 923-9310
mail@lordthompsonmanor.com
www.lordthompsonmanor.com

CHESTER BULKLEY HOUSE, Wethersfield

OVERALL ★★★½ | ROOM QUALITY ★★★ | VALUE ★★★★ | PRICE $85–95

Near a quiet inlet of the Connecticut River and a cluster of historic homes, this 1830 Greek Revival house slows the pace down to the era of Mr. Bulkley. Antique dolls, Oriental rugs, fireplaces, wide-board floors, and hand-carved woodwork create a fine period ambiance. Old Wethersfield dates to 1634 and is related to a fistful of firsts: Behind the First Church of Christ, dating to the 1600s, is the landmark cemetery where America's first slave and the first commissioned Marine are buried in somewhat ironic juxtaposition.

SETTING & FACILITIES

Location In center of historic village, amid more than 150 early 19th-century homes; I-91 to Exit 26 onto Marsh St., left onto Main St.; B&B is 4th house on left
Near Wethersfield Cove, state parks; historic home museums; yachting cove; Hartford, oldest statehouse in America, Wadsworth Atheneum museum
Building Pretty 1830 Greek Revival
Grounds Village yard, brick patio w/ English gardens

Public Space Parlor, DR, sitting room
Food & Drink Full communal breakfast; specialties: Finnish oven-baked pancakes w/ banana, blueberry, and strawberry hot sauce, corn-flake French toast; special diets avail.; tea
Recreation Antiquing, hiking trails, arts events, day trips
Amenities & Services Refrigerator, cots, chocolate-covered strawberries by bed, fax/dataport, local paper

ACCOMMODATIONS

Units 5 guest rooms
All Rooms Seating, phone, radio/alarm clock, A3 w/ priv. baths, writing desk
Bed & Bath Antique, brass, carved beds, sizes vary; priv. baths, shower-only, 2 rooms share 1 full bath, robes
Favorites Largest—king four-poster,

priv. bath
Comfort & Decor 1800s historic preservation wallcoverings. Laura Ashley and Waverly fabrics. Some carpet, some painted plank floors. Rooms sharing bath converts to 2-BR 1-bath suite. Rear rooms most quiet.

RATES, RESERVATIONS, & RESTRICTIONS

Deposit Credit card holds reservation; no charge w/ 7-day notice
Discounts Midweek corp., AAA, senior, kids
Credit Cards V, AE, MC, D
Check-In/Out 4/11
Smoking No
Pets No

Kids Welcome (no cribs)
Open All year except Dec. 24–25
Host Thomas Aufiero
184 Main St.
Wethersfield, CT 06109
(860) 563-4236
Fax: (860) 257-8266
www.choice-guide.com/ct/bulkley

ELIAS CHILD HOUSE, Woodstock

OVERALL ★★★½ | ROOM QUALITY ★★★★ | VALUE ★★★ | PRICE $95–125

Built in 1714, by the mid-1700s the Elias Child house was described in land records as "the mansion house." It had risen from humble one-room beginnings to include additions, outbuildings, and an "indoor outhouse," attached to the home's ell—a unique piece of Colonial history, now part of the current screened porch. Ask to see the well-preserved attic chimney smoke chamber, once used to cure and smoke meats. Veteran bed-and-breakfast hosts Mary Beth and Tony will ease you into a relaxing getaway at this still-emerging property, combining original elements—like nine fireplaces—with clean renovations. Over the years the Felice's specialty has been "peaceful romance."

SETTING & FACILITIES

Location Rt. 171 E to West Woodstock (through Putnam and South Woodstock), turn left onto Perrin Rd.; rural area
Near Vineyards (luncheons by res., tours); herb farms; historic homes; living Colonial museums; Old Sturbridge Village, antiquing, flea markets, arts attractions, state parks, local fairs/events, golf; private schools; UConn, casinos
Building 1714 symmetrical Colonial
Grounds Over 47 acres behind house, stone walls, wooded areas, walking paths, XC ski trails
Public Space Keeping room,
reading/conversation room, stone patio, parlor, DR, screened porch
Food & Drink Full country-style, communal breakfast; daily menu; specialties: granola, omelets, bananas Amaretto, homemade pastries
Recreation Walking trails; short drive to fine restaurants, biking, hiking, swimming, day trips
Amenities & Services Summer pool, bike storage; forgotten necessities; roll-aways; BYOB set-ups, hearth-cooking demonstrations in season, bikes; massage or reiki by appt.; see website for packages

ACCOMMODATIONS

Units 2 guest rooms, 1 suite
All Rooms Bath, fireplace, seating, reading lighting, closets
Some Rooms Add'l beds, suite w/ sep. sitting room, decorative fireplace
Bed & Bath Unusual antique bedsteads, queen and double beds; shower-only, except suite
Favorites Polly's Room—sunny southwest corner, pretty antique bed
Comfort & Decor Sunny, spacious (18′ x 14′) rooms despite home's era. All rural views. Caroline's Room double bed and ¾ bed. Suite Aimee queen and twin bed, useable antique crib. Oriental and braided area rugs. Muted colors, some hand-stenciling, original paneling and wainscoting.

RATES, RESERVATIONS, & RESTRICTIONS

Deposit Credit card holds reservation; refund (less admin. fee) w/ 14-day notice
Discounts 5+ night stays, check for packages
Credit Cards V, AE, MC, D
Check-In/Out By arrangement/11
Smoking No
Pets Small dogs by arrangement
Kids Infants, or 7 and up
No-No's Toddlers
Minimum Stay 2 nights for local
parents' weekends and graduations, some holidays
Open All year
Hosts Mary Beth Gorke-Felice and Tony Felice
50 Perrin Rd.
Woodstock, CT 06281
877-974-9836 or (860) 974-9836
Fax: (860) 974-1541
tfelice@compuserve.com

Appendix

Additional
Bed-and-Breakfasts
and Country Inns

While our profiles give you a fine range of bed-and-breakfasts and country inns, some may be fully booked when you want to visit, or you may want to stay in areas where we have not included a property. So we have included an annotated listing of additional bed-and-breakfasts and country inns, spread geographically throughout New England.

All properties meet our basic criteria: They have about 3–25 guestrooms, a distinct personality, and individually decorated guestrooms. They are open regularly, and include breakfast in the price (with a few exceptions). Prices are a range from low to high season. Most are highly recommended, but we have not visited all of these properties so we cannot recommend them across the board. We suggest you get a brochure, check the Internet, or call and ask about some of the categories that are on the profile to find out more. While some of these supplementals are famed and excellent, others may not be up to the level of the profiled properties.

Maine

ZONE 1: Downeast/Acadia

Bar Harbor
Bayview Inn $85–280
  (207) 288-5861 or
  (800) 356-3585
Black Friar Inn
  $90–145
  (207) 288-5091
Brooklin
Lookout $80–105
  (207) 359-2188

Calais: St. Andrews
Kingsbrai Arms $380–500
  (506) 529-1897
Windward House $99–235
  (207) 236-9656

Castine
Pentagoet Inn $99–139
  (207) 326-8616 or
  (800) 845-1701

The Manor Inn $95-205
  (877) MANORINN

Corea
The Black Duck Inn on
  Corea Harbor $80–155
  (207) 963-2689 or
  (877) 963–2689

ZONE 1: Downeast/Acadia (continued)

Eastport
Todd House $45–80
  (207) 853-2328

Jonesport
Tootsies $50
  (207) 497-5414

Lubec
Peacock House $70–80
  (207) 733-2403

Northeast Harbor
Harbourside Inn $125–195
  (207) 276-3272
Maison Suisse Inn
  $115–195
  (207) 276-5223 or
  (800) 624-7668

Southwest Harbor
Claremont Hotel &
  Cottages $89–225

(207) 244-5036 or
  (800) 244-5036
Island House $65–145
  (207) 244-5180
The Lindenwood Inn
  $75–255
  (207) 244-5835 or
  (800) 307-5335

ZONE 2: Midcoast Maine

Bailey Island
Captain York House Bed
  & Breakfast $75–95
  (207) 833-6224
Tower Hill B&B (Orr's
  Island) $80–155
  (207) 833-2311 or
  (888) 833-2311

Boothbay
Hodgdon Island Inn
  $105–135
  (207) 633-7474
Kenniston Hill Inn
  $80–120
  (207) 633-2159 or
  (800) 992-2915

Boothbay Harbor
Lawnmeer Inn $95–195
  (207) 633-2544 or
  (800) 633-7645

Brunswick
Brunswick Bed and
  Breakfast $95–200
  (207) 729-4914 or
  (800) 299-4914
Captain's Watch B&B and
  Sail Charter $110–175
  (207) 725-0979

Camden
A Little Dream $120–250
  (207) 236-8742
Maine Stay Inn $100–150
  (207) 236-9636
Nathaniel Hosmer Inn
  $85–160
  (207) 236-4012
Swan House $90–145
  (207) 236-8275 or
  (800) (207) 8275

Damariscotta
Brannon-Bunker Inn
  $65–75
  (207) 563-5941 or
  (800) 563-9225

Damariscotta Mills
Mill Pond Inn $95
  (207) 453-8014

Rockland
Lakeshore Inn $125–145
  (207) 594-4209 or
  (877) 783-7371

Searsport
Watchtide $85–155
  (207) 548-6575 or
  (800) 698-6575

**Spruce Head (Clark
  Island)**
Craignair Inn $83–125
  (207) 594-7644 or
  (800) 320-9997

Vinalhaven
Fox Island Inn $45–105
  (207) 863-2122

ZONE 3: Southern Maine Coast and Greater Portland

Eliot
High Meadows $80–120
  (207) 439-0590

Freeport
Anita's Cottage Street Inn
  $75–110
  (207) 865-0932
Isaac Randall House
  $65–175
  (207) 865-9295 or

Kennebunk
The Waldo Emerson Inn
  $100
  (207) 985-4250
Kennebunkport
1802 House B&B Inn
  $179–369
  (207) 967-5632 or
  (800) 932-5632

Captain Fairfield Inn
  $125–275
  (207) 967-4454 or
  (800) 322-1928
Inn at Harbor Head
  $130–330
  (207) 967-5564

Phippsburg
Popham Beach $90–160
  (207) 389-2409

Portland
The Danforth
$139–289
(207) 879-8755 or
(800) 991-6557
Inn at St. John $65–155
(207) 773-6481 or
(800) 636-9127

West End Inn $99–199
(207) 772-1377 or
(800) 338-1377

Saco
Crown 'n' Anchor Inn
$75–125
(207) 282-3829 or
(800) 561-8865

York Harbor
The Admiral Olsen Inn
$125
(207) 363-1900
Inn at Harmon Park
$79–109
(207) 363-2031

ZONE 4: MAINE—Inland & Lakes

Augusta
Maple Hill Farm $65–165
(207) 622-2708 or
(800) 622-2708

Bridgton
Noble House $90–149
(207) 647-3733

Dedham
Lucerne Inn $59–199
(207) 843-5123 or
(800) 325-5123

Dexter
Brewster Inn $59–95
(207) 924-3130

Fayette
Home-Nest Farm $60–120
(207) 897-4125

Kingfield
Inn on Winter's Hill
$68–138
(207) 265-5421 or
(800) 233-9687

Stratton
Putt's Place Bed &
Breakfast $55
(207) 246-4181

New Hampshire

ZONE 5: Southern New Hampshire

Alstead
Darby Brook Farm $60–70
(603) 835-6624

Bedford
Bedford Village Inn
$200–300
(603) 472-2001 or
(800) 852-1166

Chesterfield
Chesterfield Inn $150–250
(800) 365-5515

Dover
Highland Farm Bed and
Breakfast $145–295
(603) 743-3399
Payne's Hill Bed and
Breakfast $80
(603) 740-9441

Durham
University Guest House
$70–90
(603) 868-2728

East Andover
Highland Lake Inn
$85–125
(603) 735-6426

Exeter
Inn by the Bandstand
$110–299
(603) 772-6352 or
(877) 2EX-ETER

Greenfield
Greenfield Inn
$49–139
(603) 547-6327 or
(800) 678-4144

Henniker
Meeting House Inn &
Restaurant $65–115
(603) 428-3228

Jaffrey
Benjamin Prescott Inn
$75–150
(603) 532-6637

Portsmouth
Inn at Strawbery Banke
$145–150
(603) 436-7242 or
(800) 428-3933
Martin Hill Inn $90–130
(603) 436-2287

Rindge
Grassy Pond House $60–70
(603) 899-5167

Sullivan
Post and Beam $70–115
(603) 847-3330 or
(888) 3-ROMANCE

ZONE 5: Southern New Hampshire *(continued)*

Walpole
Inn at Valley Farms
$105–160
(603) 756-2855

Wilton Center
Stepping Stones $60–65
(603) 654-9048

ZONE 6: Central New Hampshire and Lakes

Canaan
Inn on Canaan Street
$85–115
(603) 523-7310

Center Harbor
Watch Hill Bed and
Breakfast $65–75
(603) 253-4334

Charlestown
Maple Hedge Bed and
Breakfast $90–115
(603) 826-5237 or
(800) 9-MAPLE–9

Cornish
Chase House $115–150
(603) 675-5391 or
(800) 401-9455

Enfield
Shaker Inn at the Great
Stone Dwelling $105–155
(603) 632-7810 or
(888) 707-4257

Hanover
Moose Mountain Lodge
$80–100
(603) 643-3529

Holderness
Inn on Golden Pond
$125–155
(603) 968-7269

Lyme
Breakfast on the
Connecticut $110–300
(603) 353-4444
Loch Lyme Lodge $56–90
(603) 795-2141 or
(800) 423-2141

Meredith
Inn at Bay Point $229–269
(603) 279-7006 or
(800) 622-6455

New London
Inn at Pleasant Lake
$110–165
(603) 526-6271 or
(800) 626-4907

Northwood
Meadow Farm Bed
and Breakfast $70–80
(603) 942-8619

Sunapee
Inn at Sunapee
$60–140
(603) 763-4444 or
(800) 327-2466

Wakefield
Wakefield Inn $75–90
(603) 522-8272 or
800) 245-0841

West Franklin
The Maria Atwood Inn
$65–90
(603) 934-3666

ZONE 7: Northern New Hampshire and White Mountains

Bretton Woods
Bretton Arms Country Inn
$99–219
(603) 278-1000 or
(800) 258-0330

Campton
Mountain Fare Inn
$75–125
(603) 726-4283

Colebrook
Rooms With a View
$65–80
(603) 237-5106
or (800) 449-5106, ext. 1

Franconia
Hilltop Inn $75–250
(603) 823-5695 or
(800) 770-5695
Inn at Forest Hills $85–145
(603) 823-9550 or
(800) 280-9550
Lovett's Inn by Lafeyette
Brook $125–450
(603) 823-7761 or
(800) 356-3802

Jackson
Ellis River House $89–289
(603) 383-9339 or
(800) 233-8309

Paisley and Parsley $85–135
(603) 383-0859
Village House $60–120
(603) 383-6666 or
(800) 972-8343

Jefferson
Jefferson Inn $100–120
(603) 586-7998 or
(800) 729-7908

Meredith
Inn at Bay Point $229–269
(603) 279-7006 or
(800) 622-6455

New London
Inn at Pleasant Lake
$110–165
(603) 526-6271 or
(800) 626-4907

North Conway
Cabernet Inn $75–225
(603) 356-4704 or
(800) 866-4704
Farm by the River $70–185
(603) 356-2694 or
(888) 414-8353
1785 Inn $69–299
(603) 356-9025 or
(800) 421-1785
Stonehurst Manor $96–196
(603) 356-3113 or
(800) 525-9100

Victorian Harvest Inn
$80–200 (603) 356-3548
or (800) 642-0749
Wyatt House Country Inn
$55–199
(603) 356-7977 or
(800) 527-7978

Northwood
Meadow Farm Bed
and Breakfast $70–80
(603) 942-8619

North Woodstock
Wilderness Inn $60–140
(603) 745-3890 or
(800) 200-WILD

Snowville
Snowvillage Inn $99–201
(603) 447-2818 or
(800) 447-4345

Sunapee
Inn at Sunapee
$60–140
(603) 763-4444 or
(800) 327-2466

Tamworth
The Tamworth Inn
$95–140
(603) 323-7721 or
(800) 642-7352

Wakefield
Wakefield Inn $75–90
(603) 522-8272 or
800) 245-0841

West Franklin
The Maria Atwood Inn
$65–90
(603) 934-3666

Vermont

ZONE 8: Southern Vermont

Andover
Inn at High View
$115–155
(802) 875-2724

Arlington
Arlington Inn $115–265
(802) 375-6784
Hill Farm Inn $80–186
(802) 375-2269
West Mountain Inn
$155–261
(802) 375-6516

Bennington
South Shire Inn $105–160
(802) 442-3547

Chester
Inn at Cranberry Farm
$150–225
(802) 463-1339 or
(800) 854-2208

Night with a Native $60–85
(802) 875-2616

Danby
Silas Griffith Inn $199–299
(802) 293-5567 or
(800) 545-1509

Dorset
Barrows House $130–265
(802) 867-4455 or
(800) 639-1620
Inn at West View Farm
$135–215
(802) 867-5715 or
(800) 769-4903
Weddingham Farm
$130–150
(800) 310-2010

Jamaica
Three Mountain Inn
$125–295
(802) 874-4140

Landgrove
Landgrove Inn $95–235
(802) 824-6673 or
(800) 669-8466

Londonderry
Frogs Leap Inn $113–195
(802) 824-3019

Manchester
Inn at Manchester
$104–180
(802) 362-1793 or
(800) 273-1793

Manchester Village
Charles Orvis Inn at
the Equinox $169–559
(802) 362-4700 or
(800) 362-4747
Village Country Inn
$129–295
(802) 362-1792

ZONE 8: Southern Vermont *(continued)*

Old Bennington
Four Chimneys Inn
  $125–205
  (802) 447-3500 or
  (800) 649-3503

Peru
Johnny Seesaw's $120–180
  (802) 824-5533

Saxton's River
Inn at Saxton's River $120
  (802) 869-2110

Weston
Wilder Homestead Inn
  $75–150
  (802) 824-8172

Wilmington
The White House
  $110–225
  (802) 464-2135

ZONE 9: Midstate Vermont/Champlain

Bolton Valley
Black Bear Inn $79–195
  (802) 434-2126 or
  (800) 395-6335

Chittenden
Mountain Top Inn
  $168–268
  (802) 483-2311 or
  (800) 445-2100

Cuttingsville
Maple Crest Farm $55–75
  (802) 492-3367

Fair Haven
Maplewood Inn $80–145
  (802) 265-8039 or
  (800) 253-7729

Fairfield
Tetreault's Hillside View
  Farm $40–55
  (802) 827-4480

Goshen
Blueberry Hill $130
  (802) 247-6735 or
  (800) 448-0707

Killington
Mountain Meadows Lodge
  $85–140
  (802) 775-1010
Peak Chalet $61–259
  (802) 422-4278
Vermont Inn $50–205
  (802) 775-0708 or
  (800) 541-7795

Mendon
Red Clover Inn $130–350
  (802) 775-2290 or
  (800) 752-0571

Montgomery Center
Inn on Trout River
  $86–125
  (802) 326-4391

Randolph
Placidia Farm Bed
  & Breakfast $90–115
  (802) 728-9883
Three Stallion Inn $80–155
  (802) 728-5575 or
  (800) 424-5575

Shrewsbury
High Pastures $65–75
  (802) 773-2087 or
  (888) 686-4453

Smuggler's Notch
Mannsview Inn $65–95
  (802) 644-8321 or
  (888) 937-6266
Smuggler's Notch Inn
  $60–125
  (802) 644-2412 or
  (800) 845-3101

South Burlington
Willow Pond Farm Bed
  & Breakfast $85–120
  (802) 985-8505

Waitsfield
Lareau Farm Country Inn
  $70–150
  (802) 496-4949 or
  (800) 833-0766

ZONE 10: Vermont—Upper Valley/Northeast Kingdom

Chelsea
Shire Inn $110–200
  (802) 685-3031 or
  (800) 441-6908

Craftsbury
Craftsbury Inn &
  Restaurant $150–170

  (802) 586-2848 or
  (800) 336-2848

Craftsbury Common
Craftsbury Bed &
  Breakfast on Wylie Hill
  $60–85
  (802) 586-2206

Fairlee
Silver Maple Lodge &
  Cottages $59–89
  (802) 333-4326

Greensboro
Highland Lodge $195–250
  (802) 533-2647

Lyndonville
Branch Brook Bed &
  Breakfast $70–90
  (802) 626-8316 or
  (800) 572-7712

Montpelier
Inn at Montpelier $104–177
  (802) 228-2727

North Troy
Rose Apple Acres Farms
  $55–65 (802) 988-4300

Quechee
The Quechee Inn at
  Marshland Farm $80–240
  (802) 295-3133

South Woodstock
Kedron Valley Inn
  $109–248
  (802) 457-1473 or
  (800) 836-1193

Stowe
Butternut Inn at Stowe
  $55–170
  (802) 253-4277
Fitch Hill Inn $89–199
  (802) 888-3834 or
  (800) 639-2903
Ski Inn $45–65/person
  (802) 253-4050

Taftsville
Applebutter Inn $75–145
  (802) 457-4158
  (800) 486-1734

Williamstown
Autumn Harvest Inn
  $79–139
  (802) 433-1355

Wolcott
Golden Maple Inn and Fly-
  Fishing Bed & Breakfast
  $74–89
  (802) 888-6614 or
  (800) 639-5234

Massachusetts

ZONE 11: Boston Region

Andover
Andover Inn $105–195
  (978) 475-5903

Boston
The Charles Street Inn
  $220–340
  (617) 314-8900

Cambridge
A Cambridge House Bed
  & Breakfast Inn $89–275
  (617) 491-6300

Middleborough
1831 Zachariah Eddy
  House $69–125
  (508) 946-0016

Newburyport
The Morrill Place Inn
  $72–95
  (978) 462-2808

Rehobeth
Five Bridge Inn Bed &
  Breakfast $79–109
  (508) 252-3190
Perryville Inn Bed &
  Breakfast $75–105
  (508) 252-9239

Rockport
The Captain's House
  $80–125
  (978) 546-3825

Inn on Cove Hill $55–135
  (978) 546-2701
Old Farm Inn $83–130
  (978) 546-3237 or
  (800) 233-6828

Salem
The Salem Inn $139–229
  (978) 741-0680 or
  (800) 446-2995

Sudbury
Longfellow's Wayside Inn
  $80–130
  (978) 443-1776

ZONE 12: Central/Western Massachusetts

Amherst
Black Walnut Inn
  $105–135
  (413) 549-5649

Belchertown
Bed and Breakfast at
  Ingate Farms $60–90
  (413) 253-0440 or
  (888) ingate-b

Mucky Duck $80–100
  (413) 323-9657

Greenfield
Brandt House Country
  Inn $100–195
  (413) 774-3329 or
  (800) 239–3329

Lee
Chambery Inn $75–275
  (413) 243-2221 or
  (800) 537-4321

Lenox
Garden Gables Inn
  $95–225
  (413) 637-0193

ZONE 12: Central/Western Massachusetts (continued)

Lenox (continued)
Gateways Inn $130–400
    (413) 637-2532 or
    (888) 492-9466
The Summer White
    House $160–195
    (413) 637-4489

New Salem
Bullard Farm B&B
    $75–85
    (978) 544-6959

Plymouth
Plymouth Bay Manor
    $95–110

(508) 830-0426 or
(800) 492-1828

Richmond
Inn at Richmond $110–275
    (413) 698-2566 or
    (888) 968-4748

South Egremont
Weathervane Inn $125–243
    (413) 528-9580 or
    (800) 528-9580

Stockbridge
Inn at Stockbridge
    $115–285
    (413) 298-3337

The Whitney House
    $85–145
    (413) 298-3345

Ware
Wildwood Inn Bed &
    Breakfast $50–90
    (413) 967-7709 or
    (800) 860-7798

West Stockbridge
Williamsville Inn &
    Restaurant $120–185
    (413) 274-6118

ZONE 13: Cape Cod

Barnstable
Ashley Manor $135–195
    (508) 362-8044 or
    (888) 535-2246
Beechwood Inn $150–180
    (508) 362-6618 or
    (800) 609-6618
Charles Hinckley House
    $119–149
    (508) 362-9924

Brewster
Bramble Inn $115–145
    (508) 896-7644
Brewster Farmhouse Inn
    $100–225
    (508) 896-3910 or
    (800) 892-3910
Candleberry Inn $85–195
    (508) 896-3300 or
    (800) 573-4769
Pepper House Inn $89–139
    (508) 896-4389
Ruddy Turnstone Bed &
    Breakfast $110–165
    (508) 385-9871

Chatham
Captain's House $165–350
    (508) 945-0127 or
    (800) 315-0728

Chatham Town House
    $165–335
    (508) 945-2180 or
    (800) 242-2180
Cranberry Inn $100-260
    (508) 945-9232 or
    (800) 332-4667
Moses Nickerson House
    $149–199
    (508) 945-5859

Dennis
Isaiah Hall B&B Inn
    $89–163
    (508) 385-9928 or
    (800) 736-0160
Captain Nickerson Inn
    $85–160
    (508) 398 5966

Eastham
Penny House Inn $170–225
    (508) 255-6632

East Orleans
Nauset House Inn $75–140
    (508) 255-2195
Parsonage Inn
    $105–135
    (508) 255-8217

Falmouth
Captain Tom Lawrence
    House $90–165
    (508) 540-1445 or
    (800) 266-8139
Woods Hole Passage
    $95–165
    (508) 548-9575 or
    (800) 790-8976

Hyannis
Inn on Sea Street $85–135
    (508) 775-8030

Sandwich
Belfry Inne & Bistro Drew
    House $95–165
    Abbey House $135–165
    (508) 888-8550 or
    (800) 844-4542
Isaiah Jones Homestead
    $85–165
    (508) 888-9115 or
    (800) 526-1625

West Falmouth
Inn at West Falmouth
    $115–300
    (508) 540-7696

West Yarmouth
Olde Schoolhouse Bed and
    Breakfast $99–155
    (508) 778-9468

ZONE 14: Martha's Vineyard/Nantucket

Chilmark
The Inn at Blueberry Hill
$161–735
(508) 645-3322 or
(800) 356-3322

Edgartown
The Charlotte Inn
$295–795
(508) 627-4751
The Daggett House
$100–575
(508) 627-4600 or
(800) 946-3400

Hob Knob Inn $125–375
(508) 627-9510 or
(800) 696-2723

Nantucket
Cliff Lodge $165–235
(508) 228-9480
Seven Sea Street Inn
$75–295
(508) 228-3577
Sherburne Inn $85–295
(508) 228-4425 or
(888) 577-4425
The Wauwinet $230–1,020
(508) 228-0145 or
(800) 426-8718

Tisbury
Lambert's Cove Country Inn
$90–250
(508) 693-2298

Vineyard Haven
Greenwood House
$119–269
(508) 693-6150
Tuckerman House
$175–285
(508) 693-0417

Rhode Island

ZONE 15: Newport and Little Compton, Rhode Island

Newport
Admiral Farragut Inn
$75–285
(401) 849-7397 or
(800) 524-1386
Beech Tree Inn $125–275
(401) 847-9794 or
(800) 748-6565

Bluestone $80–150
(401) 846-5408
Elliot Boss House $95–180
(401) 849-9425
Melville House $110–175
(401) 847-0640

Middletown
Inn at Shadow Lawn
$90–225
(401) 847-0902 or
(800) 352-3750
Lindseys' Guest House
$70–105
(401) 846-9386

ZONE 16: Block Island

Block Island
Anchor House Inn
$105–165
(401) 466-5021 or
(800) 730-0181

Atlantic Inn $99–225
(401) 466-5883 or
(800) 224-7422
Barrington Inn $75–185
(401) 466-5510 or
(888) 279-9400

Maizie de Mars
$75–100
(401) 466-8833
Rose Farm Inn $155–235
(401) 466-2034
Sasafrash $115–125
(401) 466-5486

ZONE 17: Mainland Rhode Island/Providence

Bristol
Rockwell House Inn
$85–150
(401) 253-0040 or
(800) 815-0040
William's Grant Inn
$95–180
(401) 253-4222

Narragansett
The Canterbury $70–110
(401) 783-0046
The Old Clerk House
$75–125
(401) 783-8008
Windermere $80
(401) 783-0187

North Kingstown
Country House $75–90
(401) 294-4688
The Haddie Pierce House
$95–110
(401) 294-7674 or
(866) 4HADDIE

North Kingstown
(continued)
The John Updike House
$90–225
(401) 294-4905
Mount Maple of Wickford
$90–130
(401) 295-4373

Providence
Old Court $155–175
(401) 751-2002

Richmond
Country Acres $80–90
(401) 364-9134
Inn the Woods $70–95
(401) 539-6021

South Kingstown
Cottrell Homestead $75
(401) 783-8665
The King's Rose $110–150
(401) 783-5222
VirJess Farm $75
(401) 783-3464

Wakefield
Larchwood Inn
$50–150
(401) 783-5454 or
(800) 275-5450
Sugarloaf Hill
$65–125
(401) 789-8715

Warren
Nathaniel Porter Inn
$85–105
(401) 245-6622

Warwick
Enchanted Cottage $70–90
(401) 732-0439

Waverly
Polly's Place
$90–135
(401) 847-2160

West Kingstown
The Metcalfs
from $75+
(401) 783-3448

Westerly
Grandview $75–105
(401) 596-6384 or
(800) 447-6384

Connecticut

Bristol
Chimney Crest Manor
$105–165
(860) 582-4219

New Preston
Birches Inn $95–300
(860) 868-0563 or
(800)-lake-inn
Hopkins Inn
$70–90
(860) 868-7295

Norfolk
Greenwoods Gate
$215–265
(860) 542-5439

Ridgefield
Stonehenge $75–200
(203) 438-6511
West Lane Inn $125–185
(203) 438-7323

Riverton
Old Riverton Inn $85–195
(860) 379-1796 or
(800) EST-1796

Salisbury
The Earl Grey B&B at
Chittenden House
$140–160
(860) 435-1007

The White Hart $99–199
(800) 832-0041

Waterbury
House on the Hill
$100–175
(203) 757-9901

Watertown
The Clarks $50
(860) 274-4866

Bolton
Jared Cone House $50–75
(860) 643-8538

Bozrah
Fitch Claremont House
$65–165
(860) 889-0260

Clinton
Captain Dibbell House
$65–115
(860) 669-1646

ZONE 19: Eastern Connecticut *(continued)*

Coventry
Maple Hill Farm $75–90
  (800) 742-0635

Essex
The Griswold Inn
  $120–195
  (860) 767-1776

Glastonbury
Butternut Farm $70–99
  (860) 633-7197

Madison
Tidewater Inn $80–185
  (203) 245-8457

Mystic
Adams House $85–175
  (860) 572-9551
Pequot Hotel Bed &
  Breakfast $95–175
  (860) 572-0390

Whitehall Mansion
  $90–350
  (860) 572-7280

New London
Queen Anne Inn $130–315
  (860) 447-2600 or
  (800) 347-8818

North Stonington
High Acres $110–145
  (860) 887-4355

Old Saybrook
Deacon Timothy Pratt
  $95–225
  (860) 395-1229

Pomfret
Clark Cottage $70–95
  (860) 928-5741

Putnam
Felshaw Tavern $90
  (860) 928-3467
Thurber House $80
  (860) 928-6776

South Woodstock
Inn at Woodstock Hill
  $90–155
  (860) 928-0528

Tolland
Tolland Inn $75–150
  (860) 872-0800

Windsor
Charles R. Hart House
  $95–105
  (860) 688-5555

Index of Profiled Bed-and-Breakfasts and Country Inns

Subject Index

460   Subject Index